**EVERYTHING YOU NEED TO KNOW THOROUGHLY COVERED IN ONE BOOK**

**Five ASVAB Practice Tests — Answer Keys — Tips to Boost Scores — Military Enlistment Information — Study Aids**

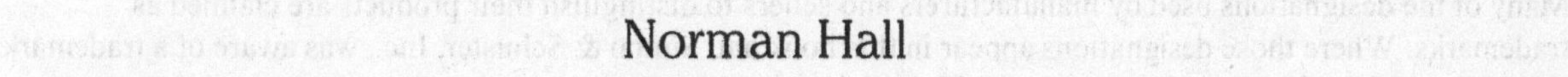

Norman Hall

**Adams Media**

**New York London Toronto Sydney New Delhi**

**Adams**media

Adams Media
An Imprint of Simon & Schuster, Inc.
57 Littlefield Street
Avon, Massachusetts 02322



For information about special discounts for bulk purchases, please contact Simon & Schuster Special Sales at 1-866-506-1949 or business@simonandschuster.com.

The Simon & Schuster Speakers Bureau can bring authors to your live event. For more information or to book an event contact the Simon & Schuster Speakers Bureau at 1-866-248-3049 or visit our website at www.simonspeakers.com.

Interior illustrations by Kurt Dolber, Eric Andrews, and Shannon Hall.

Manufactured in the United States of America

10 9 8 7 6

Library of Congress Cataloging-in-Publication Data has been applied for.

ISBN 978-1-4405-6975-3
ISBN 978-1-4405-6996-8 (ebook)



Contains material adapted and abridged from *Norman Hall's Police Exam Preparation Book, 2nd Edition* by Norman Hall, copyright © 2003 by Norman S. Hall, ISBN 978-1-58062-842-6; *Norman Hall's Firefighter Exam Preparation Book, 2nd Edition* by Norman Hall, copyright © 2003 by Norman S. Hall, ISBN 978-1-58062-932-4; *Small-Business Ownership for Creative People* by Jennifer Lawler, copyright © 2000 by Jennifer Lawler, ISBN 978-0-96392-609-8; *Songs of Life: The Meaning of Country Music* by Jennifer Lawler, copyright © 1996 by Jennifer Lawler, ISBN 978-1-88065-409-5.

# Contents

**Preface (from Norman S. Hall)** .......... 4

Introduction .......... 5

***PART 1: The Low-Down on the ASVAB*** .......... 7
CHAPTER 1: ASVAB 101 .......... 9
CHAPTER 2: Study Tips .......... 13
CHAPTER 3: Test-Taking Strategies .......... 17

***PART 2: Diagnostic Test*** .......... 21
CHAPTER 4: Diagnostic Test .......... 23
CHAPTER 5: Using the Results to Guide Your Studies .......... 81

***PART 3: Review*** .......... 83
CHAPTER 6: Word Knowledge (WK) .......... 85
CHAPTER 7: Paragraph Comprehension (PC) .......... 105
CHAPTER 8: Arithmetic Reasoning (AR) .......... 119
CHAPTER 9: Mathematics Knowledge (MK) .......... 141
CHAPTER 10: General Science (GS) .......... 165
CHAPTER 11: Electronics Information (EI) .......... 201
CHAPTER 12: Automotive and Shop Information (AS) .......... 217
CHAPTER 13: Mechanical Comprehension (MC) .......... 249
CHAPTER 14: Assembling Objects (AO) .......... 261

***PART 4: The Practice Tests*** .......... 265
CHAPTER 15: Practice Test #1 .......... 267
CHAPTER 16: Practice Test #2 .......... 331
CHAPTER 17: Practice Test #3 .......... 393
CHAPTER 18: Practice Test #4 .......... 453

**Refund Policy** .......... 510

# Preface

Congratulations on taking your first step to become part of the United States military. Your desire to enlist in the military and serve this country and its citizens is an honorable aspiration I truly respect and appreciate. It is because of people like you that we are able to enjoy our democratic form of government and the freedoms we are guaranteed by our Constitution. Thank you for choosing this book to help you achieve your goals.

Your commitment to the military can open a wide range of opportunities for your future. You may choose the military as a full-time career, or as a means of obtaining the higher education or training necessary to become employed in a well-paying profession once back in the civilian sector. The military even has programs to help cover the expenses for secondary education and specialized technical training. The key to taking advantage of what the military has to offer is highly dependent upon your performance on the Armed Services Vocational Aptitude Battery (ASVAB), particularly the group of subtests that make up the Armed Forces Qualification Test (AFQT).

Test applicants who achieve high scores have the best chance of securing their career preferences. Average to mediocre test performance can substantially restrict your options, if not preclude your admission into the military altogether. The fact that you purchased this study guide demonstrates your strong desire to succeed. My intent is to provide you with the most thorough and up-to-date information to enable you to score in the upper percentiles of applicants. You may find some of the content to be basic review; however, it can also serve to highlight potential weaknesses in given areas. Additional study will help strengthen your areas of concern, giving you the confidence for a greater chance of a successful outcome.

I have a personal stake in your success, too, and to demonstrate my commitment to you, I am offering Guaranteed Test Results—not something offered anywhere else. After using this study guide and completing your Armed Forces Qualification Test, I am guaranteeing that you will achieve a Category IIIA rating (the top 50–64 percentile) or higher, or the full purchase price of this study guide will be refunded by the publisher. (See the Refund Policy at the end of this book for further details.)

Thank you for your desire and commitment to serving in the United States military. The benefits to both you and your community are immeasurable. I am confident you will succeed in your endeavors.

—Norman S. Hall

# Introduction

The Armed Services Vocational Aptitude Battery, known as the ASVAB, is a test that predicts your likelihood of succeeding in various types of jobs, particularly those related to the military. You are required to take this exam if you plan to enlist in any branch of the United States military.

If you are planning to enlist in the military, you need to understand how your ASVAB score affects your eligibility to do various jobs. The ASVAB is a collection of subtests, and your scores on those subtests are combined in various ways to determine not just whether you're able to enlist, but what types of jobs you'll be eligible to do in the military once you have enlisted. You can read more about this in Chapter 1.

Note that in addition to your ASVAB score, your gender plays a role in the types of jobs you can qualify for in the military. The Coast Guard is the only branch of the military that does not restrict certain job categories by gender.

## MILITARY ENLISTMENT REQUIREMENTS

Your performance on the ASVAB is not the only criterion used to judge whether you can enlist in the military. Each branch of the military has specific demands. In general, you will need to:

- have at least a high school diploma. A GED is sometimes, but not always, an accepted substitute.
- be at least 17 years old. Your parents will have to agree to your enlistment if you are under 18.
- be younger than an upper-age-limit. The limit varies between 27 and 40 years of age, depending on the branch and whether you're active duty or reserve. Additional leeway is granted for former service members who are re-enlisting.
- be a U.S. citizen or resident alien.
- meet certain height requirements and body fat restrictions. If you're too tall or too short or too fat or too skinny, you won't be eligible to enlist.
- pass a physical exam. If you have certain medical conditions, you will not be eligible to enlist.

Additional considerations include marital status and parental responsibilities. If you are married to a member of the military and you have children, you may not be able to enlist. If you are a single parent, it is highly unlikely that you will be able to enlist. Other factors also play a role, such as your arrest record (if one exists), your credit record, and the state of your finances (if you can't pay your obligations with your military pay, you won't be eligible for enlistment). Drug and alcohol abuse can also prevent you from being eligible to enlist.

You can be rejected by the military if for any reason it is believed that you cannot do the job, or that you do not have the security and the best interests of the United States at heart.

## RESEARCHING MILITARY OPTIONS

If you are healthy, within the appropriate age range, and are not otherwise precluded from enlisting in the military, you can meet with a recruiter to discuss your options, although in general you will want to decide which branch of the military you wish to enlist in before talking with a recruiter. Then use an initial meeting with the recruiter to make sure that your understanding of what you can expect is accurate.

You may first want to explore the various opportunities by talking with current and former members of the military and by researching online, particularly the official sites of the military:

- U.S. Air Force: *www.af.mil*
- U.S. Army: *www.army.mil*
- U.S. Coast Guard: *www.uscg.mil*
- U.S. Marines: *www.marines.mil*
- U.S. Navy: *www.navy.mil*

The Department of Defense oversees all branches of the military and can be found at *www.defense.gov*. The DOD produces the website *www.todaysmilitary.com*, which includes a wealth of information about various branches of service. The Military.com site is also a useful clearinghouse for information, though it is not an official military site.

## GETTING READY FOR THE ASVAB

Once you decide to enlist, you will be required to take the ASVAB. Doing well on the ASVAB means you have greater options and opportunities, although just because you are eligible to do a certain job does not mean the job will be available when you enlist.

The focus of this book is to prepare you to do well on the ASVAB. If you earned good grades in high school, you should be able to do well on the ASVAB. If you had areas of difficulty, though, it is in your best interest to carefully review the information you will need to know to do well on the test.

First, read Chapters 1, 2, and 3 in Part 1. They will help you understand what the ASVAB is about and how it is used by the military. Then, take the diagnostic exam in Chapter 4 and use Chapter 5 to grade the exam and understand what your results mean.

Then, use the various review chapters in Part 3 to brush up on the areas where you have weaknesses. Take the first practice exam, grade it, and see where you've improved and where you need further work. Take the next practice exam and continue the process. By the time you've taken the fourth practice exam—which will be the fifth time you've taken the test—you should be fairly confident about your ability to succeed come test day.

So let's get started!

# PART 1
# The Low-Down on the ASVAB

In this part, you'll get all the details on how the ASVAB is used by the military, what each of the various subtests covers, how the ASVAB is scored, and how to use this book. Let's get started!

# CHAPTER 1

# ASVAB 101

The Armed Services Vocational Aptitude Battery (ASVAB) is designed to determine whether you have the knowledge and ability to succeed in the military and then to help the military place you in an appropriate job. The battery consists of a number of subtests that determine your general knowledge of subjects like math and vocabulary, as well as more specific knowledge of technical material such as basic electricity and shop materials and practices.

The type of career you wish to pursue should be in mind as you study for the ASVAB. If you'd like a technical job, you will need to be sure that you do well on the technical portions of the exam. If you'd like to be a communications specialist, you will have to do well on the verbal subtests.

## WHAT'S ON THE ASVAB

Let's break it down, starting with the fact that you may be taking any one of three different ASVAB tests. There is a student test that many high school students take for career-counseling purposes. That one is not used for enlistment purposes, so you can pretty much disregard it. The other two ASVAB versions test the same material, but in slightly different ways. There is the pencil-and-paper version of the ASVAB, which is given—you guessed it—on paper, with you marking the correct answers with a pencil. Then there is a computer version, called the Computer Adaptive Test, or CAT-ASVAB. You take this one on a computer.

Why two different versions? Not all testing sites are equipped to offer the computer version. Sometimes a Military Entrance Test (MET) site is a high-school cafeteria. If you're sent to take the ASVAB at a Military Entrance Processing Station (MEPS), you'll most likely take the computer version, and you may also complete other aspects of enlistment at the same time, such as getting a physical exam.

### The Subtests and What They Measure

For you to be eligible to enlist in the military, you must score well on the Armed Forces Qualifying Test (AFQT). This is a composite of the scores you achieve on four of the subtests of the ASVAB. You can score poorly on the other subtests and yet be eligible to enlist as long as you do well on the subtests that make up the AFQT. But if you fail the AFQT, you can't enlist regardless of how well you do on the other subtests.

Thus, doing well on the AFQT is your main goal. The AFQT is made up of math and verbal subtests:

- Word Knowledge (WK). This is basically a vocabulary test.
- Paragraph Comprehension (PC). This is a reading comprehension test.
- Arithmetic Reasoning (AR). This tests your basic math skills using word problems.
- Mathematics Knowledge (MK). This determines your understanding of algebra and geometry.

In addition, there are technical subtests that measure your knowledge of other subject areas. Doing well on these subtests will go a long way towards helping you get the job you want in the military.

- General Science (GS). This test covers chemistry, biology, and basic physics.
- Electronics Information (EI). This one covers basic electricity and electronics.

- Automotive and Shop Information (AS). This test covers information about motor vehicles, engines, and tools.
- Mechanical Comprehension (MC). This test covers the principles of machinery—how machines work and mechanical principles.
- Assembling Objects (AO). This is a test of your spatial relations abilities.

### Paper Test Versus Computer Test

In addition to the paper test being on paper and the computer test being on computer, the pencil-and-paper ASVAB differs from the CAT-ASVAB in a couple of important ways. One of these ways is in how many questions you have to answer and how much time you have to answer them. Generally speaking, you have fewer questions and more time (per question) on the computer version than on the paper version.

On the pencil-and-paper version, the Automotive and Shop Information subtest is given as one subtest with 25 questions. On the CAT version, it is given as two subtests with 11 questions each. There are other similar variations: On the pencil-and-paper version, you have 25 questions on the General Science subtest and 11 minutes to answer them, whereas on the CAT version you have 16 questions and 8 minutes to answer them.

But the main difference is that the computer version is adaptive. It changes the questions it asks based on how well you are answering. So, the first question of each subtest will be of medium difficulty. If you answer it correctly, the next question will be harder. But if you answer that harder question correctly, it's worth more on your final score. If you answer the first (medium-difficulty) question incorrectly, then the next question you are asked will be easier. If you answer it correctly, great, but an easier question is worth less in the scoring. You will do better to be sure that you're answering the first few questions correctly, to get a higher score. The total number of questions doesn't vary, just their difficulty.

On the pencil-and-paper version, everyone gets the same questions to answer.

### How the ASVAB Is Scored

The question of how the ASVAB is scored is more complex than you'd think. The pencil-and-paper test is scored somewhat differently from the CAT-ASVAB (as described in the section on "Paper Test Versus Computer Test," the computer test will give you harder questions if you can answer them, and thus you'll get higher scores).

There are raw scores, which are how many questions you got right and how many you got wrong. There are standard scores, which are weighted according to the difficulty of the questions you answered correctly. There are composite scores, which are your scores on various subtests added together. And there are percentile scores, which compare your efforts to those of the control group of many thousands of people who took the ASVAB as part of a survey about 20 years ago. Add to that the fact that every branch of the military requires different scores for enlistment and for various jobs, and that these scores can change depending on the military's needs, and you have a confusing situation indeed!

However, keep in mind that your AFQT score is what matters to enlistment. At the time that this book went to press, if you have a high school diploma, and a percentile score of 50 or higher on the AFQT, then you would be eligible for enlistment (assuming that you had no other problem that would disqualify you). If you have a GED, you will need to score higher than that, and may not be eligible to enlist at all. One way around this problem is to succeed at a semester or two of college.

The scores of the various subtests are used to determine your eligibility for certain jobs. For example, you might need to score well on General Science, Electronics Information, and Mechanical Knowledge to do a certain job.

Suppose, for example, that you want to repair airplanes for the army. There is a specific job, called a "military occupational specialty" (MOS), for this role. For instance, Aircraft Electrician is a job you can do in the army. To be eligible for it, you have to score well on the following subtests: Automotive and Shop, Mechanical Comprehension, and Electronics Information. If you want to be an Intelligence Specialist in the Marine Corps, you would need to do well on Paragraph Comprehension, Word Knowledge, and Arithmetic Reasoning. You would also need to do well in an entry course and pass a security check. Your recruiter can help you understand the demands of various military occupations.

## WHERE AND HOW TO TAKE THE TEST

You can take the ASVAB when you are in high school. As long as you were at least a junior when you took the test, it can be used for your enlistment in the military. However, if you took the test more than two years ago, you will have to retake it. Your high school career counseling center or guidance counselor should be able to tell you if your school offers the ASVAB and when you can take it. There is no fee for taking the test.

If the ASVAB is not offered at your high school, the counselor should be able to arrange for you to take it elsewhere. If that's not possible, or you're not in high school, then you'll simply need to contact a military recruiter and he or she will be able to schedule your ASVAB.

If your recruiter does set up a time for you to take the ASVAB, you are not required to enlist in the military. But you can expect the ASVAB to be required if you do decide to enlist.

The recruiter may send you to a Military Entrance Processing Station (MEPS) for you to take the ASVAB. If one isn't nearby, you may be sent to a Military Entrance Test (MET) site.

If you do not do well enough on the ASVAB to enter the military, or you cannot get the job you desire based on your scores, you can retake the test a month later. You can actually retake the test more than once, although after the first two retakes, you will have to wait six months between attempts, instead of one. Your recruiter or high school counselor can help you set up a retake.

# CHAPTER 2

# *Study Tips*

The ASVAB is not the kind of exam where you can hope for a high test score by conducting a study marathon the night before. You picked up this book, so you probably already know that fact.

How much time you spend preparing to take the ASVAB depends on how familiar you are with the material that will be covered. If, for example, you didn't study electronics in school but would like to have a military job where a high score on the Electronics Information subtest is required, it's better to start sooner and to consider taking a course at a local community college or at a continuing education center. If you're familiar with all of the information that might be covered on the ASVAB, then a few weeks of study before the test will help ensure that you remember everything you need to do well on the test.

## IDENTIFYING PROBLEM AREAS

The best way to plan your study program for the ASVAB is to take the diagnostic test in this book (see Chapter 4). Take it without reviewing anything first. You want a baseline read on your strengths and weaknesses. See Chapter 1 for information on how the ASVAB is scored, and the types of scores you'll need to qualify for enlistment and to be considered for various job opportunities.

Once you've taken the test and scored it, you'll have a better idea of what areas of review you need to focus on. If your Word Knowledge attempt was weak, then you can plan to spend more time improving your vocabulary. If you felt overwhelmed by the Mathematics Knowledge subtest, then it would be wise to invest additional time in reviewing that material.

If you know ahead of time that you're not interested in certain fields that require you to do well on specific subtests, then don't worry about reviewing for those portions of the exam. Spend that time on reviewing the material that more directly impacts the subtests you do need to do well on. However, be aware that many of the more desirable jobs require solid technical knowledge, which will be tested on subtests such as Mechanical Comprehension and Electronics Information.

Don't forget that the four subtests that make up the Armed Forces Qualifying Test (AFQT) are the most crucial. These subtests are Word Knowledge, Paragraph Comprehension, Arithmetic Reasoning, and Mathematics Knowledge. The AFQT determines your eligibility to enlist in the military. It doesn't matter how well you score on, say, the Automotive and Shop Information subtest if you don't do well enough on the AFQT subtests to enlist. If you struggle with any of the material on these four subtests, you will want to invest additional time in mastering the material.

## PLANNING A STUDY STRATEGY

Regular study times should be established and tailored to your comfort. Each person's schedule is different. Some people prefer to study for one or two hours at a time with intermittent breaks, while others prefer several hours of straight study. Regardless of how you study, it is important that you do it regularly, and not rely on cramming. You will remember the subject matter more easily and comprehend it better by establishing regular study habits.

*Where* you study is important, too. Eliminate any distractions that can disrupt your studies. The television, the telephone, and children can hinder quality study time. Set aside one of the rooms in your home as a study place and use it to isolate yourself from distractions. If you elect to use a bedroom as a study area, avoid lying in bed while you read. Otherwise, you may find yourself more inclined to sleep than to learn.

It is important to have a good desk, a comfortable chair, and adequate lighting; anything less can hamper studying. If studying in your home is not feasible, go to your local library or some other place that offers an environment conducive to study.

Again, be sure to get plenty of rest. It is counterproductive and slows learning if you try to study when you are overly tired. It is also important not to skip meals. Your level of concentration during the exam can suffer if you lack proper nutrition. Coffee and/or other stimulants are not recommended.

Good study habits can have a significant impact on how well you do on the exam. If you follow these few simple guidelines, you can approach the exam more relaxed and confident, two essential ingredients for top performance on any exam.

## CREATING A STUDY SCHEDULE

It's easy to put off studying if you just think, "I should review that material before I'm scheduled to take the ASVAB." Instead, create a calendar that includes time set aside for studying. Consider how well you did on the practice test, and make sure you include ample review times for those areas where you feel you need improvement. Also be sure to schedule time to take all of the practice exams. Be sure to do each exam in one sitting, as that's how you'll have to take the exam on the day of the ASVAB. Practicing ahead of time will help you be ready to sit through the entire test and do well even at the end.

See Figure 2.1 for a sample study schedule.

**Sample Study Schedule**

| Time | Monday | Tuesday | Wednesday | Thursday | Friday |
|---|---|---|---|---|---|
| 8:00 A.M. | | | | | |
| 8:30 A.M. | | | | | |
| 9:00 A.M. | | | | | |
| 9:30 A.M. | | | | | |
| 10:00 A.M. | | | | | |
| 10:30 A.M. | | | | | |
| 11:00 A.M. | | | | | |
| 11:30 A.M. | | | | | |
| 12:00 noon | | | | | |
| 12:30 P.M. | | | | | |
| 1:00 P.M. | | | | | |
| 1:30 P.M. | | | | | |
| 2:00 P.M. | | | | | |
| 2:30 P.M. | | | | | |
| 3:00 P.M. | | | | | |
| 3:30 P.M. | | | | | |
| 4:00 P.M. | | | | | |
| 4:30 P.M. | | | | | |
| 5:00 P.M. | | | | | |
| 5:30 P.M. | | | | | |
| 6:00 P.M. | | | | | |

Figure 2.1

## WHAT TO DO BEFORE, DURING, AND AFTER THE TEST

The night before test day, be sure you get plenty of sleep. Staying up late and reviewing all the study material is actually counterproductive. Cramming does not improve test performance and can increase your own nervous tension. Make sure you eat a good breakfast, but don't overdo it or you'll find yourself napping instead of answering questions. Also make sure to dress appropriately—you want to be able to focus on the test, not on the fact that the exam room is freezing, too hot, your clothes are too tight, or your feet hurt.

Give yourself plenty of time to arrive at the test site; twenty to thirty minutes early is desirable. Unforeseen events could detain you at home, or traffic congestion en route to the exam could make you late. Once the exam has been started, latecomers will not be permitted to take the test. If you haven't been to the testing site before, consider taking a practice run a day or two ahead of schedule at the same time as the exam to review traffic issues and the like.

Before you arrive to take the test, be sure to have some form of identification such as a valid driver's license. If you wear glasses or contacts, don't forget them. No personal items like bags, backpacks, calculators, or notes will be permitted in the examination room.

During the test, remember to follow the proctor's instructions carefully. If you're taking the pen-and-pencil version of the test, he or she will tell you when to start and when you can go on to the next test. If you're taking the CAT version, then you'll be able to go at your own pace, although you will have a maximum amount of time allotted for each test.

As with any standardized test, make sure you fill out the answer form correctly as you go. See Chapter 3 for more information on test-taking strategies.

After the test is over, congratulate yourself for getting through it! If you're taking the test through your high school, you'll get the results within a few weeks. If a military recruiter has arranged for you to take the test, he or she will tell you when and how you can expect to receive the results.

If you find that you did not do as well on the exam as you had hoped, you may retake the test after a one-month waiting period. Your military recruiter can help you reschedule your exam.

# CHAPTER 3

# Test-Taking Strategies

Don't let test-taking nerves result in you scoring lower on the ASVAB than you should. If you've prepared ahead of time by reviewing the information you'll need to know for each of the subtests and taken all of the practice exams in this book, you should feel confident. Remember to get enough sleep the night before and allow yourself plenty of time to get to the testing center (see Chapter 2 for more information). Keep in mind that the questions you encounter on the practice tests in this book will not be exactly the same as the ones you'll find on the actual ASVAB. However, you should be confident that if you have done well on the practice tests, you'll do well on the ASVAB itself.

Throughout this chapter, you'll find some additional tips to remember for the day of the exam.

## WATCHING THE CLOCK

Each of the subtests on the ASVAB is timed. If you're taking the pen-and-pencil version, the proctor supervising the exam will tell you when to start and when to finish. If you're taking the exam by computer, you can go at your own pace, but there is a maximum amount of time that you can spend on each subtest. Therefore, you need to be sure to give yourself enough time to answer each of the questions.

That doesn't mean you should constantly check the clock; in fact, you would do better to focus on answering the questions as carefully as you can. However, if you are not aware of how quickly time is passing, you may find that the proctor calls "Time!" before you've finished the subtest you're working on.

Good time management on the day of the test means you need to be aware of how much time you have for each subtest, and how many questions you'll need to answer in that amount of time. If you have 25 questions to answer and 11 minutes to answer them (as, for example, on the General Science subtest), then you know you can't spend much more than about twenty seconds answering each question. You can't consider the question and possible answers for very long. You simply need to pick what you think is the best answer and move along. For other subtests, you have more time per question, so you can take more time thinking over your answer before making your choice. It is better to guess at an answer and move along than to leave a lot of answers blank because you didn't have time to answer them.

## BASIC STRATEGIES

You may have a firm grip of the subject matter on the test, but if you make mistakes filling in the answer sheet, the resulting test score will not truly reflect your knowledge. It is not uncommon for test-takers to discover that they received a poor score because they made a mistake on the answer sheet or otherwise failed to follow instructions.

For pencil-and-paper versions of the ASVAB, make sure not to leave stray marks on the answer sheet, because the machine that scores the exams can misconstrue a mark as an incorrect answer. If you change your mind about any answer, be certain to erase the original answer completely. If two answers are apparently marked, the scoring machine will consider the answer incorrect. One costly mistake is marking answers that do not correspond to the question you are working on. As a simple rule, check every ten questions or so to make sure you are marking the matching answers for the corresponding question.

For the computer (CAT) version of the ASVAB, make sure that you're clicking on the correct answer choice and not accidently marking the wrong selection.

When the examiner (the proctor) gives any kind of instruction, pay attention. The examiner will explain how to properly fill in personal information that will be used to identify your exam results. He or she will explain how and when to proceed on the exam. Do not deviate in any manner from the established test procedure. If you do, you may disqualify yourself altogether.

### Using the Process of Elimination

The ASVAB is a multiple-choice exam. This type of test makes your task a bit less difficult; you know that *one* of the choices has to be correct. Even if the answer isn't immediately apparent, you may be able to eliminate some choices immediately, increasing your chances of selecting the right answer. For example, common sense or experience may tell you that a certain answer is incorrect even if you're not specifically sure why it's wrong.

When you look over test questions, be sure to read them carefully and completely. It is easy to read the first or second choice and select one of them as the correct answer without bothering to examine the remaining options. Read the entire question thoroughly and then mark your answer sheet accordingly. Pay close attention to conjunctions such as *and, but, or, when, if, because, though, whereas*, and *besides*. These key words can completely alter the meaning of a question. If you overlook one of these words, there is a good chance that you will select the wrong answer.

Try reading the answers before you read the question so that when you read the question you'll know the type of answer being sought. A math question with answers in square feet will tell you that you're looking for the area of an object, whereas one with answers in cubic feet will tell you you're looking for volume.

### Picking the Best Answer

For all of the questions on the ASVAB, you are supposed to pick the *best* answer. That means more than one possible answer could be correct, but one of them is *most* correct. For example, on the Word Knowledge subtest, two possible answers for the definition of a word could be close in meaning to the word, but one of them will be a better answer than the other. Your job is to make sure you pick the better answer.

This is also one of the reasons why you need to carefully read all of the answer choices before selecting one. Sometimes answer "A" may be correct, but answer "D" is *more* correct. Sometimes two answers are correct (for example "A" and "B") and one answer choice spells this out ("Both A and B"). Be sure you understand all of your options before picking the best one.

For the computer (CAT) version of the ASVAB, remember that you're likely to score higher on the test if you answer the first several questions correctly, because you'll be given harder questions worth more as you go along. So it's worth taking a little extra time to get those right.

### Guessing the Answer

When you don't know the answer to a question, guessing can be a good strategy. However, the effectiveness of this approach changes depending on which version of the test you're taking.

Remember that for the paper-and-pencil version, you can go back to earlier questions in the subtest, so if Question #6 stumps you, move on to Question #7, and then go back to Question #6 at the end. That way you'll have the chance to get as many right as possible. If you're running out of time, you can try guessing the likely answer and then moving on to the next question. There is no penalty for wrong answers on the pencil-and-paper version of the ASVAB.

For questions you skip and intend to go back to, as a timesaver, you can cross out in the test booklet the options that you know are wrong. When you return to that question, you can quickly focus on the remaining selections. If you skip a question, be sure to skip the corresponding answer blank, too.

For the pencil-and-paper version, it makes sense to answer the questions you know the answers to first, then go back and solve those that you're less familiar with. If word problems give you trouble, save them for the end so that you can be sure to get as many questions right as possible.

If you're taking the computer (CAT) version of the ASVAB, you can't go back to questions you've skipped. So, if you find that you're spending too long trying to decide on the answer to a question, pick your best guess and go on. Guessing on the CAT-ASVAB doesn't penalize you per se (some tests penalize you for guessing by subtracting more for a wrong answer than for no answer at all), but the test is designed so that if you answer a question incorrectly, the next question is easier. That next question is also worth less in computing your score than a harder question. If you get a question right, the next question is harder, and you get a higher score for answering harder questions than you do for answering easier questions.

As a rule, the first choice you select is the correct one. Statistics show that answers changed are typically wrong. All too frequently, people read too much into a question and obscure the proper choice. Mark the first answer that seems apparent.

Be sure you carefully read word problems to make sure you are solving the right question. Word problems often contain extra information that isn't needed to solve the problem. Be aware that answers will often include several possibilities that are almost right, which will make it harder to estimate the correct answer. However, estimating is still an option to help you rule out obviously wrong answers, especially if you are running short on time.

# PART 2
# Diagnostic Test

In this part, you'll take a diagnostic test before beginning your ASVAB review (Chapter 4). Once you've graded the test, you'll have a better sense of what areas require the most attention (see Chapter 5). You can plan your study program based on what the diagnostic test tells you about your skills.

See Chapters 1, 2, and 3 to find out more about the various subtests and how they impact your ability to enlist in the military and your eligibility for various jobs.

# CHAPTER 4

# *Diagnostic Test*

Take the diagnostic test just as you would any standardized test. Use the answer sheet at the end of this chapter to record your answers. Set a timer for the amount of time allotted for each subtest, take them in the order in which they're given, and try to do your best. Then turn to Chapter 5 to grade your efforts and understand how to use the results.

## GENERAL SCIENCE

You have 11 minutes to answer the 25 questions on this subtest.

1. Astronomy is the study of

   A. asteroids
   B. matter and energy
   C. space and the universe
   D. the earth's atmosphere

2. Absolute zero is the same as

   A. 0°F
   B. 0°C
   C. 32°F
   D. 0 K

3. A microgram (μg) is equivalent to

   A. one millionth of a gram
   B. one billionth of a gram
   C. one tenth of a gram
   D. one thousandth of a gram

4. Of the answers below, which is *not* a requirement for natural selection?

   A. Production of more offspring than are likely to survive
   B. Inheritance of traits from parents
   C. A hospitable environment
   D. Traits varying from offspring to offspring

5. The process of moving fluids into and out of a cell membrane is called

   A. osmosis
   B. mitosis
   C. fluid transfer
   D. ionization

6. An ecosystem is another word for a(n)

   A. habitat
   B. food chain
   C. biological community
   D. adaptable environment

7. Blood cells are produced in your body's

   A. liver
   B. pancreas
   C. heart
   D. bone marrow

8. The most accurate word to describe a state of not taking in any oxygen at all is

A. hypothermia
B. apoxia
C. hypoxia
D. aerobia

9. Hemoglobin is a protein in your blood that

A. gives white blood cells their color
B. tries to eliminate disease-causing bacteria
C. binds to oxygen and carries it throughout your circulatory system
D. clots your blood

10. If one parent has a pair of genes Aa, and the other has the pair AA, what is the likelihood that the offspring of these parents will have the pair aa?

A. 100%
B. 25%
C. 50%
D. 0%

11. Good food sources for calcium include

A. beef, chicken, leafy vegetables
B. citrus, green vegetables, nuts
C. vegetable oil, fish, chicken
D. dairy, tofu, spinach

12. In geologic time, we are currently living in which epoch?

A. Holocene
B. Pleistocene
C. Eocene
D. Paleocene

13. Seawater possesses which of the following properties?

A. greater buoyancy than fresh water
B. poor conduction of electricity, making it a good insulator
C. good conduction of electricity, making it a good conductor
D. both A and C

14. A tsunami is a type of

A. wind
B. wave
C. current
D. tide

15. When an air mass become unstable and starts rising in the atmosphere, what weather event is likely to result?

    A. Massive snowfall
    B. Thunderstorm
    C. Sunny, warm day
    D. Sudden frost

16. The smallest planet in the solar system is

    A. Earth
    B. Venus
    C. Mercury
    D. Neptune

17. Water is an example of a(n)

    A. element
    B. atom
    C. particle
    D. compound

18. An element with a different number of neutrons than protons is

    A. an isotope of that element
    B. the inverse of that element
    C. a molecule
    D. not chemically possible

19. A reaction that causes A + BC to become AB + C is called

    A. combustion
    B. synthesis
    C. displacement
    D. decomposition

20. Newton's Second Law, also called the Law of Force, can be represented by the following mathematical formula:

    A. Force = Mass × Acceleration
    B. Acceleration = Force × Mass
    C. Force = Mass ÷ Acceleration
    D. Force = Acceleration × Trajectory

21. A signal with a wave frequency of 10 Hertz produces how many cycles per minute?

    A. 10
    B. 100
    C. 60
    D. 600

22. The absence of light waves creates the color

A. white
B. black
C. blue
D. red

23. Some sound-canceling headphones produce sound waves in order to "cancel out" incoming sound waves. They do this by producing:

A. sound waves that are inverted from the incoming waves
B. sound waves that are in phase with the incoming waves
C. lower-pitched waves that cover up the sound of the incoming waves
D. higher-pitched waves that distract you from the sound of the incoming waves

24. A hypothesis differs from a theory in that

A. hypothesis is a question and a theory is a statement
B. theory cannot be proven but a hypothesis can
C. hypothesis cannot be proven but a theory can
D. theory is a hypothesis that has been proven to be true

25. According to classical taxonomy classification, forms of life can be grouped into categories such as

A. kingdoms, phyla, and species
B. phyla, families, and troops
C. animal, vegetable, and bacterial
D. organic and inorganic

## ARITHMETIC REASONING

You will have 30 questions and 39 minutes to answer them.

1. Given $17\frac{3}{4} - 8\frac{1}{4} = x$, which of the following equals $x$?

   A. $9\frac{3}{4}$
   B. $9\frac{1}{8}$
   C. $9\frac{1}{2}$
   D. 9

2. According to the directions on a bottle of liquid fertilizer, it is supposed to be mixed in water at the rate of 3 tablespoons per gallon before applying to a garden. How many tablespoons of fertilizer would be required for 20 gallons of water?

   A. 20
   B. 40
   C. 60
   D. 80

3. If a screw has a pitch that requires it to be turned 30 times to advance it two inches, what ratio correctly reflects the relationship?

   A. 2:30
   B. 30:1
   C. 2:15
   D. 15:1

4. Assume a test-taker scored a 95% on the exam and answered 152 questions correctly. How many test questions were on the exam?

   A. 175
   B. 160
   C. 157
   D. 152

5. If $9\frac{1}{4} + 18\frac{1}{2} + 20\frac{1}{4} = x$, which of the following equals $x$?

   A. $48\frac{1}{4}$
   B. $48\frac{1}{2}$
   C. $43\frac{1}{4}$
   D. 48

6. If someone were to withdraw $237.00 from a savings account that totaled $3,000.00, what percent of money is left in the account?

   A. 92.1%
   B. 83.7%
   C. 94.1%
   D. 89.7%

7. Brian was recently promoted at his job. He now earns twice the hourly wage he was earning last year. If Brian's current wage is $23.50 per hour, what was his hourly wage 3 years ago?

   A. $11.75
   B. $11.25
   C. $10.75
   D. $9.25

8. It takes Fred 3 hours to prep 125 sandwiches at the sandwich shop. When John performs the same task, however, it takes him an extra hour. If both of these individuals were assigned to do the job together, how long would it take both of them to produce 125 sandwiches?

   A. 1 hour and 35 minutes
   B. 1 hour and 43 minutes
   C. 2 hours and 15 minutes
   D. 2 hours and 22 minutes

9. A 600-mile trip could be driven by a motorist in 10 hours with an average speed of 60 mph. On the presumption that this motorist wanted to make the same trip in 8 hours, how much faster would he/she have to drive?

   A. 13.3 mph
   B. 14.7 mph
   C. 15 mph
   D. 20 mph

10. A water tank has a maximum capacity of 600 cubic meters. However, internal corrosion is responsible for significant leakage. It is assessed that a constant half-cubic meter of water leaks every minute. If a 3-inch water line can recharge the tank at the rate of 12 cubic meters per minute, how much time would be required to fill the tank to its capacity?

    A. 45.25 minutes
    B. 48.6 minutes
    C. 52.17 minutes
    D. 59.7 minutes

11. A taxi was dispatched from the yard to the train station at 9:30 A.M. and traveled 45 mph along State Highway 101. At 11:00 A.M., a hired van was dispatched from the same location and traveled the same route, averaging 60 mph. At what time would the van catch up to the taxi?

    A. 3:30 P.M.
    B. 4:45 P.M.
    C. 5:00 P.M.
    D. 6:00 P.M.

12. Assume two individuals live 350 miles apart. Both people get into their cars at 8:00 A.M. and travel toward one another, with Driver A going 15 mph faster than Driver B. If they pass each other at 11:00 A.M., how fast was Driver A going?

    A. 70.12 mph
    B. 68.75 mph
    C. 67.15 mph
    D. 65.83 mph

13. How many liters of pure benzene must be added to 20 liters of solution that is currently 60% benzene to strengthen it to a solution of 75% benzene?

A. 12 liters
B. 13.25 liters
C. 14.1 liters
D. 15 liters

14. What is the area of a rectangle if its dimensions are 6 feet long by 4 feet wide?

A. 10 square feet
B. 64 square feet
C. 24 cubic feet
D. 24 square feet

15. $8\frac{3}{4} \div 2\frac{1}{2} = x$. Which of the following equals $x$?

A. $1\frac{7}{8}$
B. $3\frac{1}{8}$
C. $3\frac{1}{2}$
D. $4\frac{1}{10}$

16. The number 13 is 75% of what number?

A. 15.49
B. 16.35
C. 16.99
D. 17.33

17. If a township is a square section of territory and one side is known to be 6 miles in length, how many square miles would the township occupy?

A. 16 square miles
B. 18 square miles
C. 36 square miles
D. 42 square miles

18. In town, three gas stations charge slightly different prices for a gallon of gas. At Station A, it costs \$3.99, at Station B, it costs \$3.79, and at Station C, it costs \$3.89. What is the mean cost of gas in town?

A. \$3.89
B. \$3.99
C. \$3.79
D. \$3.85

19. If the houses in the Sutcliffe neighborhood sold for the following prices, what is the median price of a house in that neighborhood?

1100 Oak: $180,000
1215 Pine: $223,000
1315 Elm: $225,500
1032 Ash: $220,000
1205 Oak: $187,000

A. $200,000
B. $207,100
C. $225,500
D. $220,000

20. If Anna invests $1,000 in an investment that returns an annual rate of 4.5% interest, what will her investment be worth in 12 months?

A. $1450
B. $1045
C. $1540
D. $45

21. Mikayla's car gets 22 miles per gallon of gas used. Gas costs $3.89 per gallon, and her tank is empty. If she needs to drive to her grandmother's house 350 miles away, how much will the gas to get there cost her?

A. $35.00
B. $85.58
C. $15.91
D. $61.85

22. $15.75 \div 4.12 = x$. Which of the following equals $x$?

A. 3.822
B. 3.283
C. 3.023
D. 3.803

23. A rectangular garden plot has a perimeter of 14 meters. If the width is 2.5 meters, then how long is it?

A. 5 meters
B. 14 meters
C. 4.5 meters
D. 9 meters

24. The fraction $\frac{3}{7}$ represents what percentage?

A. 41.85%
B. 42.85%
C. 48.25%
D. 43.35%

25. Military recruit Morris was working out to get into shape for enlistment. The exercise regimen included sit-ups, pull-ups, and push-ups. If he can currently do 58 push-ups, which is 7 more than three times the number of push-ups he did when he started the program, how many push-ups could he do originally?

A. 14
B. 15
C. 16
D. 17

26. $9 \bullet 5.2 \div 18.76 = x$. Which of the following equals $x$?

A. 0.40
B. 15.75
C. 28.06
D. 2.49

27. $6.75 + 8.372 \bullet 3.14 = x$. Which of the following equals $x$?

A. 47.48
B. 33.04
C. 37.48
D. 34.03

28. Coty has a Malamute and an Irish Setter. The Malamute eats more than the setter in a ratio of 3:2. If Coty feeds the dogs a total of 12.5 cups of dry dog food, how much does the Malamute get in his bowl?

A. 7.5
B. 2.5
C. 12.5
D. 5

29. Last year, 15 workers received a 5% merit raise. This year, 18 workers received the merit raise. What is the percent change in the number of workers receiving raises this year versus last year?

A. 30%
B. 120%
C. 1.2%
D. 20%

30. What is the prime factorization of 18?

A. $9 \times 2$
B. $3 \times 3 \times 2$
C. $6 \times 3$
D. 1,8

## WORD KNOWLEDGE

**You'll have 35 questions and 11 minutes to answer them.**

1. Exigent most nearly means
   A. broad and far reaching
   B. extenuating
   C. requiring immediate action
   D. unfortunate

2. James made a cursory search of the classroom for out-of-place materials before leaving for the day. Cursory most nearly means
   A. extensive
   B. thorough
   C. superficial
   D. detailed

3. Regina used a question about a work assignment as a pretext for calling a friend from work. Pretext most nearly means
   A. precondition
   B. means
   C. rule
   D. excuse

4. Integrity most nearly means
   A. moral character
   B. superiority
   C. fairness
   D. improbity

5. Imminent most nearly means
   A. justifiable
   B. impending
   C. remote
   D. irrelevant

6. The landmark case would serve as a precedent for future court rulings. Precedent most nearly means
   A. source of confusion
   B. majority view
   C. visible reminder
   D. none of the above

7. Intangible most nearly means
   A. insignificant
   B. invaluable
   C. not corporeal
   D. white collar

8. When deciding on a course of treatment, Janine told her doctor that cost was immaterial. Immaterial most nearly means
   A. not pertinent
   B. admissible
   C. substantive
   D. relevant

9. Indifferent most nearly means
   A. attentive
   B. apathetic
   C. intolerant
   D. indignant

10. Cheryl was quite overt in her sexual advances toward her client. Overt most nearly means
    A. shy
    B. blunt
    C. conspicuous
    D. slow

11. There can be fairly substantial disparities in what engineers earn depending on where they live and work. Disparities most nearly means
    A. penalties
    B. similarities
    C. compensations
    D. differences

12. Misconstrued most nearly means
    A. misinterpreted
    B. judged
    C. criticized
    D. analyzed

13. Incompetence most nearly means

A. inability
B. inhibition
C. incongruity
D. disregard

14. It is imperative that instructors clearly state their course objectives. Imperative most nearly means

A. unimportant
B. immaterial
C. compulsory
D. considerate

15. Mr. Miller experienced some degree of trepidation every time he had to talk with an employee about his or her performance. Trepidation most nearly means

A. having power
B. hesitation
C. quandary
D. trembling

16. The buildings in the downtown core were pretty dilapidated. Dilapidated most nearly means

A. modern
B. tall
C. neglected
D. new

17. Ambiguous most nearly means

A. infallible
B. uncertain
C. argumentative
D. interesting

18. Lawyers should be taught not to act condescendingly toward their clients. Condescending most nearly means

A. discourteous
B. harsh
C. unprofessional
D. patronizing

19. The building inspector confirmed that there were insufficient means of egress in the case of a fire. Egress most nearly means

A. entrance
B. exit
C. approach
D. attack

20. Expedite most nearly means

A. deter
B. speed the progress of
C. prevent congestion
D. monitor

21. Her neighbor's abhorrent behavior made Cecily want to move. Abhorrent most nearly means

A. loud
B. intrusive
C. repulsive
D. crabby

22. Matthew didn't want to broach the subject of finances with his wife. Broach most nearly means

A. bring up
B. argue about
C. lie about
D. respond to

23. Transact most nearly means

A. conduct business
B. camouflage
C. count
D. create

24. Melinda gave a sophisticated presentation. Sophisticated most nearly means

A. complicated
B. simplistic
C. colorful
D. experienced

25. <u>Vitality</u> most nearly means

A. importance
B. livelihood
C. liveliness
D. optimism

26. The citizens felt veracity was the most important quality in a political representative. <u>Veracity</u> most nearly means

A. wisdom
B. truthfulness
C. intelligence
D. diplomacy

27. <u>Surreptitious</u> most nearly means

A. open
B. clear
C. covert
D. amid

28. Mandy filled out the requisite forms to register her car. <u>Requisite</u> most nearly means

A. necessary
B. extra
C. excessive
D. complex

29. Rafael was known for his mordant wit. <u>Mordant</u> most nearly means

A. depressing
B. inappropriate
C. gentle
D. sharp

30. <u>Juncture</u> most nearly means

A. complication
B. intersection
C. point
D. connection

31. Simon's lapse wasn't noticed by his coworkers. <u>Lapse</u> most nearly means

A. omission
B. absence
C. forgetfulness
D. attention

32. The series was on hiatus for the time being. <u>Hiatus</u> most nearly means

A. schedule
B. record
C. notice
D. break

33. Michael's uncle was garrulous in company. <u>Garrulous</u> most nearly means

A. talkative
B. reserved
C. silly
D. quiet

34. Some actors are notorious for their lifestyles. <u>Notorious</u> most nearly means

A. notable
B. infamous
C. well-regarded
D. pitied

35. <u>Intrinsic</u> most nearly means

A. infallible
B. worth
C. inside
D. inherent

## PARAGRAPH COMPREHENSION

You'll have 15 questions and 13 minutes to answer them.

1. Ethylene oxide is a clear, colorless, volatile liquid with an ethereal odor. The vapors may burn inside a container. The vapors are irritating to the eyes, skin, and respiratory system. Prolonged contact with the skin may result in delayed burns. It is lighter than water and soluble in water. The vapors are heavier than air.

   According to this paragraph, which of the following choices is not recognized as a symptom stemming from ethylene oxide vapor exposure?

   A. Eye irritation
   B. Skin irritation or burns
   C. Irritation of the respiratory system
   D. Loss of muscular function

2. According to the National Safety Council, each year twenty times more deaths within the United States are caused by fires than by tornadoes, floods, earthquakes, and hurricanes combined.

   What can we deduce from this statement?

   A. Fires are more lethal by comparison.
   B. Tornadoes, floods, earthquakes, and hurricanes are taken for granted by most people.
   C. People are better able to cope with natural weather phenomena than fire.
   D. Statistically there are many more fires than natural weather or geophysical disasters.

3. The position of office manager requires an applicant to have good communication skills (written and oral), strong computer aptitude, the ability to work well under pressure, the ability to work with others and to follow direction, plus self-motivation and a willingness to work hard. Three years' previous experience is desired but not mandatory.

   According to this passage, an applicant must

   A. have three years' experience to apply
   B. have a strong math background
   C. be self-motivated
   D. pass a drug-screening test

4. A general partnership is a business with two or more principle partners. The partners, called general partners, agree on each person's financial responsibility, each person's duties, and each person's compensation. A general partnership doesn't protect the owners from business-related lawsuits. If one partner gets sued while acting in any capacity for the business, the other partner is equally at risk. Since personal wealth and income is not protected, the spouses of partners can be affected by a lawsuit or bankruptcy.

   According to this passage, a general partnership

   A. protects personal wealth
   B. leverages tax loopholes
   C. includes at least one partner
   D. doesn't protect the owners from business-related lawsuits

5. One possible investment to consider is a CD (a certificate of deposit). When you invest in a CD, the bank guarantees you a specified interest rate if you promise to leave your money in the bank for a set period of time. You decide what this period is up front. The longer the period, the higher the interest rate. You can invest in thirty-day CDs, sixty-day CDs, five-year CDs, ten-year CDs, and others. At the end of the set period of time, the maturity date arrives, which means you can withdraw your money and the interest it earned, or you can reinvest the money and its interest in another CD or another investment type. If you need your money before the maturity date, you can withdraw it, but you have to pay a penalty and probably won't see any of the interest you had been promised.

   A good title for this passage would be

   A. Investing Basics
   B. The ABCs of CDs
   C. Comparing Investment Options
   D. How to Withdraw Money from a CD

6. In some cultures, dancing, chanting, and pantomime are rituals designed to influence the spirits, gods, or nature by imitation. Some so-called "sympathetic magic" is based on the correspondence of items. A wax image, for instance, imitates the real person. Such magic can be strengthened by adding an actual part of the real person to the wax image—hair or nails or pieces of clothing. The theory of correspondence also means that if, for instance, a plant leaf is shaped like a human liver, it will somehow be efficacious if you used the plant by eating it or applying it to the body.

   Based on this passage, you can assume that "sympathetic magic" is

   A. a type of imitative magic
   B. based on caring about other people
   C. a way to generate a common feeling among a group
   D. a method for creating harmony

7. The Middle Ages in Europe covered a lengthy period of time, from about A.D. 500 to A.D. 1500. We are used to a fast-paced world with revolutions in science and technology happening almost overnight. With those changes come rapidly changing social attitudes. But it was different in the Middle Ages. Generation after generation lived in much the same way, with the same tools, the same attitudes, and the same beliefs. Thus, the peasant in the twelfth century sat down to an evening meal much like the laborer in the fifteenth century. They ate the same bread, drank the same ale, even said the same blessing.

   According to this passage, social change

   A. comes slowly
   B. is connected with revolutions in science and technology
   C. was discouraged in the Middle Ages
   D. can be detrimental to social order

8. When she wrote what would become a wildly popular and successful book on military ethics, her editor changed her name so that her book would appear to have been written by a man. Widowed at age twenty-five, she turned to writing as a way to support herself and her three young children, writing numerous works in many genres. She became a well-known poet and the official biographer to the king. Her name is Christine de Pizan, and she was born in 1365.

   The author wrote the passage using this method of organization because

   A. the impact of the last sentence is heightened by including that information at the end
   B. who the name of the person is and when she lived is unimportant
   C. chronological order is a common way to organize information
   D. comparison/contrast is a good way to highlight differences

9. During the Renaissance, neoclassical ideas were the fashion. The works of Aristotle and Plato were copied and circulated. This taste for Greco-Roman classics endured for two hundred years.

   According to this passage,

   A. after the end of the Renaissance, no one was interested in Aristotle and Plato
   B. Aristotle and Plato were much-admired Renaissance writers
   C. the Renaissance lasted for two hundred years
   D. Neoclassical ideas were favored during the Renaissance

10. An effective persuasive paper is one that argues the author's position using outside sources of information to support his or her claims. Other elements of an effective persuasive paper include a clearly stated thesis, main points that support the argument, and a logical response to counter-claims.

    According to this passage, an effective persuasive paper

    A. does not include the author's opinion
    B. uses outside information to support points
    C. should ignore counter-claims
    D. should not go on too long

11. A ballad tells a story with a beginning, a middle, and an end, while a lyric song tries to capture a moment, an emotion, or a mood. The lyric tends to supersede the ballad in technique, sophistication, and creativity.

    The author of this passage used

    A. comparison and contrast to discuss ballads and lyric songs
    B. chronological order to explain the information
    C. a step-by-step organization to show how the process is accomplished
    D. an inverted pyramid style to write the piece

12. Self-defense strategies come in four basic varieties: planning and setting boundaries; nonviolent actions; basic physical techniques (which require little or no preparation); and advanced physical techniques (which require some practice).

    According to this passage,

    A. self-defense strategies involve physical violence
    B. nonviolent actions are never useful
    C. some physical techniques require practice
    D. the types of strategies are organized by order of effectiveness

13. Alchemy is an ancient science dedicated to finding the substance that would turn base metal into gold, and finding the substance that would extend life. Although based on suspect theories, alchemy is the forerunner of modern chemistry. Alchemy derived from the Aristotelian belief that all matter tended toward perfection. Since gold was seen as the most perfect of metals, it was assumed that other metals turned into gold as they became more perfect. It was believed that with sufficient expertise, alchemists could duplicate this process. The substance or object that was believed to bring about this change was called the philosopher's stone. Alchemists also believed that if they combined the right substances in the right quantities they would discover the elixir of life that would prolong human life for many years.

    According to this passage,

    A. the two main goals of alchemy were to turn metals into gold and prolong life
    B. volatile substances were used in alchemy
    C. alchemy was a type of quackery that made no significant contribution to human knowledge
    D. alchemy is a fairly recent invention

14. The Aztec empire existed in central and southern Mexico, and flourished from the fourteenth to the sixteenth century. The Aztecs created sophisticated military and government administrations. They allied with other groups, creating an extensive empire. A number of provinces, petty kingdoms, and tribes were subsumed under the empire as the Aztecs expanded their territories throughout the fifteenth century.

    According to this passage,

    A. it can be assumed that Aztecs created an empire through alliance and war
    B. the arrival of the Spanish destroyed the Aztec empire
    C. Aztecs were indifferent about expanding their territory
    D. overzealous territorial expansion explains the failure of the Aztec empire

15. Boëthius was a Roman philosopher born around 480, who at first found favor with Theodoric, the Ostrogothic king of Italy, and was granted the title of patrician. By 510, he also held a consulship and served as head of Theodoric's civil service. In 523, he was accused of treason and imprisoned. While awaiting his trial and subsequent execution, he wrote *The Consolation of Philosophy*, a much-admired classic. He was executed in 524.

    According to this passage,

    A. Boëthius was imprisoned and executed for treason.
    B. Roman philosophers often challenged the status quo.
    C. Theodoric never liked Boëthius and had it in for him from the start.
    D. the Ostrogoths invaded Rome in 510.

## MATHEMATICS KNOWLEDGE

You'll have 25 questions and 24 minutes to answer them.

**1. What is the circumference of a gear that has a $5\frac{7}{8}$ inch diameter?**

A. 18.05 inches
B. 16.57 inches
C. 19.45 inches
D. 18.46 inches

**2. If a triangle has a base of 8 feet and a height of 3.5 feet, what is its area?**

A. 12 square feet
B. 14 square feet
C. 16 square feet
D. 20 square feet

**3. If a rectangular object is 20 feet long by 15 feet wide and has a height of 4 inches, what is its approximate volume?**

A. 1,200 cubic feet
B. 1,200 square feet
C. 100 cubic feet
D. 100 square feet

**4. If one side of a cube measures 36 inches, what is its volume?**

A. 46,000 square inches
B. 46,656 cubic inches
C. 46,656 cubic yards
D. 1.5 cubic yards

**5. If a fully inflated basketball has a diameter of 12 inches, how much volume would it contain?**

A. 904.78 cubic inches
B. 673.54 cubic inches
C. 509.78 cubic inches
D. 475 cubic inches

**6. If a can has a height of 16 inches and a volume of 1,256.64 cubic inches, what is its diameter?**

A. 10 inches
B. 11 inches
C. 12 inches
D. 12.5 inches

**7. The polynomial $x+3y^2-9+3y^3$ written in standard form would be:**

A. $x=6y^5-9$
B. $-9+x+3y^2+3y^3$
C. $x-9+6y$
D. $3y^3+3y^2+x-9$

8. If $10y < 40$, which of the following is true?

A. $y = 10$
B. $y = 4$
C. $y < 4$
D. $y \leq 4$

9. What is the product of $(x+3)(x-2)$?

A. $x^2 + 1$

B. $x^2 + x - 6$

C. $x^2 + 3x - 2$

D. $2x + 1$

10. Solve for $x$: $8x - 24 = -8$.

A. $x = 2$
B. $x = 4$
C. $x = -2$
D. $x = 1$

11. Which of the following equations will form a straight line when graphed?

A. $2n + 3 = y$
B. $2n^2 = y$
C. $\sqrt{x} + 32 = y$
D. $x^3 + x = y$

12. Solve the inequality $-3x > 6$.

A. $x = 2$
B. $x > -2$
C. $x < -2$
D. $x \geq 2$

13. Evaluate the expression $2x + (3x)^2 - x + 7x^3$.

A. $7x^3 + 6x^2 + x$

B. $7x^3 + (5x)^2 - x$

C. $13x^3$

D. $7x^3 + (3x)^2 + x$

14. Solve for $x$: $3x - 9 = 27$.

A. $x = 3$
B. $x = 12$
C. $x = 36$
D. $x = 18$

15. Solve for $x$: $\frac{1}{3}x = 9$.

    A. $x = 9$
    B. $x = 3$
    C. $x = 27$
    D. $x = 36$

16. Solve for $x$: $\frac{x}{8} = \frac{2}{x}$.

    A. $x = 4$
    B. $x = \frac{1}{2}$
    C. $x = 3$
    D. $x = 16$

17. A recipe requires flour and sugar in a 3:1 ratio. If the flour required is $2\frac{3}{4}$ cup, how much sugar is required?

    A. $\frac{1}{4}$ cup
    B. 1 cup
    C. $\frac{11}{12}$ cup
    D. $\frac{3}{4}$ cup

18. Add the fractions $\frac{x}{3} + \frac{2}{5}$.

    A. $\frac{2+x}{8}$
    B. $\frac{6}{5x}$
    C. $\frac{5x}{6}$
    D. $\frac{5x+6}{15}$

19. Divide the fractions $\frac{x+3}{x^3} \div \frac{6}{x-3}$.

    A. $\frac{6}{x^3}$
    B. $\frac{x^2-9}{6x^3}$
    C. $\frac{3x-9}{6x^3}$
    D. $\frac{2x}{6x^3}$

20. Given $y = 4x + 4$ and $y = 5x + 1$, solve for $x$ and $y$.

    A. $x = 3, y = 16$
    B. $x = 1, y = 8$
    C. $x = 5, y = 24$
    D. $x = -3, y = 9$

21. Factor $2x^2 + 4x$.

A. $x^2 + 2x$

B. $2x(x+2)$

C. $8x^3$

D. $2x + 2x + 4x$

22. Solve the inequality $\frac{x}{5} > 4$.

A. $x = 20$
B. $x < 20$
C. $x > 20$
D. $x > \frac{4}{5}$

23. In a deck of cards with an equal number of red and black cards, what is the probability of picking a red card three times in a row?

A. $\frac{1}{2}$

B. $\frac{1}{6}$

C. $\frac{1}{8}$

D. $\frac{3}{52}$

24. Factor $x^2 + 3x - 28$.

A. $(x+3)(x-4)$
B. $(x+6)(x-3)$
C. $(x+7)(x-4)$
D. $(x+3)(x+1)$

25. Solve for $x$: $x^2 - 14 = 2$.

A. $x = 3$
B. $x = 9$
C. $x = 5$
D. $x = 4$

## ELECTRONICS INFORMATION

You'll have 20 questions and nine minutes to answer them.

1. If an ammeter registers 0, what does that tell you?

   A. There is too much resistance to complete a circuit.
   B. There must be a short somewhere.
   C. The wire in question is considered hot.
   D. No electrical current is flowing.

2. When it is not actively flowing, electricity is said to have

   A. potential
   B. limitations
   C. inductance
   D. capacitance

3. An example of a material that makes a good insulator is

   A. glass
   B. wood
   C. water
   D. both A and B

4. The measure of electric charge passing a specific point in a specific measure of time is called a(n)

   A. ampere
   B. watt
   C. volt
   D. ohm

5. 10 kilowatts is the same as how many watts?

   A. 1,000
   B. 100
   C. 10,000
   D. 1,000,000

6. The symbol Ω on a schematic means:

   A. ohms
   B. volts
   C. watts
   D. joules

7. An accurate representation of Ohm's Law would be:

   A. $V = \frac{I}{R}$
   B. $I = \frac{V}{R}$
   C. $I = VR$
   D. $R = \frac{1}{2}I$

8. A 60-watt bulb is left on for 15 minutes. How much energy does it use?

A. 60 joules
B. 900 joules
C. 54,000 joules
D. 13,500 joules

9. 1 mA can be expressed as

A. $10^{-3}$ A
B. 10 A
C. 1,000 A
D. $10^{3}$ A

10. An electromagnet can be used to

A. convert mechanical energy into electric energy
B. create power without electricity
C. convert electric energy into mechanical energy
D. shield small electronic devices

11. In the series circuit, what is <u>not</u> true about the second light bulb in the series?

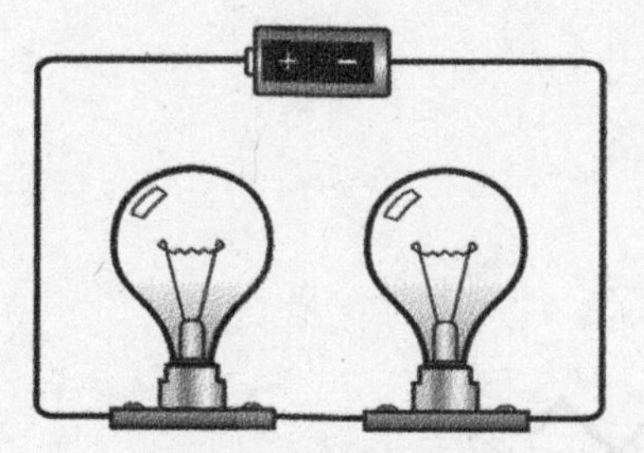


A. It won't work if the first light bulb breaks.
B. It will cast a weaker light than the first bulb.
C. The first light bulb must be on for the second light bulb to work.
D. The second light bulb is more likely to break.

12. A component in a circuit that impedes the flow of electricity is called a

A. conductor
B. inductor
C. capacitor
D. resistor

13. Grounding is the process of

A. tying down electrical equipment
B. removing a charge (or excess charge)
C. creating a complete circuit
D. cleaning electrical equipment

14. What is the total resistance in the series circuit shown in the following figure if $R_1 = 900$ ohms and $R_2 = 700$ ohms?

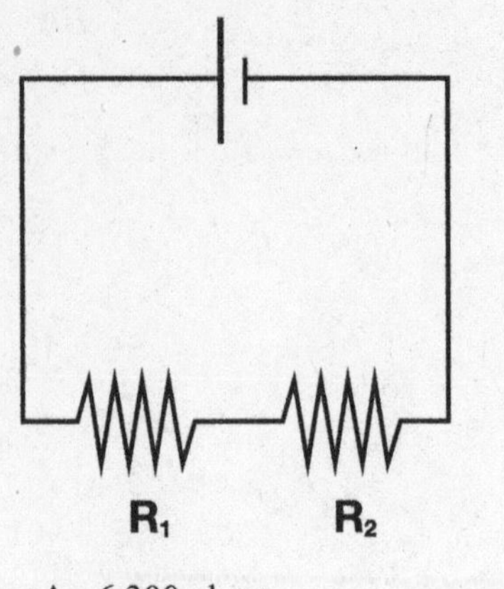


A. 6,300 ohms
B. 1,600 ohms
C. 200 ohms
D. 700 ohms

15. What is the total current in a series circuit powered by a 12-volt battery when $R_1 = 2\Omega$ and $R_2 = 3\Omega$?

A. 12 A
B. 3 A
C. 2.4 A
D. 5 A

16. What is the schematic symbol indicating an open switch?

A.
B.
C.
D.

17. What type of circuit is shown in the figure below?

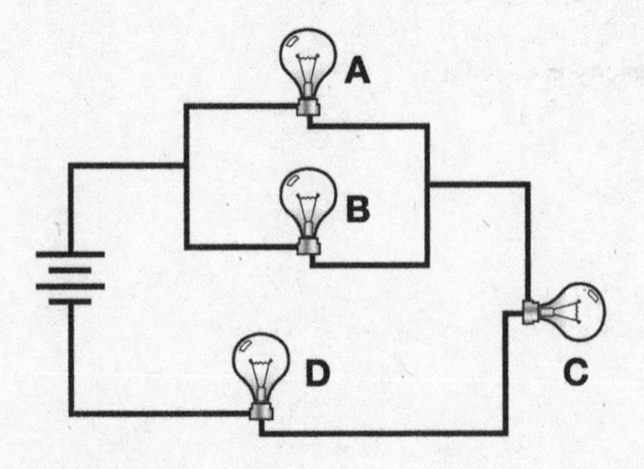


A. parallel
B. series
C. series-parallel
D. none of the above

18. In the figure below, what is the purpose of S?

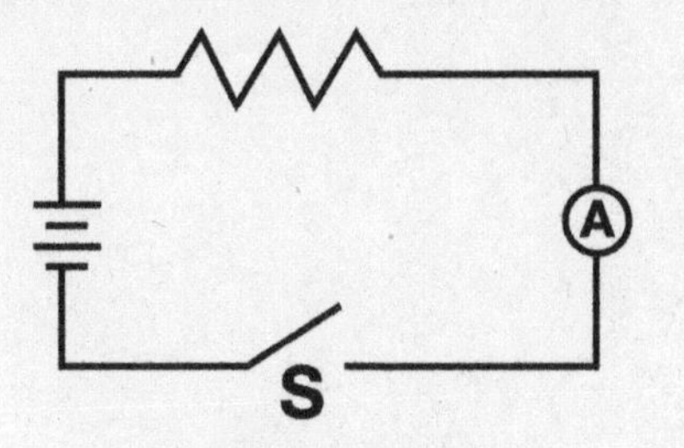


A. to amplify the current
B. to interrupt the current
C. to change the flow of current
D. to store electricity

19. In the figure below, $R_1$ and $R_2$ could represent:

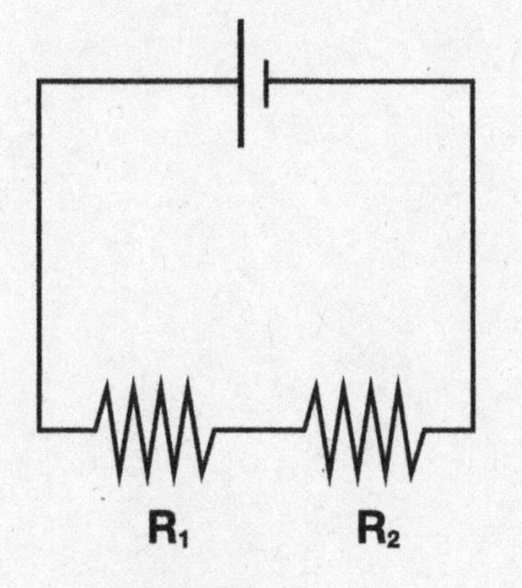


A. light bulbs
B. switches
C. power sources
D. connectors

20. The symbol stands for what component on a schematic?

A. capacitor
B. diode
C. inductor
D. power source

## AUTOMOTIVE AND SHOP INFORMATION

You'll have 25 questions and 11 minutes to answer them.

1. The device pictured below is an example of what engine device?

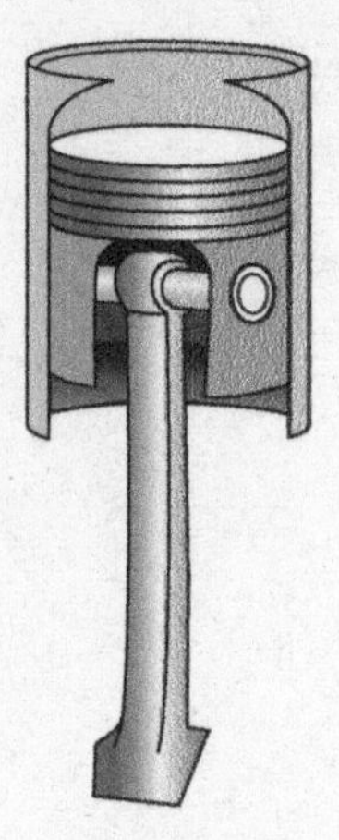

A. a cylinder and piston
B. a flywheel
C. a spark plug
D. an intake manifold

2. A four-stroke engine refers to which of the following?

A. an engine with four cylinders
B. the four main drive gears (forward, reverse, park, and neutral)
C. the four-strokes a piston goes through to power the engine
D. a malfunctioning engine

3. The intake and exhaust valves are opened and closed with which of the following?

A. the spark plugs
B. the cylinder block
C. the crankshaft
D. the camshaft

4. The purpose of the radiator is which of the following?

A. to use air to cool the hot coolant
B. to bathe the hot coolant with cold coolant (freon)
C. to power the heater (radiate heat throughout the car)
D. to amplify the power of the crankshaft

5. The device which directs the engine's torque in different ways is called which of the following?

A. a differential
B. a piston
C. an axle
D. a driveshaft

6. A front-wheel drive car has which of the following advantages over a rear-wheel drive car?

   A. It makes the car lighter.
   B. It provides better fuel economy.
   C. Under some circumstances, it allows for better traction.
   D. All of the above.

7. The alternator serves which of the following purposes?

   A. It starts the car.
   B. It supplies electricity as needed.
   C. It ignites the fuel mixture.
   D. It opens the intake valves.

8. The device in a carburetor that controls the ratio of fuel to air is called which of the following?

   A. the fuel line
   B. the throttle
   C. the venturi or choke
   D. the fuel filter

9. PCV means which of the following?

   A. Precarburetor Vehicle
   B. Positional Camshaft Vertex
   C. Positive Crankcase Ventilation
   D. Pilot Core Valve

10. Which of the following is not a type of spring found in a car?

    A. torsion bars
    B. leaf springs
    C. air springs
    D. filtration spring

11. A vehicle with power-assisted steering and brakes means which of the following?

    A. less force is required to operate the steering and brakes
    B. the vehicle has an electric starter
    C. the vehicle can be used on rough terrain
    D. sensors in the body of the car locate obstacles and alert the driver to them

12. The master cylinder contains which of the following?

    A. ball bearings
    B. brake fluid
    C. engine coolant
    D. lubricating oil

13. Which of the following tools would be used to get precise metric dimensions of a pipe's interior diameter?

    A. micrometer calipers
    B. Vernier calipers
    C. depth gauge
    D. push-pull tape measure

14. Which of the following tools would best be used to determine the gauge or thickness of a thin sheet of metal?

A. carpenter's square
B. depth gauge
C. inside calipers
D. micrometer calipers

15. A combination square is versatile because it can be used in which of the following ways?

A. as a miter square
B. to measure
C. to level
D. all of the above

16. The figure shown below is that of which of the following?

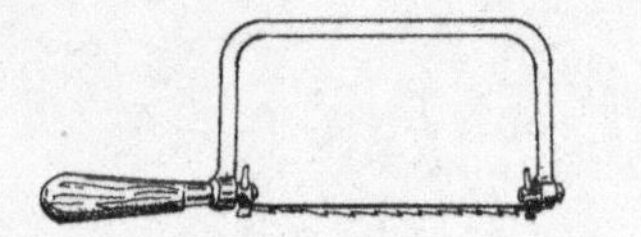

A. miter saw
B. crosscut handsaw
C. coping saw
D. portable circular saw

17. What kind of blade would be recommended to cut a plank of wood lengthwise (with the grain)?

A. rip cut
B. cross cut
C. dado blade
D. abrasive disk

18. A wood chisel is best used with what kind of hammer?

A. claw hammer
B. ball peen hammer
C. sledge hammer
D. rubber mallet

19. What kind of tool would have to be used to tighten the screws shown in the diagram?

A. Torx screwdriver
B. Allen wrench
C. Phillips screwdriver
D. socket wrench

20. If a painted metal pipe needed to be turned to thread it into a fixed coupling, what kind of wrench would probably be most suitable?

    A. Stilson wrench
    B. torque wrench
    C. strap wrench
    D. crocodile wrench

21. What kind of tool would probably be used to eliminate internal burrs or rough edging on a pipe that has just been cut?

    A. ream
    B. flat file
    C. orbital sander
    D. expansive drill bit and brace

22. What kind of drill bit would be necessary to drill a hole into concrete flooring?

    A. spade bit
    B. auger bit
    C. ream
    D. masonry bit

23. Which of the following wrenches is not adjustable?

    A. crescent wrench
    B. crocodile wrench
    C. monkey wrench
    D. Stilson wrench

24. If two angled pieces of wood were to be glued together as shown in the diagram below, what kind of clamps would probably be used?

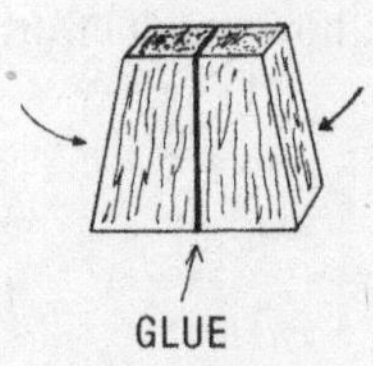


    A. parallel clamps
    B. C-clamps
    C. machinist's vise
    D. pipe clamps

25. The tool portrayed in the diagram below is which of the following?

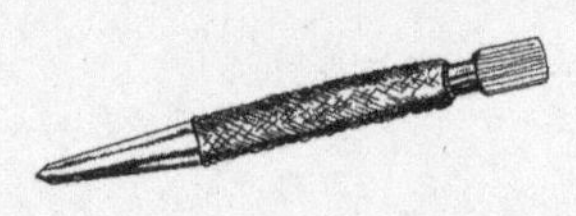

    A. awl
    B. sheet metal punch
    C. center punch
    D. mail punch

## MECHANICAL COMPREHENSION

You'll have 25 questions and 19 minutes to answer them.

1. If someone used a 10-foot-long lever to move a $2\frac{1}{2}$-ton rock, which location of the fulcrum would provide the greatest lift?

   A. 2 feet from the rock
   B. 4 feet from the rock
   C. 6 feet from the rock
   D. The end of the lever held by the user

2. A crate weighs 3,000 pounds and measures $3\frac{1}{2}$ feet by 4 feet. The fulcrum of a lever is placed 2 feet from the crate. The lever itself is 10 feet long. Effort will be applied at the very end of the lever opposite the load. How much effort would be required to lift the crate?

   A. 675 pounds
   B. 700 pounds
   C. 725 pounds
   D. 750 pounds

3. A crate weighs 3,000 pounds and measures $3\frac{1}{2}$ feet by 4 feet. The fulcrum of a lever is placed 2 feet from the crate. The lever itself is 10 feet long. Effort will be applied at the very end of the lever opposite the load. What mechanical advantage is gained by using the lever as opposed to lifting the crate directly?

   A. 1:4
   B. 3:2
   C. 4:1
   D. 2:3

4. If a wrecking bar is used to pry apart laminated framework as shown in the figure below, how much effort would be required to do the job?

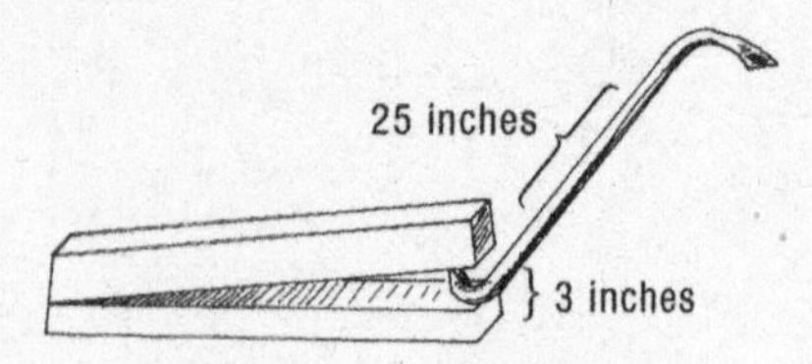


   A. 50 pounds
   B. 60 pounds
   C. 65 pounds
   D. 70 pounds

5. Three people are struggling to raise a 30-foot flagpole that measures 3 inches in diameter. The total weight of the flagpole is 95 pounds. If one person served as the fulcrum by anchoring the end of the flagpole to the ground, and the other two people attempted to lift the flagpole at a point 12 feet from the fulcrum, how much resistance would they encounter?

   A. 95 pounds
   B. 160.35 pounds
   C. 118.75 pounds
   D. 250 pounds

6. If a 30-foot flagpole measuring 3 inches in diameter and weighing 95 pounds is lifted 12 feet by 3 people, one of them serving as the fulcrum by anchoring the end of the flagpole to the ground, what mechanical advantage is afforded by lifting the flagpole as described?

   A. 1:1
   B. 2:1
   C. can't be determined with the information provided
   D. There is no advantage gained by using leverage in this manner.

7. Which pulley in the figure below can offer the most amount of lift?

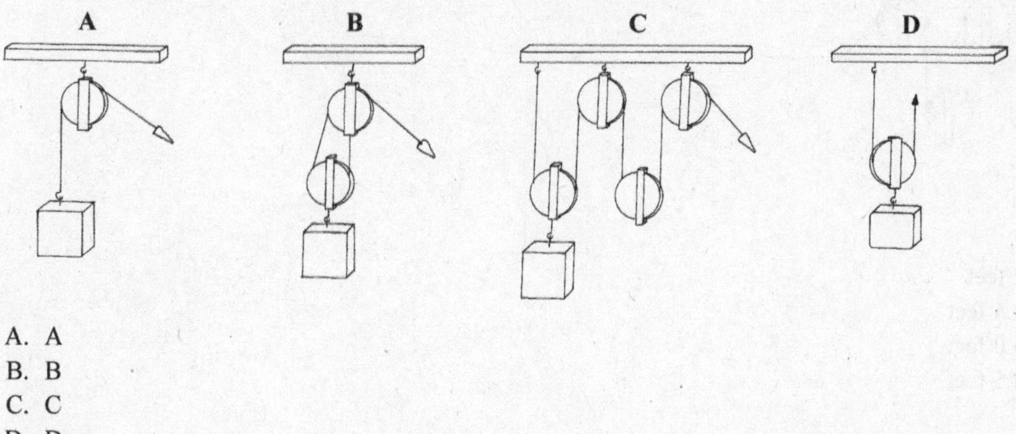


   A. A
   B. B
   C. C
   D. D

8. Of the pulley arrangements shown in the figure below, which one does not provide any mechanical advantage?

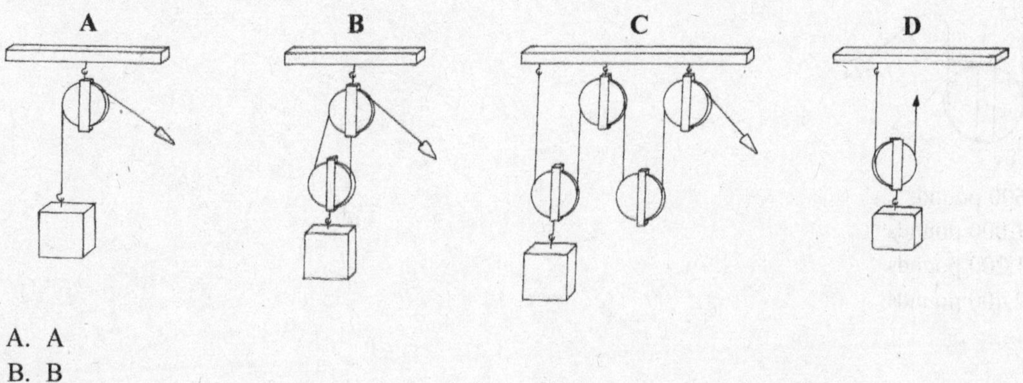


   A. A
   B. B
   C. C
   D. D

9. Examine the diagram in the figure below. How much effort would be required, using this set of pulleys, to lift the 1,600-pound weight?

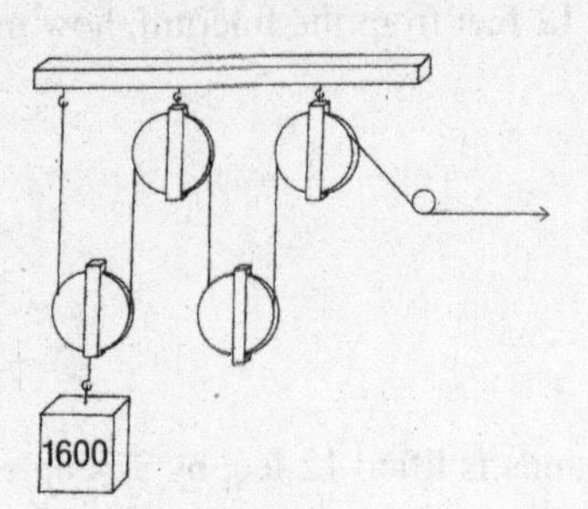


A. 300 pounds
B. 400 pounds
C. 500 pounds
D. 550 pounds

10. Examine the diagram below. If the cable were pulled 10 feet, how high would the 1,600-pound weight rise?

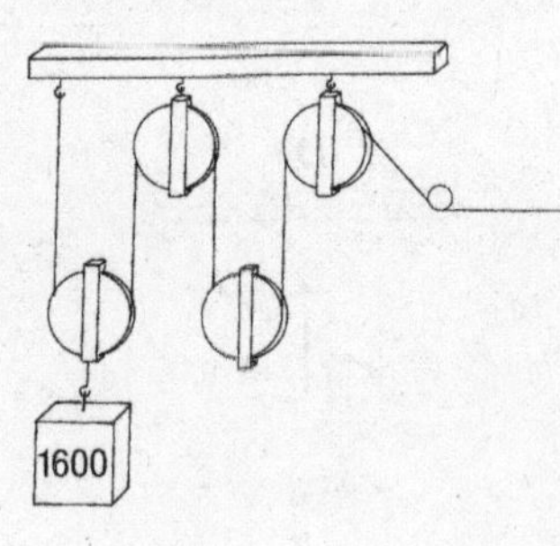


A. 2 feet
B. 2.5 feet
C. 3.0 feet
D. 3.5 feet

11. Refer to the diagram below. If 600 pounds of pulling force were exerted on the cable, what would be the maximum load this pulley could lift?

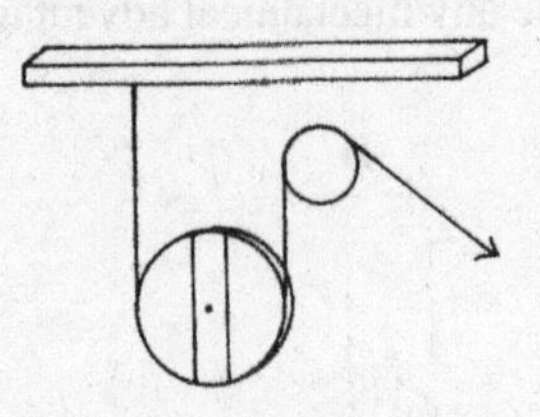

A. 600 pounds
B. 1,000 pounds
C. 1,200 pounds
D. 2,400 pounds

12. How much pulling force will be required to lift the 1,000 pounds of resistance in the diagram below?

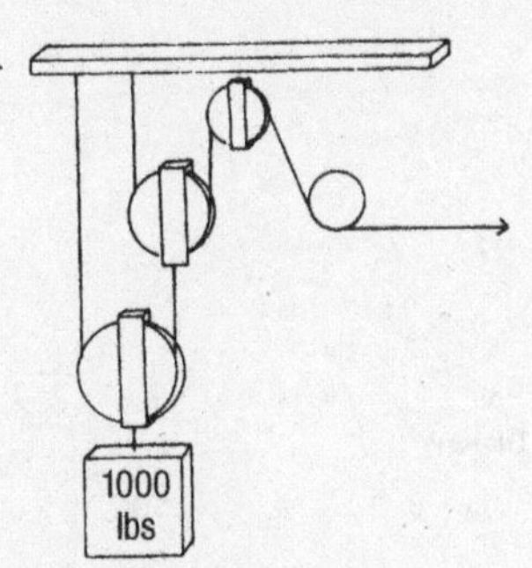


A. 1,000 pounds
B. 500 pounds
C. 350 pounds
D. 250 pounds

13. Which of the inclined plane diagrams in the figure below demonstrates the best mechanical advantage in lifting a heavy object to the height of the platform?

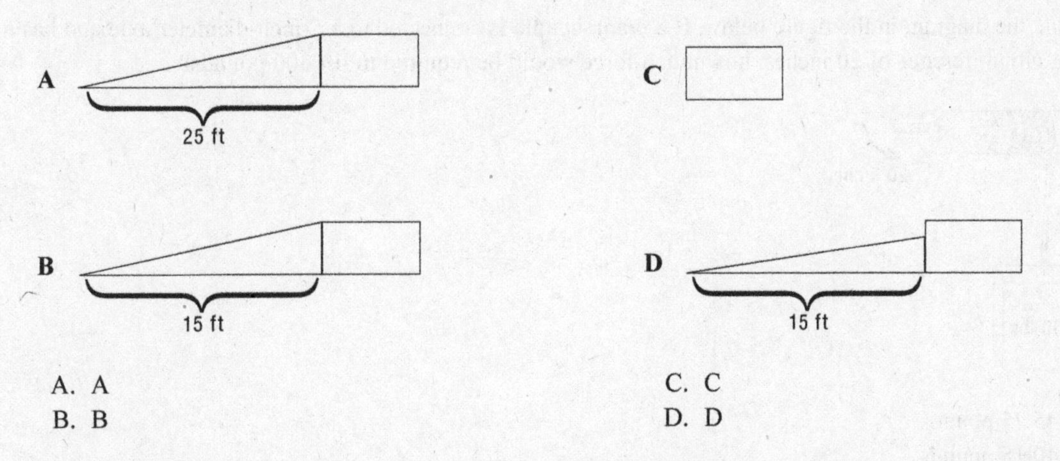


A. A
B. B
C. C
D. D

14. What is the mechanical advantage of the figure below if the height of the platform is 10 feet?

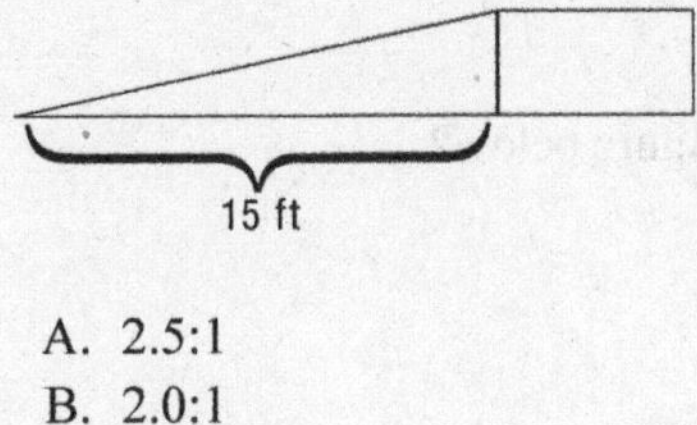


A. 2.5:1
B. 2.0:1
C. 1.75:1
D. 1.5:1

15. If someone needed to load a 425-pound fuel barrel into the back of a truck with a bed height of 4 feet, how much effort would be required if a 10-foot plank were used as an inclined plane?

A. 150 pounds
B. 170 pounds
C. 180 pounds
D. 185 pounds

16. What would be the height that a 500-pound barrel could be lifted if a 20-foot inclined plank having a mechanical advantage of 2:1 was used and only 150 pounds of force is available?

A. 4 feet
B. 5 feet
C. 6 feet
D. 7 feet

17. What is the mechanical advantage of the inclined plane shown in the figure below?

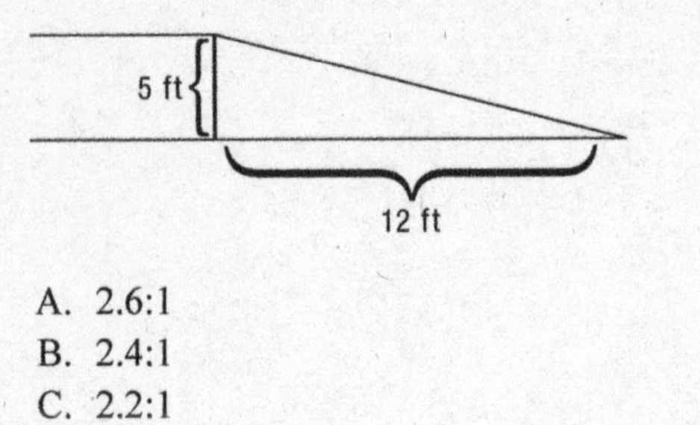


A. 2.6:1
B. 2.4:1
C. 2.2:1
D. 2.0:1

18. Examine the diagram in the figure below. If a crank handle is connected to a 5-inch-diameter axle and has a turning circumference of 20 inches, how much force would be required to lift 300 pounds?

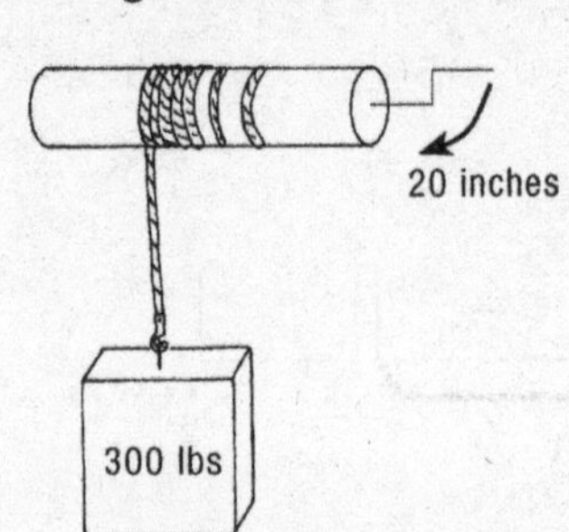


A. 245.75 pounds
B. 240.15 pounds
C. 237.80 pounds
D. 235.65 pounds

19. What mechanical advantage is gained by using the crank shown in the figure below?

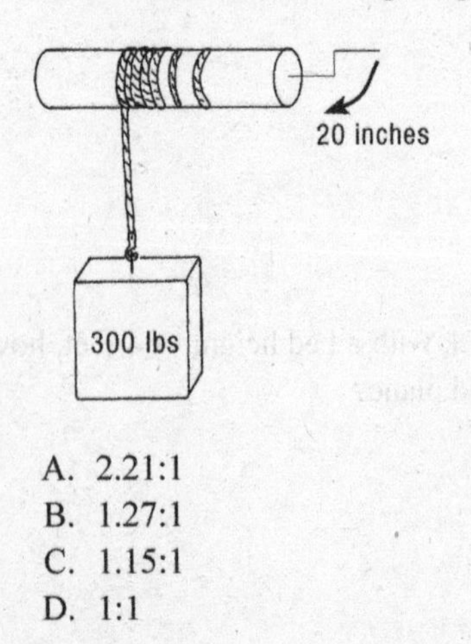


A. 2.21:1
B. 1.27:1
C. 1.15:1
D. 1:1

20. How much weight could be lifted if 150 pounds of force were exerted on a crank connected to an axle with a known circumference of 8.5 inches?

A. 615.27 pounds
B. 631.65 pounds
C. 637.65 pounds
D. 665.29 pounds

21. What is the mechanical advantage if resistance is 700 pounds and force is 180 pounds?

A. 3.71:1
B. 4.22:1
C. 3.89:1
D. 4.71:1

22. Refer to the diagram below. Gear A has 10 teeth, B has 40 teeth, C has 10 teeth, D has 20 teeth. If Gear A turned one full revolution, how much would Gear D turn?

NOTE: Gears B and C are keyed to the same shaft.

A. $\frac{1}{5}$ of a revolution

B. $\frac{1}{8}$ of a revolution

C. $\frac{1}{9}$ of a revolution

D. $\frac{1}{10}$ of a revolution

23. Refer to the diagram in the figure below. Gear A has 10 teeth, B has 40 teeth, C has 20 teeth, and D has 30 teeth. If Gear A turned 6 revolutions, how much would Gear D turn?

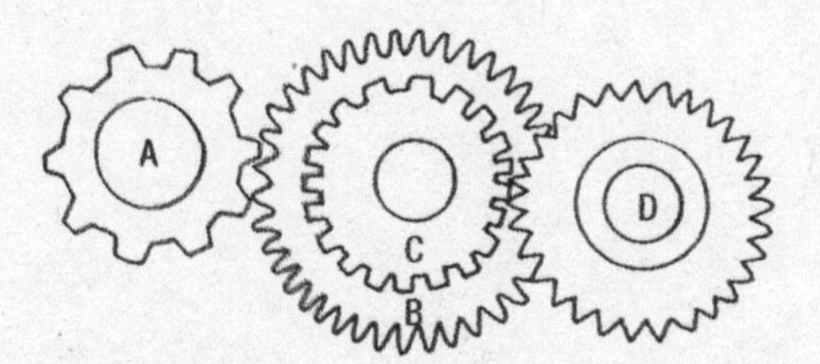


NOTE: Gears B and C are keyed to the same shaft.

A. 1 revolution
B. 1.5 revolutions
C. 1.75 revolutions
D. 2 revolutions

24. Assuming that a V-8 350 engine could yield 250 horsepower creating a maximum torque of 175 foot-pounds, and the drive train gear ratio was 1:6, what would be the maximum torque output of $G_L$?

A. 1,000 foot-pounds
B. 1,050 foot-pounds
C. 1,100 foot-pounds
D. 1,150 foot-pounds

25. Belt drives can do which of the following?

A. decrease torque
B. decrease speed
C. change drive direction
D. All of the above

## ASSEMBLING OBJECTS

You'll have 16 questions and 15 minutes to answer them.

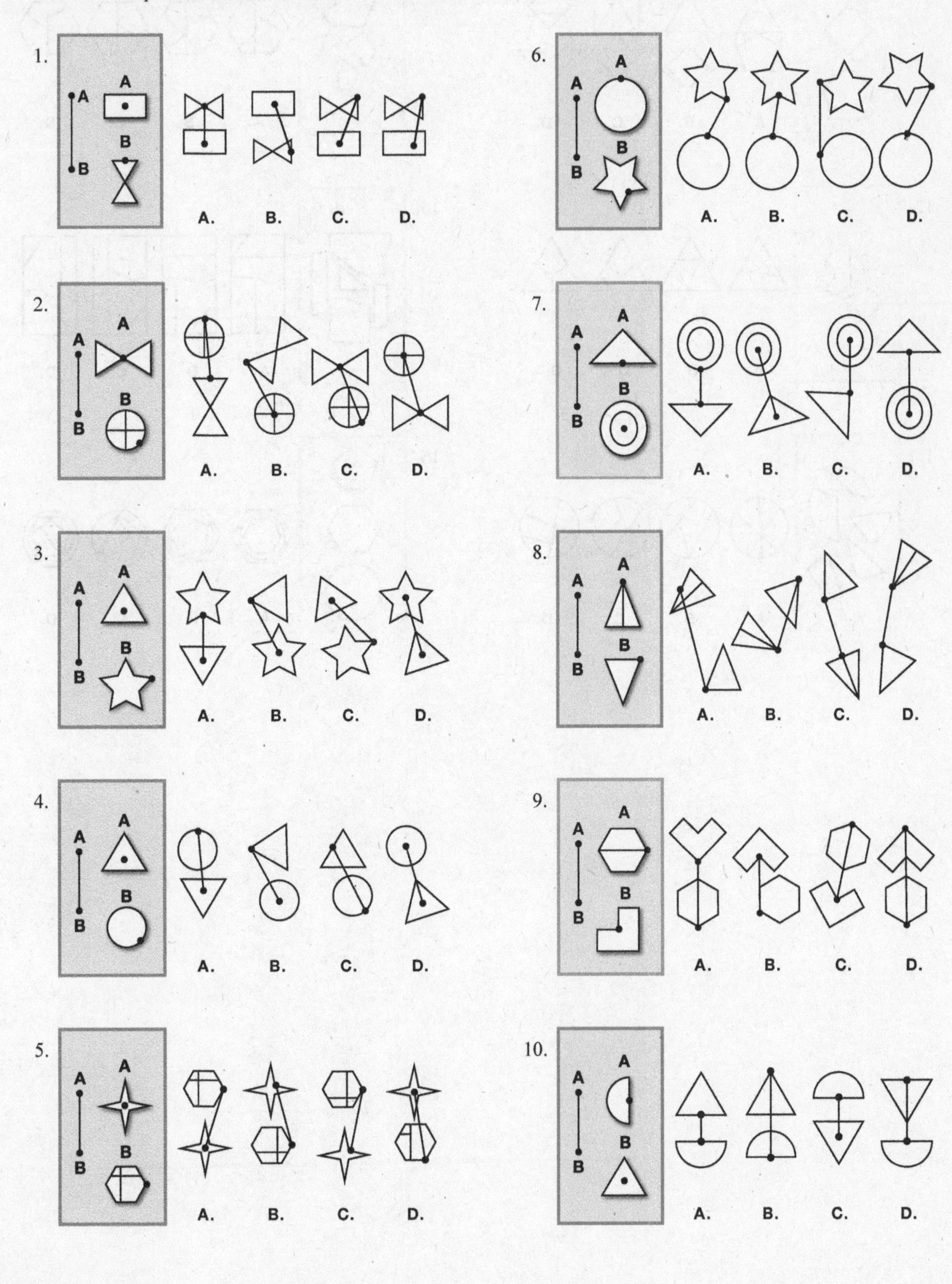

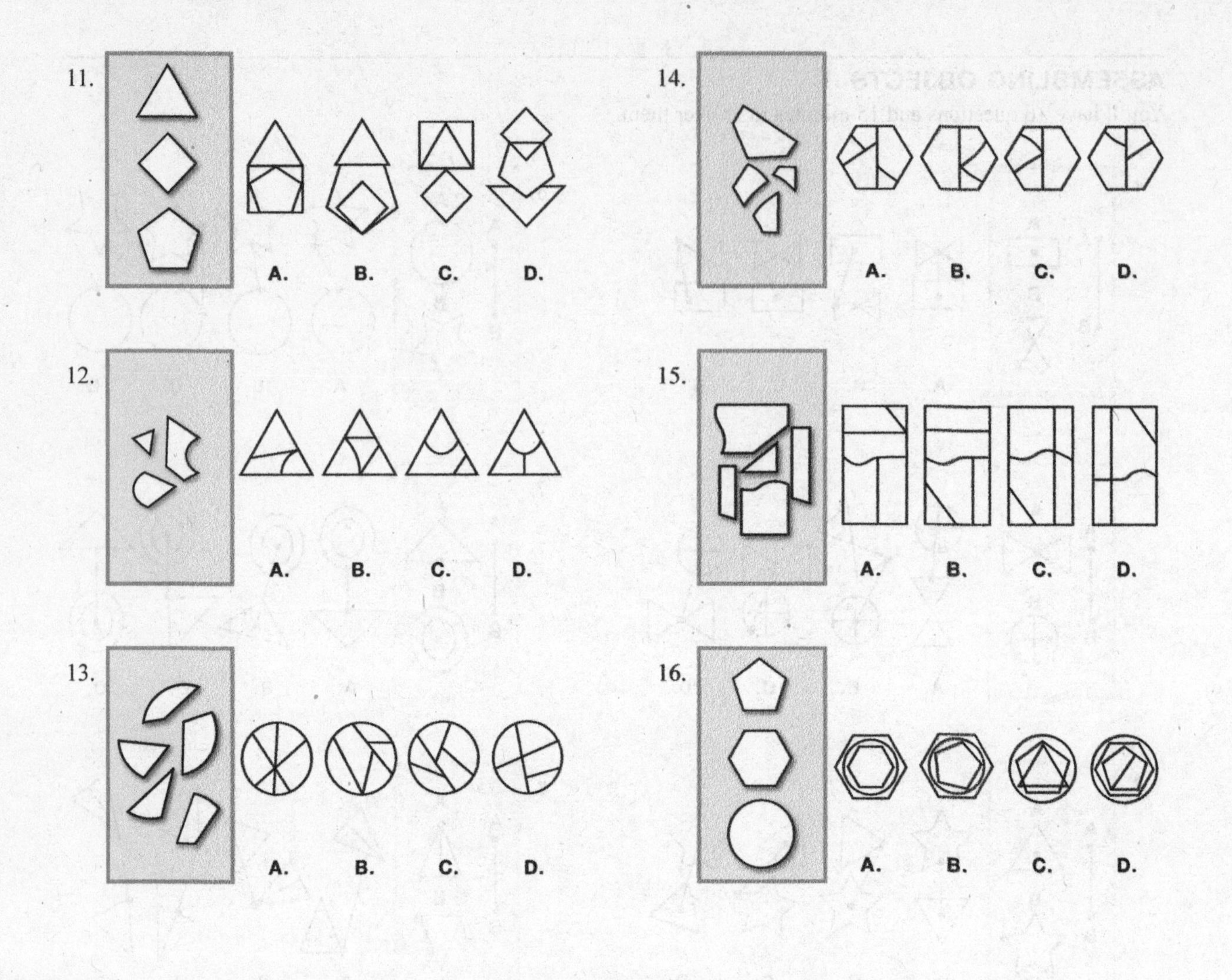
11.
A.
B.
C.
D.
12.
A.
B.
C.
D.
13.
A.
B.
C.
D.
14.
A.
B.
C.
D.
15.
A.
B.
C.
D.
16.
A.
B.
C.
D.

## ANSWER SHEET

### GENERAL SCIENCE

1. (A) (B) (C) (D)
2. (A) (B) (C) (D)
3. (A) (B) (C) (D)
4. (A) (B) (C) (D)
5. (A) (B) (C) (D)
6. (A) (B) (C) (D)
7. (A) (B) (C) (D)
8. (A) (B) (C) (D)
9. (A) (B) (C) (D)
10. (A) (B) (C) (D)
11. (A) (B) (C) (D)
12. (A) (B) (C) (D)
13. (A) (B) (C) (D)
14. (A) (B) (C) (D)
15. (A) (B) (C) (D)
16. (A) (B) (C) (D)
17. (A) (B) (C) (D)
18. (A) (B) (C) (D)
19. (A) (B) (C) (D)
20. (A) (B) (C) (D)
21. (A) (B) (C) (D)
22. (A) (B) (C) (D)
23. (A) (B) (C) (D)
24. (A) (B) (C) (D)
25. (A) (B) (C) (D)

### ARITHMETIC REASONING

1. (A) (B) (C) (D)
2. (A) (B) (C) (D)
3. (A) (B) (C) (D)
4. (A) (B) (C) (D)
5. (A) (B) (C) (D)
6. (A) (B) (C) (D)
7. (A) (B) (C) (D)
8. (A) (B) (C) (D)
9. (A) (B) (C) (D)
10. (A) (B) (C) (D)
11. (A) (B) (C) (D)
12. (A) (B) (C) (D)
13. (A) (B) (C) (D)
14. (A) (B) (C) (D)
15. (A) (B) (C) (D)
16. (A) (B) (C) (D)
17. (A) (B) (C) (D)
18. (A) (B) (C) (D)
19. (A) (B) (C) (D)
20. (A) (B) (C) (D)
21. (A) (B) (C) (D)
22. (A) (B) (C) (D)
23. (A) (B) (C) (D)
24. (A) (B) (C) (D)
25. (A) (B) (C) (D)
26. (A) (B) (C) (D)
27. (A) (B) (C) (D)
28. (A) (B) (C) (D)
29. (A) (B) (C) (D)
30. (A) (B) (C) (D)

### WORD KNOWLEDGE

1. (A) (B) (C) (D)
2. (A) (B) (C) (D)
3. (A) (B) (C) (D)
4. (A) (B) (C) (D)
5. (A) (B) (C) (D)
6. (A) (B) (C) (D)
7. (A) (B) (C) (D)
8. (A) (B) (C) (D)
9. (A) (B) (C) (D)
10. (A) (B) (C) (D)
11. (A) (B) (C) (D)
12. (A) (B) (C) (D)
13. (A) (B) (C) (D)
14. (A) (B) (C) (D)
15. (A) (B) (C) (D)
16. (A) (B) (C) (D)
17. (A) (B) (C) (D)
18. (A) (B) (C) (D)
19. (A) (B) (C) (D)
20. (A) (B) (C) (D)
21. (A) (B) (C) (D)

22. (A) (B) (C) (D)
23. (A) (B) (C) (D)
24. (A) (B) (C) (D)
25. (A) (B) (C) (D)
26. (A) (B) (C) (D)
27. (A) (B) (C) (D)
28. (A) (B) (C) (D)
29. (A) (B) (C) (D)
30. (A) (B) (C) (D)
31. (A) (B) (C) (D)
32. (A) (B) (C) (D)
33. (A) (B) (C) (D)
34. (A) (B) (C) (D)
35. (A) (B) (C) (D)

## PARAGRAPH COMPREHENSION

1. (A) (B) (C) (D)
2. (A) (B) (C) (D)
3. (A) (B) (C) (D)
4. (A) (B) (C) (D)
5. (A) (B) (C) (D)
6. (A) (B) (C) (D)
7. (A) (B) (C) (D)
8. (A) (B) (C) (D)
9. (A) (B) (C) (D)
10. (A) (B) (C) (D)
11. (A) (B) (C) (D)
12. (A) (B) (C) (D)
13. (A) (B) (C) (D)
14. (A) (B) (C) (D)
15. (A) (B) (C) (D)

## MATHEMATICS KNOWLEDGE

1. (A) (B) (C) (D)
2. (A) (B) (C) (D)
3. (A) (B) (C) (D)
4. (A) (B) (C) (D)
5. (A) (B) (C) (D)
6. (A) (B) (C) (D)
7. (A) (B) (C) (D)
8. (A) (B) (C) (D)
9. (A) (B) (C) (D)
10. (A) (B) (C) (D)
11. (A) (B) (C) (D)
12. (A) (B) (C) (D)
13. (A) (B) (C) (D)
14. (A) (B) (C) (D)
15. (A) (B) (C) (D)
16. (A) (B) (C) (D)
17. (A) (B) (C) (D)
18. (A) (B) (C) (D)
19. (A) (B) (C) (D)
20. (A) (B) (C) (D)
21. (A) (B) (C) (D)
22. (A) (B) (C) (D)
23. (A) (B) (C) (D)
24. (A) (B) (C) (D)
25. (A) (B) (C) (D)

## ELECTRONICS INFORMATION

1. (A) (B) (C) (D)
2. (A) (B) (C) (D)
3. (A) (B) (C) (D)
4. (A) (B) (C) (D)
5. (A) (B) (C) (D)
6. (A) (B) (C) (D)
7. (A) (B) (C) (D)
8. (A) (B) (C) (D)
9. (A) (B) (C) (D)
10. (A) (B) (C) (D)
11. (A) (B) (C) (D)
12. (A) (B) (C) (D)
13. (A) (B) (C) (D)
14. (A) (B) (C) (D)
15. (A) (B) (C) (D)
16. (A) (B) (C) (D)
17. (A) (B) (C) (D)
18. (A) (B) (C) (D)
19. (A) (B) (C) (D)
20. (A) (B) (C) (D)

## AUTOMOTIVE AND SHOP INFORMATION

1. (A) (B) (C) (D)
2. (A) (B) (C) (D)
3. (A) (B) (C) (D)
4. (A) (B) (C) (D)
5. (A) (B) (C) (D)
6. (A) (B) (C) (D)
7. (A) (B) (C) (D)
8. (A) (B) (C) (D)
9. (A) (B) (C) (D)
10. (A) (B) (C) (D)
11. (A) (B) (C) (D)
12. (A) (B) (C) (D)
13. (A) (B) (C) (D)
14. (A) (B) (C) (D)
15. (A) (B) (C) (D)
16. (A) (B) (C) (D)
17. (A) (B) (C) (D)
18. (A) (B) (C) (D)
19. (A) (B) (C) (D)
20. (A) (B) (C) (D)
21. (A) (B) (C) (D)
22. (A) (B) (C) (D)
23. (A) (B) (C) (D)
24. (A) (B) (C) (D)
25. (A) (B) (C) (D)

## MECHANICAL COMPREHENSION

1. (A) (B) (C) (D)
2. (A) (B) (C) (D)
3. (A) (B) (C) (D)
4. (A) (B) (C) (D)
5. (A) (B) (C) (D)
6. (A) (B) (C) (D)
7. (A) (B) (C) (D)
8. (A) (B) (C) (D)
9. (A) (B) (C) (D)
10. (A) (B) (C) (D)
11. (A) (B) (C) (D)
12. (A) (B) (C) (D)
13. (A) (B) (C) (D)
14. (A) (B) (C) (D)
15. (A) (B) (C) (D)
16. (A) (B) (C) (D)
17. (A) (B) (C) (D)
18. (A) (B) (C) (D)
19. (A) (B) (C) (D)
20. (A) (B) (C) (D)
21. (A) (B) (C) (D)
22. (A) (B) (C) (D)
23. (A) (B) (C) (D)
24. (A) (B) (C) (D)
25. (A) (B) (C) (D)

## ASSEMBLING OBJECTS

1. (A) (B) (C) (D)
2. (A) (B) (C) (D)
3. (A) (B) (C) (D)
4. (A) (B) (C) (D)
5. (A) (B) (C) (D)
6. (A) (B) (C) (D)
7. (A) (B) (C) (D)
8. (A) (B) (C) (D)
9. (A) (B) (C) (D)
10. (A) (B) (C) (D)
11. (A) (B) (C) (D)
12. (A) (B) (C) (D)
13. (A) (B) (C) (D)
14. (A) (B) (C) (D)
15. (A) (B) (C) (D)
16. (A) (B) (C) (D)

## ANSWER KEY

### GENERAL SCIENCE

1. **C.** While the study of asteroids (answer A) is part of astronomy, it is only a small part of the science. Answer C is more accurate and is therefore the correct answer. (Keep in mind that many of the questions on the ASVAB will have more than one answer that could be accurate, and you have to pick the one that is most correct.)
2. **D.** This question requires you to understand the different ways temperature is measured, in Fahrenheit, Celsius, and Kelvin. Absolute zero is not the same as zero degrees Fahrenheit or Celsius, so answers A and B are incorrect. It is also not the same as the freezing point in Fahrenheit, so C is incorrect. However, 0 on the Kelvin scale corresponds with absolute zero, so D is correct.
3. **A.** A microgram is one millionth of a gram.
4. **C.** Natural selection requires three basic qualities, but a hospitable environment is not one of them. While it may be necessary for an individual to be in a hospitable environment to survive, it is not considered one of the components of natural selection.
5. **A.** Osmosis is the process of moving fluid into and out of cells. Mitosis (answer B) is a type of cell division, and while fluid transfer (answer C) is a reasonable description of what happens, that is not the term scientists use, so A is a more correct answer. Ionization (answer D) is the process of acquiring an electrical charge.
6. **C.** The phrase "biological community" is another way to say "ecosystem." An ecosystem is all of the elements of a specific environment, including landscape. A habitat (answer A) is where a particular organism naturally lives. A food chain (answer B) is a relationship among organisms in an ecosystem. Answer D is a made-up phrase that is designed to sound possible but is wrong.
7. **D.** Blood cells are produced in your body's bone marrow.
8. **B.** "Apoxia" is the term used to describe the situation of not taking in any oxygen (for organisms that respire). Hypothermia (answer A) has to do with lowered body temperature. Hypoxia (answer C) is a state of reduced oxygen intake, not the state of no oxygen intake at all. Aerobia (answer D) refers to organisms that can live in environments with oxygen in them.
9. **C.** Hemoglobin binds to oxygen and carries it throughout your circulatory system. It gives blood cells their *red* color, which is why answer A is incorrect. White blood cells, not hemoglobin, work to eliminate disease-causing bacteria (making answer B incorrect). Platelets, not hemoglobin, help clot your blood (making answer D wrong).
10. **D.** There are no circumstances under which AA and Aa can combine to produce aa.
11. **D.** The other series are more suitable for obtaining different minerals.
12. **A.** We live in the Holocene epoch. The Pleistocene (answer B) began 2.588 million years ago. The Eocene (answer C) began 55.8 million years ago, and the Paleocene (answer D) began 65.5 million years ago.
13. **D.** Seawater possesses greater buoyancy than fresh water and is a good conductor of electricity. When you encounter a "both," "all," or "neither" answer possibility on the ASVAB, it's a good idea to carefully evaluate all of the answers and pick not just one that is correct but the one that is *most correct.* In this case, answers A and C are both correct, but you would be wrong if you'd chosen either of those answers, as D ("both A and C") is the most correct.
14. **B.** A tsunami is a type of wave.
15. **B.** A thunderstorm is likely to result when an air mass become unstable and starts rising in the atmosphere.

16. **C.** The smallest planet in the solar system is Mercury. It is also closest to the sun.

17. **D.** Water is an example of a compound, which is a substance that contains two or more elements. Water consists of the elements hydrogen and oxygen.

18. **A.** While elements usually have the same number of protons, neutrons, and electrons, it is possible for an element to have different numbers of protons and neutrons. When that happens, the result is called an isotope of that element.

19. **C.** A reaction that causes A + BC to become AB + C is called displacement. Combustion (answer A) is a reaction that involves burning. Synthesis (answer B) is the combination of elements to create a new element. Decomposition (answer D) creates substances with smaller parts.

20. **A.** Newton's Second Law, also called the Law of Force, can be represented by the formula Force = Mass × Acceleration. The other options are incorrect.

21. **D.** A signal with a wave frequency of 1 Hertz produces 1 cycle per second, so a frequency of 10 Hertz produces 600 cycles per minute.

22. **B.** The absence of light waves creates the color black. We tend to think the color white is the absence of color, but white is actually the presence of all the light waves.

23. **A.** Sound waves can be "canceled" by mixing them with inverted sound waves. Sound waves that are in phase (answer B) create a higher amplitude, while sound waves that are different (answers C and D) combine to create a new sound.

24. **D.** A hypothesis is a step in the scientific method that eventually may result in a proven theory.

25. **A.** Kingdoms, phyla, and species are accepted groups in classical taxonomy. In answer B, "troops" is not used in science. Answer C is not a generally accepted list of groups. In answer D, inorganic substances are usually not living, so scientists do not divide living organisms this way.

## ARITHMETIC REASONING

1. **C.** $\frac{3}{4}-\frac{1}{4}=\frac{2}{4}$ which should be reduced to $\frac{1}{2}$. Then, 17 – 8 = 9. Therefore, $x=9\frac{1}{2}$.

2. **C.** To find *x*, we just need to know that for every 1 gallon of water we need 3 tablespoons of fertilizer. Therefore multiply 3 tablespoons by 20 (the number of gallons of water) to get 60 tablespoons.

3. **D.** The ratio is simple: 30 screws to gain 2 inches = 30:2 or $\frac{30}{2}$. Reduce as you would any fraction to get $\frac{15}{1}$ or 15:1.

4. **B.** You know that 152 is 95% of the unknown quantity, or *x*. 95% can be written as a decimal, or 0.95. So, $\frac{152}{.95}=160$. $x$ = 160 test questions.

5. **D.** Add the whole numbers to get 47. Then convert the fractions to the same denominator: $\frac{1}{4}$, $\frac{2}{4}$, $\frac{1}{4}$ and add together to get $\frac{4}{4}$ or 1. Then, 47 + 1 = 48.

6. **A.** First, 3000 – 237 = 2763. Then 2763 ÷ 3000 (the original amount in savings) = 0.921. Then, convert 0.921 to a percentage (0.921 × 100) for an answer of 92.1%.

7. **A.** Brian was earning half of what he is earning now, or $\frac{23.50}{2}$. That works out to $11.75 an hour.

8. **B.** First, we need to figure out how much Fred and John can each produce in an hour—but the number of sandwiches is a red herring. We don't need to use that number anywhere in our calculations. Fred can produce $\frac{1}{3}$ of the sandwiches in 1 hour, and John can produce $\frac{1}{4}$. Add the fractions together to determine how many sandwiches they can produce together in 1 hour (first find a common denominator): $\frac{4}{12}+\frac{3}{12}=\frac{7}{12}$. In 1 hour they can produce $\frac{7}{12}$ or about 58%. Thus, we know it will take less than 2 hours to produce all of the sandwiches. To find out more precisely how long it would take to produce all of the sandwiches, divide 12 by 7 to get about 1.714 hours, or just about 1 hour, 43 minutes.

9. **C.** First, $8(60+x)=600$. Which is the same as $480+8x=600$. Next, subtract 480 from each side:

$$480-480+8x=600-480$$

Thus, $8x=120$.
Then, divide both sides by 8 to isolate $x$:

$$\frac{8x}{8}=\frac{120}{8}$$

$x = 15$ mph

10. **C.** If the tank can be filled at a rate of 12 cubic meters per minute, then the 600 cubic meter tank can be filled up in 50 minutes ($600 \div 12 = 50$). However, don't forget to account for the leak! First, determine how long it will take for the leak to empty the tank. If it leaks at $\frac{1}{2}$ cubic meter per minute, then 600 cubic meters will be drained in 1200 minutes. So, to account for the leak we'd set up the following calculation:

$$\frac{1}{50}-\frac{1}{1200}=\frac{1}{x}$$

Give the fractions a common denominator:

$$\frac{24}{1200}-\frac{1}{1200}=\frac{1}{x}$$

Then:

$$\frac{23}{1200}=\frac{1}{x}$$

If we cross-multiply the fractions, we get $23x = (1)1200$ or $23x = 1200$. Then divide 1200 by 23 to get an answer of (rounded down) 52.17.

11. **C.** The taxi is traveling 45 miles per hour for an unknown amount of time, so $45x$. The van is going 60 miles an hour and started $1\frac{1}{2}$ hours later than the taxi, so $60(x-1.5)$ or $60x-90$. We make these two quantities equal and solve for $x$: $60x-90=45x$.

    Add 90 to both sides of the equation:

    $$60x-90+90=45x+90$$

    So that:

    $$60x=45x+90$$

    Subtract $45x$ from both sides of the equation:

    $$60x-45x=45x-45x+90$$

    Or $15x = 90$. Divide both sides by 15 to find $x$:

    $$\frac{15x}{15}=\frac{90}{15}$$

    Therefore, $x = 6$. It will take 6 hours for the van to catch up with the taxi. Since the van left the dispatch yard at 11:00 A.M., it would be 5:00 P.M. when the two vehicles caught up to each other.

12. **D.** Driver A is represented by $3(x+15)$ which is the unknown speed of Driver B plus the 15 mph that Driver A exceeded that speed, multiplied by the number of hours it took Driver A to pass Driver B. This can also be represented as $3x + 45$.

    Driver B is represented by $3x$
    The total distance involved was 350 miles. Therefore:
    $3x + 3x + 45 = 350$
    $6x + 45 = 350$
    $6x = 305$
    $x = 50.83$ mph.

    Driver A was traveling at 50.83 + 15 mph (or 65.83 mph)

13. **A.** The 20 liters of 60% benzene can be represented as $0.60 \bullet 20$. The problem can then be set up as $(0.60 \bullet 20)+x=0.75(20+x)$.

    Then, $12 + x = 15 + 0.75x$
    $1200 + 100x = 1500 + 75x$
    $1200-1200+100x=1500-1200+75x$
    $100x=300+75x$
    $25x=300$
    $x=12$ liters of pure benzene must be added to the solution to acquire a 75% concentration.

14. **D.** A rectangular area as determined by the following equation: area = length × width. Therefore, 6 feet × 4 feet = 24 square feet.

15. **C.** $8\frac{3}{4}=\frac{35}{4}$; $2\frac{1}{2}=\frac{5}{2}$

So, we know that to divide fractions we can multiply by the inverse of one of the fractions: $\frac{35}{4} \div \frac{5}{2} = \frac{35}{4} \bullet \frac{2}{5}$

Or, $\frac{70}{20}$. This is the same as $3\frac{10}{20}$ or, when reduced, $3\frac{1}{2}$.

16. **D.** Set this problem up as a proportion to find the solution. We know that $\frac{75}{100} = \frac{13}{x}$. Cross-multiply and you have $75x = 1300$. Divide both sides by 75 to find $x$:

$$x = \frac{1300}{75}$$

Or, $x = 17.33$

17. **C.** Since the area of a square is equal to the length of one side squared, we simply square 6 miles (that is, $6^2$), giving us 36. Therefore, the township occupies 36 square miles.

18. **A.** To determine the mean price, just add up all the prices and divide by the number of prices you have. So:

$$\frac{3.99 + 3.79 + 3.89}{3}$$

Or $3.89.

19. **D.** The median price is the price in the middle. So, arrange the prices lowest to highest: $225,500; $223,000; $220,000; $187,000; $180,000. Thus, $220,000 is the median price.

20. **B.** Simple interest is calculated as **Interest = Principal • Rate • Time**. In this case, that would be: **Interest = 1000 • 0.045 • 1**, or Interest = $45. But the question doesn't ask how much interest she'll accrue, it asks how much her investment will be worth. So the interest needs to be added to the principal to come up with the correct answer: $1,000 + $45 = $1,045.

21. **D.** First determine how many gallons of gas Mikayala will need to travel 350 miles: $350 \div 22 \approx 15.91$. Then multiply the number of gallons needed by the price of gas $15.91 \times \$3.89 = \$61.85$.

22. **A.** Move the decimal points over so that you're dividing 1,575 by 412. Then reinsert the decimals. The answer is 3.8228, or 3.823 rounded off to thousandths.

23. **C.** The perimeter of a rectangle is found by adding up all the sides. So, we know that the perimeter = 14 meters. If the width of one side is 2.5 meters, then the width of both sides is 5 meters. 14 meters − 5 meters = 9 meters, which means that the remaining 2 sides must add up to 9 meters. Since they must be the same length, we can divide 9 by 2 to get our answer: 4.5 meters.

24. **B.** 3.0 divided by 7 = 0.4285; then $0.4285 \bullet 100 = 42.85\%$.

25. **D.** If 58 pushups is three times the amount of pushups Morris originally did, plus 7, that can be represented at $3x + 7 = 58$. Then, subtract 7 from each side of the equation: $3x + 7 - 7 = 58 - 7$. Then $3x = 51$. Divide by 3 to get the result:

$$\frac{3x}{3} = \frac{51}{3}$$

Or 17 pushups.

26. **D.** When multiplication and division occur together, do them in the order from left to right. Multiply 9 by 5.2, then divide the product by 18.76; 46.8 divided by 18.76 = 2.49.

27. **B.** Multiplication and division are always carried out before addition or subtraction. When several multiplications and divisions occur together, you should do them in the order they are given. In this case, we first multiply 8.372 by 3.14, giving us 26.29. Now, add 26.29 to 6.75. Therefore, $x = 33.04$.

28. **A.** If $x$ equals one share of the food, then together the Malamute and the Irish setter received $3x + 2x = 12.5$. So, $5x = 12.5$. Divide both sides by 5 to determine $x$:

$$\frac{5x}{5} = \frac{12.5}{5}$$

Or, $x = 2.5$

Since the Malamute's share of the food is $3x$, the answer is $3 \bullet 2 \bullet 5$ or 7.5 cups of food.

29. **D.** To determine percent change, you need to follow three steps: Divide the new value by the old value, or $18 \div 15 = 1.2$. Then convert the resulting decimal value by multiplying by 100 to determine the percent: $1.2 \bullet 100 = 120\%$. Then subtract 100% to determine the difference, which is the percent change. $120 - 100 = 20\%$.

30. **B.** The smallest prime numbers that will divide evenly into 18 are 3 and 2.

## WORD KNOWLEDGE

Note: The answers have been provided for the vocabulary section without explanation. If further reference is needed, consult a dictionary.

| | | | |
|---|---|---|---|
| 1. **C.** | 10. **C.** | 19. **B.** | 28. **A.** |
| 2. **C.** | 11. **D.** | 20. **B.** | 29. **D.** |
| 3. **D.** | 12. **A.** | 21. **C.** | 30. **C.** |
| 4. **A.** | 13. **A.** | 22. **A.** | 31. **A.** |
| 5. **B.** | 14. **C.** | 23. **A.** | 32. **D.** |
| 6. **D.** | 15. **D.** | 24. **D.** | 33. **A.** |
| 7. **C.** | 16. **C.** | 25. **C.** | 34. **B.** |
| 8. **A.** | 17. **B.** | 26. **B.** | 35. **D.** |
| 9. **B.** | 18. **D.** | 27. **C.** | |

## PARAGRAPH COMPREHENSION

1. **D.** The passage states that the vapors are irritating to the eyes, skin, and respiratory system, and that prolonged contact with the skin may result in delayed burns. Thus, answers A, B, and C are incorrect. The passage says nothing about loss of muscular function, so answer D is correct.

2. **D.** Though the article doesn't explicitly state it, it's likely that the increase in deaths is caused by the fact that more fires occur than do weather events. None of the other possible answers are supported by the passage, so common sense must prevail in interpreting the information. Choice A may seem to be the correct response; however, it's not. When the destructive capabilities of fire are compared to those of tornadoes, hurricanes, earthquakes, and floods, it is a misconception to think that fire is the worst. In fact, the destructive energy of the other phenomena discussed is significantly greater.
3. **C.** The passage doesn't say the applicant needs a strong math background or that a drug-screening test will be given, so answers B and D are incorrect. The passage says that three years' experience is preferred but not required, so answer A is incorrect. Answer C, self-motivated, is specifically stated in the paragraph, so it is the correct answer.
4. **D.** A general partnership doesn't protect the owners from business-related lawsuits, as the paragraph specifically states. A is incorrect because the paragraph states that a partnership doesn't protect personal wealth. B is incorrect because the passage says nothing about taxes. C is incorrect because a general partnership is defined as having two or more participants.
5. **B.** The passage discusses basic information about CDs, making this the most appropriate title. A is incorrect because the passage doesn't discuss investing generally but CDs specifically. C is incorrect because no comparison is being made. D is incorrect because while withdrawing money from a CD is mentioned in the piece, that is not the main point.
6. **A.** The passage uses the words "by imitation" and the word "imitates" to describe this type of magic, so A is most correct. B is incorrect, because while someone in sympathy with someone else may care about them, that is not how sympathetic magic is defined in the passage. C and D are incorrect for the same reason; they may have something to do with "sympathy," but not specifically with the definition of "sympathetic magic."
7. **B.** The passage specifically connects revolutions in science and technology with rapidly changing social attitudes. While social change did come slowly in the Middle Ages, the passage is not arguing that social change comes slowly, so A is incorrect. C is incorrect for the same reason. How social change affects social order is not addressed in the passage, making D incorrect.
8. **A.** The author organized the paragraph to lead to a surprising ending, that the person being written about was a woman who lived in the fourteenth century. Most readers would assume that a later time period is being discussed. B is incorrect because the time period is important. C is incorrect because the paragraph does not use chronological order to organize ideas. D is incorrect because the paragraph does not use comparison/contrast.
9. **D.** A is incorrect because the paragraph doesn't say "no one" was interested in Aristotle and Plato, though it can be surmised that interest in them diminished. B is incorrect because Aristotle and Plato were not Renaissance-era writers. C is incorrect because the paragraph says that interest in Greco-Roman classics endured for two hundred years, not that the Renaissance lasted for two hundred years.
10. **B.** The paragraph clearly states that an effective persuasive paper is one that argues the author's position using outside sources of information to support his or her claims. A is incorrect because the paragraph doesn't say anything about the author's opinion, just that claims must be supported using outside sources of information. C is incorrect because the paragraph directly contradicts it. D is incorrect because length is not addressed in the paragraph at all.
11. **A.** The author compares and contrasts ballads and lyric songs by describing how they are different. B is incorrect because chronological order is not used. Nor is a step-by-step organization used, meaning C is wrong. The inverted pyramid style is what journalists use to write newspaper stories describing who, when, what, and where, and that is not the method the author of this paragraph used, meaning D is incorrect.

12. **C.** The passage clearly states that some types of techniques require practice. A is incorrect because not all strategies discussed involve physical violence. B is incorrect because nonviolent actions are included in the list of self-defense strategies. D is incorrect because nothing in the passage says that the strategies are ranked by effectiveness.

13. **A.** The passage explains that alchemy was dedicated to finding the substance that would turn base metal into gold and finding the substance that would extend life. Although B may be true, it is not addressed in the paragraph, so it is incorrect. C is incorrect because the paragraph states that alchemy is the forerunner of modern chemistry. D is incorrect because alchemy is called "ancient" in the paragraph.

14. **A.** The passage specifically states that the Aztecs allied with other groups, and it also says that the provinces, petty kingdoms, and tribes were "subsumed" under the empire, implying some type of warfare was probably involved, making this answer the most accurate. While it is true that the arrival of the Spanish destroyed the Aztec empire, this is not discussed in the passage, making B incorrect. C is incorrect because the passage describes how the Aztecs acquired a significant amount of territory, and the implication is that doing so was important to them. D is incorrect because there is nothing in the passage to support it.

15. **A.** The passage states that Boëthius was accused of treason and imprisoned and later executed. B is incorrect because while it may be true, nothing in the passage is about that. C is incorrect because the passage states that Boëthius found favor with Theodoric at first. D is incorrect because the passage describes 510 as a year in which Boëthius held a consulship and served as head of the civil service, not as a year in which the Ostrogoths invaded Rome.

## MATHEMATICS KNOWLEDGE

1. **D.** The first step in this problem is to change the fraction $\frac{7}{8}$ into a decimal, since $\pi$ is in decimal form. Thus, we divide 7 by 8 giving us 0.875. The gear's diameter is then 5.875 in decimal form. The equation is Circumference = Diameter($\pi$). $\pi \approx 3.1416$. Therefore, $\mathbf{5.875 \bullet 3.1416 = 18.4569}$ inches, or 18.46 inches rounded to hundredths.

2. **B.** Since the area of a triangle is equal to $\frac{1}{2} \times \text{base} \times \text{height}$ we can plug in the numbers accordingly. That gives us the following: $\frac{1}{2}(8)(3.5) = 14$. The area is 14 square feet.

3. **C.** The volume of a rectangle is found by using the formula V = lwh, or volume = length × width × height. Before we use this equation, all units must be the same (that is, inches or feet). In this case, it is easier to convert the height to feet than to convert the other measures to inches. 4 inches = $0.3\overline{3}$ feet. Thus, volume = 20 × 15 × 0.33. Volume = 99.90 cubic feet, or approximately 100 cubic feet.

4. **B.** Since volume = lwh, and each side is of equal length, the answer is $36^3$, which works out to 46,656 cubic inches.

5. **A.** A basketball fully inflated can be thought of as a sphere. The equation for the volume of a sphere is $V = \frac{4}{3}\pi r^3$. The diameter is given as being 12 inches. Radius = $\frac{1}{2}$ diameter. Therefore, $r = 6$ inches. So:

$$V = \frac{4}{3}(3.1416)6^3$$

Then, calculate exponents: $6^3 = 216$.

So,

$$V = \frac{4}{3}(3.1416)216$$

Or, $4.1888 \times 216 = 904.78$ cubic inches rounded to hundredths

6. **A.** Since the geometric shape in the question concerns a cylinder, the equation we need to use is $V = \pi r^2 h$. If we plug our known values into this equation, it would read:

$$1256.64 = \pi r^2(16)$$

We can rewrite the equation to make it easier to solve:

$$\frac{1256.642}{3.1416 \bullet 16} = r^2$$

Or $\frac{1256.642}{50.2656} = r^2$. Which is to say, $25 = r^2$. The square root of 25 is 5, so $r = 5$.

Remember, 5 inches represents only the radius. The diameter is twice the radius, so $5 \times 2 = 10$ inches.

7. **D.** When you write a polynomial in standard form, you start with the term with the largest exponent, then the next largest, until you get to the constant, which is the last term.
8. **C.** To answer the question, simply solve the inequality. Do this by dividing both sides by 10. Therefore, $y < 4$.
9. **B.** Use the distributive property to determine the product. $(x+3)(x-2)$ can be written as:

$$x(x-2)+3(x-2)$$

That can be simplified as $x^2 - 2x + 3x - 6$. Or $x^2 + x - 6$.

10. **A.** To solve for $x$, add 24 to both sides to isolate the unknown on one side. Therefore, $8x = 16$. Then divide both sides by 8 to isolate $x$. $x = 2$.
11. **A.** A linear equation does not have an exponent or a square root (or a cube root, etc.) in the unknown.
12. **C.** To solve the inequality, you divide both sides by $-3$. But when you divide an inequality by a negative number, you have to reverse the direction of the inequality sign.
13. **D.** To simplify the expression, do whatever operations you can. In this case, you can subtract $x$ from $2x$, leaving $x$. Then arrange the terms in standard polynomial form, with the term having the highest exponent coming first.
14. **B.** To solve the equation, start by adding 9 to both sides to isolate the unknown on one side of the equation:

$$3x - 9 + 9 = 27 + 9$$

Then $3x = 36$, so it's a simple matter of dividing both sides of the equation by 3 to find that $x = 12$.

15. **C.** To solve this equation, you would have to divide both sides by $\frac{1}{3}$. To do that, you simply multiply by the inverse, so that:

$$\frac{3}{1} \bullet \frac{1}{3} x = 9 \bullet \frac{3}{1}$$

Or, $x = 27$.

16. **A.** We know that $\frac{a}{b}=\frac{c}{d}$ can be expressed as $ad=bc$. So if we restate this equation, we come up with $x^2=8\bullet 2$, or $x^2=16$. The square root of 16 is 4, so $x = 4$.

17. **C.** The ratio 3:1 means that $\frac{1}{3}$ as much sugar is needed as flour. So to find how much sugar is needed, multiply $2\frac{3}{4}\bullet\frac{1}{3}$. The easiest way to do this is to convert the mixed number to a fraction: $2\frac{3}{4}=\frac{11}{4}$. Then, $\frac{11}{4}\bullet\frac{1}{3}=\frac{11}{12}$. So the amount of sugar needed for this recipe is $\frac{11}{12}$ cup.

18. **D.** To add algebraic fractions, remember that $\frac{a}{b}+\frac{c}{d}=\frac{ad+bc}{bd}$. Then just plug in the relevant numbers: $\frac{5x+6}{15}$.

19. **B.** To divide fractions, remember that $\frac{a}{b}\div\frac{c}{d}=\frac{ad}{bc}$. So, $\frac{(x+3)(x-3)}{6x^3}$. That fraction can be further simplified to $\frac{x^2-9}{6x^3}$. You could also multiply by the reciprocal to come up with the same answer.

20. **A.** When solving for two unknowns with two true equations, start by substituting one equation for one unknown. In this case, we'll restate the equation as $5x+1=4x+4$. Then subtract 1 from both sides to come up with $5x=4x+3$. Then subtract $4x$ from each side to find that $x = 3$. Once you know that, you can plug in the answer to $x$ in the original equations to find $y$. So, $y=4(3)+4$ yields an answer of $y = 16$. You can confirm that by checking to be sure that $y = 16$ in the second formula, which it does.

21. **B.** To factor this equation, you're going from $ab+bc$ to $a(b+c)$. That means finding a common factor in the unknown and moving it to the front of the parenthesis. Thus, $2x$ is the common factor. In other words, this equation could be restated as $2x\bullet x+2x\bullet 2$ which can be represented as $2x(x+2)$.

22. **C.** Solve this as you would any equation with an unknown. Multiply both sides by 5 to isolate $x$ and determine $x > 20$.

23. **C.** To determine the probability of an independent event, you multiply the likelihood of each event. Since picking a red card in a deck that has an equal number of red and black cards has a probability of 1 in 2, or $\frac{1}{2}$, then the probability of picking a red card three times in a row can be expressed as $\frac{1}{2}\times\frac{1}{2}\times\frac{1}{2}$ or $\frac{1}{8}$.

24. **C.** Factors of 28 (the value of the $c$ variable) that add up to 3 (the value of the constant in the $b$ variable) are 7 and −4. Thus, the factors are $(x+7)(x-4)$. You can double check this answer by multiplying the factors: $x(x-4)+7(x-4)$. That is, $x^2-4x+7x-28$, which (after some addition) is $x^2+3x-28$.

25. **D.** Start by adding 14 to both sides to isolate the unknown. Then, $x^2=16$. To find $x$, you just need to determine the square root of 16, which is 4.

## ELECTRONICS INFORMATION

1. **D.** A reading of 0 means no current is flowing.

2. **A.** Electricity that isn't actively flowing is said to have potential.

3. **D.** Both glass and wood make reasonable insulators, so D is the best answer. Water is a good *conductor* of electricity, so C is incorrect.

4. **A.** 1 coulomb (unit of charge) per second equals 1 ampere. The other answers measure electricity in other ways.

5. **C.** A kilowatt is the same as 1,000 watts per hour, so 10 kilowatts is the same as 10,000 watts.

6. **A.** The horseshoe-shaped symbol indicates ohms.

7. **B.** Ohm's Law says: Current (I) is equal to voltage (V) divided by resistance.

8. **C.** 1 watt = 1 joule per second. So a 60-watt bulb uses 60 joules per second. Energy use is found by multiplying power by time, so 60 joules times 900 seconds (the number of seconds in 15 minutes) = 54,000 joules.

9. **A.** 1 mA is a milliampere or one thousandth of an ampere.

10. **C.** An electromagnet (and the power of electromagnetism) can be used to convert electrical energy into mechanical energy.

11. **D.** The second bulb's position has no bearing on how long it is likely to stay unbroken. The other options are all true of the second bulb.

12. **D.** A resistor impedes the flow of electricity in a circuit.

13. **B.** Grounding is the process of safely removing a charge (or an excess charge) from an object.

14. **B.** The total resistance in a series circuit is the sum of the resistance of each resistor.

15. **C.** The current of a circuit is voltage divided by resistance. So, the total resistance is 5 ohms and the total voltage is 12 volts. Thus, I = 2.4 A.

16. **D.** A is the symbol for a battery, B is the symbol for a closed switch, and C is the symbol for a resistor.

17. **C.** Part of the circuit is wired in series and part in parallel, so it is a series-parallel circuit.

18. **B.** S is a switch, so its purpose is to interrupt the flow of current.

19. **A.** A resistor can be the object a circuit is powering, like a light bulb. But the symbol shown is not for a switch or any of the other options.

20. **C.** This is the symbol for an inductor.

## AUTOMOTIVE AND SHOP INFORMATION

1. **A.** The illustrated device is a cylinder and piston.

2. **C.** During the process of internal combustion, a small amount of fuel (liquid gasoline) is turned into a gas (a spark creates a small explosion). The process creates energy that is used to power the engine. Most cars use a four-stroke engine cycle to operate their engines. What this means is that the pistons in the engine go through four different strokes in a cycle.

3. **D.** The camshaft opens and closes the valves. Spark plugs (answer A) are used to combust the fuel mixture. The cylinder block (answer B) is where the pistons and cylinders are located, but it doesn't do the actual opening and closing of valves. The crankshaft (answer C) turns the linear motion of the pistons to rotating force that powers the engine.

4. **A.** The radiator is the part of a car that uses air from the outside to cool the hot coolant mixture. Thus the radiator is situated where airflow can be used to cool the fluid. The radiator itself is typically made of a core with a lot of surface area over which air can flow to cool down the water. Generally, tubes carry the water and aluminum fins provide the surface area to cool it down.

5. **A.** A differential directs the engine's torque in different ways. A car may have more than one differential. The piston (answer B) provides linear force to power the engine but does not direct the engine's torque. The drive-shaft and the axles (answers C and D) are part of the drive train (as is the differential) but they are not the components that alter the torque.

6. **D.** All of the choices are true of a front-wheel drive car.

7. **B.** Once the car engine is running, the alternator takes over the process of supplying electricity to whatever needs electricity.

8. **C.** The venturi or choke regulates the fuel-to-air ratio. The fuel line (answer A) brings the fuel to the engine but doesn't regulate it. The throttle (answer B) controls the amount of fuel mixture going to the engine. The fuel filter (answer D) serves to keep dirt out of the engine.

9. **C.** PCV means Positive Crankcase Ventilation.

10. **D.** A filtration spring is not a type of spring found in a vehicle.

11. **A.** Less force is required to operate the steering and brakes.

12. **B.** The master cylinder is tied into the hydraulic brake system and is filled with brake fluid.

13. **B.** Vernier calipers have calibrated internal jaws that can precisely measure the inside diameter of pipe.

14. **D.** Micrometer calipers are used to determine very fine measurements of flat workpieces.

15. **D.** All of the above. A combination square can act as a miter square or try square, measure, and level.

16. **C.** Coping saw.

17. **A.** The rip cut blade is primarily used to cut lumber parallel to the grain. A dado blade is primarily used to cut grooves for various forms of joints.

18. **D.** The rubber mallet is less prone to damage the wood chisel's handle.

19. **B.** Allen wrench—an Allen set screw is set apart from others by its characteristic hexagonal slot, thus requiring an Allen wrench for tightening or loosening.

20. **C.** The strap wrench is designed not to harm the exterior finish of the pipe. The Stilson and crocodile wrenches would probably leave tooth marks and chip the paint.

21. **A.** Reams are used for this purpose as well as beveling. A flat file is more appropriate for flatter kinds of stock instead of pipe.

22. **D.** Masonry bits are designed with carbide tips that allow penetration of hard materials like stone, marble, and concrete. Reams are not meant for drilling holes.

23. **B.** The crocodile wrench is the only wrench listed without an adjustable feature.

24. **A.** Parallel clamps have the versatility to secure or clamp angled woodwork. A machinist's vise is not meant for wood.

25. **C.** Center punch.

## MECHANICAL COMPREHENSION

1. **A.** The closer a fulcrum is moved to a heavy object (resistance), the easier it is to apply leverage to move the object.

2. **D.** Effort is determined by multiplying the resistance to lift by the resistance distance, then dividing that product by the effort distance. In this case:

$$\text{Effort} = \frac{3000 \text{ pounds} \times 2 \text{ feet}}{8 \text{ feet } (10 \text{ feet } - 2 \text{ feet})} = 750 \text{ pounds}$$

3. **C.** Mechanical advantage is arrived at by dividing resistance by the amount of force required to lift it.

$$\frac{3000}{750} = 4$$

Or a 4:1 mechanical advantage.

4. **B.** Effort is determined by multiplying the resistance to lift by the resistance distance, then dividing that product by the effort distance. In this case:

$$\text{Effort} = \frac{500 \text{ pounds} \times 3 \text{ inches}}{25 \text{ inches}} = 60 \text{ pounds}$$

Or, 60 pounds of force is required to pry the framework apart.

5. **C.** Effort is determined by multiplying the resistance to lift by the resistance distance, then dividing that product by the effort distance. Since the fulcrum point is at the base of the pole, the entire length of the flagpole is considered the resistance distance. Therefore:

$$\text{Effort} = \frac{95 \text{ pounds} \times 15 \text{ feet}}{12 \text{ feet}}$$

Effort = 118.75 pounds of force is required at that point to lift the flagpole.

6. **D.** Since mechanical advantage is determined by dividing resistance by the amount of force required to lift (95 pounds ÷ 118.75 pounds) we arrive at a mechanical advantage of less than 1 (0.80). In other words, leverage is actually working against the two individuals trying to raise the flagpole. In fact, the closer they come to the fulcrum to attempt lift, the greater the resistance.

7. **C.** The pulley apparatus shown in choice C has a mechanical advantage of 4:1. Therefore, it can lift more weight as compared to the others; they have smaller mechanical advantages.

8. **A.** The pulley shown in choice A affords no mechanical advantage. It only changes the direction of pull. If you were to lift 500 pounds of weight, it would require 500 pounds of pull or effort. Answers B and D both offer a mechanical advantage of 2. If 500 pounds were lifted by either of these two pulley arrangements, the effort required would be only 250 pounds.

9. **B.** Since this example shows a pulley that has a mechanical advantage of 4:1, we simply divide the weight (that is, resistance) by the mechanical advantage to obtain the amount of effort required to lift it. 1600 ÷ 4 = 400 pounds of effort.

10. **B.** The length of the pull divided by the mechanical advantage gives the amount of lift. So, 10 feet ÷ 4 = 2.5 feet of lift.

11. **C.** The pulley has a 2:1 mechanical advantage. Therefore: 600 pounds of force × 2 = 1,200 pounds of potential lift.

12. **D.** The mechanical advantage demonstrated by this kind of pulley configuration is 4:1. The smaller wheel closest to the source of pull serves only to change the direction of that effort.

    This device is referred to as a snatch block. It does not contribute to mechanical advantage. In this case, Effort = Resistance ÷ Mechanical Advantage. Or:

$$\frac{\textbf{1000 pounds}}{4} = \textbf{250 pounds of effort}$$

13. **A.** The mechanical advantage is determined by the length of the plane divided by the height it is elevated. Since choice A has the longest plane and the height is the same for all selections, plane A would have the greater mechanical advantage. Both choices C and D still require direct lift.

14. **D.** In this case, the mechanical advantage is the length of inclined plane divided by the height of inclined plane, or:

$$\frac{\text{15 feet}}{\text{10 feet}} = 1.5:1$$

15. **B.** The formula for effort in this case is Effort = the product of resistance times height divided by the length of the inclined plane. Or:

$$\frac{\text{425 pounds} \times \text{4 feet}}{\text{10 feet}} = \text{170 pounds}$$

16. **C.** Effort times effort distance (length of the inclined plane) equals resistance times height (resistance distance). We know the effort, the effort distance, and the resistance. We don't know the height (lift). Thus the problem can be stated as:

$$150(20) = 500h$$

    Then, 3000 divided by 500 (to isolate $h$, or height) equals 6. So, the amount of lift possible is 6 feet.

17. **A.** Since we must first determine the length of the plane, we have to use the Pythagorean theorem applied to geometric right triangles ($a^2 + b^2 = c^2$). The square root of the resulting number will give us the length of the third side (that is, the inclined plane). So,

$$a^2 = 12^2 = 144$$
$$b^2 = 5^2 = 25$$

$$144 + 25 = 169, \text{ or } c^2.$$

    To find c, we need to determine the square root of 169, which is 13. Now we know the length of the inclined plane. To determine the mechanical advantage, we divide the length of the plane by the height (13 feet ÷ 5 feet) and determine that the advantage is 2.6:1.

18. **D.** First we need to determine the circumference of the axle. The circumference of a circle is π times diameter. In this case (π = 3.1416)(5 inches) = 15.7075 inches. We round to 15.71 inches. The following formula can be used to determine force:

    Force × Large-wheel circumference = Resistance × Axle circumference
    Since we know the amount of resistance and both circumferences, we can plug those numbers in:
    Force × 20 inches = 300 pounds × 15.71 inches
    20F = 4713. Divide both sides by 20 to isolate F: 235.65 pounds.

19. **B.** Divide the resistance by the force required to lift it. In the previous problem (#18), the force was determined to be 235.65, and resistance equals 300 pounds, so 300 ÷ 235.65 = 1.27 or a mechanical advantage of 1.27:1.

20. **D.** We need to first determine the crank handle's turning circumference. The length of handle that protrudes from the axle's axis is not important. What is important is the measurement of that portion of the handle that constitutes the radius of circular movement. Circumference is π times diameter. When we only know the radius, we have to multiply that number by 2, as the radius is half the diameter. In this case, since the radius is 6 inches, the diameter is 12 inches. The circumference is 12 × 3.1416 (π). Thus the circumference of the handle is equal to 37.70 inches. We know that Force × Large-wheel circumference = Resistance × Axle circumference.

    So, 150 pounds of force × 37.7 inches = R × 8.5 inches, or 5,655 = 8.5R. Divide both sides by 8.5 to isolate R: 665.29 pounds (rounded down).

21. **C.** Divide the resistance by the amount of force used to determine mechanical advantage. 700 divided by 180 rounds up to 3.89, or a mechanical advantage of 3.89:1.

22. **B.** Gears A and C are the drive gears shown in the diagram. Note that gears B and C are on the same shaft. The speed of the last gear, the unknown, can be called $G_L$. Its value can be determined by multiplying the speed of Gear A times the quotient of the product of the teeth of Gear A and C divided by the product of the teeth of Gear B and D, or:

    $$G_L = G_A\left(\frac{10\times 10}{40\times 20}\right)$$

    Since it is given in the problem that $G_A$ makes only 1 revolution, its value is 1. So $1\left(\frac{100}{800}\right)$ or $\frac{1}{8}$ of a revolution.

23. **A.** Gears A and C are the drive gears; B and D are the driven gears. As in Question #22:

    $$G_L = G_A\left(\frac{\text{product of teeth of Gears A and C}}{\text{product of teeth of Gears B and D}}\right)$$

    Or:

    $$G_L = 6\left(\frac{10\times 20}{40\times 30}\right)$$

    Then, $6\left(\frac{1}{6}\right)=1$, so $G_1 = 1$ revolution.

24. **B.** Since we know the gear ratio is a 1:6 reduction, its mechanical advantage is 6. Therefore, 6 × 175 foot pounds = 1050 foot pounds. 1,050 foot pounds is the maximum torque output possible under the conditions given.

25. **D.** Depending on how belt drives are set up, they can increase or decrease speed and torque as well as change drive direction.

## ASSEMBLING OBJECTS

1. B.
2. C.
3. C.
4. A.
5. A.
6. B.
7. D.
8. B.
9. C.
10. C.
11. B.
12. C.
13. C.
14. C.
15. D.
16. B.

# CHAPTER 5

# Using the Results to Guide Your Studies

Use the answer key following each practice exam, including the diagnostic exam, to grade your exam. Then turn to the section called "What the Results Mean" in this chapter to find out how to use the results to plan how to study for the ASVAB.

## WHAT THE RESULTS MEAN

Once you've scored your answer sheet using the answer key given, you'll need to use your results to help you determine your plan of attack for studying to take the ASVAB. Chapter 2 gives general information on setting up a study schedule and how to plan your studies, but before you set up a schedule you need to know *what* to study. We're going by raw scores in this section, which is to say that we're looking at how many you got right, rather than looking at how hard the questions were that you got right. That means these scores are a little different than the ones that you'll get on the ASVAB. However, keep in mind that on the practice tests, the harder questions tend to be later, so pay attention to where you're getting incorrect answers. If most of them are coming at the end of the subtest, you are not going to score as well on the test versus if your incorrect answers are scattered throughout.

For each subtest, you'll simply count up the number you answered correctly, and compare it to the chart for that subtest. "Good" means that you should have no trouble with the material on that section of the ASVAB, and that you should be able to qualify for a job that requires a good score on that subtest. "Acceptable" means that you'll probably do fine on that section of the subtest, but it's possible that your score won't be high enough to get the best of the jobs that require a good score on that subtest. A "Needs Work" score indicates that you will want to review the material on that subtest in order to bolster your score. A "Poor" score means that you may not pass at all.

So, let's look at each of the sections in turn, starting with the subtests that make up the AFQT. You have to score well on these four subtests in order to enlist, so it makes sense to pay the most attention to them.

### AFQT Subtests

#### Arithmetic Reasoning (AFQT)

**Subtest Results**

| Good | Acceptable | Needs Work | Poor |
|---|---|---|---|
| 27 | 24 | 21 | 15 |

#### Word Knowledge (AFQT)

**Subtest Results**

| Good | Acceptable | Needs Work | Poor |
|---|---|---|---|
| 32 | 28 | 24 | 16 |

**Paragraph Comprehension (AFQT)**

Subtest Results

| Good | Acceptable | Needs Work | Poor |
|---|---|---|---|
| 13 | 11 | 9 | 7 |

**Mathematics Knowledge (AFQT)**

Subtest Results

| Good | Acceptable | Needs Work | Poor |
|---|---|---|---|
| 23 | 20 | 17 | 14 |

**Technical Subtests**

The following subtests determine your eligibility to enlist in different types of military occupations. You will need to do well on the subtests that correspond with your desired occupation. See Chapter 1 for more information.

**General Science**

Subtest Results

| Good | Acceptable | Needs Work | Poor |
|---|---|---|---|
| 23 | 20 | 17 | 14 |

**Electronics Information**

Subtest Results

| Good | Acceptable | Needs Work | Poor |
|---|---|---|---|
| 18 | 16 | 14 | 10 |

**Automotive and Shop Information**

Subtest Results

| Good | Acceptable | Needs Work | Poor |
|---|---|---|---|
| 23 | 20 | 17 | 14 |

**Mechanical Comprehension**

Subtest Results

| Good | Acceptable | Needs Work | Poor |
|---|---|---|---|
| 23 | 20 | 17 | 14 |

**Assembling Objects**

Subtest Results

| Good | Acceptable | Needs Work | Poor |
|---|---|---|---|
| 14 | 12 | 10 | 8 |

Use the information in the "Using the Results to Guide Your Studies" section of this book after each practice test. Score each test, then review your results with the charts in this section, and revise your study schedule to reflect that material that you most need to review.

# PART 3
# Review

The chapters in this part will help you review the material that you will find on the various subtests that make up the ASVAB. It is strongly recommended that you take the Diagnostic Test first (Part 2, Chapters 4 and 5) to identify areas where you are not performing as well as you could. Then focus your review on those weaker areas.

Once you've done an initial review, take one of the practice tests (Part 4) to assess your improvement. You may need to do additional study, such as reading books on science or math (check your local library) if you have areas of particular concern. Continue alternating review with taking practice tests to ensure the best results on the day you take the ASVAB.

The first four chapters of this part (Chapters 6, 7, 8, 9) cover the subtests (Word Knowledge, Paragraph Comprehension, Arithmetic Reasoning, and Mathematics Knowledge) that make up the AFQT, which is the core test that determines whether you can enter the armed forces. It is particularly important to do well on these four subtests. See Chapter 1 for more information about the AFQT.

# CHAPTER 6

# *Word Knowledge (WK)*

The Word Knowledge section of the ASVAB is one of the four subtests that are combined together to create the Armed Forces Qualification Test (AFQT), which is the core test that determines whether you're eligible for entrance into the military. For that reason, it's crucial to do well on this subtest. See Chapter 1 for more information on the AFQT and how it's scored, including minimum requirements for acceptance into the military.

The Word Knowledge section is basically nothing more than a big vocabulary test. You probably remember how to study for vocab tests: Invest in a pack of index cards and start making flash cards! That old standby is still one of the best ways to master new vocabulary. Read further for more strategies that will help you do well on the Word Knowledge material.

## WHAT THE TEST MEASURES

It might surprise you to learn just how important paperwork—or at least written communication—is to the military, but practically nothing can be done without it. Everything from orders to training manuals to operations recaps is written down. Being able to communicate with others and to understand what others are communicating to you is fundamental to success in your military career. So you need to have the appropriate vocabulary. That's what this subtest is all about.

The subtest measures your vocabulary in two ways:

- Definition
- Context

For the first type of question, you'll be given a word and asked to choose the definition that most closely matches it.

For example:

***<u>Incensed</u> most nearly means:***

***A. smelly***
***B. angry***
***C. unhappy***
***D. lacking feeling***

Then you'll pick the answer that most accurately defines the word. In this case, that's answer B. While you're definitely unhappy (C) if you're incensed, "angry" is a better, more accurate answer.

For the second type of question, you'll be asked to pick the definition of a word used in context. Again, you'll be picking the "most nearly means" answer, so while there may be more than one answer that could be correct, you'll pick the one that is most accurate.

For example:

***The luxury high-rise apartment building boasts oak wood floors, granite countertops, and state-of-the-art green technology. Luxury most nearly means:***

*A. cheap*
*B. new*
*C. essential*
*D. extravagant*

Here, answer D—"extravagant"—most accurately defines the word "luxury."

Remember that words can have more than one meaning, so for the context questions you have to be sure you're defining the word according to the way in which it's being used, not necessarily according to the most commonly used definition. (More on words with multiple meanings later in this chapter.)

## DEVELOPING A BETTER VOCABULARY

In order to improve your vocabulary, you should make an effort to read more on a daily basis. If you're not a big reader now, you'll be surprised at how quickly your vocabulary will improve if you give reading some focused concentration every day over a few months. Even an extra half hour a day can make a big difference.

While it's best if the reading challenges you (thereby improving your vocabulary), you should pick material that interests you so that you're more likely to do the reading. And you don't have to haul heavy books around; reading blogs, online sites, and magazines can also do the trick.

As mentioned at the start of this chapter, you can use flash cards to help you memorize vocabulary words (rote memorization is ideal for this). Later in this chapter, we'll talk about learning the parts of words so that you can pick a word apart to arrive at its definition even if you've never seen the word before. This is an extremely helpful skill that won't just benefit you on the ASVAB, but will be useful throughout your life. We'll also talk about games you can play by yourself or with others to improve your vocabulary.

Try to make building your vocabulary an interesting part of your day rather than a painful chore and you'll be more likely to do it.

- Buy a word-a-day calendar or subscribe to a daily vocabulary list like the A.Word.A.Day list, which e-mails subscribers a new word (and its definition) every day: *www.wordsmith.org/awad/*.
- Challenge your friends to stump you with words from the dictionary.
- Use your new vocabulary words in conversation—make it a point to use one new word each day.

Polishing your vocabulary skills doesn't have to be something you do just to pass a test. It can become an enriching part of your daily life.

### Reading for Vocabulary

If you follow the suggestion above and begin doing more challenging reading on a daily basis, you'll encounter words that are unfamiliar to you. While it's tempting, don't skip over such words. The whole point of doing the reading is to come across such words and to figure out what they mean. Here are some steps to take when you do meet up with a word you don't know:

1. First, use the context to give you a clue to the word's meaning. See the section called "Using Context to Determine Meaning" in this chapter for pointers on how to do this.

2. Then, use a dictionary to verify the meaning of the word. You can keep a dictionary handy as you read, or you can use a dictionary app for your phone or tablet. Either way, get into the habit of looking up unfamiliar words as you encounter them to build your vocabulary.

3. Make a mental note of the word and its definition before going on with your reading.

### Creating an Unknown Word List

Some people find it helpful to write each unknown word on a small card as a reminder (or you can use a notebook or your phone's note-taking app to make a list). By jotting down the unfamiliar word and its definition, you'll reinforce its meaning and are more likely to recall it later. Such a list can be used in memory drills as you prepare for the ASVAB.

You can also use this method when you don't want to stop your reading to look up the meaning of a word. Write down the unknown word on your list, leaving a space to record its definition later. If you chose to take this approach, it's important that you do the research as soon as possible after your reading in order for the material to stay fresh in your mind.

## USING ROOTS, SUFFIXES, AND PREFIXES TO DETERMINE MEANING

In addition to using a dictionary to look up the meaning of a word, you can use basic word derivations or etymology to understand what a word means. This skill is particularly helpful for taking the ASVAB because if you encounter an unfamiliar word on the test, you can make some solid guesses about what it might mean and improve your score.

Word derivations can provide a partial, if not complete, meaning for a term. For example, take a look at the word "injudicious." The first two letters, in-, are a prefix that means "not" or "lack of." The root of the word, -judiei-, means "judgment." The last portion of the word, -ous, is the suffix, and means "characterized by." Therefore, "injudicious" may be interpreted as a characterization of someone who lacks judgment.

Look at the word "malicious." If you knew the root, "malice," then you'd know that it means "spite" or "ill will." The suffix -ous means (as mentioned above) "characterized by." So you can determine that "malicious" means "characterized by spite." But even if you didn't know the word malice, you might know the prefix mal-, which means "bad." So you'd be able to come up with a pretty good guess about the meaning of the word.

Having some familiarity with prefixes, suffixes, and roots can help you score well on the Word Knowledge subtext. See the tables of common roots, suffixes, and prefixes included in this chapter to help you study.

### List of Common Roots

| Root | Meaning | Example |
|---|---|---|
| acou | hearing | acoustical—pertaining to sound |
| acro | furthest or highest point | acrophobia—fear of heights |
| acu | needle | acupuncture—puncturing of body tissue for relief of pain |
| aero | air or gas | aeronautics—study of the operation of aircraft |
| alt | high | altitude—a position or a region at height |
| ambi | both | ambidextrous—capable of using both hands equally well |
| anter | in front | anterior—toward the front |
| anthrop | human being | anthropology—science of mankind |
| aqueo, aqui | water | aquatic—living in water |
| audio | hearing | audiology—science of hearing |
| auto | self | autocratic—ruled by a monarch with absolute rule |
| avi | bird, flight | aviary—large cage for confining birds |
| bio | life | biography—written history of a person's life |
| bona | good | bona fide—in good faith |
| capit | head | capital—involving the forfeiture of the head or life (as in capital punishment) |
| carb | carbon | carboniferous—containing or producing carbon or coal |
| carcin | cancer | carcinogen—substance that initiates cancer |
| carn | flesh | carnivorous—eating flesh |
| cent | a hundred | centennial—pertaining to 100 years |

### List of Common Roots

| Root | Meaning | Example |
|---|---|---|
| centro, centri | center | centrifugal—movement away from the center |
| cepha | head | hydrocephalus—condition caused by excess fluid in the head |
| chron | time | synchronize—to happen at the same time |
| citri | fruit | citric acid—sour-tasting juice from fruits |
| corpor, corp | body | corporate—combined into one body |
| crypt | covered or hidden | cryptology—art of uncovering a hidden or coded message |
| culp | fault | culprit—criminal |
| cyclo | circular | cyclone—a storm with strong circular winds |
| demo | people | democracy—government ruled by the people |
| doc | teach | doctrine—instruction or teaching |
| dox | opinion | paradox—a self-contradictory statement that has plausibility |
| dyna | power | dynamometer—device for measuring power |
| eco | environment | ecosystem—community or organisms interacting with the environment |
| embry | early | embryonic—pertaining to an embryo or the beginning of life |
| equi | equal | equilibrium—balance |
| ethn | race, group | ethnology—study of human races or groups |
| exter | outside of | external—on the outside |
| flor | flower | florist—dealer in flowers |
| foli | leafy | defoliate—to strip a plant of its leaves |
| geo | earth | geophysics—the physics of the earth |
| geri | old age | geriatrics—division of medicine pertaining to old age |
| graphy | write | autograph—a person's own signature |
| gyro | spiral motion | gyroscope—rotating wheel that can spin on various planes |
| horti | garden | horticulture—science of cultivating plants |
| hydro | water | hydroplane—form of boat that glides over the water |
| hygi | health | hygiene—practice of preservation of health |
| hygro | wet | hygrometer—instrument used to measure moisture in the atmosphere |
| hypno | sleep | hypnology—science that treats sleep |
| ideo | idea | ideology—study of ideas |
| iso | equal | isotonic—having equal tones or tension |
| jur | swear | jury—body of persons sworn to tell the truth |
| lac, lacto | milk | lacteal—resembling milk |
| lamin | divided | laminate—bond together layers |
| lingui | tongue | linguistics—study of languages |
| litho | stone | lithography—art of putting design on stone with a greasy material to produce printed impressions |
| loco, locus | place | locomotion—act or power of moving from place to place |
| macro | large | macrocosm—the great world; the universe |
| man | hand | manual—made or operated by hand |
| medi | middle | mediocre—average or middle quality |

### List of Common Roots

| Root | Meaning | Example |
|---|---|---|
| mega | large | megalopolis—urban area comprising several large adjoining cities |
| mero, meri | part or fraction of | meroblastic—partial or incomplete cleavage |
| micro | small or petty | microscopic—so small as to be invisible without the aid of a microscope |
| mini | small | miniature—an image or representation of something on a smaller scale |
| moto | motion | motive—what moves someone to action |
| multi | many | multimillionaire—person with several million dollars |
| navi | ship | navigation—to direct course for a vessel on the sea or in the air |
| neo | new | neonatal—pertaining to the newborn |
| noct, nocti | night | nocturnal—occurring in the night |
| oct, octo, octa | eight | octagonal—having eight sides |
| olig, oligo | scant or few | oligarchy—a government which is controlled by a few people |
| oo | egg | oology—a branch of ornithology dealing with bird eggs |
| optic | vision or eye | optometry—profession of testing vision and examining eyes for disease |
| ortho | straight | orthodontics—dentistry dealing with correcting the teeth |
| pent, penta | five | pentagon—having five sides |
| phob | panic or fear | arachnophobia—fear of spiders |
| phon | sound | phonograph—instrument for reproducing sound |
| pod | foot | podiatry—the study and treatment of foot disorders |
| pseudo | false | pseudonym—fictitious name |
| psyche | mental | psychiatry—science of treating mental disorders |
| pyro | fire | pyrotechnics—art of making or using fireworks |
| quad | four | quadruped—animal having four feet |
| quint | five | quintuple—having five parts |
| sect | part or divide | bisect—divide into two equal parts |
| spiri | coiled | spirochete—spiral-shaped bacteria |
| stasi | to stand still | hemostatic—serving to stop hemorrhage |
| techni | skill | technician—skilled person in a particular field |
| terri | to frighten | terrible—capable of exciting terror |
| tetra | four | tetrahedron—a shape with four faces |
| therm | heat | thermostat—device that automatically controls desired temperatures |
| toxi | poison | toxicology—science concerning the effects, antidotes, and detection of poisonous substances |
| uni | single | unilateral—involving one person, class, or nation |
| urb | city | suburb—outlying part of a city |
| uro | urine | urology—science of studying the urinary tract and its diseases |
| verb | word | proverb—a name, person, or thing that has become a byword |
| veri | truthful | verify—to prove to be truthful |
| vit | life | vitality—liveliness |
| vitri | glass or glasslike | vitreous—resembling glass |

### List of Common Roots

| Root | Meaning | Example |
|---|---|---|
| vivi | alive | viviparous—giving birth to living young |
| vol | wish | volunteer—to enter into or offer oneself freely |
| zo, zoi, zoo | animal | zoology—science of studying animal life |

### List of Common Suffixes

| Suffix | Meaning | Example |
|---|---|---|
| -able, -ible | capacity of being | readable—able to be read; eligible—qualified to be chosen |
| -ac | like or pertaining to | maniac—like a mad person |
| -age | function or state of | mileage—distance in miles |
| -ally | in a manner that relates to | pastorally—in a manner that relates to rural life |
| -ance | act or fact of | cognizance—knowledge through perception or reason |
| -ary | doing or pertaining to | subsidiary—serving to assist or supplement |
| -ant | person or thing | tyrant—a ruler who is unjustly severe |
| -ar | of the nature or pertaining to | nuclear—pertaining to the nucleus |
| -ation | action | excavation—act or process of excavating |
| -cede, -ceed | to go or come | intercede—to go or come between; succeed—to follow |
| -cide | destroy or kill | homicide—the killing of a person by another |
| -cy | quality | decency—the state of being decent |
| -dy | condition or character | shoddy—pretentious condition, or something poorly made |
| -ence, -ery | act or fact of doing or pertaining to | despondence—loss of hope; confectionery—place of making or selling candies or sweets |
| -er | one who does | lawyer—one who practices law |
| -ful | abounding or full of | fretful—tending to fret or be irritable |
| -ic | like or pertaining to | artistic—having a talent in art |
| -ify | to make | magnify—to make large |
| -ious | full of | laborious—full of labor, or requiring a lot of work |
| -ise | to make | devise—to create from existing ideas |
| -ish | like | childish—like a child |
| -ism | system or belief | capitalism—an economic system that revolves around private ownership |
| -ist | person or thing | idealist—a person with ideals |
| -ize | to make | idolize—to make an idol of |
| -less | without | penniless—without a penny |
| -logy | the study of | archaeology—the study of historical cultures using artifacts of past activities |
| -ly | in a manner | shapely—well formed |
| -ment | the act of | achievement—the act of achieving |
| -ness | state of or quality | pettiness—state of being petty or small-minded |
| -or | person who acts | legislator—person who enacts legislation |
| -ory | place | dormitory—building that provides living quarters |

### List of Common Suffixes

| Suffix | Meaning | Example |
|---|---|---|
| -ship | condition or character | censorship—overseeing or excluding items that may be objectionable to those concerned |
| -tude | state of or result | solitude—state of being alone or apart from society |
| -ty | condition or character | levity—lightness in character |
| -y | quality or result | hefty—moderately heavy or weighty |

### List of Common Prefixes

| Prefix | Meaning | Example |
|---|---|---|
| a- | not or without | atypical—not typical |
| ab- | away from | abnormal—deviating from normal |
| ac- | to or toward | accredit—to attribute to |
| ad- | to or toward | adduce—to bring forward as evidence |
| ag- | to or toward | aggravate—to make more severe |
| at- | to or toward | attain—to reach |
| an- | nor or without | anarchy—a society with no government |
| ante- | before or preceding | antenatal—prior to birth |
| anti- | against or counter | antisocial—against being social |
| auto- | self or same | automatic—self-acting |
| bene- | good or well | benevolence—an act of kindness or goodwill |
| bi- | two or twice | bisect—to divide into two parts |
| circum- | around | circumscribe—draw a line around or encircle |
| com- | together or with | combine—join |
| contra- | against or opposite | contradict—opposed, or against what someone else says |
| de- | removal from | decongestant—relieves or removes congestion |
| dec- | ten | decade—a ten-year period |
| demi- | half | demigod—partly divine and partly human |
| dis- | apart, negation, or reversal | dishonest—a lack or negation of honesty |
| dys- | diseased, bad, difficult, faulty | dyslexia—impairment of reading ability |
| e-, ex- | from or out of | evoke—draw forth or bring out |
| extra- | beyond | extraordinary—outside or beyond the usual order |
| hemi- | half | hemisphere—half of the globe |
| hyper- | excessive or over | hyperactive—excessively active |
| hypo- | beneath or under | hypodermic—something introduced under the skin |
| im- | not | impersonal—not personal |
| in- | not | inaccessible—not accessible |
| ir- | not | irrational—not having reason or understanding |
| inter- | among or between | interdepartmental—between departments |
| intra- | inside or within | intradepartmental—within departments |
| kilo- | thousand | kiloton—one thousand tons |
| mal- | bad or ill | malcontent—dissatisfied |

List of Common Prefixes

| Prefix | Meaning | Example |
|---|---|---|
| mis- | wrong | misinterpret—to interpret wrongly |
| mono- | one or single | monochromatic—having only one color |
| non- | not | nonresident—person who does not live in a particular place |
| ob- | against or opposed | object—declared opposition or disapproval |
| omni- | all | omnivore—an animal that eats all foods, either plant or animal |
| per- | through or thoroughly | perennial—continuing or lasting through the years |
| poly- | many or much | polychromy—an artistic combination of different colors |
| post- | after or later | postglacial—after the glacial period |
| pre- | before or supporting | preexamine—an examination before another examination |
| pro- | before or supporting | proalliance—supportive of an alliance |
| re- | again, former state or position | reiterate—do or say repeatedly |
| retro- | backward or return | retrogressive—moving backwards |
| self- | individual or personal | self-defense—act of defending oneself |
| semi- | half or part | semifinal—halfway final |
| sub- | below or under | submarine—reference to something underwater |
| super- | above or over | superficial—not penetrating the surface |
| tele- | distance | telegraph—an instrument used for communicating at a distance |
| trans- | across, over or through | transparent—lets light shine through |
| ultra- | beyond or excessive | ultraconservative—beyond ordinary conservatism |
| un- | not | unaccountable—not accountable or responsible |

## USING CONTEXT TO DETERMINE MEANING

To do well on the Word Knowledge subtest, you'll need to be able to understand the meaning of a word by its context. Practicing this skill ahead of time will help you succeed. While you may not be able to memorize every possible word you could encounter on the test, if you use context (the surrounding words) as cues, you can often determine the meaning of the word in question, or at least make a good guess as to its meaning.

As you're reading and you run across a word you're not familiar with, start by looking at how the word is used within the sentence before you look it up in the dictionary. That will give you practice in determining meaning from context.

When you see an unfamiliar word in context, try to identify whether it's a noun (person, place, or thing), a verb (an action word), or an adjective/adverb (descriptive words). That will help you narrow down the possibilities.

For example, look at the following sentence:

***The <u>nominee</u> ran a brutal campaign. <u>Nominee</u> most nearly means:***

***A. candidate***
***B. money-lender***
***C. employee***
***D. criminal***

You can guess that "nominee" is a noun, even if you don't know its exact meaning, because if you substitute another noun, like "teacher," the sentence still makes sense. So you know the word in question is a person, place, or thing.

Then consider the other words in the sentence and see if they give clues to the meaning. Since "campaign" generally has to do with working toward a goal, such as being elected to a political office, you can guess that a nominee is someone who wants to be elected. Thus A, candidate, would be the most accurate answer.

Another example:

***The restaurant patron was extremely vexed when the waiter accidently spilled coffee on his lap. Vexed most nearly means:***

*A. pleased*
*B. irate*
*C. bored*
*D. surprised*

Here, "vexed" is an adjective being used to describe how the patron is feeling. Obviously, the customer would not be happy under such circumstances, so we know the word "vexed" implies a degree of dissatisfaction. So B, "irate," would be most accurate.

## DEALING WITH MULTIPLE DEFINITIONS

The Word Knowledge subtest asks you to look at words in context in order to decide which of the possible answers is nearest its meaning. So it's important to pick the answer for the word as it's used in the sentence, not necessarily for its most common meaning. You will also find that for the questions that simply ask you to pick the correct definition of a word, sometimes you'll need to demonstrate your knowledge of alternate definitions of a word.

For example, if you were asked to pick the answer that most nearly defines "pupil" you might immediately think "student." But what if your choices were:

A. desk drawer
B. eye part
C. small figure
D. shoe insert

None of those possible answers is close to "student" so you will need to consider other meanings of the word. Since "pupil" also means the aperture in the iris that allows light to enter one's eye, answer B, "eye part," is correct.

If the word is used in context, it's easier to see when it's being used with its alternate meaning:

***The pupil put away her books.***
***Her pupil was dilated.***

In both cases, "pupil" is spelled the same way, but it has vastly different meanings.

Sometimes two definitions of a word are exact opposites: You can clip pages (attach them) and clip coupons (separate them).

There are also words that sound the same, but are spelled differently and have different meanings (one/won, shone/shown). This can trip you up if you're accustomed to hearing a word but not to seeing it spelled out.

What does this mean for taking the Word Knowledge subtest?

- First, remember that many words have more than one meaning, so if you don't see an answer that matches what you think the word means, ask yourself if that could be because you need to use a different meaning of the word.
- Second, determine the part of speech. Sometimes the definition of a word is related to its function in a sentence. For example, you might scale a mountain (verb) but weigh yourself on a scale (noun). If you know a scale weighs things, but the question uses scale as a verb, you will need to consider alternate meanings; in other words, you need to be aware that scaling a mountain may have nothing to do with how much the mountain weighs.
- Finally, as with any word you see in context, you can use the surrounding words to help you determine an alternate meaning. For example, consider the sentence:

***The emergency message was of grave <u>import</u>.***

You probably know that an import can be a product that comes from another country, but here the words "emergency" and "grave" signal that perhaps "import" is being used with an alternate meaning.

## WORD MEMORIZATION GAMES

To help memorize the meanings of words you're studying, you can play some word games that go beyond just drilling with flash cards. Grab a study partner to make the experience more entertaining and memorable. Teamwork is an important part of military life, so don't be shy about building a network of people who will help you succeed on the ASVAB—being part of a team is exactly what you'll be expected to do once you've joined the armed forces.

Studies show that you may need to see a word ten or twenty times before you'll remember its meaning, so don't get discouraged if you don't recall a vocabulary word right away. Just keep working at it and the knowledge will come. This is also why it's so important to start studying for the ASVAB at least several weeks before you take it—skills take time to build.

### Games with a Partner

Have you recruited your study partner? Here are a couple of memorization games you can play together.

#### Guess Which Word

For this game, Player A picks a word from the Words to Know list (see "Words to Know" in this chapter) and gives the definition. Player B has to name the word Player A is defining. Spell it correctly for bonus points. You can also do the more straightforward approach of having Player A give the word and Player B has to define it.

#### One Word Two Ways

Player A picks a word from a list of words that have multiple meanings (try any handy dictionary). Player B uses the word in a sentence. Player A uses an alternate meaning of the word in a second sentence.

#### Word Game Workout

Play a word game with a friend, like Scrabble. But don't just play it the ordinary way. Add a special studying-for-the-ASVAB twist: Every time you use a word, you have to define it correctly in order for your score to count. Player A uses the dictionary to check Player B's definitions, and vice versa.

### Games to Play Solo

Studying by yourself can be more interesting if you mix up your approaches. Sure, using flash cards over and over can help you improve your vocabulary, but that's not the only way to learn. In fact, taking a variety of approaches to learning can help you master the material more quickly than if you just rely on one tried-and-true method.

#### Word Association Sentences

Pick a word you're having trouble memorizing the definition for, say it out loud (you can hear the correct pronunciation of any word at *www.merriam-webster.com*), and then create a sentence that will help you remember its meaning. For example, "zenith" means "high point." But instead of memorizing the dictionary definition, create a personally meaningful sentence. For example:

> ***The <u>zenith</u> of my life was when I graduated from high school*** (or bought a puppy or won an award—whatever is personally relevant).

Then when you review the sentence, you'll remember that graduating from high school (or buying that puppy) was a high point in your life, thus helping you recall the definition of the word "zenith." This approach works much better than just making up some random sentence that has no personal connection to you.

**Memorize in Clusters**

Many words have similar meanings, so look for words that you can associate together. For example, "alluring," "prepossessing," "ravishing," "exquisite," and "winsome" all have to do with beauty. When you memorize the definition of a word, write down as many synonyms for that word as you know. You can also Google synonyms to broaden your scope.

You can do a variation on this theme by looking up all the antonyms (opposites) of a word. You can use a dictionary or *www.Thesarus.com* for this game.

For example, some antonyms for "beautiful" are:

- ugly
- repulsive
- hideous
- grotesque
- unsightly
- repellant

By memorizing synonyms and antonyms in clusters, you're more likely to recall their meanings when you encounter them again.

**Substitute Teaching**

Use the word you're trying to memorize in a catchphrase or adage that has a word with a similar meaning. For example, suppose you're trying to memorize the meaning of the word "canine." You'd swap it for "dog" in the following adage:

***You can't teach an old dog new tricks***

becomes

***You can't teach an old canine new tricks.***

Try some of these others and see if you can guess the meaning of the substituted word:

1. Avians of a feather flock together.
2. The attire makes the man.
3. Curiosity killed the feline.
4. Seek and ye shall procure.
5. There's no such thing as a complimentary lunch.
6. He who temporizes is lost.
7. Two transgressions don't make a right.

The correct answers are:

1. birds
2. clothes
3. cat
4. find
5. free
6. hesitates
7. wrongs

**Practice with Paragraphs**

One fun game is to write a paragraph or two using as many of the words on the word list in the "Words to Know" section (in this chapter) as you can. The caveat? The paragraph has to make sense. Another way to play is to pick five words at random and create a few sentences around them.

Here's an example with the words abnormal, controversial, equilibrium, guerilla, and oasis pulled at random from the list:

***The abnormal test result caused the guerilla to lose his equilibrium and seek an oasis away from the controversial struggle he was involved with.***

You can also play this game with a partner. In that case, Player A assigns Player B five words to use in a limited number of sentences, then vice versa.

## WORDS TO KNOW

The following word list includes vocabulary words that are commonly found on tests like the ASVAB. This list doesn't include every word you might encounter, and it only gives one common definition (many words have more than one definition), but it gives you a place to start. Review the list and identify words you're unfamiliar with, then use those in your studying. Remember, you'll need to see a word and its definition a number of times before it's "yours," so don't be afraid to try the different study aids and games described in this chapter to help you out.

You can find additional vocabulary words to study by checking out vocabulary books from your library, and by using online sites like *www.vocabulary.com*.

### Word List

| Word | Definition |
|---|---|
| abnormal | deviating from normal |
| accessible | within reach |
| acclimated | accustomed to |
| accredit | to attribute to |
| accumulate | to gather or gain |
| achievement | the act of achieving |
| acoustic | pertaining to sound |
| acquitted | freed from |
| acrophobia | fear of heights |
| acute | sharp or severe |
| adjacent | sharing a border |
| aerial | of the air |
| aerobic | occurring in the presence of oxygen |
| aggravate | to make more severe |
| allege | to claim without proving |
| alliance | connection between groups |
| amateur | one who pursues a study as a hobby |
| ambidextrous | capable of using both hands equally well |
| analogy | assumption that if two things are alike in some ways they will be alike in others |
| analysis | the act of breaking a whole into its parts |
| anarchy | a society with no government |
| anecdote | a short narrative |
| annihilate | to utterly destroy |
| annul | to make into nothing |
| antagonist | one who opposes |
| antenatal | prior to birth |
| anterior | toward the front |
| antisocial | against being social |
| antithesis | contrast of ideas |
| apparatus | equipment meant for a specific use |
| aquatic | living in water |

**Word List**

| Word | Definition |
|---|---|
| attain | to reach to |
| atypical | not typical |
| audiology | science of hearing |
| autocratic | ruled by a monarch with absolute rule |
| automatic | self-acting |
| auxiliary | providing help |
| beneficial | helpful to well-being |
| benevolence | an act of kindness or goodwill |
| bisect | to divide into two parts |
| bona fide | in good faith |
| buoyant | able to float |
| bureaucrat | an administrator or government official |
| calculation | the act of determining by mathematic process |
| carcinogen | substance that initiates cancer |
| caricature | distortion by exaggeration |
| carnivorous | eating flesh |
| cartographer | map-maker |
| catalyst | a substance that creates a reaction |
| catastrophe | a momentous, tragic event |
| censorship | overseeing or excluding items that may be objectionable |
| chagrin | distress because of failure or humiliation |
| changeable | able or likely to vary |
| characteristic | typical or distinctive quality |
| chastise | to punish |
| circumscribe | draw a line around or encircle |
| circumstantial | dependent on a situation |
| cognizance | knowledge through perception or reason |
| coherence | the state of sticking together |
| coincide | to be in the same place at the same time |
| colossal | big enough to astonish |
| comparative | relating to the examination of similarities |
| composite | a whole made up of discrete parts |
| concede | to yield |
| conceit | excessive self-regard |
| conceive | to become pregnant |
| conciliate | to be united or drawn together |
| condemn | to state something is wrong |
| condescend | to become less formal |
| confer | to give |
| congruent | consistent with |
| conjunction | the state of being connected |
| connoisseur | an expert judge |

### Word List

| Word | Definition |
|---|---|
| conscientious | adhering to rules of moral goodness |
| consensus | agreement in general |
| consistency | firmness of character |
| contradict | to oppose or be against what someone else says |
| controversial | causing opposing views |
| coordinates | sets of numbers used to indicate a place |
| corollary | related to a main idea |
| correlate | to establish a relationship between |
| culprit | criminal |
| curriculum | courses offered by a school |
| curtail | cut short |
| debacle | complete disaster |
| decadent | characterized by overindulgence |
| deceit | the practice of lying |
| deferential | showing respect |
| deferred | put off |
| defoliate | to strip a plant of its leaves |
| democracy | government ruled by the people |
| depose | to remove from a high position |
| despondence | loss of hope |
| detrimental | harmful to |
| devastation | ruin created through violence |
| devise | to create from existing ideas |
| dilettante | one who dabbles |
| diligence | energetic effort |
| disastrous | creating suffering |
| disdainful | filled with scorn |
| dispensable | something that can be done away with |
| disservice | an unhelpful behavior |
| diversified | balanced among various classes |
| doctrine | instruction or teaching |
| ecosystem | community or organisms interacting with the environment |
| ecstasy | a state beyond one's control |
| efficiency | characterized by productivity |
| elevation | the height to which something is raised |
| eligible | able to be chosen |
| emigrate | to leave one's residence to live in another country |
| eminent | standing out as notable |
| endeavor | concentrated effort |
| equilibrium | balance |
| evoke | draw forth or bring out |
| exhaustion | the state of being drained or fatigued |

**Word List**

| Word | Definition |
|---|---|
| exhibition | the act of showing |
| exhilarate | to make excited |
| external | on the outside |
| extinct | no longer in existence |
| extraneous | not needed |
| exuberance | the state of being excessive or uncontained |
| fallacy | a false or erroneous belief |
| feasible | capable of occurring |
| federation | a larger political entity formed from smaller ones |
| feisty | full of lively energy |
| fictitious | something made up or pretend |
| fiscal | having to do with finances |
| forcibly | using violence against opposition |
| foreshadowing | hinting at what is to come |
| forfeit | to give up, usually as a penalty |
| geriatrics | division of medicine pertaining to old age |
| grandeur | a state of magnificence |
| graphic | related to the visual arts |
| grievous | causing deep suffering |
| guerrilla | a fighter engaged in irregular warfare |
| gyration | spiral motion |
| harass | to persistently annoy or create hostility |
| hefty | moderately heavy or weighty |
| heinous | wrongful in a shocking or evil degree |
| heist | an armed robbery |
| hemisphere | half of the globe |
| hemorrhage | to bleed profusely |
| hierarchy | the arrangement of levels according to ability or authority |
| hygiene | practice of preservation of health |
| hyperactive | excessively active |
| hyperbole | overstatement for rhetorical effect |
| hypocrite | one who puts on a false appearance |
| hypothesis | an idea to be tested |
| idealist | a person with ideals |
| ideology | study of ideas |
| idiom | the language or dialect of a specific group of people |
| idiosyncrasy | a peculiar characteristic |
| idolize | to make an idol (hero) of |
| impersonal | without a specific subject in mind |
| implement | to put into use |
| inaudible | not able to be heard |
| indicted | charged with a crime |

### Word List

| Word | Definition |
|---|---|
| indispensable | cannot be done without |
| influential | holding sway over others |
| initiative | ability to take charge |
| innocuous | not able to harm |
| instantaneous | done immediately |
| insurgency | a state of revolt against authority |
| intercede | to go or come between |
| interfere | to insert in a way that hinders |
| interjection | the act of throwing something in between |
| interminable | seemingly without end |
| intermittent | happening only occasionally |
| interrogate | to question in a formal way |
| introvert | one who turns inward |
| invertebrate | without a spinal column |
| irony | using words to convey the opposite meaning |
| irrational | not having reason or understanding |
| irrelevant | something that is not applicable |
| irresistible | impossible to deny |
| judicial | relating to justice |
| kinetic | relating to the movement of bodies |
| laborious | full of labor or requiring a lot of work |
| lapse | a small error owing to inattention |
| latitude | allowing scope or range |
| legislator | person who enacts legislation |
| lenient | not rigidly adherent to rules |
| levity | lightness in character |
| liaison | one who maintains communication between various parties |
| lineage | line of descent from an ancestor |
| linguistics | study of languages |
| liquefy | to reduce to a liquid state |
| luxury | characterized by ease and indulgence |
| lyric | expressing intense emotion |
| macrocosm | the great world; the universe |
| magistrate | an official who administers the law |
| magnificence | a state of greatness |
| malcontent | dissatisfied |
| malicious | marked by the desire to cause pain |
| manual | made or operated by hand |
| median | the middle or intermediate position |
| medieval | relating to the Middle Ages |
| mediocre | average or middle quality |
| melancholy | a state of depression |

### Word List

| Word | Definition |
|---|---|
| melodious | an appealing arrangement of sounds |
| metaphor | figurative language that uses analogy to create an image |
| mien | appearance and bearing |
| migratory | characterized by moving from one location to another |
| millennium | one thousand years |
| mischievous | having the tendency to cause annoyance or to pester |
| misinterpret | to interpret or understand wrongly |
| misnomer | named in a wrong or inappropriate way |
| monochromatic | having only one color |
| motive | what moves someone to action |
| mundane | characterized by worldly concerns |
| municipal | relating to local government |
| myriad | a great many |
| naïve | lacking worldly wisdom |
| narrative | a story or account |
| neonatal | pertaining to the newborn |
| neurotic | one who suffers a mild mental or emotional disorder |
| neutral | not taking sides |
| nocturnal | occurring in the night |
| nucleus | the central point of a collection |
| nuisance | an annoyance or pest |
| oasis | a place of pleasant refuge |
| obsolete | out of date and no longer useful |
| obtuse | blunt, not sharp |
| omnivore | an animal that eats all foods either plant or animal |
| opaque | a condition that obscures light |
| oppression | the unjust exercise of power against others |
| optometry | profession of testing vision and examining eyes for disease |
| originate | to stem from |
| panorama | a complete view |
| paradox | a situation in which a contrary understanding might be true |
| patronage | support or influence of a person of power |
| penniless | without a penny |
| perennial | continuing or lasting through the years |
| permissible | that may be allowed |
| permutation | a major change of existing elements |
| perseverance | the quality of not giving up |
| personification | the representation of a nonhuman thing as having human qualities |
| pettiness | state of being petty or small-minded |
| phenomenon | a fact or event of meaning |
| placebo | an inert substance that provides comfort rather than producing an effect |
| plagiarism | representing another's work as one's own |

## Word List

| Word | Definition |
|---|---|
| plausible | something that could happen |
| postscript | an addition to the main idea |
| precede | to go ahead of someone or something else |
| precipitation | the state of being hasty |
| precocious | mature or able beyond one's years |
| prelude | an introduction to the main event |
| prestige | standing or esteem |
| presumption | an attitude of expectation or assumption |
| prevalent | commonly in use |
| privation | a state of lack |
| probation | the condition of being subject to testing or examination |
| prognosis | the prospect of a specific condition occurring in the future |
| propaganda | spreading ideas in order to confirm a specific viewpoint |
| propagate | to increase through reproduction |
| proximity | nearness to |
| pseudonym | fictitious name |
| pyrotechnics | art of making or using fireworks |
| quadrant | one quarter of a circle |
| quadruped | animal having four feet |
| qualm | feeling of uneasiness about the rightness of a particular action |
| quandary | a situation that creates doubt |
| quarantine | enforced isolation of a subject or community to contain a disease |
| quell | to put down or stop |
| querulous | the characteristic of constantly complaining |
| quiescent | at rest |
| quintessence | the purest expression of a thing |
| quintuple | having five parts |
| quorum | the number of people in an elected body required to conduct business |
| rampage | a period of violent behavior |
| rampant | characterized by absence of restraint |
| rarefy | to make less dense |
| recede | to return to a former position |
| recession | a time of economic downturn |
| reciprocal | something shared by both sides |
| rectify | to put right |
| refraction | the deflection of an energy wave from a straight path |
| reign | to hold royal power |
| reiterate | do or say repeatedly |
| reminiscence | recalling to mind a forgotten fact or experience |
| remittance | a sum of money sent elsewhere |
| repugnant | an object of distaste or revulsion |
| reservoir | a storage place |

**Word List**

| Word | Definition |
|---|---|
| retaliate | to pay back an injury or injustice |
| sacrilege | a violation of what is hallowed or consecrated to God |
| sanitize | to remove unpleasant elements |
| saturate | to wet thoroughly |
| scalene | possessing three unequal sides |
| scholastic | relating to school |
| segregate | to place apart |
| segue | to flow uninterrupted from one activity to another |
| shrewd | characterized by cleverness |
| solitude | state of being alone or apart from society |
| spasmodic | characterized by sudden violent action |
| spontaneous | done without thinking |
| stalemate | a condition in which none of the opposing parties can make a move |
| strenuous | using considerable energy |
| succession | the process of following a series or order of steps |
| superficial | not penetrating the surface |
| supersede | to take the place of |
| supposition | something that is believed |
| sustenance | one's means of nourishment or support |
| symmetrical | having corresponding parts on opposite sides |
| taciturn | not talkative |
| tangent | moving away from an original or main point |
| tariff | a tax imposed on imported goods |
| tertiary | of third rank; that is, of less importance |
| toxicology | science concerning the effects, antidotes, and detection of poisonous substances |
| transcend | to go beyond ordinary experience |
| transitory | not permanent |
| transparent | lets light shine through |
| tyrant | a ruler who is unjustly severe |
| unaccountable | not accountable or responsible |
| unanimous | agreed by all |
| unilateral | involving one person, class, or nation |
| unscrupulous | without scruple or conscience |
| veneer | a thin outer layer |
| veracity | characterized by truthfulness |
| verify | to prove to be truthful |
| versatile | easily changed |
| vestige | leftover trace or sign of something that came before |
| vitality | liveliness |
| wreak | to inflict upon |
| zenith | the upper limit |

## STRATEGIES FOR SUCCEEDING ON THE WORD KNOWLEDGE SECTION

This chapter describes a number of strategies you can use to study for the Word Knowledge section of the ASVAB, and you would do well to begin your study at least a few weeks ahead of test-taking day in order to improve your results.

But as you're taking the test itself, there are some strategies you can use to improve your chances of scoring well. Review these pointers just before you take the ASVAB. Also, review the general test-taking tips in Chapter 1. Keep them in mind as you work. Remember that your overall test-taking strategy will depend to some degree on whether you're taking the CAT (computer) version or the paper-and-pencil version. (More on this in Chapter 1.)

If you're taking the CAT version of the ASVAB, the Word Knowledge section has sixteen questions and you'll have eight minutes to answer them. For the paper-and-pencil version, you'll have thirty-five questions and eleven minutes to answer them. That means, depending on which version you're taking, you'll have only twenty to thirty seconds to answer each question. That doesn't give you a lot of time to ponder. So when you study, focus on both speed and accuracy. That goes for test-taking day as well.

### CAT Specific Tips

Remember that each section of the CAT starts with a question of average difficulty. If you answer it correctly, then you'll get a harder question (that doesn't seem like much of a reward, does it?). But answering harder questions means you score more points and more points are key to success, which is especially important on the subtests that make up the AFQT (and Word Knowledge is one of those subtests).

So, for the CAT, the key is to make sure you're correctly answering the first few questions. If that means you take a little extra time, so be it. But remember to finish the complete section before time expires, even if that means guessing at the end. It's better to guess than to not answer a question.

### Paper-and-Pencil Specific Tips

For the paper-and-pencil version, the questions are the questions and they don't change no matter how you answer the first couple of questions. So for the paper-and-pencil version, it makes sense to go through and answer the questions you know the answers to as quickly as possible before going back to those that are more difficult for you. Again, answer all the questions even if you have to guess.

### Overall Tips

Whether you're taking the CAT or the paper-and-pencil version, you may encounter questions for which you're not sure of the answer. Remember these steps to help you get as many of those questions right as possible:

1. Look for clues about the word's meaning based on context.
2. Guess at the meaning of the word. Pick the answer closest to that guess. If you're not sure, decide which answers you know are wrong and eliminate those, then pick among the remaining answers.
3. Don't forget to use prefix, suffix, and root word clues to help you determine the meaning of a word.

# CHAPTER 7

# Paragraph Comprehension (PC)

Throughout your military career, you'll have to study, interpret, and understand a vast amount of information—and you'll have to apply it correctly to various situations. How efficiently you acquire that knowledge and how well you understand how to use it is largely dependent upon your reading comprehension abilities. That's precisely what the Paragraph Comprehension subtest tests you on.

The Paragraph Comprehension subtest of the ASVAB is one of the four subtests that are combined together to create the Armed Forces Qualification Test (AFQT), which is the core test that determines whether you're eligible for entrance into the military. For that reason, it's crucial to do well on this subtest.

## WHAT THE TEST MEASURES

The Reading Comprehension subtest includes written passages of various lengths (usually one paragraph, but sometimes more than one). For each passage, you will be asked anywhere from one to five questions. But don't assume that if you can read and remember, you'll do fine. Reading comprehension isn't just the ability to recall what you've read or simply to summarize it. You will need to be able to determine a passage's main point, recall details about the material, draw conclusions, and identify sequences of events.

The subtest helps the military determine your ability to read and understand written communications, even when some of the information is implied rather than stated. The ability to do this is pivotal to your career success.

## READING COMPREHENSION TIPS

Some people find it easier than others to comprehend written material. Some people attribute this to inherited ability, but for the most part it is directly related to the kind of reading habits acquired in basic education. Of course, if those habits serve to impede rather than enhance a person's ability to read, it's a safe assumption that comprehension will suffer as well.

Let's examine some poor reading habits that were and still are indoctrinated in many English and reading classes.

One such misconception is the belief that subvocalizing what you read (moving your lips or other parts of your mouth or throat as you read silently) is detrimental to your comprehension. Some teachers have even gone to the extent of passing out candy in class to prevent students from subvocalizing. In truth, subvocalizing has been proven to be beneficial in various studies. The groups of students that did subvocalize their reading were shown to have a better understanding of most material studied. This was especially true when difficult or technical information was read.

Another widespread fallacy is that you should not read word for word. Rather, it is suggested that reading should be done by looking at several words as a unit. Some say that these units lend sufficient insight into the article's content. The idea is that time is saved and reading comprehension improved. Studies demonstrate that the opposite is true.

Some teachers also believe that if a student does not fully understand the material presented, it is better to continue on instead of rereading. The line of reasoning here is that if a student does not learn what is read the first time, repetitive reading only proves to be unproductive and a waste of time. Many studies have disproved this belief. In fact, rereading can be a necessity when the material being studied is complicated or abstract. Articles should be reread as many times as necessary to get the full meaning of the text before continuing.

Another misguided belief is that any text can be completely and quickly comprehended if key words are discerned. This very concept has given rise to the speed reading industry. Speed reading "experts" claim that reading at 250 to 300 words per minute is too slow when it is entirely possible to skim at a rate of three to six times that. What they fail to mention is that comprehension is sacrificed for the sake of speed. This raises the question: What gain is there if a fair share of information is not fully understood or comprehended?

Additionally, the major shortcoming of skim reading practices is that key words may be taken out of context and may cause you to misconstrue the underlying meaning of the article. Verbs and prepositions linking nouns can dramatically alter the tenor of the material being studied. If they, too, are not given attention as key words, a passage may be taken to mean one thing when, in fact, it actually means something entirely different.

You can be assured that college students studying for the LSAT, VCAT, MCAT, or other professional entrance exams do not skim their reading. Subject matter expected to be on these exams is closely scrutinized without regard to speed. There is no acceptable substitute for full and accurate reading comprehension.

So, to better hone your reading skills, practice reading as much material as possible and avoid the bad ideas just discussed. You will find it is easier to do this if the articles you read are on topics of interest.

### Read What You Enjoy

Nothing will discourage reading more than a dull or boring article. Reading of any kind is beneficial. Newspapers, magazines, and fiction and nonfiction books are a few possible sources for material. If you like sports, then read books about how to participate, or about great athletes. If you're interested in personal development, then check out blogs, articles, and books by people who are interested in teaching others how to make the best of themselves. It can be anything. Also, try something you've never read before. If you don't normally read fiction, pick up a novel from the local library and give it a try. You may discover something you enjoy.

### Read for Review

If you're in school, use your textbooks to practice reading for comprehension. It'll help you in your current classes as well as on the ASVAB. Even if you're out of school, cracking a textbook or two will help you review for the ASVAB. If you're still in school your school library is a great place to find textbooks for classes you may not be taking but for which you may want to study. If you're not in school, your local library can help you out with this.

### Read for Comprehension

As you read an article or book, try to discern the underlying meaning of the content. What is it that the author is trying to say? Are there ideas or other information that support any conclusions? If so, which are the most important? In this respect, certain concepts can be prioritized. You will find, over time, that by following such an inquisition into all your reading, your comprehension and reading efficiency will improve immensely.

## PARAGRAPH COMPREHENSION QUESTION TYPES

Most paragraph comprehension questions will ask you to demonstrate one of five basic reading comprehension skills:

1. Identifying the main idea
2. Finding specific details
3. Determining the author's purpose, tone, style, or technique
4. Making an interpretation or drawing a conclusion
5. Identifying a sequence of events, cause-and-effect, or other relationship

### Identifying the Main Idea

What is the basic underlying theme of the passage, or what would be a suitable title or heading that summarizes the article? In most cases, this is an inferential question. In other words, you have to assimilate all the information given and select one of four possible options (A through D) which best encompasses the meaning of the article. There will not be a singular sentence taken directly out of the article to serve as a potential option. This is more of a judgment decision on your part.

Note that the main idea is often found in the first or last sentence of a paragraph. A writer will often summarize the topic (or the main idea) of the paragraph in either the opening or the concluding sentence.

Here's a sample passage with a typical "main idea" question:

***A recent study found that U.S. employees spent nearly 3 hours per week dealing with workplace conflict. That is about $3.6 billion in paid hours (based on average hourly earnings of $17.95) or the equivalent of almost 400 million working days.***

***What does this study show?***

- ***A. U.S. employees average an hourly wage of $17.95.***
- ***B. Employees spend time on work other than their jobs.***
- ***C. Most people work hard.***
- ***D. Workplace conflict takes up time and productivity.***

The correct answer is D. While it's true that the passage reports the average hourly earnings as $17.95, answer A is not correct because that is not the point of the piece; it's merely a detail given to show how the calculations were made. While the passage doesn't come out and say "the study showed that workplace conflict takes up time and productivity," you can reach that conclusion by recognizing that the various points made all have to do with how much time and money is used up by employees dealing with workplace conflict.

Here's another example:

***One of the most common problems human resources professionals encounter in the hiring process is a resume that stretches the truth. When verifying previous employment, an HR professional may find that the job title given on the resume doesn't match the applicant's actual job title, or that dates of employment don't line up. Some applicants indicate that they've earned a diploma that they haven't. When this happens, an applicant is generally not considered for the job.***

***What would be a good title for this passage?***

- ***A. How to Verify Employment***
- ***B. Resume Dos and Don'ts***
- ***C. A Day in the Life of a Human Resources Professional***
- ***D. Resume Mistakes You Shouldn't Make***

The foregoing is an example of another type of main idea question you may be asked—one in which you're asked to come up with a good title or heading for the piece you've been asked to read. This can be a little trickier since a title isn't a topic sentence. However, if you can grasp the main idea of a paragraph, you shouldn't have any trouble picking an appropriate title for the piece.

In this case, the best answer is D. While the piece does talk about human resources professionals, it doesn't describe how to do the job, so A is incorrect. C is also incorrect since verifying the information on an applicant's resume is only part of what an HR professional does—and the piece isn't organized in a way that would suggest the reader is following along as the HR professional does her job. Although B is close, the focus of the piece is on resume errors; it doesn't discuss "dos." So D is the most accurate answer.

### Find Specific Details

Some questions you encounter on the Paragraph Comprehension subtest may concern literal reading comprehension. In other words, questions about certain details, ideas, or facts will be asked. If the answer is not immediately apparent, it can simply involve going back to the applicable part of the reading and picking out the correct answer directly.

***The adoption tax credit, which was permanently extended, has a maximum amount of $12,970, which you can use to reduce your tax bill. However, if your modified adjusted gross income exceeds $234,580, you cannot take the credit.***

***What is the maximum adoption tax credit?***

***A. $234,580***
***B. $12,970***
***C. It depends on your income.***
***D. The amount is not indicated in the passage.***

In this case, the answer is B. While it's true that the tax credit is phased out or eliminated at certain income levels (C), the question merely asks what the maximum credit is, so B is correct.

***Some women develop gestational diabetes during pregnancy. Gestational diabetes is a result of the pregnant woman's body not being able to make and use insulin as needed. High blood glucose levels in a pregnant woman who did not have diabetes previously indicate that she may have gestational diabetes. Gestational diabetes occurs in about twenty percent of pregnancies.***

***Gestational diabetes is:***

***A. a disease that inhibits a pregnant woman's ability to produce insulin.***
***B. a disease that results from a poor diet.***
***C. a type of diabetes that occurs equally in women and men.***
***D. another term for hypoglycemia.***

The above example shows one common type of question about details, and that is a question that asks you to define a word (or phrase) in context. In this case, the correct answer is A. Chapter 6, which covers the Word Knowledge section of the ASVAB, discusses ways to understand the meaning of words in context, so the information you learn there can also help you on the Paragraph Comprehension subtest. But on the Paragraph Comprehension subtest, the word or phrase you need to define is actually defined in the passage; you just have to make sure that your answer is supported by what is said in the passage.

### Determining the Author's Purpose, Tone, Style, or Technique

Some questions may ask you to consider aspects of a passage that go beyond the facts presented. You may be asked to identify the author's purpose, tone, style, or technique. For example, you may need to decide whether an author has written a passage to explain how to do something, or to entertain the reader, or to share a opinion. These are all different purposes.

You may also be asked to identify what tone the author is using—the emotion he or she is attempting to express. The tone could be humorous or angry or sentimental. (Or many other possibilities.)

You may be asked questions meant to consider how the author creates the effect he or she creates (style or technique questions).

***It never fails. You've just set the table for the twenty guests who are starting to arrive for Thanksgiving dinner when your eight-year-old comes into the kitchen and says, "Mom, the toilet won't flush." The best way to prevent a clogged toilet is to be careful what you put in it, but the time comes in every person's life when she is faced with the dreaded task of trying to unstop the toilet. First, don't flush the toilet five times, hoping that will solve the problem. You'll just end up flooding the bathroom. Instead, use a plunger to see if you can clear the clog that way. Remember to put the plunger gently into the bowl so you don't splash dirty water all over. Then, make sure the plunger covers the whole and press down slowly. If that doesn't clear the clog, try using an unbent coat hanger to clear any obstruction that may be causing the pile-up.***

***1. The purpose of this passage is***

***A. to tell a funny story about a time the toilet was clogged***
***B. to persuade people to use a plumber***
***C. to show the reader how to unclog a toilet***
***D. to describe for the reader the many uses of a coat hanger***

***2. The tone of this passage is***

***A. lighthearted***
***B. angry***
***C. ironic***
***D. formal***

On the Paragraph Comprehension section, you may be asked more than one question about the passage, as has been done in the above example. In this case, the answer to question #1 is C. Although the story starts with a hypothetical story about Thanksgiving dinner, the ultimate purpose of the passage isn't to tell that story, but to explain how to unclog a toilet.

The answer to question #2 is A, lighthearted. Even though the author's purpose is serious, she doesn't use a formal tone to communicate it.

### Making an Interpretation or Drawing a Conclusion

Another type of question may concern interpretation. After studying the information within a passage, a comparable or hypothetical situation may be posed and it will be left to you to interpret how what you have read applies to it. For example:

***Winter weather can be extremely dangerous. Subfreezing temperatures can cause people to suffer from hypothermia, a condition in which your body is unable to maintain a normal temperature. That means your organs, including your heart, can't work correctly. Hypothermia can cause heart failure and eventually death.***

***Based on this passage, it can be assumed that:***

***A. Hypothermia is a leading cause of death in the winter months.***
***B. The elderly are more susceptible than younger adults to the effects of hypothermia.***
***C. Heart failure is a preventable problem.***
***D. Hypothermia can be avoided by keeping warm.***

In this case, answer D is the one assumption you can make from the information in the passage. While the passage doesn't say that keeping warm will prevent hypothermia, it does say that subfreezing temperatures are what cause hypothermia, so a logical conclusion to reach is that staying warm will prevent it. The passage doesn't say anything about how many deaths are caused by hypothermia, so A is incorrect. Nor does the passage say anything specifically about elderly adults, so B is incorrect. It may be a common sense conclusion (that the elderly are more susceptible to the effects of hypothermia), but it isn't supported anywhere in the passage. By the same token, while heart failure is mentioned in the passage (answer C), it's only in relation to the problems hypothermia can cause. D is the better answer.

***A recent report showed that the CEOs of major corporations didn't just make a lot more money than an average worker at their company. They made* a lot *more money. For example, one corporate CEO makes as much as* six thousand *people in his company combined. Granted, running a company requires a skillset that most people don't have, but the outsized pay doesn't necessarily correspond with stellar results. In fact, most studies show there's little connection between a CEO's salary and the performance of his or her company in the long run.***

***Based on this passage it can be assumed that:***

*A. The author feels that corporate CEOs are paid inflated salaries.*
*B. The author wishes that workers were paid more.*
*C. The author thinks that CEOs are paid a lot but they produce results.*
*D. The author believes that running a company can be hazardous to your health.*

For this question, A is the best answer. While B may be true, the focus of the article is on CEO pay, not worker pay. C is flatly contradicted in the passage. And D, while it may be true, is not supported by anything the passage says.

***Someone who commits a crime under a threat against his or her person ("duress"), will not be held accountable for the criminal act (murder being the exception). In the courts' view of the matter, the conduct of the person actually committing the crime is justifiable under such circumstances. However, once the threat ceases to exist, any further acts contributing to the commission of a crime can no longer be justifiable. The courts further point out that the threat perceived by anyone forced into conducting criminal activity must be in the present, not the future. The prospect of the threat of force being carried out at some future time if the individual in question doesn't cooperate is not reason enough for criminal behavior to continue. Any criminal act under such circumstances is committed with intent and is therefore subject to prosecution.***

***Which of the following is a situation under which "duress" would apply and the person committing the crime would not be subject to prosecution?***

***A. In a bank, Steve is forced at gunpoint to fill a sack with money from a teller's drawer.***
***B. Margaret is forced at gunpoint to bash her next-door neighbor's head in with a shovel, killing the neighbor.***
***C. Arnold got a call on the phone telling him to steal the payroll cash from his employer or photos of Arnold in a compromising position would be sent to his wife.***
***D. Janice was forced under threat of death to put expensive electronics in her purse at a store. The thief was recognized by security and ran from the store. Janice later left with the electronics in her purse.***

In this case, you have to extrapolate from the general information given to a specific incident. That means you have to compare the various scenarios against the definition of "duress" and how it applies, and decide which alternative satisfies the requirements as laid out. For this example, A is the correct answer. The law specifically says that murder is not excused, so B is not a correct answer. The law requires a threat against one's person, so C is not correct (the threat of blackmail is not considered duress). In answer D, Janice was no longer under duress once the thief fled the store, so she should not have taken the electronics with her.

### Identifying a Sequence of Events, Cause-and-Effect, or Other Relationship

Some questions on the Paragraph Comprehension subtest have to do with identifying a sequence of events, figuring out cause-and-effect, or determining some other relationship between ideas given in a passage, such as comparison/contrast.

***As populations in the western United States grow, providing water to support them is becoming an increasingly complex—and politically heated—challenge. Cities, states, and other municipalities wrangle over how to use rivers, lakes, and other bodies of water that run through their territories. Litigation over water rights is increasing exponentially and there are no clear answers. Soon, politicians will not be able to avoid taking on this problem.***

***According to the passage,***

***A. population growth in the western United States should be restricted.***
***B. water rights litigation is easily settled, if precedence is relied on.***
***C. litigation over water rights should be restricted so as not to unnecessarily tie up judges with pointless proceedings.***
***D. politicians will need to devise regulations to deal with conflict over water rights.***

Here, answer D is the correct answer. It's clear that "politicians will not be able to avoid taking on this problem" has something to do with politicians needing to devise regulations. Again, there are other answers that *could* be true, for example A, but D is the one best supported by the information given in the passage.

***To install the light fixture, first make sure the power is turned off at the breaker. It isn't enough to turn the light switch off. Use a voltage detector to verify the power is off. Then connect the wires. Use a wire stripper to remove about three-quarters of an inch of the wire sheathing. Next, bend the wires into a U shape and wrap them around the screws. The black wire is the current. Sometimes the current wire is red. The white is neutral. The green is ground. Sometimes the ground is copper. Be sure to attach the black wire to the gold screw, the white wire to the silver screw, and the green wire to the green screw.***

***Based on this passage, to install the light fixture,***

- ***A. shut the power off at the switch, then strip the wires and connect them to the screws, making sure you connect the right wires to the right screws.***
- ***B. shut the power off at the breaker, connect the wires to the screws, then make sure the sheathing is stripped.***
- ***C. shut the power off at the breaker, then strip the wires and connect them to the screws, making sure you match the right wires to the right screws.***
- ***D. shut the power off, wrap the wires around the screws, then use the voltage detector to make sure everything is working correctly.***

For this question, you're being tested on your ability to identify the correct sequence of events. In this case, the most accurate answer is C. The passage reminds the reader that turning the power off at the switch isn't sufficient, so A is incorrect. B is incorrect because the wires need to be stripped before they're connected to the screws. D is not necessarily wrong—no harm in using the voltage detector after installation—but that's not what the passage says. So C is the best answer.

## UNDERSTANDING PARAGRAPH ORGANIZATION

When you were in high school, your teacher may have taught you to write paragraphs—and indeed essays—with a topic sentence, a few supporting points such as details or examples, and a concluding sentence. If only paragraphs on the ASVAB were all written like that, you'd know exactly where to find the main idea and the details!

But they're not. Passages on the ASVAB are written a lot like paragraphs you encounter in the real world—in blogs, newspapers, books, and magazines articles. In other words, you'll see all kinds of paragraphs providing all kinds of information in all kinds of ways. For that reason, it's a good idea to expose yourself to different varieties of writing instead of just limiting yourself to a few specific magazines you subscribe to or a couple of your favorite blogs.

It's true that a paragraph generally covers just one main idea, but that isn't always the case. So it's a mistake to assume that you can count on a given paragraph to be organized in a certain way.

However, that doesn't mean you can't learn to identify certain types of paragraph structures, which will help you identify where to find the information you'll need to answer the questions on the test. Let's take a look at some of the more common ways to organize a paragraph.

### Main Idea with Supporting Points

To illustrate a paragraph that's organized around a main idea with supporting points, let's look at a paragraph we saw earlier in the chapter.

***A recent study found that U.S. employees spent nearly 3 hours per week dealing with workplace conflict. That is about $3.6 billion in paid hours (based on average hourly earnings of $17.95) or the equivalent of almost 400 million working days.***

This is a paragraph that gives a main point in the first sentence. Note that it doesn't say, "In this passage, I will be discussing workplace conflict." No one writes that way except in English class. But that first sentence sets up the topic that is being discussed (the cost of workplace conflict). Everything else in the passage goes to support that point.

You can identify this type of organization because the body sentences all offer facts or evidence to support the main point (which you may have heard called a topic sentence or thesis statement).

While any of the question types you may find in the Paragraph Comprehension section could be asked over any of the passages, a "main idea with supporting points" organization lends itself to questions about (not surprisingly) the main idea. They are also often used for questions about finding specific details, since these paragraphs generally include a lot of details to support the main idea.

Paragraphs that are organized to include a main idea and supporting points can also be paragraphs that define a word or phrase, such as the gestational diabetes passage you read earlier in this chapter. Main idea + definition, where the definition takes the place of supporting points.

### How-To Organization

To illustrate a paragraph organized as a how-to, let's look at the first part of the installing light fixtures passage again.

> ***To install the light fixture, first make sure the power is turned off at the breaker. It isn't enough to turn the light off. Use a voltage detector to verify the power is off. Then connect the wires. Use a wire stripper to remove about three-quarters of an inch of the wire sheathing. Next, bend the wires into a U shape and wrap them around the screws.***

Notice that a lot of transitional words are used in this passage. "First," "then," "next." These words are clues that you're being shown how to do something in a step-by-step fashion. These types of paragraphs are, logically, often used for questions that test your understanding of sequencing. In that case, look for the transitional words in order to make sure you're identifying the correct order of steps.

### Chronological Order

A paragraph organized in chronological order is similar to one organized as a how-to. That is, information is given in a sequential way, and you're likely to see a lot of transitional words, such as "next," "then," "afterwards," "later."

### Comparison-Contrast Organization

In this type of organization, two (or more) things are likened to each other and their similarities and differences listed. Here's an example:

> ***Ash trees are different from other trees because they have opposite branching and compound leaf structures. A mountain ash is not a true ash tree (and is often called a rowan), though its leaves bear some resemblance to those of a true ash. Ash trees usually have anywhere from five to nine leaflets per leaf, unlike other trees such as the box elder, which may have three leaflets per leaf, or the maple, which has one leaf, or the walnut, which has many leaflets. Older ash trees have a characteristic diamond pattern on their bark.***

In this passage, you can see that the ash tree is being compared and contrasted to other trees like the mountain ash, the box elder, the maple, and the walnut. You'll see words such as "like," "unlike," "compared to," "the same as."

When you see a paragraph like this, you may be asked a question about the relationship between two objects, or a question about details.

While there are many types of paragraph organization, these are among the most common. Recognizing them when you see them can help you correctly respond to questions about the material.

## WHEN IDEAS ARE IMPLIED

Some of the more difficult questions on the Paragraph Comprehension subtest have to do with implied ideas. If a main idea isn't directly stated, it can be hard to know exactly what it is. If a conclusion is one you have to draw yourself, you might just go off in the wrong direction. So how can you prevent that from happening?

1. First, give yourself credit. You've inferred a lot of information over the years without anyone having to outright tell you what they mean. When the teacher says, "Don't forget to review Chapter 7 before next week's test," you can probably assume (infer from the teacher's implied point) that material in Chapter 7 will be on the test.

2. Figure out what you're being asked to do. Do you need to find a main idea? Do you need to draw a conclusion about the information? Do you need to apply the information to a different situation?
3. Next, focus on what is in the passage. You don't have to have special knowledge of the subject under discussion in order to be able to make an inference about what the main idea is or to draw a conclusion. In fact, you have to be careful not to make assumptions based on outside knowledge. Focus on what is stated in the passage, then draw your conclusions from that.
4. Identify the topic of the passage. You can often find clues to this in the first or last sentence of the paragraph, even if the main idea is not explicitly stated. What would you tell someone if they asked you, "What's that about?"
5. Determine what the various sentences in the passage have in common. What makes them relate together? Superficially they may not have a clear connection, but something must tie them together or they wouldn't all be in the same passage.
6. Summarize the message of the passage. Here's where you make a tentative conclusion about the main idea (or about whatever other inference you're being asked to make). Put the message into your own words. Then look at the possible answers and pick the one closest to the inference you've made.

Here's an example that will help you see how this is done.

***Who doesn't love a puppy? Well, other than cats. And cat people. But I've always been convinced that even cat people love puppies under all that eye-rolling and mean-spirited comments about blind obedience and lack of smarts. Puppies can be a pain, I'll admit that, what with their accidents in the kitchen, and in the living room, and the bedroom, and pretty much anywhere that isn't outside, and their yapping, and their nipping, and their inability to heel. But they're so darned cute. The cute factor definitely weighs in their favor. On the other hand, I'm starting to see the appeal of cats.***

***What is the main idea of this passage?***

What's the main idea? It's not specifically stated—nowhere does it say, "Dogs make great pets" or "Dogs are better pets than cats, for three reasons."

So you're looking for an implied main idea. But that's not so easy to grasp because the author seems to be undercutting her own point about how wonderful puppies are by listing what's annoying about them. So, work through the steps to figure this one out.

1. *First, give yourself credit.* Okay, done.
2. *Figure out what you're being asked to do.* This is pretty straightforward: What's the main idea?
3. *Focus on what is in the passage.* Can do. You're not being asked for your opinion about cats versus dogs, or what have you. What's in the passage is a rhetorical question, some examples of puppy behavior, and a concluding sentence that indicates that maybe the author isn't as sold on puppies as she thought she was.
4. *Identify the topic of the passage.* This one's pretty obvious; the passage seems to be about the appeal of puppies, which is implied in the "Who doesn't love puppies?" question that starts it off.
5. *Determine what the various sentences in the passage have in common.* We've got a sentence about how everyone loves puppies, and one that makes an exception for cats, and a sentence about how cat people really do like puppies even though they criticize them, then a sentence about the annoying things puppies do . . . in general, these sentences are about the characteristics of puppies. But not all of these characteristics are flattering, so while the topic seems to be about the appeal of puppies, the body of the paragraph doesn't actually support this conclusion.
6. *Summarize the message of the passage.* Now that we've analyzed the passage, we can see that the message of the piece is more "puppies can be a handful" and less "puppies are adorable!" So, using that summary, you can choose the most accurate answer from the ones given.

Suppose the possible answers are:

***What is the main idea of this passage?***

- **A.** ***Dogs make better pets than cats.***
- **B.** ***Cat owners actually prefer dogs to cats.***
- **C.** ***Puppies are a joy to be around.***
- **D.** ***Though adorable, puppies can be a challenge.***

Try this technique out an various paragraphs that you read in a newspaper or magazine article to help you study for the ASVAB.

## SAMPLE PARAGRAPHS WITH QUESTION TYPES

In this section of the chapter, we'll look at some passages and a series of questions that are asked about them. On the Paragraph Comprehension subtest, you're not going to be told which question type you're answering, or how the paragraph is organized, so you'll want to practice reading passages and answering questions about them without knowing what to expect. On the ASVAB, you'll need to ascertain for yourself what information is being asked in order to select the correct answer.

Let's get started.

***PASSAGE #1***

***All crimes, regardless of their nature, leave some degree of evidence behind. How an officer goes about gathering physical evidence can make the difference between offering evidence that is material and relevant in a trial versus that which is bound to be thrown out under cross-examination.***

***Preservation of the crime scene is the number one priority before and during the actual investigation. The number of investigators or specialists surveying the crime scene should be kept to an absolute minimum. Unauthorized persons should be removed from the premises until the investigation is complete. Bystanders can inadvertently step on or otherwise destroy or remove valuable evidence. In fact, some people have been known to obstruct justice willfully by destroying evidence in the hope of protecting a friend or relative.***

***For obvious reasons, efforts should also be made to protect evidence from the elements, such as wind, sun, rain, or snow.***

***Not only is minimizing the potential for evidence contamination very important, but so is the way an officer proceeds with the search for and collection of evidence. The mechanics of the search itself, if conducted in a careful and orderly manner, can preclude duplication (i.e., covering the same area twice) in the investigation. This search and collection needs to be carried out within a reasonable time because certain kinds of evidence are perishable (principally organic compounds such as blood and semen) and begin to deteriorate quickly. In addition to the time element, temperatures higher than 95°F or below freezing can also have a detrimental effect on such evidence.***

***In the course of the actual search itself, officers should be on the lookout for any evidence prior to actually entering the crime scene. Normally, searches are begun by scanning the floor and walls, finally proceeding to the ceiling. When marking and securing evidence, investigators should be extremely careful not to destroy any of it. Dropping a delicate article or accidently marking or scratching items are two examples of how evidence can be damaged. All evidence, once located, should be cataloged (recorded), listing a description and relative location where found in the crime scene. This compiling of records essentially provides the chain of evidence prosecutors can use at trial to secure a conviction.***

***1. What would be an appropriate title for this passage?***

- **A.** ***How Best to Secure Criminal Convictions Through Evidence Handling***
- **B.** ***What an Officer Should Not Do During the Investigation of a Crime Scene***
- **C.** ***The Intricacies of Evidence Gathering***
- **D.** ***Procedural Guidelines and Cautions for Crime Scene Investigations***

***2. What two words would be considered suitable adjectives in summarizing the content of this article?***

***A. Prudent and compulsory***
***B. Intelligent and inquisitive***
***C. Circumspect and expeditious***
***D. Attentive and compliant***

***3. Which type of evidence given below is most prone to deterioration with time and temperature extremes?***

***A. Blood stains***
***B. Fired casings and bullets***
***C. Hairs and fibers***
***D. Dirt and soil particles***

***4. Which of the following is not considered an underlying objective for investigators in sealing off a crime scene?***

***A. To prevent willful obstruction of justice by persons close to the investigation***
***B. To prevent persons outside of the investigative unit from inadvertently destroying evidence***
***C. To illustrate to the public that police know what they are doing***
***D. To preserve the crime scene as is***

For Passage #1, the best answer to question #1 is D. Only D best describes the scope of the article. Selections A and C are, at best, ambiguous in defining the content of the reading. Selection B was, in fact, mentioned in the passage, but it only addresses what an officer is not to do rather than providing a more complete overview of what is involved in evidence collection, as the passage does.

For question #2, the best answer is C. Circumspect and expeditious are the correct selections. The article points out that an officer has to look around a crime scene carefully and then be expeditious or prompt in gathering the evidence found in order to avoid potential contamination.

For question #3, the best answer is A. Selection A is the correct answer because the article mentioned that organic compounds are more prone to deterioration with time and temperature extremes and cites blood as an example. Hair is considered organic in nature as well, but it does not have the same kind of enzymatic or bacterial breakdown as blood. The remaining selections are inorganic and not subject to the same kind of degradation from the elements.

For the final question, #4, C is the correct choice. Only C is considered as being false. The rest of the alternatives provided are, in fact, underlying objectives for authorities to rope off a given crime scene.

***PASSAGE #2***

***Thermal energy flows from a hot material to a cooler material until an equilibrium is established (that is, until the temperatures of the two materials involved become the same). This is accomplished through one or a combination of three processes. The first process is conduction.***

***Thermal energy flows from one material to another by direct contact of the two materials. This can be accomplished indirectly as well, if there is a thermal conducting medium involved. A second form of thermal energy flow is convection. As a gas or liquid within a defined air space is heated, expansion occurs, and thermal energy moves in an upward current, displacing cooler air. An example of convection would be a fire that originates at the base of a wall. As the fire builds in intensity by ascending, the cumulative heat trapped in the ceiling eventually ignites the ceiling. The third process of thermal energy flow is radiation. Thermal energy is comparable to light energy in the respect that both travel in waves. However, when radiated thermal energy is absorbed by an opaque, nonreflective material, the material involved becomes heated. If the thermal energy absorbed surpasses the material's ignition point, a fire occurs.***

***1. What would be an appropriate title for this passage?***

A. *Thermal Energy and Its Effects on Structures*
B. *The Three Types of Heat Transfer*
C. *The Physical Dynamics of Heat Transmission*
D. *The Intrinsic Properties of Conduction, Convection, and Radiation*

2. ***A two-story home has a vertical heating duct common to both floors. If a basement fire heated this duct to the point that the floorboards around the heat duct upstairs caught fire, what form of heat transmission can we surmise is responsible?***

A. *Conduction*
B. *Convection*
C. *Radiation*
D. *Combination of radiation and convection*

3. ***The reason for the parapets between adjoining rooftops, is to serve as a protective barrier against which form of heat transmission?***

A. *A combination of convection and conduction*
B. *Convection*
C. *Conduction*
D. *Radiation*

4. ***Every time you heat food on an electric range, you are essentially using which form of thermal energy transfer?***

A. *A combination of convection and conduction*
B. *Convection*
C. *Conduction*
D. *Radiation*

5. ***According to the passage, which of the following is not true?***

A. *Heat and light are basically the same in thermodynamic terms.*
B. *As a given material is heated, it expands.*
C. *When thermal energy flows from a heated source to a cooler surface, an equilibrium of temperature is reached, provided the ignition point of the material involved is not surpassed.*
D. *Heated substances have the proclivity of displacing cooler substances.*

For Passage #2, the best answer for question #1 is C. Choices B and D are unsatisfactory because these titles only imply discussion of the three methods of heat transmission. The basic principle of heat flow is not included in either. Choice A is incorrect because there is no discussion in the passage about heat transfers and consequent effects on structures.

For question #2, the best answer is A. The heating duct common to both floors of the home can serve as a thermal energy conductor. The increasing flow of heat through this medium eventually reaches an equivalent ignition point for wood. The floorboards that directly contact the heat duct consequently ignite, resulting in fire in separate quarters of the home.

For question #3, the best answer is D. A parapet is essentially an extension of a fire wall above the roof level. If an adjacent building's roof were on fire, the thermal energy radiated would not affect surfaces shielded behind a parapet.

For question #4, the best answer is C. Pots and pans serve as mediums for conducting thermal energy from the electric range heating elements to the food being cooked.

For question #5, the best answer is A. Heat and light were described in the passage as being similar only in the respect that they both travel in waves. These energy forms exhibit different properties because of their differences in frequency.

***PASSAGE #3***

***In 1969, the Supreme Court made a landmark decision in overturning a lower California Appeals Court and California Supreme Court ruling. The case in question involved Ted Chimel, who was arrested for the burglary of a local coin shop. Incidental to his arrest, authorities thoroughly searched his residence against his wishes. Officers were successful in locating evidence that implicated Mr. Chimel in the coin shop robbery. That evidence was used in the trial to convict Mr. Chimel. Both the California Appeals Court and the California Supreme Court upheld the decision. It was, however, reversed by the Supreme Court, which held that Mr. Chimel's Fourth and Fourteenth Amendment rights were violated when the search (incident to the arrest and without a warrant) went beyond that area of his person or the area within his reach from which he might have obtained a weapon. Consequently today, how and what is searched is rigidly defined. Incident to arrest, an officer is only allowed to search the person and area within proximate reach for a potential weapon. Searches cannot be expanded further unless there is a warrant issued by a magistrate specifying exactly what can be searched or the arrested person gives permission or an officer has reasonable belief that another person's life may be in danger. The word "reasonable" is and has been subjected to various interpretations in the courts. The most dependable way of conducting a search without the "color of authority" potentially affecting the outcome of a trial is with a written warrant from an impartial magistrate.***

1. ***What would be an appropriate title for this passage?***
   - **A.** ***Chimel vs. California (1969)***
   - **B.** ***Search and Seizure Guidelines as Established by the Supreme Court***
   - **C.** ***The Consequences of an Unreasonable Search***
   - **D.** ***The Disadvantages of Not Utilizing a Warrant***

2. ***The word "incident" (as in "incident to arrest") as it is applied in the reading most nearly means:***
   - **A.** ***as a preliminary***
   - **B.** ***dependent on***
   - **C.** ***in the course of***
   - **D.** ***preparatory***

3. ***Which of the following factors could ultimately determine the legality of a warrantless search in the court's view?***
   - **A.** ***The position of the arresting officers in relation to the arrestee***
   - **B.** ***The degree of physical restraint placed on the arrestee***
   - **C.** ***The relative degree of ease or difficulty of the arrestee reaching a given area***
   - **D.** ***All of the above***

4. ***According to the reading, which of the following statements is the most accurate?***
   - **A.** ***Mr. Chimel's Fourteenth Amendment rights were violated in the landmark case of*** **Chimel vs. California.**
   - **B.** ***Warrants give a broad definition as to what area can be searched during criminal investigations.***
   - **C.** ***Warrants, in effect, remove the prospect of a court's consideration of whether "color of authority" may have in any way biased the case.***
   - **D.** ***The California Supreme Court overturned Mr. Chimel's conviction on the basis that his civil rights were neglected.***

For Passage #3, the best answer for question #1 is B. Selection A was indeed discussed, but it fails to include the entire content of the article. Selections C and D touch only on specifics and do not properly summarize the passage's underlying meaning.

For question #2, the best answer is B. Selection B is the correct interpretation of the word "incident" as used in the reading.

For question #3, D is the best answer. Selections A, B, and C are all factors that limit areas that an arrestee may reach, albeit for a weapon or just the fact that it is within their area of control. After the *Chimel vs. California* decision, courts take three factors into consideration when determining what a reasonable search without a warrant may entail.

For question #4, the best answer is C. Selection A is correct, but the question asks for the most accurate statement of the four given. This selection would have been more complete had it specified that his Fourth Amendment rights were violated as well. Selection B is incorrect because warrants are very specific with regard to what can be searched. They are not broad in definition. Selection D is incorrect because it was the Supreme Court of the United States, not the California Supreme Court, that reversed a lower court's decision in Chimel's case.

## STRATEGIES FOR SUCCEEDING ON THE PARAGRAPH COMPREHENSION SUBTEST

This chapter describes a number of strategies you can use to study for the Paragraph Comprehension section of the ASVAB, and you would do well to begin your study at least a few weeks ahead of test-taking day in order to improve your results.

But as you're taking the test itself, there are some strategies you can use to improve your chances of scoring well. Review these pointers just before you take the ASVAB. Also, review the general test-taking tips in Chapter 2. Keep them in mind as you work.

Remember that your overall test-taking strategy will depend to some degree on whether you're taking the CAT (computer) version or the paper-and-pencil version. (More on this in Chapter 1.)

### CAT Version Information

If you're taking the CAT version of the ASVAB, the Paragraph Comprehension section has eleven questions and you'll have twenty-two minutes to answer them.

### Paper-and-Pencil Version Information

For the paper-and-pencil version, you'll have fifteen questions and only thirteen minutes to answer them. That's a big difference, so you're definitely at an advantage if you take the CAT version.

### Overall Tips for Success

Either way, you'll have to read quickly but carefully in order to do well on this subtest. It's ironic, but you may find it easier to read the questions before reading the passage presented. It's somewhat of a backward approach to reading comprehension questions, but it will alert you to what is considered important, hence what to look for within the article, thus saving time. In other words, it's a time-saving strategy that will help you accomplish what you need to accomplish in the short amount of time you have.

Remember: Read the questions first, then try to answer the questions as you read the passage, looking for clues in the passage that will answer the questions.

Some additional tips for doing well on this test:

1. Remember, your answer needs to be supported by what the passage says. An answer may be logical, or you may know it to be true because of specific knowledge about the topic that you have, but that doesn't matter. The answer must be one that the passage states or implies.
2. Keep track of time as you read. If you're taking the CAT version and you're ten minutes into the test, you should have answered five questions. If you're taking the pen-and-paper version, by the time you're ten minutes into the test, you should have answered about twelve questions. Don't spend too much time on any one question.
3. Guess if you don't know the answer, but try to eliminate obviously wrong answers first.

# CHAPTER 8

# Arithmetic Reasoning (AR)

The Arithmetic Reasoning subtest of the ASVAB is one of the four subtests that are combined together to create the Armed Forces Qualification Test (AFQT), which is the core test that determines whether you're eligible for entrance into the military. For that reason, it's crucial to do well on this subtest.

In addition, many of the jobs you may be interested in pursuing in the military will require a solid understanding of math concepts, so getting a good score on this subtest will enhance your opportunities. The Arithmetic Reasoning score is often combined with Mathematics Knowledge and/or General Science in order to determine your eligibility for various military jobs. Some technical and clerical jobs require a solid Arithmetic Reasoning score as well as a good showing on the verbal subtests (Word Knowledge and Paragraph Comprehension).

## WHAT THE TEST MEASURES

The Arithmetic Reasoning subtest measures your basic math skills. This includes simple operations such as addition, subtraction, multiplication, and division, but also more complicated skills like dividing fractions, converting fractions into decimals (and vice versa), and calculating percent change.

If your math skills are shaky, a thorough review is in order since this is such a crucial component of success in the military. Work through the material in this chapter (as well as Chapter 9, Mathematics Knowledge) and take the practice tests. If you're still struggling, consider working with a tutor or taking a refresher course at a local community college.

## NUMBER SYSTEMS

While the term "number systems" can mean the symbols we use to indicate numbers, it also means that different types of numbers are used in different types of calculations, and number systems are just groups of those numbers. For example:

- *Natural numbers* are a number system that includes positive numbers (such as 1, 2, 3, 4, etc.). Sometimes 0 is considered part of the natural number system.
- *Whole numbers* are those numbers that contain no fraction. 1 is a whole number; $1\frac{1}{3}$ is not.
- *Integers* are whole numbers but can include negative numbers as well, such as 1 and −1.
- *Rational numbers* are numbers that can be written as a fraction. The number 5 is the same as $\frac{5}{1}$ so it qualifies as a rational number. The fraction $\frac{1}{5}$ is also a rational number. The decimal 0.25 is a rational number because it can be written as a fraction: $\frac{1}{4}$. But the decimal 0.2734592 is not a rational number, since it cannot be written as a fraction.
- *Irrational numbers* are numbers that can't be written as fractions. Since 0.2734592 can't be written as a fraction, it qualifies as an irrational number.

- *Real numbers* is a set that includes rational and irrational numbers, but not imaginary numbers.
- *Imaginary numbers* are numbers that don't actually exist, except that we can pretend they do. The accepted definition of an imaginary number is a number that, when squared, produces a negative number. That's because there's no number that, when squared, produces a negative number. To square a number, you multiply it by itself, so $3^2 = 3 \times 3 = 9$. If you had $-3^2$ the answer would still be 9, not $-9$. That's because a negative number multiplied by a negative number is a positive number: $-3 \times -3 = 9$. In other words, $-3 \times -3 \neq -9$. (The equal sign with a slash through it, $\neq$, means "does not equal.")

But if we imagine a number exists that could do this, we can solve some complicated math problems that we couldn't otherwise solve. Fortunately, math problems requiring the use of imaginary numbers don't pop up on the ASVAB.

## PLACE VALUE

*Place value* is the way we recognize the meaning of various digits in a number. For example, in the number 473, we know that the 4 is in the hundreds column, so we are talking about four hundreds. The number 7 is in the tens column, so we know we're talking about 7 tens, or 70. And the 3 is in the ones column, so we know we're talking about 3 ones. We would say the number as "four hundred seventy-three."

In other words, we're not talking about thousands. Nor are we talking about 7 hundreds or 3 tens. The position of the digit tells us its value.

The same is true on the other side of the decimal point. The number 473 could also be written as 473. or 473.0; they all mean the same thing. To the right of the decimal point, place values are in fractions. The first value is tenths, then hundredths, then thousandths. In our whole number 473, we have zero tenths (we also have zero hundredths and zero thousandths).

On the other hand, in the number 12.659, there are 6 tenths, 5 hundredths, and 9 thousandths. The 6 tenths could be represented as $\frac{6}{10}$, the 5 hundredths could be represented as $\frac{5}{100}$, and the 9 thousandths could be represented as $\frac{9}{1000}$.

We use commas in numbers to help us identify the place value of a given number. 1,000,000 is easier to identify as 1 million than 1000000 is.

## NUMBER LINE

A concrete way to visualize how numbers work is through the use of a number line, a straight line with points corresponding to numbers, usually (but not always) integers. The numbers on a number line increase in value moving to the right and decrease in value moving to the left. See Figure 8.1.

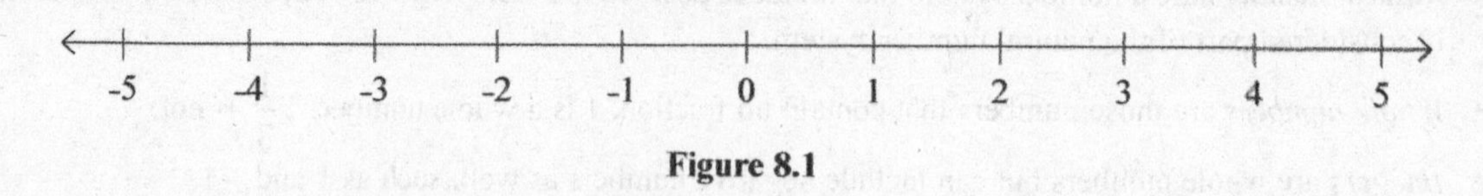


**Figure 8.1**

A number line is especially helpful when dealing with negative numbers. A number line can help you determine comparative values, and can help you easily figure out differences, such as "What is the difference between $-6$ and 6?" You might at first glance think the answer is 0, but counting on the number line will show you the answer is 12. A number line can also help you figure out how to add negative numbers. Use the number line to determine the sum of $-6 + -6$. (You should have come up with the answer $-12$.)

## OPERATIONS REVIEW

We can manipulate integers by combining them together or taking some amount away. This manipulation is accomplished through operations that you're familiar with: addition, subtraction, multiplication, and division. We'll look at whole numbers first (that is, those numbers without fractions). Then we'll look at how to manipulate fractions.

### Addition

Addition is the simplest of the operations. If you have 2 apples in your basket, and you pick 3 more, you now have 5 apples. The numbers being added together are called addends, and the result is called the sum.

If you're adding together a negative number and a positive number, then you disregard the signs, subtract the smaller number from the larger number, then use the sign of the larger number in the result:

$$-9+4=-5$$

In this case, you subtract the smaller number (4) from the larger number (9), then use the sign of the larger number (–) in the answer.

It also works if the larger number is positive:

$$9+(-4)=5$$

You still subtract the smaller number (4) from the larger number (9) for a result of 5. Then you use the sign of the larger number. In this case, the 9 is positive, so the answer is, too. As you can see, $9+(-4)$ is the same as $9-4$.

#### Commutative Property

When you add numbers together, it doesn't matter what order you add them, you still get the same result.

$$2+3=5$$

$$3+2=5$$

This is true no matter how many numbers you're adding together:

$$1+2+3+4+5=15$$

$$5+4+3+2+1=15$$

$$1+3+5+2+4=15$$

This property of addition is called the commutative property (also sometimes called the commutative law). The commutative property is true of multiplication as well (since multiplication is just another method of addition).

#### Additive Identity

When you add 0 to a number, the number stays the same.

$$2+3=5$$

$$2+3+0=5$$

This is the additive identity. Unlike the commutative property, though, the additive identity is *not* also true of multiplication. If you multiply anything by 0, the answer is 0.

**Associative Property**

In a series of numbers to be added, it doesn't matter which numbers you add together first, the answer will always be the same. So, if you have $1 + 2 + 3 + 4 + 5 = ?$ you could add $1 + 2$ first, or you could add $2 + 3$ first, or you could add $2 + 5$, and it wouldn't matter. The answer would still be 15.

This is a useful tool because sometimes it's easier to add together certain numbers first. For example:

$$18+26+4=?$$

If you add $26 + 4$ together first, as the associative property says you can, you get 30; $30 + 18 = 48$, a calculation you can make more quickly than you can make if you add $18 + 26$ together first.

This property of addition is called the associative property (it is also true of multiplication).

**Additive Inverse**

The additive inverse is a number's opposite. The sum of the two numbers always equals 0. So, the additive inverse of 9 is $-9$. The additive inverse of $-9$ is 9 (9 is the same as $+9$, but we usually drop the plus sign in front of positive numbers).

**Addition Property of Equality**

The addition property says that if the same amount is added to each side of an equation, then the equation remains equal.

For example, suppose you have the equation:

$$3+2=5$$

You could add 4 to each side and the equation would still be equal:

$$3+2+4=5+4$$

In this case, $3 + 2 + 4 = 9$ and $5 + 4 = 9$.

Note that this property doesn't mean the values somehow remain the *same*. It just means they remain equal.

**Subtraction**

Subtracting is the operation of taking an amount away. So if you had 5 apples in your basket, and Joelle stole 3, you'd have 2 apples left. The difference (2 apples) is the amount that is left over.

$$5-3=2$$

Unlike addition, though, you can't move the numbers around when you're subtracting and still get the same result. If you said $3-5=2$, you'd be wrong.

When you subtract a larger number from a smaller one, the answer is a negative number:

$$2-9=-7$$

When you subtract a negative number from a positive number, you're actually adding:

$$3-(-2)=5$$

Or:

$$3+2=5$$

That's also true if you're subtracting a negative number from a negative number:

$$-3-(-2)=-1$$

Or:

$$-3+2=-1$$

If the negative number you're subtracting is larger than the number you're subtracting from, the difference is positive:

$$-2-(-9)=7$$

Or:

$$-2+9=7$$

If you're subtracting a positive number from a negative number, the answer is a negative.

$$-3-4=-7$$

Another way to say that would be:

$$-3+(-4)=-7$$

**Subtractive Identity**

When you subtract 0 from a number, the number stays the same.

$$9-0=9$$

This is the subtractive identity.

**Subtraction Property of Equality**

The subtraction property says that if the same amount is taken from each side of an equation, the equation remains equal.

Suppose you have the equation:

$$9-4=5$$

You could subtract a number from both sides of the equation, and the equation would still be equal.

$$9-4-3=5-3$$

In this case, $9-4-3=2$ just as $5-3=2$.

As with the addition property of equality, we're not saying the values don't change, we're just saying they remain equal.

### Multiplication

Multiplication is basically repeated addition. You could write:

$$2+2+2+2+2+2+2=14$$

Which is just a way of saying "2 seven times." Or you could write:

$$2 \times 7 = 14$$

It's much easier to write and much easier to answer correctly. (The more times you have to perform an operation, the more opportunities you have for making a mistake.)

Because the times symbol (×) can be confused with a variable (such as $x$), a dot is often used to indicate multiplication:

$$2 \bullet 7 = 14$$

Sometimes an asterisk is used:

$$2 * 7 = 14$$

But you're unlikely to encounter that on the ASVAB, and we don't use asterisks to indicate multiplication in this book.

Multiplication can also be indicated when a number is next to an unknown:

$2a$ means "2 times $a$."

Two unknowns (also called variables) next to each other also indicate multiplication:

$$xy = x \bullet y$$

Parentheses can also be used to indicate multiplication. Sometimes two sets are used:

$(2 + 2)(3 + 2)$ is the same as $(2 + 2) \times (3 + 2)$

And sometimes just one set is used:

$2(2 + 3)$ is the same as $2 \times (2 + 3)$

**Commutative Property**

As in addition, multiplication has the commutative property. That means that you can multiply a series of numbers in any order and the answer is still the same. So:

$$2 \bullet 9 \bullet 5 = 90$$

And:

$$9 \bullet 2 \bullet 5 = 90$$

And:

$$5 \bullet 2 \bullet 9 = 90$$

And so on.

**Associative Property**

As with addition, multiplication has the associative property. That means you can multiply a series of numbers according to whatever groups you like and the answer is still the same. So, given:

$$9 \bullet 2 \bullet 5 = ?$$

You can multiply $9 \bullet 2$ first, then multiply the result (18) by 5 to reach 90. Or you can multiply $2 \bullet 5$ first, then multiply the result (10) by 9 to reach 90. As you can see, the second way of multiplying this series would be faster and easier to do in your head than the first way.

**Distributive Property**

The distributive property says that if you have a number that you need to multiply by a group of numbers, such as $9 \bullet (2+6)$, the answer is the same whether you add that group first or multiply each number in the group separately, then add the results together.

In other words:

$$9 \bullet 8 = 9 \bullet 2 + 9 \bullet 6$$

Either way, the answer is 72. This property is a useful one to know in order to solve for unknowns in algebra.

**Multiplicative Identity**

If you multiply a number by 1, the number stays the same.

$$9 \times 1 = 9$$

This is the multiplicative identity.

**The Zero Property of Multiplication**

This is also called the zero-product property, the property of zero, and the multiplicative property of zero.

If you multiply a number by 0, that number becomes 0:

$$9 \times 0 = 0$$

**Multiplicative Inverse**

This is also called a reciprocal. The multiplicative inverse of a number is the number it can be multiplied by to reach a product of 1. For example, if you multiplied $2 \times \frac{1}{2}$ the product is 1. The inverse is basically a fraction turned upside down. This is easier to see if we make the number 2 into a fraction:

$$\frac{2}{1} \times \frac{1}{2} = 1$$

Here are a few other examples:

$$\frac{2}{3} \times \frac{3}{2} = 1$$

Or:

$$1\frac{1}{4} \times \frac{4}{5} = 1$$

### Division

Division is the operation that breaks a number into equal parts. It's the inverse operation to multiplication. Division problems are expressed in different ways:

$$7\overline{)31} = ?$$

Or:

$$31 \div 7 = ?$$

Or:

$$31/7 = ?$$

Or:

$$\frac{31}{7} = ?$$

The dividend is the number that is being divided. In this case, that's 31. The divisor is the number that it is being divided by, or, in this case, 7. Doing the math, you can see that 7 goes into 31 four times, so the quotient is 4. But 31 does not divide evenly by 7, so there are numbers left over. These leftovers are called the remainder. In this case, there's a remainder of 3.

The dividend and the divisor must always be of the same type of unit. For example, you can divide miles by miles, but not miles by feet (unless you do some other calculations first). You can't divide 31 apples into 4 groups of oranges, right?

**Divisive Identity**

Any number divided by 1 stays the same:

$$31 \div 1 = 31$$

This is the divisive identity.

**The Zero Property of Division**

There are two parts to this rule. The first is that dividing 0 by any number equals 0:

$$0 \div 7 = 0$$

That's because you can't split nothing into groups.

The second rule is that if you divide any number by 0 ($7 \div 0$), the answer is undefined. Note that this is not the same as the answer being 0. It just means you can't solve the problem.

## ORDER OF OPERATIONS

Often when you need to solve a problem, you have to do several operations in order to arrive at the correct answer. For example:

$$3^2 + 4 + (6 \times 5) \div 2 = ?$$

Where do you begin? There's a handy rule of thumb: PEMDAS.

That means:
*Parenthesis* first.
Then *exponents*.
Next, *multiplication* and *division* (moving from left to right).
And finally *addition* and *subtraction* (moving from left to right).
So, let's solve that problem one step at a time. Parenthesis first:

$$3^2 + 4 + 30 \div 2 = ?$$

Then exponents:

$$9 + 4 + 30 \div 2 = ?$$

Then multiplication and division:

$$9 + 4 + 15 = ?$$

Then addition and subtraction:

$$9 + 4 + 15 = 28$$

## ROUNDING AND ESTIMATION

Often in calculations you simply need to have a basic estimate of an answer. For example, suppose you need to buy three things at the grocery store and want to know if the twenty in your wallet is enough to cover them. Instead of breaking out the calculator and adding $2.37, $4.99, and $8.79 then figuring out the sales tax and adding it in, you could round up the numbers ($2.50, $5, and $9), add 10 percent to cover the sales tax (if applicable), and quickly determine that you have enough.

Rounding, which is reducing or increasing a number to make calculations easier, generally follows this rule of thumb: if the number is under 5, you round down, and if the number is 5 or over, you round up.

Usually you round to the next place value. For example, 4.577 would round up to 4.58, dropping the thousandths place. By the same token, 4.322 would round down to 4.32. Usually you just round up by one increment. So we went from 4.577 to 4.58 (moving up one hundredth) instead of 4.59 (which would be two hundredths).

But the rule of thumb isn't set in stone. You could round up more than one place value. For example, 4,492,173 could be rounded to 4,492,170, but it might be more usefully expressed as "about 4.5 million." (Note that when rounding or estimating, you always want to use "about" or "approximately" in your answer.)

In our grocery store example, rounding up the $2.37 to $2.50 (rather than rounding to $2.40) and the $8.79 to $9 (rather than $8.80) makes the calculation easier.

Being able to quickly estimate an answer means you can immediately exclude wrong answers, which can be convenient (keep this in mind for when you take the Arithmetic Reasoning subtest).

## SERIES, SETS, AND SEQUENCES

A sequence is a series of things (for our purposes, numbers) placed in some sort of order. So, 1, 2, 3, 4 . . . is a sequence. When the three periods (which you might recognize as an ellipsis) are used in math, they mean "infinity." So, that sequence of whole numbers is a sequence that goes on forever.

When we say "placed in some sort of order" we mean that someone is deciding what that order is. So, a sequence might be odd numbers only, or it might be a sequence where every number after the first has 3 added to it: 1, 4, 7, 10 . . . . It could be backwards: 10, 9, 8, 7 . . . . It could be practically any order you can think of.

This organizational principle is called a rule. If you know the rule, you can figure out what the next number in the sequence is going to be. However, a sequence can have more than one rule, or it may be impossible for you to know the exact rule given limited information. A sequence of 2, 4 might be even numbers, or it might be numbers with two added to them, or it might be numbers multiplied by two. With the limited information you have available, you can't know for certain.

Some sequences are finite. For example, you could have a sequence of single-digit even whole numbers, and that would be limited to 2, 4, 6, 8.

The numbers in a sequence are called terms, and are named according to position: first term, second term, etc.

Like a sequence, a set is a collection or group, but don't confuse the two! A set has only one of each thing. In a sequence, you could have 1, 2, 3, 1, 2, 3 . . . , but a set would not repeat the numbers. The parts of a set are called its elements, and in math sets are often used to define like elements (the first ten negative integers, for example, or whole numbers greater than zero but less than 100).

Curly brackets $\{\ \}$ (also called braces) are used to indicate a sequence or a set.

A series is the value of the terms of a sequence added together. So if you have a sequence of $\{2,4,6,8\}$ then the series can be written as $\{2+4+6+8\}$ and the sum, or value, would be 20.

A sequence is often given a letter as its name. So a sequence might be called *a*. A term in that sequence can be indicated generically as a subscript *n*: $a_n$

Therefore, if you wanted to refer to the second term in that sequence, you would call it $a_2$.

In a formula or a problem, you might see a term in a sequence written as $x_n$ or with any variable in the place of *x*.

If you have a rule for a sequence, you can figure out what the various terms are without having to write out the entire sequence manually. You can see that this might be handy if you have to figure out what the fifteenth term is—or the fiftieth!

For example, if a sequence has the formula $3_n + 1$, then you'll always be able to figure out what value a specific term should be. If you wanted to find out the fifteenth term, then you would just calculate this way: $3(15) + 1 = 46$.

## FRACTIONS

Fractions are essentially parts of a whole. If you have $\frac{1}{2}$ of something, this means you have 1 of 2 equal parts.

If you have $\frac{7}{8}$ of something, this means you have 7 of the 8 equal parts available.

The 1 of $\frac{1}{2}$ is the numerator, which tells the number of parts used. The 2 is the denominator, which tells how many parts the whole has been divided into. As a general rule, if the numerator is less than the denominator, the fraction is called "proper." On the other hand, if the numerator is greater than or equal to the denominator, the fraction is called "improper." See the examples below:

$\frac{1}{3}$ is a proper fraction

$\frac{2}{3}$ is a proper fraction

$\frac{3}{3}$ is an improper fraction (note: this fraction has a value of 1)

$\frac{7}{3}$ is an improper fraction

### Mixed Numbers

A mixed number is simply a whole number with a fractional part. For example, $2\frac{1}{3}$ is a mixed number. If you need to change a mixed number into an improper fraction, simply multiply the whole number by the denominator of the fraction and add the resulting product to the numerator. The result is placed over the original denominator. For example:

$$2\frac{1}{3}=\frac{(2\bullet 3)+1}{3}=\frac{7}{3}$$

If you need to change an improper fraction into a mixed number, simply divide the numerator by the denominator. The quotient is the whole number, the remainder is left over the denominator, and the remaining fraction reduced to its lowest terms. For example:

$$\frac{15}{10}=1\frac{5}{10}=1\frac{1}{2}$$

The fraction $\frac{15}{10}$ is improper, and $15\div 10$ is 1 with 5 left over, so $1\frac{1}{2}$ is the resulting mixed number reduced.

When you reduce (or simplify) a fraction, you're making a fraction easier to understand. You can picture $\frac{1}{2}$ much easier than you can picture $\frac{5}{10}$. And you probably have a $\frac{1}{2}$ cup measuring cup, but not a $\frac{5}{10}$ cup measuring cup.

To reduce a fraction, find the largest number that divides evenly into the numerator and the denominator (the greatest common factor), and divide the numerator and the denominator by that number.

For example, the largest number that divides into the numerator and denominator of $\frac{5}{10}$ is 5. So, $5\div 5=1$ and $10\div 5=2$, so the reduced fraction is $\frac{1}{2}$.

### Adding and Subtracting Fractions

To add or subtract fractions, you are adding or subtracting numerators. But for the operation to work correctly, the fractions you're adding or subtracting must always have a common denominator.

For example, you can't add $\frac{1}{4}+\frac{1}{2}$. They have to have the same denominator. Since $\frac{1}{2}$ is the same as $\frac{2}{4}$, you can substitute $\frac{2}{4}$ in the equation:

$$\frac{1}{4}+\frac{2}{4}=\frac{3}{4}$$

In the same way, you can't subtract $\frac{1}{2}-\frac{1}{6}$ but you can make a substitution:

$$\frac{3}{6}-\frac{1}{6}=\frac{2}{6}$$

Notice that the denominators in the solutions remain the same, while the variable is the numerator. That is, $\frac{1}{4}+\frac{2}{4}$ does not equal $\frac{3}{8}$, nor does $\frac{3}{6}-\frac{1}{6}$ equal $\frac{2}{0}$ or 0.

The same thing applies to mixed numbers as well.

$$2\frac{1}{4}+1\frac{3}{4}=3\frac{4}{4}$$

The fraction $\frac{4}{4}$ is an improper fraction that can be reduced to 1. Therefore:

$$2\frac{1}{4}+1\frac{3}{4}=4$$

But what happens when you have to add or subtract two fractions that have different denominators—and you can't make a simple substitution, such as $\frac{1}{2}$ is the same as $\frac{2}{4}$?

Look at an example:

$$\frac{3}{7}+\frac{1}{2}=x$$

Before you can start adding, you have to find the least common denominator (LCD, also called lowest common denominator); that is, you have to find a denominator that is the same for both fractions, and you want it to be the smallest number possible for ease of calculations. For this example, we need to find the LCD for 7 and 2.

In this case, it happens to be 14 (that is, 7 and 2 each divide evenly into 14, and 14 is the smallest number for which that is true). Now that we are working the problem in units of fourteenths, it is easy to figure the proportional values of the numerators involved. For example:

$$\frac{3}{7}=\frac{x}{14}$$

To find $x$, you need to divide 7 into 14.

$$14\div 7=2$$

Then, multiply the quotient (2) by the numerator (3):

$$2\bullet 3=6$$

Therefore:

$$\frac{3}{7}=\frac{6}{14}$$

Work in a similar manner for the other fraction in the equation:

$$\frac{1}{2}=\frac{x}{14}$$

Find $x$:

$$14\div 2=7$$

Multiply numerator by the quotient:

$$7\bullet 1=7$$

Therefore:

$$\frac{1}{2}=\frac{7}{14}$$

Now that we have a common denominator, we can add or subtract numbers as we please. In this case:

$$\frac{6}{14}+\frac{7}{14}=\frac{13}{14}$$

This is a proper fraction that cannot be reduced any further.

The same process is used for subtraction. Let's look at another example:

$$\frac{5}{8}-\frac{1}{3}=x$$

The least common denominator is 24. You can multiply the denominators to find a common denominator, but it won't always be the smallest one possible. In this case, it is. Here's the math in a snapshot:

$\frac{5}{8}=\frac{x}{24}$. Then, $24\div 8=3$, and $3\bullet 5=15$. Therefore, $\frac{5}{8}=\frac{15}{24}$. For the other fraction:
$\frac{1}{3}=\frac{x}{24}$. Then, $24\div 3=8$, and $8\bullet 1=8$. Therefore, $\frac{1}{3}=\frac{8}{24}$.

Now we can solve the original problem:

$$\frac{15}{24}-\frac{8}{24}=\frac{7}{24}$$

This is a proper fraction which cannot be reduced further.

To add or subtract mixed numbers with different fractions, the same rule applies. The only difference is that whole numbers can be treated as fractions themselves if they need to be borrowed from. See the example below:

$$5\frac{2}{8}-3\frac{3}{4}=x$$

First we need to convert the fractions separately. The LCD for both fractions is 8. Therefore, $\frac{3}{4}=\frac{6}{8}$.

Since $\frac{2}{8}-\frac{6}{8}$ would leave us with a negative number, we need to add some more eighths to the $\frac{2}{8}$.

To do that, we borrow from the whole number (that is, 5). To imagine this, consider that we can write the number 5 as 5, or as $\frac{5}{1}$, or as $\frac{25}{5}$, or as $4\frac{8}{8}$. Therefore, we can look at $5\frac{2}{8}$ as the same thing as $4\frac{10}{8}$.

Thus, the problem now reads:

$$4\frac{10}{8}-3\frac{6}{8}=x$$

As the problem now reads, we can subtract the whole numbers (4 and 3) separately. Thus, 4 – 3 = 1.

The fractions $\frac{10}{8}$ and $\frac{6}{8}$ can be subtracted separately as well:

$$\frac{10}{8}-\frac{6}{8}=\frac{4}{8} \text{ or } \frac{1}{2}.$$

Now, put the whole number answer and the fractional answer together, and we arrive at the total solution of $x=1\frac{1}{2}$.

### Multiplying Fractions

To multiply fractions or mixed numbers, it is not necessary to determine an LCD. Rather, the product of the numerators is divided by the product of the denominators. Here's an example:

$$\frac{6}{7}\bullet\frac{5}{8}=\frac{6\bullet 5}{7\bullet 8}=\frac{30}{56}$$

Which is equivalent to (or "reduces to") $\frac{15}{28}$.

Here's another example:

$$4\bullet 7\frac{1}{3}=\frac{4}{1}\bullet\frac{22}{3}=\frac{4\bullet 22}{1\bullet 3}=\frac{88}{3}=29\frac{1}{3}$$

### Dividing Fractions

When you need to divide fractions or mixed numbers, convert the divisor to its reciprocal (reverse the numerator and denominator) and then multiply. For example:

$$\frac{7}{8}\div\frac{1}{2}=x$$

Convert the divisor to its reciprocal:

$$\frac{2}{1}\text{ is the reciprocal of }\frac{1}{2}$$

Then multiply:

$$\frac{7}{8}\bullet\frac{2}{1}=\frac{14}{8}=1\frac{3}{4}\text{ (reduced)}$$

Another example involving mixed numbers is shown below:

$$6\frac{5}{8}\div 3\frac{1}{3}=x$$

If we convert both mixed numbers to fractions and then find the reciprocal of $3\frac{1}{3}$, we can calculate:

$$\frac{53}{8}\bullet\frac{3}{10}=\frac{159}{80}=1\frac{79}{80}$$

## DECIMALS

Decimals are basically another means to represent fractional numbers. The difference is that all the fractions are expressed in factors of 10. The placement of the decimal point determines if it is a measure concerning tenths, hundredths, thousandths, ten thousandths, etc., and it will directly influence the size of the whole numbers involved. Look at the example below that depicts the same number with different decimal placements and examine the consequent change in value:

4,459.1340 = Four thousand, four hundred fifty-nine and one hundred thirty-four thousandths.
44,591.340 = Forty-four thousand, five hundred ninety-one and thirty-four hundredths.
445,913.40 = Four hundred forty-five thousand, nine hundred thirteen and four tenths.
4,459,134.0 = Four million, four hundred fifty-nine thousand, one hundred thirty-four.

### Adding and Subtracting Decimals

When conducting addition or subtraction of decimals, the place values (that is, decimal points) of decimals must be in vertical alignment. Just as mixed numbers require a common denominator, so decimals require this alignment. In this respect, the common denominator is that tenths are under tenths, hundredths are under hundredths, etc. For example:

$$\begin{array}{r} 6.5432 \\ +73.43 \\ \hline 79.9732 \end{array}$$

Or:

$$\begin{array}{r} 50.432 \\ -12.07 \\ \hline 38.362 \end{array}$$

### Multiplying Decimals

When multiplying decimals, it is necessary to treat them as whole numbers. Once you have determined the product, the decimal point is moved to the left the same number of places as there are numbers after the decimal point in both the decimals being multiplied.

For example, suppose you need to multiply 5.678 and .02. You would multiply them as if you were multiplying 5,678×2. The product is 11,356.

But because you're dealing with decimals, you have to add the decimal point back in. You do that by counting the number of places in each number being multiplied and adding them together. The number 5.678 has 3 decimal points and the number .02 has 2 decimal points. Together they have 5 decimal points. So, count 5 decimal points to the left in the product and you have .11356, or 0.11356 if you want to make it clearer.

### Dividing Decimals

Dividing decimals is as simple as multiplication. If you're dividing a decimal by a whole number, simply ignore the decimal and perform long division. Then, in your answer, place the decimal point in the quotient above the decimal point in the dividend. For example:

$$4\overline{)1.5}$$

Treat this like 15÷4. But line up the decimal points in the quotient:

$$\begin{array}{r} 0.375 \\ 4\overline{)1.5} \end{array}$$

If the divisor is also a decimal, simply move both place values to the right so that the divisor becomes a whole number. The decimal point then needs to be placed in the quotient above the place it has been moved to in the number being divided. At that point, each of the numbers can be treated as whole numbers and ordinary long division can be used.

Let's work through an example:

$$7.62 \div 3.11 = x$$

Which can be written as:

$$3.11\overline{)7.62} = x$$

We need to move the decimal point over two places to render the divisor a whole number. We move the decimal point over the same number of places in the dividend, too.

$$311.\overline{)762.} = x$$

Note the placement of the decimal in the quotient:

$$\begin{array}{r} 2.45 \\ 3.11\overline{)7.62} \end{array}$$

### Converting Fractions to Decimals

Converting fractions to decimals is just a matter of dividing the numerator by the denominator. So, $\frac{1}{2}$ is $1 \div 2$, or 0.50. This works for any fraction, although, depending on what you're calculating, it may be worthwhile to round your answer. For example, the fraction $\frac{16}{23}$ can be converted to a decimal by dividing 23 into 16. The quotient is 0.69565217391, but you may find it just as useful to round up to 0.696 or even 0.7.

## PERCENT

The term "percent" or "percentage" by itself means "divided by one hundred." For example, 15% means $15 \div 100$. A percentage shows what portion of 100 a given number constitutes. For example, if an individual had 100 plants and gave away 20 to a friend, that would mean he or she gave away $\frac{20}{100}$ or 0.20 of the stock. To determine the percentage of plants given away, we would simply multiply 0.20 by 100, giving us 20%.

Let's look at another problem and determine the percentages involved.

If a fire truck had 300 feet of $1\frac{1}{2}$-inch hose and three firefighters took 100 feet, 75 feet, and 125 feet respectively to attend to a fire, what percentage did each firefighter carry?

Since we already know the total length of hose involved, it is a simple matter to solve for percentages.

Firefighter A:

$$\frac{100}{300} = 0.3\overline{3} \text{ and } 0.3\overline{3} \times 100 = \text{ about } 33\%$$

Firefighter B:

$$\frac{75}{300} = 0.25 \text{ and } 0.25 \times 100 = 25\%$$

Firefighter C:

$$\frac{125}{300} = 0.41\overline{6} \text{ and } 0.41\overline{6} \times 100 = \text{ about } 42\%$$

When you total these percentages together, you get 100% of hose used. (Note that the dash over the top of a number [like this: $\overline{6}$] means the number is repeated forever.)

### Converting Percents to Decimals

Just as you can convert decimals to percents, you can convert percents to decimals simply by using the inverse operation. To convert decimals to percents, you multiply by 100. The inverse of multiplication is division. Thus, to convert percents to decimals, you divide by 100.

For example, $15\% \div 100 = 0.15$.

### Percent Change

A percent increase or decrease is a relative change in amount. If last year 10% of students got an A on their social studies final, and this year 15% got an A, the number of students receiving As has increased by 50%. It's easy to think that the increase is the difference between 10% and 15% (which is 5%), but that is a percentage point change, not a percent change (see "Percentage Point Change" in this chapter for more information).

To determine percent change, you need to follow three steps:

1. Divide the new value by the old value.
2. Convert the resulting decimal value by multiplying by 100 to determine the percent.
3. Subtract 100% to determine the difference, which is the percent change.

Let's do an example.

The cost of a movie ticket has gone up from \$9 to \$11.50. What is the percent change?

1. Divide the new value by the old value, so: $11.50 \div 9 \approx 1.28$ (Note that the symbol $\approx$ means "about.") $11.50 \div 9$ actually equals 1.27777777778, but rounding up a little makes our calculation much easier.
2. Convert the resulting decimal value by multiplying by 100 to determine the percent.

$$1.28 \times 100 = 128\%$$

3. Subtract 100% to determine the difference, which is the percent change:

$$128\% - 100\% = 28\%$$

As with many math problems, there's more than one way to solve this problem. You could also subtract the old value from the new value, divide the difference by the old value, and multiply by 100 to get the percent change. Let's try that with the same problem:

The cost of a movie ticket has gone up from \$9 to \$11.50. What is the percent change?

1. Subtract the old value from the new value:

$$11.50 - 9 = 2.50$$

2. Divide the difference by the old value:

$$2.50 \div 9 \approx .28$$

3. Multiply by 100 to get the percent change:

$$0.28 \times 100 = 28\%$$

### Percentage Point Change

A percentage point change is simply the difference between two percentages. For example, if inflation has gone from 5% to 7%, it has increased by 2 percentage points, but that is not the same as a 2% increase. It's actually a 40% increase, which you can determine by using one of the calculations in the "Percent Change" section in this chapter.

## EXPONENTS

Exponents are simply a way of expressing a type of multiplication. An exponent is the number of times a number is multiplied by itself. If you wanted to multiply the number 3 by itself, you could say $3 \times 3 = 9$, or you could represent that as $3^2 = 9$. The superscript 2 (the tiny number above and to the right of the number being multiplied) indicates an exponent. In this case, the exponent indicates the multiplication of $3 \times 3$. If you wanted to multiply $3 \times 3 \times 3$, or 3 three times, then you'd indicate that as $3^3$. An exponent can be any number, and it can also be negative. Exponents are often used as a shorthand method of representing very large numbers or very small numbers, such as $10^{100}$ or $10^{-100}$.

You will sometimes hear people refer to exponents as raising a number to the *n*th power, e.g., "5 raised to the 7th power," which would be expressed as $5^7$.

A number multiplied by itself is called squared while a number multiplied three times is called cubed.

Remember that a negative number squared is a positive number: $-3 \times -3 = 9$.

A perfect square is the square of a whole number (for example, $1^2, 2^2, 3^2$, etc.).

## SQUARE ROOTS

The square root of a number is the number that when squared (multiplied by itself) yields that number. So if $3 \times 3$ $(3^2) = 9$, then the square root of 9 is 3. The square root of 9 also happens to be $-3$ because $-3 \times -3 = 9$. The square root symbol is $\sqrt{\ }$ and is called a radical. It's used like this:

$$\sqrt{49} = 7$$

It's pretty easy to determine the square root of a perfect square. For example, if given $\sqrt{81} = x$, you can quickly determine that the square root is 9. If you multiply 9 by itself, you get 81. But other numbers are much more difficult to find the square root of. For example, consider $\sqrt{85}$. If $\sqrt{81} = 9$ and $\sqrt{100} = 10$, then $\sqrt{85}$ must fall between 9 and 10. But where?

- If we multiply 9.5 by 9.5 we get 90.25, which is too much.
- If we multiply 9.1 by 9.1, we get 82.81, which is too little.
- So we might try $9.25 \times 9.25$, but that yields 85.5625, which is still too much.

As you can see, while we keep getting closer, we could be at this all day. So, using the handy square root function on your calculator, you would find that $\sqrt{85} \approx 9.22$. We're using the "approximately equals" sign because the answer is actually 9.219544, etc. (an irrational number).

If you don't have a handy calculator, the above process of guessing will help you narrow down possible answers quickly. We started with square roots on both sides of the one we needed, then adjusted our search as we determined whether our answers were too large or too small.

## PRIME NUMBERS

A prime number is a number greater than 1 that can only be evenly divided by itself and 1. For example, 3 can only be evenly divided by itself and by 1. The number 2 is the only even number that is also a prime number. The number 9 is not a prime number because it can be evenly divided by 3.

As you can imagine, as the numbers increase, we find fewer primes. For example, in the numbers 1 through 10, we find four primes: 2, 3, 5, and 7 but from 60 through 70, there are only two prime numbers: 61 and 67. And there are no prime numbers between 800 and 810. You might think that eventually we'd run out of primes, but that's not true. There are an infinite number of primes, just as there are an infinite number of numbers.

Primes are important in advanced mathematics because they are basically the building blocks of other numbers. You can use primes to produce any other number. For example, the number 14 is the product of the primes 7 and 2.

## FACTORS

Factors are numbers you can multiply together to get another number. For example, in the equation $2\times3=6$, the factors are 2 and 3. You can also multiply $6\times1$ to get 6. That means 6 and 1 are also factors of 6. (A prime number can only be factored as $1 \times$ itself.)

And don't forget that multiplying negative numbers by negative numbers results in a positive number, so $-2\times-3$ also equals 6, meaning $-2$ and $-3$ are factors of 6. If you guessed that this means $-6$ and $-1$ are also factors of 6, you'd be correct.

Factors must be able to divide evenly into a number to be a factor of that number. So, 2 is a factor of 6 but not a factor of 13.

Prime factorization is figuring out the factors (of a number) that are also prime numbers. So in the case of 6, 2 and 3 are the prime factors, but not 6 and 1 (because 6 and 1 are not prime numbers).

Often, you need more than two prime numbers as factors of a given number to produce that number. For example, 36 can be produced by multiplying the factors 18 and 2, but 18 is not a prime number. So, the prime factorization of 36 would be $2\times2\times3\times3$. If you recognized that this could also be written as $2^2\times3^2$, you're correct.

To find the prime factor of a number, start by finding the smallest prime that can be evenly divided into it. For example, 15 cannot be evenly divided by 2, but it can be evenly divided by 3. The quotient, 5, is a prime number itself, so the prime factorization of 15 is $3\times5$.

Let's try another number. 18 can be evenly divided by the prime number 2, with a quotient of 9. 9 is not a prime number. It can be evenly divided by the prime number 3, with a quotient of 3. So, $2\times3\times3$ (or $2\times3^2$) would be the prime factorization of 18.

### Greatest Common Factor

Sometimes you need to find common factors among a set of integers. For example, if you have the numbers 15 and 27, and you factor them, you'd see that the factors for 15 are 1, 3, 5, and 15 while the factors for 27 are 1, 3, 9, and 27. If you compare those two sets of factors, you'd see that they share common factors of 1 and 3. The greatest (largest) of these is 3, so you can say that the greatest common factor for 15 and 27 is 3.

## MULTIPLES

A multiple is a number produced by multiplying a number by an integer. In the section on "Factors" in this chapter, we learned that 2 and 3 are factors of 6. We could turn that around and say that 6 is a multiple of 2. That means you can multiply 2 by another integer and produce 6. (6 is also a multiple of 3. You can also multiply 3 by another integer and produce 6.)

### Least Common Multiple

As with common factors, you may be asked to find common multiples of two or more numbers. If you came up with the first ten multiples of 4, you'd see a set like this: {4, 8, 12, 16, 20, 24, 28, 32, 36, 40}

Compare that to the first ten multiples for 7: {7, 14, 21, 28, 35, 42, 49, 56, 63, 71}

In this list, they share one common multiple: 28.

The least common multiple (also called lowest common multiple) would be the smallest of the common multiples of any two or more numbers. In this case, 28 is the least common multiple of 4 and 7.

## FACTORIALS

A factorial is the product of a given number (a positive integer for our purposes) and all of the smaller integers below that number. It's symbolized as *n*! So 5! would be $5\times4\times3\times2\times1$, or 120. It's accepted that 0! =1, although we also know that 0 multiplied by anything is 0. However, accepting this makes certain calculations a lot easier to do.

A helpful factorial formula says:

$$n! = n(n-1)!$$

In other words, if you know that $5! = 120$, then you can easily determine what 6! is without having to go through the whole process of multiplying $6\times5\times4\times3\times2\times1$. You would just multiply $6\times120$.

Factorials are used to calculate probabilities, combinations, and permutations. For example, if you wanted to know the number of ways in which 4 horses could cross the finish line, finding 4! would tell you the answer (24).

## AVERAGES

We often use averages to make comparisons. For example, to know if we're being paid a fair wage for our work, it's helpful to know what the average salary in our field is for someone with our education and experience. We can use averages for many purposes in daily life, such as determining a course grade (weighing a number of scores together).

However, sometimes we're not very scientific in the way we use the word "average," and we think it means one thing when it can mean another. That's why the terms "mean," "median," and "mode" are often used in math instead of the word "average."

### Mean

The mean is what we normally think of when we think of the word "average." It's the number you arrive at if you add up all the numbers in a set and divide by the number of items in the set. So, for example, if you wanted to find out the average ticket price for a movie, you might call up all the local theaters and learn that Cinema A charges $9.00, Cinema B charges $10.00, and Cinema C charges $9.50.

To determine the mean price, add up the ticket prices (all the numbers in the set) and divide by three (the number of prices in the set).

$$\frac{9+10+9.5}{3} = 9.5 \text{ or } \$9.50$$

### Median

The median is the middle number in a set of numbers. An equal amount of numbers are above this number as below it. You just line up the numbers in order and pick the one in the middle. To continue our movie ticket example, if you put the numbers in order of value, the middle one would be the median:

**$9.00, $9.50, $10.00**

So, $9.50 is the median as well as the mean. (This isn't always the case.)

If you have an even set of numbers, then you would find the mean of the middle two numbers in order to find the median. For example, if we added Cinema D, charging $9.75, to our example, we'd have a series that looks like this:

**$9.00, $9.50, $9.75, $10.00**

Since this is an even number of items, you'd simply take the two middle numbers and find their mean:

$$\frac{9.50+9.75}{2} = 9.625 \text{ or about } \$9.63$$

In this case, the median is $9.63. (But the mean is about $9.56.)

### Mode

The mode is the number that appears most often in a set of numbers. This is useful if outliers on either end of a series is likely to skew the mean or the median. For example, suppose that of ten houses in your neighborhood, 9 sold for about $200,000 but one sold for $1 million. The mean sale price would be $280,000, considerably above the $200,000 most homes in the neighborhood are worth. Suppose the property tax on your $200,000 home were based on the mean sale price. You'd be understandably upset! It also wouldn't be fair to claim to a potential buyer that your home is worth $280,000.

So, to recap, in this set: {2, 4, 4, 4, 6, 6, 7, 9, 9, 10}, the mode is 4, since it is represented the most often.

## SOLVING WORD PROBLEMS

Don't expect the Arithmetic Reasoning questions of the ASVAB to be all, "What is the least common multiple of 5 and 6?" You will also get a number of word problems, where you will have to figure out what numbers to plug into what formula to find the correct solution.

For example:

***Tom, Joe, and Wayne pay the electric bill for their shared apartment based on usage. If Tom uses 35%, Joe uses 40%, and the bill is $130, how much does Wayne owe?***

*A. $25*
*B. $33.75*
*C. $32.50*
*D. $55*

You might be tempted to answer A, $25, because if you subtract Tom's 35% and Joe's 40% from 100, you get 25. That's incorrect.

You might also be tempted to subtract 35% and 40% from $130 to get answer D, $55, but that would also be incorrect.

First, you have to determine what percent of the bill Wayne pays. If Tom and Joe pay in total 75%, then Wayne pays 25%. The next step is to determine how much of $130 equals 25%. So, $130 \times 0.25 = \$32.50$. Answer C is correct.

Remember that when you're solving a word problem that you need to identify exactly what the question is asking you to do. Then you need to figure out the steps you need to take to solve the problem. As with the above example, you may need to take more than one step.

A good rule to remember is to check the answers first before you start trying to solve the problem. That will indicate exactly what you need to be looking for and can prevent you from making the time-wasting mistake of solving for the wrong problem, then having to go back and solve for the right problem.

## STRATEGIES FOR SUCCEEDING ON THE ARITHMETIC REASONING SUBTEST

Doing well on the Arithmetic Reasoning subtest is crucial to your eligibility to enter the military. For that reason, it's essential to review ahead of time in order to do your best. But there are some strategies you can use during the actual test-taking itself to improve your chances of success.

### CAT Version Tips

There are 16 questions on the CAT version of the ASVAB, and you'll have 39 minutes to answer them. That gives you a little over two minutes for each question. Given that you may encounter a number of multistep problems, this is not as much time as it first appears! But do remember that you're likely to score higher on the test if you answer the first several questions correctly because you'll be given harder questions worth more as you go along. So it's worth taking a little extra time to get those right.

### Pencil-and-Paper Version Tips

The pencil-and-paper version of the ASVAB has 30 questions and you'll have 39 minutes to answer them. That means a little over a minute per question. For the pencil-and-paper version, it makes sense to answer the questions you know the answer to first, then go back and solve those that you're less familiar with. If word problems give you trouble, save them for the end so that you can be sure to get as many questions right as possible.

### Overall Tips

**Be sure you carefully read word problems to make sure you are solving for the right question. Word problems often contain extra information that isn't needed to solve the problem.**

**Be aware that answers will often include several possibilities that are almost right, which will make it harder to estimate the correct answer. However, estimating is still an option to help you rule out obviously wrong answers, especially if you are running short on time.**

# CHAPTER 9

# *Mathematics Knowledge (MK)*

The Mathematics Knowledge subtest of the ASVAB is one of the four subtests that are combined together to create the Armed Forces Qualification Test (AFQT), which is the core test that determines whether you're eligible for entrance into the military. For that reason, it's crucial to do well on this subtest.

In addition, many of the jobs you may be interested in pursuing in the military will require a solid understanding of math, so getting a good score on this subtest will enhance your opportunities. Mathematics Knowledge is often combined with Arithmetic Reasoning and/or General Science and/or Electronics Information to determine your eligibility for specific military jobs. Some clerical and technician jobs require solid Mathematics Knowledge and good verbal skills (Paragraph Comprehension and Word Knowledge).

## WHAT THE TEST MEASURES

In the military, you will need to have good mathematical aptitude to do most jobs, but mathematics will prove important outside your career as well. The implications can be as far reaching as calculating depreciation values on real estate for tax purposes to simply balancing your checkbook.

This section of the book is designed with the purpose of reviewing only those aspects of math that have been predominantly seen on past exams. If you find areas of weakness in any of these (especially after completing the diagnostic test in Chapter 4), it would be in your best interest to get additional reference material from your library.

The problems you'll find on this test include algebraic operations, equations, geometry, and probability, among others. Your understanding of math, as well as your ability to think logically, are measured with this test.

## WHAT ALGEBRA IS

Mathematics treats exact relations existing between quantities in such a way that other quantities can be deduced from them. That is an algebraic equation. In other words, you may know the basic quantity of a given item, but to derive further use from that quantity, it is necessary to apply known relationships (that is, formulas).

For example, let's say you wanted to know how many revolutions a tire would have to make to roll a distance of exactly 20 feet. Outside of physically rolling the tire itself and using a tape measure, it would be impossible to solve such an unknown without mathematics. However, by applying math, we can exploit known relationships to derive the answer.

If we know that the diameter of the tire is 40 inches, we can easily determine the tire's perimeter or, in other words, its circumference. In geometric terms, the tire is a circle, and the known formula for determining the circumference of a circle is to multiply the diameter by $\pi$ (which is 3.1416). The symbol $\pi$ is referred to in mathematics as *pi*. Therefore, our tire's circumference is $40 \times 3.1416 = 125.66$ inches.

Since we now know that the circumference of the tire is 125.66 inches, we can learn how many revolutions a tire with this circumference would need to go exactly 20 feet. However, we cannot simply divide 125.66 inches into 20 feet, because we are dealing with two entirely different units of measurement, inches and feet.

Therefore, we need to convert feet into inches. We know that there are 12 inches in 1 foot, 20 feet $\times$ 12 inches $=$ 240 inches. Now, we can divide 125.66 inches into 240 inches to find the answer we need. In this case, the tire would have to make 1.91 revolutions to roll exactly 20 feet. You can see by this example how known relationships can help find an unknown.

## NUMBER THEORY

The questions you're likely to run into on the Mathematics Knowledge section of the ASVAB largely (but not exclusively) have to do with number theory, which is sometimes called higher arithmetic. It deals with the properties of integers and how they relate to each other. That means you won't be dealing with advanced mathematical concepts such as you might find in calculus. But you will need to have a solid understanding of algebra and geometry in order to do well.

## EQUATIONS

An equation is a mathematical statement that two values are equal, using the equal sign (=) to indicate this equivalence.

So, $2 + 2 = 4$ is an equation. So is $2n = 4$. That second equation is what we think of when we think of algebra, because in algebra we often have to solve for unknowns.

*Linear equations* are those that form a straight line on a graph. They don't have exponents in the unknown (also called the variable). They also don't have square roots or cube roots. $2n = 4$ is a linear equation.

So what does it mean to say that a linear equation forms a straight line on a graph? Let's look at the equation $y = 5$. (It's still an equation even though there's nothing to solve.) See Figure 9.1 to see what it looks like graphed.

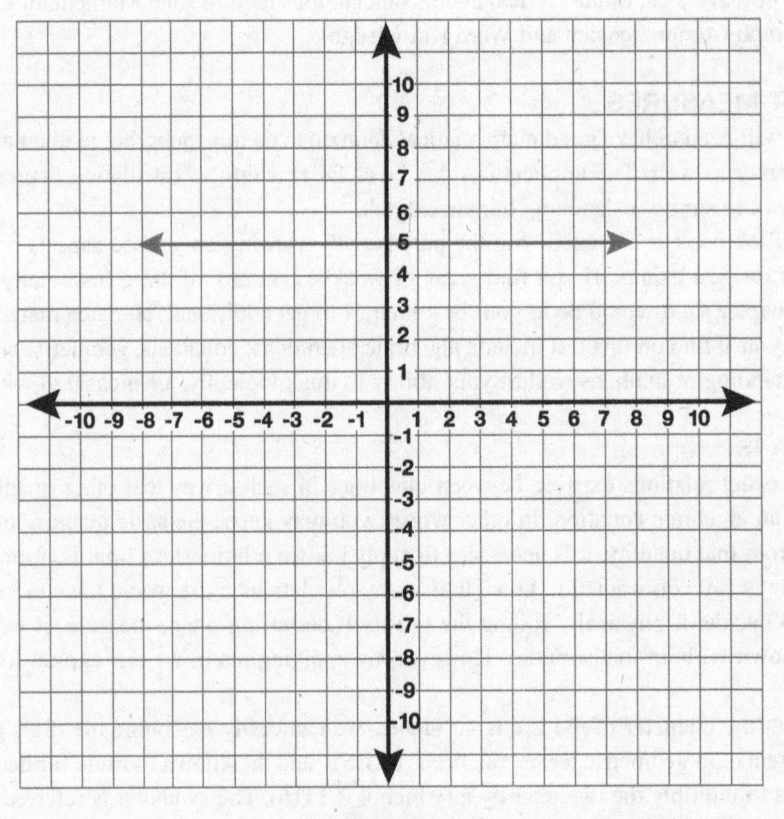


**Figure 9.1**

Linear equations often have more than one variable (for example, $y = 3x + 3$). That means there can be several possible answers. Those possible answers, when graphed, form a straight line. If they don't, either you don't have a linear equation, or you've solved it incorrectly.

In this case, $x$ could equal 1, or 2, or 3, or 0, or $-1$, or $-2$, or $-3$. (And lots of other numbers as well).

Let's see what $y$ would be if we plug in those answers for $x$:

$$6 = 3 \bullet 1 + 3$$
$$9 = 3 \bullet 2 + 3$$
$$12 = 3 \bullet 3 + 3$$
$$3 = 3 \bullet 0 + 3$$
$$0 = 3 \bullet -1 + 3$$
$$-3 = 3 \bullet -2 + 3$$
$$-6 = 3 \bullet -3 + 3$$

We could show these points as:

$(x = 1, y = 6)$
$(x = 2, y = 9)$
$(x = 3, y = 12)$
$(x = 0, y = 3)$
$(x = -1, y = 0)$
$(x = -2, y = -3)$
$(x = -3, y = -6)$

We can plot them on a graph. See Figure 9.2.

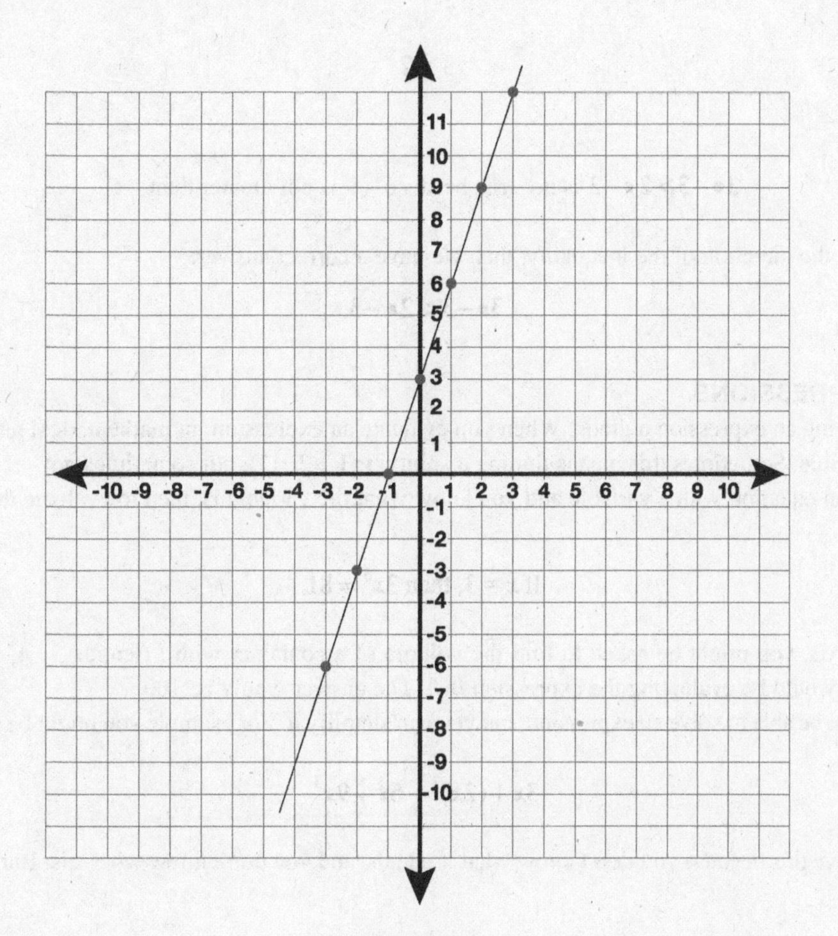


Figure 9.2

*Nonlinear equations* are (not surprisingly) those that don't form a straight line on a graph. They have exponents in the unknown (such as $x^2$), or square roots, or cube roots, etc. For example, $x^2 + y^2 = 34$ is a nonlinear equation. When graphed, nonlinear equations might form a circle, a parabola, an ellipse, or another shape, but they don't form a straight line.

## INEQUALITIES

Inequalities are mathematical expressions where the numbers being compared are not equal. Thus we do not use the equal sign. We also do not call them equations; we call them expressions. So the expression $3 > 2$ ("3 is greater than 2") is an inequality and uses the "greater than" symbol. $2 < 3$ ("2 is less than 3") is another inequality, using the "less than" symbol. We could also say $2 \neq 3$ ("2 does not equal 3"). Sometimes we use "greater than or equal to," symbolized by $\geq$, and sometimes we use "less than or equal to," symbolized by $\leq$.

If you think about it, we use inequalities all the time. "I won't spend more than ten thousand dollars on a used car" could be stated as "$x \leq \$10{,}000$" where $x$ is the amount you're willing to spend.

How could you state "I want to earn a salary of \$45,000 or more" as a mathematical expression? If you came up with something like $s \geq \$45{,}000$, where $s$ is your acceptable salary, then you are correct.

You solve inequalities basically the same way as you solve equations, by isolating the variable. (More on that in "Solving for Variables" in this chapter.) However, you have to be careful! We know that $2 + 1 = 3$, and we could state that as $3 = 2 + 1$, but we can't do the same for inequalities. $2 < 3$, but $3 < 2$ is incorrect.

In addition, some of the properties of equality do not hold true for inequalities. For example, in Chapter 8, we described how you could multiply or divide both sides of an equation with the same number and both sides would remain equal (for example, $2 = 2$ could be $2 \times 2 = 2 \times 2$ and the equation would still be true). But you can't multiply or divide an inequality by a negative number *unless* you change the direction of the inequality.

For example:

$$3 > 2$$

But:

$$3 \bullet -3 > 2 \bullet -3 \text{ is not true because } -9 \text{ is not greater than } -6$$

If we change the direction of the inequality, then we have a correct answer:

$$3 \bullet -3 < 2 \bullet -3$$

## EVALUATE EXPRESSIONS

No, you're not giving an expression a grade. When you evaluate an expression, in mathematical terms, you simplify it as much as possible. Sometimes this means finding a solution ($1 + 2 = 3$), but sometimes not.

If you have an equation with a variable and you know what the variable is, then to evaluate the expression you just do the math:

$$\text{If } x = 3, \text{ then } 3x^3 = 81$$

On the ASVAB, you might be asked to find the volume of a container with $l$ (length) $= 4$, $w$ (width) $= 5$, $h$ (height) $= 5$. You would be evaluating the expression $lwh$. The answer would be 100.

You might not be able to solve an expression, but you can simplify it. For example you might be asked to evaluate:

$$3x + (2x)^3 - 6x + 9x^3$$

You can't solve this because you don't know what it equals, and you don't know what $x$ is. But you can simplify it to:

$$17x^3 - 3x$$

## SOLVING FOR VARIABLES

Solving for variables will show up on the ASVAB. Algebra is essentially a mathematical expression that employs the use of one or more variables that have an unknown value. Typically, algebra expressions are set up in an equation whereby both expressions are established as being equal. The variable component(s) to the problem can be solved through the operations of subtraction, addition, multiplication, and/or division.

Whatever mathematical function is used to isolate and determine the value of the variable (often but not always called $x$), it is important to note that both sides of the equation should be treated equally. By making sure to treat both sides the same, you're simply restating the equation in different form rather than changing the equation.

In Chapter 8, we described the Addition Property of Equality. The addition property says that if the same amount is added to each side of an equation, then the equation remains equal. This is also true of subtraction, multiplication, and division. (Note that this is not necessarily true of inequalities. See "Inequalities" in this chapter for more information.)

We can use these properties of equations to find an unknown in an equation.

Look at the following examples that demonstrate this principle:

### Subtraction

Here's an example of using subtraction to find $x$.

$$x+6=20$$
$$x+6-6=20-6$$
$$x=14$$

### Addition

Here's an example of using addition to find $x$.

$$x-14=5$$
$$x-14+14=5+14$$
$$x=19$$

### Multiplication

Here's an example of using multiplication to find $x$.

$$\frac{x}{4}=10$$

$$\frac{x}{4}\bullet 4=10\bullet 4$$

$$x=40$$

### Division

Here's an example of using division to find $x$.

$$3x=39$$
$$\frac{3x}{3}=\frac{39}{3}$$

$$x=13$$

### Using Inverses to Solve for *x*

In Chapter 8, when we discussed the operation of multiplication, we mentioned multiplicative inverses (sometimes called the reciprocal), the number by which a number can be multiplied to produce 1. We also learned that 1 times any number is that number. So, we can use these properties to help solve for *x* in fractions.

Here's an example:

$$\frac{1}{3}x+8=15$$

$$\frac{1}{3}x+8-8=15-8$$

$$\frac{1}{3}x=7$$

In the following step we multiply by the inverse to solve for *x*:

$$\frac{1}{3}x\bullet\frac{3}{1}=7\bullet\frac{3}{1}$$

$$x=21$$

Here's another example:

$$\frac{2}{5}x-3=9$$

$$\frac{2}{5}x-3+3=9+3$$

$$\frac{2}{5}x=12$$

$$\frac{2}{5}x\bullet\frac{5}{2}=12\bullet\frac{5}{2}$$

$$x=30$$

### Cross-Multiplication

Cross-multiplication is used to solve for *x* in fractions, particularly when you have 2 unknowns. Just as you can multiply both sides of an equation by the same amount without changing the equation, you can multiply the numerator and the denominator of a fraction without changing the fraction ($\frac{2}{3}$ is the same as $\frac{4}{6}$, right? We've multiplied both the numerator and denominator by 2).

When you cross-multiply, you're using this property. Let's use some variables to show what this means. We can say:

$$\frac{a}{b}=\frac{c}{d} \text{ and } ad=bc$$

Now let's try it on some actual fractions.

$$\frac{2}{3}=\frac{4}{6}$$

and

$$2 \bullet 6 = 3 \bullet 4$$
***or***
$$12 = 12$$

Here's an example of putting cross-multiplication into practice:

$$\frac{x}{9}=\frac{4}{x}$$

If $ad = bc$, then $x^2 = 9 \bullet 4$, or $x^2 = 36$. To solve, we just need to find the square root of 36, which is 6. So $x =$ 6 (the answer could also be $-6$, since a negative number multiplied by a negative number equals a positive number). To check the answer, just plug in the solution for $x$:

$$\frac{6}{9}=\frac{4}{6}$$

Is this correct? Since both fractions are equal (both are the same as $\frac{2}{3}$), the answer is yes.

## RATIOS AND PROPORTIONS

A ratio is simply two items compared by division. For example, if you say Quantity A is 1 and Quantity B is 2, you could say they have a ratio of 1:2. In practical terms, a recipe might need 1 cup of water and 2 cups of milk; the ratio of water to milk is 1:2. If you needed to change the recipe to produce a larger or smaller serving, the ratio would tell you how to do this. 2 cups of water would require 4 cups of milk to keep the ratio in balance. $\frac{1}{2}$ cup of water would require 1 cup of milk; $\frac{1}{3}$ cup of water would require $\frac{2}{3}$ cup of milk. It's easy if you know the ratio.

A proportion is an equation that shows that two ratios are equal. One of the more common types of questions seen on past exams concern speed and distance proportions. For example, if a car can travel 5 miles in 6 minutes, how far can it travel in 30 minutes, assuming the same speed is maintained? This kind of problem would first be set up as two separate ratios and then placed in a proportion to determine the unknown.

$$\text{Ratio 1: } \frac{5\text{ miles}}{6\text{minutes}} \qquad \text{Ratio 2: } \frac{x\text{ miles}}{30\text{ minutes}}$$

Create a proportion:

$$\frac{5\text{ miles}}{6\text{ minutes}}=\frac{x\text{ miles}}{30\text{ minutes}}$$

Then cross-multiply the proportion figures and obtain this:

$$6x = 5 \bullet 30$$

Then divide both sides of the equation by 6 to solve for $x$:

$$\frac{6x}{6}=\frac{150}{6}$$

$$x=25$$

When working with direct proportions like this, you have to be careful not to confuse them with inverse proportions. An example would be two gears with differing numbers of teeth that run at given rpm. Let's say one gear has 30 teeth and runs at 60 rpm, while the other gear has 20 teeth and runs at $x$ rpm. Find $x$.

Since we recall from mechanical principles that a gear with fewer teeth turns faster than a gear with more teeth, using a direct proportion would be incorrect. Rather, it should be inversely proportional.

Therefore, it is important when coming across a question of this nature to utilize the reciprocal of one of the ratios in the equation to set up the proportion. For example:

$$\frac{20\text{ teeth}}{30\text{ teeth}}=\frac{60\text{ rpm}}{x\text{ rpm}}$$

Or:

$$\frac{30\text{ teeth}}{20\text{ teeth}}=\frac{x\text{ rpm}}{60\text{ rpm}}$$

Both of these ways are correct proportions.

Let's solve the first one:

$$\frac{20x}{20}=\frac{30\bullet 60}{20}$$

$$x=\frac{1800}{20}$$

$$x=90\text{ rpm}$$

## ALGEBRAIC FRACTIONS

You can use the same operations on algebraic fractions as you do regular fractions. Review the section "Fractions" in Chapter 8 if needed. A few formulas will help you remember how to do operations on algebraic fractions.

### Addition

To add algebraic fractions, remember:

$$\frac{a}{b}+\frac{c}{d}=\frac{ad+bc}{bd}$$

Here's an example:

$$\frac{x}{2}+\frac{3}{5}=\frac{5x+2(3)}{2(5)}=\frac{5x+6}{10}$$

### Subtraction

Subtraction uses a formula similar to the one used for addition, except that you're subtracting, so the formula reflects that:

$$\frac{a}{b}-\frac{c}{d}=\frac{ad-bc}{bd}$$

Here's an example:

$$\frac{x+3}{6}-\frac{4}{x-2}=\frac{x^2-6-24}{6x-12}=\frac{x^2-30}{6x-12}$$

### Multiplication

To multiply, just multiply numerators together and denominators together. Here's the formula:

$$\frac{a}{b}\times\frac{c}{d}=\frac{ac}{bd}$$

Here's an example:

$$\frac{x}{x-2}\times\frac{x+3}{6}=\frac{x^2+3x}{6x-12}$$

### Division

For division, you're doing cross-multiplication. So here's the formula:

$$\frac{a}{b}\div\frac{c}{d}=\frac{ad}{bc}$$

And here's an example:

$$\frac{x+2}{x^2}\div\frac{6}{x-3}=\frac{x^2-6}{6x^2}$$

## SOLVE FOR TWO UNKNOWNS

So far we've discussed finding variables when we have only one variable to find, such as $3n = 9$. Find out what $n$ is and the problem is solved.

But many equations have more than one unknown. In the section called "Equations" in this chapter, we talked about one type of equation with two variables: $y=3x+3$. With this type of equation, we plug in any number for $x$ and we get $y$. The points can be plotted on a graph. However, sometimes we are given two expressions or equations and asked to solve for the variables. These are given in groups of two (or more) expressions called systems. You use both expressions (in this case, but not always, they're equations) to solve for the unknowns. For example:

$$y=3x+5$$
$$y=4x+2$$

In this example, we can't plug whatever we want for $x$. Both equations are true, and so we have to solve for both $x$ and $y$.

One way to do this would be to plot the possible answers for each equation on a graph. Where they intersect is the correct answer. Another way is to use one equation to solve the other. How? Well, if the second equation tells us $y = 4x + 2$ then we can plug that answer into the first equation:

$$4x + 2 = 3x + 5$$

Next, we subtract 2 from both sides:

$$4x = 3x + 3$$

Then we subtract $3x$ from both sides:

$$4x - 3x = 3$$

Or, $x = 3$

Now we can go back to the original equations and solve for $y$. We had $y = 3x + 5$. Plug in 3 for $x$ and you get $y = 14$. We can verify this with the second equation: $14 = 4(3) + 2$. Since this is true, we know our answers for $x$ and $y$ are also true.

Sometimes we can use the equations to cancel out one of the variables. For example:

$$3x + 3y = 15$$
$$-3x + 9y = 21$$

In this case, we could add the equations together to eliminate the $x$ variable.

$$3x + 3y + (-3x) + 9y = 15 + 21$$

Then we can do a little addition and subtraction:

$$12y = 36$$

Then,

$$\frac{12y}{12} = \frac{36}{12}$$

Or $y = 3$.

If we know $y$, we can solve for $x$. Give it a try.

If you came up with $x = 2$, you are correct.

Sometimes you have to multiply both sides of one equation first to make this addition process work.

For example, if you have:

$$2x + 2y = 18$$
$$-4x + y = -11$$

You wouldn't be able to eliminate any variables by adding them together. However, if you multiplied both sides of the first equation by 2, you'd get:

$$4x + 4y = 36$$

Now you can add the first equation to the second equation to eliminate a variable.

$$4x+4y+(-4x)+y=36+(-11)$$

We can do a little adding and subtracting to simplify matters:

$$4y+y=25$$

Or

$$5y=25$$

Then divide both sides by 5 to determine that $y = 5$. Then go back and solve for $x$ by plugging $y$ into either equation. If you came up with $x = 4$, you're correct.

Sometimes we run into a situation where the two unknowns are on one side of the equation. For example:

$$3x+y=15$$
$$2x+5y=23$$

If both equations are true, then we can solve for $y$, then for $x$.

$$3x+y-3x=15-3x$$

Or:

$$y=15-3x$$

Then plug the solution for $y$ into the second equation.

$$2x+5(15-3x)=23$$

The distributive property of multiplication tells us we can turn this into:

$$2x+5(15)-5(3x)=23$$

We can simplify a little:

$$2x+75-15x=23$$

And do some subtraction so that we only have one $x$ to deal with:

$$-13x+75=23$$

Then subtract 75 from both sides:

$$-13x=-52$$

And finally divide both sides to isolate $x$:

$$\frac{-13x}{-13}=\frac{-52}{-13}$$

Which means $x = 4$.
Now that we know this, we can simplify $y$, which was $15-3x$. Since we can plug in $x$, we can find out that $y$ is 3. We try these answers in our original set of equations to make sure they are correct.

$$3(4)+3=15$$
$$2(4)+5(3)=23$$

And the answers prove to be correct.
Sometimes we can also use the variable elimination process on these types of equations. Suppose you have:

$$2x-8y=-10$$
$$x+4y=11$$

Multiply both sides of the second equation by 2:

$$2x+8y=22$$

Then add the two equations together:

$$2x-8y+2x+8y=-10+22$$

Do a little addition and subtraction:

$$4x=12$$

And just a bit of division will yield $x = 3$. Then we can determine $y$ by plugging the value for $x$ into either equation. So:

$$3+4y=11$$
$$4y=8$$
$$\frac{4y}{4}=\frac{8}{4}$$
$$y=2$$

We check our answers by putting them into the two equations:

$$2(3)-8(2)=10$$
$$3+4(2)=11$$

Since both equations are true, our answers are correct.

## MONOMIALS, BINOMIALS, AND POLYNOMIALS

Mathematical expressions come in a variety of flavors. A polynomial is an expression that has (or can have) constants, variables, and non-negative integer exponents. (It doesn't have to have all these things.) The terms in a polynomial can include the operations of addition, subtraction, multiplication, and division, with the exception of division by a variable. So $2x^3-2y^2+y$ is a polynomial, but $\frac{2x^3-2y^2+y}{x}$ is not. The expression $\frac{2x^3-2y^2+y}{2}$ is a polynomial because it's being divided by a constant, not a variable.

A monomial is a type of polynomial that has just one term, like $2x^3$. A binomial is a polynomial that has two terms, like $2y^2+y$. And a trinomial is a polynomial that has three terms, like $2x^3-2y^2+y$.

You can add and multiply polynomials and get a polynomial.

### Standard Form of Polynomials

When polynomials are written out, the standard notation or standard form is to write them with the largest exponent first, then the next largest, until you get to the constant, which is the last item. So, a polynomial written in standard form would look like this:

$$2x^3 - y^2 + 3x - 9$$

If we wanted to write the following equation in standard form, how would we do it?

$$x + 2y^3 - 7 + 3y^2$$

If you came up with $2y^3 + 3y^2 + x - 7$ you are correct.

### Factoring Polynomials

In Chapter 8, we discussed how to factor numbers by identifying those numbers that could evenly divide into them. So the factors of 12 would be 1, 2, 3, 4, 6, and 12. The prime factors would be 2 and 3.

Factoring polynomials is similar because you're simplifying the polynomial in much the same way that you simplify a number when you factor it. And in the same way, being able to factor polynomials can help you solve mathematical problems.

For example, you can factor an exponent by breaking it into its component parts. If $x^2 = x \bullet x$, then the factor of $x^2$ is $x$, or more specifically $(x, x)$.

In Chapter 8, we covered the distributive property of multiplication, which tells us that if you have a number that you need to multiply by a group of numbers, such as $9(2+6)$, the answer is the same whether you add that group first or multiply each number in the group separately, then add the results together. We could state this property as:

$$a(b+c) = ab + ac$$

When we factor a polynomial, we can factor it by going from $ab + ac$ to $a(b+c)$ instead of from $a(b+c)$ to $ab + bc$.

If you see a polynomial that is expressed as $ab + ac$ then you can easily factor it by moving $b + c$ back into the parenthesis. You do this by dividing. So, given:

$$3x^2 + 6x$$

You can see that $3x^2$ and $6x$ have a common factor. That is $3x$. We can say that $3x^2$ is the same thing as $3x \bullet x$ and that $6x$ is the same thing as $3x \bullet 2$. So we move the $3x$ to the outside of the parenthesis and the $x$ and the 2 to the inside of the parenthesis. In other words, we factor the expression to:

$$3x(x+2)$$

You can see that these two expressions are the same thing, since $3x \bullet x = 3x^2$ and $3x \bullet 2 = 6x$, which are the terms of the original expression.

Here's another example. Suppose we needed to factor $6x - 12$. We're just putting that back into the $a(b+c)$ form, although in this case we have a negative sign to deal with. The answer would be $6(x-2)$, since 6 is a common factor. We can check our factoring by putting the expression in $ab + ac$ form: $6 \bullet x$ and $6 \bullet -2$ or $6x - 12$.

When the constants in the terms of a polynomial don't cooperate by being divisible by a common factor, you can factor a polynomial by dividing out the variable.

For example:

$$6x^2 + 7x = x(6x+7)$$

## QUADRATIC EQUATIONS

A quadratic equation is one in which the variable is squared. We have worked with some quadratic equations in this chapter, we just didn't happen to call them that. Quadratic equations are always polynomials.

The standard form of a quadratic equation is:

$$ax^2 + bx + c = 0$$

In a quadratic equation, we know what *a*, *b*, and *c* are, but we don't know *x*. In a quadratic equation, *a* can't be zero. So $3x+5=0$ is not a quadratic equation (although it is a polynomial). But do remember that *b* can = 1, so sometimes the second term in a quadratic equation can be written as just *x* (because *x* is the same as 1*x*). Or sometimes it is 0, in which case it isn't written down at all. And like *b*, *c* can also equal zero, so sometimes it's not shown, either.

An example of a quadratic equation would be:

$$3x^2 + 4x + 5 = 0$$

Sometimes we don't recognize a quadratic equation right off. For example, $x^2 = 2x + 5$ is a quadratic equation; it's just not written out as one. To put it in recognizable form, we'd just subtract $2x + 5$ from each side. Then we'd have:

$$x^2 - 2x - 5 = 2x + 5 - 2x - 5$$

Or:

$$x^2 - 2x - 5 = 0$$

Let's look at this polynomial, which has been factored as we described in "Factoring Polynomials" in this chapter:

$$x(2x - 3) = 6$$

We can express that as a quadratic equation:

$$2x^2 - 3x - 6 = 0$$

So just because an equation doesn't look like a quadratic equation that doesn't mean it isn't one. The solution to a quadratic equation is called the *root*. (The inverse operation to an exponent is a root operation, for example, finding a square root or cube root, and thus the name.)

Quadratic equations may have more than one root (usually two).

So, how do we solve them? We use the same approach as we do for any polynomial. Suppose we have this equation:

$$x^2 - 4 = 0$$

Using the addition property of equations we know that we can add 4 to each side to isolate *x*.

$$x^2 - 4 + 4 = 4$$

Or:

$$x^2 = 4$$

Then we just need to find the square root of 4, which is 2 or −2, and we can say that $x = 2$ or $x = -2$.

Sometimes the equation is more complex than this, in which case we will often need to factor the equation.

### Factoring Quadratic Equations

Factoring the quadratic can help you solve it. Just as we can factor polynomials (as described in the "Factoring Polynomials" section in this chapter) we can factor quadratic equations. Then we can solve the equation.

So, let's look at this quadratic equation:

$$x^2+4x-5=0$$

The common factors are $x+5$ **and** $x-1$. These are factors of 5 (our *c* variable) that add up to 4 (our *b* variable). We can verify that this is true by multiplying the factors together:

$$(x+5)(x-1)$$
$$x(x-1)+5(x-1)$$
$$x^2-x+5x-5$$
$$x^2+4x-5$$

Which is our original expression, so we have factored correctly and have solved the problem. The solution is written as:

$$x^2+4x-5=(x+5)(x-1)$$

## DETERMINE PROBABILITY

Probability is the likelihood that some event will occur. We can say with some certainty that the sun will rise in the east tomorrow, but not all events are equally probable. Math helps us codify this likelihood. In general, we can say that:

$$\text{Probability} = \frac{\text{number of selected/preferred outcomes}}{\text{number of possible outcomes}}$$

Sometimes the category of "selected/preferred outcomes" is called "favorable outcomes" but we don't necessarily have to want something to happen to need to know how likely it is to occur.

Starting with a simple example, let's imagine that you have two poker chips in your hand. One is red and the other is green. If someone randomly picked one (without looking), two events could occur. The red chip (R) might be picked, or the green chip (G) might be picked. So we can say that the likelihood of $R=\frac{1}{2}$. The likelihood of G is also $\frac{1}{2}$.

You can see how this works for even somewhat more complicated possibilities. Suppose you have a penny, a nickel, a dime, and a quarter in your pocket. If you randomly pull one out, what is the likelihood that it will be a dime? If you said $\frac{1}{4}$, you were correct.

You can make this slightly more complicated by changing the selected outcomes. For example, you might ask what the likelihood is that the coin you pick will be worth ten cents or more. There are two coins that meet that criteria, so your revised probability would be $\frac{2}{4}$ or $\frac{1}{2}$.

Remember that you can convert this probability fraction to a decimal (0.5) or a percent (50%). It may also sometimes be called "a one-in-two chance."

Probability is always between 0 and 1, with 0 being that the event is impossible (like the sun rising in the west) and 1 being that the event is certain (like the sun rising in the east).

But just because the probability that you'll pick a penny is $\frac{1}{4}$, that doesn't mean that for every four tries, you'll pick the penny once. You might go twenty tries without picking the penny at all, or you might pick the penny six times in a row. However, over time, you'll find that you pick the penny about 25% of the time. That doesn't mean you can know with more certainty than $\frac{1}{4}$ which coin you'll pick next time, even if you seem "due" to pick the penny. Thinking that probability changes in a random event like this is called the Gambler's Fallacy, and casinos love it.

As you might imagine, though, how we calculate probability depends on a number of factors. One of the most important is whether the event is independent or dependent. Picking a coin out of your pocket is an independent event. Nothing influences it; it's random. If you put the coin back in your pocket after every try, the probability that you will pick it again doesn't change. However, if you pick the penny, then remove it from your pocket, the probabilities change for the remaining coins. This is called a dependent event.

You can determine the likelihood of a series of independent events by multiplying the probability of each event. So, for example, if you want to calculate the probability of picking the penny twice in a row, you'd multiply the probability of picking the penny on try #1 ($\frac{1}{4}$) with the probability of picking the penny on try #2 ($\frac{1}{4}$), for a probability of $\frac{1}{16}$. If you wanted to know the likelihood of picking the penny three times in a row, you'd multiply $\frac{1}{4} \times \frac{1}{4} \times \frac{1}{4}$ for a probability of $\frac{1}{64}$.

Here's another example. Suppose one person from each of three income groups is randomly chosen for a telephone tax audit. In your income group, there are 10 people (we'll make it simple for our purposes). Then suppose one of those three people chosen for telephone audits is randomly picked for an in-person audit. Before the audits begin (that is, before anyone has been selected for anything), what is your likelihood of being picked for the in-person audit?

You would multiply your chance of being picked for the first group ($\frac{1}{10}$) by your chances of being picked for the second group ($\frac{1}{3}$), making the probability that you will win the in-person audit $\frac{1}{30}$.

Of course, the probabilities change once the audits are underway. If you're not chosen for the first audit (the telephone audit) then you can't be chosen for the in-person audit, so your probability becomes 0. But if you're picked for the telephone audit (a $\frac{1}{10}$ chance), then the likelihood that you'll receive the in-person audit becomes $\frac{1}{3}$.

Review the section called "Factorials" in Chapter 8 for more information on how factorials are used in probability (particularly permutations, which show us the likelihood of events happening in a certain order).

## GEOMETRY 101

Any object that requires space has dimensions which can be measured in length, width, and height. If all three of these measurements are used to quantify the area of a given object, it can be said that it is three-dimensional, or solid. If only two measurements, such as length and width, can be determined, it is considered to be two-dimensional, or a plane. A line is essentially a one-dimensional figure because it has no height or width, only length.

Geometry is the study of how points, lines, and shapes interact. In two dimensions, it is called plane geometry, and in three dimensions it is called solid geometry.

You'll be expected to know the basics of geometry for the Mathematics Knowledge subtest on the ASVAB.

## POINTS

In geometry, a point is a specific location, although it doesn't have any mass or substance. Think about an intersection of streets. On a map, 23rd and Pine is a different point than 15th and Main. You could graph these two points if you wanted (see Figure 9.3).

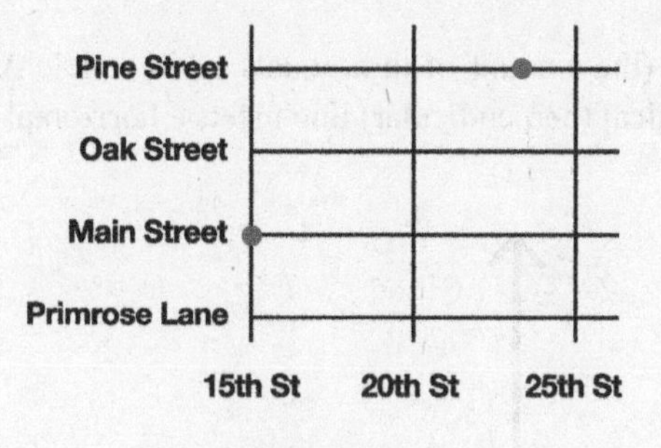


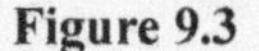
Figure 9.3

In geometry, the information you need to locate a point on a graph is its coordinates. The vertical axis of the graph is the *y*-axis, and the horizontal is the *x*-axis. The coordinates 10, 5 would indicate the position of 10 on the *x*-axis and the position of 5 on the *y*-axis. In Figure 9.3, our coordinates are 23 (corresponding to the *x*-axis) and Pine (corresponding to the *y*-axis) and {15, Main}. Locate the point {20, Oak} on Figure 9.3. Fairly straightforward, right?

## LINES

Lines have no height or width, only length. In geometry, they connect points together. Lines that can go on forever in one or both directions are indicated using an arrow: →,←, or ↔. When a line (or a section of a line being studied) has a starting point (call it *A*) and a direction (a second point often indicates this direction, usually labeled *B*) but then goes on forever, we call it a ray and give it this symbol: $\overrightarrow{AB}$.

On our map, we could draw a line connecting our points {23, Pine} and {15, Main}. See Figure 9.4.

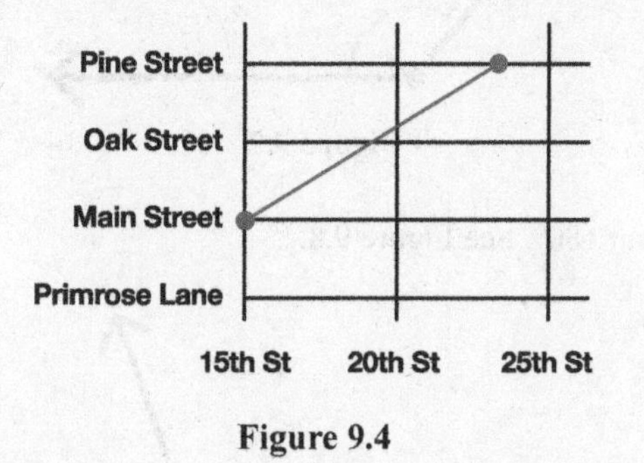


Figure 9.4

## ANGLES

Angles are simply the place where two intersecting lines meet. This is not the point where they meet, but rather the space between the lines, or what is called the amount of turn. See Figure 9.5.

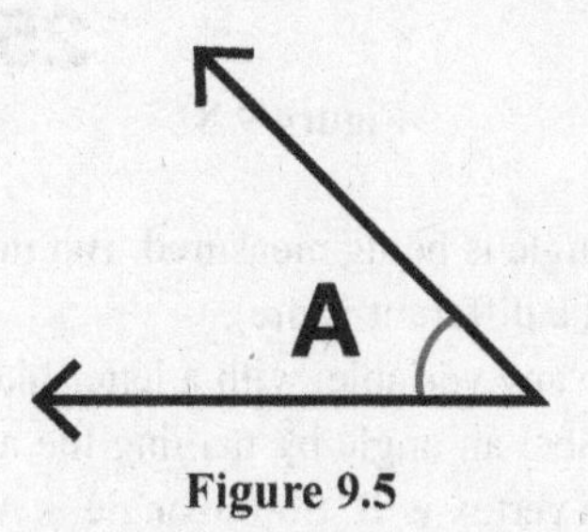


Figure 9.5

The point where the two lines of an angle intersect is called the vertex. The lines that intersect are called the arms of the angle. In Figure 9.5, the area indicated with A is the angle. It is measured in degrees (°).

An angle with 360° is a circle (the amount of turn equals a full rotation). An angle with 180° is a line (also called a straight angle). Where a vertical (perpendicular) line meets a horizontal line, and the angle is 90°, it's called a right angle. See Figure 9.6.

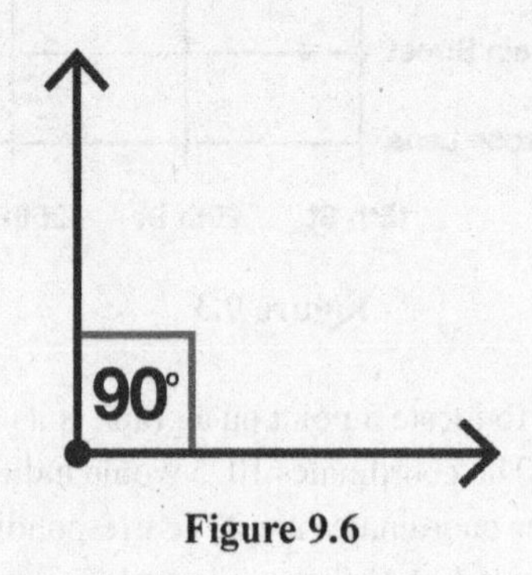


**Figure 9.6**

Angles have various names, depending on the size of the angle.

- An acute angle is less than 90°. (Figure 9.5 is an acute angle.)
- An obtuse angle is greater than 90° but less than 180°. See Figure 9.7.

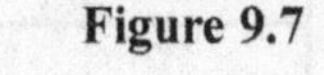

**Figure 9.7**

- A reflex angle is greater than 180°. See Figure 9.8.

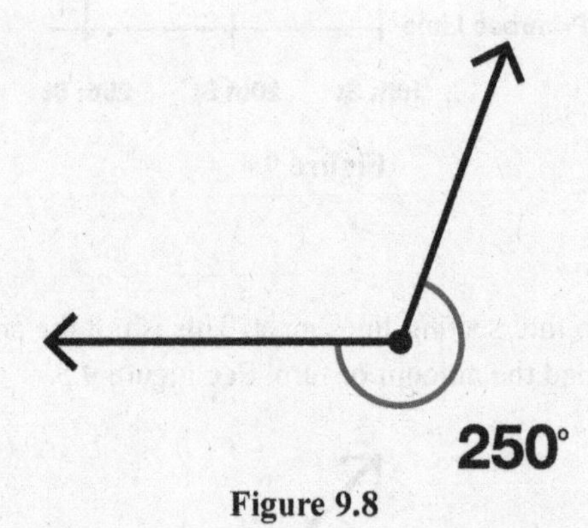


**Figure 9.8**

Notice that in Figure 9.8, the outside angle is being measured. But the inside angle could also be measured, and it would have a different measurement (and a different name).

You can label an angle the way you do any variable, with a letter like *a*. Sometimes people use Greek letters to label angles, like $\theta$ (theta). You can also label an angle by naming the arms and vertex with letters (like A, B, C). In Figure 9.9, the arms are A and C and the vertex is B. So the angle is ABC (the vertex is always the middle letter when an angle is labeled this way).

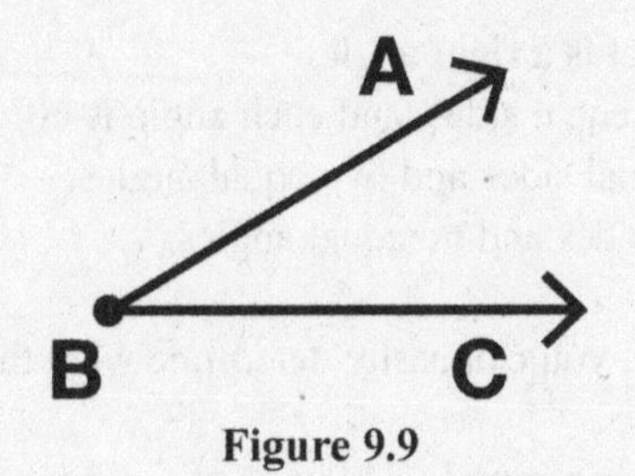


Figure 9.9

Complementary angles are two angles whose angles add up to 90°. So one angle might be 40° and the other 50°, or any combination that adds up to 90°. This is a useful fact to remember because you might be asked to find the value of a complementary angle. Given one angle's measurement you can easily deduce what the other angle's measurement needs to be.

Look at Figure 9.10. The symbol that looks like a little box in the angle indicates that the complete angle is a right angle. It is bisected by a line, resulting in two angles that add up to one complementary angle. If we know that $b = 65°$, then we can easily determine that $a = 25°$.

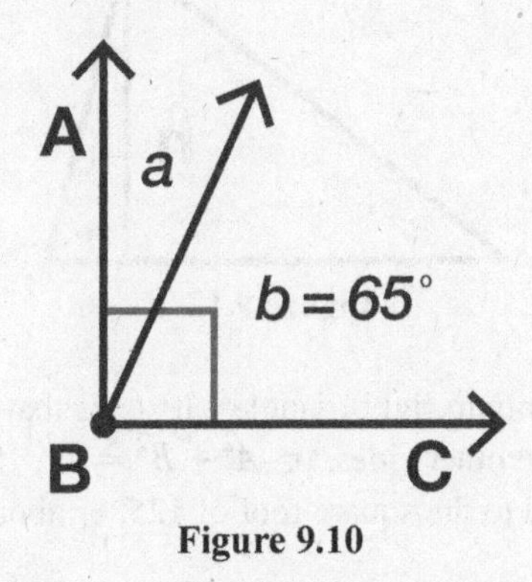


Figure 9.10

Supplementary angles add up to 180°. Again, if you know one angle's measurement, you can deduce the other's.

Note that the symbol $\angle$ means angle. So $\angle ABC$ means "angle ABC." The measurement of that angle is often indicated as $m\angle ABC$. In other words, the measurement is distinct from the angle itself. However, you may come across questions that use $\angle ABC$ to mean both the measurement as well as the object itself.

## TRIANGLES

A triangle is a closed plane shape that has three sides. It also has three angles. The three angles always add up to 180°. See Figure 9.11.

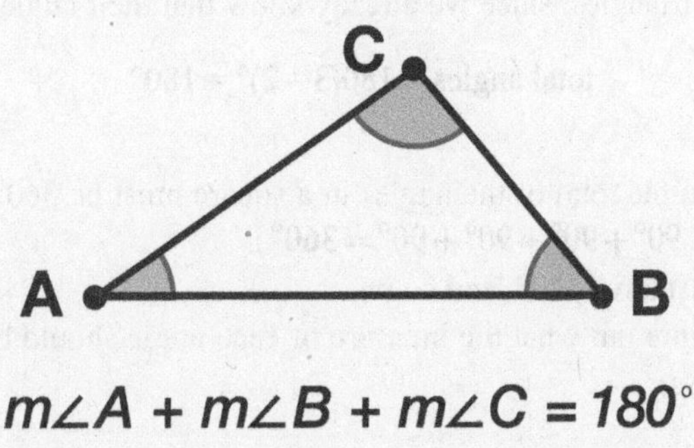


$$m\angle A + m\angle B + m\angle C = 180°$$

Figure 9.11

You can use that fact to find the missing measurement of one of the angles of a triangle. If you know that $\angle A = 60°$ and $\angle B = 65°$, then $\angle C = 55°$.

- A right triangle has one angle that is a right angle.
- An equilateral triangle has three equal sides, and each angle is 60°.
- An isosceles triangle has two equal sides and two equal angles.
- A scalene triangle has no equal sides and no equal angles.

If you have a right isosceles triangle, you can easily determine what the measure of all the angles are.

To determine the perimeter of a triangle, simply add up the measurements of the three sides.

The area of a triangle can be determined by multiplying $\frac{1}{2}$ times the base times the height, or $\frac{1}{2}bh$.

For example: A triangle with a 10 foot base and 5 foot height has an area of 25 square feet, or $\frac{1}{2}(10 \bullet 5)$.

One way this can be confusing is if you mistake the height of a triangle for the length of the vertical side. This is not necessarily the height. The height is the measure of altitude at a right angle to the base. See Figure 9.12.

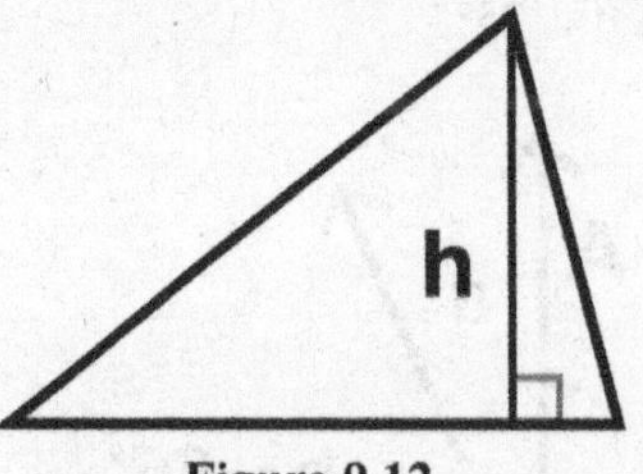


**Figure 9.12**

The Pythagorean Theorem applies only to right triangles. It states that the square of the side opposite the right angle equals the sum of the squares of the other sides, or $A^2 + B^2 = C^2$. If Side A = 5 feet and Side B = 10 feet, then $25 + 100 = C^2$. Therefore, $C$ is equal to the square root of 125, or about 11.2.

## POLYGONS

Polygons are plane figures (that is, two dimensional figures) with three or more straight sides. Triangles, rectangles, squares, hexagons, octagons—all these and more are polygons.

The sum of the interior angles of a polygon can be determined by this formula:

$$\textbf{total angles} = 180(n-2)^\circ$$

$n$ = number of sides of the polygon

Let's test out this formula on triangles, since we already know that their angles always add up to 180°.

$$\textbf{total angles} = 180(3-2)^\circ = 180^\circ$$

Okay, then! If that's true, then the total of the angles in a square must be 360° (and that makes sense, because a square has four right angles, and $90^\circ + 90^\circ + 90^\circ + 90^\circ = 360^\circ$).

A pentagon (with 5 sides) must have 540°, and so on.

If that is true, then we can figure out what the measure of each angle should be in a regular polygon (that is, a polygon with equal sides and angles):

$$\frac{180(n-2)^\circ}{n}$$

Let's find out what each angle would be for an octagon:

$$\frac{180(6)^\circ}{8} = \frac{1080^\circ}{8} = 135^\circ$$

So this formula tells us first that an octagon has a total of 1080°, and that each angle is 135°.

The perimeter of a polygon is simply the sum of the length of each of its sides.

## QUADRILATERALS

Quadrilaterals are a type of polygon with four sides and four angles. The angles add up to 360°.

### Rectangles

Rectangles are a type of quadrilateral. A rectangle is a plane shape formed from two pairs of parallel lines that are perpendicular to one another. All four angles are right angles. Opposite sides are of the same length.

A square is a type of rectangle (and a type of quadrilateral) with all four sides equal in length.

The area of a rectangle can be determined by multiplying length by width. For example, a rectangle measuring 9 feet by 6 feet would have an area of 54 square feet.

### Parallelogram

A parallelogram is a type of quadrilateral having opposite sides that are parallel and equal in length. However, the angles are not necessarily 90° angles. So, a rectangle is a parallelogram, but a parallelogram isn't necessarily a rectangle.

You find the area for a parallelogram that same way as you do for a rectangle:

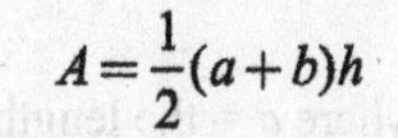

$$A = bh$$

### Rhombus

A rhombus is a quadrilateral with all sides of equal length. As with a rectangle, opposite sides are parallel. Angles are not necessarily right angles, but opposite angles are equal. The area of a rhombus is the same as for a parallelogram and a rectangle: $A = bh$.

### Trapezoid

A trapezoid is a quadrilateral that has one pair of opposite sides that are parallel. To find the area of a trapezoid, you first find the parallel sides ($a$, $b$). You find the height in the same way as you do for a triangle. Then:

$$A = \frac{1}{2}(a+b)h$$

See Figure 9.13.

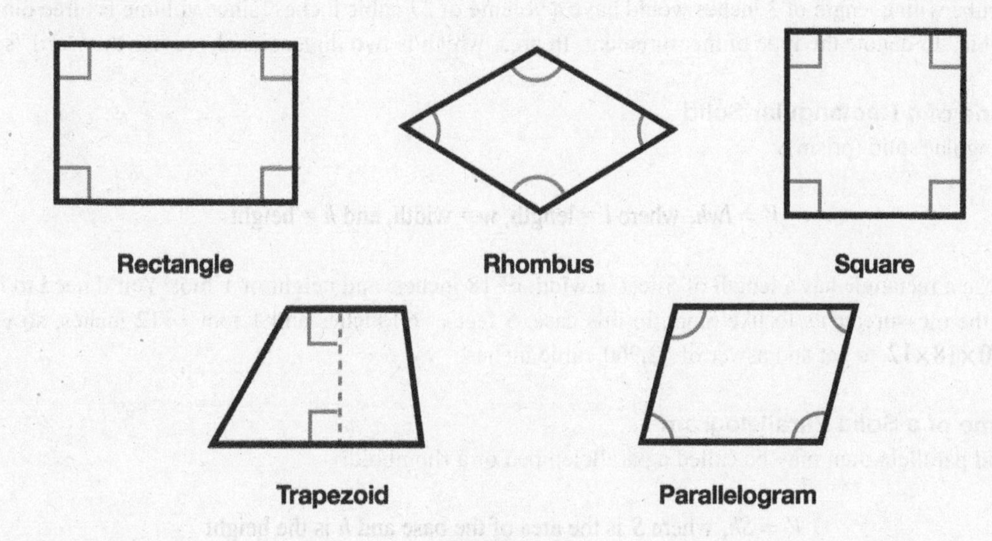


Figure 9.13

## CIRCLE

A circle is a closed plane curve whose circumference is equidistant from the center. A segment of the circumference is called an arc. The segment of lines from the center of the circle to its circumference represents the radius.

See Figure 9.14.

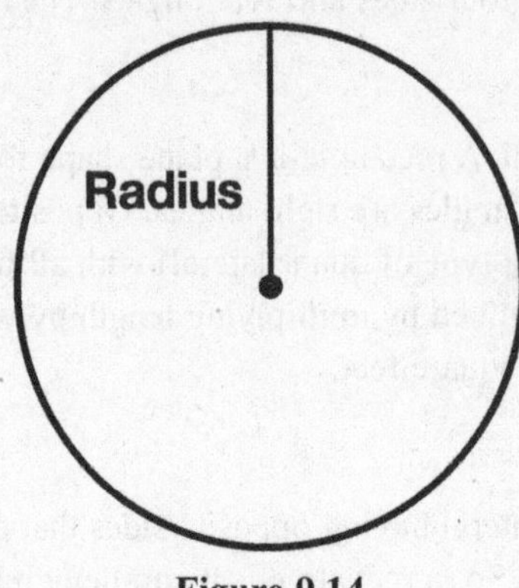

**Figure 9.14**

The diameter of a circle is the length of a line through the midpoint of the circle. It is equivalent to the radius times two ($2r$). A circle with a radius of 10 feet has a diameter of 20 feet.

The area of a circle is equal to $\pi r^2$ ($\pi = 3.1416$). For example, a circle with a radius of 10 feet has an area of $3.1416 \times 10^2$ or 314.16 square feet.

If, on the other hand, we wanted to determine the circumference, we multiply $\pi$ by the diameter, or $\pi\, 2r$. In this particular case, Circumference $= 3.1416 \bullet 10 \bullet 2$ or 62.83 feet.

## THREE-DIMENSIONAL FIGURES

In geometric terms, the space of a three-dimensional object is called its volume. You may be asked to find volume for various three-dimensional objects on the ASVAB. Here's what you need to know:

### Volume of a Cube

Cube (three-dimensional square):

$$V = a^3, \text{where } a = \text{the length of a side}$$

So a cube with a length of 3 inches would have a volume of 27 cubic inches (since volume is three dimensional, we use "cubic" to denote the type of measurement. In area, which is two dimensional, we use the word "square.")

### Volume of a Rectangular Solid

Rectangular solid (prism):

$$V = lwh, \text{ where } l = \text{length}, w = \text{width, and } h = \text{height}$$

Suppose a rectangle has a length of 5 feet, a width of 18 inches, and height of 1 foot. You'd need to remember to convert the measurements to like units. In this case, 5 feet = 60 inches and 1 foot = 12 inches, so you would multiply $60 \times 18 \times 12$ to get an answer of 12,960 cubic inches.

### Volume of a Solid Parallelogram

A solid parallelogram may be called a parallelepiped or a rhomboid:

$$V = Sh, \text{ where } S \text{ is the area of the base and } h \text{ is the height}$$

If a solid parallelogram has a base with a width of 6 inches, a length of 5 inches, and a height of 8 inches, then $S = 30$ square inches and $h = 8$ inches, so $V = 30 \bullet 8$, or 240 cubic inches.

### Volume of a Sphere

A sphere:

$$V = \frac{4}{3}\pi r^3, \text{ where } r = \text{radius}$$

For example, if the radius of a ball was 3 inches, what would be the ball's volume?

$$(\frac{4}{3})(3.1416)3^3$$

Or 113.10 cubic inches.

### Volume of a Cylinder

A tube with parallel circles.

$$V = \pi r^2 h, \text{ where } r = \text{radius and } h = \text{height}$$

For example: if a tin can has a radius of 4 inches and a height of 8 inches, what is its volume?

$$V = 3.1416(4^2)(8) \text{ or } 402.12 \text{ cubic inches.}$$

## WORD PROBLEMS

As with the Arithmetic Reasoning subtest (see Chapter 8), you'll be expected to be able to answer word problems in the Mathematics Knowledge subtest. For example, you might have a question like this:

***Fernando has a business selling collectibles. He pays a shipper $1\frac{1}{2}$ cents per cubic inch to pack and mail his packages. The average package is a small cube that's 6 inches long. Fernando has 50 packages that need to go out this week. How much will he have to pay his shipper to fill this order?***

*A. $216*
*B. $3.24*
*C. $162*
*D. $324*

To find the answer to this question, first you'll need to determine the volume of the package. The volume of a cube is $a^3$, so $6^3 = 216$ cubic inches. Then you'll need to determine how much it will cost to ship one package. That's $216 \times 1.5$, or 324 cents ($3.24). Then you'll need to multiply that amount by 50 to arrive at the correct answer, or $162.

## STRATEGIES FOR SUCCEEDING ON THE MATHEMATICS KNOWLEDGE SUBTEST

Doing well on this subtest is crucial to your eligibility to enter the military. For that reason, make sure to review ahead of time in order to do your best. But there are some strategies you can use during the actual test-taking itself to improve your chances of success.

### CAT Version Tips

There are 16 questions on the CAT version of the ASVAB, and you'll have 18 minutes to answer them. That gives you just over a minute for each question (if you're thinking you had a lot longer for the Arithmetic Reasoning questions, you'd be right!). Given that you may encounter some complex questions requiring multiple steps, you'll have to work quickly. But do remember that you're likely to score higher on the test if you answer the first several questions correctly because you'll be given harder questions worth more as you go along. So it's worth taking a little extra time to get those right.

### Pencil-and-Paper Version Tips

The pencil-and-paper version of the ASVAB has 25 questions and you'll have 24 minutes to answer them. That means a little under a minute per question. For the pencil-and-paper version, it makes sense to answer the questions you know the answer to first, then go back and solve those that you're less familiar with. If word problems give you trouble, save them for the end so that you can be sure to get as many questions right as possible.

### Overall Tips

Be sure you carefully read word problems to make sure you are solving for the right question. Word problems often contain extra information that isn't needed to solve the problem. These questions often have illustrations that go with them. The illustration may contain information you need to answer the question, so make sure you understand what you're seeing.

For either version, answer all of the questions, even if you have to guess. You aren't penalized more for a wrong answer than for no answer.

# CHAPTER 10

# General Science (GS)

The General Science subtest does not count toward the Armed Forces Qualification Test (AFQT) score that you need to achieve to be eligible for military service. However, the score is used to help determine what jobs you may be able to perform in the armed forces. A strong showing on the General Science subtest can ensure a greater number of opportunities for you.

## WHAT THE TEST MEASURES

The test measures your basic understanding of the major fields of science, including biology, chemistry, physics, earth science, and space science. You aren't expected to have an advanced knowledge of any area of science, but you will need to know basic concepts and definitions. Most high school graduates will have the required knowledge, although a careful review is always in order.

Remember that the approaches described in Chapter 6, covering Word Knowledge, will help you practice breaking a word into its parts in order to understand its meaning without having to look the word up in the dictionary, a useful skill when you're taking the General Science test.

Because the range of questions can vary so greatly—all of science is a pretty big category!—your best approach here is to focus on the fields where you have the least amount of knowledge and try to improve your understanding of these areas by using this review section. In addition, you may need to do further study at your public library. This is especially true if you're hoping for a military career that requires a good score on the General Science subtest, such as a meteorological specialist, environmental health and safety specialist, space operations specialist, or medical technician (among many others).

Keep in mind that most of the material on the General Science subtest will cover the areas of biology, chemistry, and physical science, and that you will be unlikely to receive many questions on areas like astronomy and oceanography.

## MAIN FIELDS OF SCIENCE

The General Science subtest can cover everything from anatomy to zoology, so let's start with a quick overview of what these various fields cover:

- Anatomy: the study of bodily structures. For the General Science subtest, the focus is generally on the human body.
- Astronomy: the study of space, objects in space (including planets, comets, etc.), and the universe itself.
- Biology: the study of living things. Many branches of biology deal with specific aspects of life, such as behavior (behavioral biology) or how characteristics are passed from generation to generation (genetics).
- Botany: a branch of biology that focuses on the study of plant life.
- Chemistry: the study of matter, including its composition, structure, and other properties; many subdisciplines exist within the overall field of chemistry.
- Ecology: the study of the environments of living organisms and how they interact with each other.
- Geology: the study of the earth's physical structure, including rock and soil.

- Mechanical principles (force and motion mechanics): a branch of physics that focuses on the study of physical bodies and how they respond to force/motion.
- Meteorology: the study of the earth's atmosphere, with an emphasis on understanding weather processes in order to create forecasts.
- Oceanography: the study of bodies of water (usually the ocean) to understand their properties and processes.
- Physics: the study of the interaction between matter and energy.
- Physiology: the study of the systems and processes of living organisms and how they function.
- Zoology: the study of animals, including their biology, anatomy, physiology, and natural habitats.

## HOW SCIENTISTS WORK

Understanding the scientific process is the first step toward understanding scientific concepts. Science is, essentially, the study of the world (or the universe) and how it works. This study is conducted through the use of observation and testing. In other words, it is fact-based. Scientists also have to be able to reproduce each other's work. This process verifies the accuracy of research.

### The Scientific Process in Five Easy Steps

An overly simplistic presentation of this process goes something like this:

1. Scientist observes something.
2. Scientist tries to explain why that something happened.
3. Scientist tests her explanation.
4. Explanation is proved or disproved.
5. Scientist shares her results with the world.

### The Scientific Process as It Actually Works

Let's look at the scientific process in a somewhat more nuanced way. Bear in mind that entire books have been written on the subject of the scientific process, so this is still a somewhat simplified version of how it works.

#### The Hypothesis

When trying to understand some corner of the world, a scientist begins with an idea—an explanation for something that is happening or has happened. This is called a *hypothesis*, which is just a starting point. It has to be proven—shown to be true through examination and testing. For that reason, a hypothesis must be testable. For example, you may be interested in finding out whether mother tigers feel love for their offspring, but you can't actually test for love. It's not provable. Among other considerations, you can't ask a tiger how she's feeling.

But you could test for certain behaviors that might indicate affiliation or affection. For example, your observations might have shown you that tiger mothers bump or rub the heads of their offspring. You know from your pet cat that this is a way he shows affection. So you could create a hypothesis based on extrapolation of behavior from one type of feline to another.

#### Characteristics of a Good Hypothesis

A good hypothesis indicates the reason for the research as well as the variables that are being tested. Ideally you would test just one variable at a time, although in practice that can be difficult to do. The classic high-school science example is, "If I talk to a plant, it will grow faster." Here the only variable being tested is whether or not you are talking to a plant. Everything else remains the same.

An hypothesis is a statement, not a question. So we say, "If I talk to a plant, it will grow faster." We don't say, "Will talking to a plant make it grow faster?" Although that question is a good place to start, it is not a hypothesis.

A good hypothesis is also clearly stated—a person reading it understands what is being proposed.

**Testing the Hypothesis**

The way you would test the high-school science hypothesis is to have one group for which you're testing the variable, and another group for which you are not. The first group is the variable group, and the second is the control group. If you have a measurable difference in results between the variable group and the control group, you can say that there is a relationship between the variable and the results. This is also called a relationship between the independent variable (the input you're testing, which is talking to the plant) and the dependent variable (the outcome you've gotten, which is a faster-growing plant).

So, for the high-school science experiment, you would plant seeds of a fast-germinating plant (because you don't have three years to do this), like a zinnia, from the same seed packet (to reduce the effect of outside factors, like having one seed come from a healthy parent and one seed from an unhealthy parent).

You'd then divide the plants into Group A, the group you talk to, and Group B, the group you don't talk to. You'd have several plants in each group to give you a more reliable result. (If you only plant one seed in the variable group, and it dies, there could be many reasons for it, not just hating to listen to your voice.) Then you'd treat both groups exactly the same, in terms of amount of sunlight they get, how you feed and water them, and so on, the only exception being that you would talk to the plants in Group A and be totally silent with the plants in Group B.

Each day you'd record your observations and at the end of the research period, you'd compare your results. So, Group A might have grown 10 percent more than Group B, or maybe 10 percent less, or maybe there was no difference at all. You would write up your results, reach a tentative conclusion about what you learned, and share that information with your teacher, the Science Club, or the science fair judges.

**Why Blind Studies Are Used**

Because scientists have biases in favor of their hypothesis (they want their hypothesis to be true), they can sometimes skew the results even without meaning to. For this reason, blind studies are often done to correct for this skewing. So, to do a blind study on the high-school science fair project, the person doing the caring (the watering, the feeding, and the talking) would be different from the person measuring the results. The person measuring the results would not know which plant is in which group until after the study is complete.

A double-blind study is one in which neither the tester nor the subject being tested knows which group he or she is in until after the test is over. Many drug studies are done this way, with the subject taking either the active drug or an inert substance (placebo) and the tester recording the data without knowing whether the subject is taking the active or inert substance.

**Other Ways to Test a Hypothesis**

You can't always conduct a study in a controlled clinical environment. So, scientists have to use other methods. Let's look at how that might play out.

In the case of the affectionate tiger, you have formed a hypothesis. As stated, a hypothesis usually includes a reason for the research. You might wish to conduct the research in order to have a better understanding of tiger behavior. Perhaps if a mother tiger stops bumping or rubbing the head of her offspring, it indicates something has gone wrong with the bonding process, putting the offspring at greater risk of being abandoned and dying. So that would be a useful purpose for doing the research.

Your hypothesis, then, might be that if a mother tiger rubs or bumps the head of her offspring, that means a bond is established and she is likely to protect the cub from dangers, such as from adult males who might kill it in order to mate with the mother.

**Reviewing Other Research**

Before you get started testing your hypothesis, you'd want to research the literature to see what other studies have been done that relate to your hypothesis. Since scientists don't work in isolation chambers, they often refine each other's ideas (either working together or independently), to help prove or disprove a hypothesis. You might find that your hypothesis about tiger behavior has already been examined, or that an idea similar to yours has been proposed but no actual research has taken place. You might build on work another person has been doing—you might even join your efforts together to be more effective.

**Testing the Hypothesis**

Once you've established your hypothesis and done some preliminary research about it, you would need to consider how to test it. This might include further observation. For example, if, after additional observation, you note that mother tigers are shown to bump or rub heads with adversaries, then it may not be the sign of affection you think it is (or it may be a more complex behavior than you've given it credit for being). So, that would be a sign that you need to head back to the drawing board with your hypothesis. (One of the most important characteristics of a good scientist is the willingness to let his or her hypothesis be proven wrong!)

Suppose that once you've done additional observation you're convinced that mother tigers only bump or rub heads with their offspring, and on occasion with other tigers they're not in competition with, then you might create a more complex experiment to more thoroughly prove or disprove your hypothesis. For example, you might set up an extended study that counts the number of head bumps/rubs a group of mother tigers give their cubs, then watch the mothers' behavior toward each cub as it reaches adulthood, noting the outcome for each cub. Did it survive to adulthood? Did the mother engage in protective behaviors? What is the correlation between head bumps/rubs and outcome? (There may not be one! That doesn't mean your hypothesis is wrong, it just means you might need to do additional study.)

All of this is complicated by the fact that tigers in captivity (which might be easy enough to observe) may behave very differently from tigers in the wild (which are a lot harder to observe). So you would have to decide which group you want to research.

**Correlation Is Not Causation**

It's important to remember that correlation is not causation. Even some scientists forget this! Just because one fact is related to another does not mean that one causes the other. For example, it may be that overweight people are more likely to have, say, migraine headaches than people of normal weight. But that does not mean that being overweight *causes* migraine headaches. It may seem like common sense, but common sense is not necessarily scientifically accurate. Another example would be something like "nearsighted people are more likely to have brown eyes than any other eye color." But that doesn't prove that having brown eyes causes nearsightedness. Most people have brown eyes, so therefore most people with nearsightedness would by default have brown eyes.

It is particularly difficult to pinpoint causation when there are many variables in a problem. That's why complex problems are complex! It's hard to pinpoint what is causing them or what can cure them. When a problem has multiple causes or multiple factors that impact it, the solution usually must include multiple approaches.

**Next Steps in the Process**

Once a scientist has tested a hypothesis and shared the results with others, other scientists will work to further prove or disprove the hypothesis. A hypothesis that is generally accepted by scientists is called a law. Once a hypothesis or law has been repeatedly tested and proven, it is called a *theory*. That's why we have a theory of gravity, not a hypothesis of gravity. But many people confuse hypothesis and theory, leading them to think that some scientific theories have not been proven when they have.

## Measurements in Science

Scientists rely on the metric system to make and communicate measurements. Thus, they use meters, liters, and grams rather than inches, gallons, and pounds. Metric units allow for more precise measurements that can be expressed based on a system of tens. For example, there are 12 inches in a foot, 4 quarts in a gallon, and 16 ounces in a pound, which can create considerable confusion when trying to multiply and divide measurements. But in the metric system, 10 millimeters make up 1 centimeter, and 10 centimeters make up 1 decameter, and 10 decameters make up 1 meter. The same is true of liters and grams.

**Metrics and Mass**

In science, the word "mass" is normally used as opposed to *weight*. Weight measures the pull of gravity, and so is different depending on gravitational pull. Mass is the same on the moon as it is on earth. Scientists use balances to make measurements of mass.

### Very Small Amounts and Very Large Amounts

Because some science deals with very small amounts, very tiny units of measure are needed. One common one is the microgram, denoted by the symbol μg. One microgram is one millionth of a gram. A nanogram (ng) is one billionth of a gram.

These measurements can also be indicated by using the exponent value. One microgram could also be represented as 10-6 g.

Since some scientists measure massive amounts, they also use exponents to indicate these massive amounts. A megagram (one million grams) would be represented as $10^6$ g.

### Measuring Temperature

Scientists use either Celsius or Kelvin scales for measuring temperature. The Kelvin scale uses Celsius increments but begins at absolute zero (the lowest possible theoretical temperature). Thus, a Celsius temperature is the same as Kelvin minus 273.15 degrees. If the Kelvin temperature is 0 degrees (absolute zero), then the equivalent Celsius temperature is -273.15 degrees.

## BIOLOGY

Earlier in this chapter, we gave a definition for biology that called it "the study of living things." That sounds straightforward enough, but because scientists have to nail down exactly what everything means, they can't call it the study of living things without defining what a living thing is. Think about that for a minute. What differentiates a person from a rock? What makes a person similar to a potted plant? You might say that a person changes but a rock doesn't, yet that wouldn't be completely accurate. A rock might erode, or moss might start growing on it, or it might get kicked down the hill. You might say living things breathe, but that potted plant doesn't have lungs. So what do living things have in common and what makes them different from nonliving things?

Scientists actually disagree about this, but in general, living things are said to have functions such as metabolism, growth, and reproduction. They respond to stimuli and/or adapt to the environment from within. Thus, the rock being kicked down the hill is responding to stimuli, but only in a mechanical sense of being displaced by an outside force. It is not responding from within. If you're kicked down a hill, you might respond by getting back up again after you fall, charging up the hill to punch the person who kicked you, or some other action that comes from within.

## Evolution Theory

The theory of evolution states that life on earth originated from a universal ancestor billions of years ago, and that a process of change based on variations in the genetic code led to the creation of multiple types of living organisms. Evolution is a slow process occurring over many generations that continues to the present day.

### Advantageous Adaptation

Any given population (of field mice, people, algae, anything living) undergoes this process of change over time, sometimes but not always as a result of *advantageous adaptation* (those organisms with characteristics that enable them to survive in a particular environment are more likely to pass their genetic code on through reproduction). Occasionally, however, random genetic mutation is responsible for a change in a population.

### Natural Selection

Charles Darwin is best known for proposing his theory of evolution, though his work was based on the work of earlier scientists. Darwin's theory explains the role of *natural selection* in evolution (often called "survival of the fittest"—which is basically the idea of advantageous adaptation described above). Natural selection depends on more offspring being produced than can survive (think of the number of kernels on an ear of corn), offspring having varying traits, and such traits being inherited. Out of these conditions, the individual most likely to survive and reproduce will do so, thus passing on its genes. The individual less well adapted will not survive to pass on its genetic code. To put it in simplistic terms: Giraffes with short necks didn't reproduce as well as giraffes with long necks (because they couldn't reach the food available to them); thus the giraffe population became long-necked. Competition for resources (including mates) is a key part of evolution.

### Cell Structure

Cells are the building blocks of living things. Usually cells are too small to be seen without a microscope. Some organisms are so small they contain only one cell; others are so complex they contain billions or trillions of cells.

Cells are the smallest functional component of any living organism. Smaller units of matter (such as atoms) are more properly the study of chemistry and physics, so look for that information in those sections later in this chapter.

Cells usually contain a nucleus and a cytoplasm within a membrane; the nucleus carries out the work of the cell. See Figure 10.1 for an example of a cell structure.

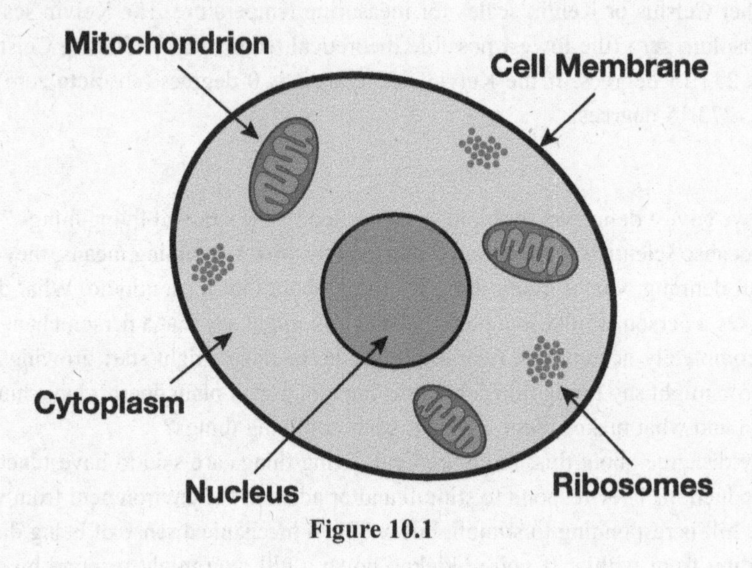


**Figure 10.1**

Cells can range from the simple to the complex, and may have many structures playing different roles. The function of a cell can vary dramatically. A human, for example, has many kinds of cells: skin cells, bone cells, neurons (which convey electrical information throughout the body), and heart muscle cells, to name just a few (depending on how you classify them, there are as many as several hundred different kinds of cells in the human body). Different cells combine together to create organs (eyes, liver, kidneys).

Note that some cells, like bacteria, have no interior cell membranes (such as generally surround the nucleus and other organelles). They are called *prokaryotic*. Cells that do have these interior cell membranes are called *eukaryotic*.

Some common structures you'll find in a cell are:

#### Cell Membrane

The outer covering of a cell that protects the cell. Certain materials can move in and out of the membrane through processes such as osmosis (the mechanism for the transfer of fluids between molecules).

#### Nucleus

The cell nucleus contains the genetic code and is responsible for cell reproduction and growth. The DNA (deoxyribonucleic acid) within a cell replicates itself and carries a cell's genetic code. RNA (ribonucleic acid) is also contained within the nucleus and is the messenger that carries out the DNA's instructions.

#### Cytoplasm

The material in a cell within the cell membrane, but not including the nucleus. (Think of an egg, with the white as the cytoplasm and the yolk as the nucleus.)

**Ribosomes**

These structures help RNA carry out its instructions; they bind to RNA and help in the production of the proteins that carry out the cell's work.

**Mitochondria**

They are the fuel centers of a cell; they do the work of respiring and producing energy.

## Classification

Biologists group similar organisms together as an aid to understanding and study. This process of classification ("scientific taxonomy") is complicated; do you group organisms based on physical similarity or shared descent? What of organisms that are similar at the molecular level?

You may have been taught the "kingdom" method of classification, in which organisms are grouped according to major categories, then further subdivided into groups that share similar characteristics. This is the approach that you'll see on the ASVAB. Here are the categories from largest (containing the most organisms) to narrowest (members are most like each other).

- Kingdom
- Phylum (the plural is "phyla")
- Class
- Order
- Family
- Genus
- Species

So your pet dog is of the kingdom *Animalia*, the phylum *chordata* (true vertebrates), the class *mammalia*, the order *carnivora*, the family *canidae* (containing wolf- and fox-like animals), the genus *canis*, the species *canis lupis* (gray wolf), and the subspecies *canis lupis familiaris*.

Humans share a kingdom, phylum, and class with dogs; we part ways at order and join the *primates*. Our family is *hominidae*, genus *homo*, species *sapiens* (usually called *homo sapiens*).

**Plants and Animals**

Traditionally, all living organisms were divided into one of two categories, plant or animal. In this traditional classification, you distinguished a plant from an animal by whether it could move or not. While this method of categorization is overly simplistic, we do tend to see organisms in the world as either plant-like or animal-like.

***Plants***

Botany is a branch of biology that focuses on the study of plant life. Generally, plants are multicellular organisms that *photosynthesize* (use the energy of the sun to fuel their processes). This includes everything from moss to redwood trees. (Many people also considered one-celled organisms, like algae, to be a plant.)

Botanists use the same "kingdom" classification as other biologists (see "Classification" in this chapter), although they generally use the word "division" instead of "phylum." The kingdom of plants, *Plantae*, has thousand and thousands (and thousands) of species; an international joint effort to list all of the various plant species contains nearly 300,000 accepted species (not to mention subspecies—think of all the varieties of roses there are in the world!).

All of these plants helpfully produce oxygen for the *animalia* of the world to breathe. How does that work? Photosynthesis occurs when the *chlorophyll* (a pigment) in a plant's green leaves collects the energy of the sun (plus carbon dioxide and water) and the plant turns the energy into carbohydrates. This process releases oxygen.

***Animals***

The study of animals (excluding humans) is called zoology. Animals (including humans) differ from plants in that we have to catch our own food. No matter how much sun and rain we soak up, it's not enough to keep us going.

We also move about (plants can move, of course, but generally that's either according to the whims of the wind or because of *heliotropism*, an innate orientation toward the sun).

*Vertebrates* are animals that have a backbone (a spine made up of vertebrae). Animals without backbones are *invertebrates*. Most of the animals in the world are invertebrates (about 95%). Animals can be categorized into *cold-blooded* (taking on the temperature of the environment) or *warm-blooded* (generating body heat). Most vertebrates are cold-blooded.

### Ecology

All of these organisms (plants and animals) exist in the natural world—that is to say, they do their respiration and reproduction, living and dying, in relationship to a place. The study of these environments is called *ecology*.

Some organisms can live practically anywhere, whereas others are restricted to a relatively small area based on the conditions they need to survive. For example, a whale can't live on land, nor can it survive in your backyard swimming pool.

The place where an organism can naturally flourish (and reproduce!) is called its *habitat*. Different kinds of organisms can be found in each habitat (although some organisms may be able to live almost anyplace, such as humans).

All of the elements of a particular habitat or environment, including living organisms and inanimate objects such as rivers and mountains, make up an *ecosystem (*sometimes called a *biological community*). But an ecosystem is more than a collection of things. It includes how those things interact. So an ecosystem can be upset by the introduction of a new element that affects those interactions (or relationships). If an ecosystem has a wolf as a top predator and humans kill all the wolves, then the ecosystem is upset. Animals that would normally have been killed by the wolves aren't, meaning more competition for resources. This might result in more aggression among those animals, or perhaps migration. Such a shift can play out in many different ways.

One of the ways in which organisms interact in an ecosystem is called the *food chain*, often called a *food web*. You might call it who-eats-whom. At one end are organisms called *producers*, like plants. They take sun and water and turn it into energy. Then there are *consumers*: various animals that eat the plants, such as people, cows, mice, and insects. These consumers are sometimes consumed themselves. People eat cows, and foxes eat mice, and birds eat insects. Snakes eat birds and are sometimes eaten by birds.

At the end of all this eating are dead leftovers, often called carrion. Carrion-eaters like vultures help these leftovers decompose or break down into smaller parts. Then other organisms like bacteria and fungi get to work to further break down the leftovers. The decomposed materials enrich the soil, and plants take sun and water and start the whole process over again.

Collections of ecosystems that share similar traits are called *biomes*. Major biomes are aquatic, desert, forest, grassland, and tundra.

## PHYSIOLOGY

The branch of biology that deals with the human body's parts, its functions, and its bodily processes is called physiology. A human is a complicated organism; understanding how it works can help you understand how other organisms work. Your body consists of a number of different organ systems that work together to keep you alive and well.

### The Five Senses

A human takes in a tremendous amount of information about the world around him or her through the five senses. Special organs (an organ is a collection of cells and tissue with a specific function) allow us to experience this sensory input. Your five senses include:

- Vision. Light waves (discussed later in this chapter) activate *photoreceptors* in your eye. These photoreceptor cells (located in your retina) send nerve impulses to your brain via the *optic nerve*. Your brain then figures out what you're looking at.
- Smell. Objects emit molecules that can sometimes be sensed by the nose (if there are enough of them). These molecules are called *odorants*. Nerve cells in your nose, called *olfactory cells*, or sometimes *olfactory receptors*, send a signal to your brain, and your brain connects the dots. Humans and other animals are

sensitive to *pheromones*, which are chemicals released by members of a species that affect the behavior of other members of the same species. You may not be aware of smelling these chemicals, but they can still affect you.

- Hearing. Sound waves (discussed later in this chapter) enter your ear and reach your inner ear. The *cochlea* there has little hairs that vibrate with the sound waves. The hairs create an electrical signal that your brain translates. Your ears also have a *vestibular system* that helps you maintain your balance.
- Touch. While your other senses are located in specific parts of your body (eyes, ears), your sense of touch is all over. Your skin is full of nerve endings that tell you whether you've just encountered a burning hot coal or an ice cube. While touch may seem less important than other senses, it's crucial for your body to move through space. Touch allows you to tell where your foot is as you walk, where your tongue is as you eat, and so on. Touch is necessary to human growth and development.
- Taste. Your mouth and tongue has thousands of taste receptors that send information to your brain, which figures out what you're eating. Your sense of smell is important to your sense of taste. If you don't smell the difference between, for example, an onion and an apple, your taste receptors are unlikely to tell the difference. Smelling the onion (or the apple) provides a context clue your brain needs to help interpret the information the taste receptors are sending it. Your sense of touch also contributes to taste; your tongue and mouth can feel the texture of a food as well as detect its taste.

A disruption in any of these senses can create considerable difficulties for a human.

In addition to the organs related to the five senses, humans have a number of other important organs required to sustain the processes of life. Organs work together to create organ systems, which we'll cover in this chapter.

### Skeletal System

You would be just a blob on the floor without your skeleton. All of your bones connect together to give your body stability and support. Other important facts to remember:

- The skeleton protects your body.
- Your bones produce blood cells in the bone marrow.
- Your bones also store minerals that your cells need to perform their functions.
- You have 206 bones.

Your skeleton is mostly bone but it also contains *cartilage*, a hard connective tissue. You'll find cartilage in your nose and ears, under your knee cap, and in other places throughout your body. An infant has more cartilage than a grown adult; the maturation process replaces some of this cartilage (most notably in the skull) with bone.

Your skeleton is articulated so that you can move. In other words, your bones are joined in such a way that allows you to move more easily. (Imagine if you had no knees or elbows!) These points of articulation are called *joints*. Your bones are held together at these points with *ligaments*, which are tough strips of tissue. *Tendons* attach muscle to bone (see "Muscular System" in this chapter).

The tendons and ligaments allow your bones to move within a specific range. Not all of your joints work in the same way. There are four different kinds of movable joints, and one kind of joint that doesn't move once you're an adult:

1. Hinge joints. These work like a door opening and closing. Your knee is a hinge joint.
2. Pivot joints. These joints allow your bones to move in an arc, to twist, and to move up and down as well as side to side. Your elbow is a pivot joint.
3. Ball-and-socket joints. These joints allow you to move your bones in a circular way. Your hip is a ball-and-socket joint.

4. Sliding joints (sometimes called gliding joints). These joints allow you to move your ankles and wrists in a circular motion (as well as up and down) but they are not ball-and-socket joints like your hip.
5. Immovable joints. Your skull has places of articulation where bones meet, but you can't move these joints.

Some scientists add another type of joint, the semi-movable joint, such as the joint that attaches your ribs to your vertebrae. Your rib cage is flexible so that you can breathe.

### Muscular System

You wouldn't be able to walk without your muscles. You wouldn't be able to carry the groceries into the kitchen. You wouldn't be able to talk (your tongue is a muscle!) or write a note. In fact, you wouldn't be able to do much of anything your brain thinks up, because almost everything a human does requires the use of muscle.

A muscle is made up of fibrous tissue that contracts and relaxes in order to carry out whatever task it needs to carry out. Muscles can repair themselves, grow stronger, and convert food energy into movement. Strong fibrous strips of tissue called *tendons* attach muscle to bone.

Sometimes you don't notice your muscles moving, such as when your body is moving food through its digestive system. Once you swallow whatever you're eating, your body takes over and you don't have to make a conscious effort to do anything until it gets to the other end and you have to eliminate it.

The vast majority of your body heat (about 85 percent) is generated by muscle, which is why moving around helps you feel warmer in cold weather.

- *Voluntary* muscles are the ones over which you have conscious control. For example, lifting a box, walking across the room, bending to pick up a dropped object.
- *Involuntary* muscles are the ones you don't consciously control. For example, you don't consciously make your heart beat.

Some muscles, like those involved in breathing, can be both voluntary and involuntary. You breathe without thinking about it, but you also can control your breathing if you decide to do so.

Depending on who's counting, you have about 650 muscles in your body.

### Skin System

The skin system, also called the *integumentary* system, is an organ system. In fact, your skin is the largest organ in your body. It's an organ because it's tissue organized to carry out a function—in fact, it carries out a number of functions.

- Communicating sensory information. Your skin has special nerve cells that send information to your brain. (See "The Five Senses" in this chapter for more about the sense of touch.) Touch is one of the most important functions of your skin.
- Protecting you from infection. Your skin keeps outside microorganisms like bacteria and viruses from entering your body and causing disease. It's a physical barrier to anything that might try to penetrate from outside. When your skin is cut, you are more prone to infection because your skin can't protect you from those outside microorganisms.
- Cooling and warming your body. Your skin has glands that help protect it and your body. For example, sweat glands help keep your body cool (remember that muscle generates heat, so when you exert a lot of effort, you generate a lot of heat, and your body has to get rid of the excess somehow). Your skin can also expand or constrict blood vessels, which helps raise or lower your body's temperature. Hairs on your skin can also be raised (think goose bumps) to help insulate your body and keep it warm.
- Waterproofing your body. Your skin keeps water from escaping your body (your body is mostly made up of water) in several ways. One way is by being a physical barrier. Oil from secretory glands is also used to prevent water from evaporating from our bodies and to keep us from absorbing all the water in the bathtub.

### Respiratory System

Your body's cells need oxygen to carry out their functions; they produce carbon dioxide as waste, which must be eliminated. Thus, your respiratory system functions to bring in oxygen and get rid of carbon dioxide. When you inhale, you take in oxygen, which goes to your blood, which brings it throughout your body (see "Circulatory System" in this chapter for further information on this aspect of oxygen transportation). When you exhale, you expel carbon dioxide.

Picture yourself taking a breath and you'll have a good sense of how the mechanical part of the process works. Keep in mind that the act of breathing (inhaling and exhaling) isn't exactly the same as the process of respiration (using the oxygen and getting rid of the carbon dioxide). When you breathe, you use muscles like the *diaphragm*, a dome-shaped, flat muscle that works as a partition and which is located between the chest cavity and abdomen, to physically move the air into and out of your lungs. Sudden, involuntary contractions in your diaphragm are hiccups, which can be caused by eating too quickly or by an irritant.

As you inhale, you take in air that goes into your lungs. There, small sacs in the lungs called *alveoli* collect the oxygen and pass it to tiny blood vessels called *capillaries*. The capillaries take the oxygen and whisk it off into the bloodstream while at the same time depositing carbon dioxide in the alveoli. The alveoli send the waste back up through the system until you exhale it out into the world.

The respiratory tract includes all the organs involved in respiration, including the nasal cavity, the trachea (throat), and the bronchial tubes that lead to the lungs. An upper respiratory infection is one that occurs in the area above the larynx (the larynx is where your vocal cords are located).

You yawn when you're tired because you're not getting enough oxygen into your body. It's extremely dangerous for your body to go more than a few minutes without oxygen. Brain cells begin to die when you go more than about four minutes without breathing, and irreversible cell and tissue damage can occur. A state of decreased oxygen intake is called hypoxia. No oxygen intake at all is called apoxia.

The average adult takes between twelve and twenty breaths every minute at rest.

### Circulatory System

Your circulatory system is connected to your respiratory system—they do closely related jobs. The blood vessels that make up the circulatory system could be likened to a network of roads—from interstate highways to tiny country lanes that connect all the parts of the country. The circulatory system, like a roadway system, is concerned with transporting materials. In this case, blood is used as the method of transportation, and the blood carries everything from oxygen and nutrients to waste.

Let's look at the main features of your circulatory system:

- *heart*, which is the pump that moves blood throughout your vessels
- *blood vessels*, which are the tubes that carry your blood throughout your body
    - arteries, which are larger blood vessels that take oxygen-rich blood from the heart to bring it throughout the body
    - veins, which are larger blood vessels that bring oxygen-depleted blood to the heart for recirculation
    - capillaries, which are smaller blood vessels (as described in the section "Respiratory System" in this chapter) that move blood throughout your body and are involved in moving oxygen out of your lungs and moving carbon dioxide into them
- *blood*, which moves oxygen and nutrients into your cells and takes waste out of them. Some of this waste, like carbon dioxide, is eventually expelled by the lungs. Some is brought by blood to the kidneys, where it is expelled in the urine. Blood also fights disease. *Blood plasma* is a liquid substance that helps the blood cells move through blood vessels. Plasma also stores protein. Your blood has three main types of blood cells (*hematocytes*):
    - red blood cells, also known as erythrocytes, which drop off nutrients and oxygen and whisk away waste. Hemoglobin, a protein in red blood cells, binds to oxygen and carries it around. Hemoglobin is what gives red blood cells their color.

- white blood cells, also called leukocytes, which try to eliminate disease-causing microorganisms. There are several different types of white blood cells, each of which targets different types of microorganisms. A healthy adult has about 1% white blood cells in his or her blood. Higher concentrations indicate that the body is trying to fight a disease.
- platelets, also called thrombocytes, aid in the process of blood clotting, a vital function that prevents blood loss. Too few platelets can lead to excessive bleeding while too many can cause blood clots that restrict blood flow.

**Blood Movement in a Nutshell**

Your heart is a muscle that contracts in a rhythm that moves blood throughout your circulatory system. Your heart sends oxygen-rich blood out through the aorta, the biggest artery in your body. A system of blood vessels stemming from the aorta brings this oxygen-rich blood throughout your body. Oxygen-depleted blood is brought back to the heart through veins. The heart sends this oxygen-depleted blood to the lungs through the pulmonary artery. The lungs oxygenate the blood and return it to the heart via the pulmonary vein (see "Respiratory System" in this chapter for further information). The oxygen-rich blood goes out to the body through the aorta and the cycle continues.

**Heart Beat**

An adult heart beats 60 to 100 times per minute.

- A slow heart beat is called *bradycardia.*
- A fast heart beat is called *tachycardia.*
- An irregular heart beat is called *arrhythmia.*

Any of these variations can indicate a problem with the heart.

**Blood Pressure**

Blood pressure is a measurement of how hard your heart works to do its job. There are two numbers that form a ratio, such as 120/80 (read as "one-twenty over eighty"). The top number is the pressure that's measured when the heart beats, or the systolic pressure. The bottom number is the pressure that's measured when the heart rests, or the diastolic pressure. Systolic pressure is always higher than diastolic pressure. The difference between systolic pressure and diastolic pressure is known as pulse pressure. A normal blood pressure reading is one in which the systolic pressure is less than 120 and the diastolic pressure is less than 80. You are considered to have high blood pressure if your systolic pressure is over 140 or the diastolic pressure is over 90. Extremely low blood pressure can also be a cause of concern. High or low pulse pressures (large or small differences between systolic and diastolic pressure) can also indicate heart problems.

**Heart Disease**

Coronary artery disease, sometimes just called heart disease, is the build up of plaque (cholesterol that sticks together, forming lumps) on the walls of the heart's blood vessels, and is the number one cause of death in the United States. Plaques interfere with the flow of blood into and out of the heart (sometimes blocking it completely). This can lead to heart attack.

## Digestive System

Your digestive system turns food into energy. Digestion actually starts the moment you catch a whiff of dinner, and your mouth starts salivating (glands in your mouth secrete the liquid). The saliva in your mouth is necessary to the digestive process.

1. When you take a bite, your teeth begin grinding the food into smaller pieces. Saliva mixes with these small pieces and begins breaking them down into their constituent parts. Saliva also works as a lubricant, making the chewing and swallowing process easier.

2. Once you swallow, the food moves through your *pharynx*, the cavity behind your nose and mouth, to the *esophagus*, the tube that connects your throat to your stomach. While it may seem that food just shoots down your esophagus, it is actually pushed along by a series of contractions in the esophagus. An organ at the bottom of your esophagus called a *sphincter* functions like a valve and keeps food from coming back up (although if you've ever vomited you know that this is an imperfect system).

3. Food then enters the *stomach*, an organ that's something like a sack about the size of your fist. This is where the real work of digestion begins. Your stomach has strong muscles that grind food down. Acid and enzymes in your stomach also work to break food into its constituent parts.

4. Once the stomach has done its job, it sends the food, now in a paste or liquid form, to the *small intestine*. The small intestine is a coiled tube about twenty feet long that continues the process of breaking food down. Nutrients are absorbed into the bloodstream at this stage and blood cells transport the nutrients throughout the body.

5. The food passes from the small intestine to the *large intestine*, where much of the water is absorbed. Microorganisms stationed here also help in the breakdown process. You'll find lots of beneficial bacteria in the large intestine. The large intestine works mainly to eliminate waste, those parts of the food that can't be used by the body to produce energy. For example, human digestive systems cannot break down cellulose (which makes up plant cell walls), so it must be eliminated from the body.

6. Solid waste travels through the *colon*, yet another tube-like organ. Waste is stored in the *rectum* (more tubing) until it can be eliminated through the *anus*, another sphincter.

You can envision the digestive tract (also called the alimentary canal) as a long tube that stretches from mouth to anus.

### Immune System

Your immune system is the way your body defends itself from outside attack. All kinds of microorganisms and other threats would love to find a home in your body—everything from bacteria and viruses to parasitic worms and toxins. Your body tries to expel all of these unwelcome intruders. For example, if bacteria enters a cut in your skin, your body sends white blood cells to the site to fight off the bacteria. (Your skin functions as part of your immune system.)

Other microbes are killed off in your saliva, filtered out by your cilia (tiny hairs that attach to various surfaces in your body, like your nasal cavity), trapped by mucus in various parts of your body, or destroyed by your stomach's strong acid.

Your body's strong immune system is why it's difficult for organ transplants to succeed—the body recognizes the organ as a foreign invader and tries to destroy it. Allergies—an overreaction to a substance—are basically just your immune system working incorrectly.

In the "Circulatory System" section in this chapter, we discussed how white blood cells fight off infection.

The lymphatic system, which carries nutrients between the bloodstream and tissues, also filters out waste and traps microbes, which helps your immune system keep your body healthy.

- *Lymph nodes*, small bodies located at various places throughout the body, collect these microbes, which is why swollen lymph nodes can be a sign of infection.
- The *tonsils* and *thymus*, organs associated with the lymph system, produce *antibodies*, proteins that combine with foreign substances and help to eliminate them.
- The *spleen*, an organ located in the abdomen that removes damaged blood cells from the bloodstream, also destroys bacteria and other microbes.

## Nervous System

The nervous system processes internal and external stimulus and reacts to it. It has been compared to an extensive electrical system. The major parts of the nervous system are the brain, the spinal cord, and the nerves. Special cells called neurons communicate information throughout the nervous system. Bundles of neurons make up nerves that funnel information to the brain and/or spinal cord. For example, the optic nerve funnels information from the eyes to the brain.

The central nervous system is the brain and the spinal cord; the peripheral nervous system includes all the parts of the nervous system that lie outside the central nervous system. The peripheral nervous system exists to communicate information to the central nervous system.

### Types of Neurons and Nervous System Cells

A sensory neuron perceives a stimulus, such as a touch. It signals other cells through axons, tiny fibers. The place where two neurons meet is called the synapse. A neurotransmitter converts the electrical impulse to a chemical response, and a message is sent to the next cell. The information travels to the brain, which decides what to do, and sends the response down the line in the same way. The whole process takes less than a millisecond.

A motor neuron communicates with muscles, glands, and other tissues. These neurons project their axons outside the central nervous system to control other tissues.

Interneurons, also called associative neurons, translate information between sensory neurons and motor neurons.

Glial cells keep neurons in place, feed them, and remove dead ones. They produce myelin, a fatty substance that protects and insulates axons. Glial cells could be called caretaker cells.

### The Brain

The brain is your body's computer. It's responsible for everything from maintaining your mood to making sure you look both ways before you cross the street. The brain helps us make meaning of the world around us—and helps us create meaning. The five senses are processed here, and it's where we store memories. An adult brain weighs about three pounds, pretty small for all it can do.

Like the rest of the central nervous system, the brain is made of neurons and glial cells (sometimes called neuroglia or just glia).

The brain is housed in the cranium, which is part of the skull. This bony structure protects your brain from injury. A cushiony layer between the cranium and your brain is called the meninges.

Cerebrospinal fluid (CSF) circulates around the brain and spinal cord, and helps protect both organs. Channels in the brain called ventricles produce CSF. There are four ventricles.

Your brain has three main areas:

The brainstem, which is the lower part of your brain and connects to the spinal cord. This is the part of brain that controls functions essential to life, such as breathing. It also regulates hormones.

The cerebellum, found behind the brainstem, controls some motor functions and maintains balance.

The cerebrum is what we often think of when we think of the brain. It controls conscious action and thought. Two hemispheres make up the cerebrum, with each half of the brain generally responsible for motor function on the opposite side. For example, the right side of the cerebrum controls motor function on the left side of your body.

Each hemisphere of the brain has areas called lobes that control different functions but they are extremely interdependent. These lobes come in pairs, so there's one on each side of the cerebrum. The lobes include:

- Frontal lobe, which is the seat of the intellect, and many behaviors as well as voluntary motor movements. Memory and personality are formed and maintained here.
- Temporal lobe, which is associated with visual memory and language and with the ability to recognize objects and faces.
- Parietal lobe, which helps give meaning to sensory information.
- Occipital lobe, which processes visual information.

### The Spinal Cord

The spinal cord is a thin tube of nerve tissue that extends from your brain down your back and usually ends at the top of the lumbar region. The spinal column (sometimes called your backbone) which supports and protects the spinal cord extends below the spinal cord and ends at the coccyx. The bones that make up the spinal column are called vertebrae.

The spinal cord has 31 segments and each segment has a pair of spinal nerves that extend from it to bring impulses to and from the spinal cord.

## Reproductive System

The reproductive system is responsible for creating and bearing live offspring. Two sex cells, called gametes, one from the male parent (the sperm cell or spermatozoa) and one from the female parent (egg or ovum) combine to create a fertilized egg called a zygote. Each gamete contains half the genetic code of its parent (so that combined together in the zygote they contain a complete genetic code for a human).

The zygote becomes a cluster of cells, which become an embryo (offspring in the process of development) with organ systems beginning to differentiate. At about eight weeks the embryo is said to be a fetus, as it begins to resemble an actual human baby. At forty weeks, the fetus is born live.

The process of reproduction requires both a male and a female partner. Each has very different reproductive systems.

### Male Reproductive System

In an adult male, the main reproductive organs include:

- the *testicles*, two roundish organs (about 2 inches big) that produce sperm cells as well as hormones like testosterone. These are part of the *genitalia*, the external organs of reproduction.
- the *vas deferens*, a small tube that transports sperm to the urethra.
- the *epididymis*, a tube that transports sperm from the testicles to the vas deferens.

The testicles and the epididymis are contained in the scrotum, a sack-like structure that maintains proper temperature.

- the *penis*, which serves as the organ of copulation, made up mostly of erectile tissue. In addition to delivering sperm, it contains the urethra, for the elimination of urine.

### Female Reproductive System

Most of the female reproductive system is internal, located within the pelvis. In an adult female, the main reproductive organs include:

- the *vulva*, which covers the opening to the vagina and contains an opening for the urethra.
- the *labia*, two skin flaps covering the opening to the vagina.
- the *clitoris*, a sensory organ.

These three organs are located externally and contribute to female arousal during intercourse. The other reproductive organs are internal:

- the *vagina*, a small tube, about 3–5 inches long, where the penis is inserted during intercourse. It's also where menstrual blood leaves the body, and the way a baby leaves the body.
- the *cervix*, an organ that connects the vagina and the uterus. It has a very small opening (about the size of a straw), allowing sperm to move through it. It dilates during childbirth to allow the baby to pass through.

- the *uterus*, the organ where gestation takes place. It's small, about 3 inches long, when a woman is not pregnant. During the *menstrual cycle* (a recurring monthly process during which eggs are released in a woman's body), the *endometrium*, the mucous membrane that lines the walls of the uterine, thickens. If the woman does not get pregnant, the endometrium sheds, which is the source of a woman's menstrual blood.
- the *ovaries*, two small organs about 2 inches in size, which produce, store, and release eggs. The ovaries are located above the uterus, one on the right side and one on the left.
- the *fallopian tubes*, two small (about 4 inches long) tubes connect the ovaries to the uterus. An egg travels from an ovary through a fallopian tube to the uterus. If the egg is fertilized, it attaches to the wall of the uterus and begins the process of developing into a fetus. Otherwise, it is eliminated from the body.

## Other Systems

There are other organ systems in the body, including the urinary system and the endocrine system.

### Urinary System

Liquid waste is filtered out of the blood by the kidneys, a pair of organs located in the back part of the abdominal cavity, which also maintain a proper balance of water in your body. Waste liquid is sent through ureters to the bladder, a sack-like organ that can expand to hold about 16 ounces of urine until it can be eliminated from the body through the urethra, a small tube with an outside opening.

### Endocrine System

The endocrine system helps organs in the body function by releasing hormones, substances that stimulate cells to take certain actions. Parts of the endocrine system are located throughout the body. For example, the testicles are part of the male reproductive system, but they are also part of the endocrine system, as they produce the hormone testosterone. The female ovaries are part of the female reproductive system, but they are also part of the endocrine system, as they produce the hormone estrogen.

The endocrine system regulates human growth and metabolism as well as helping maintain mood and other functions.

## Genetics

Genetics is the study of inherited characteristics or traits. Each cell in a human body has a function. In general, the function of a cell is governed by its genes. A gene is a unit of heredity that is also something like an instruction booklet. Chromosomes, which are strands of DNA (See "Cell Structure" in this chapter for more information about DNA), carry genes.

Most cells have 46 chromosomes. The sex cells (eggs and sperm) have half this many, 23. They combine together to create a zygote (see "Reproductive System" in this chapter for more information). That zygote now has 46 chromosomes.

Since each parent contributes chromosomes, the offspring will have some traits that are similar to each parent, but will be a unique individual, not a clone (which would have the exact same genetic code as its parent).

### How Genes Are Expressed

In general and somewhat simplistic terms the offspring gets two genes for each trait but only one gene will be used. Which gene will be expressed (that is, which gene will dictate the individual's trait) depends on how dominant the gene is.

Take, for example, eye color. If an individual has one gene that says "brown eyes" and a second gene that says "brown eyes" then the individual will have brown eyes, because whichever gene is expressed, what it will express is brown eyes.

But what if one gene says "brown eyes" and one gene says "blue eyes"?

### Dominant and Recessive Genes

What happens in this instance is that one gene is dominant; it gets expressed at the expense of the other. Blue eyes is a recessive gene; that is to say, it is not expressed if the dominant gene is present. So if you have one brown-eyes gene and one blue-eyes gene, you'll have brown eyes. However, just because your mother has blue eyes and your father has brown eyes, it doesn't mean you'll have brown eyes. Here's why.

Each parent also has two genes for eye color. Your mother has blue eyes, which means that she has only genes for blue eyes or she would have brown eyes. We might label her genes as bb. Someone with two of the same genes, like your mother, is called homozygous.

Your father has brown eyes, but that doesn't mean he only has genes for brown eyes. In fact, he could have a gene for blue eyes, but his brown eyes gene was expressed because it's the dominant gene. So he could have one brown eyes gene, capital B because it's dominant, and one blue eyes gene, lower case b because it's recessive. His genes are Bb. Someone like your father who has two different genes for a trait is called heterozygous.

Your mother will give you a gene. She has to give you a b gene because that's all she has. But your father could give you a B gene or a b gene. If he gives you B gene, you will have the genes Bb, and you'll have brown eyes, since brown is the dominant gene. But if he gives you his b gene, that will combine with your mother's b gene, and you'll have bb, or blue eyes.

To figure out the likelihood of having blue eyes, you'd make a little table that will show all the possibilities. See Figure 10.2.

**Determining Trait Likelihood: Eye Color**

| From Mother | From Father | Baby |
|---|---|---|
| b | b | bb |
| b | B | Bb |

**Figure 10.2**

You can see that half the time you'll end up with brown eyes, and half the time you'll be blue-eyed. That means some of the children of your mother and father could have blue eyes, and some could be brown-eyed.

What about green eyes? Well, green eyes are dominant over blue, but brown is dominant over green. So it's possible that your father has a gene for green eyes, and you could have green eyes, even though your mother is blue-eyed and your father is brown-eyed. That's because he might have genes Bg (instead of Bb) and if his g (green) gene combines with your mother's b gene, then you'd have green eyes.

## Nutrition

Nutrition is the process of supplying your body with the substances it requires to maintain life. In general we think of this as "food" or "diet," but water and sunlight are also needed. Proper nutrition is necessary for your body to function at an optimum level.

The energy you need to perform tasks (including thinking) comes primarily from carbohydrates (as well as fat and protein). Processes like building muscle require protein. Fiber helps your digestive system eliminate wastes effectively. Other nutrients, like minerals and vitamins, help you build bones and support other functions.

- Carbohydrates can be found in grains and cereal, like rice or oats.
- Fat can be found in dairy products as well as vegetable oils, like olive oil.
- Protein can be found in meats, eggs, fish, and legumes (like lentils).
- Fiber can be found in fruits, vegetables, and whole grains.

### Vitamins and Minerals

Vitamins and minerals are nutrients that your body cannot make and so must obtain them from food sources.

### Vitamin and Minerals

| Vitamin or Mineral | Source | Function |
|---|---|---|
| A | green and yellow vegetables | skin, eyesight |
| B vitamins | whole grains, dairy, potatoes, tomatoes | energy, blood cells |
| C | citrus, leafy green vegetables, tomatoes | immune function, skin |
| D | milk, fish | bone health |
| E | vegetable oil, nuts, seeds | antioxidant, immune function |
| K | green vegetables | blood clotting, bone health |
| Calcium | dairy, tofu, spinach | bone health |
| Iodine | iodized salt, seafood | hormone balance, skin |
| Iron | beef, chicken, spinach | blood cells |
| Magnesium | soybeans, nuts, whole grain | bone health, muscle function |
| Phosphorus | seeds, cheese, fish | bone health, metabolism |
| Sodium | occurs naturally in most foods | muscle function, fluid balance |
| Potassium | beans, dark leafy greens | muscle and nerve function |
| Selenium | garlic, seafood | cellular health |
| Zinc | beef, lentils, sesame seeds | antioxidant, metabolism |

### Calories

A calorie measures the amount of energy a food will produce. Your body, even at rest, burns energy (and therefore calories). So you need to eat a sufficient quantity of calories to maintain health. However, if you only focus on calories and not nutrition, you can become very unhealthy (imagine if you only ate cookies). Many people eat too many calories, causing them to gain weight. Lowering calorie intake and increasing exercise (use of energy) helps maintain a healthy weight.

According to the USDA, an active male, age 20, needs about 3,000 calories a day. An active woman of the same age needs only 2,400 calories. Of course, you may need more or less depending on your height, weight, and activity level.

## GEOLOGY

Geology is the study of the earth's physical structure, including rock and soil. Geologists are interested in the processes that have shaped the earth, and study natural resources like oil and gas—including finding out where it is. They also study how to forecast and reduce harm from events such as earthquakes. They may also be involved in studying global warming, pollution, and ground-water contamination.

### History of the Earth

The earth is about 4.5 billion years old. That's a very long time, and a lot has happened to the earth in that period. So geologists use "geologic time" to talk about what was happening in various periods. Geologic time corresponds to the layers of rock that make up the earth's structure. Thus the oldest geologic time corresponds to the oldest layers of rock.

This time is divided into a series of increasingly smaller units. Very broad units of geologic time are called eons. Eons are subdivided into smaller chunks of time called eras. Eras are subdivided into periods, periods into epochs, and epochs into ages. Thus an age is the smallest chunk of time and an eon the largest.

A particular unit of time might have early, mid, and late aspects which correspond to lower, middle, and upper in terms of layers of rock.

## Geologic Time*

| Eon | Era | Period | Epoch | Time (start) |
|---|---|---|---|---|
| PHANEROZOIC | Cenozoic | Quaternary | Holocene | 11,700 years ago (to present) |
| | | | Pleistocene | 2.588 million years ago (mya) |
| | | Neogene | Pliocene | 5.332 mya |
| | | | Miocene | 23.03 mya |
| | | Paleogene | Oligocene | 33.9 mya |
| | | | Eocene | 55.8 mya |
| | | | Paleocene | 65.5 mya |
| | Mesozoic | Cretaceous | Late | 99.6 mya |
| | | | Early | 145.5 mya |
| | | Jurassic | Late | 161.2 mya |
| | | | Middle | 175.6 mya |
| | | | Early | 199.6 mya |
| | | Triassic | Late | 228.7 mya |
| | | | Middle | 245.9 mya |
| | | | Early | 251 mya |
| | Paleozoic | Permian | Lopingian | 260 mya |
| | | | Guadalupian | 270.6 mya |
| | | | Cisuralian | 299 mya |
| | | Carboniferous | Pennsylvanian | 318.1 mya |
| | | | Mississippian | 359 mya |
| | | Devonian | Late | 385.3 mya |
| | | | Middle | 397.5 mya |
| | | | Early | 416 mya |
| | | Silurian | Pridoli | 418.7 mya |
| | | | Ludlow | 422.9 mya |
| | | | Wenlock | 428.2 mya |
| | | | Llandovery | 443.7 mya |
| | | Ordovician | Late | 460.9 mya |
| | | | Middle | 471.8 mya |
| | | | Early | 488.3 mya |
| | | Cambrian | Furongian | 499 mya |
| | | | Series 3 | 510 mya |
| | | | Series 2 | 521 mya |
| | | | Terreneuvian | 542 mya |
| PRECAMBRIAN-PROTEROZOIC | Neoproterozoic | | | 1 billion years ago (bya) |
| | Mesoproterozoic | | | 1.6 bya |
| | Paleoproterozoic | | | 2.5 bya |
| PRECAMBRIAN-ARCHEAN | Neorarchean | | | 2.8 bya |
| | Mesoarchean | | | 3.2 bya |
| | Paleoarchean | | | 3.6 bya |
| | Eoarchean | | | 4 bya |
| HADEAN | Early Imbrian | | | 4.1 bya |
| | Nectarian | | | 4.3 bya |
| | Basin Groups | | | 4.5 bya |
| | Cryptic | | | 4.6 bya |

*ages are not listed on this chart, as that level of detail is not present on the ASVAB

## Structure of the Earth

Think of the earth as a big ball around which various layers have been wrapped. Scientists believe that as the earth cooled, heavier material sank to the interior of the earth while lighter material remained on top.

- The ball in the center is the *inner core.* The inner core is thought to be made of nickel and iron and is believed to be solid. It's about as hot as the surface of the sun.
- Surrounding this is the *outer core,* which is thought to be liquid. It is also believed to be made of nickel and iron. It's believed to be liquid because while it is extremely hot it is not under as much pressure as the inner core. Additionally, certain seismological studies have shown that waves move through the earth in a way that indicates a liquid outer core. The outer core is thought to help create the earth's magnetic fields.
- Above the outer core lies *the mantle* (sometimes divided into the upper mantle and lower mantle), a rocky layer that makes up most of the earth's volume.
- The final layer is the *crust.* The crust is where we live. Like the mantle, it is made of rock. The rocks of the crust tend to be not as dense as those of the mantle. Together, the crust and upper mantle are called the *lithosphere.*

Around the outside of this layered ball is the atmosphere, which we'll get to a bit later in this chapter (see "Atmosphere").

See Figure 10.3.

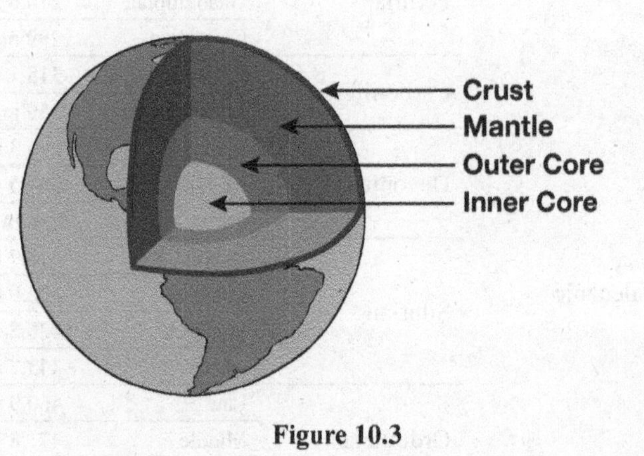


**Figure 10.3**

## Building Blocks of the Earth

The earth's crust is made of a combination of igneous, sedimentary, and metamorphic rocks.

- *Igneous* rocks are made from the magma or lava of a volcano. Obsidian and basalt are examples of igneous rocks.
- *Sedimentary* rocks are formed when deposits collect on the earth's surface or within water. Over time and under pressure, the deposits become solid rock. Sandstone and shale are common sedimentary rocks.
- *Metamorphic* rocks are rocks that were once igneous or sedimentary rocks but which have undergone a change ("metamorphosis"), such as being subjected to intense heat or immense pressure. Marble and slate are examples of metamorphic rocks.

## Weathering and Erosion

Weathering happens to a rock when outside forces act on it to break it down. For example, the process of freezing and thawing can cause parts of a rock to break away. A plant's roots can break up rock. Chemicals in water and from plants can also cause weathering. The constant action of water can also break up or wear down rock; think of a cliff wall at a seashore.

Erosion is the process by which those broken-away parts of the rock are moved by wind, water, or other forces.

Weathering and erosion are natural processes but they can be accelerated by human actions. When this happens, land can become difficult to farm (nutrient-rich soil is washed away) and waterways can become clogged.

### Fossils

Fossils are the physical remains of organisms that lived on earth a long time ago. In general, remains have to be several thousand years old before they're considered fossils.

Most living creatures decompose and eventually leave no trace of their existence, but sometimes the processes of decomposition are arrested, and the physical remains are protected in some way. Occasionally, the physical remains left behind are merely an impression—like tracks (for example, one famous fossil is of a human-like primate's footprints in volcanic ash), or the outline of a shell that has since decomposed. These impressions are also part of the fossil record and help scientists understand what life on earth was like during different periods.

Of all the organisms that have lived on earth, very few of them have become fossils. For a fossil to be formed, certain conditions must usually be met.

- The organism must have been buried quickly. For example, a sudden landslide could have buried an organism.
- The burial must be permanent (or at least for a very long time). If an avalanche buried an organism, but the snow melted the next year, the organism would not be permanently buried and could be destroyed. By the same token, an animal foraging for food might root up the remains. Also, the process of erosion might wash away the remains. That can't happen if a fossil is to form.
- The buried organism must not be exposed to too much oxygen, heat, or pressure, as these forces are likely to ruin it.

These conditions are more easily met in water than on land, which is why most fossils are found where water once was.

Once an organism dies and is permanently buried, its soft tissue will decompose, and its skeleton will undergo a process called perimineralization, where the bone material is replaced with minerals. The fossil will retain the shape of its skeleton, but it will be a rock (or rock-like) rather than a bone (it may retain some of its original bone material). Fossils can be formed in other ways (think of insects trapped in amber), but this is the most common.

### Plate Tectonics

Plate tectonics is the idea that the earth is made of plates that have moved (and do move), which explains why mountains, volcanoes, and islands form and why earthquakes occur. Geologists theorize that at one time all of the land mass on earth was one enormous continent, but that the horizontal shifting of plates broke this land mass apart.

Heat from inside the earth creates pressure that causes these plates to move. Gravity also plays a role. Although there are many plates, geologists identify seven major ones:

- African plate
- Antarctic plate
- Eurasian plate
- Indo-Australian (sometimes just called Australian) plate
- North American plate
- Pacific plate
- South American plate

Some of these plates include land and ocean, such as the Pacific plate.

Where the edges of plates come together, geologic events can happen or formations can be made.

- *Convergent boundaries* are places where plates are coming together or colliding.

- *Divergent boundaries* are places where plates are moving apart.
- *Transform boundaries* are places where plates are sliding past each other.

## OCEANOGRAPHY

Oceanography, also called marine science, is the study of bodies of water (not surprisingly, this is usually oceans) to understand their properties and processes. Oceanographers draw on research and methodologies from many scientific disciplines, including geology, biology, and physics to do their studies and aid their understanding.

### Characteristics of Salt Water Versus Fresh Water

Salt water (seawater) makes up most of the water found on earth, about 96%. Salt water, found in oceans, seas, and some large lakes, as well as tide pools, bays, estuaries, and some marshes and wetlands, is just water with salt in it. Simple, right? Most of this salt is plain old sodium chloride (table salt). But other salts are found in sea water as well.

How much salt is in a given body of salt water varies. In general the salinity (proportion of salt in a solution) is about 3.5%, although it can be considerably more than that.

This salt gives density to seawater, which means that it is easier for an object to float in seawater as compared to fresh water. (The more salt, the greater the buoyancy.) It also means that salt water conducts electricity better than fresh water.

All the salt in salt water is what makes it dangerous to drink. If you found yourself in the middle of the Atlantic Ocean with no fresh water, you could literally die of dehydration, even though you'd be surrounded by salt water. The salt in salt water would leach the water from your body. You'd be better off not drinking at all than to drink salt water. The organisms that live in salt water generally cannot tolerate fresh water conditions, and vice versa. For example, if you tried to keep a clownfish in an aquarium you filled with tap water, it would not survive.

A body of water that is partly salty (not enough salt to be salt water and too much salt to be fresh water) is called brackish.

### Marine Zones

Marine zones, also called oceanic zones or ocean regions, are distinct habitats scientists have identified in oceans. They are:

- *Epipelagic zone* (the sunlight zone), sometimes called the *euphotic*, which is the layer that goes down about 200 meters (656 feet) from the surface of the water. Enough sunlight penetrates this layer that photosynthesis can occur. Most marine life lives in this layer.
- *Mesopelagic zone* (the twilight zone), which is the layer from about 200 meters (656 feet) to 1000 meters (3281 feet). Many fewer marine animals live here, although a number of them visit. Some marine organisms that live at this level *fluoresce,* that is, they emit light that they have absorbed from the sun and stored.
- *Bathypelagic zone* (the midnight zone), which is the layer from about 1000 meters (3281 feet) to about 4000 meters (13,120 feet). Here no sunlight can penetrate. Some marine organisms at this level are capable of *bioluminescence*, which is light they produce in their own bodies (in contrast to fluorescence).
- *Abyssopelagic zone* (the abyss), which is the layer from about 4000 to 6000 meters (13,120 to 19,686 feet). The water temperature here is very near freezing, and the pressure is immense. There is very little marine life at this level, and most of it is very small invertebrates.
- *Ocean basin,* which is basically the floor of the ocean. There are geological features here not unlike those found on land, including mountains and valleys. The average depth of the ocean is 4.3 kilometers (2.65 miles).
- *Hadalpelagic zone* (the trenches), which are deep cuts in the ocean floor where some marine organisms live. The deepest so far discovered is the Mariana Trench near Japan, which is 10,911 meters deep (35,797 feet), or nearly seven miles deep. The cold and pressure at this level is beyond intense, but there are still some organisms that live here!

See Figure 10.4.

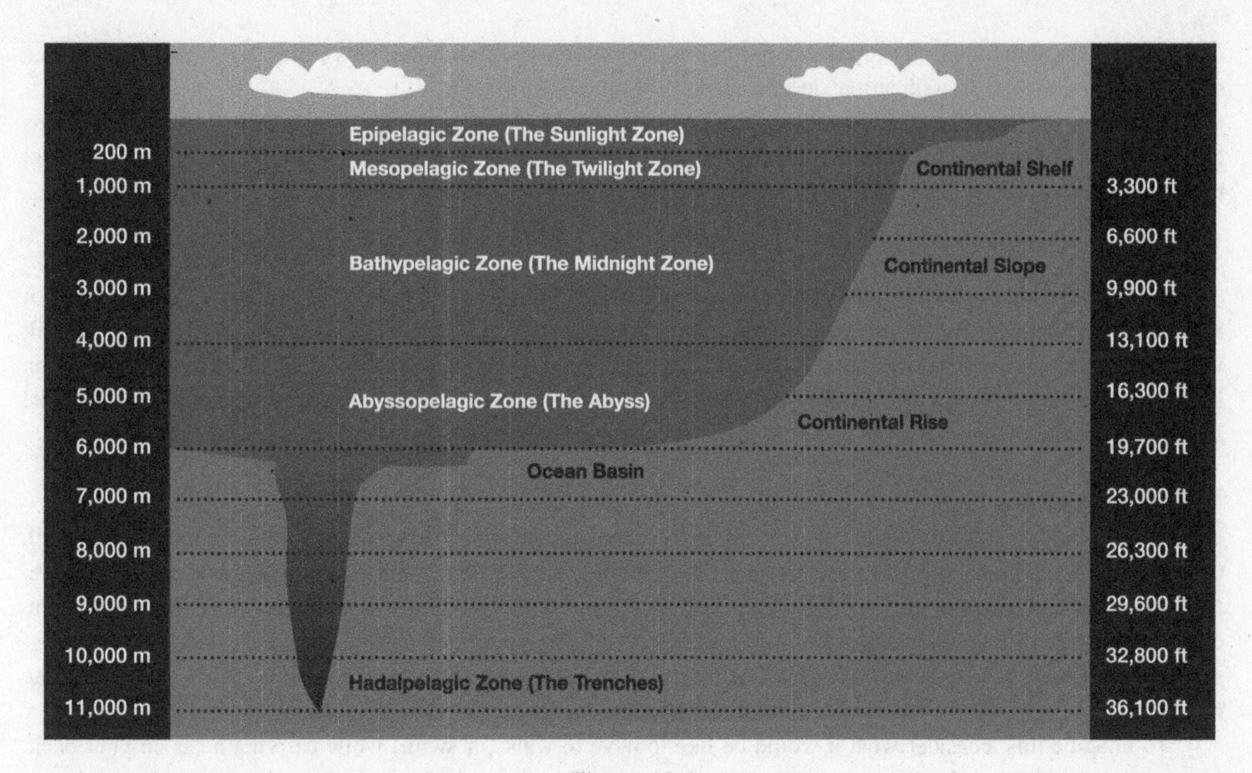


**Figure 10.4**

Note that marine zones can also refer to the distance of water from land—coastal, offshore, and high seas. People also use the phrase "marine zones" in the same way they refer to zoning on land—setting up regulations about what can be done where.

## Tides, Waves, Currents

If you've ever stood on the shore of an ocean, you noticed two distinct features: tides and waves. If you've ever gone swimming in the ocean, you might also have encountered a current.

- *Tides* are the predictable rise and fall of sea levels on the coastline that happen on a daily basis. The gravitational pull of the moon causes tides. Two high tides and two low tides happen about every 24 hours. A *neap tide* is when the difference in sea level between high tide and low tide is the smallest. These happen twice a month. A *spring tide* is when the difference is greatest ("spring" in the sense of "jump"; not related to the season). *Storm surges*, caused by climate occurrences, can create unpredictable sea levels and are not properly tides.
- *Waves* are the rolling motion of the water that builds into crests and descends into troughs. Wind is what drives waves, which is why they can vary from one day to the next, or even from one hour to another. A *tsunami* is a type of very big wave, or series of waves, that displaces a large volume of water and which can be very destructive, as the waves and water reach much farther inland than normal. They are generally caused by earthquakes or undersea volcanic activity.
- *Currents* are the continuous movement of ocean water in one direction. Wind, tides, even the shape of the shoreline all affect currents.

The energy of all this water action can sometimes be turned into fuel such as electricity.

## Marine Life

Oceanographers use the same system of classification as other biologists do. Thus, the bottle-nosed dolphin is of the kingdom *Animalia*, the phylum *chordata* (having a spinal cord), the class *mammalia*, the order *cetacea* (which includes whales, dolphins, and porpoises), the family *Delphinidae* (oceanic dolphins), the genus *Tursiops*, and the species *truncatus*. See "Classification" in this chapter for more information.

Biologists theorize that all life evolved from one-celled organisms that lived in water. Some of these organisms left the oceans and became land plants and animals, but others stayed in the water. Just as land organisms had to adapt to the conditions of living on the land, sea organisms ("marine life") have had to adapt to living in their watery habitats.

#### Buoyancy

Early in the chapter, we discussed the difference between fresh water and salt water. (See "Characteristics of Salt Water Versus Fresh Water" for more information.) Many marine organisms have adapted to the buoyancy of salt water, which allows them to have large bodies that do not require the same energy to maintain as a similar body on land (they also do not have to have strong limbs, like arms and legs; think squid). Many marine animals have special adaptations that allow them to maintain buoyancy (or lose it in order to dive).

#### Water Pressure

Because water exerts a considerable pressure on organisms, they've had to adapt to those conditions as well. One of the reasons humans have to use machines to help them go deep down into water is because of the pressure. On land, at sea level, air pressure is about 14.5 pounds per square inch (psi). For every 33 feet (10.06 meters) that you dive, the pressure of the water increases another 14.5 psi. On land, your body has mechanisms to deal with the pressure, which is why you don't notice it. But under water, too much pressure creates problems for your body. Marine mammals have lungs that collapse under pressure, and their bodies are more flexible than ours.

To imagine this, consider what it would be like to have to walk (or swim) while carrying a car on your back. Impossible, right? That's similar to the effect of water pressure on your body. But marine organisms have adapted to it.

#### Using Oxygen

Just as on land, animals in the water need to breathe (that is, to get oxygen from their surroundings to fuel their bodily processes). Special organs, such as gills, help them to get oxygen from the water. Some marine animals are able to take in oxygen through their skin. They give off carbon dioxide, just as we do on land, and sea plant life uses that carbon dioxide to fuel their processes, again just as on land.

#### Variations of Adaptations

Not all marine life can survive in all areas of a body of water. Closer to the surface, water has less pressure, allows in more light, and is warmer. Nutrients are easier to find. Going deeper, the water becomes colder and much more highly pressurized. Different types of organisms thrive in these different areas (see "Marine Zones" in this chapter for more information). Consider that you wouldn't expect to see the same organisms living on a grassy plain as in a rain forest, and this difference makes sense.

## ATMOSPHERE

Atmospheric science studies the atmosphere and its interaction with other systems. The atmosphere is, basically, the air that surrounds earth (other celestial bodies also have atmospheres). The atmosphere is held in place by gravity. Our atmosphere contains the oxygen we need to survive as well as the carbon dioxide plants need to photosynthesize. The atmosphere also protects us from the most damaging effects of solar radiation. As with the ocean, there are tides and waves in the atmosphere.

An atmosphere (atm) is also a unit of measure: 14.696 pounds per square inch equals one atmosphere.

### Atmosphere Layers

The earth's atmosphere has five distinct layers.

- *Troposphere*, which is the lowest layer, the one we live in and where weather occurs. Its height varies throughout the world, ranging from less than 9 kilometers (about 5.6 miles) to more than 17 kilometers (about 10.5 miles). Latitude and season affect the height. Air pressure gets less as you move higher into the troposphere. At the top of this layer, it's one-tenth what it is at sea level. The temperature at the bottom of this layer is warmer than at the top.

- *Stratosphere*, which is the next layer, is colder on the bottom and warmer on the top (an inversion of what happens in the troposphere). It's just below freezing at the top of the stratosphere. When you've reached cruising altitude in a commercial airliner, you're in the bottom of the stratosphere. At the top of the stratosphere is the *ozone layer*, which insulates the earth from the sun's radiation.
- *Mesosphere*, which is the next layer, starts about 50 kilometers (31 miles) above the surface of the earth, although this varies. It extends to about 85 km (53 miles) high. The temperature grows increasingly colder. At the top of the mesosphere, the temperature is about minus 90 degrees Celsius (minus 130 degrees Fahrenheit). It is difficult to study the mesosphere since airplanes can't reach it (neither can tools like weather balloons). Satellites and orbiting spacecraft go above this layer. One thing we do know about this layer is that most of the meteors that approach the earth are destroyed here.
- *Thermosphere*, which is the next layer, is the biggest layer, extending from the top of the mesosphere (about 85 km/53 miles above the earth's surface) to 500 to 1000 km (311 to 621 miles). Temperature varies greatly here, with one spot fluctuating as much as 500 degrees Celsius (900 degrees Fahrenheit), depending on the time of day and activity on the sun. Temperatures can run from 500 degrees Celsius (1932 degrees Fahrenheit) to 2000 degrees Celsius (3632 degrees Fahrenheit). The thermosphere is also where *auroras* occur, those electrical light shows sometimes observed near the North and South Poles. The International Space Station orbits in the thermosphere.
- *Exosphere*, which is the final and outermost layer, extends from the top of the thermosphere to about 10,000 km (6200 miles). Here the atmosphere merges into outer space. (Some scientists consider the thermosphere the outer layer of the earth's atmosphere, and the exosphere as part of outer space.)

The thermosphere and the exosphere are together called the ionosphere.
See Figure 10.5, Atmosphere Layers.

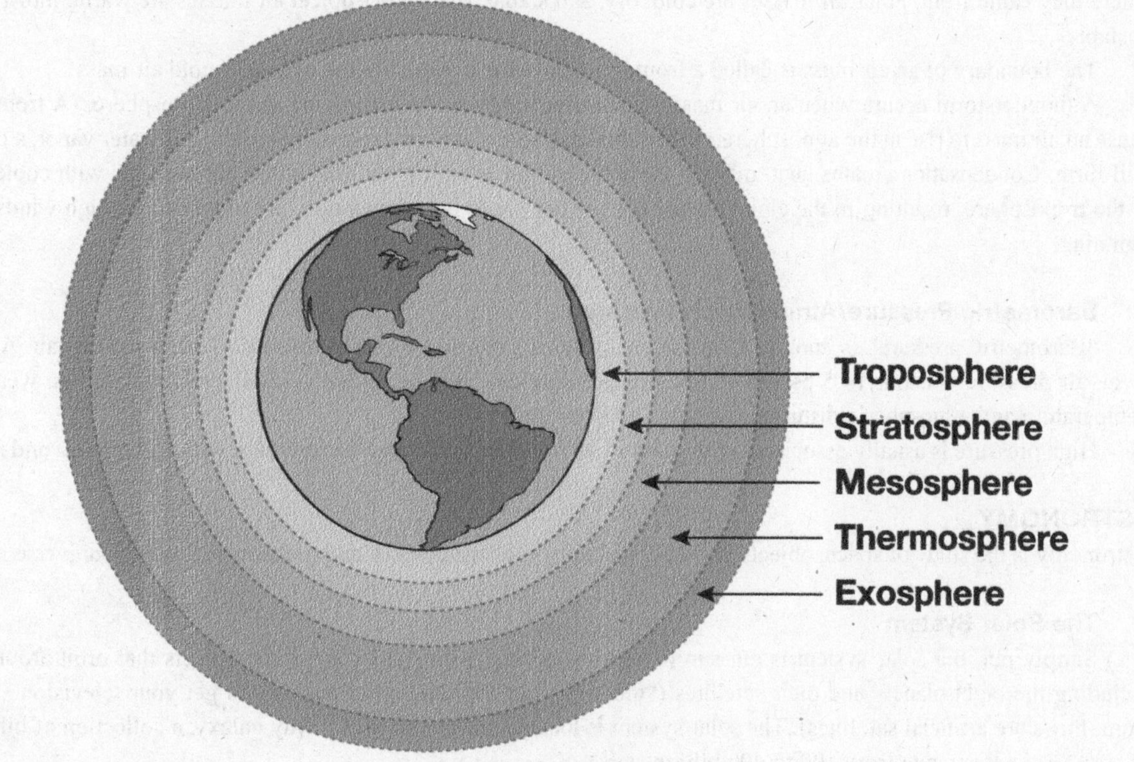


**Figure 10.5, Atmosphere Layers**

### Meteorology

Meteorology deals with the study of the atmosphere, but more specifically with how weather occurs. Predicting the weather, which is closely tied with describing weather events and how they happen, is a main focus of meteorologists.

### Climate and Weather

Weather can be described as local atmospheric conditions over a relatively brief period of time, whereas climate is the general atmospheric conditions in an area over long periods of time. So parts of Nevada are subtropical desert, meaning they are hot and dry year-round (the climate), but on a given day the weather might include rain. Climate in the United States ranges from tundra and subarctic climates in Alaska to tropical savanna in South Florida.

Long-term climate change can occur when the general conditions in a specific place change over a period of years. For example, the midwest experienced much heavier snowfalls in the early nineteenth century as compared to the early twenty-first century. Global warming, an overall trend toward warmer temperatures, is an example of a long-term climate change.

Short-term climate change can be caused by geological events, such as volcanic eruptions.

When people think of the weather, they tend to think of elements such as temperature (high or low, especially as compared to what's expected for the season), precipitation (rain, snow, sleet), wind conditions (high winds or calm), humidity, and sunniness/cloudiness. Weather phenomena like blizzards, tornadoes, and hurricanes are also of concern. Meteorologists study both weather and climate to help them understand weather events.

### Clouds and Air Masses

Clouds are visible collections of water vapor that float in the atmosphere. When the water vapor in a cloud gets large enough, it will precipitate out and fall to the ground as rain or snow (or sleet or hail).

Air masses are bodies of air with a uniform temperature and amount of moisture. Together clouds and air masses are responsible for a considerable amount of what we consider weather.

Air masses can cover hundreds, even thousands, of miles. Air masses are generally categorized depending on where they came from. Polar air masses are cold, dry, and stable. Maritime tropical air masses are warm, moist, and unstable.

The boundary of an air mass is called a front. So a cold front would be the edge of a cold air mass.

A thunderstorm occurs when an air mass becomes unstable and begins rising in the atmosphere. (A front can cause an air mass to rise in the atmosphere.) When this updraft is combined with condensation of water vapor, a cloud will form. Condensation creates heat, making the air mass rise even higher. This warm air connects with cooler air in the troposphere, resulting in the cloud releasing its water vapor in precipitation, accompanied by high winds and lightning.

### Barometric Pressure/Atmospheric Pressure

"Barometric pressure" is another term for atmospheric pressure, which is, basically, the weight of air. At sea level, air pressure is about 14.5 psi. However, this pressure can vary and it has a considerable impact on weather. Temperature and atmospheric disturbances affect air pressure.

High pressure is usually associated with good weather (clear skies) and low pressure with bad (clouds and rain).

## ASTRONOMY

Astronomy is the study of space, objects in space (including planets, comets, and meteoroids), and the universe itself.

### The Solar System

Simply put, our solar system is our sun (where we get the word "solar") and the objects that orbit around it, including the eight planets and their satellites ("moons"—not the same satellites as you get your television signal from; those are artificial satellites). The solar system is located within the Milky Way galaxy, a collection of billions of stars (estimates range from 100 to 400 billion stars).

The eight planets in our solar system are (starting closest to the sun and moving out):

- Mercury. The smallest planet in the solar system.
- Venus. Venus is similar to earth in structure and mass but it's the hottest of all the planets (even though Mercury is closer to the sun). This is because Mercury has considerably less atmosphere to trap heat.
- Earth. So far, the only place where we know life exists.
- Mars. Called "the red planet" because the iron oxide in its soil gives it a rusty shade. An asteroid belt lies between Mars and Jupiter.
- Jupiter. Next to the sun, Jupiter has the greatest mass of all the objects in our solar system.
- Saturn. Distinguished by its ring system; the rings surrounding Saturn are made of rock and ice.
- Uranus. Orbited by 27 satellites.
- Neptune. Scientists calculated that Neptune must exist before it was ever observed by telescope.

See Figure 10.6 for a visual representation of the solar system.

**Figure 10.6**

Comets are essentially chunks of rock and ice that get pulled into a gravitational field and start moving toward the sun. Heat from the sun melts some of the ice to create a tail.

Asteroids are basically planets too small to be called planets. Think of them as extremely large rocks orbiting the sun. Some asteroids have their own gravitational pull. Many asteroids are contained in the asteroid belt that lies between Mars and Jupiter.

Meteoroids are orbiting rocks that are smaller than asteroids, but in all other respects are similar. Scientists do not use a specific measurement of size to define meteoroids versus asteroids.

Meteors are pieces of space debris that enter the earth's atmosphere. Sometimes meteors are asteroids or parts of asteroids. As they pass through earth's atmosphere they burn, giving them their characteristic illumination. Meteors are sometimes called "shooting stars."

Meteorites are meteors that land on the earth's surface (that is, they are not burned up in the atmosphere).

### Planetary Motion

Early in the seventeenth century, the scientist Johannes Kepler described the motion of planets around the sun. His laws are still considered accurate by scientists today.

1. *The law of ellipses* says that objects in orbit follow an elliptical (egg-shaped) path.
2. *The law of equal areas* says that a planet moves across ("sweeps out over") the same amount of area in every time period, even though sometimes the planet is moving faster and sometimes slower, and sometimes it is closer to the sun and sometimes it is farther away. This is because the times when it is closer to the sun it is moving faster, thus covering the same amount of area as when it is farther away and moving slower.
3. *The law of harmonies* says that the time it takes for a planet to complete its orbit, and the radius of that orbit, is a ratio that holds true for all orbiting planets.

An lunar eclipse occurs when the light of the moon is obscured as the earth passes between it and the sun. A solar eclipse occurs when the light of the sun is obscured as the moon passes between it and the earth.

### Sun and Stars

A star is a massive sphere of hydrogen and helium capable of sustaining nuclear fusion, a chemical reaction that creates massive amounts of energy. This sphere has enough mass to create its own gravity, which is why it doesn't fly apart into little tiny pieces.

The sun is a star, but stars come in other shapes and sizes. The sun's surface is often called plasma because it is not a solid, liquid, or gas. See "States of Matter" in this chapter for more information.

## CHEMISTRY

Chemistry is the study of the properties of matter, how they interact, how they change, and how new substances can be created. *Matter* is a physical substance that has mass and can be measured. *Energy*, which might be called the ability to do work, can also be measured but does not have mass.

### Building Blocks of Matter

Everything except energy is made of matter. A ladder, a person, a slice of apple pie; all are made of matter.

- *Atoms* are the basic building blocks of matter. Although an atom is made up of smaller particles (more on that in a moment), it cannot be reduced without fundamentally altering how it behaves.
- You can add like atoms together to create an *element*, which are substances that contain only one type of atom. An element is like a bowl of brown rice, with the brown rice grains being atoms. Add something else and it's not just a bowl of brown rice anymore. Take the outer coating (bran) off a grain of brown rice, and it's not brown rice anymore. (Same with an atom; reduce it to its parts and it's not the same thing it was.)
- Two atoms put together create a *molecule*.
- A compound is two or more *different* elements put together, so all compounds are molecules but a molecule is not necessarily a compound. Water (made of the elements hydrogen and oxygen) is an example of a compound.

#### Structure of Atoms

Atoms are made up of particles called protons, neutrons, and electrons. A proton is a positively charged particle, a neutron has no charge, and an electron has a negative charge. Protons and neutrons together form the nucleus of an atom, while protons orbit around the nucleus (think of the sun and the planets in the solar system).

Every element has a different number of protons. Change the number of protons in an atom, and you change what it is. For example, carbon has 6 protons. Add a seventh, and now you have nitrogen.

Normally, an atom has the same number of protons and electrons, making it neutral (the positive charge of the proton is canceled out, so to speak, by the negative charge of the electron). So if you know that carbon has 6 protons, you also know it has 6 electrons. An atom generally has the same number of neutrons as well, but this can vary a bit. An element with a different number of neutrons than protons is still that element (although it's called an isotope), and it has a different mass.

If an atom has a different number of protons and electrons, it is said to be an ion. If it has more protons than electrons, it is a positive ion; if it has more electrons than protons, it is a negative ion.

### Periodic Table

The Periodic Table of Elements shows the elements arranged by their atomic number, which is the number of protons the atom has. The common abbreviation for each element is given, as its common name. See Figure 10.7.

| 1 | 2 | 3 | 4 | 5 | 6 | 7 | 8 | 9 | 10 | 11 | 12 | 13 | 14 | 15 | 16 | 17 | 18 |
|---|---|---|---|---|---|---|---|---|---|---|---|---|---|---|---|---|---|
| hydrogen 1 H 1.008 | | | | | | | | | | | | | | | | | helium 2 He 4.003 |
| lithium 3 Li 6.941 | beryllium 4 Be 9.012 | | | | | | | | | | | boron 5 B 10.811 | carbon 6 C 12.011 | nitrogen 7 N 14.007 | oxygen 8 O 15.999 | flourine 9 F 18.998 | neon 10 Ne 20.180 |
| Sodium 11 Na 22.990 | Magnesium 12 Mg 24.305 | | | | | | | | | | | aluminium 13 Al 26.982 | silicon 14 Si 28.086 | phosphorus 15 P 30.974 | sulfur 16 S 32.066 | chlorine 17 Cl 35.453 | argon 18 Ar 39.948 |
| potassium 19 K 39.098 | calcium 20 Ca 40.078 | scandium 21 Sc 44.956 | titanium 22 Ti 47.88 | vanadium 23 V 50.942 | chromium 24 Cr 51.996 | manganese 25 Mn 54.938 | iron 26 Fe 55.933 | cobalt 27 Co 58.933 | nickel 28 Ni 58.693 | copper 29 Cu 63.546 | zinc 30 Zn 65.39 | gallium 31 Ga 69.732 | germanium 32 Ge 72.61 | arsenic 33 As 74.922 | selenium 34 Se 78.09 | bromine 35 Br 79.904 | krypton 36 Kr 84.80 |
| rubidium 37 Rb 85.468 | strontium 38 Sr 87.62 | yttrium 39 Y 88.906 | zirconium 40 Zr 91.224 | niobium 41 Nb 92.906 | molybdenum 42 Mo 95.94 | technetic 43 Tc 98.907 | ruthenium 44 Ru 101.07 | rhodium 45 Rh 102.906 | palladium 46 Pd 106.42 | silver 47 Ag 107.868 | cadmium 48 Cd 112.411 | indium 49 In 114.818 | tin 50 Sn 118.71 | antimony 51 Sb 121.760 | tellurium 52 Te 127.6 | iodine 53 I 126.904 | xenon 54 Xe 131.29 |
| cesium 55 Cs 132.905 | barium 56 Ba 137.327 | 57-71 | hafnium 72 Hf 178.49 | tantalum 73 Ta 180.948 | tungsten 74 W 183.85 | rhenium 75 Re 186.207 | osmium 76 Os 190.23 | iridium 77 Ir 192.22 | platinum 78 Pt 195.08 | gold 79 Au 196.967 | mercury 80 Hg 200.59 | thallium 81 Tl 204.383 | lead 82 Pb 207.2 | bismuth 83 Bi 208.980 | polonium 84 Po 208.982 | astatine 85 At 209.987 | radon 86 Rn 222.018 |
| francium 87 Fr 223.020 | radium 88 Ra 226.025 | 88-103 | rutherfordium 104 Rf [261] | debnium 105 Db [262] | seaborgium 106 Sg [266] | bohrium 107 Bh [264] | hassium 108 Hs [269] | meitnerium 109 Mt [268] | darmstadtium 110 Ds [269] | roentgenium 111 Rg [272] | copernicium 112 Cn [277] | ununtrium 113 Uut Unknown | flerovium 114 Fi [289] | ununpentium 115 Uup unknown | livermorium 116 Uuh [298] | ununseptium 117 Uus unknown | ununoctium 118 Uuo unknown |

| | | | | | | | | | | | | | | |
|---|---|---|---|---|---|---|---|---|---|---|---|---|---|---|
| La | Ce | Pr | Nd | Pm | Sm | Eu | Gd | Tb | Dy | Ho | Er | Tm | Yb | Lu |
| actinium 89 Ac 227.028 | thorium 90 Th 232.038 | protactinium 91 Pa 231.036 | uranium 92 U 238.029 | neptunium 93 Np 237.048 | plutonium 94 Pu 244.064 | americium 95 Am 243.061 | curium 96 Cm 247.070 | berkelium 97 Bk 247.070 | californium 98 Cf 251.080 | einsteinium 99 Es [254] | fermium 100 Fm 257.095 | mendelevium 101 Md 258.1 | nobelium 102 No 259.101 | lawrencium 103 Lr [262] |

Figure 10.7

### States of Matter

In general, matter can take on three different forms.

- A *solid* has a defined volume and shape.
- A *liquid* has a defined volume but not a defined shape; it will take on the contours of its container.
- A *gas* has no defined volume or shape.

Think of water. Frozen solid, it is an ice cube of defined volume and shape. As a liquid, you can pour it into a cup and it will take on the shape of the cup. Pour too much and the cup will overflow (defined volume but not defined shape). As a gas (water vapor), it has neither volume nor shape. It will expand to fill the available space. However, gas does have mass, so there is a limit of how small a space it can be compressed into.

Scientists sometimes include a fourth state of matter, plasma, which doesn't occur very often. It's similar to a gas but its atoms are made up of free electrons and ions. In other words, the electrons don't move around the atomic nucleus in an orbit the way they normally do. The sun is a good example of plasma. There aren't a lot of other natural plasmas, but there are a number of human-made plasmas. For example, in a fluorescent light, electricity running through the gas in the tube creates a plasma.

### Mixtures

In chemistry, a mixture is the blending of two or more materials without a chemical change occurring. For example, you can mix spinach leaves and romaine lettuce leaves together to make a salad without changing the chemical nature of the spinach or the romaine.

Once a mixture is made, its component parts can sometime be separated back out (you could pick out the spinach leaves from your spinach-romaine salad without too much trouble). However, sometimes it is difficult, if not impossible, to separate a mixture into its component parts once they've been blended. Think of a milk shake: It's got ice cream and milk, but once it's been blended, it's hard to separate out the ice cream again.

Mixtures can be homogeneous or heterogeneous. In a homogeneous mixture, different parts of the mixture are all the same. A cup of coffee is an example of a homogeneous mixture. An homogeneous mixture is also called a solution. In a heterogeneous mixture, different parts of the mixture may be different from each other. For example, rocky road ice cream has marshmallows in some parts and not in others.

A suspension is a mixture with liquid and solid components (thus it is heterogeneous). A cup of hot chocolate with tiny marshmallows in it is a suspension. If you mix it so the marshmallows are evenly distributed throughout the chocolate, eventually they will fall out of the mixture. This process is called sedimentation. (Generally the heavier substance will settle to the bottom of the container, but since marshmallows float they will bob to the top.)

A colloid is a homogeneous mixture in which particles are suspended in a second substance but do not fall out of the mixture. These can be gels, aerosols, emulsions, and foams. Milk is a colloid, as is mayonnaise.

In a solution, the component that exists in a greater amount is called the solvent. The component that exists in a lesser amount is called the solute. It is dissolved in the solvent. Liquids, solids, and gases can all form parts of a solution.

### Chemical Reactions

A chemical reaction changes the structural or energetic properties of the atoms and/or molecules involved in the process. This change creates a new substance. You can physically change a substance without creating a chemical reaction (for example, think of melting ice).

Chemical reactions occur outside the chemistry lab all the time. Think of the way iron rusts. The iron reacts with oxygen to create a new substance. The substances that come together to create the reaction are called reactants; the resulting substance is the product.

1. Reactions can occur that combine substances to create new substances (*combination* or *synthesis*).
2. They can decompose substances to create new substances made of smaller parts (*decomposition* or *analysis*).
3. *Displacement* occurs when one element in a reaction is replaced by another element: $A + BC = AB + C$.
4. If two elements are involved in a displacement reaction, it's called *double displacement*: $AB + CD = AC + BD$.
5. A *combustion* reaction is one that involves burning.

A catalyst is a substance that assists a chemical reaction (usually causing it to happen more quickly). The catalyst itself does not undergo a chemical change.

### Acids and Bases

Chemically speaking, acids and bases can be defined in different ways, and in fact the same substance can act as an acid or a base depending on the chemical reaction it's involved in. (Water is an example of this.)

According to one common definition, an acid is a substance that gives away ("donates") hydrogen ions and a base is a substance that accepts them. If, after a chemical reaction, a substance has fewer hydrogen ions than it did before, it's an acid (because it donated its hydrogen ions); if it has more, it's a base.

Another definition says that acids are those substances that accept electron pairs and bases are those that donate them during a chemical reaction.

People sometimes think of acid substances as corrosive and base substances as not, but lye is a base and is extremely caustic. Citric acid, which is found in citrus juices, is a common acid.

Some base substances are called alkali. A pH test measures how alkaline or acidic a substance is. A measurement of 7 is considered neutral; a higher number indicates higher alkalinity and a lower number indicates higher acidity.

Acid-base reactions are a sixth type of chemical reaction.

### Types of Chemistry

The field of chemistry includes a number of disciplines and subdisciplines:

- *Organic* chemistry is the study of the chemistry of carbon and its compounds. Carbon is the building block of living organisms and at one time the study of organic chemistry focused solely on living organisms. Organic chemistry now includes the study of nonliving carbon compounds as well. Chemists use the principles of organic chemistry to make useful substances like medications and plastics.
- *Inorganic* chemistry is essentially the study of everything that isn't organic chemistry. It is particularly concerned with nonbiological substances.
- *Biochemistry* studies chemistry in biological systems. These chemists tend to work in medicine-related fields. *Clinical* chemistry is a subdiscipline.
- *Analytical* chemistry is the study of the properties of mixtures—essentially, how to identify what is in a mixture. Chemists in forensics labs, for example, work with the principles of analytical chemistry.
- *Physical* chemistry is concerned with the physical behavior of atoms and other substances.
- *Nuclear* chemistry is the study of radioactive substances (which do not have stable nuclei), of the nuclear properties of atoms and other substances, and of nuclear reactions.

Many other subfields exist, including polymer chemistry, water chemistry, environmental chemistry, and others.

## PHYSICAL SCIENCE

Physical science focuses on the natural laws that govern how the world works. Physics, which is the study of the properties of matter and energy, is different from biology and chemistry, although biology and chemistry follow the laws of physics. While biologists might ask, "How did life begin?" physicists ask, "How did the universe begin?" Of course there is crossover among these disciplines.

### Laws of Motion

Early physicists were particularly interested in how things move (or don't move), which is often called mechanics. Sir Isaac Newton first formulated three rules of motion in the late seventeenth century, which scientists continue to accept as generally true:

1. Newton's First Law, sometimes called "The Law of Inertia": an object at rest stays at rest unless acted on by an outside force; an object in motion maintains its direction and velocity unless acted on by an outside force. In other words, objects will tend to continue doing what they're doing (or not doing) unless interrupted.

2. Newton's Second Law, sometimes called "The Law of Force" or "The Law of Acceleration": acceleration occurs when a force acts on a mass. The greater the mass, the more force needed to cause acceleration. In other words, it requires more effort to move something heavy versus something light. This law is expressed in the formula Force = Mass times Acceleration, or $F = MA$.

3. Newton's Third Law, sometimes called "The Law of Action/Reaction": Every force causes an equal (but opposite) reaction force or, as it is commonly put, "For every action there is an equal and opposite reaction." In other words, and importantly, forces mutually interact.

In honor of Newton, his name is given to a unit of force. A newton is the amount of force that produces an acceleration (on a one-kilogram object) of one meter per one second, each second.

### Speed/Acceleration/Velocity

In order to understand the various laws of physics, especially of mechanics, it's important to understand what we mean by various units of measure.

Scalar measures are those that quantify magnitude (that is, size) but not direction.

Vector measures are those that quantify magnitude and direction.

Distance is a measure of how much ground has been covered. For example, if you're walking the dog and you stop at every tree and hydrant, you may be moving in a zigzag that covers a lot of ground, even if you don't end up that far, physically speaking, from your own backyard. (See Figure 10.8, Distance and Displacement in Dog-Walking.) If it's 0.5 mile from your house to the end of your block, but you cover a lot of ground visiting those trees and hydrants, you may in total have covered 3 miles in distance.

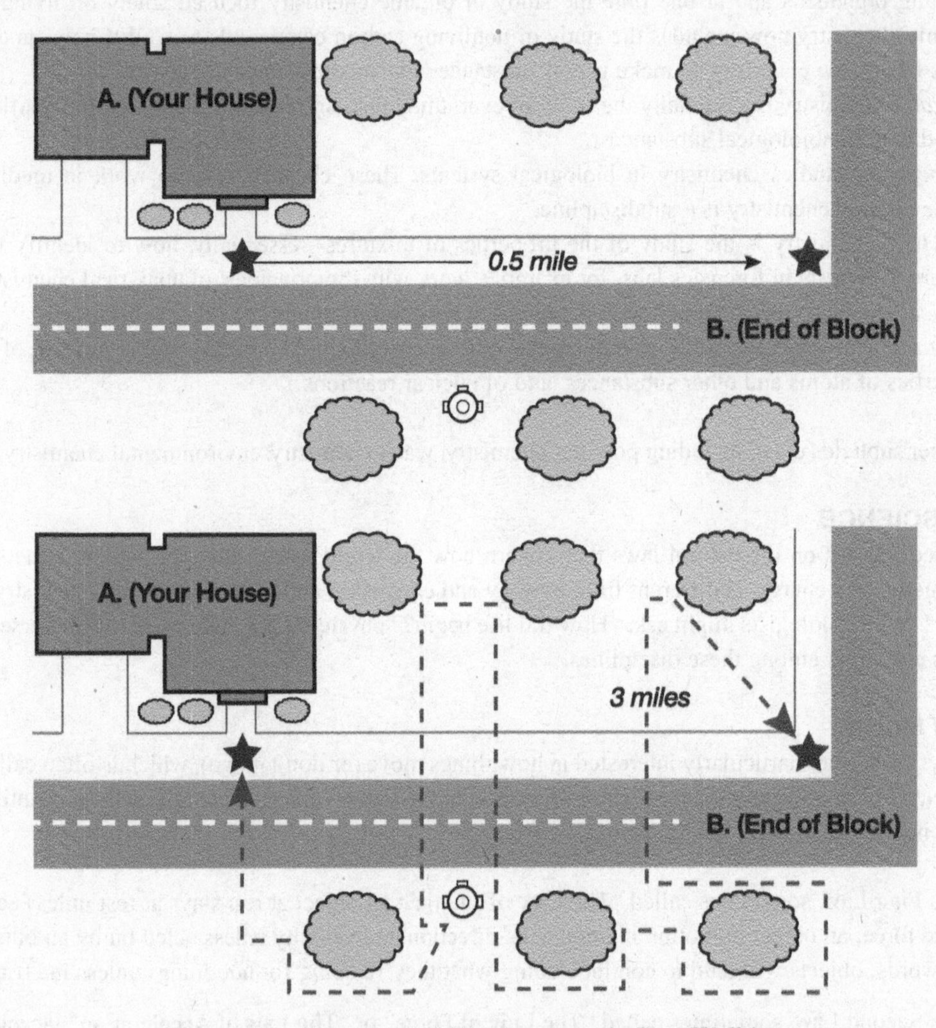


**Figure 10.8, Distance and Displacement in Dog-Walking**

Displacement refers to how far away from its starting point an object moves (or is moved). No matter how many trees and hydrants you visit with your dog, if you wind up at the end of the block, you've only put ("displaced") 0.5 mile between you and your starting point. In other words, displacement also measures direction.

Speed is the rate of motion. It is a matter of distance moved in a certain amount of time. For example, you might walk at a speed of about 3 miles per hour. If you walked in a circle, it would still be measured as 3 miles per hour. An object at rest has no speed. An object covering the same distance in less time would be going faster; an object covering the same distance in more time would be going slower.

Velocity is the rate of motion in a particular direction. It is still a measure of speed in terms of distance moved in a certain period of time, but that distance must all be in the same direction for it to be called velocity. If you took your walk by moving one step forward, then one step back, you might still reach a speed of 3 mph, but you'd be going nowhere so you would be said to have no velocity.

Acceleration is a change in velocity. (Speeding up velocity is called acceleration, while slowing down velocity is called deceleration.) The rate of change of velocity is the measure of acceleration. You can change an object's acceleration by changing its speed or by changing its direction. In either case, force is required. Acceleration equals the change in velocity divided by time:

$$a = \frac{vf - vi}{t},$$

where *vf* is the final velocity, *vi* is the initial velocity, and *t* is the time.

## Work/Energy/Power

Newton's ideas about motion aren't the only way to talk about motion. Work and energy are also ways we can talk about motion.

Work is what happens when a force causes an object to be displaced. It's important to remember that the force has to cause the displacement. Work happens all the time without our thinking of it as work: you shut a door or open the lid of your laptop. Both of those activities meet the definition of work. In formulas describing work, the angle between the force and the displacement is also considered.

Sometimes a force doesn't cause a displacement, but actually gets in the way of the displacement. That is called negative work.

Work is measured in joules. A joule is equal to one newton of force causing the displacement of 1 meter.

Energy is the ability to do work. So potential energy is stored energy that could be used. Potential energy is based on an object's position. A common example of this is a bow and arrow. When the string of the bow is pulled back, the bow string has potential energy. Once the bow string is released and returns to its usual position, it has no potential energy. Gravity also creates potential energy; think of a ball on the ground versus a ball perched on the top of a hill. The ball at the top of the hill has potential energy.

An object that has motion has kinetic energy. Kinetic energy takes three main forms, vibrational (vibrating energy, or oscillating energy, like that of a pendulum), rotational (spinning or turning energy, like the earth turning on its axis), and translational (energy moving in a straight line). The amount of translational energy an object has depends on its speed and its mass but not its direction.

Power is the rate at which work is done, which can be measured as the amount of energy used per unit of time, usually joules per second (J/s), also known as a watt.

$$\text{Power} = \frac{\text{work}}{\text{time}}$$

An object in motion has momentum.

$$\textbf{Momentum} = \textbf{mass} \bullet \textbf{velocity}$$

## Types of Forces

If you remember Newton's First Law, an object in motion will stay in motion unless acted on by an outside force. It will also stay at rest unless acted on by an outside force.

Let's look at some of these forces. They're roughly divided into two types, those that require contact between objects, and those that do not.

Examples of forces that don't require physical contact include gravitational force, electrical force, and magnetic force.

Types of forces that do require contact include frictional force (one object rubs against the other), spring force (the force of a coiled spring), tension force (rubber band pulled back), air resistance force (a type of friction), and others.

## Waves

A wave moves energy through space and matter. Some waves can move through empty space, but not all. There are a number of different kinds of waves, many of which have different properties (a wave on the surface of the ocean is somewhat different from a sound wave that allows you to hear what the teacher is saying). Waves have a repeating pattern that allow scientists to measure them.

Mechanical waves move through a medium and have a source. They cannot move through empty space. When a mechanical wave reaches the end of its medium, it will often undergo reflection, which means it reverses direction and travels back through the medium. Think of an echo.

A wave on the surface of the ocean and a sound wave are both types of mechanical waves.

Electromagnetic waves can move through empty space. They are created by the movement of charged particles (the vibration makes waves). Light waves are an example of electromagnetic waves. So are microwaves and X-rays.

### Wavelength

Think of waves crashing on the shore of the beach. The distance between one peak and the next is the wavelength. Wavelength affects our perception of a wave. For example, in light waves, the color violet has the shortest wavelength, red the longest. We're not able to perceive some light wavelengths at all with our eyes.

### Amplitude

A wave's height is called its amplitude. The more amplitude, the more intensity. A sound wave with a larger amplitude would be louder than one with a smaller amplitude.

### Wave Speed

Wave speed is measured like other speed:

$$\text{Speed} = \frac{\text{distance}}{\text{time}}$$

You would find a fixed point of the wave, such as the peak, and measure the distance it travels in a certain unit of time.

### Wave Frequency

Wave speed and wave frequency are related. Wave frequency is the number of cycles in a unit of time, usually given in hertz (Hz). One hertz equals one cycle per second. For example, you would count how many wave peaks passed a fixed point in a period of time. In other words, it is how often a specific event occurs.

### Wave Period

Wave period is how long a cycle takes, for instance, how long it takes for a peak to move down and all the way back up again. In other words, it is how long it takes a specific event to occur.

### Light Waves

Light is a kind of electromagnetic wave—in fact, it's the only electromagnetic wave we can see. We can only see some colors within a certain wavelength. Special equipment helps scientists see other colors, like infrared and ultraviolet.

When we see the color of an object, we are looking at the light wave the object reflects. All the other light waves are absorbed and we don't see them. All light waves seen together create white light. No light waves at all (the absence of light) makes black.

In light, a larger amplitude of the wave increases the intensity or brightness of the light.

Light waves are measured in nanometers (nm); we can see wave lengths between about 400 to 700 nm.

The speed of light in a vacuum (299,792,458 meters per second or about 186,000 miles per second) is thought to be the maximum speed at which any matter can travel.

### Sound Waves

Sound is a type of mechanical wave. Because waves can interfere with each other, wave interference can create a problem in acoustics—and it can also create interesting sound effects. Sound waves can silence each other (sound waves exactly inverted cancel each other out). Sound waves that are in sync ("in phase") combine to create a larger amplitude. Two different waves create a new wave.

Sound travels more slowly through air than through water.

## STRATEGIES FOR SUCCEEDING ON THE GENERAL SCIENCE SUBTEST

Although the General Science subtest can cover a wide range of material, keep in mind that most questions on this section of the ASVAB are likely to cover biology, chemistry, and physical science, and fewer questions are likely to cover earth science, astronomy, and other disciplines.

### Strategies for Succeeding on the CAT Version

The CAT version of the General Science subtest has 16 questions, and you'll have 8 minutes to answer them. That's thirty seconds per question, so you don't have a lot of time to ponder. Taking a little extra time with the first few questions to get them right means you'll probably score higher (because you'll be asked harder questions that are worth more points). Be sure to answer all questions, though.

### Strategies for Succeeding on the Paper-and-Pencil Version

The paper-and-pencil version of the General Science subtest has 25 questions and you'll have 11 minutes to answer them. That's fewer than thirty seconds per question, so you'll need to move fast. Try answering the questions you know the answers to first, then go back and answer those you're less sure of. It's okay to guess; there's no additional penalty for a wrong answer, and you may be able to guess correctly.

### Overall Strategies for Succeeding

A great deal of science has to do with understanding concepts and words—that is, knowing what different terms mean. So, use your Word Knowledge (Chapter 6) understanding to help you figure out the definitions of various words you may encounter on the test.

You'll encounter questions designed to test your knowledge of related concepts, so be sure to carefully read and understand each question and the possible answers before choosing one.

# CHAPTER 11

# Electronics Information (EI)

The Electronics Information subtest does not count toward the Armed Forces Qualification Test (AFQT) score that you need to achieve to be eligible for military service. But the score is used to help determine what jobs you may be able to perform in the armed forces. A strong showing on the Electronics Information subtest can ensure a greater number of opportunities for you.

Remember that some subtest scores are combined together in order to determine whether you're eligible for a particular job, so you'll need to do well on each of the related subtests in order to be considered for the position you want. It's common for Electronics Information to be combined with General Science and/or Mechanical Comprehension and/or Automotive and Shop Information. Also, be aware that some of the questions on the Electronics Information subtest may require a solid understanding of Arithmetic Reasoning and Mathematical Knowledge. You can expect to be asked questions that require the memorization of a few formulas and the ability to do some basic calculations.

## WHAT THE TEST MEASURES

The test measures your basic understanding of electricity and how it works, including circuitry, currents, materials, and tools. If you've taken vocational classes in high school, you'll probably be familiar with much of this material, but if not you will need to spend some time reviewing the material in this chapter. In addition, you may need to do further study at your public library. This is especially true if you're hoping for a military career that requires a good score on the Electronics Information subtest, such as an electronics technician, fire control technician, and many mechanical jobs (among others).

## ELECTRICITY BASICS

Electricity is, essentially, the movement of electrons. Remember that atoms consist of three different kinds of particles: protons (positively charged particles), neutrons (neutral particles), and electrons (negatively charged particles). Protons and neutrons form the nucleus of an atom, and electrons orbit around the nucleus. If an electron splits off from an atom, and is allowed to flow freely, it can form part of an electric current. (See Chapter 10, General Science, for more information on atomic structure.)

Electricity is present in everything, from your body to the clouds overhead. When it is not in active flow, electricity is considered to have potential. The electrical potential of various systems and structures is an important concept to understand.

Electricity can accumulate, such as with static electricity, or it can flow, as in an electrical current.

### Where Electricity Comes From

We can get electricity through the conversion of energy sources, such as by burning coal or gas. A water wheel or windmill can use the power of natural processes (the flowing of water and blowing of wind) to create electricity.

### Current

An electric current is the movement of electricity from one point to another. Substances that don't like to let go of their electrons don't allow the free flow of electrons, so it is difficult to get an electric current to go through them. They are called electric insulators. Some examples include glass and wood.

Some substances are more relaxed about allowing electrons to move about freely. These substances are called conductors. Some examples include wire and water. To move, electricity must have a conductor. In most cases, we use different kinds of wires to conduct electricity from one place to another. See "Conductors, Semiconductors, and Insulators" in this chapter for more information.

## UNITS OF MEASURE

People working with electricity need to measure it in a number of different ways, such as by how fast it is moving or how powerful a charge is. To understand how current is measured, you need to first understand some basic electric terms.

### Ampere

An ampere is a measure of electric charge passing a specific point in a specific measure of time. In other words, it measures the rate of flow or current. 1 coulomb per second equals 1 ampere. A coulomb is a unit of charge, and is basically a collection of electrons ready to flow.

### Watt

A watt is the measure of rate of work, or power. In other words, it tells us what an electric current can do (for example, power a light bulb to a certain degree of brightness).

$$1 \text{ watt} = 1 \text{ joule / second}$$

Work is measured in joules. A joule is equal to one newton of force causing the displacement of 1 meter. (See Chapter 10, General Science, for more information on joules, newtons, and displacement.)

### Kilowatts

Because we sometimes need to measure large amounts of energy, we can use kilowatts (kw) instead of watts. 1 kilowatt equals 1000 watts over 1 hour. A kilowatt is the equivalent of 3.6 million joules.

### Ohm

As described earlier in this chapter, some materials are more willing to let electrons flow through them than others. But all materials have some resistance to the flow of electrons. You might think of resistance as similar to friction. How much resistance is present in a conductor is measured in ohms. (The opposite of resistance is conductance. More on that later!) The symbol used to represent ohm in mathematical equations, plans, and schematics looks something like a horseshoe: $\Omega$.

### Volt

A volt measures electrical pressure. (Think of the water in your toilet. It just sits there until you flush, or apply pressure.)

### Formulas for Measuring Electricity

Various formulas are used to express the connection between power, pressure, and resistance.

### Ohm's Law

Ohm's Law tells us that current (I) is equal to voltage divided by resistance.

$$I = \frac{V}{R}$$

**Power**

Power (P) is equal to the voltage (V) multiplied by the current (I).

$$P = V \bullet I$$

**Electrical Efficiency**

As the power formula shows, increasing the voltage or the current increases the power of an electric current. To measure electrical efficiency (or the useful power output compared to the power consumed to produce the electricity), we can invert the power formula:

Current equals power divided by voltage:

$$I = \frac{P}{V}$$

You can use this formula to compare the efficiency of various voltage and wattage combinations. Using a higher voltage increases efficiency.

**Resistance**

You can measure resistance by dividing the voltage by the current:

$$R = \frac{V}{I}$$

**Conductance**

Since conductance (G) is the opposite (or inverse) of resistance, you can find it by using an inverse of the resistance formula:

$$G = \frac{I}{V}$$

**Energy**

Energy equals power multiplied by time.

$$E = P \bullet t$$

So, using a 75-watt bulb is equivalent to 75 joules per second in power. Leaving the bulb on for twenty minutes (1200 seconds) equals an energy use of 90,000 joules.

## MEASURING DEVICES AND ELECTRICAL TOOLS

A few different devices are used to measure electricity. Several tools are useful in fixing electrical problems in systems. You may be asked to identify some of these on the Electronics Information subtest, or at least know what they are used for.

### Voltmeter

Used to measure the flow of electricity through a conductor in relation to electrolytic decomposition (calibrated in volts).

### Ammeter

Used to measure the amount of electrical current flow (calibrated in amperes).

**Ohmmeter**
Used to measure the amount of resistance in a given unit or circuit (calibrated in ohms).

**Multipurpose Tool/Wire-Stripping Pliers**
Used as a pair of pliers to cut and strip insulation from wire, to crimp terminals, and to cut small screws.

**Soldering Gun**
Used to solder wire to form contact terminals and in other related light electrical work.

**Test Light/Circuit Tester**
Used to determine the presence of current in a given circuit.
See Figure 11.1.

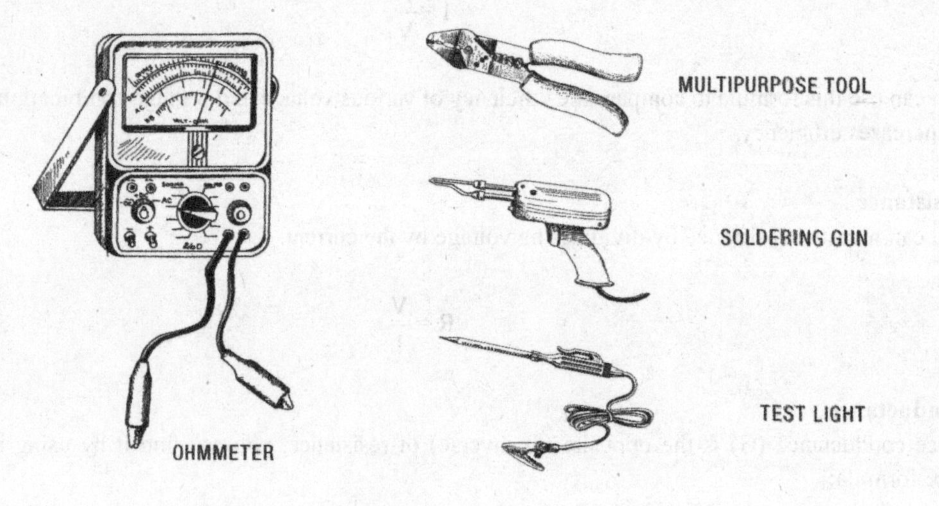


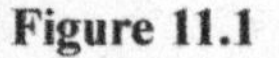
Figure 11.1

## DC AND AC TRANSMISSION

Electrical current can be delivered in one of two ways, *direct current* (DC) or *alternating current* (AC). Direct current means that the current flows in one direction. Alternating current means the current switches back and forth. In the United States, the current from a power station changes direction 60 times per second, so it's called 60-cycle AC power. A car battery uses direct current. Why the difference?

Batteries always produce direct current, because the current always flows from one terminal to the other in one direction. But your neighborhood power plant uses alternating current because it can send that current down the line at a much higher voltage. A transformer can be used to easily step up (or step down) the voltage of an AC current.

So, power companies can provide energy with greater efficiency using AC current. Since current may have to travel a very long distance to get from the power plant to your house, the power plant can send it out at a very high voltage (perhaps several hundred thousand volts) and then step it down at various points before it gets to the 120-volt outlet where you plug in your toaster. The same can't be done with direct current.

## ELECTRICITY AND MAGNETISM

To understand the connection between electricity and magnetism, we need to undertand the similarities between the two forces. Electricity is the flow of electrons that creates a charge. Static electricity is the buildup of these electrons so that a material has a different charge from its environment.

### Electric Charge

As electrons are gathered on a material or an object it becomes negatively charged (electrons contain a negative charge so naturally a collection of them will also be negative). Materials and objects that lose electrons become positively charged (because they have more protons, or positively charged particles). An object or material that is negatively charged is always attracted to (that is, drawn toward) an object or material that is positively charged. Thus, when you forget to put the dryer sheet in, your negatively charged socks are attracted to your positively charged socks, and they stick together. (The socks have gained or lost electrons by rubbing against each other as they tumbled around in the dryer.)

### Electric Discharge

When a negative charge passes through the air to unite with a positive charge, the result is an electric discharge. You've felt this when the buildup of static electricity causes a small shock when you touch something. Sometimes direct contact is not even necessary for a discharge to take place. Although air is usually a good insulator, sometimes a charge can arc across it.

### Electric Fields

Every charge has a field surrounding it—the charge extends beyond the object itself. This electric field either pushes away other fields and charges or it pulls them in. A negative field pushes away another negative field, but pulls a positive field toward it. In the same way, a positive field pushes away a positive field, but pulls a negative field toward it.

### Magnetism

Magnetism shares some similar properties with electricity. A magnet produces a magnetic field not unlike an electric field. A magnet has two poles, a north pole and a south pole, that behave not unlike electrical positive and negative electrical charges. Two unlike poles will attract each other (just as two unlike charges will attract each other in electricity). Two like poles will push each other away (repel each other).

The earth itself is like a big magnet (because of the composition of its core). So the earth is surrounded by an enormous magnetic field (which is why you can use a magnetic compass to figure out where north and south are).

### The Relationship Between Electricity and Magnetism

So, other than these similar properties, how are electricity and magnetism related? Electricity can actually produce magnetism. When an electric current goes through a wire, it creates a magnetic field around the wire.

Since certain metals make good magnets, you can create a strong magnetic field by wrapping wire around metal, such as iron, and sending an electric current through the wire. The metal core itself will become a magnet.

An electromagnet (and the forces of electromagnetism) can be used to convert electric energy into mechanical energy.

## ELECTRICITY AND HEAT

An electric current naturally creates heat. In a conductor with low resistance, an electric current generates less heat. With a higher resistance, the electrons have to work harder and so they generate more heat. Thus, if the goal is to reduce energy loss generated by heat, then the solution is to provide less resistance to the current.

But sometimes that heat is useful. For example, in an incandescent light bulb, the heat that the electric current generates creates the light. The filament inside the bulb is actually glowing from the heat given off by the current.

Other appliances also use electricity to create heat. For example, a toaster oven or a space heater uses electricity to generate heat.

You can also use heat to create electricity. For example, steam can be produced (by burning coal or through another method), and that steam can be used to turn a wheel or turbine, and the rotary motion will create electricity.

## CONDUCTORS, SEMICONDUCTORS, AND INSULATORS

To control the flow of an electric current, conductors, semiconductors, and insulators are used.

### Conductors

A conductor is a material that allows the flow of electrons. To create electrical devices, a material that does not resist the movement of charged particles is needed. Many electrical devices use conductors made of wire, especially copper wire.

### Semiconductors

A semiconductor is a material that has some properties of a conductor and some properties of an insulator. It can be used to control the flow of electric current. Silicon is the most common material for a semiconductor. Processes knowing as "doping" are used to modify the material to work as required.

### Insulators

Insulators are materials that impede the flow of atoms. Rubber is one example; it does not conduct electricity well. Glass is another, as is air. Insulators are used to contain electricity and prevent it from going where it is not wanted. For example, the wires in your laptop cord are wrapped in flexible plastic so that you're not accidentally shocked by contact with live electricity.

## CIRCUITS: SERIES, PARALLEL, AND SERIES-PARALLEL

Electric circuits are the devices we use to harness the power of electricity. As described earlier in this chapter, positive charges and negative charges attract each other. So, if you have a positively charged material and you connect it by a wire to a negatively charged material, the electrons will naturally flow down the wire from the positively charged material to the negatively charged material (you wouldn't have to do anything to make this happen). Eventually the two materials would end up with the same charge (or a very similar charge), and the flow of electrons (electricity) would stop.

However, we want the electricity to continue flowing, and that needs a loop (a circuit) that returns the positive charges to their original position. A circuit is simply a loop that allows electrical charges to continually move through it. You may have created a circuit in science lab by connecting a battery (or batteries) and a light bulb together with copper wire. When the bulb lights up, the circuit is complete. See Figure 11.2 for an example of a simple circuit.

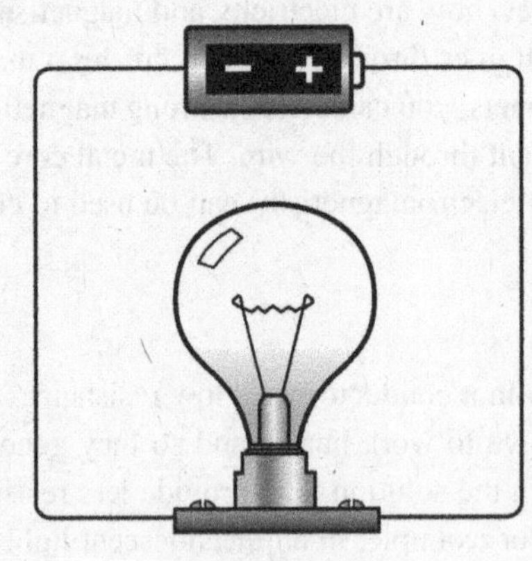


Figure 11.2

If the light bulb breaks, or the wire becomes disconnected, the circuit no longer functions. From this perspective, it's easy to imagine how a switch might be added to a loop so that sometimes the circuit is interrupted (keeping the light off) and sometimes it is not interrupted (turning the light on).

A circuit requires an energy supply. In the case of the battery-operated light bulb, the battery is supplying energy. In your house, the local electric company sends current through electric wires to your circuit panel box where it's ready for use.

### Series Circuit

So far, we've talked about a very simple closed loop system. But what if you wanted to light up more than one light bulb? You could use a series circuit to accomplish this. A series circuit is simply a loop with just one path for the current to flow along. Along that path you can have a series of electrical devices (in our example, light bulbs). See Figure 11.3 for an example of how this works.

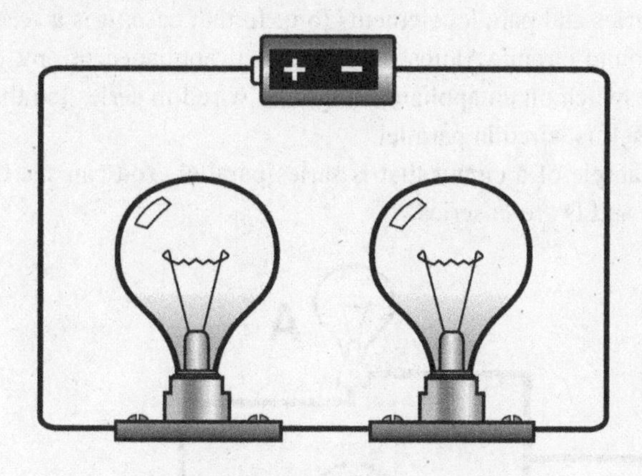


Figure 11.3

As you can see, the charge will go through each electric device in succession. The problem with this type of circuit is that as more electric devices are added, the less power each device is able to use to power itself; the overall current in the circuit decreases. Thus, in the battery-and-light-bulbs example we've been using, as more light bulbs are added, each light bulb becomes less bright. An additional problem with a series circuit is that if one electric device stops working (a bulb breaks, for example), all of the rest quit working as well because the loop is no longer closed. For the same reason, all of the devices would need to be "on" for the circuit to work. So, if all the lights in your house were connected by a series circuit, and if you wanted to have the light on in your kitchen, you'd also have to have the light on in your bedroom, the living room, and so on.

### Parallel Circuits

In order to solve the problems inherent with a series circuit, a parallel circuit can be used. In this case, separate wires branch off the main wire to connect to the electric devices. A charge passes through only one of these branches (and thus only one of the devices) before returning to the battery. But current flows to each branch, so each device is powered. See Figure 11.4 for an example of this.

## Parallel Connection

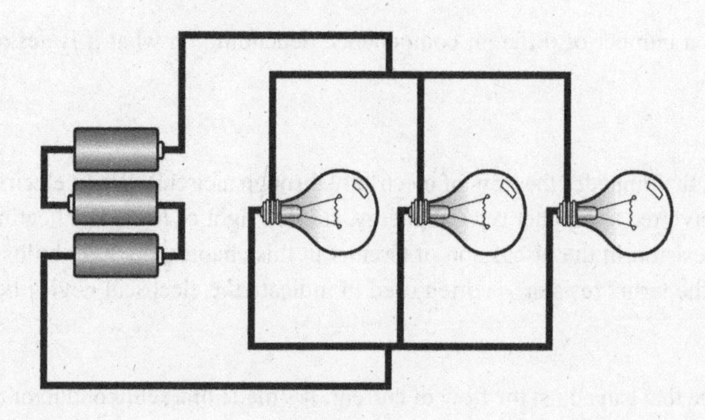

Figure 11.4

Adding devices to a parallel circuit increases the amount of current in the circuit (the bulbs therefore glow brighter). If one device stops working, the other devices are not affected; in the case of our light bulbs, they continue to be lit.

### Series-Parallel Circuit

Often a circuit has both series and parallel elements to it. In that case, it is a series-parallel circuit, sometimes called a combination or compound circuit. Almost any electrical appliance of any complexity requires a series-parallel circuit. For example, a switch on an appliance might be wired in series (so that the switch turns the device on and off) but the appliance itself is wired in parallel.

See Figure 11.5 for an example of a circuit that is series-parallel. You can see that devices A and B are on a parallel circuit while devices C and D are in series.

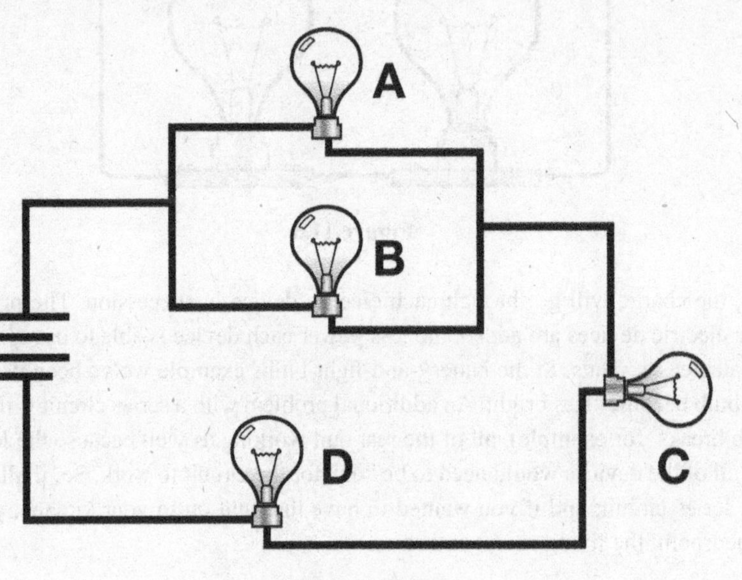


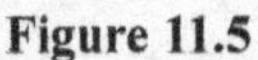

Figure 11.5

### Integrated Circuit

An integrated circuit is a collection of circuits on a chip made of a semiconductor material. Technology allows these chips to contain many circuits in a very tiny space. Most electronics today—like your computer and your smartphone—use integrated circuitry. The conducting lines in an integrated circuit (which take the place of copper wire in a regular circuit) can be measured in nanometers.

### Components

A circuit can contain a number of different components, depending on what it is designed to do. Let's look at some of these components.

#### Resistor

A resistor is anything that impedes the flow of electricity through a circuit. When electricity meets a resistor, the electric energy is often converted to another type of energy, such as light or heat. The heating element in your oven, for example, is a type of resistor. In the discussion of circuits in this chapter, the light bulbs are all resistors. In fact, when describing circuits, the term "resistor" is often used to indicate the electrical device being powered.

#### Transistor

A transistor is a device that can adjust the flow of current. It's made of a semiconductor material and can amplify a current, detect a current, or impede the flow of current. Transistors can be used like gates on a circuit, allowing the movement of current to be carefully controlled.

### Inductor

An inductor is a metal coil that contains electric potential. Current passing through the wire creates a magnetic field that produces current in a conductor, without the inductor and the conductor having to touch.

### Capacitor

A capacitor is a device capable of storing an electric charge temporarily. Essentially, a capacitor is made by placing two conductors, separated by an insulator, in close proximity to each other. One conductor collects a positive charge, the other a negative charge. A capacitor can release its charge almost immediately (making it different from a battery, which releases its charge more slowly).

A capacitor's ability to store a charge is measured in farads (F). One farad is 1 coulomb of charge at 1 volt. That would be an extremely large capacitor (although some supercapacitors are much larger), so capacity is usually measured in much smaller increments, like millifarads (one-thousandth of a farad) and microfarads (one-millionth of a farad).

### Transformer

Transformers can increase or decrease voltage in alternating current transmissions. A transformer can boost the voltage of the current coming from your electric company, then various transformers can step down the voltage at various points until it enters your house. The transformer on your laptop's power cord converts the higher-voltage AC coming from your wall outlet to a lower-voltage DC to power your computer.

### Diode

A diode is a device used to keep current flowing in one direction. It's usually made from a semiconductor material that has low resistance in one direction and high resistance in the other (which is how it moves electricity in one direction).

### Switches and Rheostats

A switch is used to turn an electric device on or off by closing a connection in a circuit (allowing current through and turning the device on) or opening the connection (and stopping the movement of current, thereby turning the device off). Switches can also be used to send current to a different place in a circuit. Sometimes switches are manual (like a light switch that you flip on or off) or automatic (like the brewing switch on your drip coffee maker that turns off when the coffee has been brewed).

A rheostat, sometimes called a dimmer switch, is used to control electrical resistance in a switch. It allows you to turn volume up or down, or to brighten or dim a light. It works by creating higher resistance as it is activated (moving some of the energy into the resistor instead of the electrical device). Higher resistance equals a dimmer light or a lower sound. But not every dimmer switch is a rheostat; many dimmer switches work by shutting the circuit on and off, supplying more or less energy to the device in each cycle. You don't actually perceive the turning on and off of the circuit.

## GROUNDING SYSTEMS

Exposure to an electrical current can be extremely dangerous. It can cause a fire or shock a person (which can be deadly), so electrical systems are designed to reduce the risk of current leaking out of the system through the use of proper grounding.

Grounding is basically the process of removing a charge or an excess charge. The ground is an object that can accept the excess charge from the object that is carrying it. A pathway must exist between the object with the excess charge and the ground. That pathway must be a conductor of electricity. What you don't want is for that pathway to be you!

The electrical system in your home is grounded to the actual ground (earth) by way of a ground rod. Any overload can be dumped in the ground where it doesn't harm anyone and will dissipate.

### Circuit Breakers

A circuit breaker is a switch that turns off the flow of current. It can be manual, so that you can turn off the current yourself, in order to fix a problem or install a ceiling fan without getting electrocuted. It can also be automatic, detecting an excess charge and shutting off the current before it can hurt anyone.

### Fuses

A fuse shuts off a current by melting (it melts if the current exceeds a certain level, thus opening the circuit and shutting off the current). A fuse has to be replaced, but a circuit breaker is usually just reset.

### Ground Fault Circuit Interrupters (GFCI)

Ground fault circuit interrupters, sometimes just called ground fault interrupters, are outlet-based circuit breakers. While fuses and circuit breakers operate from the electrical control panel in your house, the GFCI is in an outlet and so works to protect you from a shock generated by an appliance using that outlet as a source of power.

It can detect very small variations in the way the current is moving.

## ELECTRICAL SCHEMATICS AND SYMBOLS

You'll be expected to know common symbols and to be able to read electrical diagrams (schematics) on this section of the ASVAB.

See Figure 11.6 for some common symbols that are used in circuit diagrams. See Figure 11.7 for a simple schematic.

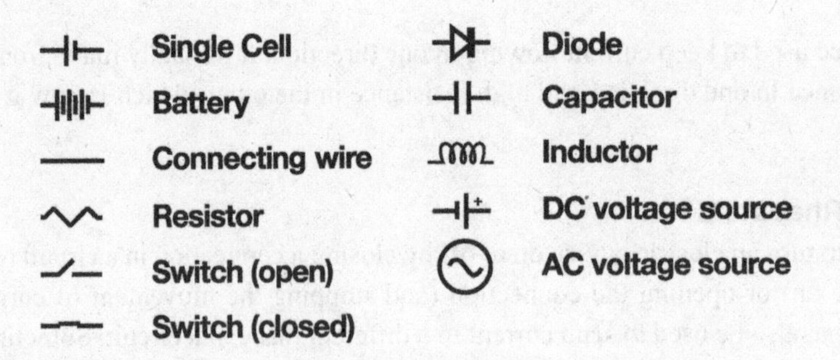


Figure 11.6

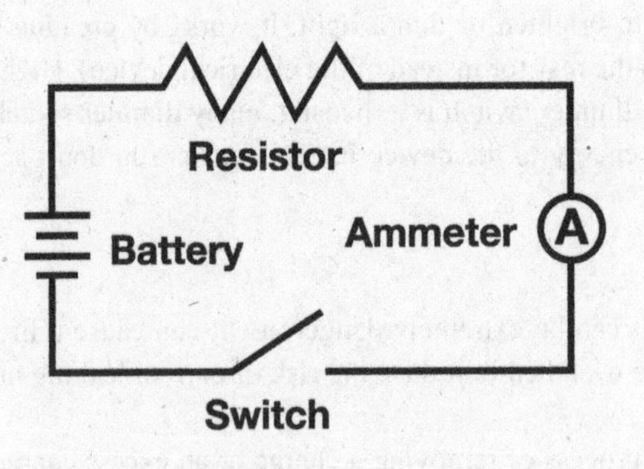

Figure 11.7

In Figure 11.6, note that for the symbol for the battery, the long line indicates the + terminal and the short line the – terminal.

In Figure 11.7, notice that a line connects the battery, resistor, ammeter, and switch. The line indicates a connection. It doesn't say what that connection is. It could be copper wire, it could be something else. If needed, other documentation would describe the types of materials used.

Diagrams are not necessarily drawn to scale. That is, the line symbolizing the connection isn't necessarily proportional to the other elements, nor is it meant to represent an actual length required between, for example, a resistor and a switch.

See Figure 11.8 for an example of a drawing of a circuit versus how that same circuit would look as a schematic.

**Drawing of Circuit**

**Schematic Diagram of Circuit**

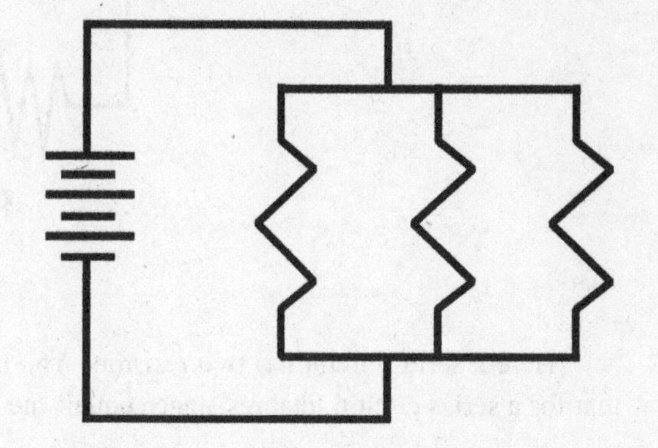

**Figure 11.8**

Components in a circuit may be labeled with an abbreviation (usually one or two letters) that indicates what they are:

- resistor: R
- capacitor: C
- diode: D
- transistor: Q
- switch: S
- inductor: L
- integrated circuit: U (sometimes IC)

If there's more than one of a type of component it may be given a number, such as R1 and R2 for resistor 1 and resistor 2, and a key used to further describe the characteristics of the components. For example, R1: 500 Ω, R2: 750 Ω. Or these characteristics may be written in the schematic itself and not in a key.

(In formulas, the numbers may be represented in subscript, such as $R_1$ and $R_2$.)

Arrows may be used to indicate the direction of the current, and + and – symbols to indicate a positive or negative charge.

## USING SCHEMATICS TO DETERMINE VALUES

You may be given a schematic and asked to find answers to questions such as "how much total resistance is in the circuit?" To do this you will need to be able to read the schematic and to remember the correct formula to use to arrive at the proper answer.

### Example 1

For example, you may be shown a schematic such as that in Figure 11.9.

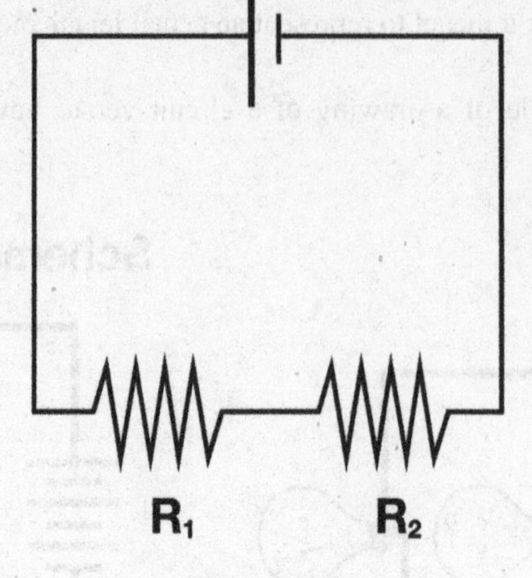


Figure 11.9

Here a series circuit has two resistors. You may be asked to find the total resistance in the circuit. Remember that for a series circuit, total resistance equals the sum of the resistance of each resistor:

$$R_t = R_1 + R_2$$

In the same way, the total voltage drop across a series circuit is the sum of the voltage drop across each individual resistor.

Now, look at Figure 11.10, which has the voltage and amount of resistance noted.

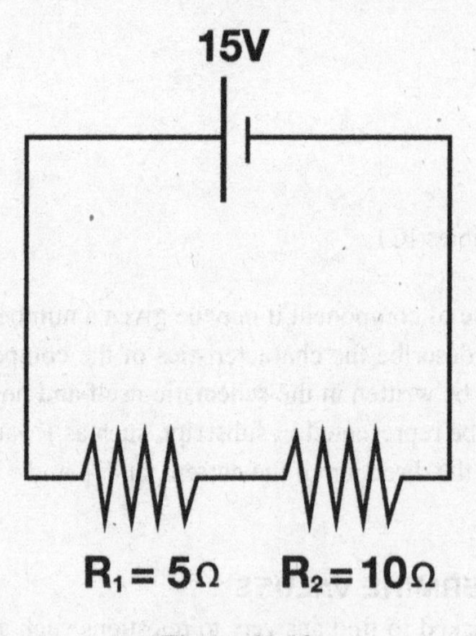


Figure 11.10

You may be asked what the current in the circuit is. To determine this, you would need to remember Ohm's Law:

$$I = \frac{V}{R}$$

You know the voltage is 15 (see the label on the battery in Figure 11.10). To find the total resistance, you'd need to add $R_1$ and $R_2$. $R_1 = 5\,\Omega$ and $R_2 = 10\,\Omega$ (as noted in the schematic), so the total resistance (Rt) is 15 $\Omega$. The current must be 1A (ampere), or 15 divided by 15.

**Example 2**

Look at Figure 11.11.

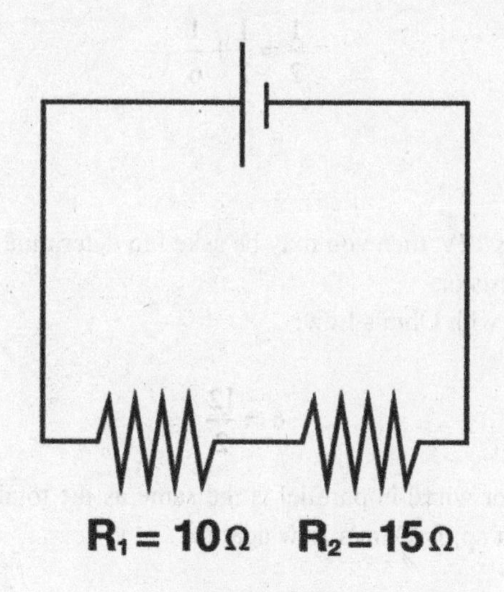


**Figure 11.11**

If you were told the total current was 2A, and asked to determine the voltage of the battery, you could once again use Ohm's Law to figure this out. To find voltage, you would just look at Ohm's Law in a slightly different way. Total voltage equals current times resistance:

$$V = IR$$

If the current is 2A and the total resistance is 25 Ω ($R_1 + R_2$) then the voltage equals 50V.

**Example 3**

Look at Figure 11.12.

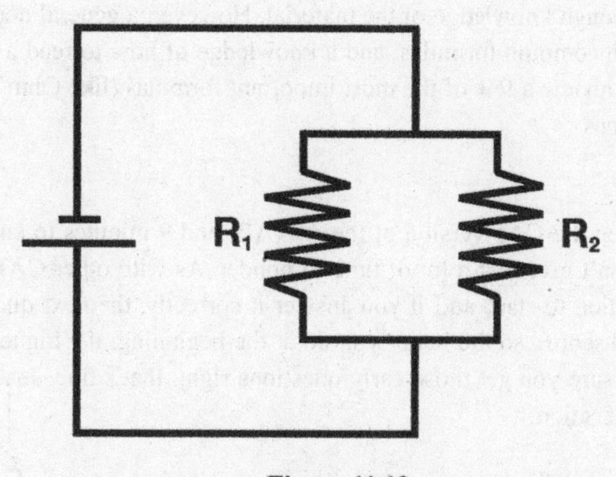


**Figure 11.12**

In this case, the circuit is wired in parallel. In a parallel circuit, total resistance is:

$$\frac{1}{R_t} = \frac{1}{R_1} + \frac{1}{R_2}$$

So you might be asked, "What is the total resistance if $R_1 = 3\,\Omega$ and $R_2 = 6\,\Omega$?"

$$\frac{1}{2}=\frac{1}{3}+\frac{1}{6}$$

Rt = $2\,\Omega$

### Example 4

If the voltage in Figure 11.12 is 12V, then you may be asked to determine the total current in the circuit as well as the current going through each resistor.

The total current can be found with Ohm's Law:

$$6=\frac{12}{2}$$

The voltage across each resistor wired in parallel is the same as the total voltage, so to determine the current going through each resistor, you just apply Ohm's Law again:

$R_1$:

$$4=\frac{12}{3}$$

R2:

$$2=\frac{12}{6}$$

## STRATEGIES FOR SUCCEEDING ON THE ELECTRONICS INFORMATION SUBTEST

It's unlikely that you'll be able to do well on the Electronics Information subtest if you don't know the material and haven't spent some time working with electronics, so there are no easy or quick fixes that will help you succeed on this test if you don't have a thorough knowledge of the material. However, a general understanding of how electricity works, some familiarity with common formulas, and a knowledge of how to read a diagram will be better than nothing. On the day of the test, review a few of the most important formulas (like Ohm's Law) to make sure you're ready for the most likely questions.

### CAT Version Tips

You'll have 16 questions on the CAT version of the ASVAB, and 9 minutes to answer them. That's just over thirty seconds each, which doesn't give you a lot of time to ponder. As with other CAT version subtests, you'll be given a medium-difficulty question to start, and if you answer it correctly, the next question will be more difficult (but worth more in your overall score), so the better you do at the beginning, the higher your score. If you need to take a little extra time to make sure you get those early questions right, that's fine. Just remember to give yourself enough time to finish the entire section.

### Paper-and-Pencil Version Tips

You'll have 20 questions and 9 minutes to answer them, so you'll have less than thirty seconds to respond to each question. You may find some of the questions easier to answer than others, so answer those first in order to get them out of the way and receive full credit for them, but don't forget to give yourself time to go back and finish the entire test. You may be able to guess some of them correctly.

### Overall Tips

Review Chapter 3 for test-taking strategies that will apply to the entire ASVAB. For the Electronics Information subtest, one key thing to remember is you don't always have to read the schematic to understand and answer the question. For example, if a schematic is shown and you're told that the voltage is 5V and the resistance is 10 $\Omega$, you don't have to read and understand the schematic to answer the question, "What is the current running through the resistor?" You just need to remember that:

$$I=\frac{V}{R}$$

Additionally, on this subtest you may be able to eliminate obviously wrong answers based on common sense if you're not otherwise sure of the answer. Some electricity-related answers may be as easy to rule out as not standing in a puddle of water when you plug in an appliance, a concept practically anyone knows even if they have no specialized knowledge of electricity.

# CHAPTER 12

# *Automotive and Shop Information (AS)*

The Automotive and Shop Information material is covered as one subtest on the pencil-and-paper version of the ASVAB, but is broken into two subtests on the CAT version of the ASVAB. See the section called "Strategies for Succeeding on the Automotive and Shop Information Subtest" in this chapter for the specifics of what to expect on the test itself, depending on which version you're taking.

Either way, you'll be expected to know basic information about how cars operate, including the major automotive systems, and basic troubleshooting. You'll also need to know basic shop class principles of construction, including what various tools are used for. If you've taken auto repair and shop classes in high school, then you'll have the necessary background to succeed on this test. Some review always helps, of course.

If you've never taken a class in either subject then you will need to set aside time for a more extensive investigation into the information.

## WHAT THE TEST MEASURES

The Automotive and Shop Information subtest does not count toward the Armed Forces Qualification Test (AFQT) score that you need to achieve to be eligible for military service. However, the score is used to help determine what jobs you may be able to perform in the armed forces. A strong showing on this subtest can ensure a greater number of opportunities for you.

Remember that some subtest scores are combined together in order to determine whether you're eligible for a particular job, so you'll need to do well on each of the related subtests in order to be considered for the position you want. It's common for Automotive and Shop Information to be combined with Electronics Information and/or Mechanical Comprehension and/or General Science subtests to determine whether you're eligible for a specific type of job.

## AUTOMOTIVE: FOUR-STROKE ENGINE CYCLE

The process of internal combustion is what drives gasoline-powered cars. A small amount of fuel (liquid gasoline) is turned into a gas during the combustion process (a spark creates a small explosion). The process creates energy that is used to power the engine. Most cars use a four-stroke engine cycle to operate their engines. What this means is that the pistons in the engine go through four different strokes in a cycle. But before we get into the details of the strokes, let's look at what a piston is in the first place. (We'll also take a look at a few other parts that are useful to understand in order to visualize the four-stroke process.)

### Cylinder and Piston

A piston is a flat disk or a small, solid cylinder that fits inside a larger tube (the tube is the "cylinder" part of "cylinder and piston"). Within the cylinder, the piston moves up and down ("strokes"), causing the process of internal combustion to power the engine. See Figure 12.1 for an example of a cylinder and piston.

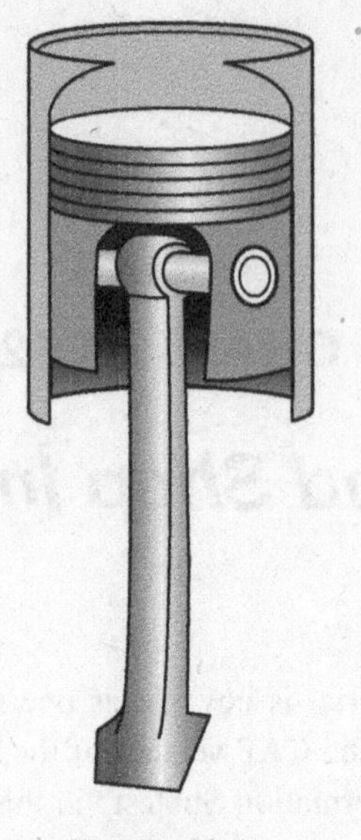

Figure 12.1

Many cars have four cylinders; cars with more (such as V6 and V8 engine configurations) are able to generate more engine power. In a four-cylinder engine, the cylinders are lined up in one row in the engine block. In a V6 or V8 engine, the cylinders form two rows opposite each other (creating a "V" shape).

### Cylinder Head

The cylinder head sits at the top of the cylinder. Generally, it allows air and fuel into the cylinder (and vents exhaust out) and closes off the top of the cylinder to allow combustion and compression to take place. Most of the time, the cylinder head for each piston is in one plate or block per row of cylinders (so a V8 engine would have two blocks).

See Figure 12.2 for an example of a cylinder head.

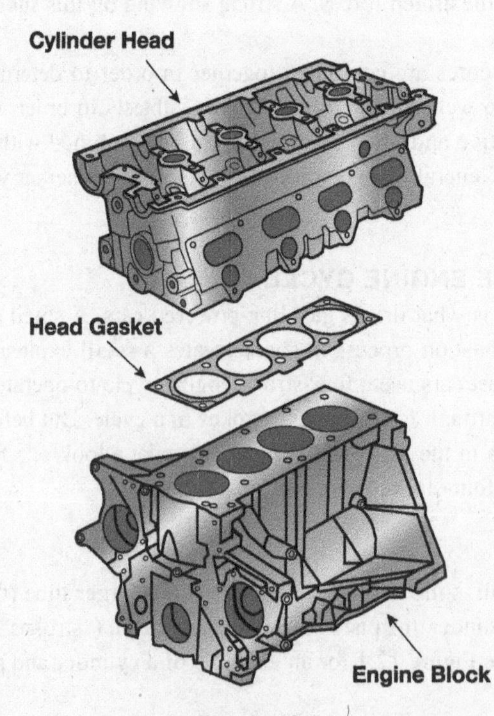


Figure 12.2

### Crankshaft

The crankshaft is a part connected to the pistons that converts the up-and-down (linear) force of the pistons into a rotating force that can be used to power the car.

See Figure 12.3 for an illustration of this part.

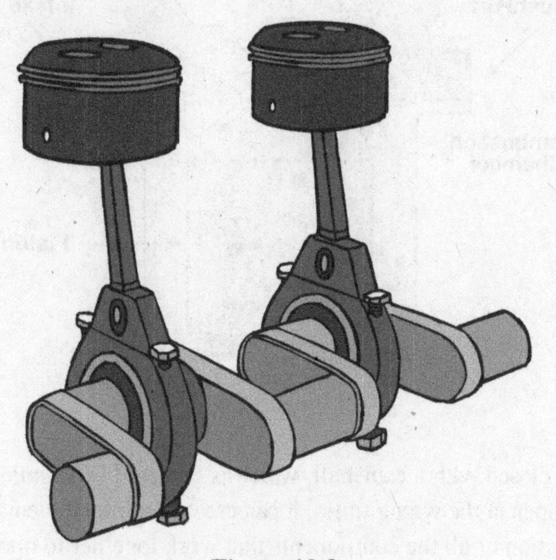

Figure 12.3

The crankshaft is generally connected to a flywheel, which translates the force throughout the engine.

See Figure 12.4 for an illustration of this.

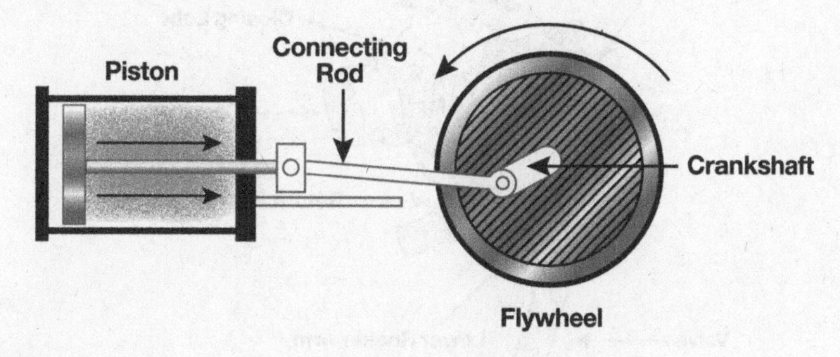


Figure 12.4

### Valves and the Valve Train

To allow fuel and air into a cylinder, intake valves are used. They open and close in timing with what the piston is doing (see "The Four Strokes" later in this chapter for more information). Exhaust valves open and close to allow the air (now called exhaust) to leave the cylinder. Valves can be located on the tops or sides of cylinders.

See Figure 12.5 for an example of valves in a cylinder.

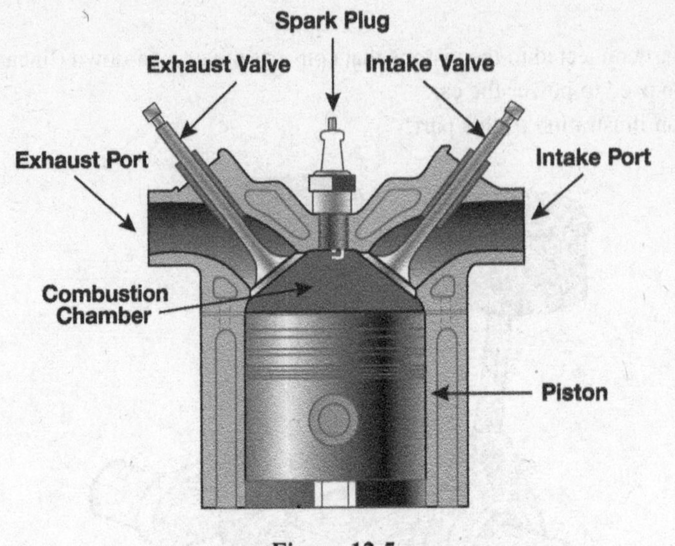


Figure 12.5

The valves are opened and closed with a camshaft, which is operated by a timing belt, timing chain, or gears. If the timing is off, and the valves open at the wrong times, it can create engine problems and difficulty powering the car.

The valve train is the collection of all the components that work together to operate the valves, and can include rocker arms, retainers, springs, and push rods.

See Figure 12.6 for an example of a valve train. Not all valve trains look or operate exactly like this.

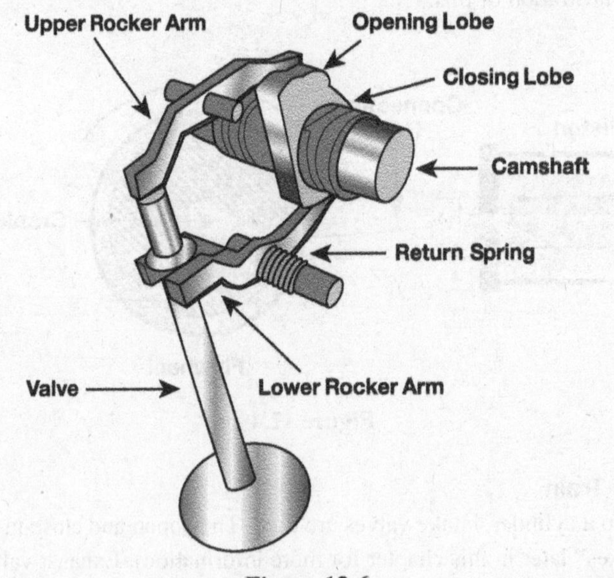


Figure 12.6

### The Four Strokes

The cylinder, piston, cylinder head, crankshaft, valves, and valve train all play important roles in the four-stroke process most internal combustion cars use. So, let's look at the parts of that process in more depth now.

The four strokes are intake, compression, combustion, and exhaust.

#### Intake

During this stroke of the engine cycle, the crankshaft pulls the piston down. At the same time, the camshaft opens the intake valve, allowing fuel and air to enter the cylinder.

**Compression**

During this stroke of the engine cycle, the intake valve closes and the piston moves up in the cylinder. This compresses, or squeezes together, the fuel-air mixture that has entered the cylinder.

**Combustion**

The fuel-air mixture is ignited, causing a small explosion. This shoves the piston back down (rotating the crankshaft).

**Exhaust**

The exhaust valve opens and as the piston moves up (because of the crankshaft's rotation), it also moves the exhaust out of the cylinder.

That completes one four-stroke cycle.

The crankshaft does two complete revolutions for each cycle. The tachometer in your car measures these revolutions as revolutions per minute. At heavier acceleration, the pistons are firing faster and the crankshaft is turning more rapidly. All engines have an RPM limit, beyond which the engine can be damaged.

## OIL LUBRICATION SYSTEM

A car has many moving parts that create friction when they rub together. Since friction can damage parts and create overheating, and since it takes energy to overcome friction (thereby lowering the overall power of the engine), an oil lubrication system is used to reduce the amount of friction between parts. It relies primarily on forcing oil through the engine. (There are other kinds of lubrication in a car, such as that used in the suspension system; adding grease to the steering system, suspension, and drive train is often called a "lube job.")

The oil starts out in the oil pan (also called the sump). A drain valve at the bottom of the oil pans allows old oil to be drained from the engine.

The oil pump sucks oil up through a tube and puts it under pressure so that it can be forced where it needs to go.

The oil is sent through the oil filter to keep dirt out of the engine. The oil filter has a bypass valve that is used if the filter gets clogged and ends up reducing the oil pressure. (Oil needs to stay under high pressure to do its job.)

The oil is used to lubricate the crankcase (the case that covers the crankshaft and some related parts), as well as the cylinders, camshaft, and other metal parts in the engine.

Gravity brings the used oil back into the oil pan, where it starts its trip all over again.

Oil leaks, which can be hard to pinpoint, will cause an engine to use up more oil than is normal, although some oil will always be consumed over time in the lubrication process. An extensive oil leak can create a lubrication problem that could cause too much friction between parts (making them quit working right, or causing the engine to overheat).

## COOLING SYSTEM

A car engine generates a lot of heat through friction, even though a car has a lubrication system to help reduce some of this friction. Too much heat would cause serious problems for the engine, so a cooling system is used to carry heat away.

This is accomplished by sending fluid (usually a mixture of coolant and water) by the hot parts of the engine, letting the coolant mixture absorb some of the heat, then putting the now-hot coolant mixture through the radiator to extract its heat. Then the coolant mixture goes back out to do its job. The coolant itself is a fluid that contains chemicals designed to lower the freezing point and increase the boiling point of water (because either frozen water or boiling water would damage your engine).

### Radiator

The radiator is the part of a car that uses air from the outside to cool the hot coolant mixture. Thus the radiator is situated where airflow can be used to cool the fluid. Usually this means putting it just behind the front grille of a car, but side radiators are common in larger vehicles. The radiator itself is typically made of a core with a lot of surface area over which air can flow to cool down the water. Generally, tubes carry the water and aluminum fins provide the surface area to cool it down. See Figure 12.7 for an example of a radiator.

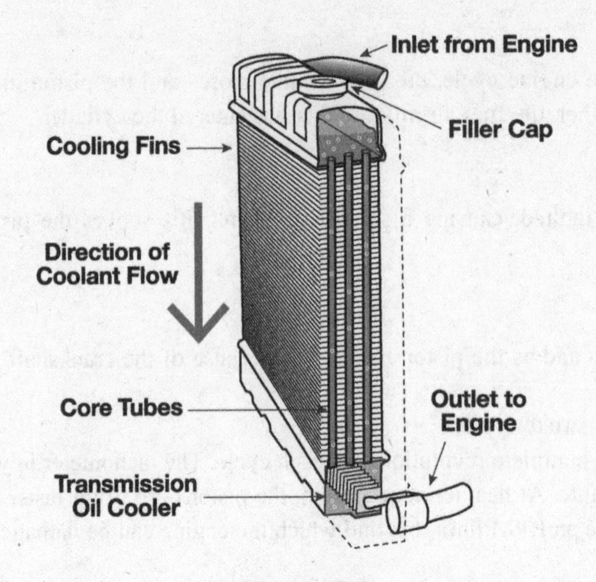


Figure 12.7

Inside the radiator is a fan that turns on as needed to help keep air moving if the airflow is insufficient to keep the engine cooled (such as when you're stopped at a light).

### Water Pump

The water pump moves the coolant throughout the cooling system. A clogged water pump will reduce the system's efficiency and may cause the engine to overheat (an overheated engine is very dangerous!).

In addition to the radiator and the pump, the cooling system requires a thermostat to keep track of the temperature (a thermostat that doesn't work correctly can cause your engine to overheat). Heat sensors also tell the radiator when the fan needs to kick on. (If they don't work right, the engine can overheat.) Hoses and clamps are used to funnel the coolant mixture throughout the engine. A worn hose or loose clamp can cause a coolant leak; if not enough coolant is circulating, the engine can overheat.

## DRIVE SYSTEM

The drive system, also called the drive train, is that collection of parts that serves to get the power of the engine out to the wheels that actually move the car along. The turning power of an engine is called its *torque*. Although there exist many different kinds of drive systems, they generally require:

- a *transmission*, which converts speeds, so that you can go faster or slower, or idle, or reverse.
- a *driveshaft*, a metal rod that's like a spine that connects the power from the transmission to the wheels of the car.
- *axles*, a metal shaft that connects the wheels of a car to the drive shaft. In a car with four wheels, there is a front axle and a rear axle, each of which connect two wheels to the driveshaft.

A drive system on a modern car also has some number of differentials, which direct the engine torque in different ways (allowing the wheels to spin at different speeds).

See Figure 12.8 for an illustration of how the piston power is converted to rotational power in a drive train.

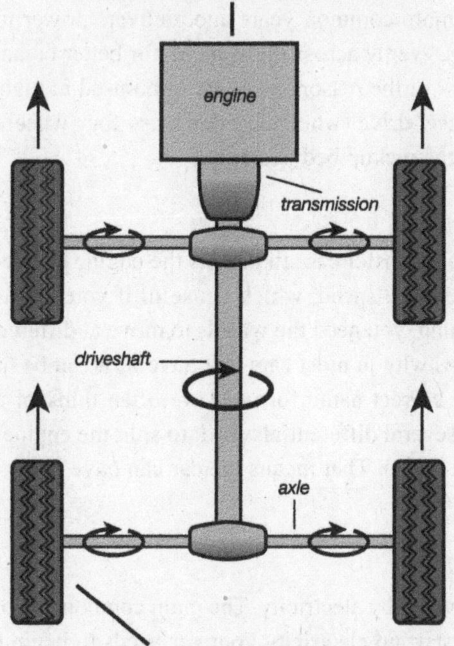


**Figure 12.8**

### Manual Transmission

A car with a manual transmission (also called a standard transmission) requires the driver to manually manipulate a clutch and a gearshift stick in order to direct the engine's torque. The clutch is essentially a connection between the transmission gears and the engine, and it keeps the engine from engaging with the transmission while gear-shifting occurs, preventing damage to the transmission.

Shifting the car into a range of forward gears (there are usually four to six of these in a manual transmission) allows the engine to work most efficiently (without generating a higher RPM than it can handle). At lower speeds, a lower gear is used, while at higher speeds, a higher gear is used. Each gear produces a different gear ratio (the relationship between input speed and output speed).

### Automatic Transmission

In an automatic transmission, the transmission automatically changes gear ratios as needed for the way the car is being driven. A torque converter is used to connect the engine and transmission (versus the clutch in a manual transmission).

A selector lever is used to choose the main forward gear ("drive"), with the transmission itself shifting gear ratios as vehicle speed increases. Most cars have between three and six gear ratios.

Other selections include "park," "reverse," and "neutral" (which basically disengages the transmission from the wheels), with a few additional gears possible depending on the vehicle. Most of these additional gears are meant to be used under very specific situations, such as driving in snow and ice, or when towing.

A continuously variable transmission is an automatic transmission that basically has any number of gear ratios (versus a regular automatic transmission, which in a regular passenger car would rarely have more than six).

### Front-Wheel Drive

A front-wheel drive vehicle uses a common type of drive system that powers the front wheels only. This allows for a lighter car, better fuel economy, and better traction (in some circumstances) than other drive choices.

### Rear-Wheel Drive

Rear-wheel drive, which was more common years ago, delivers power to the rear wheels only. This arrangement distributes vehicle weight more evenly across the vehicle, for better balance and handling. It always allows for quicker acceleration. These are a few of the reasons why it's often used in high-performance cars.

Pickup trucks also use rear-wheel drive (when they don't use four-wheel or all-wheel drive) because it allows for better traction, especially when the pickup bed is empty.

### Four-Wheel (and More) Drive

Four-wheel drive systems have a transfer case that splits the engine torque between the front and rear axle. This keeps all the wheels spinning at the same speed, which is useful if you're driving off-road as it allows for greater traction. However, when you're turning, you need the wheels to move at different speeds. That makes true four-wheel drive difficult to handle, and explains why in most cars that have it, it can be turned off.

All-wheel drive (AWD) is the correct name for what we often think of as four-wheel drive. In this case, the AWD system is on all the time, but several differentials work to split the engine torque among all the wheels (instead of just distributing it evenly to both axles). That means the car can have many of the advantages of both two-wheel drive and four-wheel drive.

## ELECTRICAL SYSTEM

Many of the systems in a car are powered by electricity. The main components of the electrical system are the *battery*, the *starter*, and the *alternator*. The start up electricity your car needs to begin operation is generated by the battery. The battery also gets the fuel system going and lights the lights (so you don't bump your head getting in the car).

### Battery

Most car batteries are 12-volt rechargeable batteries. The battery stores chemical energy, then converts it to electrical energy to start the car by sending voltage to the starter and to the fuel system.

### Starter

The starter gives a car's engine the jolt of power it needs to get moving. When the key is inserted into the ignition and turned over, a small current moves through the starter solenoid to the starter motor, and then the starter motor gets the engine cranking. Once the engine itself starts, the starter motor is no longer needed and switches off.

### Alternator

Once the car engine is running, the alternator takes over the process of supplying electricity to whatever needs electricity. The engine runs a belt that creates a magnetic field (see Chapter 11, Electronics Information, for more on electromagnetism) around a magnet in the alternator. This creates electrical energy that is sent back to recharge the battery. A voltage regulator in the alternator keeps the flow of current smooth.

## ENGINE CONTROL UNIT

Most newer cars use microprocessors to tell various systems what to do. The engine control unit (sometimes called an electronic control unit) is like the brain of your car's engine. A variety of sensors send it information. It adjusts the engine performance according to the information it receives.

Before ECUs became common in cars, adjustments to various systems were made mechanically. For example, the timing chain would be manually adjusted to correct timing problems (e.g., how often cylinder valves open and close).

The ECU can control the ratio of fuel to air in the mixture that enters a cylinder (formerly, a manual adjustment would be made to a carburetor). It can be used to control a number of other systems as well.

## FUEL SYSTEM

A car's fuel system moves gasoline from the tank of the car to the engine, where it is mixed with air and used to power the pistons that drive the engine. The *fuel tank* has sensors that indicate how full it is. It is vented to release gasoline vapors that might otherwise build up and create problems.

### Fuel Pump

The fuel pump moves the gasoline from the tank to the engine through fuel lines that can be made of steel or rubber. Generally, when the car is started, the battery gets the fuel pump going at the same time. (Sometimes the fuel pump is started by the action of the engine.) Filters prevent dirt from passing through the fuel line into the engine. Fuel filters are sometimes found in the pump. They are also found in the fuel line, though specifically where varies from vehicle to vehicle.

Before the fuel gets to the cylinders, it needs to be mixed with air in order to combust properly. This is done using either a carburetor (in older cars) or a fuel injector system (in newer cars).

### Carburetor

In the carburetor, air is mixed with fuel. Then the fuel-air mixture is sent to the cylinders and used to power the pistons. The carburetor controls the ratio of fuel to air by means of the venturi or choke. The carburetor also controls the engine speed by regulating the amount of fuel that goes to the engine by use of a throttle.

### Fuel Injector

A fuel injection system replaces the carburetor on newer cars ("newer" meaning most of those produced from around 1990 on). The fuel injector is basically a valve that squirts a specifically measured amount of fuel into the cylinder. Air intake is measured through sensors and the amount of fuel injected is adjusted accordingly. Fuel injection is a more efficient system than the carburetor and improves gas mileage.

### Accelerator

The accelerator is part of the fuel system; step on it and the car moves forward; step harder and it goes faster. Let up and the car goes more slowly. That's because the accelerator is varying the amount of fuel mixture available to power the engine.

In cars with carburetors, the pedal is tied into the throttle in the carburetor. Push the accelerator to the floor, the throttle opens, the car goes faster.

In fuel-injected cars, the process is a little more complex. Instead of a mechanical motion (pushing down on the pedal directly opening the throttle), these cars convert the mechanical motion into electrical energy. That electrical impulse communicates to the ECU, which then makes the appropriate adjustments.

## EXHAUST SYSTEM

As described in the section called "The Four Strokes" in this chapter, burning gasoline in the cylinder creates exhaust, which needs to be vented to the outside. That's what the exhaust system in a car does. Metal piping on the underside of the car takes the exhaust from the engine down the body of the car and out the tailpipe in the rear.

The exhaust manifold takes the exhaust from the cylinder heads and sends it down a pipe. The exhaust includes some dangerous chemicals, including unburned gas and carbon monoxide. The exhaust passes through the catalytic converter, which turns these dangerous chemicals into carbon dioxide and water. The exhaust passes through the muffler, which dampens the noise involved in the process. Finally, the exhaust passes to the outside through the exhaust pipe, also called the tail pipe.

See Figure 12.9 for an illustration of an exhaust system.

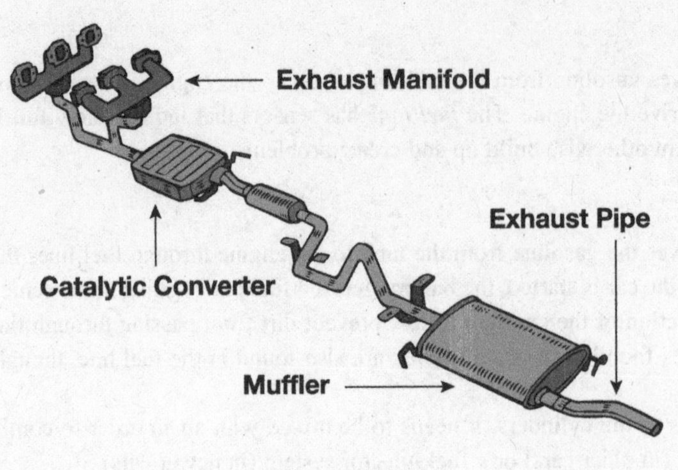


Figure 12.9

### Emission Control

Pollution laws have required car manufacturers to find ways to control the dangerous chemicals that are released during the exhaust process. Since unburned gasoline is one of those dangerous chemicals, improving engine performance (burning more of the gas in the engine) reduces emissions.

An oxygen sensor in the exhaust determines how much unburned gas is going through the exhaust system and adjusts the engine accordingly. Timing of the spark in the four-stroke cycle can also reduce the amount of unburned gasoline in the exhaust, and is controlled by the ECU.

The catalytic converter, described above, is another step in the emission control process. Air injection is used to help the catalytic converter function most effectively by helping to burn the unburned or partially burned gasoline.

A third process involves collecting the harmful gases that accumulate in the engine (specifically in the crankcase) and doing something about them at that point. Positive crankcase ventilation (PCV) takes these gases and puts them into the fuel-air injection system so that the gases will be burned during the combustion stroke. A PCV valve controls the amount of these gases that are introduced at any one time, in order to control their effect on engine performance.

Additionally, evaporative controls vent the fumes from the fuel tank into a storage container that funnels them to the engine, where they are burned.

## SUSPENSION SYSTEM

The suspension system in a car, which connects the vehicle body to the wheels, is designed to keep the tires on the road (important for control of the car), to support the vehicle while keeping an appropriate distance between the road and the body, and to minimize the roughness of a ride. *Struts*, *shock absorbers*, *springs*, and *tires* are the main parts of a suspension system.

See Figure 12.10 for an example of the suspension system in a front-wheel drive car.

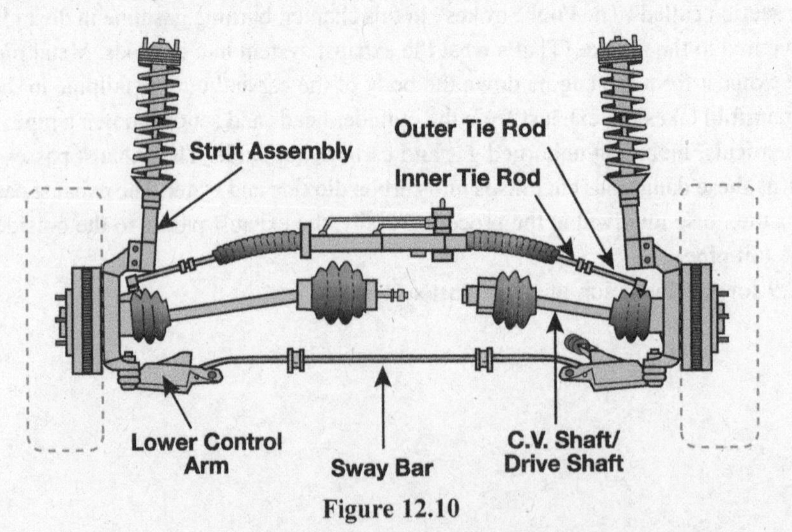


Figure 12.10

Springs are links between the frame of the car and its body. They compress to absorb bumps in the road. Struts and shock absorbers control the amount of bouncing the spring does on encountering a bump. There are several different kinds of springs, with the coil being quite common. Other types of springs include torsion bars, which are made of flexible steel, leaf springs; which are made of sheets of metal that move and slide; and air springs, which use a compressed air cylinder equipped with a piston.

Tires are a type of air spring. They also transfer the car's directional forces to the road (for example, when turning or braking). Consider how tires respond to bumps in the road. An overinflated tire will bounce more than a correctly inflated tire. An underinflated tire will not communicate the directional forces to the road as well, making it harder to stop and to corner. Time and temperature affect a tire's air pressure.

Anti-sway bars are used to create additional stability by shifting some of one wheel's motion to the parallel wheel (for example, when turning a corner).

## STEERING SYSTEM

The steering system in a car is related to the suspension system, and is designed to allow the driver to use very little force to control the car's movement. The rotation of the steering wheel is conveyed to the wheels, making them turn in the desired direction. The suspension works to reduce the impact of bumps in the road on steering.

Most cars today are equipped with power steering, in which a piston helps move the steering wheel so less force needs to be applied by the driver.

In most cars, the steering wheel connects to the steering system, which is either rack and pinion or a steering box. In a rack and pinion system, gears translate the rotational energy of the wheel to linear energy. A steering box can have several different configurations, but basically it uses a lever arm to convert the energy.

The steering system is connected to the track rod. Tie rods connect to the track rod and convey the motion to the wheels through steering arms.

See Figure 12.11 for an example of a steering box steering system. See Figure 12.12 for an example of a rack and pinion steering system.

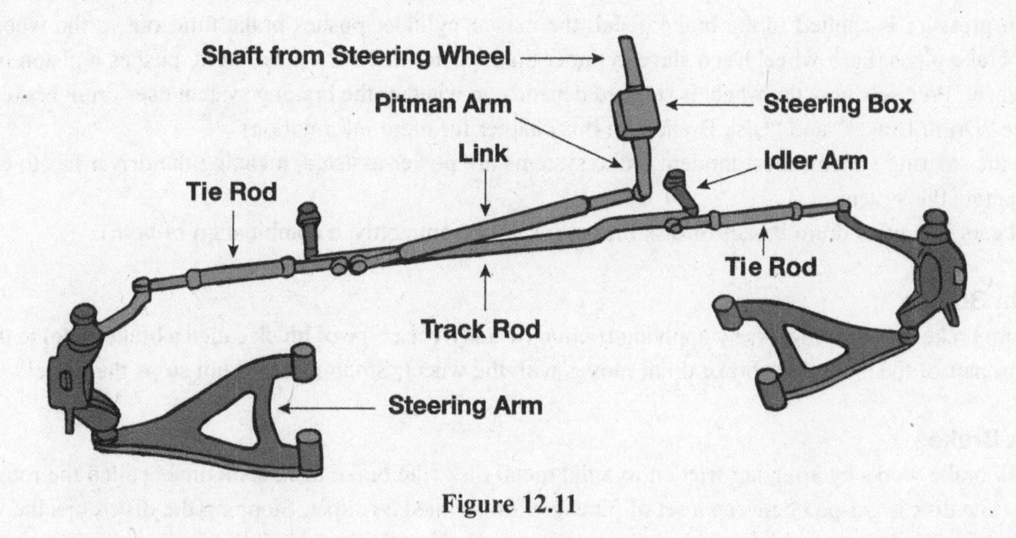


Figure 12.11

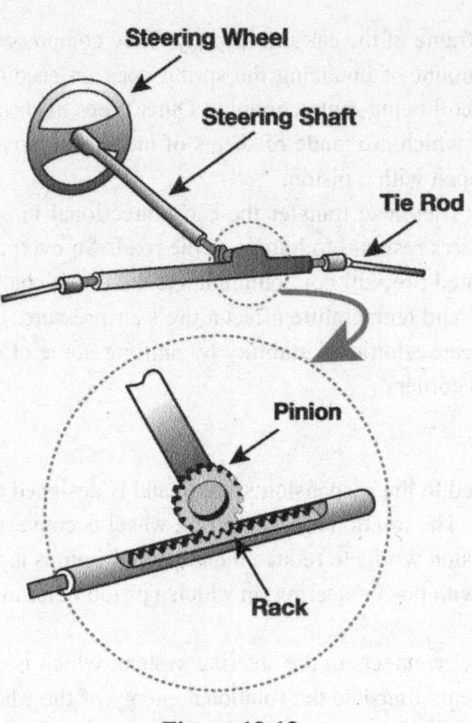

Figure 12.12

## BRAKE SYSTEM

The brake system in a car is designed to stop the forward momentum of the car safely (that is, without bouncing the car all over the road or causing the car to go into a skid). Cars have brakes on all four wheels, tied together by a hydraulic system. At the center of the hydraulic system is the *master cylinder*, which contains brake fluid.

When pressure is applied to the brake pedal, the master cylinder pushes brake fluid out to the wheels via a system of brake pipes. Each wheel has a slave cylinder that, when filled with brake fluid, pushes a piston out, stopping the wheel. Precisely how the wheel is stopped depends on whether the braking system uses drum brakes or disk brakes (see "Drum Brakes" and "Disk Brakes" in this chapter for more information).

Like the steering system, most modern brake systems are power-assisted, meaning the driver has to exert less force to operate the system.

Most cars use either drum brakes or disk brakes (or quite commonly, a combination of both).

### Drum Brakes

A drum brake is one that works by applying friction (usually via a type of block called a brake shoe) to the inside of the drum part of the brake. The brake drum moves with the wheel. Stopping the drum stops the wheel.

### Disk Brakes

A disk brake works by applying friction to a flat metal disk (the brake disk, sometimes called the rotor) inside the wheel. The disk is grasped between a set of pinching arms called a caliper. Stopping the disk stops the wheel.

The main wheels involved in stopping are the front two, since the weight of the car is thrown forward when braking. In many cars, the front two wheels are fitted with disk brakes, which are more efficient than drum brakes, and the rear two tires use drum brakes (which are less expensive). In some cases all four wheels are fitted with disk brakes. Few newer cars have all-drum brakes.

### Parking Brakes

A parking brake (sometimes called an emergency brake) is separate from the hydraulic braking system. It is a secondary or backup braking system. Usually a hand lever or foot pedal is used. When the parking brake is engaged, an entirely mechanical system of cables and levers keeps the car from moving (which is why you might engage it when parked on a steep hill) or stops its forward motion (in the case of the hydraulic system failing). In general, the parking brake pulls a steel cable attached to levers that force the brake shoes or pads in the rear tires to engage.

### Antilock Brakes

When significant pressure is applied to brakes (for example, slamming on the brakes), the brakes can "lock up," making it difficult to steer. The car is likely to skid rather than come to a complete stop. The way to prevent brakes from locking up is to pump the brake; that is, to apply pressure in quick spurts (apply-release-apply-release) rather than one hard slam.

That is basically what antilock brake systems do automatically. Most modern cars come equipped with this system, so it is only on older cars that one has to worry about the brakes locking up. In a car equipped with ABS, you can feel a slight pulsing in the brake pedal when the ABS is engaged. You may also hear a clicking noise.

Each wheel in an ABS is equipped with a sensor that can detect how fast the wheel is spinning. If the data suggests that the brake is about to lock, the master cylinder stops sending fluid to that brake (which is the equivalent of letting up on the brake).

See Figure 12.13 for an example of how antilock brake systems work.

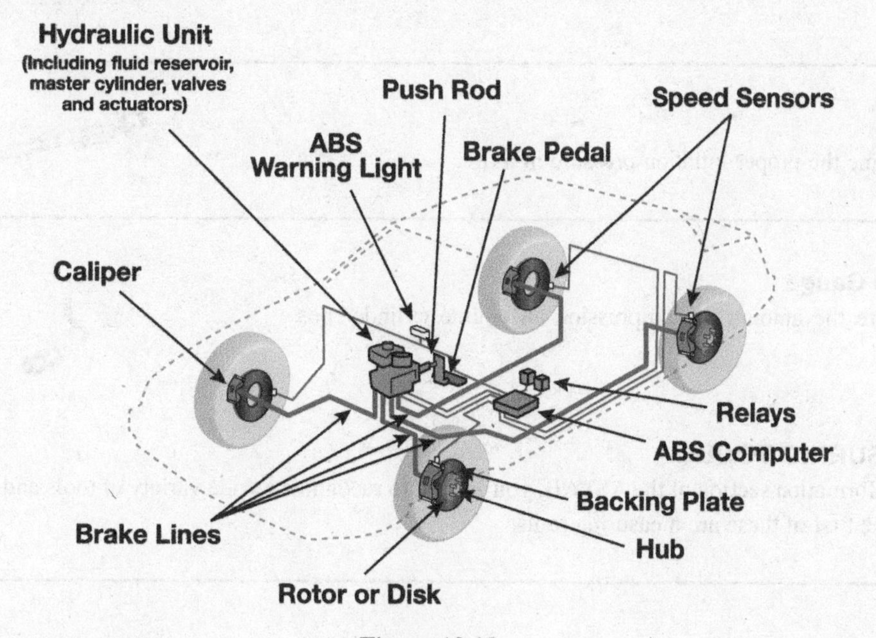


Figure 12.13

## AUTOMOTIVE TOOLS

A few tools are commonly used to do general maintenance on a car. Some of the most common are listed here.

---

### Hydrometer

A float device for determining the specific gravity of the electrolytes in a battery. This determines the state of charge.

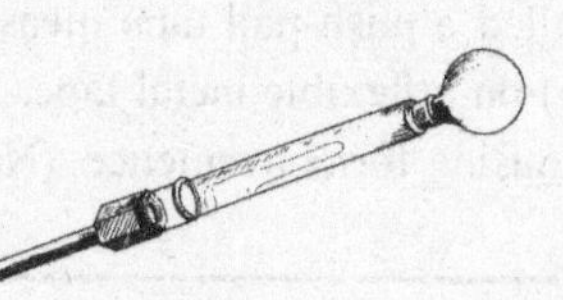

---

### Grease Gun

Used to inject lubricant into special fittings such as those found in ball joints, steering linkage, universal joints, etc.

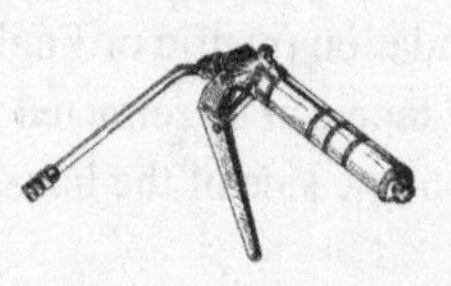

### Filter Wrench

Also called a strap wrench. Used specifically to remove or tighten oil filters.

### Spark Plug Wrench

Used specifically to remove or tighten spark plugs without damaging the insulator.

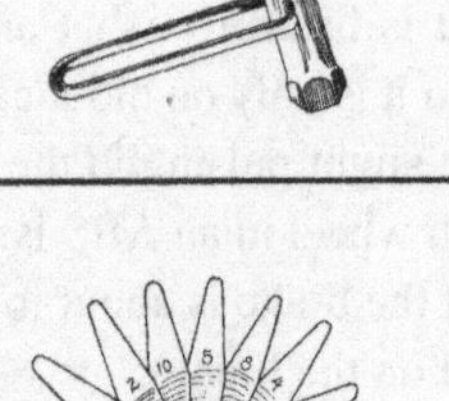

### Feelers Gauge

Used to determine gaps between electrical contacts such as those found in a spark plug. It can also measure the gap between a shaft and bearing on an engine.

### Tire Gauge

Used to determine the proper inflation pressure in a tire.

### Compression Gauge

Used to measure the amount of compression an engine cylinder possesses.

## SHOP: MEASURING TOOLS

For the Shop Information section of the ASVAB, you'll need to recognize a wide variety of tools and know what they are used for. The first of these are measuring tools.

### Steel Ruler

Has linear gradations (metric or English) to measure a workpiece; can double as a straightedge. (Average length is 12 inches.)

### Steel Tape Measure

Also called a push-pull tape measure. Has linear gradations (metric or English) on a flexible metal tape. The tape automatically retracts into a small housing for convenience. (Normal length is 3 to 16 feet.)

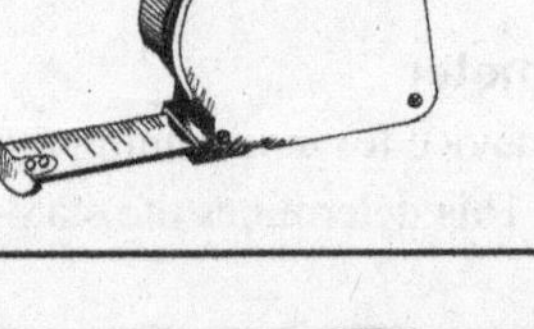

### Wind-Up Tape Measure

Has linear gradation (metric or English) on a flexible metallic tape used to measure. The tape can be retracted into a circular housing by the use of a small crank on one side of the housing. (Normal length is 30 to 100 feet.)

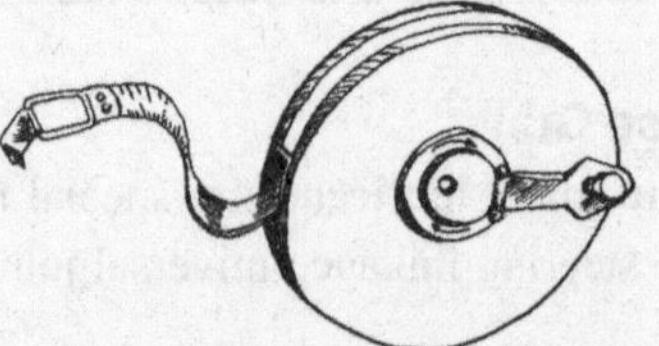

### Micrometer Calipers

Used in determining precise measurements. Calipers can measure from 0 to 12 inches or 0 to 300 millimeters, depending on the type selected.

### Vernier Calipers

Used in determining precise internal or external measurements. Measuring capacity is 6 to 72 inches or 150 to 1800 millimeters.

### Slide Calipers

Use is comparable to the vernier calipers; however, the gradations are not as precise. Its measuring capacity is up to 3 inches.

### Outside Calipers

Also called bow calipers. Used to transfer external measurements from a rule, or to match two items to fit. Measuring capacity is up to 12 inches.

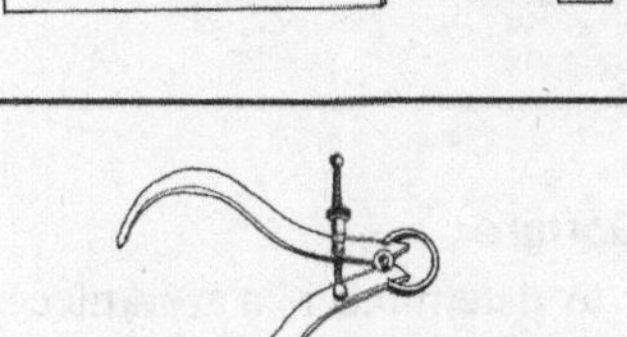

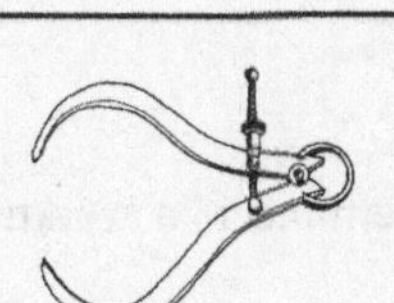

### Inside Calipers

Used to transfer internal measurements from a ruler, or to match two items to fit.

### Spring Dividers

Also called bow compass. Used to inscribe circles or arcs or to calibrate equal divisions on a line.

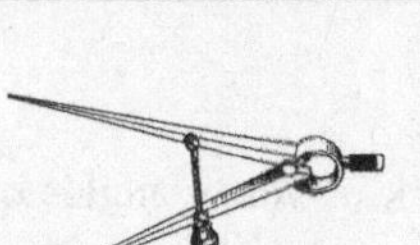

### Depth Gauge

Used to determine depths of holes, grooves, and mortises.

### Screw Pitch Gauge

Used to determine the pitch of a machined thread. Each blade is calibrated in metric units.

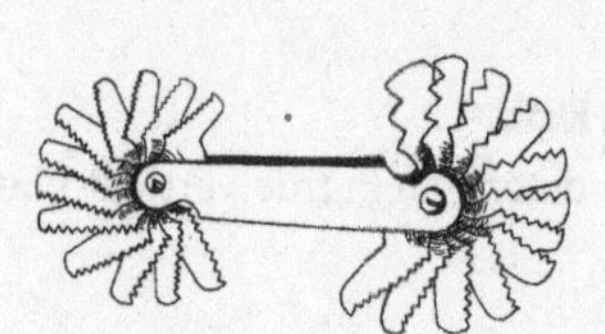

## MEASURING ANGLES

A variety of tools are used to measure angles.

### Carpenter's Steel Square

Also known as a framing square. Used to check the squareness of framing (i.e., 90-degree or right angles). There are metric or English-system gradations for measuring, as well.

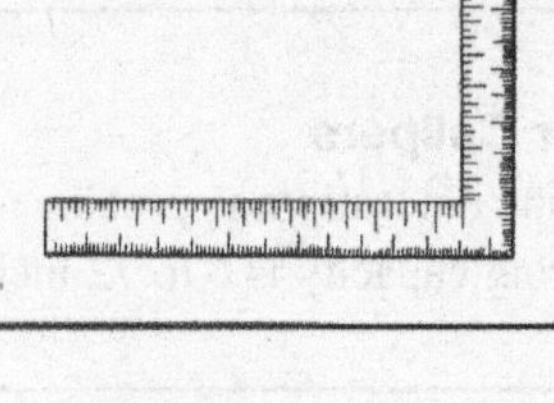

### Combination Square

An all-purpose tool that can measure and serve as a try square, miter square, and level. Measuring capacity in metric or English gradations is 12 inches.

### Try Square

Used to determine if a workpiece is square (i.e., has 90-degree right angles).

### Protractor

Used as an instrument to draw or plot angles (0 to 180 degrees) on a surface.

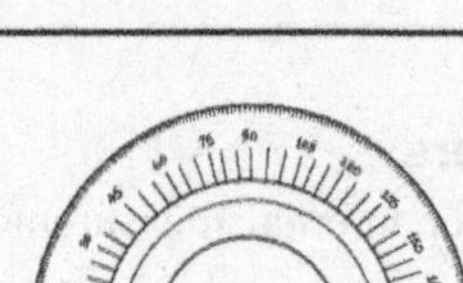

### T-Bevel

Used to mark or verify angles on a workpiece. Normally a protractor is used to serve as a point of reference.

### Level

Used to determine a true horizontal line or accurate level of a surface.

### Plumb Bob

Used to determine a true vertical line.

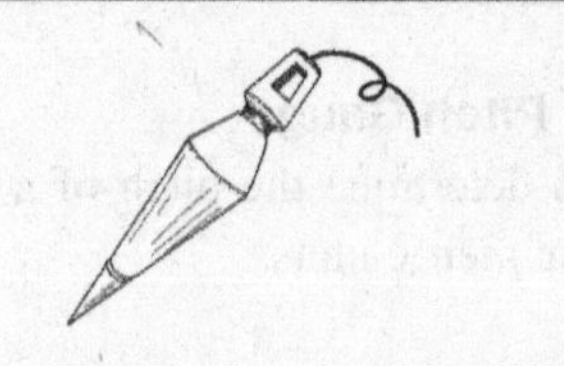

## CUTTING TOOLS

A wide variety of tools are used for cutting purposes. Among these are saws.

### Handsaw

A handsaw can be crosscut, rip, or combination. Used to cut wood planks, sheets, or panels to desired size.

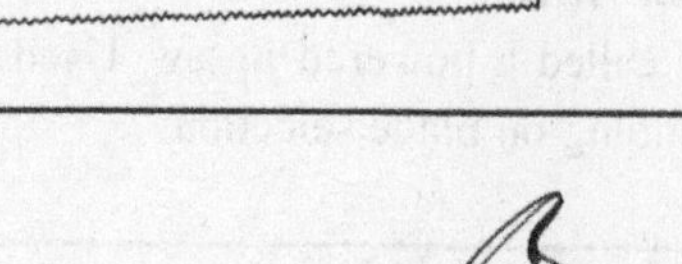

### Back Saw

Also called a tenon saw. Primarily used to cut fine joints in wood, as in a tenon, lap, or dovetail. It can also be used in conjunction with a miter box to cut accurate 45- or 90-degree angles.

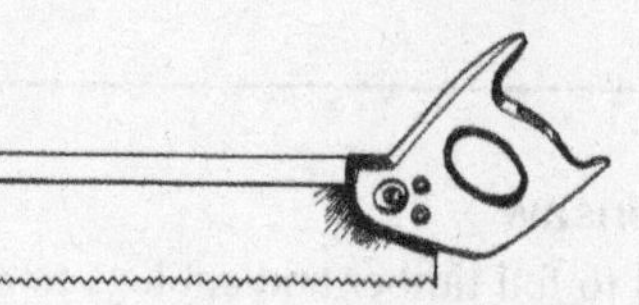

### Coping Saw

Used in making curved cuts in wood or plastic.

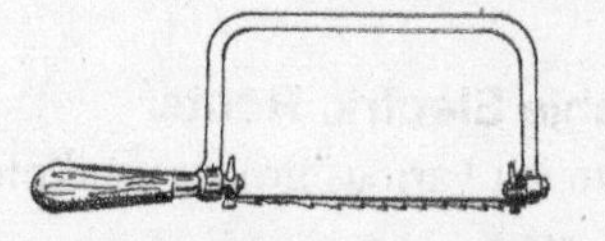

### Compass Saw

Also called a keyhole saw. Used to cut holes in a panel. This saw is not restricted to an edge of a workpiece, like the coping saw, because of the lack of a frame.

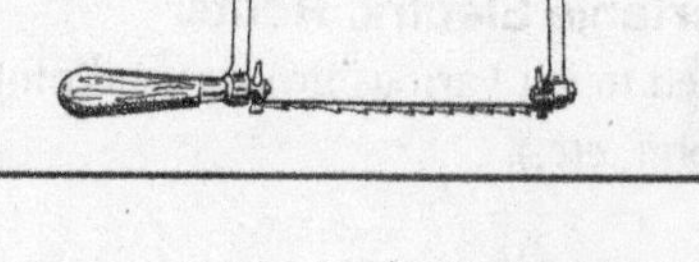

### Hacksaw

Used to cut metal sheets, pipes, plastics, etc.

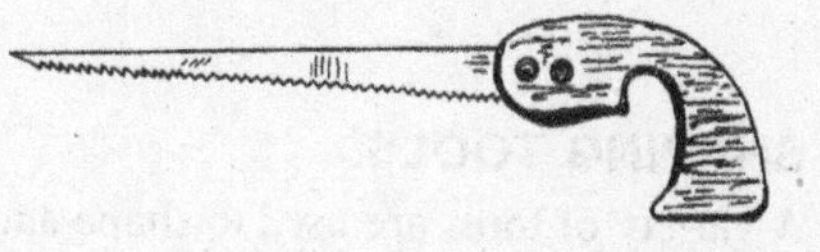

### Portable Circular Saw

Used to cut lumber or plywood to desired size. Saw blades that can be used with this tool are:

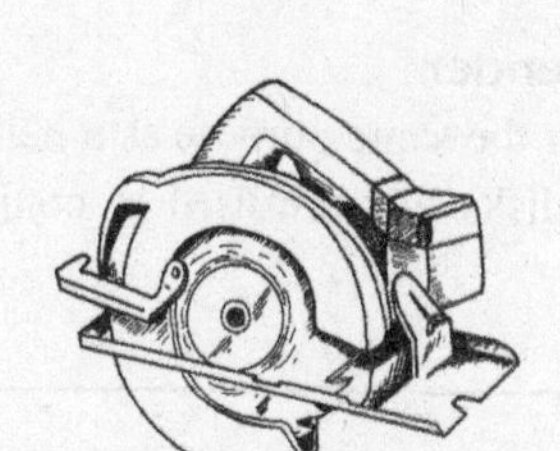

1. Cross cut—cuts across grain of lumber
2. Rip cut—cuts parallel to the grain of lumber
3. Combination—cuts lumber in any direction
4. Carbide tipped—cuts particleboard or lumber with the primary advantage of teeth remaining sharper for longer periods of time
5. Metal cutting—cuts thin sheets of copper, aluminum, and other metals
6. Friction blade—cuts corrugated sheet metal
7. Abrasive disk—cuts concrete, marble, etc.

### Reciprocating Saw

Used in much the same way as a handsaw or compass saw to cut wood, plastic, or thin-gauge metal depending on blade selection.

### Saber Saw

Also called a powered jigsaw. Used to cut curves in various materials depending on blade selection.

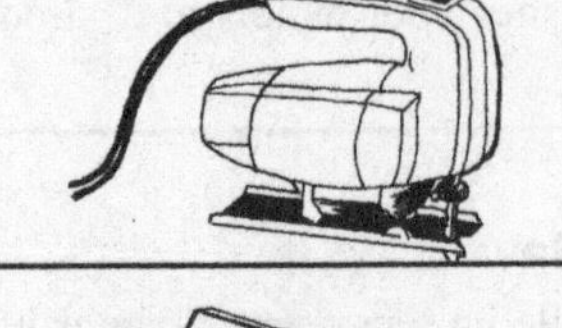

### Chainsaw

Used to fell timber and cut logs to desired lengths.

### Portable Electric Router

Used to cut various grooves and moldings (e.g., hinge mortise, dovetail, rabbit, etc.).

## SHAPING TOOLS

A variety of tools are used to shape and polish various materials.

### Belt Sander

Used to quickly sand wood, steel, or plastic. Various abrasives embedded in the belts are used on this machine in a back and forth motion.

### Disk Sander

Used for the same purpose as a belt sander, but the abrasives are embedded in disks that are used in conjunction with a drill or offset sander grinder.

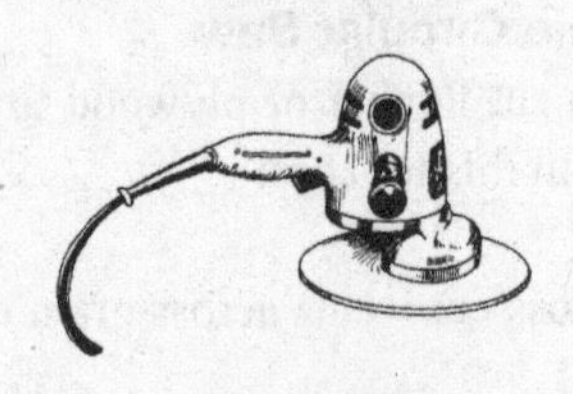

### Orbital Sander

Also called a finishing sander. Used to finish sanding with light abrasive paper.

### Flat File

Used to file flat surfaces; can be used on most types of material.

### Triangular File

Used to file angles or square corners (e.g., saw teeth).

### Round File

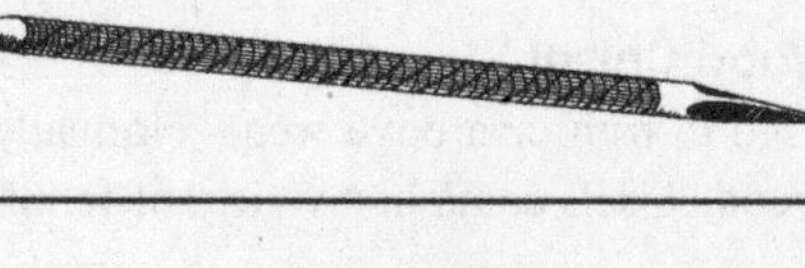

Also called a rat-tail file. Used to smooth round openings.

### Jack Plane

Also called a fore plane. Used to dimension or smooth a wooden workpiece.

## DRILLING AND BORING TOOLS

Drilling and boring tools make holes in materials, often in order to join or fasten pieces together.

### Brace

Used to manually drill holes in wood or provide extra torque in driving screws. Bits that can be used with this tool are:

1. Expansive bit—an adjustable spurred cutter, which allows holes of various sizes to be drilled in wood.
2. Auger bit (twist bit)—various sizes of helical twists and a prominent lead screw are characteristic of this form of bit for drilling holes in wood.
3. Turn screw bit—used to drive screws.
4. Ream—used only to bevel or widen the opening of a pipe.

### Power Drill

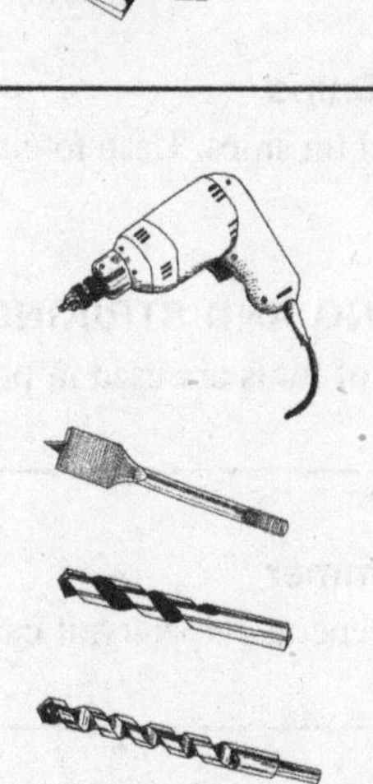

Used in principally the same way as a brace, the difference being in speed and flexibility of using various accessories (e.g., sanding disks, buffs, wire brushes, lathe, etc.). Bits that can be used with this tool are:

1. Spade bit (flat bit)—used to drill wide holes in wood or plastics.
2. Twist drill (Morse drill)—used to drill holes in wood, metal, or plastics.
3. Masonry drill—a carbide tip allows this bit to be used to drill holes in material such as concrete, marble, stone, etc.
4. Countersink bit—used to create a recess hole to accommodate the head of a countersink screw.

**Center Punch**
Used to mark and guide the placement of a drill point.

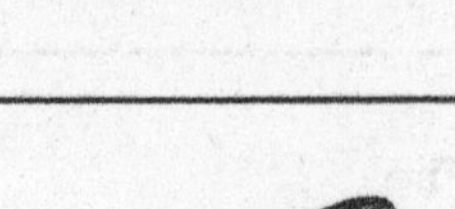

**Wood Chisel**
Used to trim or groove wood. Normally used with a soft-faced mallet. Wood chisels come in a variety of forms and sizes.

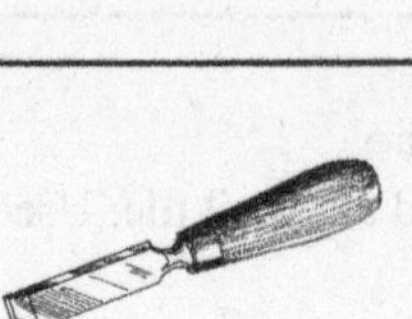

**Nail Punch**
Also called a nail set. Used as an instrument to drive nails below the surface of a wooden workpiece.

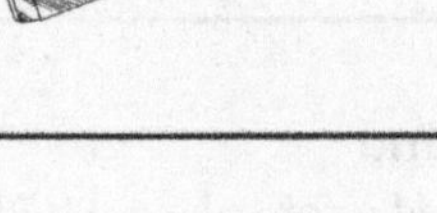

**Awl**
Used to start holes in wood to accommodate nails or screws.

**Bolt Cutters**
Used to cut steel rod, bolts, chains, and locks through the use of compound leverage.

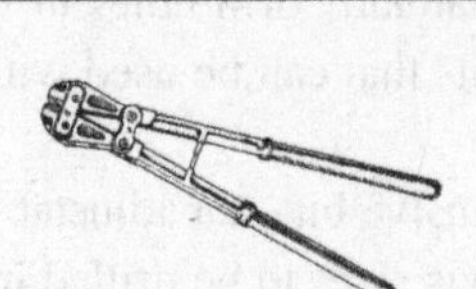

**Cold Chisel**
Also called a flat chisel. Used to chip or cut cold metal such as rivets, chain links, bolts, etc.

**Straight Snips**
Also called tin snips. Used to cut thin sheet metal.

## POUNDING AND STRIKING TOOLS

A number of tools are used in pounding and striking.

**Claw Hammer**
Used for general carpentry, it can pull and extract nails.

**Ball Peen Hammer**
Also called an engineer's hammer. Used in metalworking such as rivet setting or metal forging.

**Club Hammer**

Also called a hand-drilling hammer. Used for heavy-duty work involving masonry drills or chisels. The head can weigh up to four pounds.

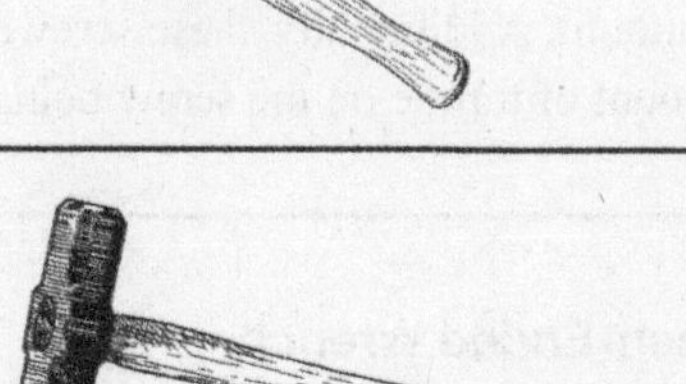

**Sledgehammer**

Used for heavy-duty work such as breaking concrete, driving posts, etc. The head can weigh from two to twenty pounds.

**Soft-Faced Mallet**

Also called a rubber mallet. Used to drive materials without causing any damage to the tools involved or to the surface of a workpiece.

## TURNING TOOLS

A number of tools are used for turning, such as to fasten screws.

**Conventional Straight-Shank Screwdriver**

Also called a standard, slotted, or flat-head screwdriver. Used to drive slotted head screws.

**Phillips Screwdriver**

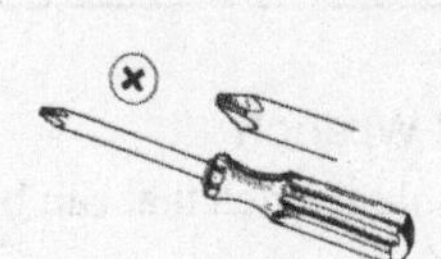

Used to drive Phillips-head screws (cross-shaped). Its design enhances one's grip compared to that achieved with conventional slotted- or flared-tip screwdrivers.

**Torx Screwdriver**

Used when a fair amount of torque is required on a screw. This design enhances your grip still more than a Phillips or flare-tipped screwdriver.

**Stubby Screwdriver**

Also called a close-quarter screwdriver. Used to drive screws where space is fairly restricted.

**Jeweler's Screwdriver**

Used in driving or loosening relatively small screws such as those found in eyeglass hinges, clocks, wristwatches, etc.

**Offset Screwdriver**
Also called a cranked screwdriver. Used when standard screwdrivers cannot fit. Additionally, these screwdrivers enable the user to place a fair amount of torque on the screw being driven.

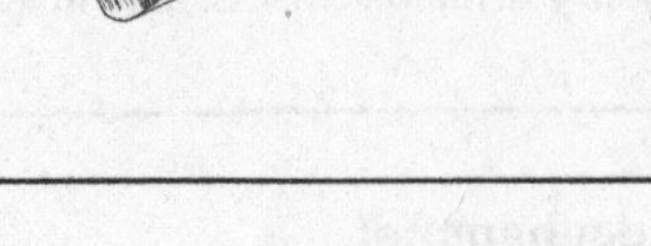

**Open-Ended Wrench**
Used to tighten or loosen nuts and bolts from the side. This is advantageous over other wrenches in cramped areas where a nut is obstructed by something directly overhead.

**Box Wrench**
Used to tighten or loosen nuts and bolts. A closed wrench of this design allows for significantly more torque to be applied without the fear of the wrench slipping and stripping the nut. Its drawback is that it takes more time to use this wrench than the open variety.

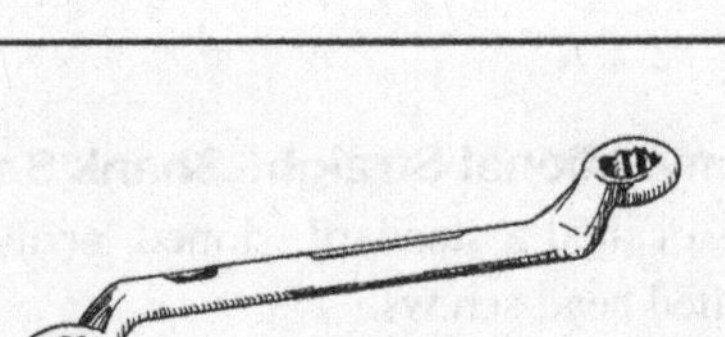

**Offset Wrench**
Designed to be able to reach a nut or bolt in a recessed area over an obstruction. These wrenches also have the advantage of allowing hand clearance when tightening a bolt or nut flush with a work surface.

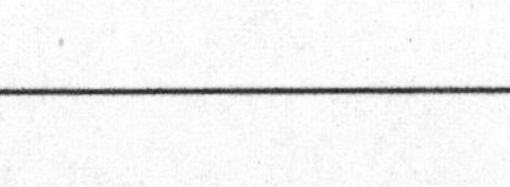
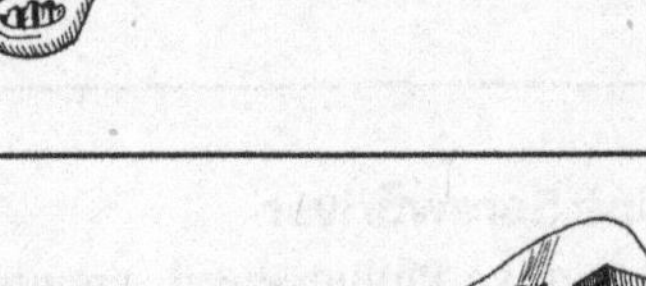
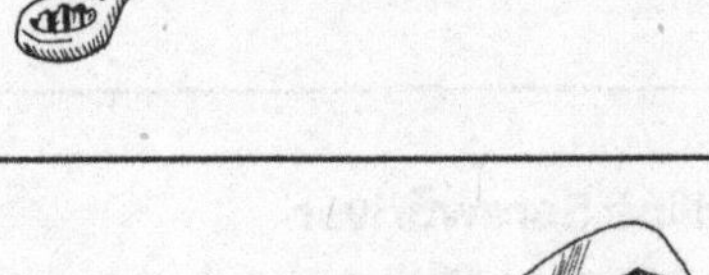

**Crescent Wrench**
An adjustable wrench that can be used to tighten or loosen nuts and bolts of varied sizes.

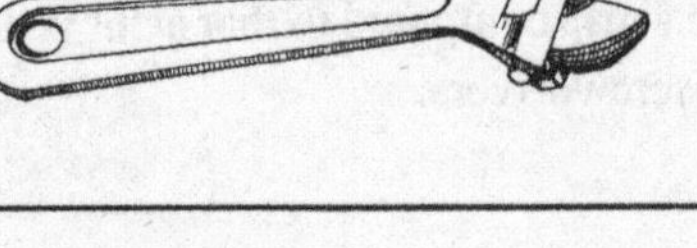

**Monkey Wrench**
Also called a screw wrench. Another adjustable wrench that can be used to tighten or loosen nuts and bolts of varied sizes. This wrench has a heavier design than a crescent wrench.

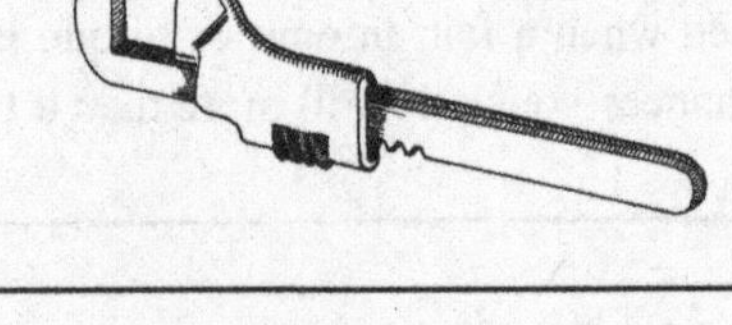

**Stilson Wrench**
Also called a pipe wrench. An adjustable wrench used to grip round objects like metal pipes or steel rods.

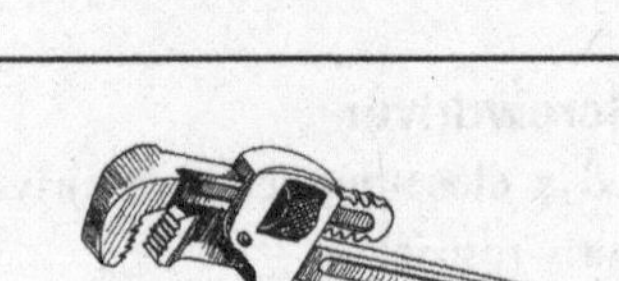
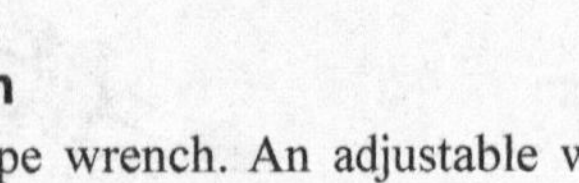

**Strap Wrench**
Used for gripping and turning pipes without harming the exterior finish.

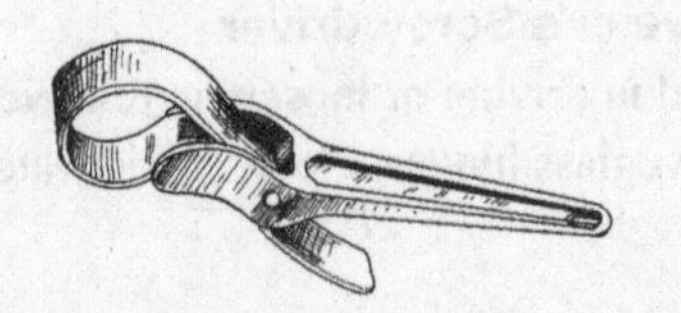

**Socket Wrench**

One of the most common wrenches used today. Nuts and bolts can be quickly tightened or loosened with the ratchet handle, thus sparing the need to readjust for another grip as with most other wrenches.

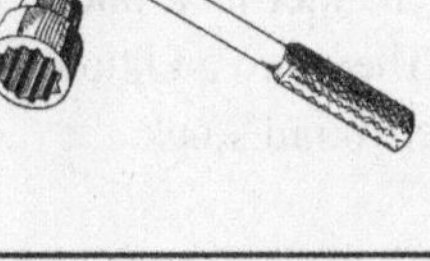

**Torque Wrench**

Used to apply a calibrated force when tightening a nut or bolt as recommended by the manufacturer.

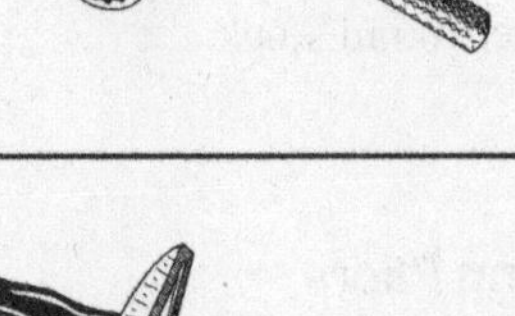

**Spanner Wrench**

Also called a hook spanner. Used to turn special nuts or hose couplings.

**Allen Wrench**

Also called a setscrew wrench. An L-shaped hexagonal key used to tighten or loosen a machined setscrew.

**Crocodile Wrench**

Also called a bulldog wrench. Used to grip and turn round stock such as pipe or steel rod.

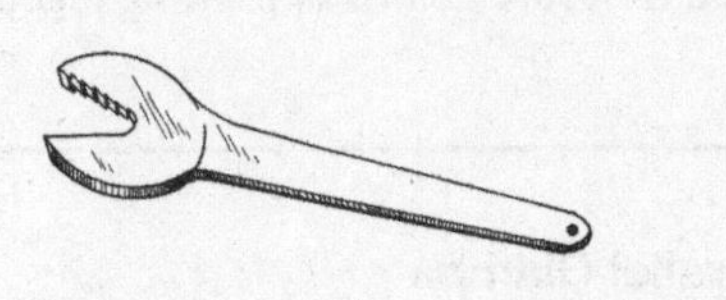

**Tap Wrench**

Used when cutting internal screw threads with a tap. It allows for a better and more even grip when applying pressure.

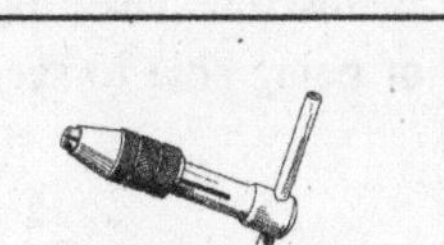

**GRABBING TOOLS**

A variety of tools are used to grab.

**Needle-Nose Pliers**

Also called snipe-nosed pliers. Used to shape or cut thin-strand wire and grip small items (e.g., washers, nuts, etc.) in confined spaces.

**Slip Joint Pliers**

Used like ordinary pliers, but a pivot allows for two different jaw settings.

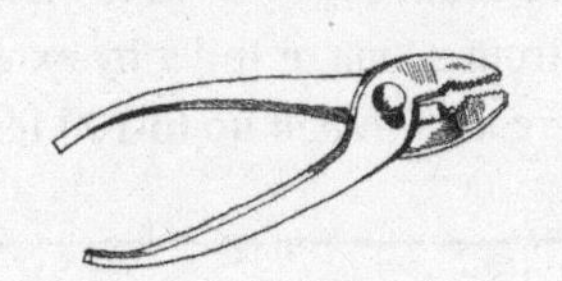

**Curved Jaw Pliers**
Also called channel lock pliers. Used much in the same manner as slip joint pliers. There are additional settings to adjust jaw widths to accommodate larger round stock.

**Side Cutting Pliers**
Used to cut metal wire.

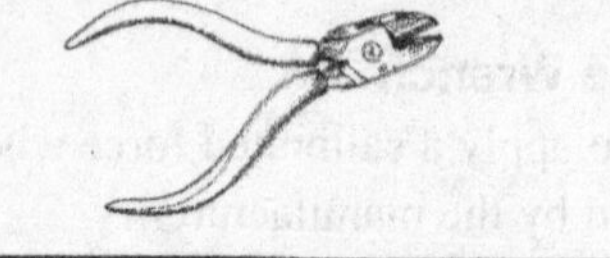

**End Cutting Pliers**
Used to crop metal wire close to a work surface.

## FASTENING TOOLS

A number of tools are use to grab and hold materials.

**Pipe Clamps**
Used to secure boards or framing together while they are bonded by glue.

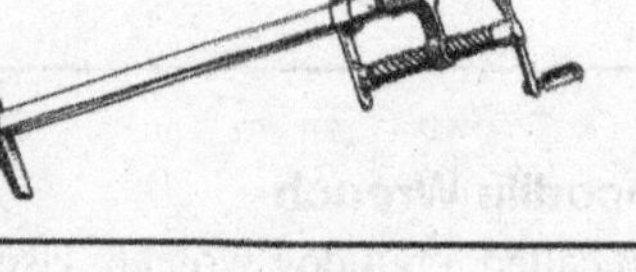

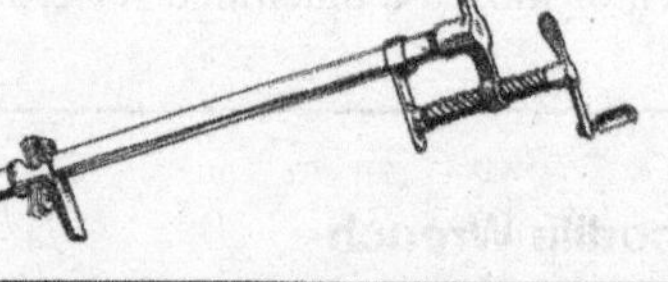

**Parallel Clamps**
Also called a handscrew. Used principally like pipe clamps with the added feature of being able to secure an angled object, whether wood or metal.

**C-Clamps**
Used to clamp wood or metal for various purposes.

## SPECIALIZED TOOLS

A number of different tools are used in various trades for different tasks.

**Drain Snake**
Also called a drain auger. Used to clear or remove debris that obstructs a drain pipe from a sink or toilet by extending into the piping. Some drain augers can reach through up to 100 feet of pipe.

**Plunger**
Used to clear debris blocking a drain trap by creating back pressure on the obstruction.

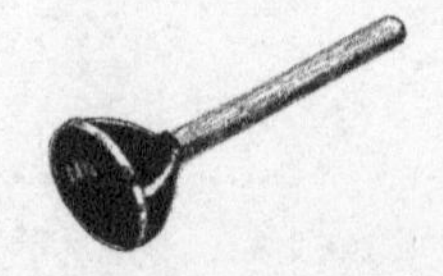

---

**Pipe Cutter**
Also called a wheel cutter. Used to cut metal pipe to the desired size.

---

**Propane Torch**
Used as a heat source for brazing and soldering pipework.

---

**Soldering Iron**
Used to heat metal and solder to form a joint.

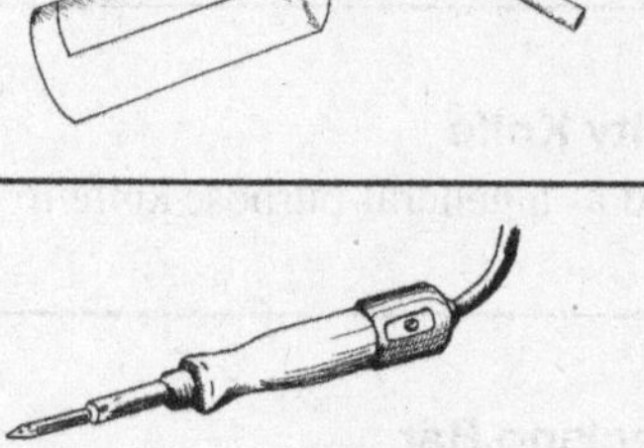

---

**Vise Grips**
Also called plier wrench. Used to grip round metal stock or sheet metal firmly without much effort.

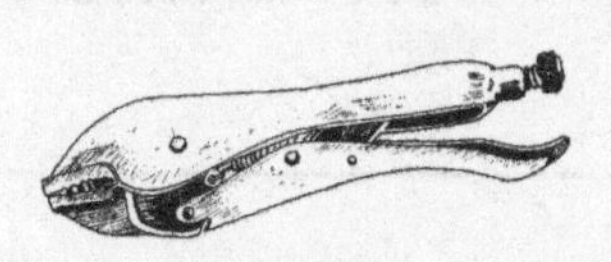

---

**Arc Welder**
Used to fuse pieces of metal together using electrical current (rated in amperage).

---

**Cutting Torch**
Also called an acetylene torch. Used to cut metal or thick steel by means of a flame generated from an oxygen and acetylene mix.

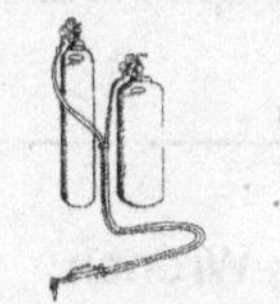

---

**Machinist Vise**
Used to secure or hold a metal workpiece.

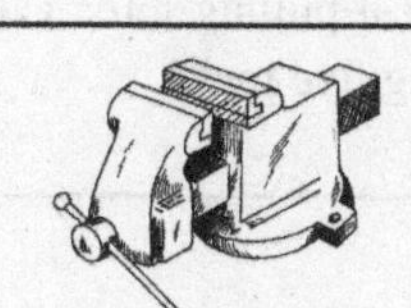

---

**Bench Grinder**
Used to sharpen tools or remove rough edging from a metal workpiece. Optional wire brush or buffer wheel can further clean and polish metal work.

---

**Whetstone**
A rectangular stone comprised of gritty abrasive that is used to sharpen tools manually.

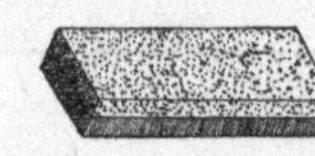

### Glass Cutter

Used to score a line across glass. Applying pressure by bending the glass then causes it to break along the scored line. The notches on the back of the cutter are designed to remove small pieces of glass from the desired cut or line.

### Utility Knife

Used as a general-purpose knife to cut various materials.

### Wrecking Bar

Also known as a crowbar. Used as a lever to pry things apart or remove nails.

### Caulking Gun

Used to apply sealants to various joints such as those found in windows, door frames, roofing vents, and bathroom tile.

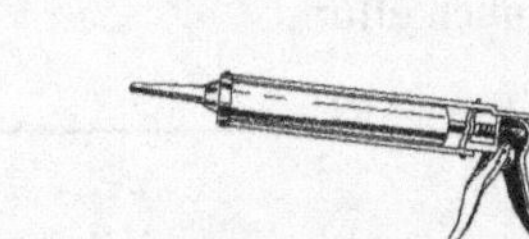

### Staple Gun

Used to drive staples in attaching various materials together.

### Come-Along Wrench

Used to exert a pulling force (vertical or horizontal) on heavy objects (not exceeding five tons).

### Mason's Trowel

Also called a brick trowel. Used to spread, shape, and smooth mortar when working with bricks or concrete block.

### Skimmer Float

Used to acquire a smooth finish when working with either wet plaster or concrete.

### Lopping Shear

Used to prune back branches of shrubs or trees.

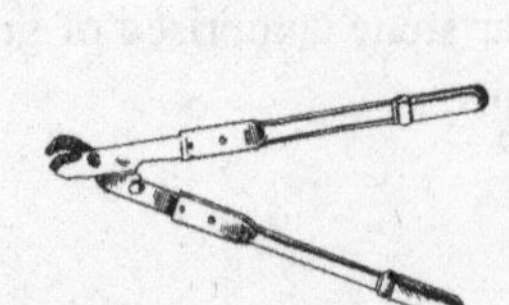

**Sickle**
Used to cut tall weeds or grass.

**Wedge Felling Axe**
A cutting tool used for felling trees and chopping or hewing wood.

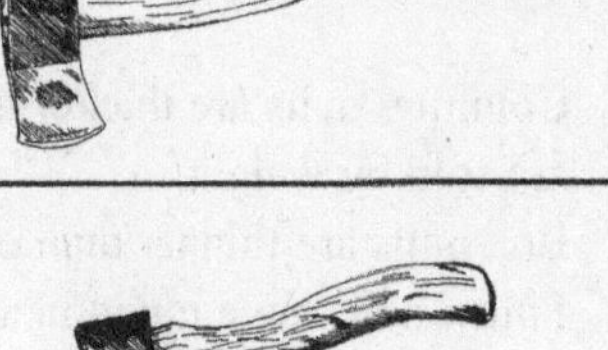

**Hatchet**
Used to trim wood and doubles as a hammer.

**Pickaxe**
Used to indent, pierce, or break up hard material such as concrete, asphalt, hardpan soils, etc.

**Shovel**
Used to lift and throw earth or other materials.

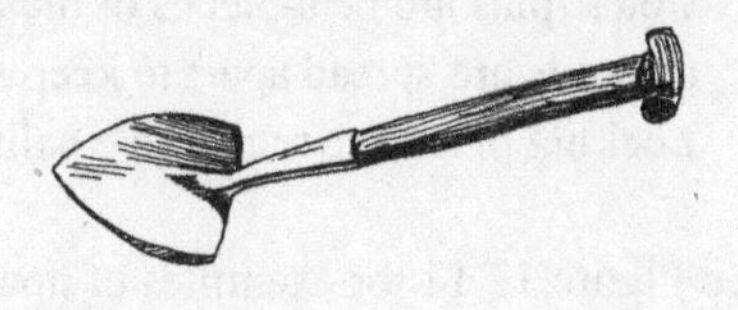

## FASTENING TECHNIQUES

Materials can be joined together in a variety of ways. Each method has strengths and weaknesses. Choosing a fastening technique (and a fastener) depends on what needs to be connected together (the types of materials and how thick they are), where (your kitchen or a hospital operating room?), and what type of join is needed. Some common fastening techniques include:

- *welding*—heating the materials, usually metal, to their melting points; as they cool they join together
- *soldering*—cementing two materials, usually metal, together by adding a thin layer of molten metal to the join and letting it cool
- *clamping*—joining materials together through the mechanical means of bracing them between a vise or a press
- *hingeing*—using a movable joint to connect two materials
- *mortise and tenon joints*—joining two materials together by creating a hole in one and a peg in the other so they fit together
- *stapling* or *clipping*—using a piece of bent wire pushed through or bent over two materials to join them together
- *crimping*—folding the two materials together in a way that keeps them from coming undone
- *tying*—using wire, rope, or another fiber to hold two materials together
- *energy forces*—using friction, suction, or magnetic force to bond materials together

Mechanical fasteners (such as bolts) and adhesives (such as glue) can also be used to join materials together. See "Mechanical Fasteners" and "Adhesives" in this chapter for more information.

## MECHANICAL FASTENERS

A huge number of mechanical fasteners are used to connect materials together. They are generally divided into two categories, *threaded* and *nonthreaded.*

### Nonthreaded Fasteners

The main nonthreaded types of fasteners are nails and rivets, plus special fasteners like cotter pins and locking pins.

- Common nails are thicker and stronger than other types of nails. They come in a wide variety of sizes and are sold by weight.
- Box nails are thinner than common nails. They do not hold as strongly as common nails do.
- Finish nails have round heads and can be made flush with the surface.
- Brads are like very small finish nails.
- Casing nails are smaller than common nails and have very small heads (for uses where you don't want the head showing)
- Spikes are very large nails used for very heavy materials.
- Double-headed nails (duplex nails) have two heads and are often used for temporary construction since they are easier to remove than other types of nails.
- Rivets are short metal pins with a head. The end (without the head) is flattened or opened to prevent the rivet from slipping out of position. Sometimes a cap is put on the end to hold the rivet in position.
- Cotter pins are bent pieces of metal with one end usually shorter than the other. Once inserted into the join, the ends are spread apart to keep the pin from slipping out of the hole.
- Locking pins have retractable balls or flanges that stick out from the end of the pin to secure the pin in place.

See Figure 12.14 for examples of nonthreaded fasteners.

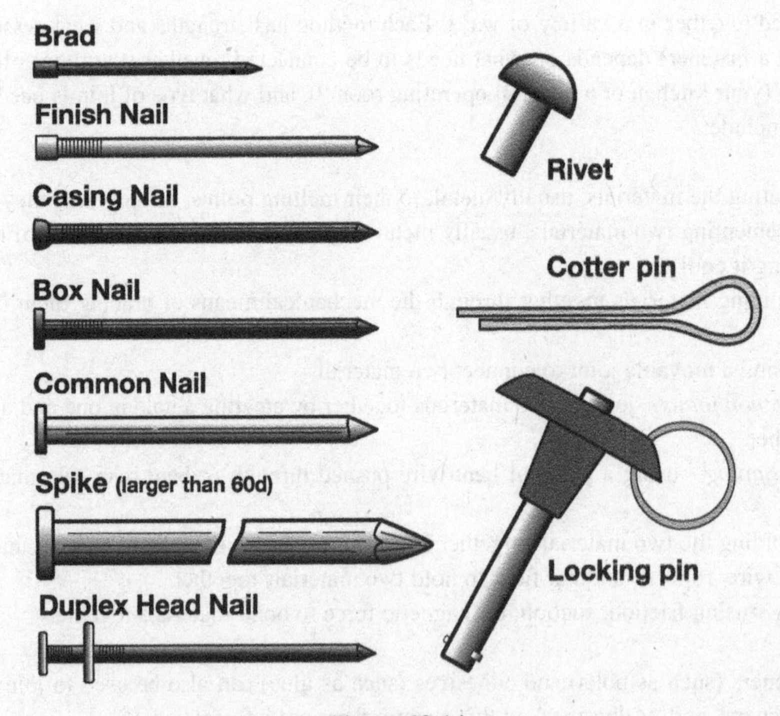


Figure 12.14

### Threaded Fasteners

Threaded fasteners include bolts and screws. Bolts and screws mainly differ in that you generally need to use a nut to fasten a bolt (although this is not true of all types of bolts). Threads measured in U.S. measurements may have thread measures in threads per inch (TPI). A smaller threaded fastener usually has smaller threads, so more fit per inch.

Threaded fasteners measured in metric use thread pitch, which is the distance between threads. Thread gauges make the measurement process easier. Threads come in coarse or fine, the difference being how tall the thread is (a taller thread has more gripping power, but a finer thread may be needed for applications with smaller tolerances).

#### Bolts

Bolts come with various types of heads, such as hexagonal or round. Some have slotted heads so that they can be driven (same as a screw). Frequently they have partially smooth shafts (the entire shaft is not threaded). Common types include:

- Carriage bolts, which generally have round heads, are used for many wood-to-wood connections. They range in diameter from ¼" to 1", and from ¾" to 20" in length.
- Machine bolts are usually used for metal-to-metal connections. They come in many head types. They come in diameters of ¼" to 3", and in lengths from ¾" to more than 30".
- Stove bolts usually have slotted heads, either flat or round, and can be used to connect metal to metal, wood to wood, or metal to wood. They have a diameter of ⅛" to ⅜", and range from ⅜" to 6" in length.
- Toggle bolts have spring-loaded flanges that unfold to secure the bolt in place. Diameters generally run from ⅛" to ⅜", and lengths from 2" to 6".
- Molly bolts, also called expansion bolts, come sheathed in a sleeve that expands as the bolt is driven into place. The sleeve secures the bolt.

See Figure 12.15 for examples of common bolts.

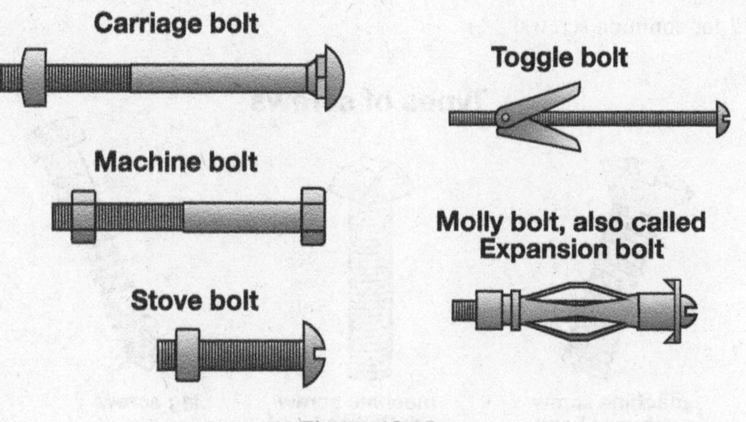

Figure 12.15

#### Nuts and Washers

Bolts are often secured in place with nuts and washers. Nuts have a threaded hole that corresponds with a bolt's threads. Nuts are often configured in the shape of a hexagon, as this allows for easy fastening, but there are many variations. Wing nuts, for example, which have two extensions or "wings," are meant to be finger tightened. Cap nuts (also called acorn nuts) have a rounded dome that covers the end of the bolt.

Washers are used to spread the load of the nut (especially to prevent damage to the surface of the material being bolted), to create spacing, and in some cases to help lock the bolt into place.

See Figure 12.16 for illustrations of common nuts and washers.

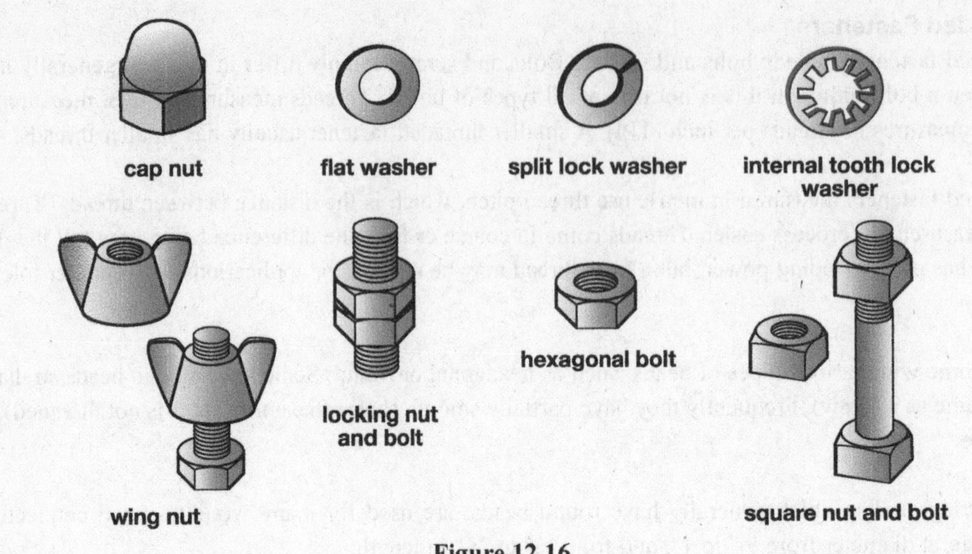


Figure 12.16

**Screws**

Screws come in a variety of sizes (diameters and lengths), with a variety of head shapes. Different types of threads are used in different applications. For example, wood screws have coarse threads, which helps them grip and prevents stripping. Some screws alternate high threads with low threads (high-low screws), and are used to fasten materials like plastic.

Screws can also be distinguished by the way they are driven. Slotted screws use a standard screwdriver; Phillips-head screws (cross-slotted) use a Phillips screwdriver.

Two other common kinds of screws are self-tapping screws, which are designed to create their own holes, and lag screws, also called lag bolts, which are used for large load-bearing pieces of wood.

See Figure 12.17 for common screws.

**Types of screws**

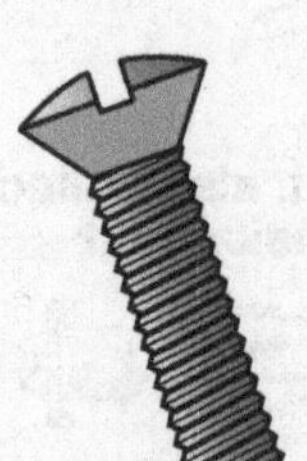

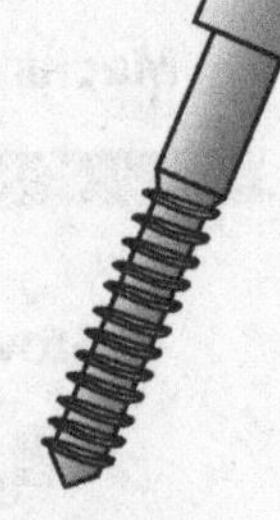


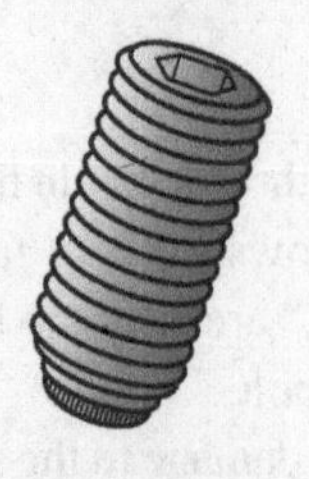


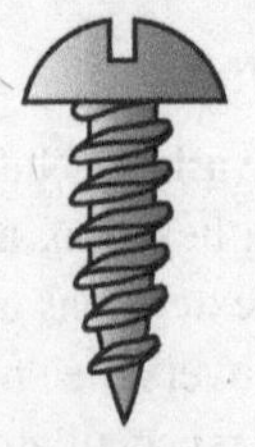


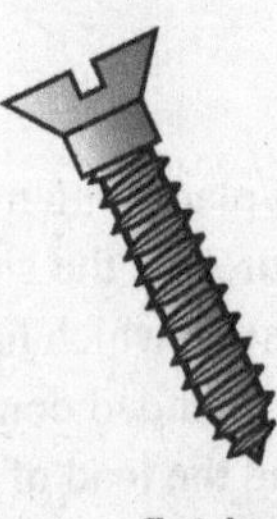


Figure 12.17

## ADHESIVES

Adhesives are another kind of fastener. Unlike many mechanical fasteners, adhesives can't be removed without damaging the joined materials, so these are generally permanent bonds. Different kinds of adhesives are used for different purposes and to adhere different kinds of materials. They each have benefits and drawbacks. A few of the most common adhesives are:

- *White glue*, like the kind you used in elementary school, is easy to use, is fairly nontoxic and easy to clean, and can bond porous materials (like paper) together. It takes a long time to set ("cure") and is not very strong.
- *Epoxy* can be used on most materials to create a strong bond. Curing time varies, but can be slow.
- *Contact adhesive* (sometimes called contact cement) can be used to bond two different types of material (like wood to plastic). It can be very strong.
- *Polyurethane* can be used on most materials. It's waterproof, an advantage in some situations. It can cure quickly.
- *Silicone* can bond a variety of materials. The bond is not strong but it is flexible.
- *Thermal adhesives* require heat to work (think of a glue gun). Different types set at different speeds; generally as the adhesive cools, the bond cures. Thermal adhesives are suitable for materials that won't be damaged by heat.

## PLANS AND PATTERNS

A basic understanding of how plans and patterns work may prove useful on this subtest. A plan is an overall illustration of how a project is intended to look. It does not include all of the details about how the project will be built (for a large project, the technical drawing that would include that information is called a blueprint).

There are several basic kinds of plans: overhead view, which is the simplest approach and shows how something would look if you were staring down at it; elevated view, which shows the project vertically from one direction; and cross-section, which shows the project as if it were cut through.

Plans use either architectural scale (feet and inches) or engineer's scale (which can use metric or feet and inches, but inches will be recorded as decimals). Be sure you know which scale the plan is using.

Common symbols represent doors, windows, etc. Most plans have a key that shows what these are.

See Figure 12.18 for a floor plan. This is an example of an overhead plan.

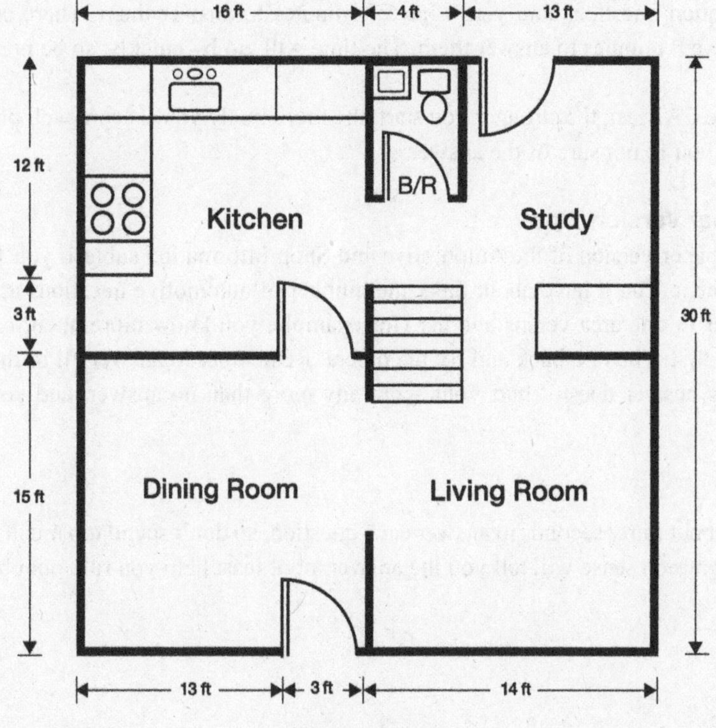


Figure 12.18

Patterns are distinguished from plans in that they are for smaller-scale projects (a doll house versus an actual house) and generally give enough detail for you to be able to build the project. See Figure 12.19 for an example of a simple plan.

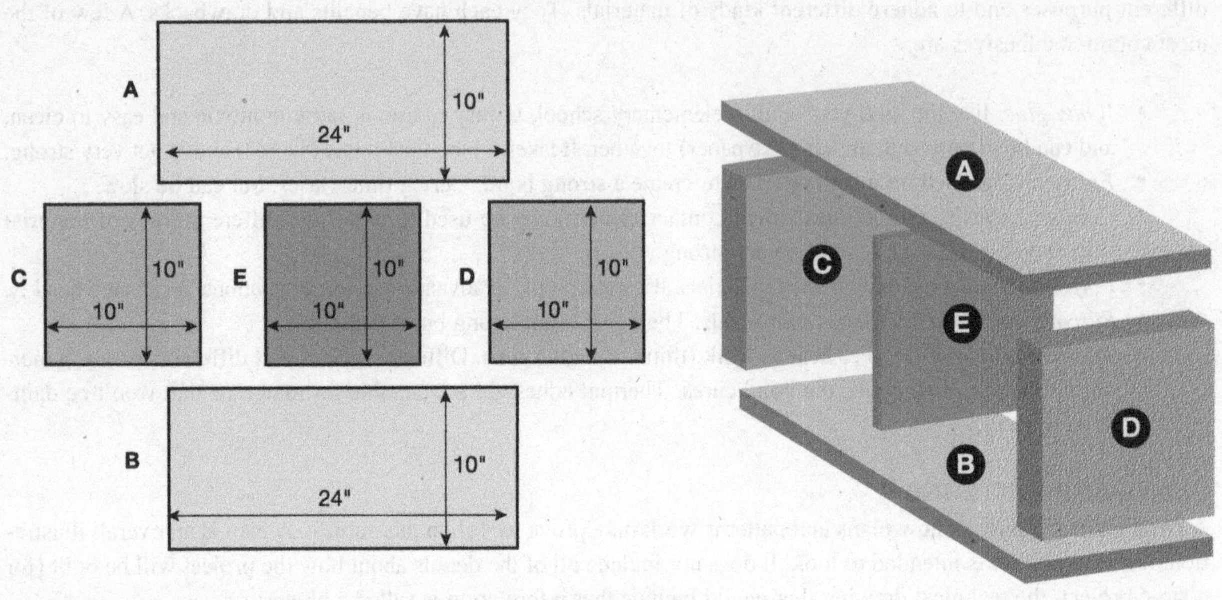


Figure 12.19

## STRATEGIES FOR SUCCEEDING ON THE AUTOMOTIVE AND SHOP INFORMATION SUBTEST

It's unlikely that you'll be able to do well on the Automotive and Shop Information Subtest if you don't have a good familiarity with the material, but there are a few strategies that can help you succeed on test day.

### CAT Version Tips

In the CAT version, the Automotive Information is on a separate subtest from the Shop Information. There are 11 Automotive Information questions and you'll have 6 minutes to answer them. There are 11 Shop Information questions and you'll have 5 minutes to answer them. The time will zip by quickly, so be prepared to jump right into each test.

As always with the CAT test, the stronger you start, the more likely you'll score well on the test. But do answer every question, even if you're not sure of the answer.

### Pencil-and-Paper Version Tips

In the pencil-and-paper version of the Automotive and Shop Information subtest, you'll have 25 questions and 11 minutes to answer them. You'll have about the same number of automotive questions as you'll have shop questions. If you're stronger in one area versus another (for example, you know more about car care than shop tools) answer those questions first. Then go back and try the others. Remember to answer all of the questions, even if you have to guess. A wrong answer doesn't hurt your score any more than no answer, and you may be able to guess correctly.

### Overall Tips

You'll only have about thirty seconds to answer each question, so don't spend too much time on any one answer. Remember that often common sense will tell you the answer, or at least help you rule out obviously wrong answers.

# CHAPTER 13

# Mechanical Comprehension (MC)

The Mechanical Comprehension subtest does not count toward the Armed Forces Qualification Test (AFQT) score that you need to achieve to be eligible for military service. But the score is used to help determine what jobs you may be able to perform in the armed forces. A strong showing on the Mechanical Comprehension subtest can ensure a greater number of opportunities for you.

Remember that some subtest scores are combined together in order to determine whether you're eligible for a particular job, so you'll need to do well on each of the related subtests in order to be considered for the position you want. It's common for Mechanical Comprehension to be combined with General Science and/or Electronics Information and/or Automotive and Shop Information to determine your eligibility for a particular job.

Also be aware that some of the questions on the Mechanical Comprehension subtest may require a solid understanding of Arithmetic Reasoning and Mathematical Knowledge. You can expect to be asked questions that require the memorization of a few formulas and the ability to do some basic calculations.

Be sure to review the "Physical Science" section in Chapter 10, General Science, to ensure you have a solid understanding of the calculations involved in physical science, some of which may be present on the Mechanical Comprehension subtest.

Many operations and mechanical jobs require a good score on the Mechanical Comprehension subtest.

## WHAT THE TEST MEASURES

The Mechanical Comprehension subtest measures your knowledge of information about mechanical principles, including mechanical motion. You'll need to know the basic properties of various materials and understand how simple machines (like levers) work, as well as compound machines (which are basically two or more simple machines put together). You'll also need to know concepts such as force, lift, and friction, and be able to make basic calculations about efficiency and mechanical advantage.

While the basic concepts can be learned through study and review, if you haven't spent much time putting the principles into action, you'll be at a bit of a disadvantage on the test. If doing well on the Mechanical Comprehension section is important to the type of job you want to do in the military, but you have little previous experience, it may be worthwhile to enroll in a vocational class or to get involved in handyman or construction projects.

## MECHANICAL PRINCIPLES

Humankind learned early that in order to create more force to perform a specific job, one of two things was needed: either more workers or the use of simple machines. Machines can basically be classified in six general groups: lever, pulley, inclined plane, wheel and axle, screw, and wedge.

Regardless of how complicated a given machine is, one or a combination of these principles is always employed.

How does this work? Using a simple machine multiplies the amount of force you can use to move an object.

### Mechanical Advantage

For purposes of illustration, think of a plank of wood balanced on a pivot point, such as a teeter-totter. (For future reference, the pivot point is called the fulcrum.) If two different weights were placed on the plank at equal distances from the fulcrum, the side bearing the heavier weight would fall to touch the ground, lifting the lighter weight. However, if the heavier weight were moved closer to the fulcrum, eventually a balance would be struck. If the heavier weight was moved even closer to the fulcrum, the lighter weight could actually have enough force to lift the heavier weight. This concept is known as leverage or mechanical advantage.

Mechanical advantage is why one person can move large rocks with a pry bar, carry heavy loads using a wheelbarrow, or apply tremendous pressure with the jaws of vise grips.

To demonstrate the benefits of leverage quantitatively, the following equation can be applied:

$$\text{Effort} \times \text{Effort Distance} = \text{Resistance} \times \text{Resistance Distance}$$

Let's apply this formula to the following example:

*EXAMPLE 1*

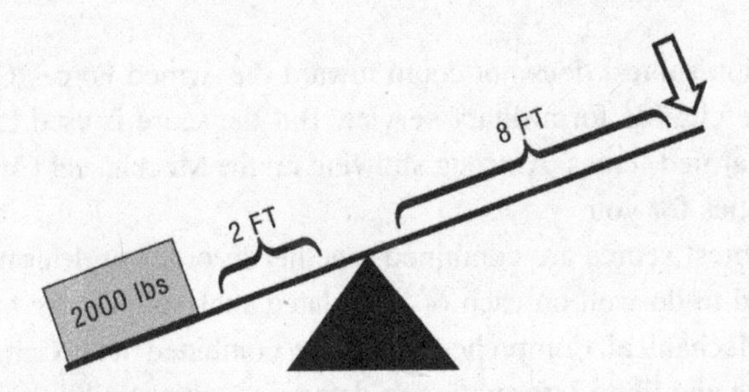


***A 2,000-pound (1 ton) weight is placed two feet from the fulcrum of the plank. How much effort would an individual have to exert on the opposite end of the plank, exactly 8 feet from the fulcrum, to balance the load?***

First, let's identify specifics as they relate to the equation. The 2,000-pound weight represents the resistance (that is, the resistance to lifting the object, or resistance to lift) and the 2-foot space between the weight and fulcrum is considered the resistance distance.

We are also told that the space between the fulcrum and where a force will be exerted is 8 feet. This is the effort distance. The unknown as represented by $x$ is the amount of force necessary to lift the weight.

If we plug this information into the equation, we are left with a simple proportion to figure:

$$x \bullet 8 \text{ feet} = 2000 \text{ pounds} \bullet 2 \text{ feet}$$

To determine $x$, divide effort distance into the product of the resistance and the resistance distance.

$$x = \frac{2000 \text{ pounds} \bullet 2 \text{ feet}}{8 \text{ feet}}$$

A quick calculation shows that $x = 500$ pounds.

Therefore, 500 pounds of force would be required. Given the proper conditions, you can see the dramatic results of leverage as opposed to trying to lift the 2,000-pound weight directly.

## SIMPLE MACHINES AND COMPOUND MACHINES

A simple machine is a mechanical device used to apply force. Simple machines may have moving parts but they do not have motors. Compound machines are two or more simple machines put together. For example, a hand-operated can opener is a compound machine. It contains a wheel and axle, gears, a lever, and a wedge.

### Levers

The example given in the "Mechanical Advantage" section in this chapter is a simple machine called a lever. Using a lever multiplies your ability to work. Let's look at another example of how a lever can multiply your force.

*EXAMPLE 2*

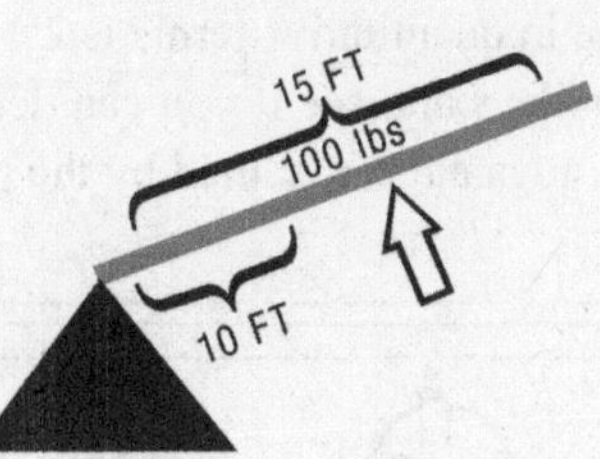


***A wooden beam 15 feet long and weighing 100 pounds needs to be moved. If lift is applied 10 feet from the fulcrum, how much effort is required to lift the beam at that point?***

Again, identify the specifics as they relate to the equation discussed earlier. The weight of the beam itself, 100 pounds, is the resistance to lift. Since the fulcrum is at the base of the beam, it would be an easy assumption to make that the beam's entire length of 15 feet would serve as the resistance distance.

However, the beam's center of mass must be taken into consideration. Since the beam would be the heaviest to lift at its middle versus either end, we must only figure $\frac{1}{2}$ the beam's length as the true resistance distance. Therefore, if we place these numbers into the equation, the lift requirement will easily be determined:

$$x \bullet 10 \text{ feet} = 100 \text{ pounds} \bullet 7.5 \text{ feet}$$

$$x = \frac{100 \text{ pounds} \bullet 7.5 \text{ feet}}{10 \text{ feet}}$$

$$x = 75 \text{ pounds of effort required to lift the beam}$$

Note that the mechanical advantage of Example 1 far exceeds that seen in Example 2. The location of the fulcrum plays a crucial role in leverage effectiveness.

### Pulleys

Pulleys are another means of gaining mechanical advantage and making a job easier. Pulleys can be used in a wide variety of ways to pull or lift heavy objects. They can either be in a fixed or movable position. For an illustration, look at the example in Figure 13.1.

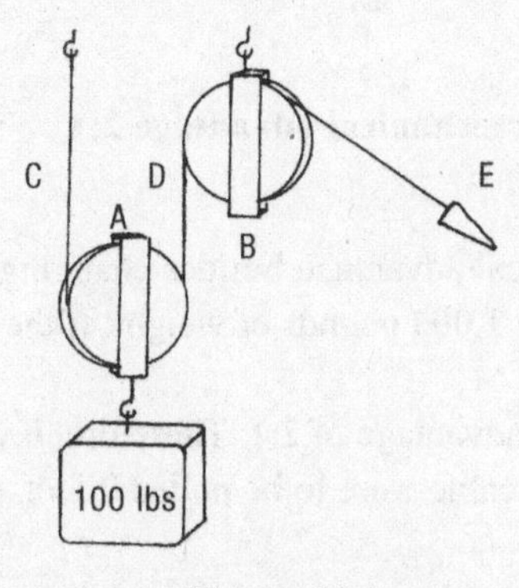


**Figure 13.1**

The pulley apparatus shown is depicted lifting a 100-pound weight. Since the weight is evenly distributed between cables C and D, each cable would be responsible for supporting 50 pounds.

Therein lies the mechanical advantage, because only 50 pounds of pulling force is needed at point E to lift the weight. Therefore, the mechanical advantage in quantitative terms is 2:1 (resistance divided by effort, or 100 ÷ 50).

Let's look at another arrangement of pulleys and see if you can determine how much force will be required to lift the weight and what kind of mechanical advantage is gained by the pulleys. Look at Figure 13.2.

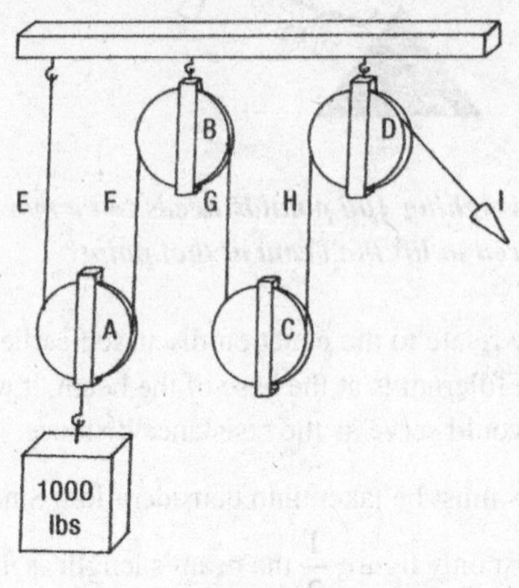

**Figure 13.2**

Since the weight is evenly distributed between cables E, F, G, and H, each cable would be responsible for supporting 250 pounds. Thus, it would require only 250 pounds of pulling force to lift the 1,000-pound weight. If you figured that the mechanical advantage was 4 you were correct. (Resistance of 1,000 pounds divided by 250 pounds of effort.)

What should be apparent at this point is that what is gained in force, we sacrifice in distance, or vice versa. This basic law applies to all forms of simple machinery. Let's look at the sample pulley arrangements below to see this principle at work:

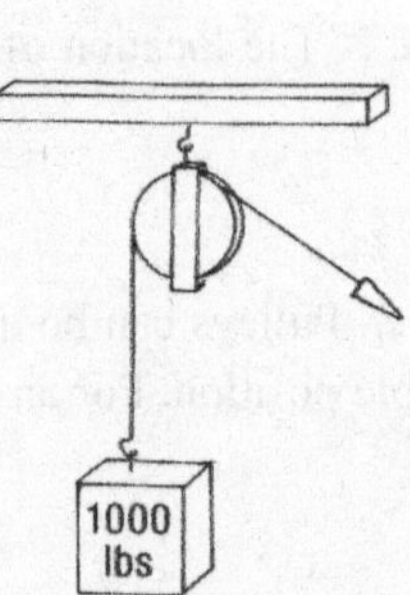


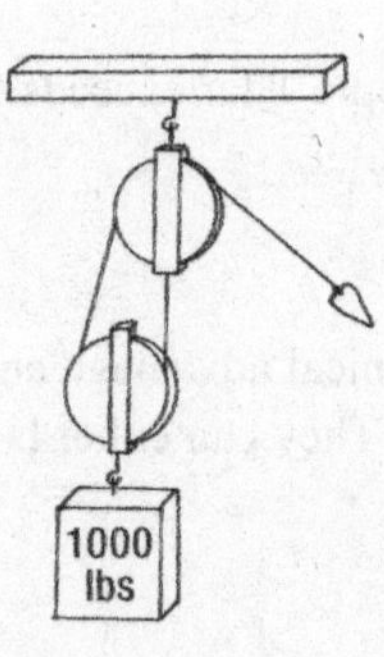


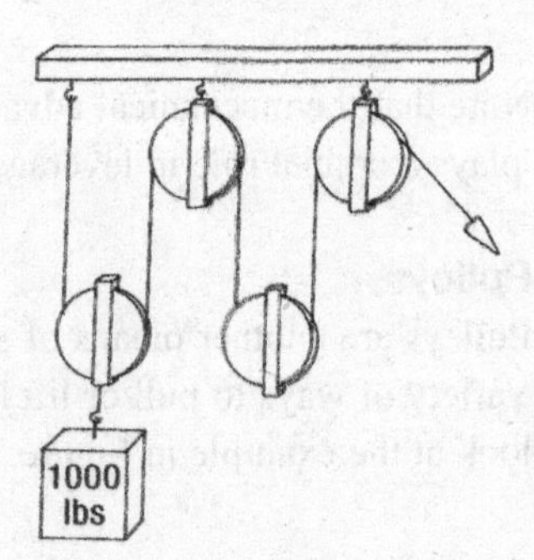


**mechanical advantage 1:1** **mechanical advantage 2:1** **mechanical advantage 4:1**

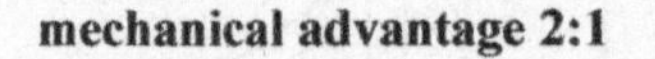

Example A does not have any mechanical advantage besides changing the direction the cable can be pulled. It would require 1,000 pounds of pull to lift the 1,000 pounds of weight. If the cable is pulled 2 feet, the weight will be lifted 2 feet. This is a 1 to 1 proportion.

Example B demonstrates a mechanical advantage of 2:1. Therefore, it would only require 500 pounds of pull to lift the 1,000-pound weight. However, if the cable were to be pulled 2 feet, the 1,000-pound weight would be raised only 1 foot.

Example C illustrates a pulley system that has a mechanical advantage of 4:1. It requires only 250 pounds of pull to lift the 1,000-pound weight. In this example, if the cable was pulled 2 feet, the 1,000-pound weight would be lifted only half a foot.

The correlation made apparent by these examples is that:

$$\text{Effort} = \frac{\text{Weight (Resistance)}}{\text{Mechanical Advantage}}$$

Also:

**Length of pull = Height (Lift) • Mechanical Advantage**

## Inclined Planes

If a truck driver had an extremely heavy barrel (300 pounds) to load, he would be considered foolish to attempt picking it up directly. Chances are the amount of force required to do that would exceed the driver's physical limitations. Back injury or rupture could result. On the other hand, if a ramp were used to load the barrel into the truck, significantly less effort would be required. Using an inclined plane such as the ramp gives the driver a distinct mechanical advantage.

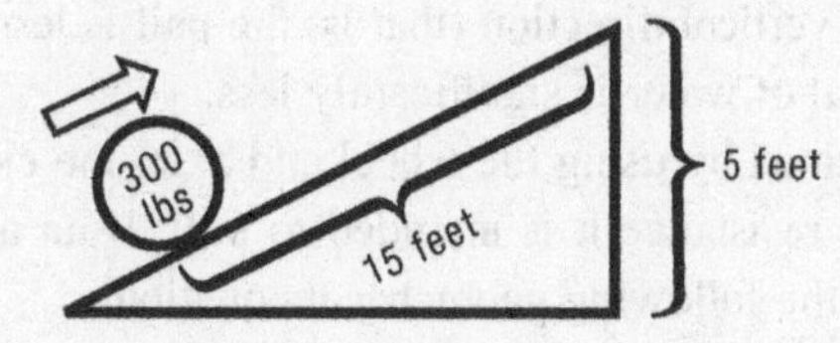


To quantify this advantage, the length of the inclined plane (effort distance) must be divided by the height of the inclined plane (resistance distance). So if the plank is 15 feet long and the truck bed is 5 feet off the ground, the mechanical advantage would be: 15 feet ÷ 5 feet, or 3:1.

To determine the amount of force required to load the barrel, use the same kind of formula applied for solving leverage problems.

**Effort • Length of Inclined Plane (Effort Distance) = Resistance • Height (Resistance Distance)**

**Effort • 15 feet = 300 pounds • 5 feet**

$$\text{Effort} = \frac{\text{300 pounds} \bullet \text{5 feet}}{\text{15 feet}} = \text{100 pounds}$$

Therefore, 100 pounds of effort is required to load the barrel.

## Wedges

In principle, wedges are similar to inclined planes. The only difference is that we use a wedge to push under or between objects that are to be moved instead of moving objects up an incline to gain mechanical advantage. A wood-splitting wedge is a good example. As the wedge is driven further into the end of the big log, more pressure is exerted against the grain, causing the log to eventually split.

See Figure 13.3 for an example.

Figure 13.3

Generally, the mechanical advantage of a wedge can be found by dividing the length of its slope by the width of the widest end, that is, the end opposite the point.

### Wheel and Axle

In general terms, a larger wheel is connected to a rod or axle that performs work, or which turns a smaller wheel that performs work. The force required to turn the larger wheel connected to the smaller wheel or axle bearing resistance is significantly less than that required to turn the smaller wheel or axle alone.

Therein lies the distinct mechanical advantage that a wheel and axle can provide.

A good example of this would be the crank mechanism or windlass positioned above an open water well. One end of the coiled rope is secured to the axle itself, while the other end is tied to a large pail. As the axle is turned by the attached crank to unwind the coil of rope, the pail is lowered into the well to retrieve water. When the crank is turned in the opposite direction, the pail of water which represents the resistance is hoisted to the surface. Outside of the advantage of directing pull in a true vertical direction (that is, the pail is less prone to drag against the sides of the well), the lift required to hoist the pail of water is significantly less.

To measure the amount of force gained by using the wheel and axle, the circumference of the wheel and axle must be given along with the weight or resistance it is intended to pull. If an axle has a diameter of 4 inches, its circumference would be found by using the following geometrical equation:

$$\textbf{Circumference} = \pi\ (3.1416) \times \textbf{Diameter}$$

Therefore, the circumference of a 4-inch diameter axle is: $\pi\ (3.1416) \bullet 4 \text{ inches} = 12.566 \text{ inches}$

Once the circumferences of a wheel and axle are known, the following equation can be applied as a proportion to determine force or effort requirements to gain lift:

Force • Circumference of the larger wheel = Resistance • Circumference of the axle or smaller wheel. For example:

How much force would be required to raise a pail of water weighing 40 pounds if the crank turns a wheel with a circumference of 30 inches and the axle it connects to has a diameter of 6 inches?

Since the circumference of the axle must first be determined, we multiply $\pi$ (3.1416) with 6 inches to get 18.849 inches.

Now that both circumferences are known, we can easily figure the lift requirement using our equations.

$$X \bullet 30 \text{ inches} = 40 \text{ pounds} \bullet 18.849 \text{ inches}$$

$$X = \frac{40 \text{ pounds} \bullet 18.849 \text{ inches}}{30 \text{ inches}}$$

$$X = 25.13 \text{ pounds of force}$$

The mechanical advantage using this kind of device would be calculated by simply dividing the resistance by the force or effort required.

$$MA = R \div E$$

In this case, 40 pounds ÷ 25.13 pounds = 1.59 or a mechanical advantage of 1.59:1.

### Screws

Screws can be thought of as being very similar to wedges. They can be used to wedge into a variety of materials such as wood, plastics, and sheet metal, or harnessed to lift heavy objects as demonstrated by the use of a jackscrew. See Figure 13.4 for an example.

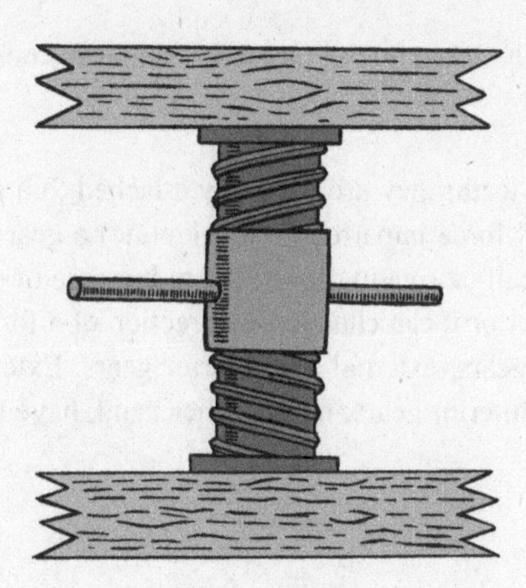

**Figure 13.4**

Screws are essentially rods with spiral threading. The distance between each two winds of the thread is called the pitch. If the screw is turned one complete revolution, the distance that the screw moves or performs work is determined by the pitch. To measure the mechanical advantage of a screw, the circumference of the circle through which the lever which moves the screw turns is divided by the pitch. For example:

***If a jackscrew handle is 16 inches long and the screw pitch is 1/□ of an inch, what is the mechanical advantage?***

First, we need to determine the potential circumference of the lever (handle) involved. Since the length of the handle is the radius of its turning circle, twice that length is the diameter. This product is multiplied by π (3.1416) to obtain the circumference.

$$16 \text{ inches} \bullet 2 \quad = 100.53$$

Divide this number by the screw pitch to determine the mechanical advantage.

$$100.53 \div \frac{1}{6}$$

Note: When dividing by a fraction, multiply both the numerator and the denominator by the inverse of that fraction as shown below:

$$\frac{100.53 \bullet 6}{\frac{1}{6} \bullet 6} = \frac{603.18}{1} = 603.18$$

So the mechanical advantage is about 603:1.

Now, if we know what kind of mechanical advantage is afforded us by using this jackscrew, it is simple to calculate its potential lift (that is, resistance). Let's assume we exert a 15-pound effort on the handle of the jackscrew. How much weight (that is, resistance) can be lifted by the jack? Since the mechanical advantage has already been determined to be 603:1, we simply set it up in the following formula:

$$\text{Resistance} \bullet \text{Effort} = \text{Lift}$$

If the resistance is 603 and the force is 15 pounds, then:

$$603 \bullet 15 = 9045$$

In other words, 9,045 pounds can be lifted by the jackscrew under the conditions given.

## Gears and Gearing

Gears are essentially wheels with teeth; they are normally attached to a shaft. Depending on the origin of the torque (that is, the twisting or torsional force imparted on a driveline) a gear may either be turned by the shaft or may turn the shaft itself. A gear is basically a rotating lever. It can increase or decrease torque by applying the same principle of leverage as discussed earlier or it can change the direction of a force.

There are two general classes of gears, external and interior gears. External gears are the most common and consist of a wheel with exterior teeth. Interior gears, on the other hand, have teeth on the inside to accommodate a smaller gear for torque enhancement.

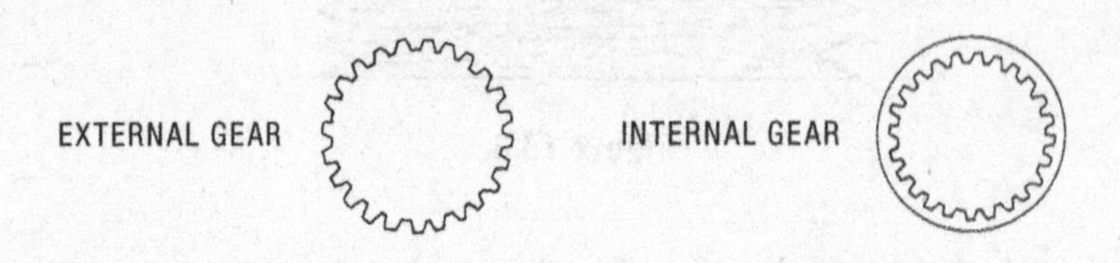


Teeth alignment serve to further classify gears. If a gear has straight teeth (that is, teeth set perpendicularly to a gear's facing), it is considered to be a spur gear. If the teeth are cut at an angle, this is a helical gear. Herringbone gears are two helical gears placed back to back. These more complex designs tend to alleviate vibration and noise.

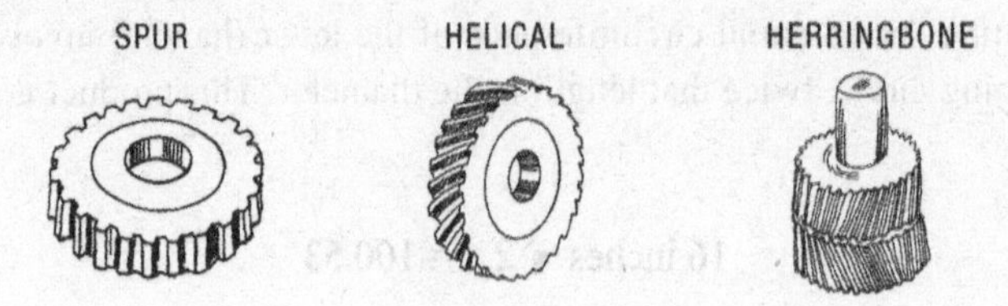


If a drive train must change direction, beveled gears are used. The teeth are not situated like those seen on an exterior spur gear. Rather, the teeth are cut into the edging of a gear to give it a beveled appearance.

BEVELED GEAR

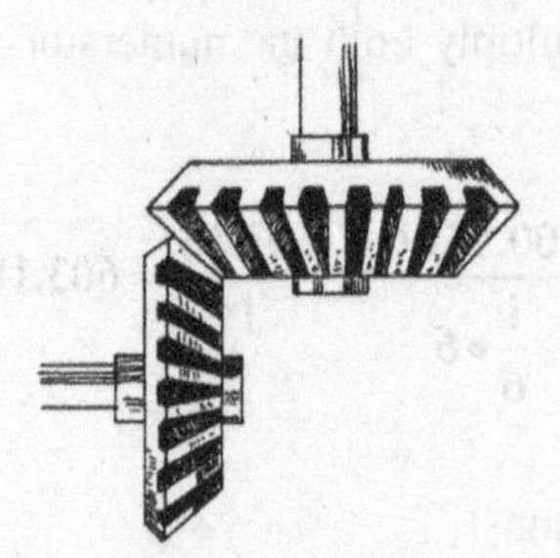

When we examine gears to see what they do, we can refer to the principles discussed in the section on the wheel and axle. The larger the wheel, the more twist or torque it can apply to a smaller wheel or axle. The same can be said of gears. A larger gear can exert far more torque on the shaft it is connected to than a smaller gear can.

However, when we examine torque output between meshing gears, an inverse relationship is seen. For instance, if the diameter of the drive gear (that is, pitch diameter) is twice the size of a connected smaller gear, the output torque is halved. If the drive gear is three times the size of the second gear, the torque would only be one third as much.

On the other hand, if the drive gear is half the size of the second gear, the output torque is doubled. The underlying principle here is that what is sacrificed in torque is gained in speed and vice versa.

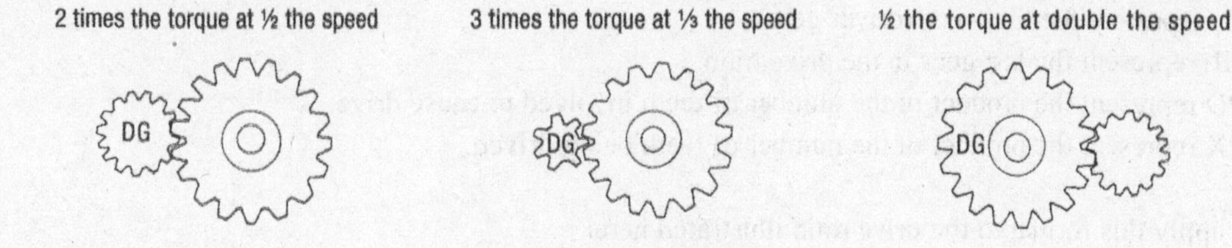


Instead of looking at pitch diameter to determine gear ratios, the number of teeth on each gear can be counted and compared. If a drive gear has 8 teeth and the second connecting gear (that is, the driven gear) has 24 teeth, we can determine that the drive gear would have to turn 3 times to turn the driven gear once.

Or, in other terms, the gear ratio (i.e., mechanical advantage) is 3:1 and the torque generated would be 3 times as much. As a basic guideline, the more teeth (hence larger pitch) a given gear has, the slower it will run, resulting in a proportionate increase in torque.

When looking at several gears in a driveline, it can be a little confusing to try and determine the direction in which any one gear will turn. It is understood that when one gear meshes with another, the direction of the driven gear is always opposite that of the drive gear. See Figure 13.5.

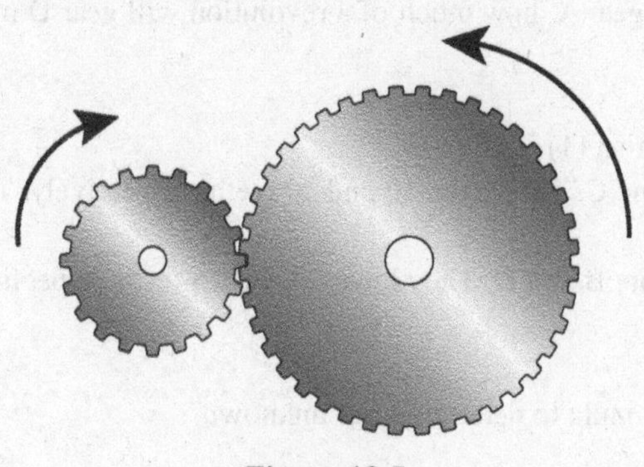

**Figure 13.5**

When several gears are shown in a driveline, the principle remains the same. Remembering which gear went in what direction may get a little confusing toward the end of the drive train; here is a simple solution to that problem: Number each gear as it falls in succession, such as shown in the example below:

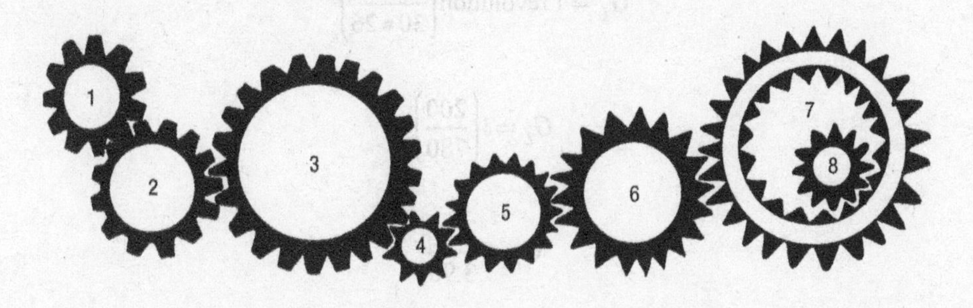


The odd-numbered gears will always turn in one direction while the even-numbered gears turn in the opposite direction. The exception to this rule is an internal gear (Gear #8 in the example shown). It always turns in the same direction as the gear surrounding it.

Now, if we desire to quantify how much of an effect the driver gear will have on the last gear of a drive train, the following procedure can help:

Let $G_1$ represent the first gear (driver gear)
Let GL represent the last gear in the drive train
Let PD represent the product of the number of teeth involved to cause drive
Let PX represent the product of the number of teeth being driven

Let's apply this format to the drive train illustrated here:

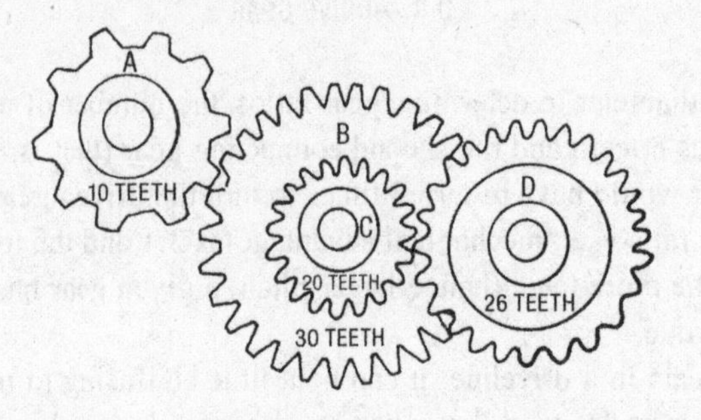


(Note: Gears B and C are situated on the same shaft. Therefore, the direction is the same for both.)
For every one revolution of gear A, how much of a revolution will gear D make?

$G_L$ is our unknown
G1 demonstrates one revolution (1)
PD: the driver gears are A and C. They have 10 and 20 teeth, respectively. Therefore, the product would be 10 • 20 = 200.
PX: the gears being driven are B and D. They have 30 and 26 teeth respectively. Therefore, the product would be 30 • 26 = 780.

We can use the following formula to determine our unknown.

$$G_L = G_1 \bullet \frac{P_D}{P_x}$$

Using this equation, we can plug in our known factors and determine GL.

$$G_L = 1 \text{ revolution}\left(\frac{10 \bullet 20}{30 \bullet 26}\right)$$

$$G_L = 1\left(\frac{200}{780}\right)$$

$$G_L = \frac{1}{3.90}$$

So, in other words, this particular gear reduction causes the last gear to turn almost $\frac{1}{4}$ of a revolution for every 1 revolution made by the first driver gear. This demonstrates a mechanical advantage of 4:1 or 4 times as much torque due to the configuration of gears involved.

This is a very simplified overview of gears and their applications. There is a host of technical information that can be discussed relating to this topic. However, the most important concept that should be learned here is that there is no such thing as perpetual motion. What we achieve in force, we lose in distance; whatever torque is gained, we lose in speed. This is assuming the source of power (e.g., an engine) is constant.

### Belt Drives

Belt drives are very comparable to gears, with the exception of the manner in which they are interconnected to perform work. Instead of various sized gears directly intermeshing, wheels are connected by means of a belt. This too, depending on the configuration of wheels, can increase or decrease speed or torque. If the belt is twisted in the manner shown below, it can directly change the direction of the opposing wheel.

In general, the mechanical principles discussed for gears and their applications are the same for belt drives.

## HYDRAULICS AND FLUID DYNAMICS

Fluid dynamics is an extremely complicated field in itself. However, there are a few basic properties that apply to all fluids and their mechanical uses.

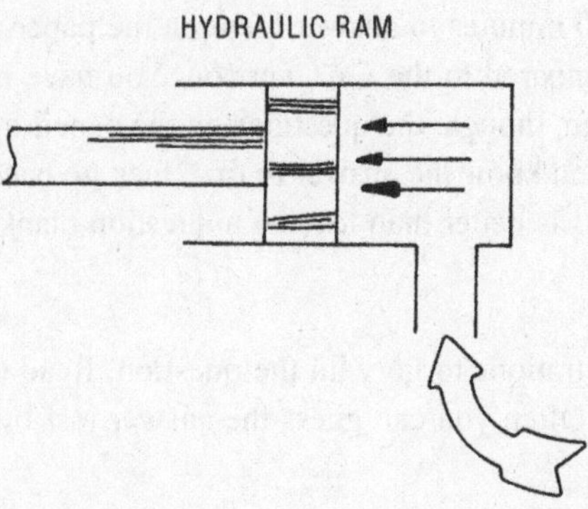


1. To begin with, fluid pressure always acts on a given surface in a perpendicular manner. A rod in the cylinder of a hydraulic apparatus would be a good example. As pressure is increased via the inlet port, there is a corresponding perpendicular force exerted on the piston to perform work.
2. Second, if pressure is exerted on a fluid trapped in a confined space, the pressure is distributed in all directions without consequent loss of power used to create the pressure. Let's look at the hydraulic ram, again. If the piston encounters an opposing force equal to that which is coming through the inlet port, the trapped fluid will exert an equal pressure at any point within its container.
3. A third property is that fluid pressure is the same at a given depth in all directions as well as being proportional to that depth (that is, in an open container). For example, if a scuba diver descends to a depth of 33 feet, regardless of where that diver swims on that plane, he or she will have to tolerate an ambient pressure of 29.4 pounds per square inch. (At sea level, it is only 14.7 pounds per square inch.) At 66 feet, it would be 44.1 pounds per square inch. At 99 feet, it would be 58.8 pounds per square inch, and at 132 feet, it would be 73.5 pounds per square inch.

Varying fluid densities play a role, too. Salt water is actually heavier than fresh water (64 pounds per cubic foot versus 62.4 pounds per cubic foot) because of the salts in suspension. Therefore, a diver at a depth of 33 feet in fresh water is subject to less pressure than a diver in 33 feet of salt water. The proportional changes of pressure as dictated by depth still occur regardless of the fluid density involved.

Finally, fluid pressure is unaffected by the dimension of open containment. For example, the ocean floor may be six miles deep in a given area. The pressure for that depth is the same regardless of the expanse of shallower water on its periphery.

These few examples demonstrate the basic guidelines that affect fluid dynamics. It is important that they be understood because they play a key role in hydraulic mechanics.

## STRATEGIES FOR SUCCEEDING ON THE MECHANICAL COMPREHENSION SUBTEST

Memorizing the mechanical advantage formula for each type of simple machine is going to be one of the most useful things you can do as you study in the days ahead of the test. But on test day, there are a few additional strategies you can employ in order to ensure a good score on the test.

### CAT Version Tips

You'll have 16 questions and 20 minutes to answer them on the CAT version of the Mechanical Comprehension subtest. This is actually more time than usual! But don't let that fool you—the time will go fast anyway. As always on the CAT version, you'll be given a medium-difficulty question to start with. Spend some time making sure you answer those first few questions correctly, and you'll likely end up with a higher score since you'll be answering more difficult questions.

### Pencil-and-Paper Version Tips

You'll have 25 questions and 20 minutes to answer them on the paper-and-pencil version of the ASVAB. This puts you at a slight disadvantage compared to the CAT version. You have more questions in total and less time to answer each particular question. Again, though, the questions on the pencil-and-paper version are the questions, so it makes sense to tackle the questions you know the answer to first, then go back and try to figure out the questions that you're not sure of. As always, a guess is better than leaving a question blank, as you may guess correctly.

### Overall Strategies

The test will often include illustrations to go with the question. Read the question and the answers, then take a moment to review the illustration. Often you can guess the answer just by the visual cues on the illustration. For example, look at Figure 13.6.

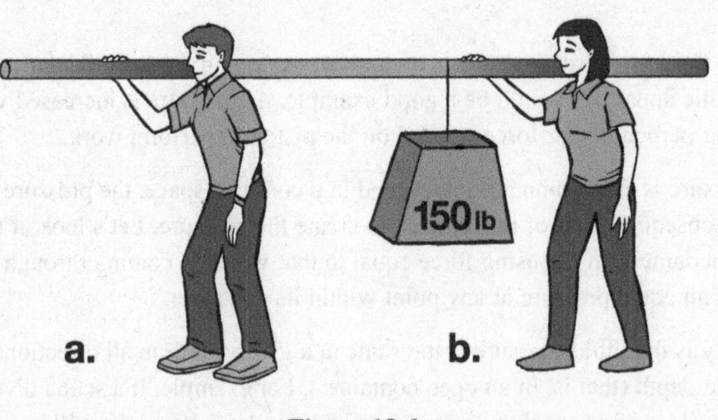


**Figure 13.6**

If the test asked you which person was carrying the heavier part of the load, you'd realize it was Person B. You wouldn't necessarily know the specific formula for why, but common sense would tell you the correct answer.

While not all of the questions on the Mechanical Comprehension subtest will be so easy to answer—be prepared to do a certain amount of math—you'll find that your familiarity with everyday activities will at least help you eliminate obviously wrong answers. For example, if you've worked with simple machines like crowbars and compound machines like wheelbarrows, you'd recognize that they all give you a mechanical advantage, so any answer that doesn't reflect at least some mechanical advantage would be incorrect.

# CHAPTER 14

# *Assembling Objects (AO)*

The Assembling Objects subtest does not count toward the Armed Forces Qualification Test (AFQT) score that you need to achieve to be eligible for military service. However, it is used in some instances to determine your eligibility for certain types of jobs.

The Assembling Objects subtest is only given on the CAT version of the ASVAB. If you will be taking the pencil-and-paper version of the ASVAB, then you don't need to worry about this test. But assuming you'll be taking the CAT version, you'll want to spend a little time becoming familiar with the types of questions you'll be asked. While there aren't lists of words to remember or concepts to review with the Assembling Objects subtest, some familiarity with how the test works will help you succeed at it.

## WHAT THE TEST MEASURES

The Assembling Objects subtest is a measure of your spatial relations skills. Basically it tests how well you visualize the way various objects fit together. It's one way to gauge your problem-solving skills because it requires abstract thinking to arrive at the best possible solution. It's also one way to test your mechanical aptitude.

The subtest score is used in part to determine your eligibility for certain operations and mechanical jobs. It is sometimes combined with your Mechanical Comprehension score to determine your eligibility for various opportunities. Currently only the Navy is using the AO score to determine eligibility for jobs but other branches may adjust their criteria at any time and beginning using these scores.

## BUILDING YOUR SKILLS

You can do some practice (besides taking the practice tests in this study guide) to improve your spatial relations skills. Here are a few things you can do to help yourself succeed on this subtest:

- You will find that playing computer games can improve your spatial relationship skills, especially games such as Tetris, which require you to fit shapes together.
- Other games, such as playing chess or putting together jigsaw puzzles, have been shown to help build better spatial relations skills.
- Some hobbies, such as photography and origami, also build visual-spatial skills.
- Also, researchers have found that people who study geometry tend to have better spatial relationship skills. Since geometry requires you to be able to think visually about shapes, this makes sense.

Obviously, this is a skill that it takes a while to build. You're not going to suddenly master spatial relations by folding one paper crane. However, research has shown that even a few hours of practice immediately ahead of test-taking can help you do better on the test. So remember that even a little bit can help!

### Types of Assembling Objects Questions

The Assembling Objects subtest is basically about solving puzzles. There are two types of questions that are asked. In both types of questions, you're shown a box containing unassembled shapes and then asked to look at a series of assembled shapes (these possible answers are labeled A, B, C, and D). You must pick the correct answer.

One type of question requires you to assemble the parts into a whole, sort of like putting a jigsaw puzzle together. However, you have to imagine how the pieces fit together, since you can't physically manipulate them.

The other type of question asks you what the unassembled shapes would look like if they were connected at certain points. You might call the two question types "some assembly required" questions and "connect the dots" questions.

### Sample Questions

Let's look at an example of the first type of question.

***In the following question, which figure best shows how the objects in the box on the left would look if they were assembled?***

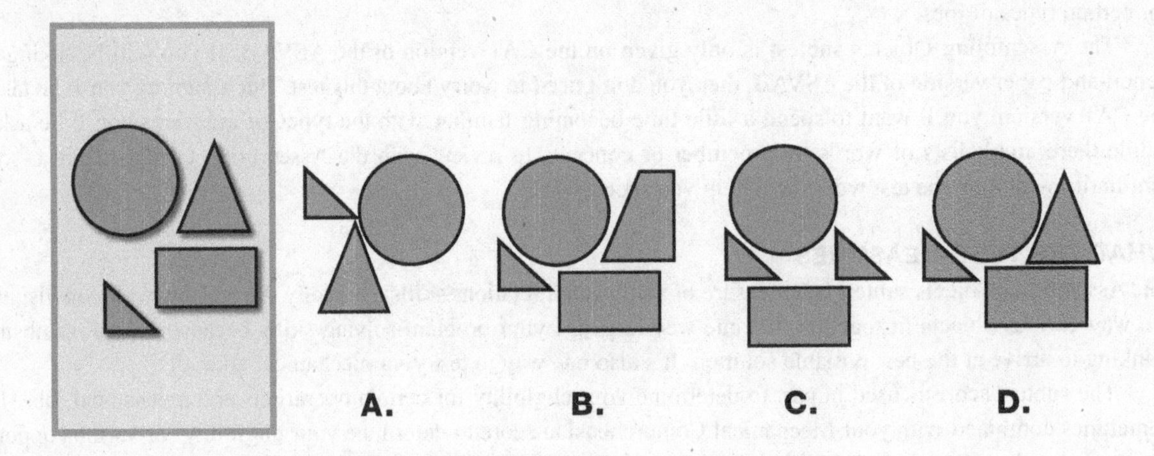


As you can see, there are any number of ways the shapes in the left-hand box could be arranged, so spending time thinking up various possibilities is actually a waste of effort. Instead, look at the possible choices and pick the answer that is most correct.

If you look at answer A, you'll see that only three of the four shapes are used. On this subtest, all of the shapes must be used, so you can immediately eliminate A.

If you look at B, you'll see that there are four shapes, and they are similar to those shown in the left-hand box, but one of them is a bit different. It's not exactly the same triangle it was. That means B can be eliminated. The shapes must be exactly the same (although they can be rotated, they must otherwise be the same).

Now, look at C. This has four shapes, but they are not the exact same four shapes. One of the shapes is a duplicate. This answer can be eliminated.

Finally, look at D. It has all four of the original shapes, and each is exactly the same shape and size as in the left-hand box. None of them has changed in any way. That makes D the best possible answer.

For a "some assembly required" question, sometimes the shapes fit together perfectly as they do in a jigsaw puzzle. Often, however, as in the sample question here, they don't. In other words, don't assume that the shapes need to fit together like a puzzle for the answer to be correct. That's not what you're looking for. You need to look for the correct shapes (size and all) and the correct number of shapes. In the sample, one of the answers had too few shapes, but you may come across an answer that has too many. That is also incorrect.

Now, let's look at the second type of question.

***In the following question, which figure best shows how the objects in the box on the left would look if the points lettered A and B were connected by line A-B?***

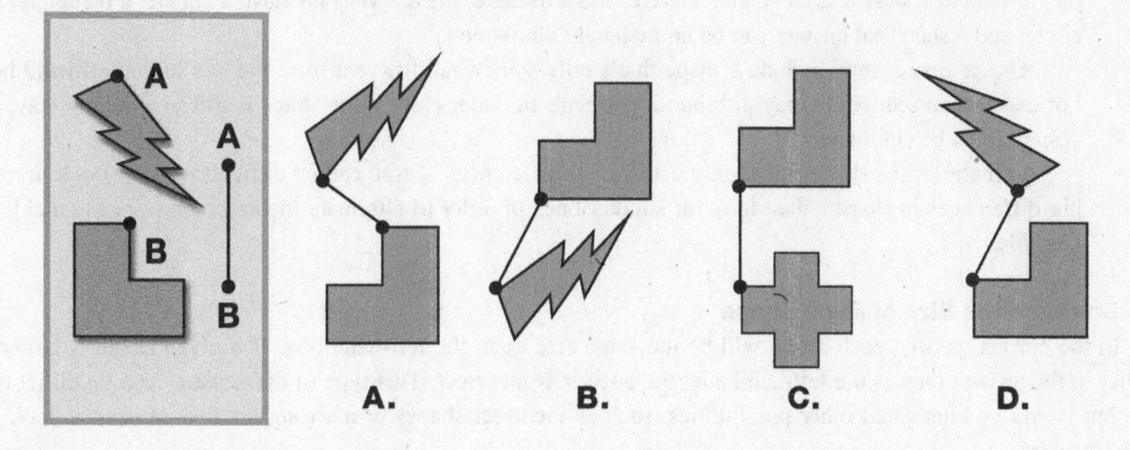


In this case, a "connect the dots" question, you're supposed to visualize what the objects would look like if they were connected with a line from point A to point B. Further, you have to imagine what the objects would look like rotated.

Again, though, as with the "some assembly required" type of question, you don't need to try to work out the right answer ahead of time. You just need to look at the possible answers and pick the best match.

If you look at answer A, you'll see that a lower corner on the L-shaped piece is connected to the top left-hand corner of the lightning-bolt shape. In neither case does the attached area correspond with points A or B as indicated in the left-hand box. Answer A can be eliminated.

If you look at B, you'll see that the correct point on the lightning bolt has been used but it is not connected to the correct spot on the L-shaped piece. Answer B can be eliminated.

If you look at C, you'll immediately note that one of the shapes is incorrect. C can be immediately eliminated.

If you look at D, you'll see that the point being connected on the lightning bolt corresponds correctly with point A on the lightning bolt in the left-hand box. You'll see that it connects to the correct spot on the L-shaped piece as well. Answer D is the correct answer.

For these types of questions, note where the points are in the shapes in the left-hand box. You can eliminate any answers that show the point in the wrong place on the shape. In the case of the sample question, just knowing where the points were on the shapes immediately eliminated two of the wrong answers.

## Solving Assembling Objects Problems

Whichever type of question you're being asked on the Assembling Objects subtest, keep in mind these following pointers.

### Count the Shapes

The correct answer will have the same number of shapes as the left-hand box (the box with the unassembled pieces). If the left-hand box has five shapes, the correct answer must have five shapes as well. Counting shapes is a quick way to eliminate incorrect answers.

### Identify the Shapes

1. The correct answer will have the same shapes as the left-hand box. That means each shape must be used once in the answer. If the left-hand box has a square, a rectangle, a circle, and a triangle, the answer must have each of those shapes as well. If an answer has two squares, a rectangle, and a circle, it may have the correct number of shapes, but not the correct type, and it should be eliminated.

2. The correct answer will have shapes that are exactly the same as those in the left-hand box (with the exception of being rotated). In some possible answers, a different shape entirely may be used. For example, instead of a square, a rectangle, a circle, and a triangle, the answer may have a square, a rectangle, a circle, and a star. That answer can be immediately eliminated.

   Or, an answer may include a shape that's only somewhat different from the one in the left-hand box. For example, a semicircle may turn into a crescent. In either case, if the shape is different in any way, the answer must be eliminated.

   Sometimes the shapes have only very minor differences. These can be difficult to spot. Look first for big differences in shapes, then look for smaller ones in order to eliminate incorrect answers as quickly as possible.

### Compare the Size of Each Shape

In the correct answer, each shape will be the same size as in the left-hand box. If a given shape is larger or smaller in the answer than in the left-hand box, the answer is incorrect. This type of discrepancy can be difficult to spot, but if you've eliminated other possibilities, such as incorrect shapes or a wrong number of shapes, look for incorrect sizes.

### Eliminate Mirrored Shapes

The correct answer never includes a mirror image of one of the shapes. If one of the answers has a shape that is the mirror image of a shape in the left-hand box, that is always an incorrect answer. Shapes may (and probably will) be rotated, but not mirrored. This is a trick that occasionally catches people off-guard. Be aware of it.

### Look for Distinct Shapes

Two other points will help you find the right answer more quickly:

- If a very distinct type of shape is given in the left-hand box, look for it in the answers. If it's not in an answer, that answer can be eliminated.
- Conversely, look to see if any of the answers have a shape that isn't in the left-hand box. If the answer contains such a shape, it can be eliminated.

## STRATEGIES FOR SUCCEEDING ON THE ASSEMBLING OBJECTS TEST

You'll have 16 questions and 9 minutes to answer them. Since the test is only given on the CAT version, you don't have to worry about it if you're taking the pen-and-pencil version. You'll have just over thirty seconds to answer each question, so you don't have a lot of time to fiddle with the solution.

The best approach is to look at the pieces presented in the question, then immediately eliminate those answers that are obviously wrong. Through this process of elimination, you'll find the correct answer. This approach works best because there could be more than one way to answer the question; you're just picking the best one based on the possible answers. So look at the possible answers first.

Don't forget to review the "Solving Assembling Objects Problems" section in this chapter immediately before the test. The pointers given there are immediately applicable on test day. Also, remember that the CAT version of the ASVAB always starts with a medium difficulty question and either goes up or down from there. You want it to go up so you can score higher on the subtest. For that reason it makes sense to be careful that your first few answers are absolutely correct. You'll be more likely to score more points this way.

Do answer all of the questions, even if you have to guess on some of them. Wrong answers do not count against you any more than an unanswered question, and you may be able to guess correctly (thus improving your score).

When possible, eliminate as many answers as you can using the steps indicated in the "Solving Assembling Objects Problems" section before guessing. If you can't eliminate them all that way, then pick the answer that seems most likely of the remaining choices.

# PART 4
# The Practice Tests

In this part, you'll have the opportunity to take four practice tests in order to measure your knowledge of the material that is likely to be found on the ASVAB.

Take each test exactly as you would take the official ASVAB (giving yourself precisely the amount of time as indicated for each subtest, recording the answers on the answer sheet, and so on). But only take one test at a time. Don't try to do all of the practice tests in a marathon study session. After you've graded the test, consider what areas require additional review (see Chapter 5 for more information on evaluating a practice test). Then do that additional review before taking another practice test.

Not only will taking the practice tests help you identify areas where you need additional study, it will get you in the habit of taking standardized tests, so when you actually take the official ASVAB, you'll be more comfortable with the approach and will be more likely to do well.

# CHAPTER 15

## *Practice Test #1*

Take the diagnostic test just as you would any standardized test. Use the answer sheet at the end of this chapter to record your answers. Set a timer for the amount of time allotted for each subtest, take them in the order in which they're given, and try to do your best. Then turn to the answer key (later in this chapter) to grade your efforts and help you plan your review before taking the next practice test.

## GENERAL SCIENCE

You have 11 minutes to answer the 25 questions on this subtest.

1. Which of the following structures are found within a cell?

   A. nucleus and mitochondria
   B. leukocytes and erythrocytes
   C. nucleoids and riboids
   D. ions and protons

2. An upper respiratory infection affects

   A. the heart and lungs
   B. the lungs only
   C. the nasal cavity
   D. the entire respiratory system

3. The earth is made up of a variety of layers. We live on the

   A. outer core
   B. mantle
   C. crust
   D. atmosphere

4. Matter without defined shape or volume is

   A. liquid
   B. gas
   C. solid
   D. none of the above

5. An example of a heterogeneous mixture is

   A. apple juice
   B. wine
   C. coffee
   D. vinaigrette dressing

6. For every 10 meters you dive down in the ocean, the water pressure will increase by about

   A. 14.5 psi
   B. 33 psi
   C. 145 psi
   D. there will be no change

7. Anatomy is the study of

   A. environments
   B. matter
   C. living things
   D. structures of living things

8. In a scientific study, the word "correlation" means

A. one event causes another
B. two conditions are related
C. two conditions are not related
D. one event can influence another

9. The metric system is based on

A. the decimal system
B. the Imperial system
C. the customary system
D. the Hellenic system

10. Scientists use the word "mass" instead of weight because

A. weight measures the pull of gravity, so it can vary based on where the item being measured is located
B. weight can only be measured in pounds and scientists use the metric system
C. scientists don't like to use words that are already in common use
D. weight cannot be measured in very small or very large increments

11. Metabolism, growth, and reproduction are characteristic of

A. inorganic matter
B. living things
C. elements
D. the scientific process

12. A change in a population may occur for any of the following reasons *except*:

A. advantageous adaptation
B. random genetic mutation
C. selective breeding
D. cloning

13. A eukaryotic cell differs from a prokaryotic cell in that a eukaryotic cell

A. has an interior cell membrane
B. glows under ultraviolet light
C. undergoes reproduction
D. contains DNA

14. Humans share the class *mammalia* with

A. geese
B. dolphins
C. tree frogs
D. snakes

15. Necessary materials for photosynthesis to occur include

    A. chlorophyll, carbon dioxide, sunlight, and water
    B. chlorophyll, carbon monoxide, sunlight, and water
    C. carbon dioxide, salt, sunlight, and water
    D. chlorophyll, oxygen, sunlight, and water

16. Vertebrates are

    A. warm-blooded animals
    B. cold-blooded animals
    C. mammals with a backbone
    D. organisms with a backbone

17. Photoreceptors are cells that are activated by

    A. sound waves
    B. smell
    C. light waves
    D. touch

18. Children have more bones than adults because

    A. some of the bones are absorbed and turned into blood cells as the child grows
    B. some of the bones fuse together as the child grows
    C. some of the bones turn into cartilage through a process of mineralization as the child grows
    D. children don't have more bones than adults

19. What is *not* one of the functions of your skin?

    A. To protect your body from infection
    B. To help regulate your body temperature
    C. To communicate sensory information to your brain
    D. To attach your muscles to your bones

20. Oxygen-depleted blood is sent to the lungs for re-oxygenation by the heart via the

    A. pulmonary artery
    B. pulmonary vein
    C. aorta
    D. lateral ventricle

21. The three types of rocks that make up the earth's crust are

    A. igneous, metamorphic, and combination
    B. igneous, sedimentary, and metamorphic
    C. obsidian, shale, and slate
    D. igneous, sedimentary, and igneous-sedimentary

22. The average depth of the ocean is about

A. 4.3 kilometers
B. 50 kilometers
C. 13 kilometers
D. 1.2 kilometers

23. Falling barometric pressure is often associated with

A. clear weather
B. cloudy skies and rain
C. high tides
D. warm weather

24. A lunar eclipse occurs when

A. the sun passes between the earth and the moon
B. the moon passes between the sun and the earth
C. a full moon happens in autumn
D. the earth passes between the moon and the sun

25. If you add a proton to an atom, you change it into a(n)

A. ion
B. isotope
C. compound
D. different element

## ARITHMETIC REASONING

You will have 30 questions and 39 minutes to answer them.

1. $9-\frac{3}{8}=x$. Which of the following equals $x$?

   A. $8\frac{3}{8}$

   B. $8\frac{5}{8}$

   C. 9

   D. $7\frac{3}{8}$

2. $6\frac{1}{3}-4\frac{5}{6}=x$. Which of the following equals $x$?

   A. $1\frac{1}{4}$

   B. $1\frac{1}{2}$

   C. $1\frac{3}{4}$

   D. $1\frac{3}{6}$

3. $4\frac{2}{3}+1\frac{1}{6}-2\frac{1}{8}=x$. Which of the following equals $x$?

   A. $3\frac{17}{24}$

   B. $3\frac{1}{4}$

   C. $3\frac{3}{16}$

   D. $3\frac{5}{18}$

4. In a training course the number of women attending are 9 more than half the number of men present. If there are 16 women in attendance, how many men are attending the course?

   A. 14
   B. 16
   C. 18
   D. 20

5. Two water lines are used to refill a 160-gallon tank. If it is known that one line can supply water at the rate of 16 gallons per minute, and the other line can supply 10 gallons per minute, how much time would be needed to fill the tank completely, assuming the tank was originally empty?

   A. 14.7 minutes
   B. 13.91 minutes
   C. 8.7 minutes
   D. 6.15 minutes

6. $12\frac{3}{8} \bullet 2\frac{5}{7} = x$. Which of the following equals $x$?

   A. $32\frac{33}{25}$

   B. $32\frac{17}{18}$

   C. $33\frac{33}{56}$

   D. $34\frac{1}{3}$

7. If a basement's floor plan had the dimensions shown, how many square feet would this basement have?

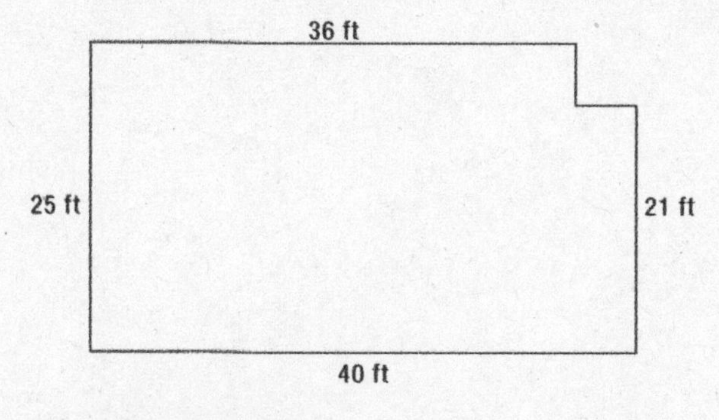


   A. 1,000 square feet
   B. 995 square feet
   C. 988 square feet
   D. 984 square feet

8. The formula for converting Celsius temperatures to Fahrenheit is °F = $\frac{9}{5}$ (°C) + 32. What is 25° Celsius in Fahrenheit?

   A. 102.6°
   B. 77°
   C. 67.3°
   D. 59.4°

9. If a brick is $23\frac{5}{8}$ centimeters in length, how many bricks laid end to end would constitute a row $283\frac{1}{2}$ centimeters long?

   A. 8 bricks
   B. 9 bricks
   C. 11 bricks
   D. 12 bricks

10. If two engines could generate 175 and 224 horsepower, respectively, but under normal conditions exert only $\frac{7}{8}$ and $\frac{6}{7}$ of their respective ratings, what would be the expected horsepower of both engines combined?

    A. 399 horsepower
    B. $367\frac{1}{5}$ horsepower
    C. $353\frac{1}{7}$ horsepower
    D. $345\frac{1}{8}$ horsepower

11. Four students are collecting donations toward a goal of new uniforms for the marching band. If Joe collected $\frac{7}{16}$ of the goal amount, Tamara collected $\frac{5}{8}$, Sam collected $\frac{1}{2}$, and Rashid collected $\frac{3}{4}$, what amount of the goal did the students achieve in total?

    A. $\frac{16}{30}$
    B. $2\frac{5}{16}$
    C. $3\frac{7}{16}$
    D. $\frac{8}{15}$

12. If someone had an 850-liter underground diesel-fuel tank filled six times during the year, how many kiloliters of fuel were consumed annually?

    A. 5.1 kiloliters
    B. 51 kiloliters
    C. 510 kiloliters
    D. 5,100 kiloliters

13. How can $1\frac{1}{3}$ yards to 16 inches be best expressed in terms of a ratio?

    A. 1.33:16
    B. 1.33:1.5
    C. 3:1
    D. 1:3

14. Delilah was able to buy a scratch-and-dent stand mixer for $49, which is 42% of the original price. What was the original price of the mixer?

    A. $20.58
    B. $79.40
    C. $116.67
    D. $136.10

15. If Fire District #9 responded to 245 fires related to accidents or negligence, and another 8% of its fires were attributed to arson, how many calls did Fire District #9 receive altogether? (All fires can be regarded as caused by arson, negligence, or accident.)

    A. 248
    B. 253
    C. 266
    D. 275

16. If a 6-foot-tall basketball player cast a shadow 7.5 feet long and simultaneously noticed that the community center building cast a shadow 35 feet long, how tall is the community center?

    A. 27.5 feet
    B. 28 feet
    C. 29.7 feet
    D. 32 feet

17. If a technician working toward a certification scored 80%, 82%, 90%, and 87% on his first four exams, what kind of grade would be required on the fifth exam to acquire an overall average of 87%?

    A. 87%
    B. 89%
    C. 96%
    D. 98%

18. If six building inspectors can inspect 25 buildings in two days, how many buildings could be inspected by five building inspectors in four days?

    A. 22
    B. 27
    C. 35
    D. 42

19. Two brothers who lived in cities 469 miles apart started traveling toward one another on the same route at rates of 57 mph and 68 mph. If both drivers departed at 6:15 A.M., what time would they reach each other?

    A. 9:15 A.M.
    B. 10:00 A.M.
    C. 10:20 A.M.
    D. 1:15 P.M.

20. On Friday night, Greg drove home from work at an average rate of 58 mph. On the return trip Monday morning, his rate was 5 mph slower, which took him an additional 30 minutes of travel time. How long of a commute is it between Greg's home and his work?

A. 261 miles
B. 292.5 miles
C. 301.7 miles
D. 307.4 miles

21. How many ounces of water should be added to 24 ounces of an alcohol/water solution containing 44% alcohol to dilute the mixture to 20% alcohol?

A. 33.1 ounces
B. 31 ounces
C. 28.8 ounces
D. 24 ounces

22. A survey of households in a neighborhood showed that 6 of them spent 4 hours a day on the computer. Three of them spent 3.25 hours a day, and 2 of them spent 1 hour per day. What is the mean number of hours spent on the computer by this group?

A. 3.25 hours
B. 3 hours
C. 4 hours
D. 3.5 hours

23. What is the next term in the sequence {3, 9, 4, 10}?

A. 3
B. 5
C. 6
D. 11

24. The cost of a ticket to a local amusement park went from $75 last year to $82 this year. What is the percent change in the cost of the ticket from last year to this?

A. 1.09%
B. 9.3%
C. 109.3%
D. 10.9%

25. $\sqrt{52}$ falls between which 2 numbers?

A. 7 and 7.25
B. 7.25 and 7.5
C. 6 and 7
D. 7.5 and 8

26. Which of the following is a factor of 12?

A. 7
B. 5
C. −2
D. 0

27. If there are 5 cars entered in a race, what are the total possible combinations of ways they could cross the finish line?

A. 5
B. 25
C. 50
D. 120

28. Jonas has $1250 invested in a CD that pays an annual rate of 4.5%. After 6 months, he decides to withdraw the money. He must pay a penalty equal to 1% of the total value of the CD to redeem it early. How much money does Jonah take from the bank?

A. $1,278.00
B. $1,265.22
C. $28.13
D. $1,306.25

29. In the formula $a^2 + b^2 = c^2$ find the value of $c^2$ if $a = 3$ and $b = 2$.

A. 5
B. 9
C. 13
D. 15

30. Gloriana earns a base pay of $9.25 an hour. She earns a commission equal to 10% of her hourly pay for each hair product she sells. Assuming she sells 10 products in an eight-hour day at an average price of $13.50, how much does she make in a normal day?

A. $74.00
B. $92.50
C. $209.00
D. $166.50

## WORD KNOWLEDGE

You'll have 35 questions to answer in 11 minutes.

1. The crop report was seemingly redundant in a couple of areas. Redundant most nearly means

   A. incomprehensible
   B. repetitious
   C. concise
   D. easy to understand

2. Facetiousness most nearly means

   A. serious nature
   B. blitheness
   C. wisecracking
   D. stubborn attitude

3. Doctors are not permitted to divulge information to a third party unless authorized. Divulge most nearly means

   A. conceal
   B. distort
   C. expose
   D. disclose

4. The minor infraction was enough to warrant permanent expulsion. Expulsion most nearly means

   A. exclusion
   B. replacement
   C. resentment
   D. subjugation

5. Anarchy most nearly means

   A. compatibility
   B. conformity
   C. disorder
   D. harmony

6. Jerry had nothing but contempt for his boss once she refused his request for time off. Contempt most nearly means

   A. disdain
   B. praise
   C. concern
   D. high regard

7. Coercion most nearly means

   A. reservation
   B. assistance
   C. stipulation
   D. intimidation

8. It was alleged that Ms. Phelps used her position on the city council to help her friends. Alleged most nearly means

   A. guaranteed
   B. credible
   C. indisputable
   D. purported

9. Verbatim most nearly means

   A. imprecisely
   B. word for word
   C. perfunctory
   D. eloquently

10. Dr. Sid Morrissey is a proficient researcher. Proficient most nearly means

    A. incompetent
    B. prodigious
    C. expert
    D. amateur

11. Asphyxiated most nearly means

    A. uncomfortable
    B. distressed
    C. suffocated
    D. restless

12. The students petitioned the principal to abrogate the new attendance rule. Abrogate most nearly means

    A. repeal
    B. reinforce
    C. lessen
    D. rethink

13. The cashier was nonchalant in the face of the customer's rudeness. Nonchalant most nearly means

    A. visibly upset
    B. calm
    C. angry
    D. unhappy

14. Monica found her seatmate vapid. Vapid most nearly means

    A. challenging
    B. pretty
    C. insipid
    D. inspiring

15. Pedro's vegetable garden grew profusely. Profusely most nearly means

A. in patches
B. without tending
C. poorly
D. abundantly

16. Dissemble most nearly means

A. conceal
B. take apart
C. repair
D. reveal

17. The president of the company preferred having sycophants on the board. Sycophants most nearly means

A. counselors
B. flatterers
C. competitors
D. friends

18. His friends were surprised when Mitchell had the temerity to contradict the football coach. Temerity most nearly means

A. inspiration
B. facts
C. time
D. bravery

19. Impute most nearly means

A. say
B. attribute
C. judge
D. believe

20. Nichole responded to the question with exasperation. Exasperation most nearly means

A. annoyance
B. patience
C. anger
D. disbelief

21. Many people have inchoate opinions about philosophical matters. Inchoate most nearly means

A. firm
B. unformed
C. decided
D. unbiased

22. Like many young adults, Francis was wary of taking on debt. Wary most nearly means

A. cautious
B. inclined
C. forced
D. unhappy

23. Acumen most nearly means

A. discernment
B. ability
C. acclimate
D. accumulate

24. Jasmine's dog was fickle in her behavior. Fickle most nearly means

A. constant
B. changeable
C. predictable
D. unresponsive

25. Members of the club ostracized outsiders. Ostracized most nearly means

A. included
B. excluded
C. invited
D. distrusted

26. Michael's father exhibited skepticism when Michael explained why he missed school three days in a row. Skepticism most nearly means

A. compassion
B. anger
C. disbelief
D. concern

27. Effusion most nearly means

A. blockage
B. infection
C. outpouring
D. process

28. The students were boisterous at graduation. Boisterous most nearly means

A. attentive
B. contrite
C. composed
D. high-spirited

29. The city council's decision was held in abeyance. Abeyance most nearly means

A. public
B. secret
C. suspension
D. distrust

30. Jerry didn't begrudge his brother's good fortune. Begrudge most nearly means

A. envy
B. deplore
C. despise
D. appreciate

31. All communities have a finite amount of resources. Finite most nearly means

A. defined
B. limited
C. taxed
D. numberless

32. Muffle most nearly means

A. enhance
B. affect
C. dampen
D. mistake

33. Stella brewed a potent cup of coffee. Potent most nearly means

A. rich
B. aromatic
C. tasty
D. powerful

34. It is imperative for professionals to be judicious when dispensing advice. Judicious most nearly means

A. gentle
B. correct
C. considerate
D. wise

35. Gertrude gave the barking dog a baleful look. Baleful most nearly means

A. impatient
B. evil
C. unhappy
D. gleeful

## PARAGRAPH COMPREHENSION

You'll have 15 questions and 13 minutes to answer them.

1. Static electricity is a natural phenomenon that by itself can pose little, if any, danger. However, if it is present in an area of stored flammable substances, a real danger exists. Normally, a nonconductive material has a charge present on its surface. Some of the time this charge can diminish by itself. Other times, if there is an insufficient electrical path for this charge to flow along, an open spark can be the consequence. Therein lies the extreme danger of the potential ignition of the flammable materials.
   This paragraph is chiefly concerned with what kind of problem?

   A. Static electricity
   B. Flammable materials
   C. The potential for electrical shock
   D. The prospect of static electricity igniting flammable materials

2. A preliminary hearing is a proceeding in which a magistrate decides whether a crime has been committed or if there is probable cause to believe the defendant committed the act. If it is decided that neither of these can be determined, it is within the magistrate's authority to have the charges dropped and the defendant released. However, if enough evidence is presented to substantiate one or both of these considerations, the defendant can be ordered held for further trial proceedings.
   According to this passage:

   A. a preliminary hearing can determine whether a crime has been committed
   B. a defendant cannot be ordered held for further proceedings during a preliminary hearing
   C. a defendant cannot be released after a preliminary hearing is held
   D. a preliminary hearing determines whether a defendant committed a crime

3. The Ming Dynasty was the last indigenous Chinese dynasty and it flourished from 1368 to 1644. It was noted for a strong central government, and for supporting navigation and exploration. The manufacture of porcelain reached a peak during this dynasty. The traditional blue-and-white pattern characteristic of Ming porcelain was imitated throughout Europe. The dynasty fell in the seventeenth century owing to military threats, civil strife, and burdensome taxes.
   This passage suggests that

   A. Ming porcelain was imported from Europe
   B. there may be a connection between the dynasty's notable achievements and its eventual collapse
   C. the dynasty was more focused on artist endeavors than on governance
   D. little is known about the Ming Dynasty

4. The practice of physiognomy, the classifying of human types based on external appearances, has been popular at various times in human history, notably during the time of ancient Greek philosophers and again in Europe in the late eighteenth century. It was used the same way as modern people use psychology, to understand the motivations and problems of people.
   According to this passage,

   A. physiognomy was popularized by ancient Greek philosophers but lost credibility in the late 18th century
   B. physiognomy is still practiced widely by psychologists
   C. there is a connection between physiognomy and psychology
   D. physiognomy relies on the theory of correspondence

5. Throughout the ages, people have believed in mythical lands and creatures, such as the lost land of Atlantis. They have also believed in a land called Ophir, where King Solomon's gold was hidden; El Dorado, a city of gold; and Rio Doro, the river of gold. They have searched for the Fountain of Youth, the Empire of Monomatapa, the Seven Cities of Cibola, St. Brendan's Isle, and the Brazil Rock. They have believed in a race of Cyclopeans—giants with one eye. They have been sure the monoceros (unicorn) was tamable only by virgins. They were convinced that a band of Amazons—fierce women warriors—existed and they knew of trees that grew wool. In some lands, they believed, snakes had gemstones for eyes.
A good title for this passage would be

   A. Mythical Lands and Creatures
   B. Ignorance Is Human
   C. The History of Pseudoscience
   D. Greed Rules Imagination

6. A caste is a hereditary social group. Societies with such social ranks have rigid rules regarding social and occupational choices, status and tribal affiliation. Members of one caste generally may not marry into another.
According to this passage,

   A. people can easily move from one caste to another
   B. caste defines one's political affiliation but little else
   C. caste should be abolished
   D. one's caste can affect all areas of life

7. The Alhambra, in Granada, Spain, is probably the most famous example of Moorish architecture. The Alhambra (or "red house") was built in the fourteenth century as a fortified palace. An outer wall surrounds the structure, with several gates controlling access. One of these gates is called the Justice Gate, because the court met there to hear cases of petty crime. In the center of the building is the Court of Lions, a courtyard built around a large fountain with sculptures of lions. An arcade supported by over one hundred marble columns runs around the perimeter of this courtyard. Stucco ornaments decorate the palace, as do inscriptions from the Koran.
According to this passage,

   A. the Alhambra is one of the largest religious structures in the world
   B. the phrase "red house" comes from the fact that criminal cases were heard here
   C. the Justice Gate is one of several gates controlling access to the Alhambra
   D. the Court of Lions is where illustrious members of the nobility met

8. Fan clubs have been around since the late forties, though the idea of supporting one's favorite artist is probably timeless. Fan clubs continue to be successful even long after the performer dies or retires from the business. For instance, late stars such as Hank Williams Sr. and Patsy Cline have very active fan clubs. Clubs exist for almost every star, and for not-so-famous performers as well.
According to this passage,

   A. Fan clubs have been around since the 1940s
   B. Patsy Cline and Hank Williams Sr. have the largest numbers of fans in their fan clubs
   C. Supporting one's favorite artist is a new idea
   D. Fan clubs are only for the famous

9. The instruments of country music may vary from none to many, but some important ones include the guitar, the banjo, and the fiddle; the harmonica and the accordion, which give country music a distinct sound; and the piano, the drums, and the electric bass, which are recent additions. Even horns have been added to give country music a more "lush" sound. The mandolin, the dulcimer, and the autoharp have also found their way into the hands of country music performers, and live performances are almost always amplified, with an occasional acoustical performance to showcase the artist's vocal talent.
   A good title for this passage would be:

   A. The Origin of Musical Instruments
   B. How Instruments Shape Music
   C. The Evolution of Country Music
   D. Musical Instruments Used in Country Music

10. Amulets and talismans are objects that have some sort of protective power. The lucky rabbit's foot is an example. Charms are collections of objects—herbs, twigs, animal parts—that are brought together in an attempt to create some powerful result.
    The author's purpose in this passage is to:

    A. define various objects used in magic
    B. teach the reader how to use magic
    C. dissuade the reader from performing magic
    D. compare magical rituals to scientific experiments

11. There are several kinds of rights to a creative work (they overlap), including reproduction, adaptation, distribution, performance, and display. For a photographer, the right to reproduce and to display their work is more important than the right to perform it. A writer is more concerned about reproduction and performance than display.
    This author of this passage used

    A. chronological order to explain the information
    B. comparison to show how different types of artists are concerned with different types of rights
    C. a step-by-step organization to show how to apply for copyright protection
    D. definitions to explain copyright law

12. Natural disasters such as fire and flood can destroy your property. Be certain to guard yourself against these risks as much as possible. For fire risk, install smoke detectors. Keep important documents and computer disks in a safety deposit box at the bank, or at least in a fireproof box in the home. Know where your fire extinguisher is. For flood risk, keep that fireproof box in the attic, not the basement. Put a flood plan into action by locating and safely storing essential materials.
    The purpose of this passage is to

    A. explain risk-reduction strategies
    B. emphasize the importance of having insurance coverage
    C. show how to keep your home safe from theft and forcible intrusion
    D. scare people into taking action

13. Traditional Individual Retirement Accounts (IRAs) are a popular investment tool. Depending on your circumstances, you can deposit a certain amount of before-tax dollars into such an account. You don't pay taxes on the money or the interest it earns until you retire. The theory is that when you retire, you'll be in a lower tax bracket so you'll pay less in taxes. IRAs are investment tools that can be linked to mutual funds or to specific stocks.
According to this passage,

    A. you can use IRAs to save for anything
    B. IRAs are the best investment strategy for anyone
    C. you can only retire if you have sufficient money in your IRA
    D. you can deposit only a certain amount of money into an IRA

14. An income statement can be used to look at financial records over the course of a specific period of time. An income statement simply totals your revenue and your expenses. Expenses are subtracted from revenue to determine net income. Knowing your net income for a given period of time allows you to see how much money your business actually generates. If your net income is a negative number, you're operating at a loss, which can cause your business to fail.
The purpose of this paragraph is to

    A. warn business owners not to operate at a loss
    B. describe what an income statement is
    C. show how to improve cash flow
    D. explain reporting requirements

15. Alexandria, a city in northern Egypt, was founded by Alexander the Great in 332 B.C. Located in the Nile River delta, it has also always served as an important port. During the Middle Ages, it was a center of commerce between East and West. It was also home to a diverse population, including Greeks, Jews, and Egyptians, allowing the free flow of ideas that made it an intellectual center.
According to this passage, Alexandria became

    A. an intellectual center because of the diversity of its population
    B. was never a center of trade
    C. was named after a type of mineral found in the Nile
    D. is only a few hundred years old

## MATHEMATICS KNOWLEDGE

You'll have 25 questions and 24 minutes to answer them.

1. If the length of Side A of a triangle is 8 feet and the length of Side C (the hypotenuse) is 12.8 feet, what is the length of Side B, assuming it is a right triangle?

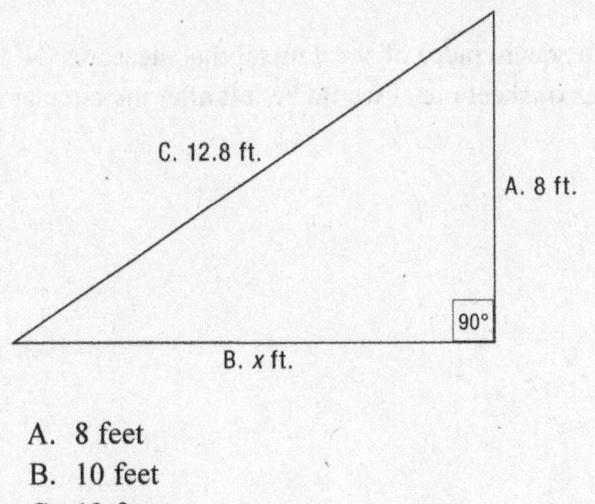


   A. 8 feet
   B. 10 feet
   C. 12 feet
   D. 12.3 feet

2. What is the area of the trapezoidal figure shown?

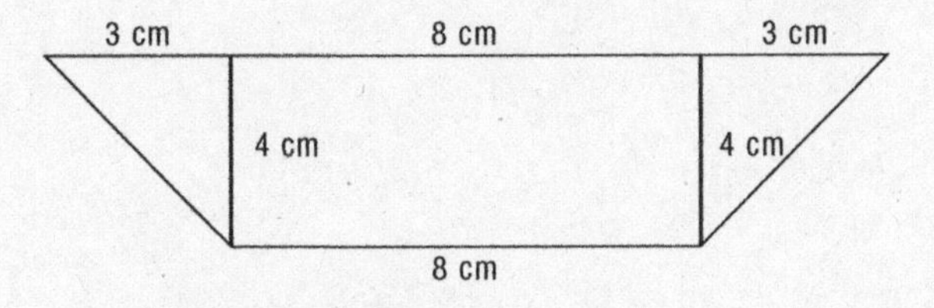


   A. 44 square centimeters
   B. 46 square centimeters
   C. 48 square centimeters
   D. 50 square centimeters

3. What is the length of a diagonal line inside a square that has the area of 81 square feet?

   A. 9.82 feet
   B. 10.38 feet
   C. 12.73 feet
   D. 14.71 feet

4. If 34 inches represents 34% of the diameter of a particular circle, what is the area of the circle?

   A. 4,891 square inches
   B. 5,432 square inches
   C. 6,971 square inches
   D. 7,854 square inches

5. If you were told that a specific tire could roll 200 yards in 27.28 revolutions, what is the radius of the tire?

A. 42 inches
B. 84 inches
C. 37.5 inches
D. 75 inches

6. Someone was told to cut a 23.5-inch-diameter circle from a square piece of sheet metal that measures 24 inches on one side. Approximately how many square inches of sheet metal would be left after the circular cut was made?

A. 142.26 square inches
B. 147 square inches
C. 159.87 square inches
D. 163.2 square inches

7. Solve for $x$: $11x < 33$.

A. $x = 22$
B. $x > 3$
C. $x = 3$
D. $x < 3$

8. What is the product of $(y+3)(y-3)$?

A. $y^2$
B. $y^2 - 9$
C. $2y$
D. $y - 9$

9. Which of the following is true about a trapezoid?

A. A trapezoid has parallel sides equal in length
B. A trapezoid has four equal angles
C. A trapezoid has one pair of opposite sides that are parallel
D. A trapezoid has four sides of equal length

10. Solve for $x$: $6x - 18 = -42$.

A. −4
B. 4
C. −24
D. 10

11. The total measurement of the angles of a polygon with 9 sides is:

A. 810°
B. 360°
C. 180°
D. 1260°

12. Evaluate the expression $x+(2x)^3-3x+6x^2$.

A. $(x)^3+6x^2$

B. $(3x)^3-3x+6x^2$

C. $(2x)^3+6x^2-2x$

D. $(2x)^3+4x^2$

13. What is the product of $(y-3)(y+4)$?

A. $2y+1$

B. $y^2+4y$

C. $y^2+1$

D. $y^2+y+12$

14. Solve the inequality $-2y<6$.

A. $y<-3$
B. $y>-3$
C. $y=3$
D. $y=-12$

15. Solve for $y$: $7y-21=-49$.

A. $y=-7$
B. $y=4$
C. $y=-4$
D. $y=28$

16. Solve for $y$: $\frac{2}{5}y=4$.

A. $y=10$
B. $y=20$
C. $y=2$

D. $y=\frac{1}{2}$

17. Solve for $x$: $\frac{1}{x}=\frac{x}{9}$.

A. $x=-9$
B. $x=9$

C. $x=\frac{1}{9}$

D. $x=3$

18. Subtract the fractions $\frac{x}{5}-\frac{2}{3}$.

A. $\frac{10}{3x}$

B. $\frac{x-2}{2}$

C. $\frac{2x}{2}$

D. $\frac{3x-10}{15}$

19. Divide the fractions $\frac{x-2}{x}\div\frac{x}{x+10}$

A. $\frac{x-2}{x+10}$

B. $\frac{x^2-8x+20}{x^2}$

C. $8x+20$

D. $\frac{x^2+8}{x^2}$

20. What is the product of $(x-2y)(x-10)$?

A. $x^2-2yx-10x$

B. $x^2-8x+8y$

C. $x^2-10x-2yx-20y$

D. $-8xy$

21. Factor $x^2+4x-12$.

A. $(x+3)(x-4)$
B. $(x+2)(x+2)$
C. $(x+4)(x-4)$
D. $(x+6)(x-2)$

22. What is the root of the equation $x^2-16=0$?

A. $x=8$
B. $x=4$
C. $x=-4$
D. Both B and C

23. Joe is about to enter a lottery. He has a 1 in 10 chance of being selected in the first round. Then he has a 1 in 5 chance of being selected in the second round. What is Joe's probability of advancing to the second round right now?

A. $\frac{1}{20}$

B. $\frac{5}{10}$

C. $\frac{1}{50}$

D. $\frac{1}{2}$

24. Of 300 students, 10 were selected to participate in a telephone survey. Maureen was one of them. Of the students selected to participate, 25% will be chosen at random to receive a free lunch at school. What are Maureen's chances of being selected to receive the free lunch?

A. $\frac{1}{4}$

B. $\frac{1}{30}$

C. $\frac{1}{120}$

D. $\frac{1}{75}$

25. Given $y = 3x - 7$ and $y = x + 1$, what are the values of $x$ and $y$?

A. $x = 3, y = 2$
B. $x = 3, y = 4$
C. $x = 4, y = 5$
D. there is not enough information to determine the answer

## ELECTRONICS INFORMATION

You'll have 20 questions and nine minutes to answer them.

1. Conductors are materials that

   A. allow current to flow freely
   B. resist the flow of current
   C. alternate the flow of current
   D. amplify the flow of current

2. The measure of electrical pressure is

   A. a watt
   B. a volt
   C. an ampere
   D. an ohm

3. The formula that represents the power equation is:

   A. $P = \frac{I}{V}$

   B. $V = PI$

   C. $P = VI$

   D. $P = \frac{1}{2}VI$

4. A circuit with 12 volts and a total resistance of 6 ohms has how much current?

   A. 48 A
   B. 0.5 A
   C. 18 A
   D. 2 A

5. A voltmeter shows 10 V on a car battery. That means the battery:

   A. is fully charged
   B. has 0% charge
   C. is 50% charged
   D. is about 75% charged

6. What is not true of direct current electricity?

   A. direct current flows from one terminal to another in one direction
   B. car batteries use direct current electricity
   C. direct current can be sent down power lines at a much higher voltage than alternating current
   D. direct current can be obtained from an alternating current through the use of a rectifier

7. Materials that gain electrons become:

   A. negatively charged
   B. positively charged
   C. either A or B, depending
   D. none of the above

8. Every charge has a field that extends beyond the charged object and which attracts or repels other charges. That field is called:

   A. an energy field
   B. a force field
   C. a magnetic field
   D. the ionosphere

9. To reduce energy lost through heat:

   A. increase the amount of current
   B. reduce the voltage
   C. use a semiconductor
   D. reduce the resistance to the current

10. The most common material used for a semiconductor is:

    A. glass
    B. copper wire
    C. silicon
    D. air

11. The figure below shows what type of circuit?

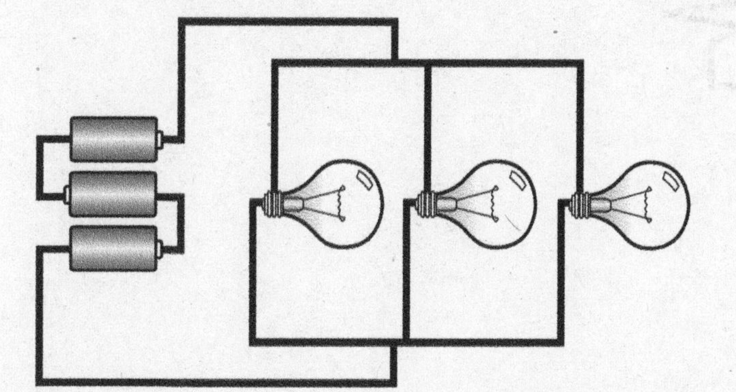

    A. parallel
    B. series
    C. series-parallel
    D. none of the above

12. The mathematical expression for 1μF is:

    A. 1,000 F
    B. 0.01 F
    C. $10^{-6}$
    D. $10^{-3}$

13. A ground rod serves as

    A. a storage unit for electric potential
    B. a conduit from a power line to a home's electric panel
    C. a pathway for an excess charge to travel harmlessly
    D. a source of electrical energy

14. If the recommended fuse size is 125% of the current in a circuit, what is an appropriate fuse size for a circuit with a voltage of 15 and a total resistance of 5 ohms?

A. 3.75 A
B. 3 A
C. 15 A
D. 18.75 A

15. If the total current of a circuit is 2.5 A and the total resistance is 4 ohms, what is the voltage?

A. 1.5 V
B. 1.6 V
C. 6.5 V
D. 10 V

16. In the figure below, if $R_1 = 3$ ohms and $R_2 = 6$ ohms, what is the total resistance?

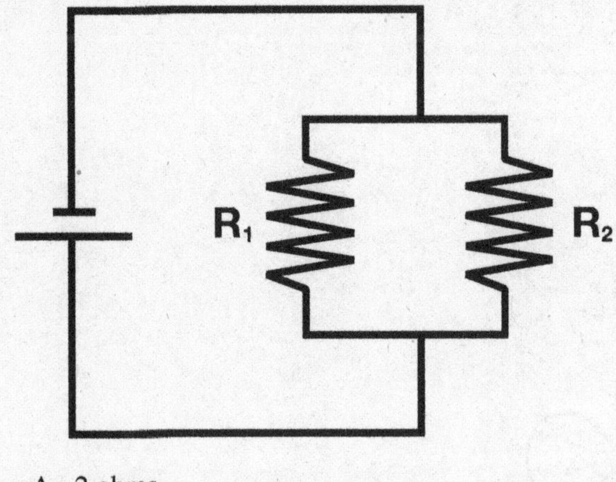


A. 2 ohms
B. 9 ohms
C. 3 ohms
D. 18 ohms

17. In the figure below, if the voltage drops 1.5 V at $R_1$ and 1 V at $R_2$, what is the total voltage drop across the circuit?

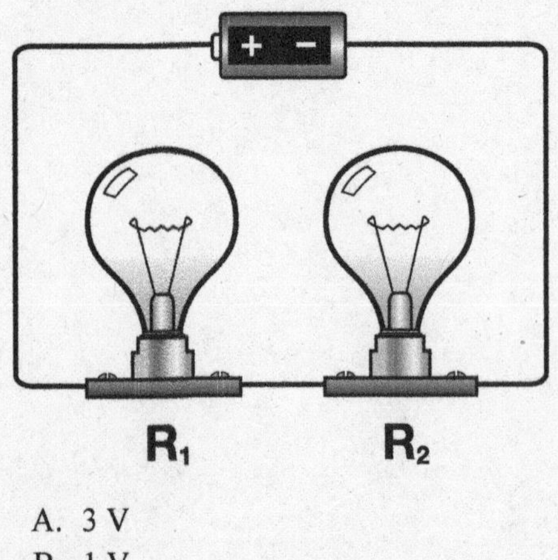


A. 3 V
B. 1 V
C. 1.5 V
D. 2.5 V

18. The symbol ⊣⊢ stands for what component in a schematic?

A. capacitor
B. resistor
C. diode
D. inductor

19. According to the schematic below, which of the following is true:

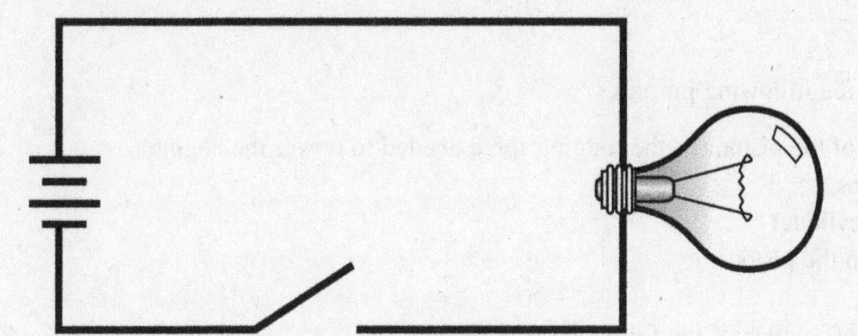

A. the light bulb is not lit
B. the connectors are copper wire
C. the circuit is wired in parallel
D. the total voltage of the circuit is 12 volts

20. What is the function of a capacitor?

A. to amplify an electric current
B. to impede an electric current
C. to allow the free flow of an electric current
D. to store an electric charge

## AUTOMOTIVE AND SHOP INFORMATION

You'll have 25 questions and 11 minutes to answer them.

1. The purpose of intake valves is which of the following?

   A. to allow fuel into the fuel tank
   B. to filter fuel in the engine
   C. to allow fuel and air into the cylinder
   D. to vent exhaust

2. The crankshaft serves which of the following purposes?

   A. to convert the linear force of the pistons to the rotating force needed to power the engine
   B. to open and close the valves
   C. to close off the top of the cylinder
   D. to ignite the fuel mixture in the piston

3. If the timing of the camshaft is off, which of the following occurs?

   A. the battery wears down
   B. the starter won't engage
   C. the valves open at the wrong time
   D. the parking brake won't operate

4. The device shown in the figure below is an example of what automotive system?

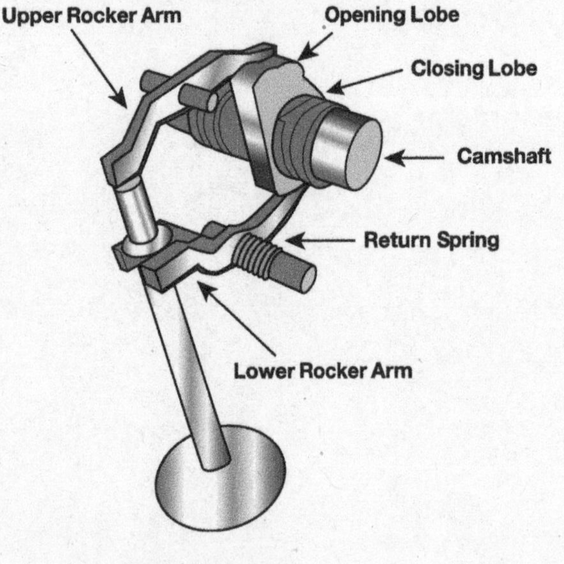


   A. the suspension system
   B. the steering system
   C. the drive train
   D. the valve train

5. In a four-stroke cycle, the first stroke is the intake stroke and the second stroke is which of the following?

   A. combustion
   B. compression
   C. exhaust
   D. elimination

6. How many revolutions does the crankshaft make per cycle in a four-stroke engine?

   A. 1
   B. 2
   C. 3
   D. 4

7. The oil lubrication system serves which of the following purposes?

   A. it cools the engine
   B. it assists with power steering and braking
   C. it reduces the amount of friction between parts
   D. it enhances the fuel efficiency of the gasoline

8. A clogged water pump can cause which of the following problems?

   A. improperly functioning brakes
   B. incorrect fuel mixture
   C. loss of acceleration
   D. engine overheating

9. Which of the following are advantages of a rear-wheel drive vehicle?

   A. it distributes weight more evenly over the vehicle
   B. it allows for better balance and handling
   C. it allows for quicker acceleration
   D. all of the above

10. The engine component that allows the car to go faster or slower, idle, and reverse is called which of the following?

    A. the throttle
    B. the transmission
    C. the venturi
    D. the governor

11. The abbreviation "ABS" stands for which of the following?

    A. Antilock Brake System
    B. Air Brake Solution
    C. Anti-Burglary System
    D. All-Band Stereo

12. If a piece of $\frac{1}{2}$-inch rebar had to be shortened, what kind of a saw would you use?

    A. portable circular saw with a combination blade
    B. back saw
    C. coping saw
    D. hacksaw

13. Prior to staining or painting furniture, what kind of power sander would be used to do the smooth finish work?

    A. belt sander
    B. disk sander
    C. orbital sander
    D. all of the above

14. A hydrometer measures what?

    A. glycerol in an automotive coolant system
    B. battery electrolyte fluid (wet cell)
    C. hydraulic fluid levels
    D. none of the above

15. What tool is commonly used in the electrical profession?

    A. multipurpose tool
    B. plunger
    C. claw hammer
    D. slip joint pliers

16. Which of the following wrenches are the slowest to use in loosening a nut?

    A. crescent wrench
    B. open-ended wrench
    C. screw wrench
    D. box wrench

17. A jack plane is associated with what profession?

    A. plumbing
    B. electrical
    C. carpentry
    D. metal fabrication

18. What kind of wrench could loosen the nut shown in the diagram in the figure below?

    A. crescent wrench
    B. open-ended wrench
    C. offset box wrench
    D. monkey wrench

19. What kind of pliers are shown in the diagram in the figure below?

A. channel lock pliers
B. slip joint pliers
C. needle-nose pliers
D. end-cutting pliers

20. If the contents of a wooden shipping crate needed to be inspected by custom officials, what one tool would probably be used to open it?

A. wrecking bar
B. wood chisel
C. sledgehammer
D. chain saw

21. Which of the following gauges are used to determine spark plug gaps?

A. screw pitch gauge
B. depth gauge
C. compression gauge
D. feelers gauge

22. If a rivet had to be removed from sheet metal, what tool could be used?

A. bolt cutters
B. lopping shears
C. hacksaw
D. cold chisel

23. When a plumber is said to be sweating a joint, what is the probable source of heat?

A. arc welder
B. oxyacetylene cutting torch
C. propane torch
D. all of the above

24. If a lawn mower blade had to be sharpened, what tool would be the quickest and most convenient to use?

A. bench grinder
B. flat file
C. whetstone
D. emery paper

25. The diagram shown illustrates what kind of a tool?

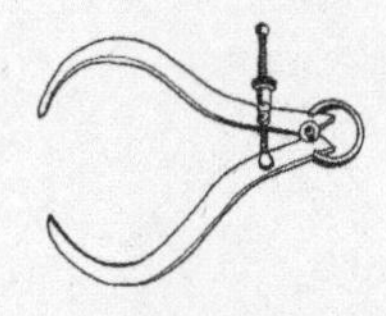

A. inside calipers
B. outside calipers
C. bow compass
D. micrometer

## MECHANICAL COMPREHENSION

You'll have 25 questions and 19 minutes to answer them.

1. Examine the diagram below. Which statement is correct, assuming that the drive gear is turning counterclockwise?

   A. All the gears are turning counterclockwise.
   B. Gears 1, 3, and 6 all turn counterclockwise.
   C. Gears 2, 4, and 6 all turn clockwise.
   D. Since gear 4 is an internal gear, it rotates in the same direction as gear 3.

2. What kind of gears are used in changing the direction of a drive train?
   A. external spur
   B. beveled gears
   C. helical gears
   D. herringbone gears

3. If a drive gear has 30 teeth and a connecting gear (that is, the driven gear) has 10 teeth, which of the following will occur?
   A. The output torque is tripled while speed is cut by $\frac{1}{3}$.
   B. The output torque and speed are tripled.
   C. The output torque is only $\frac{1}{3}$ while speed is tripled.
   D. The output torque is increased only 25%.

4. Refer to the diagram in the figure below. Assuming gears A and B have 10 teeth each and gear C has 20 teeth, what would happen if gear B were the drive gear and turned $\frac{1}{2}$ a revolution counterclockwise?

A. Gears A and C would each turn $\frac{1}{2}$ revolution counterclockwise.

B. Gear A would turn $\frac{1}{2}$ revolution counterclockwise and gear C would turn clockwise.

C. Gears A and C would respectively turn $\frac{1}{4}$ revolution and $\frac{1}{2}$ revolution clockwise.

D. Gears A and C would respectively turn $\frac{1}{2}$ and $\frac{1}{4}$ revolution clockwise.

5. If a piston exerted a pressure of 200 pounds per square inch (psi) on the water trapped in the pipe (i.e., a closed system) as in the figure below, which of the following statements is correct?

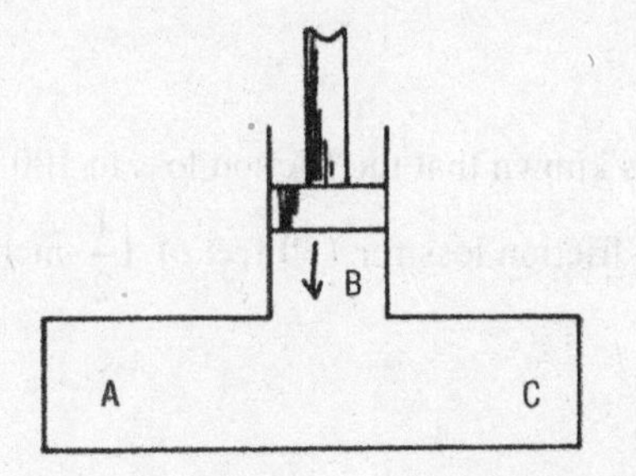


A. The pressure would be the greatest at point B.
B. The pressure is the same throughout the closed system.
C. The pressure measured at points A and C is twice that at point B.
D. The pressure is diminished at both points A and C.

6. Refer to the diagram in the figure below. Assuming the base of each container is the same and that each container is full of salt water, which of the three vessels shown would have the greatest pressure at its base?

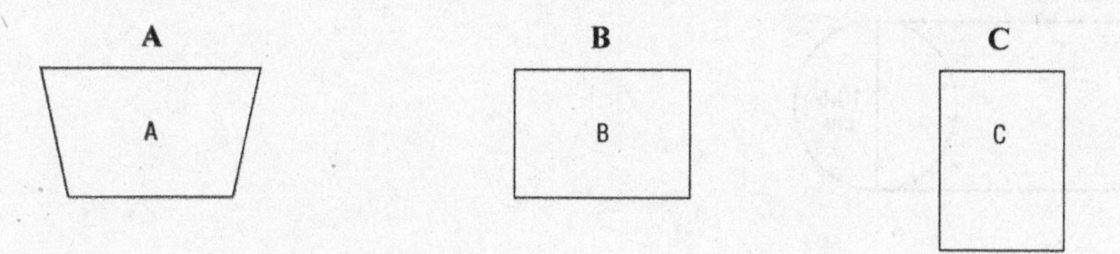


A. A
B. B
C. C
D. All vessels would have the same pressure at their base because the same kind of fluid was used (that is, fluid density is the same).

7. Which of the diagrams in the figure below demonstrates the quickest way to siphon the fluid in the container, assuming all things are equal except the length of the siphon tube itself?

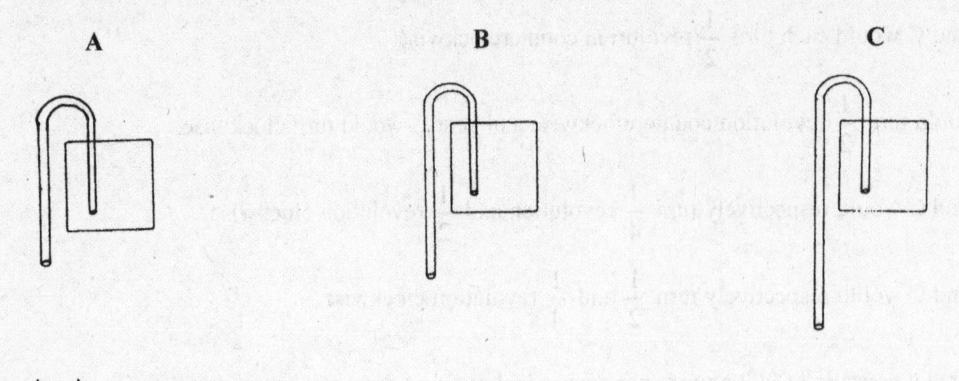


A. A
B. B
C. C
D. Cannot be determined with the information given.

8. The loss of water pressure in a hose can be attributed to friction. If it is known that the friction loss in 100 feet of $1\frac{1}{2}$-inch hose is 25 pounds per square inch, what would be the friction loss for 150 feet of $1\frac{1}{2}$-inch hose, assuming all other factors remain constant?

A. 16.67 psi
B. 37.5 psi
C. 47.3 psi
D. 52 psi

9. If the two pulleys shown in the figure below are spaced 35 centimeters apart center to center and have 10.5 centimeter diameters, what would be the length of V-belt required?

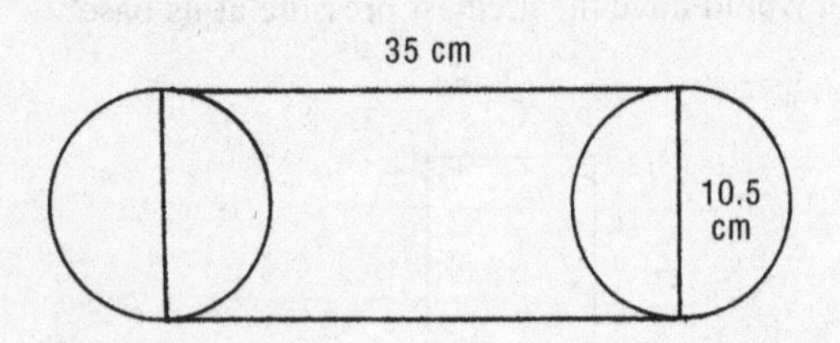


A. 95.72 cm
B. 97.691 cm
C. 100.2 cm
D. 102.987 cm

10. What would be the displacement of a piston that has a bore of 3.25 inches and a stroke of 4.75 inches?

A. 39.41 cubic inches
B. 47.59 cubic inches
C. 132.52 cubic inches
D. 157.62 cubic inches

11. According to the diagram in the figure below, at what position could a fulcrum be placed to maximize the lift capability of this lever?

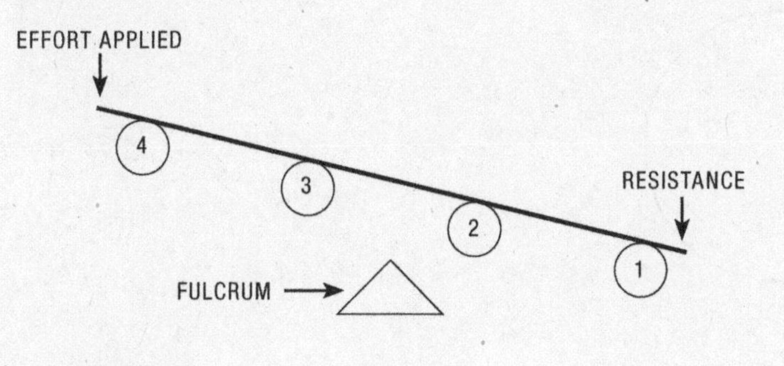


A. Position 1
B. Position 2
C. Position 3
D. Position 4

12. Assuming that the resistance of a load to be lifted is 825 pounds, the length of the lever is exactly 14 feet, and the fulcrum is placed dead center beneath the lever, what amount of effort would be required at the end opposite the load to attain lift?

A. 82.5 pounds
B. 412.5 pounds
C. 825 pounds
D. 1,000 pounds

13. Assuming that the resistance of a load to be lifted is 825 pounds, the length of the lever is exactly 14 feet, and the fulcrum is placed dead center beneath the lever, the use of the lever as described affords what kind of mechanical advantage for lift?

A. 1:2
B. 2:1
C. 1:1
D. 3:2

14. According to the illustration in the figure below, if 1,000 psi of pressure is exerted on the fluid trapped within the cylinder, which of the following statements is true?

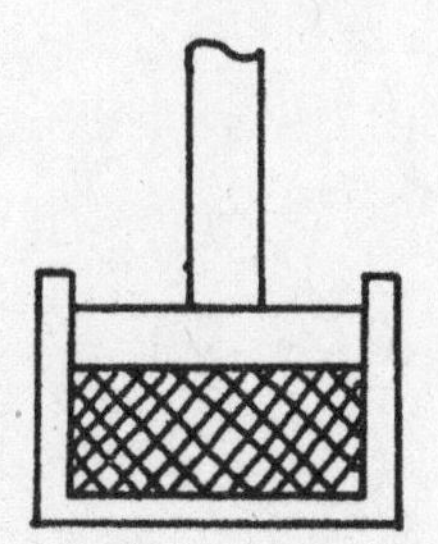

A. That portion of fluid closest to the piston or ram comes under the greatest pressure.
B. Pressure is evenly distributed through the fluid and against the cylinder's walls without consequent loss of power.
C. The portion of fluid closest to the bottom of the cylinder is subjected to the greatest pressure.
D. There is a proportional decrease in fluid volume.

15. If the two pulleys shown in the figure below have a 3:1 ratio and the smaller pulley has a 9.5 inch circumference, how fast would the larger pulley turn if the smaller pulley turned at a rate of 300 rpm?

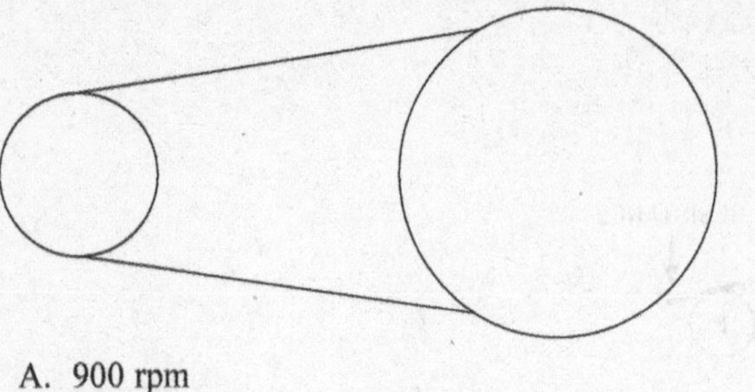

A. 900 rpm
B. 300 rpm
C. 100 rpm
D. 75 rpm

16. Which of the following statements is true with respect to the drive train illustrated in the figure below?

A. Gears 2 and 8 will turn clockwise if the first gear turns clockwise.
B. Gears 4 and 5 will turn counterclockwise if gear 2 turns clockwise.
C. Gears 3, 5, and 6 will turn the same direction that gear 2 turns.
D. Gears 3, 5, and 7 will turn counterclockwise if gear 2 turns clockwise.

17. According to the diagram shown below, how much pulling effort at point C would be required to lift the weight?

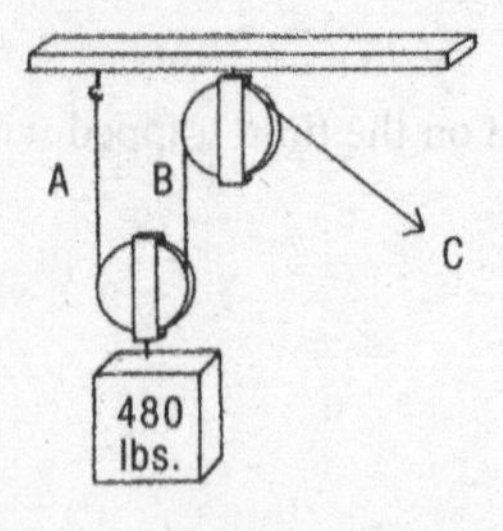


A. 960 pounds
B. 480 pounds
C. 240 pounds
D. 120 pounds

18. The pulley apparatus in the figure below demonstrates what kind of mechanical advantage?

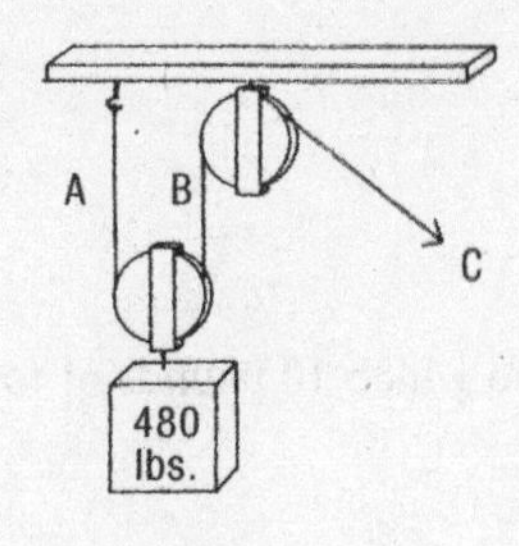


A. 1:2
B. 2:1
C. 1:1
D. 1:5

19. Which of the following is not considered in the truest form to be an example of a simple machine?
   A. A two-stroke gasoline powered engine
   B. A ramp used to lift heavy objects
   C. A wedge-shaped device used to split wood
   D. A pry bar

20. The tool illustrated in the figure below is sometimes used by firefighters to conduct a forcible entry. If the handle portion measures 28 inches in length and the distance from the base of the handle to the tip of the pointed end measures 8 inches in length, how much effort is required at the end of the handle to pry off a door lock shackle that offers 575 pounds of pry resistance?

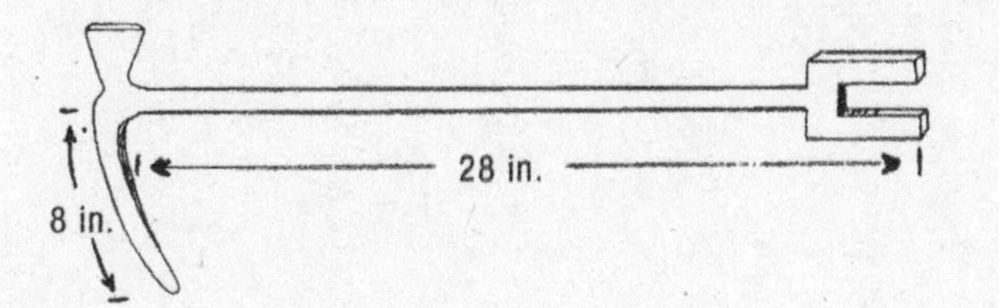


   A. 244.2 pounds of force
   B. 178.9 pounds of force
   C. 164.3 pounds of force
   D. 152.7 pounds of force

21. If a tool requires only 125 pounds of effort to move 655 pounds of resistance, what kind of mechanical advantage is gained by using it?

   A. 5.35:1
   B. 4.21:1
   C. 5.24:1
   D. 3.76:1

22. Assume a $\frac{3}{8}$-inch hole is drilled into a block of steel and later tapped to create a $\frac{1}{8}$-inch pitch. If a $\frac{3}{8}$-inch bolt with a $\frac{1}{8}$-inch pitch is screwed into the hole with a box-end wrench 6 inches long, what is the potential force of the bolt as measured at its threaded end if we apply 10 pounds of force?

A. 2,576 pounds of force
B. 3,016 pounds of force
C. 3,758 pounds of force
D. 3,982 pounds of force

23. If a jackscrew with a pitch of $\frac{1}{7}$-inch possesses a handle (lever) 20 inches long to which 10 pounds of force is applied, how much potential weight could be lifted?

A. 8,796 pounds
B. 8,875 pounds
C. 9,257 pounds
D. 9,762 pounds

24. If a jackscrew with a pitch of $\frac{1}{7}$-inch possesses a handle (lever) 20 inches long, what mechanical advantage is gained by using the jackscrew?

A. 879.62:1
B. 887.51:1
C. 925.70:1
D. 976.29:1

25. How much force or effort would be required to lift 3 tons using a jackscrew with a $\frac{1}{6}$-inch pitch and a handle 18 inches long?

A. 6.0 pounds
B. 7.62 pounds
C. 7.75 pounds
D. 8.84 pounds

## ASSEMBLING OBJECTS

You'll have 16 questions and 15 minutes to answer them.

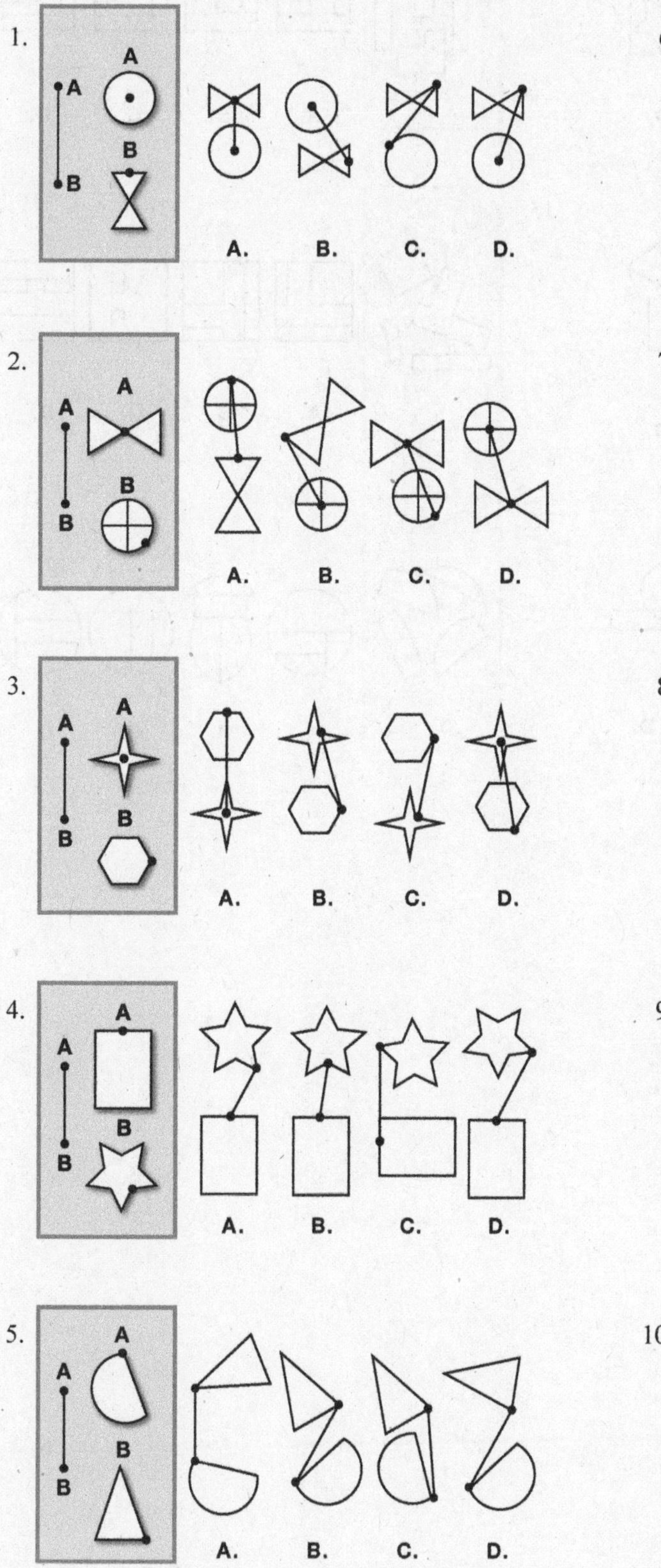


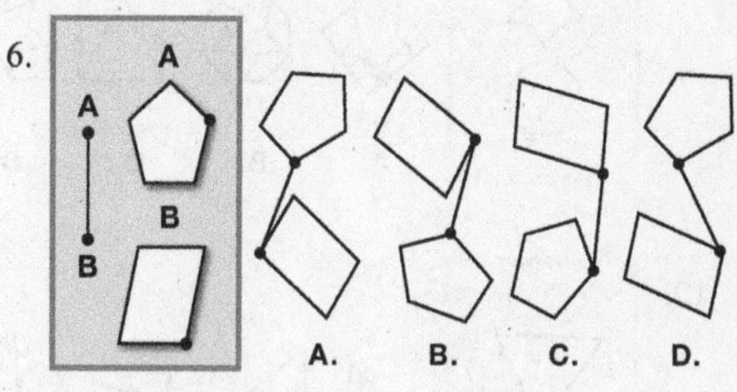


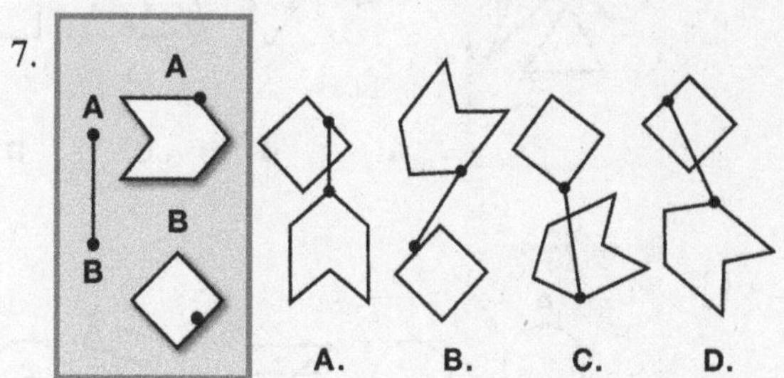


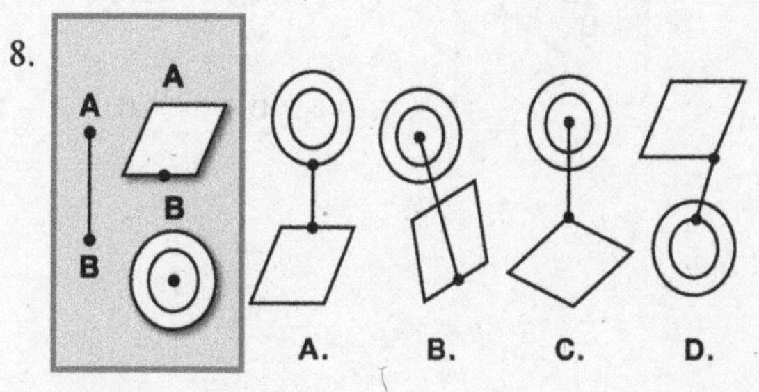


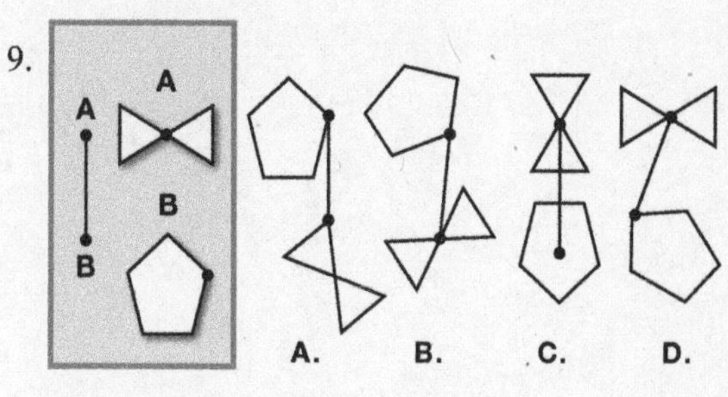


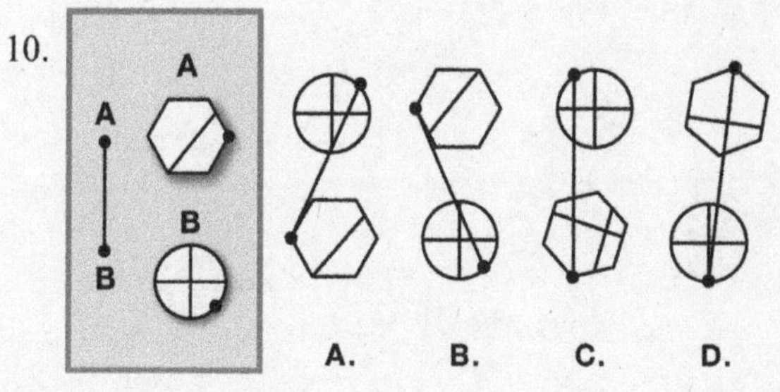

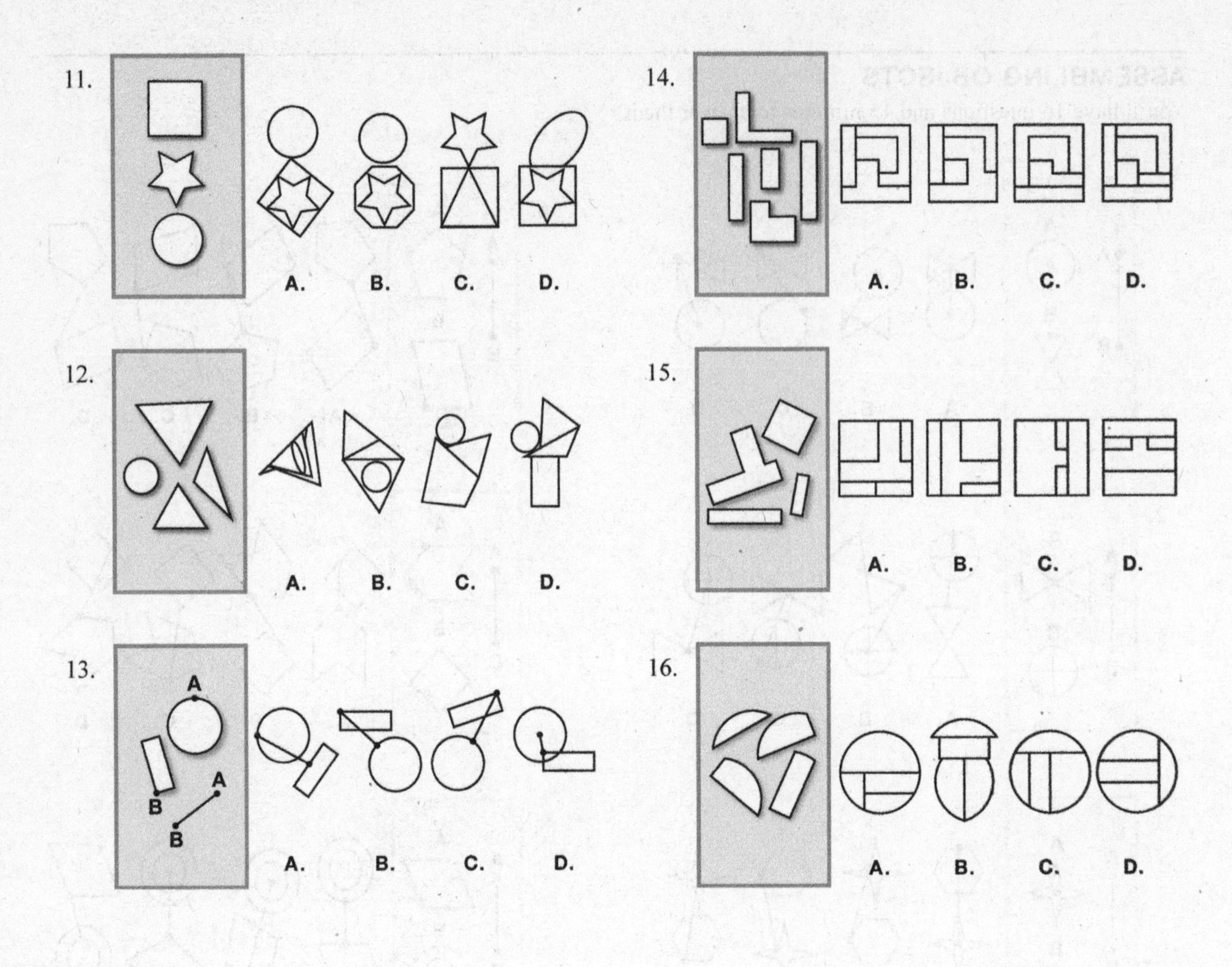
11.
A.
B.
C.
D.
12.
A.
B.
C.
D.
13.
A
B
A
B
A.
B.
C.
D.
14.
A.
B.
C.
D.
15.
A.
B.
C.
D.
16.
A.
B.
C.
D.

# ANSWER SHEET FOR PRACTICE TEST #1

## GENERAL SCIENCE

1. Ⓐ Ⓑ Ⓒ Ⓓ
2. Ⓐ Ⓑ Ⓒ Ⓓ
3. Ⓐ Ⓑ Ⓒ Ⓓ
4. Ⓐ Ⓑ Ⓒ Ⓓ
5. Ⓐ Ⓑ Ⓒ Ⓓ
6. Ⓐ Ⓑ Ⓒ Ⓓ
7. Ⓐ Ⓑ Ⓒ Ⓓ
8. Ⓐ Ⓑ Ⓒ Ⓓ
9. Ⓐ Ⓑ Ⓒ Ⓓ
10. Ⓐ Ⓑ Ⓒ Ⓓ
11. Ⓐ Ⓑ Ⓒ Ⓓ
12. Ⓐ Ⓑ Ⓒ Ⓓ
13. Ⓐ Ⓑ Ⓒ Ⓓ
14. Ⓐ Ⓑ Ⓒ Ⓓ
15. Ⓐ Ⓑ Ⓒ Ⓓ
16. Ⓐ Ⓑ Ⓒ Ⓓ
17. Ⓐ Ⓑ Ⓒ Ⓓ
18. Ⓐ Ⓑ Ⓒ Ⓓ
19. Ⓐ Ⓑ Ⓒ Ⓓ
20. Ⓐ Ⓑ Ⓒ Ⓓ
21. Ⓐ Ⓑ Ⓒ Ⓓ
22. Ⓐ Ⓑ Ⓒ Ⓓ
23. Ⓐ Ⓑ Ⓒ Ⓓ
24. Ⓐ Ⓑ Ⓒ Ⓓ
25. Ⓐ Ⓑ Ⓒ Ⓓ

## ARITHMETIC REASONING

1. Ⓐ Ⓑ Ⓒ Ⓓ
2. Ⓐ Ⓑ Ⓒ Ⓓ
3. Ⓐ Ⓑ Ⓒ Ⓓ
4. Ⓐ Ⓑ Ⓒ Ⓓ
5. Ⓐ Ⓑ Ⓒ Ⓓ
6. Ⓐ Ⓑ Ⓒ Ⓓ
7. Ⓐ Ⓑ Ⓒ Ⓓ
8. Ⓐ Ⓑ Ⓒ Ⓓ
9. Ⓐ Ⓑ Ⓒ Ⓓ
10. Ⓐ Ⓑ Ⓒ Ⓓ
11. Ⓐ Ⓑ Ⓒ Ⓓ
12. Ⓐ Ⓑ Ⓒ Ⓓ
13. Ⓐ Ⓑ Ⓒ Ⓓ
14. Ⓐ Ⓑ Ⓒ Ⓓ
15. Ⓐ Ⓑ Ⓒ Ⓓ
16. Ⓐ Ⓑ Ⓒ Ⓓ
17. Ⓐ Ⓑ Ⓒ Ⓓ
18. Ⓐ Ⓑ Ⓒ Ⓓ
19. Ⓐ Ⓑ Ⓒ Ⓓ
20. Ⓐ Ⓑ Ⓒ Ⓓ
21. Ⓐ Ⓑ Ⓒ Ⓓ
22. Ⓐ Ⓑ Ⓒ Ⓓ
23. Ⓐ Ⓑ Ⓒ Ⓓ
24. Ⓐ Ⓑ Ⓒ Ⓓ
25. Ⓐ Ⓑ Ⓒ Ⓓ
26. Ⓐ Ⓑ Ⓒ Ⓓ
27. Ⓐ Ⓑ Ⓒ Ⓓ
28. Ⓐ Ⓑ Ⓒ Ⓓ
29. Ⓐ Ⓑ Ⓒ Ⓓ
30. Ⓐ Ⓑ Ⓒ Ⓓ

## WORD KNOWLEDGE

1. Ⓐ Ⓑ Ⓒ Ⓓ
2. Ⓐ Ⓑ Ⓒ Ⓓ
3. Ⓐ Ⓑ Ⓒ Ⓓ
4. Ⓐ Ⓑ Ⓒ Ⓓ
5. Ⓐ Ⓑ Ⓒ Ⓓ
6. Ⓐ Ⓑ Ⓒ Ⓓ
7. Ⓐ Ⓑ Ⓒ Ⓓ
8. Ⓐ Ⓑ Ⓒ Ⓓ
9. Ⓐ Ⓑ Ⓒ Ⓓ
10. Ⓐ Ⓑ Ⓒ Ⓓ
11. Ⓐ Ⓑ Ⓒ Ⓓ
12. Ⓐ Ⓑ Ⓒ Ⓓ
13. Ⓐ Ⓑ Ⓒ Ⓓ
14. Ⓐ Ⓑ Ⓒ Ⓓ
15. Ⓐ Ⓑ Ⓒ Ⓓ
16. Ⓐ Ⓑ Ⓒ Ⓓ
17. Ⓐ Ⓑ Ⓒ Ⓓ
18. Ⓐ Ⓑ Ⓒ Ⓓ
19. Ⓐ Ⓑ Ⓒ Ⓓ
20. Ⓐ Ⓑ Ⓒ Ⓓ
21. Ⓐ Ⓑ Ⓒ Ⓓ

22. A B C D
23. A B C D
24. A B C D
25. A B C D
26. A B C D
27. A B C D
28. A B C D
29. A B C D
30. A B C D
31. A B C D
32. A B C D
33. A B C D
34. A B C D
35. A B C D

## PARAGRAPH COMPREHENSION

1. A B C D
2. A B C D
3. A B C D
4. A B C D
5. A B C D
6. A B C D
7. A B C D
8. A B C D
9. A B C D
10. A B C D
11. A B C D
12. A B C D
13. A B C D
14. A B C D
15. A B C D

## MATHEMATICS KNOWLEDGE

1. A B C D
2. A B C D
3. A B C D
4. A B C D
5. A B C D
6. A B C D
7. A B C D
8. A B C D
9. A B C D
10. A B C D
11. A B C D
12. A B C D
13. A B C D
14. A B C D
15. A B C D
16. A B C D
17. A B C D
18. A B C D
19. A B C D
20. A B C D
21. A B C D
22. A B C D
23. A B C D
24. A B C D
25. A B C D

## ELECTRONICS INFORMATION

1. A B C D
2. A B C D
3. A B C D
4. A B C D
5. A B C D
6. A B C D
7. A B C D
8. A B C D
9. A B C D
10. A B C D
11. A B C D
12. A B C D
13. A B C D
14. A B C D
15. A B C D
16. A B C D
17. A B C D
18. A B C D
19. A B C D
20. A B C D

## AUTOMOTIVE AND SHOP INFORMATION

1. A B C D
2. A B C D
3. A B C D
4. A B C D
5. A B C D
6. A B C D
7. A B C D
8. A B C D
9. A B C D
10. A B C D
11. A B C D
12. A B C D
13. A B C D
14. A B C D
15. A B C D
16. A B C D
17. A B C D
18. A B C D
19. A B C D
20. A B C D
21. A B C D
22. A B C D
23. A B C D
24. A B C D
25. A B C D

## MECHANICAL COMPREHENSION

1. A B C D
2. A B C D
3. A B C D
4. A B C D
5. A B C D
6. A B C D
7. A B C D
8. A B C D
9. A B C D
10. A B C D
11. A B C D
12. A B C D
13. A B C D
14. A B C D
15. A B C D
16. A B C D
17. A B C D
18. A B C D
19. A B C D
20. A B C D
21. A B C D
22. A B C D
23. A B C D
24. A B C D
25. A B C D

## ASSEMBLING OBJECTS

1. A B C D
2. A B C D
3. A B C D
4. A B C D
5. A B C D
6. A B C D
7. A B C D
8. A B C D
9. A B C D
10. A B C D
11. A B C D
12. A B C D
13. A B C D
14. A B C D
15. A B C D
16. A B C D

## ANSWER KEY TO PRACTICE TEST #1

Use the following answer key to grade your exam. Use the results to guide your review. (See Chapter 5 for strategies on how to do this.)

### GENERAL SCIENCE

1. **A.** The nucleus and mitochondria are found within a cell. Leukocytes and erythrocytes (answer B) are types of cells, not structures found within cells. While nucleoids do exist in some cells, riboids is a made-up thing and doesn't exist, making answer C incorrect. Ions and protons (answer D) relate to the chemistry of atoms, but aren't structures in a cell.
2. **C.** An upper respiratory infection affects the nasal cavity; the upper respiratory tract includes those structures above the larynx (where your vocal cords are located).
3. **C.** We live on the crust of the earth. The outer core is below the crust, and is thought to be liquid.
4. **B.** Gas is matter without defined shape or volume. Liquid (answer A) has a defined volume. A solid (answer C) has a defined shape and volume.
5. **D.** An example of a heterogeneous mixture is vinaigrette dressing. Heterogeneous mixtures are those that are not exactly the same throughout. Eventually the oil and water in a vinaigrette dressing will separate out, but coffee, apple juice, and wine (answers A, B, and C) will never separate out into their constituent parts. They are homogeneous and completely uniform throughout.
6. **A.** Water pressure increases about 14.5 psi for approximately every 10 meters.
7. **D.** Anatomy is the study of the structures of living things. Ecology is the study of environments (answer A), and chemistry is the study of matter (answer B). Biology is the study of living things (answer C) and while this is also technically true of anatomy, answer D is more accurate.
8. **B.** In a scientific study, the word "correlation" means two conditions are related. Correlation does *not* mean one event causes another (answer B). It also does not mean two conditions are not related (answer C); it means they are related. While answer D may be true of two conditions that are correlated, it also may not be.
9. **A.** The metric system is based on the decimal system. The Imperial system (answer A) and the customary system (answer C) are based on traditional British measurements of feet and pounds, while the Hellenic system (answer D) is the ancient Roman system that is the forerunner of the Imperial system.
10. **A.** Scientists use the word "mass" instead of weight because weight measures the pull of gravity, so it can vary based on where the item being measured is located. Answers B and C are incorrect because weight can be measured in various ways and to various degrees, and neither answer is the reason why measuring mass is the preferred approach. And while it may seem to be true that scientists don't like to use words already in common use (answer C) that is not the reason why "mass" is preferred.
11. **B.** Metabolism, growth, and reproduction are characteristics of living things. Answer A, inorganic matter, is incorrect because these processes do not occur in inorganic material. Answer C, elements, is incorrect because elements are groups of atoms that do not make up living systems that metabolize, grow, and reproduce. The scientific process (answer D) itself is the way in which science is conducted, not a definition for life.
12. **D.** A change in a population may occur for any of the following reasons *except* cloning, because a clone is an exact duplicate of an existing organism. Advantageous adaptation (answer A), random genetic mutation (answer B), and selective breeding (answer C) are all ways in which the genetics of a population can change over time.

13. **A.** A eukaryotic cell differs from a prokaryotic cell in that a eukaryotic cell has an interior cell membrane. Glowing under ultraviolet light (answer B) has nothing to do with whether a cell is eukaryotic or prokaryotic. Answers C and D are incorrect because these are characteristic of both types of cells.

14. **B.** Humans share the class *mammalia* with dolphins, although many people mistake dolphins for fish.

15. **A.** Necessary materials for photosynthesis to occur include chlorophyll, carbon dioxide, sunlight, and water. In answer B, carbon monoxide is incorrect. In answer C, salt is incorrect. In answer D, oxygen is incorrect.

16. **D.** Vertebrates are organisms with a backbone. Whether an animal is warm-blooded (answer A) or cold-blooded (answer B) has nothing to do with whether it is a vertebrate. While answer C is true, it is also incomplete; an organism can be a vertebrate without also being a mammal. Therefore, D is most correct.

17. **C.** Photoreceptors are cells that are activated by light waves. They're in the retina of your eye and transmit images to your brain. They are not associated with hearing, smelling, or touching (answers A, B, and D).

18. **B.** Children have more bones than adults because some of the bones fuse together as the child grows. For example, the bones of the skull fuse together.

19. **D.** Attaching your muscles to your bones is the function of your tendons, not your skin. The other three answers are all functions of your body's skin.

20. **A.** Oxygen-depleted blood is sent to the lungs for re-oxygenation by the heart via the pulmonary artery. The pulmonary vein(s) (answer B) bring oxygenated blood into the heart. The aorta (answer C) is the vein through which oxygenated blood is sent throughout the body. Lateral ventricles (answer D) are found in your brain, not your circulatory system.

21. **B.** The three types of rocks that make up the earth's crust are igneous, sedimentary, and metamorphic. "Combination" is not one of the three types of rocks, making answer A incorrect. Obsidian, shale, and slate (answer C) are types of igneous, sedimentary, and metamorphic rocks, but these are not the only types of igneous, sedimentary, and metamorphic. In answer D, igneous-sedimentary is not correct.

22. **A.** The average depth of the ocean is about 4.3 kilometers (2.65 miles).

23. **B.** Falling barometric pressure is often associated with cloudy skies and rain. Clear weather (answer A) is more associated with high barometric pressure. High tides (answer C) are not related to barometric pressure. Falling barometric pressure is more associated with cold weather than warm weather, making D incorrect.

24. **D.** A lunar eclipse occurs when the earth passes between the moon and the sun. The sun never passes between the earth and the moon, as the earth and the moon are in orbit around it, not the other way around, making answer A incorrect. Answer B is the definition of a solar eclipse. Answer C is incorrect; a full moon that happens in autumn is often called a harvest moon, but it is not a lunar eclipse.

25. **D.** If you add a proton to an atom, you change it into a different element. An ion (answer A) is the gain or loss of an electron (not a proton). An isotope (answer B) is a variation in the number of neutrons in an atom. A compound (answer C) is a mixture of elements and doesn't have anything to do with proton count in an atom.

## ARITHMETIC REASONING

1. **B.** The number 9 can be represented as $8\frac{8}{8}$. Then, subtract: $\frac{8}{8}-\frac{3}{8}=\frac{5}{8}$. Therefore, $x$ must equal $8\frac{5}{8}$.

2. **B.** $\frac{1}{3}$ can be represented as $\frac{2}{6}$, so $6\frac{1}{3}$ can be written as $5\frac{8}{6}$. Thus, $5\frac{8}{6}-4\frac{5}{6}$. $5-4=1$ and $\frac{8}{6}-\frac{5}{6}=\frac{3}{6}$. $\frac{3}{6}$ can be reduced to $\frac{1}{2}$, so therefore $x=1\frac{1}{2}$. Answer D is correct as well, but it is not in reduced form.

3. **A.** $\frac{2}{3}, \frac{1}{6}, \frac{1}{8}$ have the LCD of 24. Therefore, $\frac{2}{3}=\frac{16}{24}, \frac{1}{2}=\frac{4}{24}, \frac{1}{8}=\frac{3}{24}$. Do the operations on the fractions first:

$$\frac{16}{24}+\frac{4}{24}-\frac{3}{24}=\frac{17}{24}$$

Then, the whole numbers: $4+5-2=3$. Therefore, $x=3\frac{17}{24}$.

4. **A.** The problem can be stated as $9+\frac{1}{2}x=16$. Subtract 9 from each side:

$$9-9+\frac{1}{2}x=16-9$$

Thus, $\frac{1}{2}x=7$. To isolate *x*, multiply both sides of the equation by 2:

$$2\bullet\frac{1}{2}x=7\bullet 2$$

Or, $x = 14$.

5. **D.** The first water line can do $\frac{1}{10}$ of the fill in one minute. The second water line can do $\frac{1}{16}$ of the fill in one minute. Therefore:

$$\frac{1}{10}+\frac{1}{16}=\frac{1}{x}$$

Find the lowest (least) common denominator:

$$\frac{8}{80}+\frac{5}{80}=\frac{1}{x}$$

Or,

$$\frac{13}{80}=\frac{1}{x}$$

Cross-multiply to find $13x=80$. Then divide both sides by 13 to find $x=6.15$, which represents the amount of time it would take both water lines to completely fill the tank.

(Note: Another way of looking at this problem is that between the two inlet lines, they will fill the tank at a combined flow rate of 26 gallons per minute. Therefore: $26x = 160$; $x = 6.15$ minutes.)

6. **C.** Another way to express $12\frac{3}{8}$ is $\frac{99}{8}$; another way to express $2\frac{5}{7}$ is $\frac{19}{7}$.

$$\text{Then: } \frac{99}{8}\bullet\frac{19}{7}=\frac{1881}{56}=33\frac{33}{56}$$

7. **D.** With the dimensions given, we can assume it has a rectangular shape. The easiest way to approach this question is to determine the total area of the basement as a rectangle and subtract the area missing in the corner.

$$\textbf{40 feet} \bullet \textbf{25 feet} = \textbf{1000 square feet}$$

To measure the missing corner:
Side A = 25 feet – 21 feet or 4 feet
Side B = 40 feet – 36 feet or 4 feet

The area of the missing corner is 4 feet • 4 feet or 16 feet square. Therefore, this basement's total area is 1000 square feet – 16 square feet = 984 square feet.

8. **B.** Work the part in the parenthesis first, then do multiplication and division second, followed by any addition or subtraction. Otherwise, you will end up with an incorrect answer.

$$\frac{9}{5} \bullet \frac{25}{1} = \frac{225}{5} = 45$$

Then, 45 + 32 = 77°F.

9. **D.** To determine the number of bricks required, simply divide $23\frac{5}{8}$ into $283\frac{1}{2}$. The problem can be stated as:

$$\frac{567}{2} \div \frac{189}{8} = x$$

Multiply by the inverse:

$$\frac{567}{2} \bullet \frac{8}{189} = 12$$

10. **D.** Under normal working conditions we can expect:

$$175 \text{ hp} \bullet \frac{7}{8} = \frac{1225}{8} = 153\frac{1}{8} \text{ hp}$$

and

$$224 \text{ hp} \bullet \frac{6}{7} = \frac{1344}{7} = 192 \text{ hp}$$

This combined horsepower = $153\frac{1}{8} + 192 = 345\frac{1}{8}$ hp.

11. **B.** The lowest (least) common denominator (or LCD) for the four fractions is 16. Therefore:

$$\frac{7}{16} + \frac{10}{16} + \frac{8}{16} + \frac{12}{16} = \frac{37}{16} = 2\frac{5}{16}$$

12. **A.** If an 850-liter tank was filled six times during the year, 850 liters × 6 = the number of liters consumed annually, which in this case is 5,100 liters. However, the question asks how many kiloliters are consumed annually, not liters. Since a kiloliter is 1,000 liters, we can divide our answer by that amount to determine the number of kiloliters:

$$\frac{5100}{1000} = 5.1 \text{ kiloliters}$$

13. **C.** Since we are dealing with two different units of measure (i.e., yards and inches), it is necessary to convert one to the other. This can be done one of two ways. We know there are 36 inches in a yard, so 16 inches is equal to $\frac{16}{36}$ yard or, in reduced form, $\frac{4}{9}$ yard. Or we can change yards into inches; we simply multiply:

$$1\frac{1}{3} \text{ or } \frac{4}{3} \bullet \frac{36 \text{ inches}}{1 \text{ yard}} = \frac{144}{3} = 48 \text{ inches}$$

Let's figure the ratio on the basis of inches.

$1\frac{1}{3}$ yards : 16 inches = 48 inches : 16 inches, or 3:1 when reduced.

14. **C.** By setting up the following proportion, we can solve for $x$.

$$\frac{49}{x} = \frac{42}{100}$$

Cross-multiply:

$$42x = 4900$$

Divide both sides by 42 to determine that $x$ = $116.67.

15. **C.** Since we know 245 responses represents 92% of the total calls (i.e., 100% − 8% = 92%), we can set up the following proportion to determine how many calls were received altogether:

$$\frac{92}{100} = \frac{245}{x}$$

Cross-multiply:

$$92x = 24{,}500$$

Then divide both sides by 92 to determine that $x$ = 266 calls.

16. **B.** This problem can be solved by setting up a proportion:

$$\frac{6 \text{ feet tall}}{x \text{ feet tall}} = \frac{7.5 \text{ foot shadow}}{35 \text{ foot shadow}}$$

So, $7.5x = 210$. Divide both sides by 7.5 to determine that $x$ = 28 feet.

17. **C.** When determining the average of test scores for an applicant, it is necessary to add all test scores together and divide by the number of tests taken. Therefore, if we know what the four previous test scores were, and the desired overall average, we can solve the percent required in the last exam.

$$\frac{80\% + 82\% + 90\% + 87\% + x\%}{5} = 87\%$$

Or,

$$\frac{339\% + x\%}{5} = 87\%$$

Multiply both sides of the equation by 5 to find that $339 + x = 435$. Subtract 339 from both sides to find that $x = 96\%$.

18. **D.** This is a question that requires a compound proportion. The ratios involved are:

$$\frac{\text{6 building inspectors}}{\text{5 building inspectors}}, \frac{\text{25 buildings inspected}}{x \text{ buildings inspected}}, \text{ and } \frac{\text{2 days}}{\text{4 days}}.$$

This can be thought of as a direct proportion because obviously the more building inspectors involved, the larger the number of buildings that can be inspected. In other words, there is a direct instead of an inverse relationship. The same kind of direct relationship exists between the time and the inspections conducted (i.e., the more time involved, the greater the number of buildings that can be inspected). Therefore, the ratio can be multiplied as shown below to set up the compound proportion.

$$\frac{6}{5} \bullet \frac{2}{4} = \frac{25}{x}$$

So, $\frac{12}{20} = \frac{25}{x}$. Since $\frac{12}{20}$ can be reduced to $\frac{3}{5}$, we can say:

$$\frac{3}{5} = \frac{25}{x}$$

Cross-multiply to determine that $3x = 125$. Divide both sides by 3 to determine that $x = 41.67$ or, when rounded up, 42 buildings could be inspected.

19. **B.** The distance traveled by both drivers to the point of where they actually reach one another represents the total distance involved. Let $x$ represent the number of hours involved in traveling. Therefore $57x + 68x = 469$. Thus, $125x = 469$. Divide both sides of the equation by 125 to isolate $x$:

$$x = \frac{469}{125}$$

Therefore, $x = 3.75$ hours or 3 hours, 45 minutes. If they departed at 6:15 A.M., they would reach one another at 10:00 A.M.

20. **D.** Let $x$ represent the time it took Greg to drive home. Since the distance between the two destinations is constant, the problem is solved accordingly (note: 30 minutes should be expressed in hours):

$$58x = 53(x + 0.5)$$

Then, distribute the operations in parenthesis:

$$58x = 53x + 26.5$$

So, $5x = 26.5$ and therefore $x = 5.3$.
Since it took Greg 5.3 hours to make the commute, and it is known that his average speed was 58 mph, $5.3 \times 58 = 307.4$ miles represents the distance involved.

21. **C.** Let $x$ represent the water needed for the dilution. So, $x + 24$ represents the total mixture after dilution. The 10.56 ounces of alcohol ($24 \times 0.44$) in the original solution must equal 20% of the new mixture. Therefore $10.56 = 0.20(x + 24)$. Distribute to get $10.56 = 0.20x + 4.80$. Subtract 4.80 from both sides to get $5.76 = 0.20x$. Divide both sides by 0.20 to isolate $x$ and find that $x = 28.8$. So, 28.8 ounces of water needs to be added to the original solution to acquire a 20% alcohol concentrate.

22. **A.** Find the mean by adding all the numbers together and dividing by the total number of people represented. So:

$$\frac{4+4+4+4+4+4+3.25+3.25+3.25+1+1}{11}$$

Or $\frac{35.75}{11}$ or 3.25 hours per person.

23. **B.** For this series, it appears that every other number goes up one integer, so 5 is the next term.

24. **B.** To find the percent increase, divide the new value by the old value: $82 \div 75 = 1.09\overline{3}$. Convert to a percentage by multiplying by 100: about 109.3%. Then subtract 100% to find the percent change: 9.3%.

25. **A.** The square root of 52 must be between 7 and 8, since $7^2 = 49$ and $8^2 = 64$. The square of 7.25 is about 52.56, so we know the number must be lower than that. Thus answer A is correct.

26. **C.** Remember that two negative numbers multiplied produce a positive number. Since $-2$ is the only factor of 12 in the choices, it is correct.

27. **D.** This question asks for permutations, which can be found by finding the factorial of the number. 5! is 120 (or $5 \times 4 \times 3 \times 2 \times 1$).

28. **B.** To find how much interest Jonah has earned, we use the interest calculation:

$$\text{Interest} = \text{Principal} \bullet \text{Rate} \bullet \text{Time}$$

Or

$$1250 \bullet 0.045 \bullet 0.5 = 28.125$$

(Since the interest rate is an annual rate, and Jonah was invested for only 6 months, the time is reduced to 0.5). So, \$1,250 + \$28.13 (rounding up slightly) = \$1,278.13. That is the total of what Jonah's investment is worth. But he has to pay a penalty of 1% of the total value of the CD, which is \$12.78 (rounding down slightly). \$1,278.00 − \$12.78 = \$1,265.22.

29. **C.** The answer just requires a simple substitution. If $a = 3$ then $a^2 = 9$; if $b = 2$ then $b^2 = 4$. Then, $9 + 4 = 13$.

30. **D.** First, calculate Gloriana's base pay. At \$9.25 per hour × 8 hours, Gloriana earns a base pay of \$74.00 per day. She earns a commission equal to 10% of her hourly pay for each hair product she sells. That means she earns 92.5 cents per product she sells. Assuming she sells 10 products in a normal day, she'll earn an additional \$92.50 in commission. \$74 + \$92.50 = \$166.50. The price of the product (\$13.50) is a red herring and has no bearing on her earnings.

## WORD KNOWLEDGE

**Note: The answers have been provided for the vocabulary section without explanation. If further reference is needed, consult a dictionary.**

1. **B.**
2. **C.**
3. **D.**
4. **A.**
5. **C.**
6. **A.**
7. **D.**
8. **D.**
9. **B.**
10. **C.**
11. **C.**
12. **A.**
13. **B.**
14. **C.**
15. **D.**
16. **A.**
17. **B.**
18. **D.**
19. **B.**
20. **A.**
21. **B.**
22. **A.**
23. **A.**
24. **B.**
25. **B.**
26. **C.**
27. **C.**
28. **D.**
29. **C.**
30. **A.**
31. **B.**
32. **C.**
33. **D.**
34. **D.**
35. **B.**

## PARAGRAPH COMPREHENSION

1. **D.** Static electricity and flammable material by themselves pose no problem. However, if the two are combined as stated in choice D, a real problem can result. Choice C can pose that kind of a problem for an individual; however, it was not discussed in the passage.
2. **A.** The passage says that a preliminary hearing can determine whether a crime has been committed, so answer A is correct. Answer B is incorrect because a defendant can be ordered held for further proceedings. Answer C is incorrect because a defendant can be released after a preliminary hearing. Answer D is incorrect because a preliminary hearing doesn't determine whether a defendant committed a crime but rather if there is probable cause to believe so.
3. **B.** The passage states that the Ming Dynasty was noted for a strong central government, and for supporting navigation and exploration and that the dynasty fell owing to military threats, civil strife, and burdensome taxes. It can be posited that the dynasty's focus on the former achievements could have caused the problems that resulted in its downfall. A is incorrect, as Ming porcelain was not imported from Europe. Neither C nor D is supported by information provided in the paragraph.
4. **C.** The passage states that practice of physiognomy was used the same way as modern people use psychology. A is incorrect because physiognomy was popular during both of the stated time periods. B is incorrect as it is not commonly practiced any longer. D is incorrect because nothing in the paragraph supports such a connection.
5. **A.** Because the paragraph is basically just a list of mythical lands and creatures, this is the most appropriate title. B is less appropriate because the passage isn't about ignorance, it's about mythical lands and creatures. C is also incorrect because the passage isn't about pseudoscience. And D is incorrect because even though "gold" is at the heart of some of these mythical lands, that is not the theme of the passage.
6. **D.** The passage mentions the very many areas of life in which caste matters. A is incorrect because nothing in the passage suggests this is true. The fact that one's caste is hereditary and that such rules are rigid suggest otherwise. B is incorrect because the paragraph identifies many different areas in which caste affects one's life. C is incorrect because while it may be true, nothing in the paragraph suggests the author is making such an argument.

7. **C.** The passage states that several gates control access and that one of them is the Justice Gate. A is incorrect because nothing in the passage indicates that this is a religious structure. B is incorrect because the origin of the name is not given. D is incorrect because the passage merely states that the Court of Lions had statues of lions.

8. **A.** Fan clubs have been around since the late forties. B is incorrect because the passage doesn't say anything about how many fans are in the fan clubs of these two performers. C is incorrect because the passage states that the idea of supporting one's favorite artist is probably timeless. D is incorrect because the passage says fan clubs exist for not-so-famous performers.

9. **D.** The passage is basically a long list of instruments used in country music. A is incorrect because the passage doesn't say anything about the origin of instruments. B is incorrect because while there is a passing mention of how horns add a "lush" sound, that is not the principal concern of the piece. C is incorrect because the passage is about instruments used in country music, not how the music itself has changed over time.

10. **A.** The author simply defines amulets, talismans, and charms. B is incorrect because nothing in the passage specifically states how to create or use such objects. C is incorrect because the author does not express an opinion. D is incorrect because magic is not compared to anything.

11. **B.** The passage compared writers and photographers to show what rights matter most to them. A is incorrect because no chronological order was used. C is incorrect because the passage does not show how to apply for copyright protection. D is incorrect because definitions are not used to explain copyright law.

12. **A.** The passage states specific suggestions for reducing risk. B is incorrect because the passage says nothing about insurance. C is incorrect because the passage focuses on natural disasters such as fire and flood. D is incorrect because the passage uses a neutral tone and doesn't talk about why people should take action, it just says what those actions should be.

13. **D.** The passage says that depending on your circumstances, you can deposit a certain amount of before-tax dollars into such an account. A is incorrect because the passage mentions retirement and this investment vehicle is called a retirement account. B is incorrect because nothing in the passage says this. C is incorrect because there are other ways to save for retirement and the passage doesn't claim that this is the only way.

14. **B.** The passage described what an income statement is. While the passage does mention that operating at a loss can cause a business to fail, that is not the main point of the passage, so A is incorrect. C is incorrect because the passage does not say anything about how to improve cash flow. D is incorrect because the passage does not say anything about reporting requirements.

15. **A.** The paragraph states that Alexandria was home to a diverse population, including Greeks, Jews, and Egyptians, allowing the free flow of ideas that made it an intellectual center. B is incorrect because the passage states that the city has always served as an important port and was a center of commerce between East and West. C is incorrect because the passage doesn't say this. It does say it was founded by Alexander the Great and it can be inferred that Alexander himself is the namesake for the city. D is incorrect because the passage states that the city was founded in 332 B.C.

## MATHEMATICS KNOWLEDGE

1. **B.** The Pythagorean theorem tells us that for right triangles, $a^2+b^2=c^2$. We can determine the solution with simple algebra.
We know that Side A = 8, and Side C = 12.8, so:

$$8^2+b^2=12.8^2$$

Or, $\mathbf{64+b^2=163.84}$. Subtract 64 from both sides of the equation to get $\mathbf{b^2=99.84}$ **feet**. The square root of 99.84 can be rounded up to 10.

2. **A.** In geometric terms this is considered to be a trapezoid, which is a quadrilateral with two sides parallel and the other two sides not parallel. To figure the area, we can see it as one rectangle (A) and two triangles (B) and (C). For the rectangle, area = lw. Therefore, $\mathbf{8 \bullet 4 = 32\ cm^2}$.

   The area of a triangle is $\frac{1}{2}bh$. So, $\frac{1}{2}3(4) = 6\ cm^2$. The total area of the trapezoid is the sum of the rectangular area and the two triangular areas, which is $32\ cm^2 + 6\ cm^2 + 6\ cm^2 = 44\ cm^2$ (square centimeters).

3. **C.** The area of a square is the length of one side squared. If the square given is 81 square feet in area, then the square root of 81 will give us the length of the square's side, which in this case is equal to 9. Since we are dealing with right angles in the square, we can apply the Pythagorean theorem $(a^2 + b^2 = c^2)$ to determine the length of the diagonal. Therefore, $9^2 + 9^2 = c^2$. Or, $81 + 81 = c^2$. Additional multiplication tells us $162 = c^2$. The square root of 162 is about 12.73, so the answer is 12.73 feet.

4. **D.** First, we need to figure the diameter. If we know that 34 inches is 34% (that is, 0.34) of the diameter, we can set up a proportion to solve it. Our proportion would be:

$$\frac{34}{0.34} = \frac{x}{1.00}$$

   Then:

$$\frac{0.34x}{0.34} = \frac{34}{0.34}$$

   So, $x = \frac{3400}{34}$ or $x = 100$.

   That means the diameter is 100 inches. We can now use the formula for determining the area of a circle $(a = \pi r^2)$ to answer the question. Since the radius is half the diameter, the radius of our circle is 50 inches. So:

$$a = 3.1416(50^2)$$

   So, $a = 3.1416(2500)$, or $a = 7854$ square inches.

5. **A.** First divide 27.28 revolutions into 200 yards to determine how far this particular tire could travel after one revolution: $\frac{200}{27.28} = 7.33$ yards. Since all of the answers are in inches, the unit used needs to be converted from yards to inches. A yard has 36 inches, so $7.33 \times 36 = 263.88$ inches. In other words, for every 1 revolution this tire makes, it can travel 263.88 inches. This number is the tire's circumference. $C = D\pi$ (circumference equals diameter multiplied by pi). To determine the diameter, plug numbers into the circumference formula:

$$263.88 = D(3.1416)$$

   Then, divide both sides by pi:

$$\frac{263.88}{3.1416} = \frac{D(3.1416)}{3.1416}$$

   Or, 84 inches in diameter (rounded up). Since the question wanted the radius of the tire, we can simply divide the diameter by 2, giving us an answer of 42 inches.

6. **A.** The area of a square is equal to its side squared, so $24^2 = 576$ square inches. The area of a circle is equal to $\pi r^2$. So the area of this circle is determined by finding half the diameter (half the diameter equals the radius), or 11.75 inches, then filling in the rest of the formula:

$$A = 3.1416(11.75^2)$$

Then, $\mathbf{3.1416 \bullet 138.0625 = 433.74}$ square inches.

The area of the square minus the area of the circle that has been removed will give us how many square inches of sheet metal are left over:
$576 - 433.74 = 142.26$ square inches.

7. **D.** Solve as you would any equation. Divide both sides of the inequality by 11 to isolate the unknown. Then $x < 3$.

8. **B.** Using the distributive property, we know that $(y+3)(y-3)$ can be written as $y(y-3)+3(y-3)$. Then we can multiply to determine that $\mathbf{y^2 - 3y + 3y - 9}$. Do a little addition to determine that $\mathbf{y^2 - 9}$.

9. **C.** The definition of a trapezoid is that it has two opposite sides that are parallel. A is a parallelogram. B is a square or rectangle. D is a square.

10. **A.** Add 18 to both sides to isolate the unknown:

$$6x - 18 + 18 = -42 + 18$$

Then $\mathbf{6x = -24}$. Divide both sides by 6 to isolate $x$: $\mathbf{x = -4}$.

11. **D.** The formula for determining the total measurement of the angles of a polygon is $\mathbf{180(n-2)°}$. So, $\mathbf{180(9-2) = 1260°}$.

12. **C.** To simplify the expression, do whatever operations you can. In this case, you can add $x$ and $\mathbf{-3x}$ to get $\mathbf{-2x}$. Then arrange the terms in standard polynomial form, with the term having the highest exponent coming first.

13. **D.** Use the distributive property to rewrite the equation as $y(y+4)-3(y+4)$. Then multiply: $y^2+4y-3y+12$. Or, $y^2+y+12$.

14. **B.** To solve the inequality, you divide both sides by $-2$. But when you divide an inequality by a negative number, you have to reverse the direction of the inequality sign.

15. **C.** To solve this equation, first add 21 to both sides to isolate the unknown:

$$7y - 21 + 21 = -49 + 21$$

Then, $\mathbf{7y = -28}$. Next, divide both sides by 7 to isolate $y$: $\mathbf{y = -4}$.

16. **A.** To solve this equation, multiply both sides by the inverse of the fraction to isolate the unknown:

$$\frac{5}{2} \times \frac{2}{5} y = 4 \times \frac{5}{2}$$

Then, $y = \frac{4}{1} \times \frac{5}{2} = \frac{20}{2} = 10$.

17. **D.** We know that $\frac{a}{b} = \frac{c}{d}$ can be expressed as $\mathbf{ad = bc}$. So the equation can be restated as $\mathbf{1 \bullet 9 = x^2}$ or $\mathbf{9 = x^2}$. The square root of 9 is 3, so $x = 3$.

18. **D.** To subtract fractions, use the formula $\frac{a}{b}-\frac{c}{d}=\frac{ad-bc}{bd}$. Then just plug in the given numbers to derive the correct answer.

19. **B.** To divide fractions, you cross-multiply. So, $\frac{a}{b}\div\frac{c}{d}=\frac{ad}{bc}$. In this case we simply replace the given terms with those in the formula to derive the following:

$$\frac{(x-2)(x+10)}{x^2}$$

Then we solve the numerator to derive the correct answer:

$$x(x+10)-2(x+10)=x^2+10x-2x+20=x^2+8x+20$$

20. **C.** Use the distributive property to rewrite the expression as $x(x-10)-2y(x-10)$. Then multiply from left to right to determine the correct answer.

21. **D.** Factors of 18 (the *c* variable of the quadratic equation) that add up to 4 (the constant of the *b* variable) are 6 and −2. You can check the math by multiplying:

$$x(x-2)+6(x-2)=x^2-2x+6x-12=x^2+4x-12$$

22. **D.** To solve this equation, simply add 16 to both sides to isolate the unknown. Thus, $x^2=16$. The square root of 16 is 4, but it can also be −4, so answer D is the best answer.

23. **C.** To determine the probability, multiply the likelihood of the first event by the likelihood of the second event.

24. **A.** Because Maureen has already been chosen to participate in the survey, the only probability that matters is the probability of receiving the free lunch, which is 25% or $\frac{1}{4}$.

25. **C.** When solving for two unknowns with two true equations, start by substituting one equation for one unknown. In this case, we'll restate the equation as $x+1=3x-7$. Then, add 7 to each side to learn that $x+8=3x$. Then subtract *x* from each side to determine that $8=2x$. Divide both sides by 2 to learn that $x=4$. Now that we know what *x* equals, we can plug it into one expression to determine that *y* equals 5. We can check our work by making sure that our values for *x* and *y* work for both expressions.

## ELECTRONICS INFORMATION

1. **A.** Conductors are materials that allow the free flow of electric current.

2. **B.** Volts measure electrical pressure.

3. **C.** Power equals voltage times current.

4. **D.** Ohm's Law says that $I=\frac{V}{R}$, and since we know the total voltage and the total resistance, it is simple to determine that the current = 2 A.

5. **B.** A voltmeter reading of fewer than 12 volts on a car battery indicates less than 50% charged; 10 V means the battery has a 0% charge (and probably needs to be replaced).

6. **C.** This is true of alternating current, not direct current. All of the other answers are true of direct current. Be sure to watch for "not true" statements.

7. **A.** The accumulation of electrons creates a negative charge.

8. **A.** The field around a charged object is its energy field. C is correct some of the time, but not all charged objects create magnetic fields, so A is a more correct answer.

9. **D.** Friction creates heat, so reducing friction (resistance) reduces energy loss.

10. **C.** Silicon is the most common material used for a semiconductor. The other options are either conductors or insulators.

11. **A.** This is a parallel series; the connectors go to and from each light bulb individually.

12. **C.** 1μF is one-millionth of a farad, or $10^{-6}$.

13. **C.** A ground rod is meant to carry excess charge safely to the object that can accept the charge, often the earth itself.

14. **A.** First, determine the current in the circuit. We know that $I = \frac{V}{R}$, so our current is 3 amperes. The fuse needs to be 125% of this amount, so 3.75 A.

15. **D.** We can rewrite Ohm's Law to tell us the voltage of a circuit: $V = IR$. Since we know I (2.5 A) and R (4 ohms), we simply multiply them together to find $V = 10$.

16. **A.** To find the total resistance of a series circuit, add $\frac{1}{R_1} + \frac{1}{R_2}$ and use the reciprocal of the sum. So, $\frac{1}{3} + \frac{1}{6} = \frac{1}{2}$, or 2 ohms.

17. **D.** The total voltage drop across a series circuit is simply the sum of the voltage drop for each resistor.

18. **A.** The symbol is for a capacitor.

19. **A.** The switch is open, so the current is interrupted and the light cannot be lit.

20. **D.** A capacitor stores an electric charge.

## AUTOMOTIVE AND SHOP INFORMATION

1. **C.** Intake valves allow fuel and air into the cylinder.

2. **A.** The crankshaft converts the linear force of the pistons to the rotating force needed to power the engine. The camshaft opens and closes the valves (choice B). The cylinder head closes off the top of the cylinder (choice C). The spark plug ignites the fuel mixture (choice D).

3. **C.** If the camshaft timing is off, the valves open at the wrong time, which can cause problems powering the engine.

4. **D.** The illustration is that of a valve train, which consists of all the components that work together to operate the valves, and can include rocker arms, retainers, springs, and push rods.

5. **B.** The second stroke of a four-stroke cycle is the compression stroke. The sequence is intake-compression-combustion-exhaust. Elimination (choice D) is not part of the cycle.

6. **B.** The crankshaft makes 2 revolutions per cycle.

7. **C.** The oil lubrication system reduces the amount of friction between parts by forcing oil through the engine (which keeps the parts from rubbing directly together). While it does cool the engine (choice A) by reducing the heat generated by friction, answer C is more correct.

8. **D.** The water pump helps circulate coolant throughout the engine; if it is clogged and the coolant doesn't circulate correctly, it can cause the engine to overheat.

9. **D.** All of the options are advantages of rear-wheel drive vehicles.

10. **B.** The transmission is the engine component that allows the car to go faster or slower, idle, and reverse (this is true whether the vehicle has a standard or an automatic transmission).

11. **A.** "ABS" stands for antilock brake system.

12. **D.** Hacksaw is the only alternative given that can cut metal.

13. **C.** Orbital sanders are primarily used in finishing wood products. The other sanders are meant for coarser work and do not leave the same kind of smooth finish.

14. **B.** Battery electrolyte fluid. A hydrometer can determine if a car battery has sufficient charge or warrants replacing.

15. **A.** Multipurpose tool. Wire-stripping pliers are a must for an electrician.

16. **D.** The box wrench is slowest because it requires the wrench to be lifted off the nut, repositioned, and replaced on the nut before it can be turned. All other wrenches mentioned as alternatives are open faced and allow for quicker turning.

17. **C.** Carpentry. A jack plane smoothes and pares down lumber.

18. **C.** Offset box wrench. The nut is recessed with an overhead obstruction that effectively eliminates the use of the other straight-shanked wrenches mentioned.

19. **B.** Slip joint pliers.

20. **A.** Wrecking bar. The alternatives could potentially damage the contents.

21. **D.** Feelers gauge.

22. **D.** Cold chisel. The rivet, being practically flush with the metal surface, does not present enough workable area for either bolt cutters or a hacksaw to work effectively. Lopping shears are used only for gardening.

23. **C.** Propane torch. Blowtorches or propane torches are commonly used in plumbing to heat pipes. Arc welders and oxyacetylene cutting torches are meant to fuse and cut metal, respectively.

24. **A.** Bench grinder. The three alternatives could potentially sharpen a lawn mower blade; however, their capabilities can be used better elsewhere.

25. **B.** Outside calipers.

## MECHANICAL COMPREHENSION

1. **C.** Always remember that if external gears such as those seen in a drive train are numbered in succession, the odd-numbered gears will all spin in one direction while the even-numbered gears will spin in the opposite direction. Gear 4 is not an internal gear.

2. **B.** Beveled gears are used for directing power around a corner or angle.

3. **C.** Since the drive gear has three times as many teeth as the driven gear, there is a $\frac{2}{3}$ reduction of torque with a corresponding tripling in speed.

4. **D.** If gear B turns counterclockwise, we know that connecting gears must turn in the opposite direction. Gears A and B have a 1:1 ratio. If gear B turns $\frac{1}{2}$ revolution, so will gear A. Gear C, on the other hand, has twice the number of teeth as gear B, so it will rotate only half as much. Since gear B made only $\frac{1}{2}$ revolution, gear C will exhibit a $\frac{1}{4}$ revolution.

5. **B.** Pressure exerted on a fluid trapped in a confined space is distributed in all directions without consequent loss of force.

6. **C.** Fluid pressure is directly related to the depth and density of a given fluid. Since the density is the same because salt water is the only fluid involved, we can simply compare depth. Container C has the greatest depth; therefore it will have the greatest pressure at its base.

7. **C.** The basic procedure for determining fluid pressure is to multiply the height (depth) of a fluid and its density. We cannot quantify fluid pressure from the information given. However, choice C demonstrates the longest siphon tube of the three choices. Since it has the greatest height/depth, it can siphon fluid at a greater rate than the other two vessels.

8. **B.** This problem can be solved using a direct proportion:

$$\frac{\textbf{100 feet}}{\textbf{150 feet}} = \frac{\textbf{25 psi}}{\boldsymbol{x}\textbf{ psi}}$$

$\mathbf{100x = 3740;}$ **therefore** $\mathbf{x = 37.5}$ **psi.**

9. **D.** In this example, we already know the lengths of belts between centers (i.e., 35 cm + 35 cm = 70 cm). Now, we must account for the pulleys' circumferences to determine the length of belt required for the ends. Since each end represents $\frac{1}{2}$ the circumference, two ends would represent the whole circumference of either pulley since they are equal in diameter. The circumference of a circle equals pi times diameter, or $\mathbf{3.1416 \times 10.5 = 32.987}$; therefore, the length of V-belt required for these pulleys is equal to 35 cm + 35 cm + 32.987 cm, or 102.987 cm.

10. **A.** What is essentially being described in this question is the volume of a cylinder. The bore represents the diameter of the cylinder and the stroke represents the height of the cylinder. Since volume of a cylinder is $\boldsymbol{V = \pi r^2 h}$, we can easily figure the displacement. The radius is equal to half the diameter or, in this case, 1.6252.

    The square of 1.6252 is 2.641. Therefore, $\mathbf{(3.1416)(2.641)(4.75) = x}$, or the number of cubic inches of displacement. So, $x = 39.41$ cubic inches.

11. **A.** A fulcrum placed at Position 1 would enhance the lift capability of this lever the most. Essentially, the closer a fulcrum is placed to a load or resistance, the easier it becomes to lift with the lever.

12. **C.** Effort = the product of resistance times height divided by the length of the inclined plane. In this case, the fulcrum is at 7 feet, so that is the number used as the length of the inclined plane, versus the entire 14 feet of the lever.

$$\frac{\textbf{825 pounds} \times \textbf{7 feet}}{\textbf{7 feet}} = \textbf{825 pounds}$$

13. **C.** Since it requires 825 pounds of effort to lift 825 pounds, no mechanical advantage is gained by using the lever as described. Ratios of 1:1 do not demonstrate mechanical advantage.

14. **B.** When a fluid trapped in a confined space is submitted to pressure, that pressure is distributed evenly in all directions without sacrifice of power. In other words, liquids are not compressible as are gases. The remaining choices are false.

15. **C.** If the pulleys have a 3:1 ratio, then the larger pulley would turn at $\frac{1}{3}$ the rate of the smaller pulley, or 100 rpm.

16. **D.** Gears 3, 5, and 7 will turn counterclockwise if gear 2 turns clockwise. As a rule of thumb, if gears are directly aligned end to end as shown in the illustration, the odd-numbered gears in the sequence will always turn in the same direction while the even-numbered gears will always turn the opposite direction.

17. **C.** Since cables A and B both act to support equally the weight being lifted, the load factor is evenly distributed between the two. In other words, cable A supports 240 pounds and cable B supports the other 240 pounds. Therein lies the mechanical advantage gained by using this pulley system.

18. **B.** 2:1, because it requires only 240 pounds of effort to lift the weight depicted versus 480 pounds if it were lifted directly. The lifting advantage gained by using the pulley is doubled to 2:1. Choices A, C, and D are not reflective of any mechanical advantage.

19. **A.** Choice B is an example of an inclined plane, choice C is a wedge, and choice D is an example of a lever, all of which are classified as simple machines.

20. **C.** To calculate the effort required use the following formula:

$$\text{Effort} = \frac{\text{Resistance} \times \text{Resistance Distance}}{\text{Effort Distance}}$$

Or:

$$\frac{575 \text{ pounds} \times 8 \text{ inches}}{28 \text{ inches}} = 164.3 \text{ pounds}$$

21. **C.** The mechanical advantage is determined by dividing the amount of resistance by the force applied to the tool, or 655 divided by 125.

22. **B.** The circumference of the lever—in this case, the box-end wrench—needs to be determined first. Circumference is equal to pi times diameter. We only know the radius (6 inches), so we multiply the radius by 2 to determine the diameter (12 inches). Then multiply the diameter by $\pi$ (3.1416) to determine the circumference, which is 37.7 inches. Divide the circumference by the screw pitch to determine the mechanical advantage: $\mathbf{37.7 \div \frac{1}{8}}$. Or, 37.7 inches × 8 inches = 301.60 (multiply by the inverse to divide by a fraction). So, the mechanical advantage is 301.60: 1. Multiply that by the amount of force applied (10 pounds) to determine the force of the bolt: 3,016 pounds of force.

23. **A.** First, determine the circumference of the lever: 20 inch radius × 2 yields a diameter of 40. $40\pi$ (3.1416) = 125.66 inch circumference. Then, divide the circumference by the screw pitch ($\frac{1}{7}$-inch) to determine the mechanical advantage. Multiply by the inverse to divide by a fraction: 125.66 × 7 inches = 879.62, or a mechanical advantage of 879.62:1. Multiply by 10 pounds of force to determine that 8,796.2 pounds can be lifted by this jackscrew under the conditions given.

24. **A.** Refer to the explanation given for question 23.

25. **D.** Tons should be converted to pounds; 3 tons = 6000 pounds. The handle (which is the lever) has a potential circumference of 113.09 inches (18 inches in length is the radius; multiply that by 2 to determine the diameter, and multiply the diameter by pi to determine the circumference). The mechanical advantage is the circumference divided by the screw pitch. Multiply by the inverse to divide by fractions: 113.09 × 6 = 678.54, or 678.54:1 advantage. To determine how much effort is required, divide the resistance (6000 pounds) by the advantage (678.54). So, 8.84 pounds of effort are required.

**ASSEMBLING OBJECTS**

1. B.
2. C.
3. D.
4. B.
5. B.
6. B.
7. B.
8. B.
9. B.
10. B.
11. A.
12. B.
13. B.
14. D.
15. B.
16. B.

# CHAPTER 16

# *Practice Test #2*

Take the practice test just as you would any standardized test. Use the answer sheet at the end of the chapter to record your answers. Set a timer for the amount of time allotted for each subtest, take them in the order in which they're given, and try to do your best. Then turn to the answer key later in this chapter to grade your efforts and help you plan your review before taking the next practice test.

## GENERAL SCIENCE

You have 11 minutes to answer the 25 questions on this subtest.

1. The number $10^{-6}$g means

   A. 1 nanogram
   B. 1 microgram
   C. 10 grams minus 6 grams
   D. 1 megagram

2. The mitochondria of a cell

   A. is the powerhouse of the cell
   B. protects the cell from invasion
   C. contains the genetic code of the cell
   D. is responsible for cell reproduction

3. The food chain of an ecosystem consists of two main groups:

   A. production and decomposition
   B. predators and prey
   C. producers and consumers
   D. producers and carrion-eaters

4. Which of the following is the largest biome on earth (e.g., covering the most area)?

   A. Desert
   B. Grasslands
   C. Aquatic
   D. Tundra

5. Your sense of smell can affect your behavior even if you don't realize it because of the actions of chemicals called

   A. olfactory receptors
   B. pheromones
   C. olfactory proteins
   D. glomeruli

6. An example of an involuntary muscle is the

   A. brain
   B. trapezius
   C. biceps
   D. heart

7. Alveoli are

   A. small sacs in the lungs that aid in the process of respiration
   B. tiny capillaries that make up a significant part of the circulatory system
   C. microscopic hairs in your nose that filter out contaminants in the air you breathe
   D. nerve cells that transmit sensory information to your brain

8. Arteries are different from veins in that

   A. arteries transport oxygen-depleted blood to your heart while veins transport oxygen-rich blood throughout your body
   B. arteries transport oxygen-rich blood throughout your body while veins transport oxygen-depleted blood to your heart
   C. arteries are smaller than veins
   D. There is no difference.

9. Three common types of neurons are

   A. synapse, axon, glial cell
   B. myelin, axon, sensory
   C. all neurons are of one type, sensory
   D. motor, sensory, and associative

10. The age of earth is about

    A. 1 million years
    B. 4.5 billion years
    C. 7 billion years
    D. 100,000 years

11. Erosion is a process by which

    A. rock is broken apart through natural and human actions
    B. plant matter decomposes
    C. broken parts of rock are carried away by wind, rain, and other processes
    D. volcanoes are formed

12. Tides are caused by

    A. high winds
    B. low barometric pressure
    C. the movement of the ocean basin
    D. the gravitational pull of the moon

13. A hammer weighing 1 kilogram and a box of roofing tiles weighing 3 kilograms are knocked off the roof at the same time, falling 5 meters to the ground below. Which object reached the ground first (not factoring in air resistance)?

    A. Both objects reached the ground at the same time.
    B. The hammer reached the ground first.
    C. The box of roofing tiles reached the ground first.
    D. There is not enough information to determine the answer.

14. The lowest layer of the earth's atmosphere is the

    A. stratosphere
    B. ozone layer
    C. troposphere
    D. thermosphere

15. The tail of a comet is created by

A. the sun melting some of the ice of the comet
B. space debris trailing after the comet
C. an optical illusion
D. a special type of combustion that occurs in comets

16. Carbon dioxide contains what two types of atoms?

A. carbon and hydrogen
B. hydrogen and oxygen
C. carbon and oxygen
D. carbon and helium

17. A colloid is a type of

A. heterogeneous mixture
B. homogeneous mixture
C. mixture subject to sedimentation
D. solvent

18. In physics, displacement refers to

A. how much ground has been covered when an object moves from point A to point B
B. the rate of motion when an object moves from point A to point B
C. the acceleration of an object as it moves from point A to point B
D. how far from its starting point an object has moved when it goes from point A to point B

19. The formula for momentum is

A. Momentum = Mass × Velocity
B. Momentum = Mass ÷ Acceleration
C. Momentum = Velocity ÷ Mass
D. Momentum = Force × Distance

20. A wave's amplitude is associated with its

A. coherence
B. speed
C. intensity
D. tempo

21. The scientific process is used to

A. verify the accuracy of a hypothesis
B. prove a scientist's claims
C. categorize scientific developments into rules, laws, and theories
D. describe ideas that can't be tested

22. Through the process of photosynthesis, plants produce which useful element?

A. nitrogen
B. helium
C. oxygen
D. hydrogen

23. Microorganisms in your intestines

    A. always create illness
    B. aid with digestion
    C. are rarely found
    D. are automatically digested and excreted

24. A human zygote has

    A. 23 chromosomes
    B. 10 pairs of chromosomes
    C. 152 chromosomes
    D. 46 chromosomes

25. The energy your body needs to perform tasks (including thinking) comes primarily from

    A. fats
    B. protein
    C. carbohydrates
    D. trace minerals

## ARITHMETIC REASONING

You will have 30 questions and 39 minutes to answer them.

1. $7 \bullet \frac{1}{2} \bullet \frac{3}{7} = x$. Which of the following equals $x$?

   A. $1\frac{3}{7}$

   B. $1\frac{1}{4}$

   C. $1\frac{3}{4}$

   D. $1\frac{1}{2}$

2. If the number $5\frac{2}{3}$ was changed from a mixed number to a decimal, which of the following is correct, assuming it is rounded off to hundredths?

   A. 5.67
   B. 5.66
   C. 5.6
   D. 5.7

3. $6.71 \bullet 0.88 = x$. Which of the following equals $x$?

   A. 5.0948
   B. 5.887
   C. 5.91
   D. 5.9048

4. What is the largest area that could be covered by a salvage tarp measuring **10 feet × 15 feet** (without cutting the tarp)?

   A. 100 square feet
   B. 150 square feet
   C. 200 square feet
   D. 250 square feet

5. If a driveshaft made $40\frac{5}{8}$ revolutions every $2\frac{1}{2}$ minutes, what would be the shaft's rpm (revolutions per minute)?

   A. $13\frac{1}{3}$ rpm

   B. $15\frac{3}{7}$ rpm

   C. $16\frac{1}{4}$ rpm

   D. 87 rpm

6. Adding the various amperages together, what is the total current of a circuit that has three currents that measure $1\frac{3}{10}$ amps, $2\frac{12}{100}$ amps, and $1\frac{17}{1000}$ amps?

A. $4\frac{437}{1000}$ amps

B. $4\frac{32}{1110}$ amps

C. $4\frac{17}{1000}$ amps

D. 4 amps

7. What is the perimeter length of the trapezoid shown below?

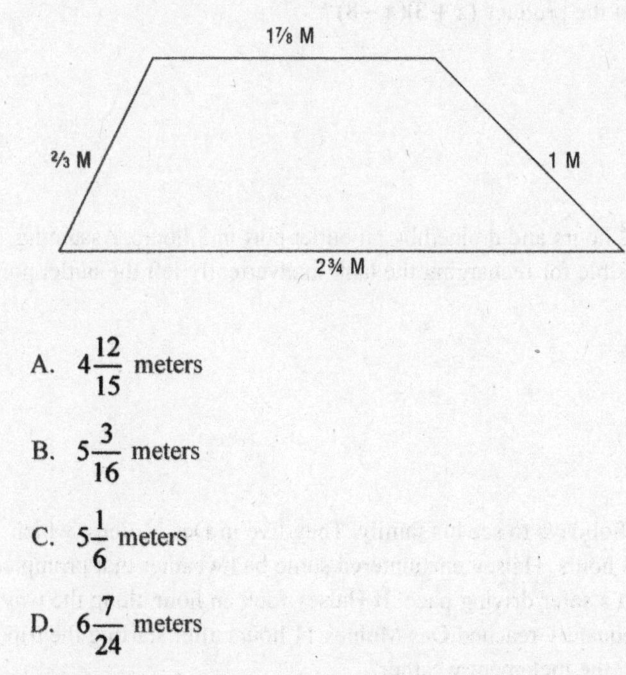


A. $4\frac{12}{15}$ meters

B. $5\frac{3}{16}$ meters

C. $5\frac{1}{6}$ meters

D. $6\frac{7}{24}$ meters

8. If a rubber hose has an internal diameter of $\frac{3}{4}$ inch and the thickness of the hose wall is $\frac{1}{16}$ inch, what is the hose's outside diameter?

A. $\frac{5}{36}$ inch

B. $\frac{13}{16}$ inch

C. $\frac{7}{8}$ inch

D. $\frac{5}{6}$ inch

9. How many centimeters are there in 2.67 meters?

   A. 2,670
   B. 267
   C. 26.7
   D. 2.67

10. A solution contains 35% benzene and 65% water. If 14 liters of this solution is diluted by adding 4.5 liters of water, what percentage of benzene would be present in the new mixture?

   A. 23.7%
   B. 26.49%
   C. 31.7%
   D. 43.55%

11. Which of the expressions below would represent the product $(x+3)(x-8)$?

   A. $x^2-5x-24$
   B. $2x-5x-24$
   C. $x^2+3x-8$
   D. $x^3-5$

12. A tanker truck can be filled via an inlet port in 2 hours and drained by an outlet port in 3 hours. Assuming the tanker truck is empty and the person responsible for recharging the tank inadvertently left the outlet port open, how long would it take to fill the tank?

   A. 4.5 hours
   B. 5 hours
   C. 5.5 hours
   D. 6 hours

13. Halsey was headed home for the Thanksgiving holidays to see his family. They live in Des Moines, which is 650 miles away. After being on the road for 4 hours, Halsey encountered some bad weather that prompted him to slow down 15 miles per hour to maintain a safer driving pace. If Halsey took an hour along the way to fill up with gas and grab a bite to eat, and subsequently reached Des Moines 11 hours after starting the trip, what speed was he driving prior to encountering the inclement weather?

   A. 65 mph
   B. 69 mph
   C. 72 mph
   D. 74 mph

14. Solve for $x$. $4^2+6+(4\bullet 5)\div 2=x$.

   A. 34
   B. 22
   C. 60
   D. 11

15. Jonathan is purchasing a flat-screen television. The cost is $799. He gets an employee discount of 10%. He will purchase a warranty for $25.00 and home delivery for $35.00. He will have to pay a sales tax of 8.85 percent on the discounted price of the television (not including the cost of the warranty and home delivery, which aren't taxed). How much will the television cost Jonathan?

A. $782.74
B. $842.74
C. $719.10
D. $63.64

16. If a sequence has the formula $2_n + 2$, what is the value of the twelfth term in the sequence?

A. 12
B. 24
C. 26
D. 16

17. $5\frac{3}{8} - 2\frac{3}{4} = x$. What is the value of $x$?

A. 3

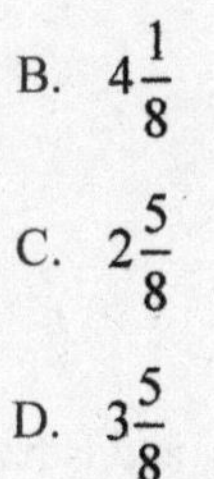

B. $4\frac{1}{8}$

C. $2\frac{5}{8}$

D. $3\frac{5}{8}$

18. Gregory made a pie and ate some of it for breakfast, leaving $\frac{7}{8}$. His friend Andrew asked for $\frac{1}{3}$ of what was left and Gregory gave it to him. What amount of the pie did Andrew receive?

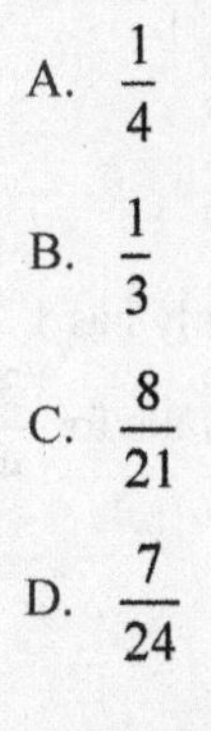

A. $\frac{1}{4}$

B. $\frac{1}{3}$

C. $\frac{8}{21}$

D. $\frac{7}{24}$

19. Meredith has allotted 25% of her departmental budget to pay for travel expenses for members of her department. She wants to share this budget out equally among the 7 employees in the department. The total departmental budget is $5,600. What amount will each employee be entitled to use for travel expenses?

A. $1,400
B. $200
C. $800
D. $140

20. Jasmine needs $3\frac{1}{3}$ yards of landscaping fabric to keep her flower bed from sprouting weeds. The fabric costs $4.29 per yard. How much will the total amount of fabric Jasmine needs cost?

A. $12.87
B. $15.74
C. $14.33
D. $15.75

21. Derrick's laptop battery can run for 3 hours and 45 minutes before it needs to be recharged. If it takes 30 minutes for his battery to recharge, what percentage of an eight-hour day must the laptop be plugged in and charging, assuming it starts with a full battery?

A. 30%
B. 62.5%
C. 6.25%
D. 0.0625%

22. Three siblings pooled their money to buy a $250 present for their parents. Martha agreed to pick up whatever cost was left over after the other two pitched in. John contributed $75 and Linda contributed $115. What percentage was Martha responsible for?

A. 24%
B. 60%
C. 10%
D. 34%

23. Ali must pay a mill levy of 3.5 on his house every year. A mill is one-thousandth of an amount, and is based on the assessed value of his home. For every thousand dollars of value, 1 mill is the equivalent of $1. If Ali's home is worth $335,000 according to the county assessor, how much will his mill levy payment be?

A. $3,500
B. $335
C. $1,172.50
D. $3350

24. Cal is making barbecue sauce for his ribs. The recipe is sufficient for 3 pounds of ribs, but he only has 1 pound of ribs, so he needs to reduce the recipe by a proportional amount. If the original recipe calls for $\frac{3}{4}$ cup of sugar, how much should he use to make the smaller amount?

A. $\frac{1}{3}$ cup
B. 1 cup
C. $\frac{1}{4}$ cup
D. $\frac{1}{2}$ cup

25. If Craig can pick $x$ number of apples in $y$ amount of time, what is the number of apples Craig can pick on his lunch break?

A. $xy$

B. $\frac{x+y}{y}$

C. $\frac{x}{y}$

D. There isn't enough information to determine the answer.

26. Federico buys collectibles at garage sales and resells them on an online auction site. He must pay the site a fee equivalent to 3.75% of the price the item sells for as its commission. If he bought a bobble-head for $4.50 and sold it for a 100% markup, what was his profit for the item (assuming shipping and taxes are handled separately)?

A. $4.50
B. $9.00
C. $8.66
D. $4.16

27. A sandwich shop employs several part-time workers, who make $7.50, $7.75, $8.15, and $8.30 an hour, respectively. What is the mean hourly wage of the workers?

A. $8.15
B. $7.75
C. $7.93
D. $7.63

28. Students in Mr. Foster's shop class earned the following grades: 99%, 83%, 94%, 77%, 97%, 82%, 69%, 50%, and 81%. What is the median grade for the class?

A. 81%
B. 82%
C. 97%
D. 77%

29. Last year, Timothy's consulting business generated $65,850 in income. This year, it generated only $57,975. What is the percent change in the amount of income this year versus last year?

A. −12%
B. 8.8%
C. 12%
D. −8.8%

30. A woman has saved $3,000 towards the down payment on a new house. If she invests it in a product returning an interest rate of 6.75% annually, how much will her down payment be worth in 9 months?

A. $3,675
B. $3,151.88
C. $3,202.50
D. $3,067.50

## WORD KNOWLEDGE

You will have 35 questions to answer in 11 minutes.

1. The ages of the students in the classroom will affect a teacher's perception of his or her role. Perception most nearly means

   A. understanding
   B. hindrance
   C. illusion
   D. veracity

2. The multijurisdictional task force represents the salutary culmination of many local agencies' efforts. Culmination most nearly means

   A. iniquity
   B. fulfillment
   C. imagination
   D. conclusion

3. Deference most nearly means

   A. compliance
   B. share
   C. honor
   D. publicity

4. There were some controversial topics in the governor's State of the State address. Controversial most nearly means

   A. arguable
   B. prejudicial
   C. unbelievable
   D. boring

5. Mr. Miller was subject to arrest for advocating civil disobedience. Advocating most nearly means

   A. supporting
   B. conducting
   C. abhorring
   D. repressing

6. Jubilant most nearly means

   A. dejected
   B. elated
   C. exonerated
   D. indifferent

7. A high standard of ethical conduct is expected of all CPAs. Integrity most nearly means

   A. name
   B. uprightness
   C. cohesiveness
   D. suitability

8. Endeavor most nearly means

   A. persevere
   B. strive
   C. refuse
   D. reconcile

9. His actions were considered flagrant violations of the team's rules and regulations. Flagrant most nearly means

   A. glaring
   B. minor
   C. inadvertent
   D. significant

10. Pervasive most nearly means

    A. costly
    B. violent
    C. elusive
    D. widespread

11. In general, attorneys seem to have a more pessimistic view of social interaction than others. Pessimistic most nearly means

    A. gloomy
    B. positive
    C. reserved
    D. enlightened

12. The patient was petulant when asked about his past drug and alcohol abuse. Petulant most nearly means

    A. cooperative
    B. querulous
    C. apathetic
    D. offended

13. Indigent most nearly means

    A. affluent
    B. neglected
    C. destitute
    D. wealthy

14. Most of what was covered in the class seemed irrelevant to day-to-day living. Irrelevant most nearly means

    A. pertinent
    B. immaterial
    C. important
    D. applicable

15. The stockbroker maintained that the trade was conducted in an aboveboard manner. Aboveboard most nearly means

A. transparent
B. impartial
C. uncomplicated
D. furtive

16. The child's defiant response angered the teacher. Defiant most nearly means

A. sarcastic
B. incorrect
C. insolent
D. complaining

17. Equivocal most nearly means

A. vague
B. equivalent
C. unhurried
D. simplistic

18. After a bad day at work, Tony eschewed after-work drinks with his coworkers. Eschewed most nearly means

A. enjoyed
B. desired
C. purchased
D. avoided

19. Solomon found the how-to guide's advice to be trenchant. Trenchant most nearly means

A. clear
B. simple
C. confusing
D. topical

20. Cajole most nearly means

A. coax
B. argue
C. create
D. imply

21. The mechanic made an ignoble suggestion. Ignoble most nearly means

A. clever
B. crude
C. insensitive
D. simplistic

22. Leniency most nearly means

A. disgust
B. obligation
C. mercy
D. kindness

23. Martha hoped never to go through such an ordeal again. Ordeal most nearly means

A. situation
B. process
C. time
D. test

24. Jeremy's teacher found his excuse plausible. Plausible most nearly means

A. ridiculous
B. believable
C. excusable
D. pointless

25. The cocker spaniel was a gregarious dog. Gregarious most nearly means

A. unhappy
B. standoffish
C. well-trained
D. friendly

26. Mickey had heard his boss's harangue before. Harangue most nearly means

A. invitation
B. perspective
C. discussion
D. rant

27. Evince most nearly means

A. imply
B. show
C. react
D. report

28. The traffic ticket was a blemish on the man's driving record. Blemish most nearly means

A. official report
B. disfiguring mark
C. distinguishing mark
D. final straw

29. Entwine most nearly means

A. depend
B. touch
C. tangle
D. send

30. The gravity of the situation grew over time. Gravity most nearly means

A. pull
B. light-heartedness
C. complicatedness
D. seriousness

31. Licit most nearly means

A. allowed
B. recognized
C. forbidden
D. preferred

32. The family faced a paucity of options. Paucity most nearly means

A. plethora
B. lack
C. confusion
D. collection

33. Yves took umbrage over the comment. Umbrage most nearly means

A. comfort
B. upset
C. anger
D. pains

34. Imperious most nearly means

A. avoidable
B. impertinent
C. impressive
D. bossy

35. The poet was laconic with his speech. Laconic most nearly means

A. respectful
B. precise
C. voluble
D. terse

## PARAGRAPH COMPREHENSION

You'll have 15 questions and 13 minutes to answer them.

1. Most witnesses to crimes are ineffective observers. Unlike a police officer, they lack the developed skill to remember in detail the people who break the law or the events involved.
Which of the statements provided below would accurately summarize the contents of this passage?

   A. Police officers have innate abilities that are over and above those of the public they serve.
   B. Most people are not truly cognizant of their surroundings.
   C. Violations of the law are not always recognized by people. Consequently, details of a crime are usually sketchy.
   D. As a general rule, witnesses to crime have lower mental capabilities.

2. The number located at the top of a driver's license consists of the first five letters of the last name, the first letter of the first name, and the first letter of the middle name. The birth year, when subtracted from 100, produces the first two numerical digits. A check digit inserted by the computer produces the third numerical digit. A code for the month of birth and a code for the day of birth are inserted toward the end.
The best title for this passage would be:

   A. The Development of the Driver's Licensing Exam
   B. Your Tax Dollars at Work
   C. How Your Driver's License Number Is Determined
   D. How to Fake a Driver's License

3. Professional liability means that people in certain professions—physicians, lawyers, writers—are personally responsible for the actions and outcomes when they practice their profession. Professional liability occurs regardless of the form of the business they own or their employer or client.
According to this passage, which of the following is <u>not</u> true:

   A. Only physicians, lawyers, and writers are personally liable for their professional outcomes.
   B. Some people can be personally sued regardless of their business type.
   C. Some people can be professionally liable for the work they do.
   D. Some people can be personally sued regardless of their employer.

4. Depending on whether you're trying to find clients or a job, you'll need to keep an up-to-date resume or bio sheet specific to your career field. A resume lists education and employment history in a format designed to highlight dates, job titles, and responsibilities. A bio sheet consists of several descriptive paragraphs about who you are and what you do. The bio sheet can reflect more of your personality, interests, and aspirations, whereas a resume is a business tool that primarily communicates facts.
The author of this passage used

   A. definitions to explain the job hunt
   B. a chronological approach to organization
   C. comparison/contrast organization to describe resumes and bio sheets
   D. a step-by-step process to describe how to write a resume or bio sheet

5. A cash-basis business records revenue when it is received and records expenditures when they are paid. It has nothing to do with whether you accept cash, checks, or credit cards.
According to this passage, if you ran a cash-basis business

A. you could only accept cash
B. you would record revenue as soon as you sent the invoice
C. you would plan how to pay for expenditures ahead of time
D. you would record expenses as soon as you paid for them

6. Many investors choose mutual funds, which are made up of groups of people investing in groups of stocks, like technology stocks or blue-chip stocks. Your investment is spread over a number of companies so if one loses money or goes bankrupt, you don't lose your entire investment. Mutual funds are very popular because they're safer than purchasing individual stocks and bonds. They may not return as much money as picking the one right stock will, but then, what are the chances of picking one right stock, anyway? Mutual funds can be started for as little as fifty or a hundred dollars a month.
A good title for this passage would be:

A. The Dangers of Irrational Investing
B. Mutual Funds Explained
C. A Comparison of Investment Options
D. Why Your Mutual Fund Is Worth So Little

7. To reduce the risk of theft, install good strong locks and exterior security lighting around your business. Invest in an alarm or security system especially if you have expensive equipment, if you've invested in an expensive inventory, if your business is in an area with a high crime rate, or if other factors place you at greater risk for theft.
According to this passage, you should invest in an alarm system

A. no matter how expensive it is
B. if your insurance requires it
C. if your business is in a high crime area
D. only if you can't afford security lighting

8. Copyright law protects the works you create from the moment you create them. No special registration is required, although you can also register for a copyright with the Library of Congress. It requires an application and a fee. This registration simply proves that the Library of Congress had a copy of your work on file at the time you registered it, which could be helpful in a lawsuit. For copyrights created since 1978, copyright protection extends for fifty years beyond the death of the creator, so remember to assign copyright ownership in your will.
According to this passage,

A. copyright only applies to works that are registered
B. copyright ends when the owner dies
C. you should assign copyright ownership in your will
D. registration is expensive

9. Many cultures use blessings to keep evil spirits away or to prevent gods or demons from destroying one's happiness. Blessing traditions are also about control. One may want one's children to grow up and be good citizens. One may want strong children, who can look after aged parents. One might want to control the behavior of one's spouse—to keep him or her from straying, or to be certain she will be a good mother, or he will remain a good provider. These concerns can be assuaged by performing ritualistic acts.
According to this passage, which of the following is not true:

   A. people use blessings for a variety of reasons
   B. blessings are ritualistic acts
   C. blessings can be about trying to control life events
   D. people call on evil spirits to perform blessings

10. The social class structure included four main groups of people: aristocracy, clergy, yeomen, and serfs. In general, serfs were much poorer than yeomen, and yeomen had fewer luxuries than members of the nobility. In each group, however, a great variety of wealth existed. Some of the clergy, for instance, lived like royalty. But some members lived more like serfs. For each group, mutual obligations existed. For example, a serf had to farm the land of his or her noble lord. In turn, the noble protected the serf from harm. At least, that was how it was supposed to work.
In this passage, the author's tone

   A. is neutral throughout
   B. is skeptical about how mutual obligations were met
   C. is sarcastic throughout
   D. expresses uncertainty about how social classes lived

11. Salads are a very popular foodstuff, and have always consisted of many of the same ingredients as we use today—lettuce, celery, onions, parsley, and watercress. For centuries, salad dressings have been made with oil and vinegar, as we make them today. But in times past, people enjoyed salads with plant material that we no longer consider food, like violet petals, primroses, daises, and dandelions.
According to this passage,

   A. people stopped eating certain plant material because it was toxic
   B. salads as we know them have been around for a long time
   C. salads are a new fashion and have only been around for a few decades
   D. only poor people used to eat salads

12. In the past, both outlawry and excommunication were used as political weapons during times of civil disturbance and widespread unrest, times in which it was difficult to force certain powerful people to do the bidding of a ruler or of a pope. Of course, outlawry was also used when it was difficult, for one reason or another, to hunt down a criminal and bring him or her to justice.
According to this passage,

   A. outlaws have always been perceived as romantic heroes
   B. only criminals were subject to becoming outlaws
   C. outlawry and excommunication were used to force compliance
   D. outlawry and excommunication are the same thing

13. Songs are used to give news and information and often serve as a way for young people to learn about their culture. In modern times, such music fosters solidarity among a social group.
According to this passage,

    A. the use of music has evolved over time
    B. music has only ever been used as entertainment
    C. music is culturally irrelevant
    D. young people love music

14. The Anasazi were Native American people who lived in a territory covering present-day southern Colorado, Utah, northern New Mexico, and Arizona from about the second century A.D. The Pueblo people are their descendants. Anasazi culture included an early Basket Maker phase, and several Pueblo periods, the last of which continued from about 1050 to 1300. After this period, they had contact with Europeans. During the late thirteenth century, they migrated southward. The Anasazi were expert at weaving, painted pottery, and stone and shell carving. They built stone apartments in caves and cliffs.
A good title for this passage would be:

    A. Who Were the Anasazi?
    B. A Study of Native American Cultures
    C. Origins of the Pueblo People
    D. Utah in the Thirteenth Century

15. Bhavabhuti was a Hindu poet who lived in the eighth century. He is considered one of the great dramatists of early Sanskrit literature. Although details of his life remain obscure, he was probably in the court of King Yasovarman. He is known for three dramas, one that depicts a love story similar to Romeo and Juliet and two that recount the adventures of the hero Rama.
According to this passage,

    A. Most Hindu poets wrote in Sanskrit
    B. Little is known about Bhavabhuti's life
    C. Bhavabhuti had little talent
    D. Shakespeare probably influenced Bhavabhuti

## MATHEMATICS KNOWLEDGE

You'll have 25 questions and 24 minutes to answer them.

1. An industrial alarm control panel is in a rectangular container that has a square base and a measured volume of 16 cubic feet. The height of this container is 16 inches. What would be the length of the base?

   A. 3.464 feet
   B. 4.125 feet
   C. 4.65 feet
   D. 5.14 feet

2. What is the diameter of a cylinder that has a circumference of $19\frac{1}{4}$ inches?

   A. 8.62 inches
   B. 7.8 inches
   C. 6.127 inches
   D. 5.911 inches

3. How high will a 25-foot ladder reach if it is placed 6 feet from the base of a building?

   A. 25 feet
   B. 24.27 feet
   C. 23.12 feet
   D. 22 feet

4. How many square feet of tarp would be needed to cover a circular area that has a radius of 7.35 feet?

   A. 46.18 feet
   B. 153.1 square feet
   C. 169.72 square feet
   D. 173 square feet

5. If someone had an A-frame attic that measured 48 feet in length and 22.5 feet in width and was 12 feet at the height of the triangle, how many cubic feet of space could be utilized for storage?

   A. 7,905.2 cubic feet
   B. 6,480 cubic feet
   C. 967 cubic feet
   D. 135 square feet

6. Solve the inequality $4x < 40$.

   A. $x < 10$
   B. $x > 10$
   C. $x \leq 10$
   D. $x = 10$

7. What is the product of $(y+4)(y+5)$?

   A. $2y+9$
   B. $y^2+9y+20$
   C. $y^2+9$
   D. $y^2+20$

8. Solve for $x$: $9x-21=6$.

   A. $x=12$
   B. $x=2$
   C. $x=3$
   D. $x=-3$

9. Solve the inequality $-2x<8$.

   A. $x=4$
   B. $x>-4$
   C. $x<4$
   D. $x<-4$

10. What is the product of $(x-2)(x+3)$?

    A. $x^2+1$
    B. $x^2-6$
    C. $2x+1$
    D. $x^2+x-6$

11. Solve the inequality $\frac{x}{3}<2$.

    A. $x=6$
    B. $x<6$
    C. $x>6$
    D. $x\leq 6$

12. Solve for $y$: $2y-8=6$.

    A. $y=-1$
    B. $y=14$
    C. $y=7$
    D. $y=1$

13. Evaluate the expression $3x+(2x)^3-2x+5x^2$.

    A. $(2x)^3+5x^2+x$
    B. $3x^3+5x^2$
    C. $(2x)^3+5x^2+5x$
    D. $7x^3$

14. Solve for $x$: $\frac{x}{5}=\frac{4}{10}$.

    A. $x=8$
    B. $x=20$
    C. $x=\frac{1}{2}$
    D. $x=2$

15. For every gallon of water he uses to water the lawn, Brian is supposed to add 3 tablespoons of fertilizer. If he uses 15 gallons of water, how many tablespoons of fertilizer does he need?

A. 45
B. 15
C. 5
D. 60

16. Add the fractions $\frac{x+1}{2}+\frac{x}{3}$.

A. $\frac{x^2+1}{5}$
B. $\frac{x^2+x}{6}$
C. $\frac{2x+1}{5}$
D. $\frac{5x+3}{6}$

17. Divide the fractions $\frac{x-2}{10}\div\frac{x}{5}$.

A. $-\frac{2}{5}x$
B. $-\frac{2x}{2}$
C. $\frac{5x-10}{10x}$
D. $\frac{x^2-2}{2}$

18. Express $3x^2=4x+13$ as a quadratic equation.

A. $3x^2+4x+13$
B. $x=3$
C. $3x^2-4x-13=0$
D. It can't be; quadratic equations don't contain exponents.

19. The total of angles of a polygon with 7 sides is:

A. 1260°
B. 900°
C. 360°
D. 180°

20. A possible solution to $y=3x+2$ is

A. $y=7, x=2$
B. $y=6, x=3$
C. $y=9, x=3$
D. $y=8, x=2$

21. Martina wants to know what the probability of getting heads in four consecutive flips of a coin. The probability is:

A. $\frac{1}{2}$

B. $\frac{1}{16}$

C. $\frac{1}{8}$

D. $\frac{1}{32}$

22. Martina has a six-sided die with each side corresponding to a number between 1 and 6. What is the likelihood that she will roll a 6 three times in a row?

A. $\frac{1}{216}$

B. $\frac{1}{36}$

C. $\frac{1}{18}$

D. $\frac{1}{6}$

23. Martina has found a second six-sided die with each side corresponding to a number between 1 and 6. If she throws both dice at the same time, what is the probability that they will both turn up 6?

A. $\frac{1}{3}$

B. $\frac{1}{6}$

C. $\frac{1}{36}$

D. $\frac{1}{72}$

24. Factor $x^2 + 2x - 8$.

A. $(x+2)(x+8)$
B. $(x+4)(x-2)$
C. $(x+4)(x+4)$
D. $(x+3)(x+2)$

25. Given $y = 2x + 5$ and $y = 3x + 8$, solve for $x$ and $y$.

A. $(x=3, y=1)$
B. $(x=2, y=9)$
C. $(x=3, y=11)$
D. $(x=-3, y=-1)$

## ELECTRONICS INFORMATION

You'll have 20 questions and 9 minutes to answer them.

1. Which of the following is <u>not</u> a type of particle?

   A. proton
   B. retron
   C. neutron
   D. electron

2. Which of the following is a good insulator?

   A. rubber
   B. aluminum cable
   C. water
   D. copper wire

3. 75 mV is the same as

   A. 75 volts
   B. 1 volt
   C. 0.0075 volt
   D. 0.75 volt

4. An integrated circuit uses which of the following to direct the flow of current?

   A. copper wire
   B. aluminum gates
   C. conducting lines
   D. electrolytes

5. Which of the following does not use a natural process to harness electricity?

   A. water wheel
   B. windmill
   C. solar panel
   D. coal-fired plant

6. 1 watt is the same as

   A. 1 volt per second
   B. 1 ampere
   C. 1 joule per second
   D. 1 ohm

7. Electrical efficiency is a measure of which of the following?

   A. how useful an appliance is
   B. how easy or difficult it is to access sources of electricity
   C. the useful power output compared to the power consumed
   D. a person's conscientiousness in turning off appliances not in use

8. 60-cycle AC power means which of the following?

A. the direction of current switches direction 60 times per second
B. each cycle requires 60 amps of power
C. 60 watts of electricity is generated per cycle
D. each cycle lasts 60 seconds

9. Static electricity is which of the following?

A. the same as free flowing electric current
B. the electric potential of an unmoving object
C. the buildup of electrons on an object gives it a charge different from the surrounding materials
D. a type of resistance found in metal objects

10. A negative energy field attracts which of the following?

A. another negative energy field
B. a neutral energy field
C. a positive energy field
D. nothing

11. Wrapping wire around metal and sending a charge through it will create which of the following?

A. a magnetic field around the wire-wrapped metal
B. a fire
C. a good semiconductor
D. a strong resistor

12. "Doping" is which of the following?

A. restricting the current
B. amplifying the current
C. a dangerous behavior when working with electricity
D. modifying the materials of a semiconductor to make it work as needed

13. A circuit has 12 volts and a current of 3 amperes. How much resistance does it have?

A. 15 ohms
B. 4 ohms
C. 9 ohms
D. 36 ohms

14. What is the correct formula to determine energy?

A. Energy equals power divided by current
B. Energy equals current divided by voltage
C. Energy equals power divided by time
D. Energy equals power multiplied by time

15. The circuit shown in the figure below is what type of circuit?

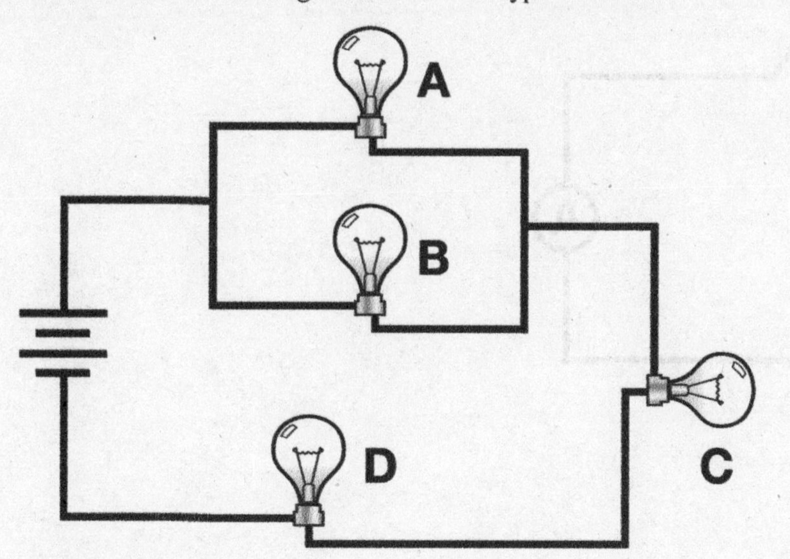


A. series
B. series-parallel
C. parallel
D. integrated circuit

16. A closed loop system does which of the following?

A. returns positive charges to their original positions
B. sends charges in one direction only
C. prevents additional resistors from being added to the system
D. uses magnets to create electromagnetic energy

17. If each of the light bulbs in the figure below has 2 ohms of resistance, what is the total resistance of the circuit?

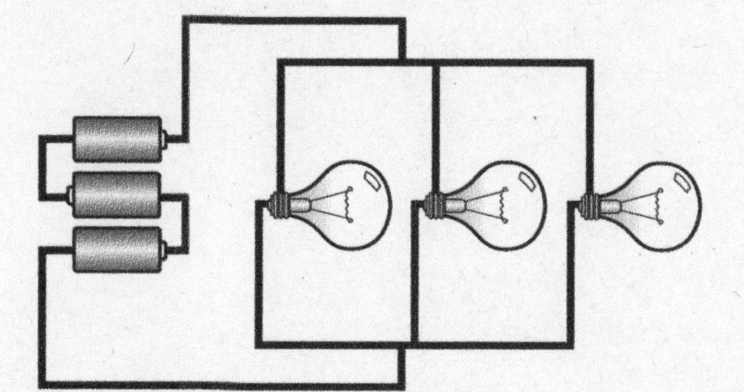

A. 2 ohms
B. 6 ohms
C. 8 ohms
D. 0.66 ohms

18. In the figure below, what is R?

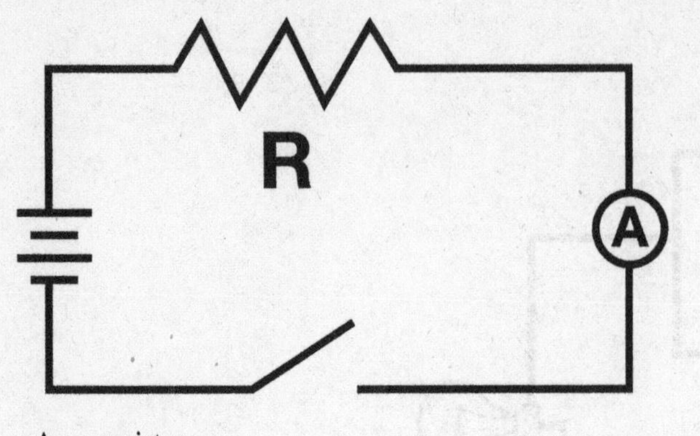


A. a resistor
B. an inductor
C. a capacitor
D. a switch

19. The symbol ⊣⊢ refers to what component on a schematic?

A. a capacitor
B. a switch
C. a battery
D. an ammeter

20. A component on a schematic is given a μF rating. What type of component is it?

A. a voltmeter
B. a resistor
C. a switch
D. a capacitor

## AUTOMOTIVE AND SHOP INFORMATION

You'll have 25 questions and 11 minutes to answer them.

1. Which of the following happens during the intake stroke of a four-stroke cycle?

   A. Coolant is taken into the engine
   B. The intake valve opens, allowing fuel and air to enter the cylinder
   C. The intake valve closes, and the fuel-air mixture is ignited
   D. Gasoline is introduced into the fuel tank

2. How many cylinders are generally found in a passenger car?

   A. 2 or 4
   B. 6 or more
   C. 4, 6, and sometimes 8
   D. 8, 10, and occasionally 12

3. Which of the following is not true of the internal combustion process?

   A. a small explosion takes place in the engine
   B. liquid fuel is turned into a gas during the process
   C. the force of combustion powers the engine
   D. the process takes place outside the engine

4. In a cylinder-and-piston component, which of the following is true?

   A. the piston is housed inside the cylinder
   B. the cylinder is housed inside the piston
   C. the piston is side-by-side with the cylinder
   D. the piston forces the cylinder forward

5. The component shown in the figure below is an example of which of the following?

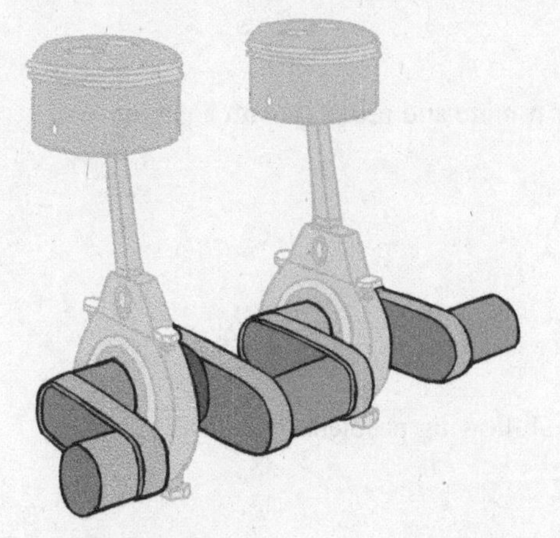

   A. crankshaft
   B. camshaft
   C. tie rod
   D. push rod

6. Exhaust valves perform which of the following functions?

   A. they vent exhaust to the outside
   B. they vent exhaust from the cylinder
   C. they recirculate unburned fuel
   D. they detect exhaust fumes in the fuel tank

7. In the figure below, the arrow is pointing to which engine component?

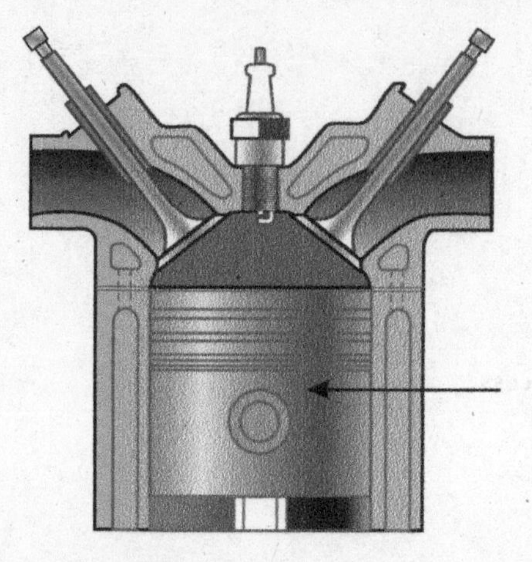

   A. a piston
   B. a flywheel
   C. a master cylinder
   D. a drum brake

8. A four-stroke cycle follows which of the following sequences?

   A. compression, combustion, intake, exhaust
   B. intake, combustion, compression, exhaust
   C. intake, compression, combustion, exhaust
   D. intake, exhaust, combustion, compression

9. The abbreviation "RPM" on a tachometer means revolutions per minute and refers to which engine component?

   A. the crankshaft
   B. the piston
   C. the camshaft
   D. the axle

10. An extensive oil leak in an engine is likely to cause which of the following problems?

   A. parts breakdown
   B. brake failure
   C. loss of steering
   D. squeaking in the suspension

11. Which of the following is not true about the coolant in a car's engine?

A. it is commonly mixed with water before being used in the cooling system
B. coolant is poisonous
C. coolant is flammable
D. it has the same qualities as water

12. In a manual transmission vehicle, the clutch serves which of the following purposes?

A. the driver uses it to select the correct gear
B. it prevents the engine from engaging with the transmission during gear-shifting
C. it applies the brakes as gears are being shifted
D. it is used to lock in the gear once it has been selected

13. A reciprocating saw can be used to cut through which of the following materials?

A. plastics
B. particle board
C. dry wall
D. all of the above

14. If a contractor needed a true vertical line of reference, what tool would be used?

A. carpenter's square
B. bevel square
C. plumb bob
D. level

15. What kind of handsaw is used specifically to cut tenon joints?

A. back saw
B. coping saw
C. hacksaw
D. saber saw

16. What kind of screwdriver would be needed to drive the screw shown in the figure below?

A. conventional straight shank
B. Phillips
C. Torx
D. close-quarters screwdriver

17. What is the reason a spark plug wrench should be used to remove spark plugs over other types of wrenches?

A. It's quicker.
B. More torque can be applied.
C. It lessens the chance of getting burned.
D. It prevents potential damage from occurring to the insulator or electrode.

18. What is shown in the figure below?

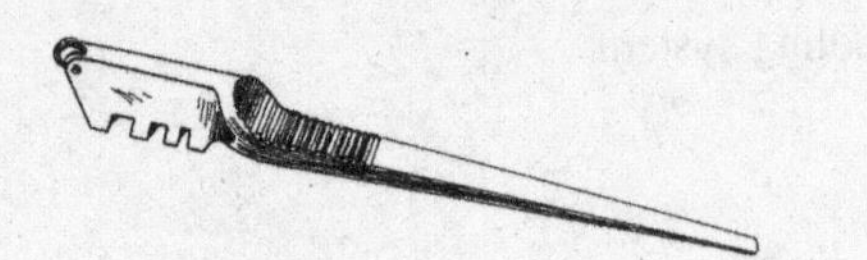

A. utility knife
B. glass cutter
C. awl
D. triangular file

19. Which of the following drill bits is not used with a brace?

A. auger bit
B. expansive bit
C. twist bit
D. masonry drill bit

20. What pair of pliers can apply a constant amount of pressure without much effort?

A. needle-nose pliers
B. curved jaw pliers
C. plier wrench
D. slip joint pliers

21. What is the measurement as shown by the micrometer caliper in the diagram below?

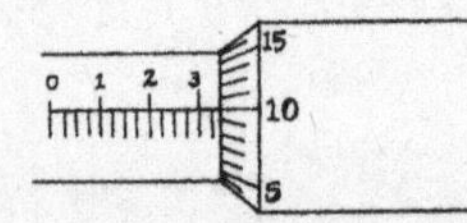


A. 0.320 inches
B. 0.335 inches
C. 0.35 inches
D. 0.275 inches

22. What is the name of the tool shown in the diagram below?

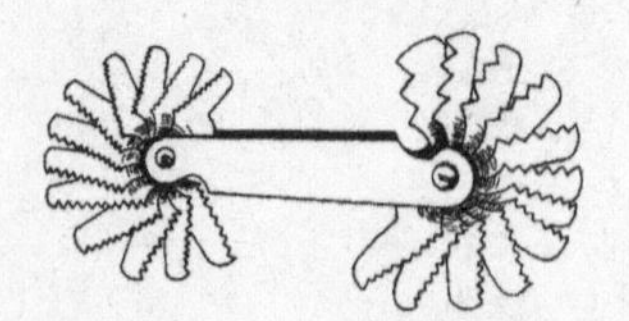

A. screw pitch gauge
B. wire gauge
C. depth gauge
D. feelers gauge

23. What is the primary advantage of a carbide-tipped saw blade?

A. It is sharper.
B. It can cut quicker with a smaller chance of kickback.
C. The hardened teeth will remain sharper longer.
D. It can cut metal and concrete.

24. What advantage does an offset screwdriver have over other screwdrivers?

A. It can tighten or loosen screws in cramped places.
B. It is quicker to use in tightening screws as compared to conventional shank screwdrivers.
C. It can exert substantially more torque than regular screwdrivers.
D. Both A and C are correct.

25. What kind of a tool is used to cut external screw threads on round metal stock?

A. taps in a tap wrench
B. round split die in a holder
C. pipe cutter
D. Stilson wrench

## MECHANICAL COMPREHENSION

You'll have 25 questions and 19 minutes to answer them.

1. Three painters attempted to lift an aluminum ladder that extended 25 feet in length and weighed 75 pounds. If one of the painters served to anchor one end of the ladder to the ground while the other two lifted the other end of the ladder at a point 10 feet from the anchorman, how much resistance would the ladder present to the two doing the actual lifting?

   A. 37.5 pounds of resistance
   B. 75 pounds of resistance
   C. 127.8 pounds of resistance
   D. 93.75 pounds of resistance

2. If three painters attempted to lift an aluminum ladder by having one of the painters serve to anchor one end of the ladder to the ground while the other two lifted the other end of the ladder, which of the following statements is true?

   A. Using leverage in this fashion makes it significantly easier for the painters to lift the ladder.
   B. The mechanical advantage gained through this kind of leverage is at least 2:1.
   C. Leverage, under the circumstances, is actually working against the two painters attempting the lift, rather than serving to their advantage.
   D. The ladder would have been harder to lift at a point farther away from the anchorman.

3. In the figure below, if gear 1 was turning at a speed of 400 rpm, how fast would gear 2 turn?

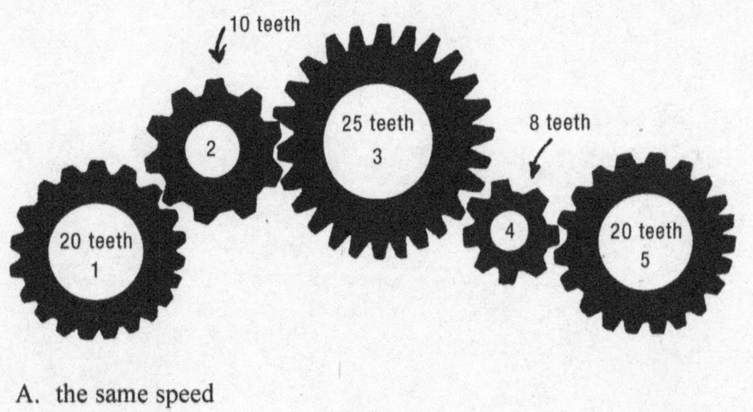


   A. the same speed
   B. twice as fast
   C. three times as fast
   D. 20% faster

4. Which of the statements below is true about the figure below?

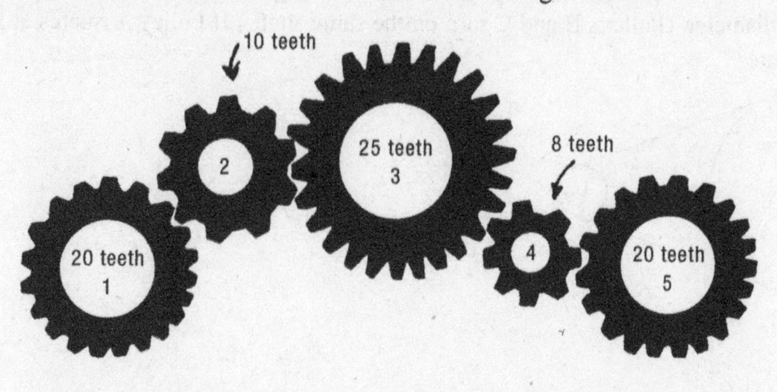


A. Gears 1, 3, and 5 will turn in the same direction, and gears 1 and 5 will turn at equivalent speeds.
B. Gears 2 and 4 will turn in the same direction at the same speed.
C. Gears 1, 2, and 3 will turn clockwise if gears 3 and 4 turn counterclockwise.
D. Gear 3 will turn the fastest of those shown in the drive train.

5. How much guy wire would be required to support a ham radio antenna if the collar to which the guy wire is connected is 23 feet off the ground and the anchor turnbuckles are evenly spaced 15 feet away from its base? (Allow an extra 8 inches for fastening the ends of each of the four wires.)

A. 112.52 feet
B. 107.5 feet
C. 101.92 feet
D. 95.78 feet

6. A 10-foot section of an 8-inch cast iron main was suspended by three metal straps from a basement ceiling. Knowing there was a strap supporting both ends and the center strap was situated closer to one end than the other, which of the statements given below would be true?

A. The strap on the end that is furthest away from the center supporting strap would bear the greatest load.
B. All three straps would bear equal load.
C. The end strap closest to the center support strap would bear the greatest load.
D. The center supporting strap would bear the greatest strain.

7. In the illustration shown in the figure below, if the drive gear is the larger gear, what overall effect does the smaller gear have on the drive train?

A. There is a proportional increase in speed.
B. There is a proportional decrease in both torque and speed.
C. There is a proportional increase in speed but a proportional decrease in torque.
D. All factors considered, it is a 1:1 gear ratio and it does not have any impact on speed or torque.

8. In the figure below, Pulley A has a 13-inch diameter. Pulley B has a 9-inch diameter. Pulley C has a 16-inch diameter. Pulley D has a 6-inch diameter. (Pulleys B and C turn on the same shaft.) If Pulley A rotates at 54 rpm, how fast does Pulley D rotate?

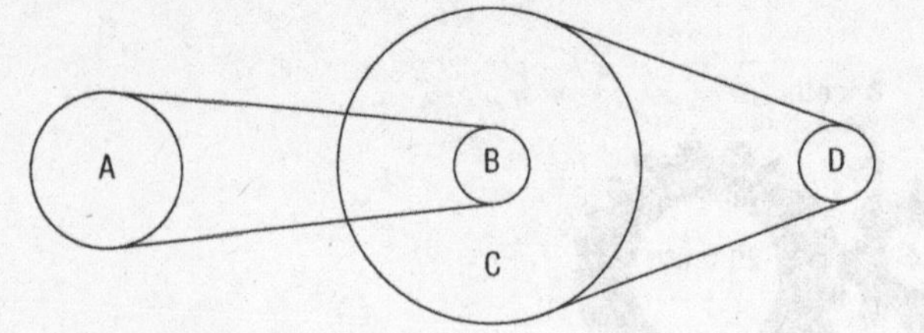


A. 407 rpm
B. 362 rpm
C. 208 rpm
D. 139 rpm

9. Which of the following statements is true with respect to the drive train illustrated in the figure below?

A. Gears 2 and 8 will turn clockwise if the first gear turns clockwise.
B. Gears 4 and 5 will turn counterclockwise if Gear 2 turns clockwise.
C. Gears 3, 5, and 6 will turn in the same direction that Gear 2 turns.
D. Gears 3, 5, and 7 will turn counterclockwise if Gear 2 turns clockwise.

10. What is the feature most responsible for the leverage gained by using a windlass (which winds a rope around a drum)?

A. The diameter of rope utilized on the drum.
B. The length of the handgrip (i.e., that portion of the handle that extends in a horizontal axis away from the drum).
C. The length of handle (i.e., that portion of the handle extending perpendicular to the drum) in relation to the drum's diameter.
D. The length of the drum itself.

11. In the figure below, if 400 pounds of tension had to be applied to the line and the windlass had a drum diameter of 6 inches, how long a handle would be necessary if only 125 pounds of potential effort is available?

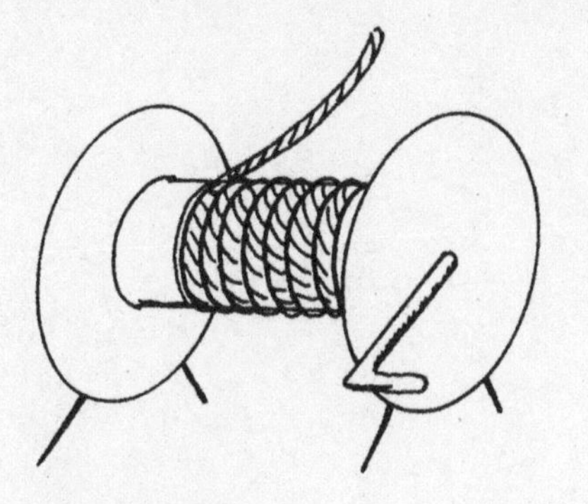

A. 60.32 inches
B. 51.7 inches
C. 25.1 inches
D. 18.85 inches

12. Two members of a cleanup crew were assisting in a toxic waste cleanup. If both people attempted to roll a 55-gallon drum of chemicals weighing 460 pounds up the inclined plane shown in the figure below in order to load it onto a disposal truck, how much effort is needed from each person?

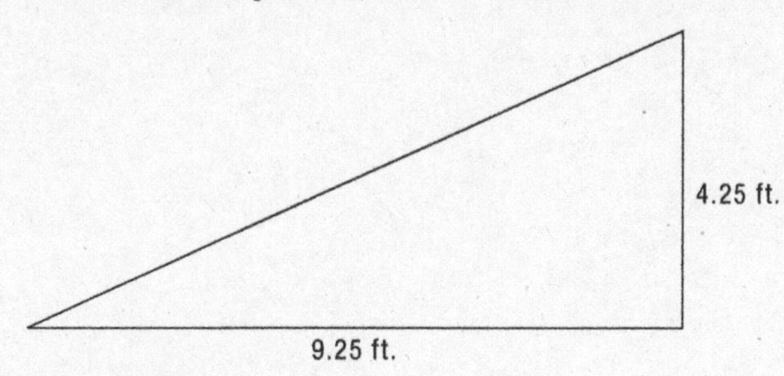


A. 192 pounds
B. 96 pounds
C. 138 pounds
D. 69 pounds

13. If two members of a cleanup crew roll a 780-pound barrel up an inclined plane, using 150 pounds of effort each, what kind of lift advantage is gained versus an individual trying to lift the barrel outright?

A. 2.4:1
B. 4.8:1
C. 5.2:1
D. 5.7:1

14. How much effort would be required using a pair of pulleys set up in the manner diagrammed in the figure below to lift the weight shown? (Assume pulley B is in a fixed position.)

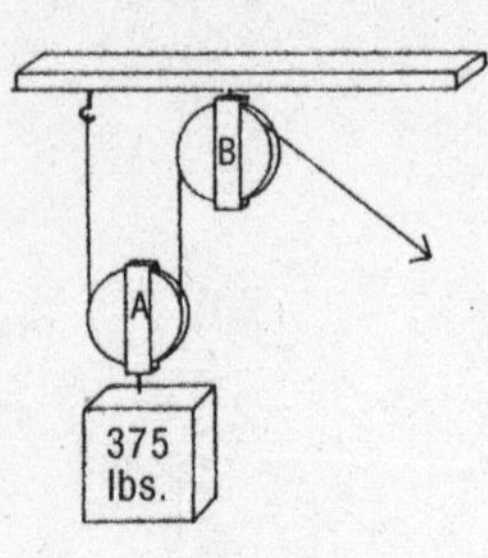


A. 187.5 pounds
B. 205.5 pounds
C. 250.5 pounds
D. 262.7 pounds

15. Referring to the figure below, if the cable in this pulley apparatus were pulled 15 feet (assuming there was enough cable present to do so), how high would this lift the weight?

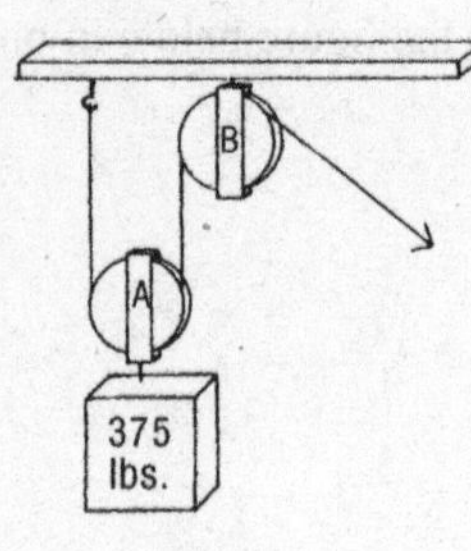


A. 7.5 feet
B. 10 feet
C. 15 feet
D. 17.5 feet

16. Which of the following statements is true with regard to the belt drive illustrated in the figure below? (Note: Wheels 3 and 4 are keyed to the same shaft.)
Wheel dimensions are as follows:
Wheel 1: 8 inches in diameter
Wheel 2: 4 inches in diameter
Wheel 3: 4 inches in diameter
Wheel 4: 8 inches in diameter
Wheel 5: 4 inches in diameter

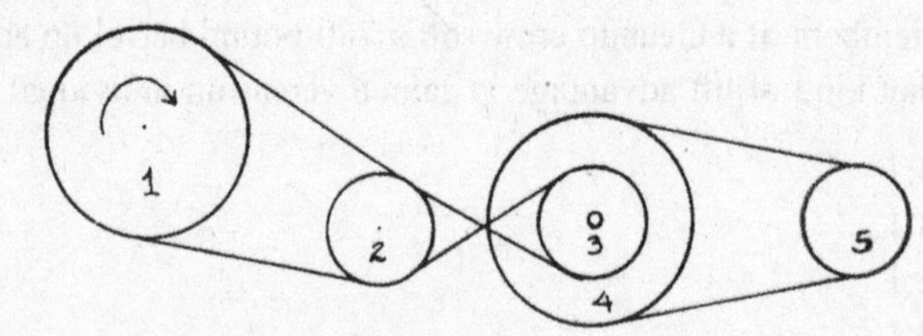


A. Wheel 4 will turn faster than wheel 2 in a counterclockwise direction.
B. Wheel 5 will turn faster than wheel 1 in a clockwise direction.
C. Wheel 2 and wheel 5 will turn in the same direction at the same speed.
D. Wheel 3 will turn faster than wheel 1 in a counterclockwise direction.

17. If the jackscrew illustrated in the figure below is needed to lift $2\frac{1}{2}$ tons and it is known the jack has a $\frac{1}{8}$-inch pitch and a handle/lever measuring 19 inches in length, how much effort is required to achieve lift?

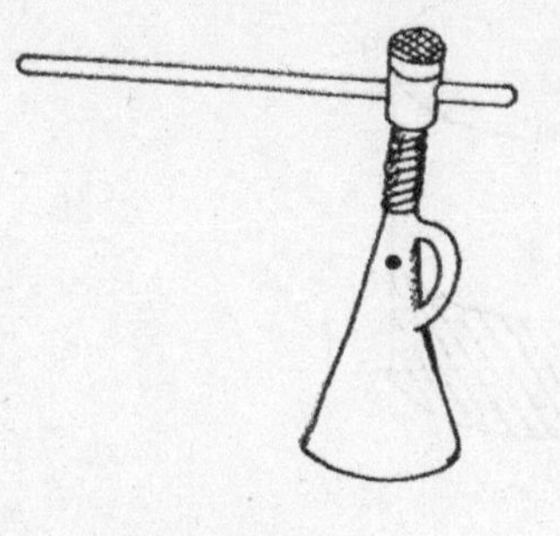

A. 3.15 pounds
B. 5.24 pounds
C. 7.9 pounds
D. 13.71 pounds

18. If a drive gear has 28 teeth and a connecting gear (i.e., the driven gear) has 14 teeth, which of the following events will occur?

A. The torque output and speed are doubled.
B. The torque output is only $\frac{1}{4}$ of that input while the speed is tripled.
C. The torque output is doubled while the speed is halved.
D. The torque output is halved while the speed is doubled.

19. Study the illustration in the figure below. Considering the fact that gears A and C are 50% the size of gears B and D in the driveline, what is the overall advantage gained by using such a gear configuration?

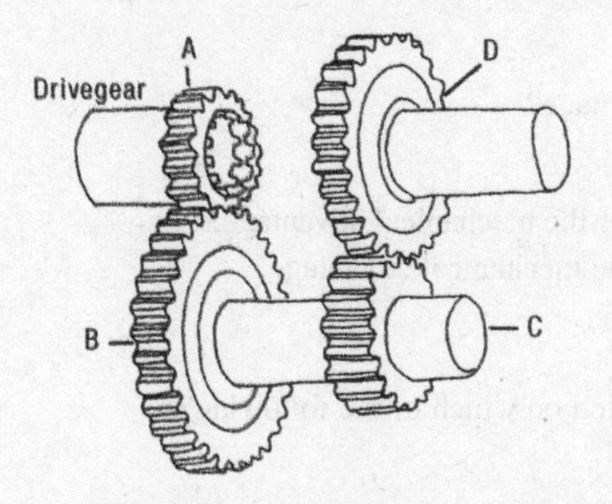


A. Speed enhancement on the order of 4:1.
B. Speed enhancement on the order of 2:1.
C. Torque enhancement on the order of 4:1.
D. Torque enhancement on the order of 2:1.

20. In the figure below, cylinders 1, 2, and 3 have 5-, 7-, and 13-liter capacities, respectively. How much water would have to be pumped through the inlet port to raise the level of cylinder 3 from 4.5 liters to 9.75 liters?

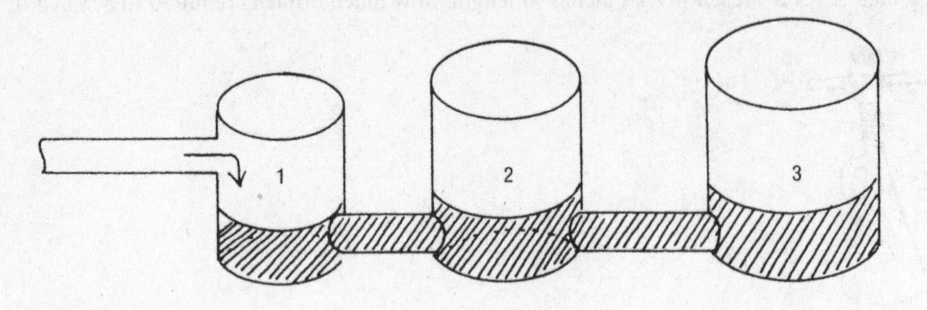


A. 10.1 liters
B. 8.7 liters
C. 5.25 liters
D. 2.423 liters

21. Which of the following is not an example of a simple machine?

A. a wheelchair ramp
B. a prybar
C. a corkscrew
D. an oven

22. Which of the following is a correct definition of a compound machine?

A. any machine with a motor
B. a simple machine with a motor
C. two or more simple machines put together
D. a lever and a screw working together

23. How does the location of the fulcrum affect mechanical advantage?

A. It doesn't.
B. The farther the fulcrum is from the resistance, the greater the mechanical advantage.
C. The nearer the fulcrum is to the resistance, the greater the mechanical advantage.
D. None of the above.

24. When using a pulley, the length of a pull has a direct correlation on which of the following?

A. the height (lift) gained
B. the length of the incline plane
C. the weight of the resistance
D. the mechanical advantage

25. A wedge is most similar to which other device?

A. a screw
B. an inclined plane
C. a wheel and axle
D. a gear

## ASSEMBLING OBJECTS

You'll have 16 questions and 15 minutes to answer them.

1.

2.

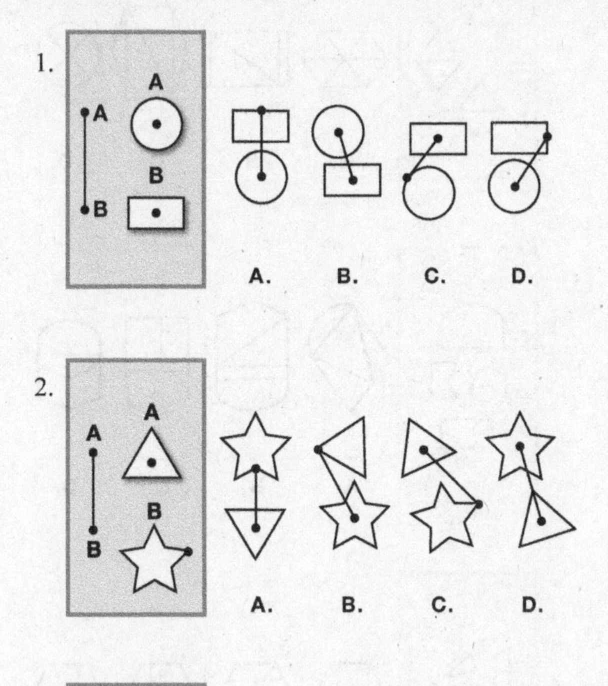


3.

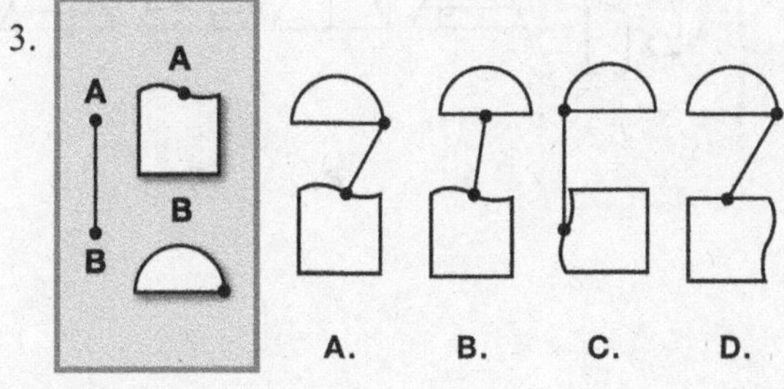


4.

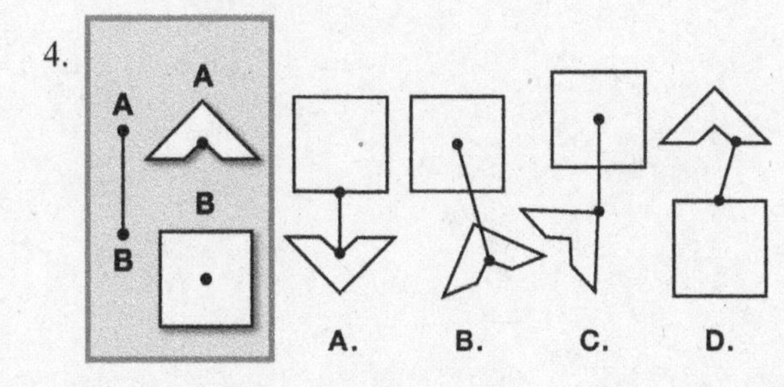


5.

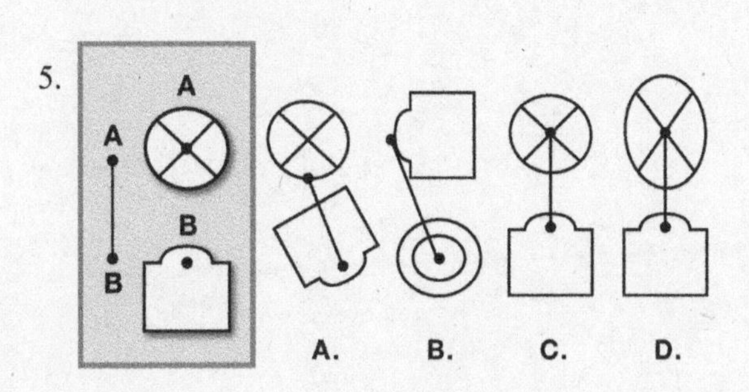


6.

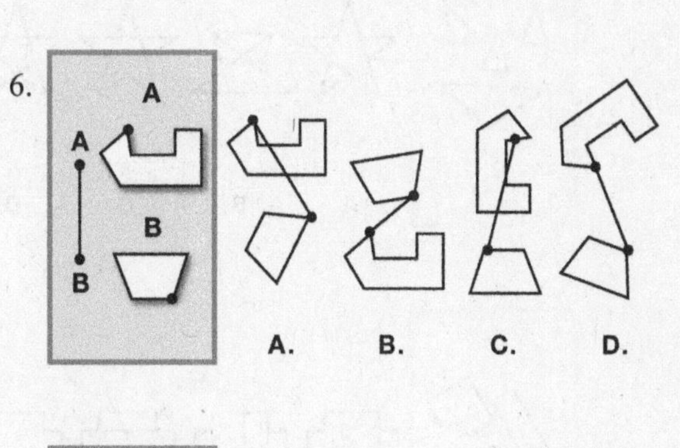


7.

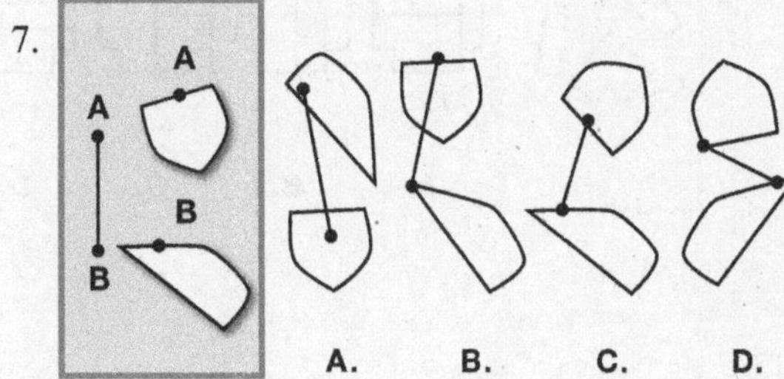


8.

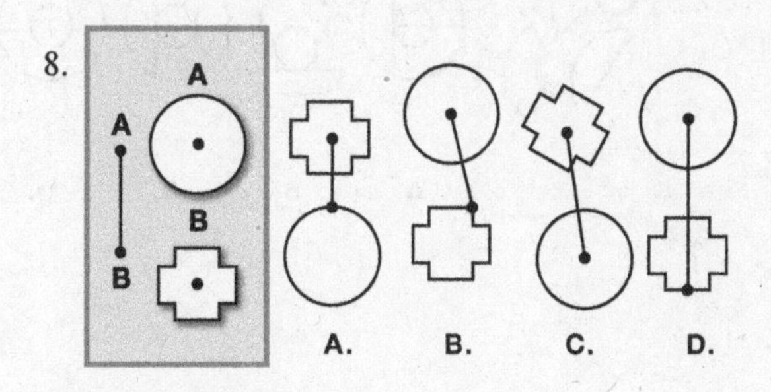


9.

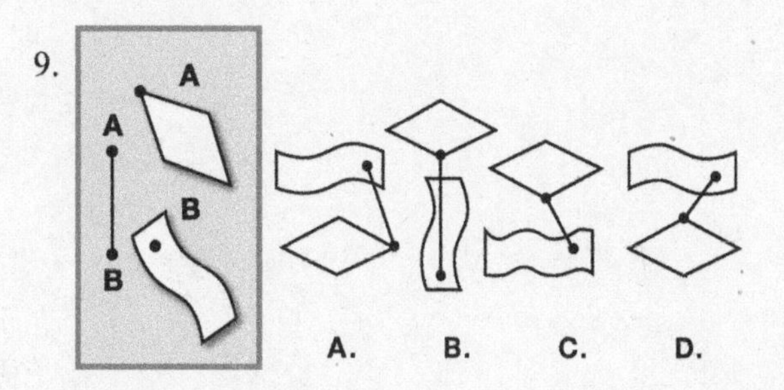


10.

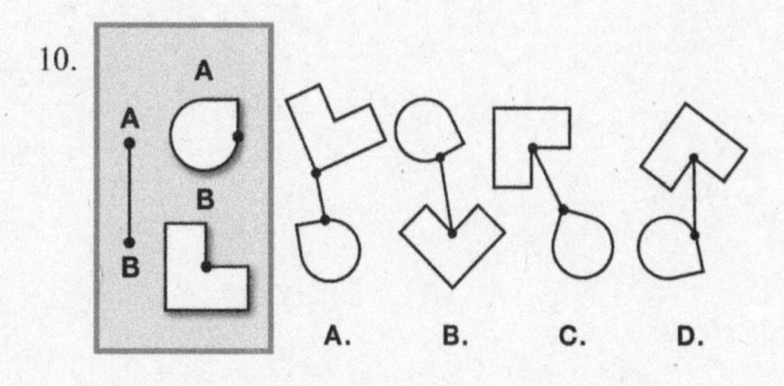

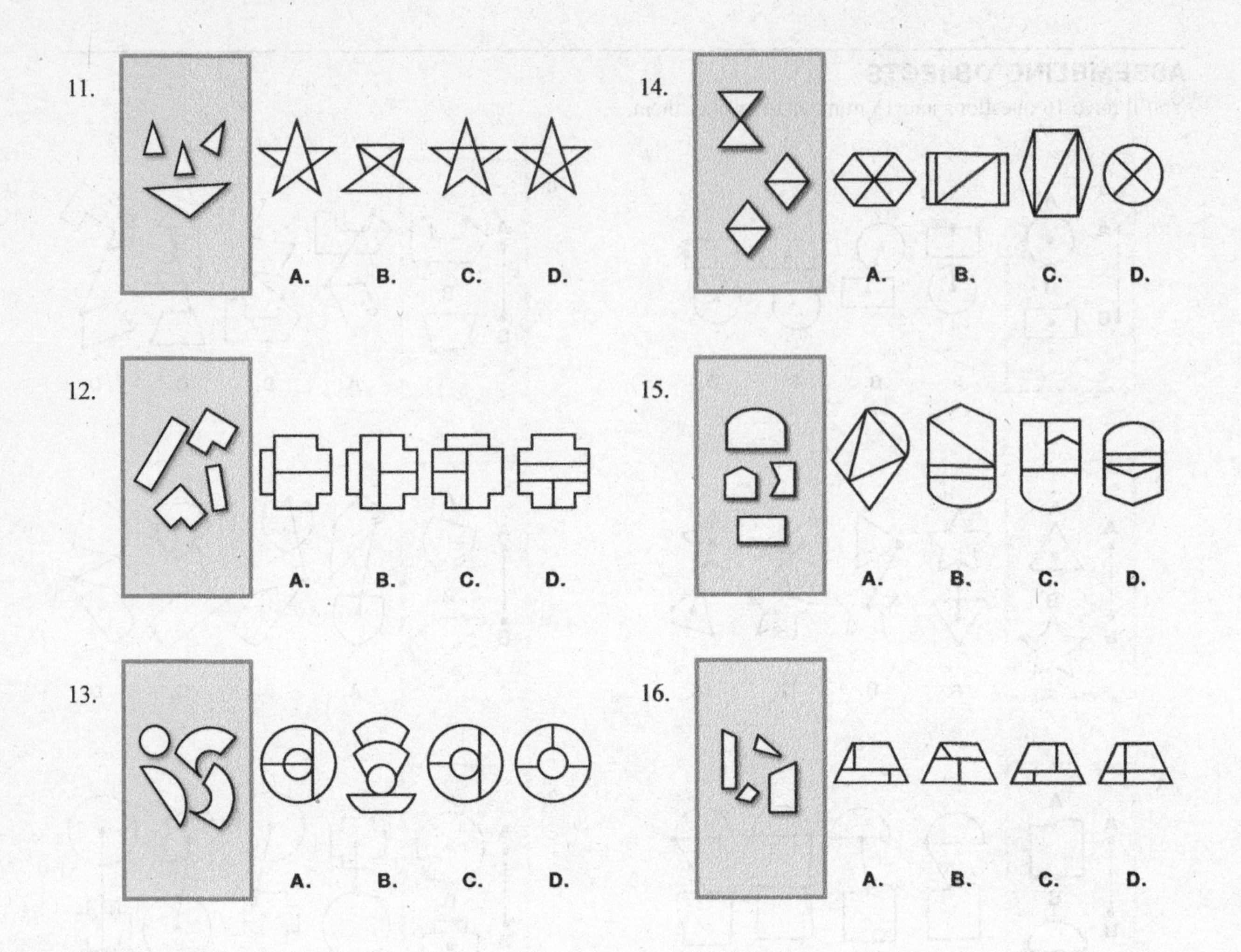
11.
A.
B.
C.
D.
12.
A.
B.
C.
D.
13.
A.
B.
C.
D.
14.
A.
B.
C.
D.
15.
A.
B.
C.
D.
16.
A.
B.
C.
D.

## ANSWER SHEET FOR PRACTICE TEST #2

### GENERAL SCIENCE

1. Ⓐ Ⓑ Ⓒ Ⓓ
2. Ⓐ Ⓑ Ⓒ Ⓓ
3. Ⓐ Ⓑ Ⓒ Ⓓ
4. Ⓐ Ⓑ Ⓒ Ⓓ
5. Ⓐ Ⓑ Ⓒ Ⓓ
6. Ⓐ Ⓑ Ⓒ Ⓓ
7. Ⓐ Ⓑ Ⓒ Ⓓ
8. Ⓐ Ⓑ Ⓒ Ⓓ
9. Ⓐ Ⓑ Ⓒ Ⓓ
10. Ⓐ Ⓑ Ⓒ Ⓓ
11. Ⓐ Ⓑ Ⓒ Ⓓ
12. Ⓐ Ⓑ Ⓒ Ⓓ
13. Ⓐ Ⓑ Ⓒ Ⓓ
14. Ⓐ Ⓑ Ⓒ Ⓓ
15. Ⓐ Ⓑ Ⓒ Ⓓ
16. Ⓐ Ⓑ Ⓒ Ⓓ
17. Ⓐ Ⓑ Ⓒ Ⓓ
18. Ⓐ Ⓑ Ⓒ Ⓓ
19. Ⓐ Ⓑ Ⓒ Ⓓ
20. Ⓐ Ⓑ Ⓒ Ⓓ
21. Ⓐ Ⓑ Ⓒ Ⓓ
22. Ⓐ Ⓑ Ⓒ Ⓓ
23. Ⓐ Ⓑ Ⓒ Ⓓ
24. Ⓐ Ⓑ Ⓒ Ⓓ
25. Ⓐ Ⓑ Ⓒ Ⓓ

### ARITHMETIC REASONING

1. Ⓐ Ⓑ Ⓒ Ⓓ
2. Ⓐ Ⓑ Ⓒ Ⓓ
3. Ⓐ Ⓑ Ⓒ Ⓓ
4. Ⓐ Ⓑ Ⓒ Ⓓ
5. Ⓐ Ⓑ Ⓒ Ⓓ
6. Ⓐ Ⓑ Ⓒ Ⓓ
7. Ⓐ Ⓑ Ⓒ Ⓓ
8. Ⓐ Ⓑ Ⓒ Ⓓ
9. Ⓐ Ⓑ Ⓒ Ⓓ
10. Ⓐ Ⓑ Ⓒ Ⓓ
11. Ⓐ Ⓑ Ⓒ Ⓓ
12. Ⓐ Ⓑ Ⓒ Ⓓ
13. Ⓐ Ⓑ Ⓒ Ⓓ
14. Ⓐ Ⓑ Ⓒ Ⓓ
15. Ⓐ Ⓑ Ⓒ Ⓓ
16. Ⓐ Ⓑ Ⓒ Ⓓ
17. Ⓐ Ⓑ Ⓒ Ⓓ
18. Ⓐ Ⓑ Ⓒ Ⓓ
19. Ⓐ Ⓑ Ⓒ Ⓓ
20. Ⓐ Ⓑ Ⓒ Ⓓ
21. Ⓐ Ⓑ Ⓒ Ⓓ
22. Ⓐ Ⓑ Ⓒ Ⓓ
23. Ⓐ Ⓑ Ⓒ Ⓓ
24. Ⓐ Ⓑ Ⓒ Ⓓ
25. Ⓐ Ⓑ Ⓒ Ⓓ
26. Ⓐ Ⓑ Ⓒ Ⓓ
27. Ⓐ Ⓑ Ⓒ Ⓓ
28. Ⓐ Ⓑ Ⓒ Ⓓ
29. Ⓐ Ⓑ Ⓒ Ⓓ
30. Ⓐ Ⓑ Ⓒ Ⓓ

### WORD KNOWLEDGE

1. Ⓐ Ⓑ Ⓒ Ⓓ
2. Ⓐ Ⓑ Ⓒ Ⓓ
3. Ⓐ Ⓑ Ⓒ Ⓓ
4. Ⓐ Ⓑ Ⓒ Ⓓ
5. Ⓐ Ⓑ Ⓒ Ⓓ
6. Ⓐ Ⓑ Ⓒ Ⓓ
7. Ⓐ Ⓑ Ⓒ Ⓓ
8. Ⓐ Ⓑ Ⓒ Ⓓ
9. Ⓐ Ⓑ Ⓒ Ⓓ
10. Ⓐ Ⓑ Ⓒ Ⓓ
11. Ⓐ Ⓑ Ⓒ Ⓓ
12. Ⓐ Ⓑ Ⓒ Ⓓ
13. Ⓐ Ⓑ Ⓒ Ⓓ
14. Ⓐ Ⓑ Ⓒ Ⓓ
15. Ⓐ Ⓑ Ⓒ Ⓓ
16. Ⓐ Ⓑ Ⓒ Ⓓ
17. Ⓐ Ⓑ Ⓒ Ⓓ
18. Ⓐ Ⓑ Ⓒ Ⓓ
19. Ⓐ Ⓑ Ⓒ Ⓓ
20. Ⓐ Ⓑ Ⓒ Ⓓ
21. Ⓐ Ⓑ Ⓒ Ⓓ

22. Ⓐ Ⓑ Ⓒ Ⓓ
23. Ⓐ Ⓑ Ⓒ Ⓓ
24. Ⓐ Ⓑ Ⓒ Ⓓ
25. Ⓐ Ⓑ Ⓒ Ⓓ
26. Ⓐ Ⓑ Ⓒ Ⓓ
27. Ⓐ Ⓑ Ⓒ Ⓓ
28. Ⓐ Ⓑ Ⓒ Ⓓ
29. Ⓐ Ⓑ Ⓒ Ⓓ
30. Ⓐ Ⓑ Ⓒ Ⓓ
31. Ⓐ Ⓑ Ⓒ Ⓓ
32. Ⓐ Ⓑ Ⓒ Ⓓ
33. Ⓐ Ⓑ Ⓒ Ⓓ
34. Ⓐ Ⓑ Ⓒ Ⓓ
35. Ⓐ Ⓑ Ⓒ Ⓓ

## PARAGRAPH COMPREHENSION

1. Ⓐ Ⓑ Ⓒ Ⓓ
2. Ⓐ Ⓑ Ⓒ Ⓓ
3. Ⓐ Ⓑ Ⓒ Ⓓ
4. Ⓐ Ⓑ Ⓒ Ⓓ
5. Ⓐ Ⓑ Ⓒ Ⓓ
6. Ⓐ Ⓑ Ⓒ Ⓓ
7. Ⓐ Ⓑ Ⓒ Ⓓ
8. Ⓐ Ⓑ Ⓒ Ⓓ
9. Ⓐ Ⓑ Ⓒ Ⓓ
10. Ⓐ Ⓑ Ⓒ Ⓓ
11. Ⓐ Ⓑ Ⓒ Ⓓ
12. Ⓐ Ⓑ Ⓒ Ⓓ
13. Ⓐ Ⓑ Ⓒ Ⓓ
14. Ⓐ Ⓑ Ⓒ Ⓓ
15. Ⓐ Ⓑ Ⓒ Ⓓ

## MATHEMATICS KNOWLEDGE

1. Ⓐ Ⓑ Ⓒ Ⓓ
2. Ⓐ Ⓑ Ⓒ Ⓓ
3. Ⓐ Ⓑ Ⓒ Ⓓ
4. Ⓐ Ⓑ Ⓒ Ⓓ
5. Ⓐ Ⓑ Ⓒ Ⓓ
6. Ⓐ Ⓑ Ⓒ Ⓓ
7. Ⓐ Ⓑ Ⓒ Ⓓ
8. Ⓐ Ⓑ Ⓒ Ⓓ
9. Ⓐ Ⓑ Ⓒ Ⓓ
10. Ⓐ Ⓑ Ⓒ Ⓓ
11. Ⓐ Ⓑ Ⓒ Ⓓ
12. Ⓐ Ⓑ Ⓒ Ⓓ
13. Ⓐ Ⓑ Ⓒ Ⓓ
14. Ⓐ Ⓑ Ⓒ Ⓓ
15. Ⓐ Ⓑ Ⓒ Ⓓ
16. Ⓐ Ⓑ Ⓒ Ⓓ
17. Ⓐ Ⓑ Ⓒ Ⓓ
18. Ⓐ Ⓑ Ⓒ Ⓓ
19. Ⓐ Ⓑ Ⓒ Ⓓ
20. Ⓐ Ⓑ Ⓒ Ⓓ
21. Ⓐ Ⓑ Ⓒ Ⓓ
22. Ⓐ Ⓑ Ⓒ Ⓓ
23. Ⓐ Ⓑ Ⓒ Ⓓ
24. Ⓐ Ⓑ Ⓒ Ⓓ
25. Ⓐ Ⓑ Ⓒ Ⓓ

## ELECTRONICS INFORMATION

1. Ⓐ Ⓑ Ⓒ Ⓓ
2. Ⓐ Ⓑ Ⓒ Ⓓ
3. Ⓐ Ⓑ Ⓒ Ⓓ
4. Ⓐ Ⓑ Ⓒ Ⓓ
5. Ⓐ Ⓑ Ⓒ Ⓓ
6. Ⓐ Ⓑ Ⓒ Ⓓ
7. Ⓐ Ⓑ Ⓒ Ⓓ
8. Ⓐ Ⓑ Ⓒ Ⓓ
9. Ⓐ Ⓑ Ⓒ Ⓓ
10. Ⓐ Ⓑ Ⓒ Ⓓ
11. Ⓐ Ⓑ Ⓒ Ⓓ
12. Ⓐ Ⓑ Ⓒ Ⓓ
13. Ⓐ Ⓑ Ⓒ Ⓓ
14. Ⓐ Ⓑ Ⓒ Ⓓ
15. Ⓐ Ⓑ Ⓒ Ⓓ
16. Ⓐ Ⓑ Ⓒ Ⓓ
17. Ⓐ Ⓑ Ⓒ Ⓓ
18. Ⓐ Ⓑ Ⓒ Ⓓ
19. Ⓐ Ⓑ Ⓒ Ⓓ
20. Ⓐ Ⓑ Ⓒ Ⓓ

## AUTOMOTIVE AND SHOP INFORMATION

1. Ⓐ Ⓑ Ⓒ Ⓓ
2. Ⓐ Ⓑ Ⓒ Ⓓ
3. Ⓐ Ⓑ Ⓒ Ⓓ
4. Ⓐ Ⓑ Ⓒ Ⓓ
5. Ⓐ Ⓑ Ⓒ Ⓓ
6. Ⓐ Ⓑ Ⓒ Ⓓ
7. Ⓐ Ⓑ Ⓒ Ⓓ
8. Ⓐ Ⓑ Ⓒ Ⓓ
9. Ⓐ Ⓑ Ⓒ Ⓓ
10. Ⓐ Ⓑ Ⓒ Ⓓ
11. Ⓐ Ⓑ Ⓒ Ⓓ
12. Ⓐ Ⓑ Ⓒ Ⓓ
13. Ⓐ Ⓑ Ⓒ Ⓓ
14. Ⓐ Ⓑ Ⓒ Ⓓ
15. Ⓐ Ⓑ Ⓒ Ⓓ
16. Ⓐ Ⓑ Ⓒ Ⓓ
17. Ⓐ Ⓑ Ⓒ Ⓓ
18. Ⓐ Ⓑ Ⓒ Ⓓ
19. Ⓐ Ⓑ Ⓒ Ⓓ
20. Ⓐ Ⓑ Ⓒ Ⓓ
21. Ⓐ Ⓑ Ⓒ Ⓓ
22. Ⓐ Ⓑ Ⓒ Ⓓ
23. Ⓐ Ⓑ Ⓒ Ⓓ
24. Ⓐ Ⓑ Ⓒ Ⓓ
25. Ⓐ Ⓑ Ⓒ Ⓓ

## MECHANICAL COMPREHENSION

1. Ⓐ Ⓑ Ⓒ Ⓓ
2. Ⓐ Ⓑ Ⓒ Ⓓ
3. Ⓐ Ⓑ Ⓒ Ⓓ
4. Ⓐ Ⓑ Ⓒ Ⓓ
5. Ⓐ Ⓑ Ⓒ Ⓓ
6. Ⓐ Ⓑ Ⓒ Ⓓ
7. Ⓐ Ⓑ Ⓒ Ⓓ
8. Ⓐ Ⓑ Ⓒ Ⓓ
9. Ⓐ Ⓑ Ⓒ Ⓓ
10. Ⓐ Ⓑ Ⓒ Ⓓ
11. Ⓐ Ⓑ Ⓒ Ⓓ
12. Ⓐ Ⓑ Ⓒ Ⓓ
13. Ⓐ Ⓑ Ⓒ Ⓓ
14. Ⓐ Ⓑ Ⓒ Ⓓ
15. Ⓐ Ⓑ Ⓒ Ⓓ
16. Ⓐ Ⓑ Ⓒ Ⓓ
17. Ⓐ Ⓑ Ⓒ Ⓓ
18. Ⓐ Ⓑ Ⓒ Ⓓ
19. Ⓐ Ⓑ Ⓒ Ⓓ
20. Ⓐ Ⓑ Ⓒ Ⓓ
21. Ⓐ Ⓑ Ⓒ Ⓓ
22. Ⓐ Ⓑ Ⓒ Ⓓ
23. Ⓐ Ⓑ Ⓒ Ⓓ
24. Ⓐ Ⓑ Ⓒ Ⓓ
25. Ⓐ Ⓑ Ⓒ Ⓓ

## ASSEMBLING OBJECTS

1. Ⓐ Ⓑ Ⓒ Ⓓ
2. Ⓐ Ⓑ Ⓒ Ⓓ
3. Ⓐ Ⓑ Ⓒ Ⓓ
4. Ⓐ Ⓑ Ⓒ Ⓓ
5. Ⓐ Ⓑ Ⓒ Ⓓ
6. Ⓐ Ⓑ Ⓒ Ⓓ
7. Ⓐ Ⓑ Ⓒ Ⓓ
8. Ⓐ Ⓑ Ⓒ Ⓓ
9. Ⓐ Ⓑ Ⓒ Ⓓ
10. Ⓐ Ⓑ Ⓒ Ⓓ
11. Ⓐ Ⓑ Ⓒ Ⓓ
12. Ⓐ Ⓑ Ⓒ Ⓓ
13. Ⓐ Ⓑ Ⓒ Ⓓ
14. Ⓐ Ⓑ Ⓒ Ⓓ
15. Ⓐ Ⓑ Ⓒ Ⓓ
16. Ⓐ Ⓑ Ⓒ Ⓓ

## ANSWER KEY TO PRACTICE TEST #2

Use the following answer key to grade your exam. Use the results to guide your review. (See Chapter 5 for strategies on how to do this.)

### GENERAL SCIENCE

1. **B.** The number $10^{-6}$g means 1 microgram, or 1 millionth of a gram (0.000001). A nanogram (answer A) is 1 billionth of a gram. A negative exponent is a multiplication problem, not a subtraction problem, making answer C incorrect. A megagram (answer D) is 1 million grams, and it is represented as $10^{6}$g.
2. **A.** The mitochondria of a cell is the powerhouse of the cell. The cell wall protects the cell from invasion, making answer B wrong. The nucleus contains the genetic code of the cell and is responsible for cell reproduction, making C and D incorrect.
3. **C.** The food chain of an ecosystem consists of two main groups, producers (like plants) and consumers (like animals). While production and decomposition are processes that take place, they are not the two main groups that make up the food chain, which means answer A is incorrect. While predators and prey (answer B) are part of the food chain, they are not the two main groups. While producers are a main group, carrion-eaters are not the other main group, making answer D incorrect.
4. **C.** Since water covers most of the earth, the aquatic biome is the largest.
5. **B.** Your sense of smell can affect your behavior even if you don't realize it because of the actions of chemicals called pheromones. Olfactory receptors (answer A) are cells that detect the presence of odors. Olfactory proteins (answer C) are located on the olfactory receptors. Glomeruli (answer D) are cells located in the brain, associated with your sense of smell. While answers A, C, and D are associated with your sense of smell, they aren't the chemicals that your body unconsciously responds to.
6. **D.** An involuntary muscle is one that works without your conscious effort. The brain (answer A) is not a muscle. The trapezius and biceps (answers B and C) are muscles but they are not involuntary.
7. **A.** Alveoli are small sacs in the lungs that aid in the process of respiration. They do not work as part of the circulatory system, making answer B wrong. The microscopic hairs that filter contaminants out of the air you breathe (answer C) are called cilia. The nerve cells that transmit sensory information to your brain (answer D) are called neurons.
8. **B.** Arteries are different from veins in that arteries transport oxygen-rich blood throughout your body while veins transport oxygen-depleted blood to your heart. Answer A is the opposite and therefore incorrect. Veins and arteries come in different sizes, but one group is not categorically larger or smaller than the other, making answer C incorrect.
9. **D.** Three common types of neurons are motor, sensory, and associative. None of the items listed in answer A are types of neurons, while in answer B only one of the items listed is a type of neuron, making both of those answers incorrect. There is more than one type of neuron, making answer C incorrect.
10. **B.** The earth is about 4.5 billion years old.
11. **C.** Erosion is a process by which broken parts of rock are carried away by wind, rain, and other processes. The process of the rock actually breaking apart (answer A) is called weather. The decomposition of plants has nothing to do with erosion, making answer B incorrect. And volcanoes are formed through the shifting of tectonic plates, not erosion, making answer D incorrect.
12. **D.** Tides are caused by the gravitational pull of the moon. The other answers have no bearing on tides.
13. **A.** Both objects reached the ground at the same time because objects of different mass fall at the same rate.

14. **C.** The lowest layer of the earth's atmosphere is the troposphere. All of the other layers (answer A, B, and D) are above the troposphere.

15. **A.** The tail of a comet is created by the sun melting some of the ice of the comet. Comets are essentially chunks of rock and ice that get pulled toward the sun by its gravitational field.

16. **C.** Carbon dioxide (chemical formula $CO_2$) contains carbon and oxygen. Neither hydrogen nor helium is part of carbon dioxide, making the other answers incorrect.

17. **B.** A colloid is a type of homogeneous mixture. It is not heterogeneous, because all parts are uniform (making answer A incorrect). Unlike a heterogeneous suspension, a colloid is not subject to sedimentation (making answer C incorrect). A solvent is one element of a mixture, not a description of the mixture itself, so answer D is incorrect.

18. **D.** In physics, displacement refers to how far from its starting point an object has moved when it goes from point A to point B. How much ground is covered could be a different amount, and is called the distance, making answer A incorrect. Rate of motion is speed, making answer B incorrect. Displacement does not measure acceleration, making answer C incorrect.

19. **A.** The formula for momentum is Momentum = Mass × Velocity.

20. **C.** A wave's amplitude is associated with its intensity. Higher amplitude in sound waves creates a more intense (louder) sound, and in light waves creates a more intense (brighter) light.

21. **A.** The scientific process is used to verify the accuracy of a hypothesis. While a scientist may hope and believe his or her ideas will prove accurate, the scientific process may disprove them, making B an incorrect process. The process is not used to categorize different types of ideas but to verify their accuracy, making answer C incorrect. While scientists may describe ideas that can't be tested, the scientific process requires that an idea be testable, making answer D incorrect.

22. **C.** Through the process of photosynthesis, plants convert carbon dioxide into oxygen.

23. **B.** Microorganisms in your intestines aid with digestion. While some microorganisms in your intestines can make you ill, they don't always do so, making answer A incorrect. Microorganisms are always found in your intestines, making answer C incorrect. They are not automatically digested, making answer D incorrect.

24. **D.** A human zygote has 46 chromosomes.

25. **C.** The energy your body needs to perform tasks (including thinking) comes primarily from carbohydrates. While it's true your body needs the other nutrients listed in answers A, B, and D, the most correct answer is C.

## ARITHMETIC REASONING

1. **D.** 7 can be written as $\frac{7}{1}$ and $\frac{7}{1} \bullet \frac{1}{2} = \frac{7}{2}$. Then $\frac{7}{2} \bullet \frac{3}{7} = \frac{21}{14}$. This answer can be made into the mixed number $1\frac{7}{14}$, which can be reduced to $1\frac{1}{2}$. Thus, $x = 1\frac{1}{2}$.

2. **A.** The whole number 5 remains unchanged; however, $\frac{2}{3}$ is the same as saying 2 divided by 3. Therefore, when rounded off to hundredths, the fraction is 0.67. Thus, the decimal should be 5.67. Choice B is correct, except that it has not been rounded off as requested. Choices C and D are not correct because both are rounded off to tenths, not hundredths.

3. **D.** Multiply as if you were dealing with the numbers 671 and 88. Then insert the decimal as the sum of the number of decimal places in the original numbers. Therefore, $x = 5.9048$.

4. **B.** The area of a rectangle is found by multiplying length times width. $\mathbf{10 \times 15 = 150}$ **square feet.**

5. **C.** The problem can be stated as:

$$\frac{40\frac{5}{8}\text{ revolutions}}{2\frac{1}{2}\text{ minutes}} = \frac{x\text{ revolutions}}{1\text{ minute}}$$

In other words, $2\frac{1}{2}x = 40\frac{5}{8}$. That can be restated as $\frac{5}{2}x = \frac{325}{8}$. To isolate $x$, divide both sides by $\frac{5}{2}$, which can be done by multiplying by the inverse, or $\frac{325}{8} \bullet \frac{2}{5}$. Thus:

$$x = \frac{650}{40} = 16\frac{10}{40} = 16\frac{1}{4}$$

Therefore, the shaft turns at $16\frac{1}{4}$ rpm.

6. **A.** The lowest (least) common denominator is one-thousandth. Thus:

$$1\frac{3}{10} = \frac{1300}{1000};\ 2\frac{12}{100} = \frac{2120}{1000};\ 1\frac{17}{1000} = \frac{1017}{1000}$$

Add the fractions together:

$$\frac{1300}{1000} + \frac{2120}{1000} + \frac{1017}{1000} = \frac{4437}{1000} = 4\frac{437}{1000}$$

So the correct answer is $4\frac{437}{1000}$ amps.

7. **D.** The perimeter length of a trapezoid is found by adding the length of its four sides:

$2\frac{3}{4}$ meter + $\frac{2}{3}$ meter + $1\frac{7}{8}$ meter + 1 meter

The lowest common denominator (LCD) for the three fractions is 24. So, convert the numbers to fractions with the same denominator:

$$2\frac{3}{4} = \frac{66}{24};\ \frac{2}{3} = \frac{16}{24};\ 1\frac{7}{8} = \frac{45}{24};\ 1 = \frac{24}{24}$$

Then add together:

$$\frac{66}{24} + \frac{16}{24} + \frac{45}{24} + \frac{24}{24} = \frac{151}{24} = 6\frac{7}{24}$$

Therefore, the perimeter length of the trapezoid shown is $6\frac{7}{24}$ meters.

8. **C.** To figure the hose's external diameter, the hose wall's thickness must be counted twice. Therefore,

$\frac{1}{16}+\frac{1}{16}+\frac{3}{4}=$ **diameter.**

The LCD is 16.

$$\frac{1}{16}+\frac{1}{16}+\frac{12}{16}=\frac{14}{16}$$

Which is reduced to $\frac{7}{8}$ inch for the outside diameter.

9. **B.** A centimeter, as the name implies, means $\frac{1}{100}$ of a meter. Another way to look at it is that there are 100 centimeters in a meter. Therefore, **2.67 • 100 centimeters = 267 centimeters.**

10. **B.** The original 14-liter solution was 35% benzene and 65% water. Therefore, there was **14•0.35** or 4.9 liters of benzene and **14•0.65** or 9.1 liters of water. If we add 4.5 liters of water to this solution, we will then end up with 4.9 liters of benzene in 18.5 liters of solution. To figure the new percentage of benzene present in solution, we divide the number of liters of benzene by the total volume of solution and multiply that quotient by 100:

$$\frac{\text{4.9 liters of benzene}}{\text{18.5 liters of solution}} \bullet 100 = 26.49\%$$

11. **A.** $(x+3)(x-8)=x^2-8x+3x-24=x^2-5x-24.$

12. **D.** Since the inlet port can fill the tank in 2 hours, it can fill $\frac{1}{2}$ the tank in 1 hour. The outlet port can drain the tank in 3 hours or $\frac{1}{3}$ of the tank in 1 hour.
Therefore:

$$\frac{x}{2}-\frac{x}{3}=\frac{1}{1}$$

Find the LCD:

$$\frac{3x}{6}-\frac{2x}{6}=\frac{1}{1}$$

Which can also be stated as:

$$\frac{3x-2x}{6}=\frac{1}{1}$$

Multiply both sides by 6 to get rid of the fraction:

$$3x-2x=6$$

Therefore, $x = 6$.

13. **D.** Halsey took 11 hours of total time to make the drive. He took 4 hours for the first part of the trip. Subtract 1 hour for gas and lunch, and that means he spent 6 hours of traveling in bad weather. Therefore:

$$4x+6(x-15)=650 \text{ miles}$$

So, $4x+6x-90=650$ miles, or $10x-90=650$ miles. Add 90 to both sides of the equation to get $10x = 740$. Divide both sides by 10 to isolate $x$, and $x = 74$ mph.

14. **A.** Remember the PEMDAS rule for solving problems with numerous operations. First, do the operation in parenthesis:

So, $4^2+6+(4\bullet 5)\div 2=x$ is $4^2+6+20\div 2=x$.

Then, find exponents: $16+6+20\div 2=x$. Next, do any multiplication (in this case, there is none) and then division: $16+6+10=x$. Finally, do any addition and subtraction: $34 = x$.

15. **B.** The cost of the television is $799. 10% (the discount) is $79.90. The discounted price of the television is $799.00 − $79.90 = $719.10. Since sales tax is calculated on that price (before warranty and delivery), multiply $719.10 by the sales tax (8.85%) to find that the sales tax will be $63.64. That means the television costs, after tax, $782.74. Next, add $60.00 (the cost of the warranty and home delivery) to find a final total price of $842.74.

16. **C.** To determine the value of a term in this sequence, multiply 2 by the place of the term (12) and add 2, resulting in 26.

17. **C.** To subtract the fractions, we need to convert them to the LCD. Thus, $5\frac{3}{8}$ and $2\frac{6}{8}$. We can't subtract $\frac{6}{8}$ from $\frac{3}{8}$. But we can borrow from the whole number (5), thus making that fraction $4\frac{11}{8}$. $4-2=2$ and $\frac{11}{8}-\frac{6}{8}=\frac{5}{8}$, so the correct answer is $2\frac{5}{8}$.

18. **D.** To multiply fractions, multiply the numerators and divide by the product of the denominators:

$\frac{7}{8}\bullet\frac{1}{3}=\frac{7\bullet 1}{8\bullet 3}=\frac{7}{24}$.

19. **B.** 25% divided by 7 can be written as $\frac{1}{4}\div 7$. To divide a fraction, multiply it by the inverse: $\frac{1}{4}\bullet\frac{1}{7}$. That means each employee can use $\frac{1}{28}$ of the total budget for travel. $\frac{5600}{28}=\$200$. Another way to determine the answer is to multiply the total budget by the percentage to be used for travel: $\$5600\bullet 0.25=\$1400$, then divide the result by 7 to determine that each employee is entitled to use $200 for travel.

20. **C.** Convert $3\frac{1}{3}$ to a decimal: 3.34 (rounded up to the nearest hundredth). Multiply 3.34 by $4.29 to find the result of $14.33 (rounding up to the nearest penny).

21. **C.** Assuming Derrick's laptop battery is full at the start of the eight-hour day, it can run for 3 hours and 45 minutes before it needs to be recharged. If it takes 30 minutes for his battery to recharge, then 4 hours and 15 minutes from the start of the day, it is recharged and can go another 3 hours and 45 minutes, which brings him right to the end of an eight-hour day. So, the battery must be plugged in for 30 minutes out of 8 hours. (Of course, he'll start the next day with a drained battery, but we don't have to worry about that.) Then we have to determine what percentage 30 minutes is of an eight-hour day. We can say that 30 minutes of an eight-hour day is $\frac{1}{16}$, or $1 \div 16$, or .0625. Multiply .0625 by 100 to determine the percentage: 6.25%.
22. **A.** The present cost \$250. So, \$250 = 100%. The other two siblings contributed \$75 + 115 = \$190, leaving \$60 left over for Martha to pay. \$60 divided by \$250 is 0.24, or 24%.
23. **C.** If a mill is \$1 per \$1,000, then on a house worth \$335,000, a mill would be \$335. Since Ali has to pay 3.5 mills, then **\$335•3.5=\$1,172.50.**
24. **C.** First, determine how much the recipe needs to be reduced. Since 1 pound is $\frac{1}{3}$ of 3 pounds, the recipe amounts need to be $\frac{1}{3}$ of their original values. In other words, $\frac{3}{4} \bullet \frac{1}{3} = \frac{3}{12}$, which can be reduced to $\frac{1}{4}$.
25. **C.** To determine a rate of speed, divide the amount by the time, or $x$ divided by $y$.
26. **D.** Federico sold the item for \$9, which is a 100% markup from the price he paid. He must pay 3.75% of that amount to the auction site, or 34 cents (rounding up to the nearest penny). **\$9.00 − 0.34 = \$8.66.** To determine his profit, you also have to subtract what he originally paid for the collectible, so **\$8.66 − \$4.50 = \$4.16.**
27. **C.** To determine the mean of a series of numbers, add them together and divide by the amount of numbers in question. So \$7.50 + \$7.75 + \$8.15 + \$8.30 = \$31.70. Then **\$31.70 ÷ 4 = \$7.925.** Round up to the nearest penny.
28. **B.** To find the median, you select the number in the middle, with an equal amount of numbers falling above and below it. So, reorder the grades from highest to lowest: 99%, 97%, 94%, 83%, 82%, 81%, 77%, 69%, 50%. The median is 82%, because an equal amount of numbers fall above and below it.
29. **A.** To determine the percent change, first divide the new value by the old value: $\frac{\$57975}{\$65850}$ or 0.880 (rounding down to thousandths). Then, multiply by 100 to determine the percentage: 88%. Then subtract 100% from that to get the percent change: **−12%.**
30. **B.** To determine interest, multiply principal by rate by time. Since 9 months is $\frac{3}{4}$ of a year, we can calculate interest = **\$3,000•0.0675•0.75 = \$151.88**, rounding up to the nearest penny. Add the interest to the principal, and she will have \$3151.88 in the account after 9 months.

## WORD KNOWLEDGE

Note: The answers have been provided for the vocabulary section without explanation. If further reference is needed, consult a dictionary.

| | | | |
|---|---|---|---|
| 1. **A.** | 6. **B.** | 11. **A.** | 16. **C.** |
| 2. **B.** | 7. **B.** | 12. **B.** | 17. **A.** |
| 3. **C.** | 8. **B.** | 13. **C.** | 18. **D.** |
| 4. **A.** | 9. **A.** | 14. **B.** | 19. **A.** |
| 5. **A.** | 10. **D.** | 15. **A.** | 20. **A.** |

21. **B.**
22. **C.**
23. **D.**
24. **B.**
25. **D.**
26. **D.**
27. **B.**
28. **B.**
29. **C.**
30. **D.**
31. **A.**
32. **B.**
33. **C.**
34. **D.**
35. **D.**

## PARAGRAPH COMPREHENSION

1. **B.** Selection C may be partially true, but B best encompasses what was meant by the passage. Most people see but do not actually observe or consciously register the actions and movements of people or objects, events, and surrounding circumstances.
2. **C.** The passage doesn't have anything to do with the licensing exam, so answer A is incorrect. Your tax dollars may be used by the department of motor vehicles, but that is not the main point of the article, so answer B is incorrect. While the information contained in the passage might be used by someone trying to fake a license, that is not the purpose of the paragraph, so answer D is incorrect. Since the passage describes how the driver's license number is created, answer C is correct.
3. **A.** The passage lists physicians, lawyers, and writers as being among those who are personally liable, but it does not say they are the only ones who are. The other options, B, C, and D, are all correct and supported by statements in the passage.
4. **C.** The author compares and contrasts resumes and bio sheets to show how they are similar and different. A is incorrect because the author does not use definitions to explain the job hunt. B is incorrect because the passage is not presented in chronological order. D is incorrect because the passage does not give a step-by-step process to describe how to write a resume or bio sheet.
5. **D.** The passage states that expenditures are recorded as soon as they are paid. A is incorrect because the passage states that a cash-basis business has nothing to do with whether you accept cash, checks, or credit cards. B is incorrect because the passage states that revenue is recorded when it is received (not when the invoice is sent). C is incorrect because while it may be wise to do this, the passage doesn't say anything about planning for expenditures.
6. **B.** The passage describes what mutual funds are, so this is the best title. A is incorrect because the passage isn't about irrational investing. C is incorrect because while mutual funds and the purchase of individual stocks and bonds are briefly compared, the main purpose of the passage is to define what mutual funds are. D is incorrect because the passage doesn't discuss this idea at all.
7. **C.** The passage specifically states that you should consider investing in an alarm system if your business is in a high crime area. A is incorrect because the passage doesn't say anything like that. B is incorrect because the passage doesn't refer to insurance at all. D is incorrect because an alarm system is discussed in addition to security lighting, not as a replacement for it.
8. **C.** The passage specifically states that you should assign copyright ownership in your will. A is incorrect because the passage states that no special registration is required. B is incorrect because the passage states that for copyrights created since 1978, copyright protection extends for fifty years beyond the death of the creator. D is incorrect because although the passage says a fee is required, it doesn't indicate how expensive that fee is.
9. **D.** The passage says that many cultures use blessings to keep evil spirits away, not that evil spirits are needed to perform the blessings. A, B, and C are all supported by statements in the paragraph, so they are not correct.

10. **B.** The closing line of the passage shows the author's skepticism. A is incorrect because while the tone is mostly neutral, there is that skeptical tone at the end, making B more correct. C is incorrect because the author is mostly factual throughout. D is incorrect because the author does not seem at all uncertain about the information.

11. **B.** The passage states that salads have been around for a long time. A is incorrect because though we don't eat some of the things people used to eat, we are not told that toxicity is the reason this is true. C is incorrect because the passage states that salads have been around for a long time. D is incorrect because the passage doesn't say anything about the wealth or social class of people who eat salads.

12. **C.** The passage states that both outlawry and excommunication were used as political weapons to force certain powerful people to do the bidding of a ruler or of a pope. A is incorrect because the passage says nothing about how outlaws have been perceived. B is incorrect because the passage states that outlawry was "also" used against criminals, meaning they weren't the only ones it was used against. D is incorrect because while the passage says that both were used it does not say that they are the same thing.

13. **A.** The passage states that songs have served a certain purpose in the past and now serve an additional purpose. B is incorrect because the passage states that songs are used to give news and information. C is incorrect because the passage states that songs often serve as a way for young people to learn about their culture. D is incorrect because while it may be true the passage doesn't say so.

14. **A.** The passage focused on describing who the Anasazi were and some characteristics about their living conditions and customs. B is incorrect because the passage is only about one culture, not "cultures" (and it can't really be called a "study"). C is incorrect because the focus is on who the Anasazi were, not on exploring the origins of the Pueblo people. D is incorrect because Utah is only part of the Anasazi's territory and the piece isn't about Utah, it's about a culture.

15. **B.** The passage states that details of Bhavabhuti's life are obscure. A is incorrect because the passage only states that Bhavabhuti wrote Sanskrit literature. C is incorrect because the passage states that Bhavabhuti is one of the great dramatists of the time. D is incorrect because nothing in the passage supports it (plus Shakespeare wasn't born until many centuries after Bhavabhuti's death).

## MATHEMATICS KNOWLEDGE

1. **A.** To determine the answer to this question, use the formula for volume of a rectangle: $V = lwh$. (volume = length × width × height). We know the height of the container is 16 inches. Since the answers are in feet, we need to convert inches to feet. 16 inches is the same as $1\frac{1}{3}$ feet. We also know that the volume is 16 cubic feet. So we know:

$$(lw)1\frac{1}{3} = 16$$

Since the base is square, we know that l is the same as $w$, so those unknowns could be represented as $x$. So,

$$(x \bullet x)1\frac{1}{3} = 16$$

Or

$$x^2 1\frac{1}{3} = 16$$

Which can be written as:

$$x^2\frac{4}{3}=16$$

To isolate $x$, divide both sides by $\frac{4}{3}$:

$$x^2=\frac{16}{1}\div\frac{4}{3}$$

To divide fractions, multiply by the reciprocal:

$$x^2=\frac{16}{1}\bullet\frac{3}{4}$$

So we know that $x^2=12$ and the square root of 12 can be rounded to 3.464. So $x=3.464$ feet.

2. **C.** The circumference of a circle is equal to diameter multiplied by $\pi$. So we know:

$$19\frac{1}{4}=d(3.1416)$$

Divide both sides by $\pi$ to isolate the variable:

$$\frac{19.25}{3.1416}=d$$

$d=6.127$ inches.

3. **B.** If you imagine a ladder against the wall of a building, the shape it represents should remind you of a right triangle. The wall of the building is perpendicular to the ground. Therefore, we can use the Pythagorean theorem $(a^2+b^2=c^2)$ to solve this problem. The base of the right triangle is 6 feet and the ladder itself can be considered the hypotenuse of the triangle. The unknown variable is the other side of the triangle. So,

$$6^2+b^2=25^2$$

Thus, $36+b^2=625$. Subtract 36 from each side to isolate the variable: $b^2=589$. The square root of 589 ($b$) is about 24.27, so the ladder reaches 24.27 feet.

4. **C.** The area of a circle is determined with the formula $A=\pi r^2$. We know that $r=7.35$, so $A=3.1416(7.35^2)$. Find the exponent first, then multiply to find $A=169.72$ square feet.

5. **B.** To solve this problem, use the formula for the area of a triangle ($a=\frac{1}{2}bh$). We know that the base is 22.5 feet (the width of the attic), and we know the height is 12 feet, so:

$$\frac{1}{2}(22.5)\bullet 12=135$$

So the area of the triangle is 135 square feet. But that's not the volume of the space. To determine that we need to multiply the area of the triangle by the length of the space (48 feet). So, 135 sq. ft × 48 feet = 6,480 cubic feet of space that can be used for storage.

6. **A.** Solve as you would any equation. In this case, divide both sides by 4 to isolate the unknown. The inequality sign remains the same.

7. **B.** Use the distributive property to rewrite the expression as $y(y+5)+4(y+5)$. Then multiply $y^2+5y+4y+20$. Do some addition to come up with the correct answer of $y^2+9y+20$.

8. **C.** To solve this equation, add 21 to both sides to isolate the unknown. Thus, $9x-21+21=6+21$ or $9x=27$. Then divide both sides by 9 to determine that $x = 3$.

9. **B.** To solve this inequality, start by dividing both sides by $-2$. That yields $x<-4$. But when you divide an inequality by a negative number, you have to reverse the sign. So, the correct answer is $x>-4$.

10. **D.** Restate the expression using the distributive property: $x(x+3)-2(x+3)$. Then, multiply and add/subtract: $x^2+3x-2x-6=x^2+x-6$.

11. **B.** Multiply both sides of the equation by the reciprocal of the fraction (3) to isolate $x$. So, $x < 6$.

12. **C.** Add 8 to both sides to isolate the unknown. Thus, $2y-8+8=6+8$. Or, $2y=14$. Then divide both sides of the equation to determine that $y = 7$.

13. **A.** To evaluate the expression, simplify as much as possible by doing whatever operations are possible, so $x+(2x)^3+5x^2$. Then put in standard form by starting with the highest exponent.

14. **D.** This problem can be solved as a proportion, or you can plug in the numbers knowing that $\frac{a}{b}=\frac{c}{d}$ is the same as $ad=bc$. So, $10x=20$. Solve by dividing both sides by 10 to determine that $x = 2$.

15. **A.** An easy way to solve this problem is to set it up as a ratio. Brian needs 3 tablespoons of fertilizer per 1 gallon of water, or 3:1. If he multiplies one side of that equation by 15 (because he is using 15 gallons of water), then he needs to multiply the other side by the same amount to keep the proportion equal. Thus, he needs 45 tablespoons of fertilizer.

16. **D.** To add fractions, remember that $\frac{a}{b}+\frac{c}{d}=\frac{ad+bc}{bd}$. So, $\frac{(x+1)3+2x}{6}$ which can be simplified to $\frac{5x+3}{6}$.

17. **C.** To divide fractions, you cross-multiply. So, $\frac{a}{b}\div\frac{c}{d}=\frac{ad}{bc}$. Thus, our fractions can be written as $\frac{(x-2)5}{10x}$ or $\frac{5x-10}{10x}$.

18. **C.** To make this a quadratic expression, subtract $4x+13$ from both sides. A quadratic expression follows this pattern: $ax^2+bx+c=0$.

19. **B.** The formula for determining the total measurement of the angles of a polygon is $180(n-2)°$. So, $180(7-2)=900°$.

20. **D.** In this case, $y$ depends on $x$, so plug in the $x$ value of each answer to determine that D is the only possible solution of those given.

21. **B.** To find the likelihood of a series of independent events happening, multiply the probability of each event by the number of occurrences, so 4 coin flips resulting in heads (a 1 in 2 chance) would be $\frac{1}{2}\times\frac{1}{2}\times\frac{1}{2}\times\frac{1}{2}$ or $\frac{1}{16}$.

22. **A.** In this case, the likelihood of a 6 appearing is 1 in 6. So the likelihood of it appearing 3 times in a row is $\frac{1}{6}\times\frac{1}{6}\times\frac{1}{6}$ or $\frac{1}{216}$.

23. **C.** Since these are two independent events, simply multiply the likelihood of each event occurring, so $\frac{1}{6}\times\frac{1}{6}$ or $\frac{1}{36}$.

24. **B.** The factors of $-8$ (the *c* variable) that equal 2 (the constant of the *b* variable) are $4,-2$. To make sure the math is correct, multiply the factors:

$$(x+4)(x-2)=x(x-2)+4(x-2)=x^2-2x+4x-8=x^2+2x-8$$

25. **D.** Substitute one of the equations for *y* to get $2x+5=3x+8$. Subtract 2*x* from each side to get $5=x+8$. Then subtract 8 from each side to isolate *x* and determine that $x=-3$. Then, plug that answer into one formula to determine that $y=-1$. To check your math, plug your values for *x* and *y* into both formulas.

## ELECTRONICS INFORMATION

1. **B.** The other three answers are all particles.
2. **A.** Rubber is a good insulator; the others are all good conductors.
3. **C.** A millivolt (mV) is one-thousandth of a volt.
4. **C.** The conducting lines on an integrated circuit are so small they can be measured in nanometers.
5. **D.** While a coal-fired plant uses a natural resource (coal) to create electricity, it does not harness a natural process, like the movement of wind or water, to create the electricity.
6. **C.** 1 watt is the same as 1 joule per second.
7. **C.** Electrical efficiency is the useful power output compared to the power used. A higher efficiency means less power is needed to produce power.
8. **A.** AC = alternating current, which switches direction (unlike direct current). Therefore, 60-cycle AC switches direction 60 times per second.
9. **C.** Static electricity is the build up of an electric charge on an object.
10. **C.** Negative charges attract positive charges (and vice versa), so negative fields attract positive fields.
11. **A.** Sending an electric charge through a wire-wrapped metal object creates a magnetic field.
12. **D.** "Doping" is the process used to turn a material into an appropriate semiconductor.
13. **B.** Resistance is voltage divided by current, so in this case 12 volts divided by 3 amperes equals 4 ohms of resistance.
14. **D.** $E=Pt$ is the standard formula for energy.
15. **B.** The circuit shown is partially wired in series and partly wired in parallel, so it is a series-parallel circuit.
16. **A.** A closed loop system (a circuit) allows the current to flow because positive charges are returned to their original position.
17. **B.** The amount of resistance in a series circuit is simply the sum of all the resistors in the circuit.
18. **A.** R is the abbreviation for resistor, and the symbol shown is the symbol used on schematics to represent resistors.
19. **A.** The symbol represents a capacitor.
20. **D.** Capacitors are measured in farads (F).

## AUTOMOTIVE AND SHOP INFORMATION

1. **B.** During the intake stroke, the intake valve opens, allowing fuel and air to enter the cylinder.
2. **C.** Many passenger cars sold today have 4-cylinder engines, but 6- and 8-cylinder engines are not entirely uncommon. Because so many cars have 4-cylinder engines, choice B is incorrect.
3. **D.** All of the other choices are correct and are things that happen during the internal combustion process. The process takes place inside the engine, meaning D is the only choice that is not true.
4. **A.** In a piston-and-cylinder arrangement, the piston is housed inside the cylinder.
5. **A.** The illustration shows a crankshaft, which drives the pistons.
6. **B.** While exhaust valves do vent exhaust, they don't directly vent it to the outside (choice A), making B a better choice than A. While some emissions control systems are designed to capture and burn unburned fuel (choice C), this isn't the function of the exhaust valves. They also don't detect exhaust fumes in the fuel tank (choice D).
7. **A.** The illustration shows a piston.
8. **C.** The correct order is intake, compression, combustion, exhaust.
9. **A.** "RPM" on the tachometer is referring to the revolutions per minute of the crankshaft. The crankshaft does two revolutions per 4-stroke cycle.
10. **A.** If too much oil leaks from the engine, the lubrication system will not work as needed and the friction of parts rubbing against each other can cause them to break down. It can also cause engine overheating, but that was not one of the choices.
11. **D.** One of the main ways coolant is different from water is that it lowers the freezing point of water and increases the boiling point (because frozen water and/or boiling water in the cooling system would be very damaging to your car's engine).
12. **B.** The clutch serves as a connection between the vehicle's transmission gears and the engine, and it prevents the engine from engaging with the transmission during gear-shifting.
13. **D.** Reciprocating saws can cut through sheet metal, wood, and a host of other materials providing the proper blade is selected.
14. **C.** A plumb bob determines a true vertical reference line while a level is used for horizontal reference. Carpenters and bevel squares are used to figure angulation.
15. **A.** Back saws have fine rip saw teeth that enable them to cut a variety of joints. Saber saws are not handsaws.
16. **B.** Phillips.
17. **D.** Prevents potential damage from occurring to the insulator or electrode.
18. **B.** Glass cutter.
19. **D.** Masonry drill bits are normally used in power drills.
20. **C.** Plier wrench is another name for vise grips; they can actually lock onto a piece of work with a minimum of effort. The other pliers exert pressure only in direct proportion to how hard they are squeezed. Vise grips utilize adjustable leverage to enhance a grip over and above what can be done conventionally.
21. **B.** 0.335 inches. Add the sleeve reading, 0.325 inches, and the thimble reading, 0.010.
22. **A.** Screw pitch gauge.

23. **C.** The hardened teeth remain sharper longer.

24. **D.** Both A and C are correct. Offset screwdrivers can work in tight places and apply more torque because of their shape.

25. **B.** Round split die in a holder. Taps with a tap wrench are used to cut interior screw threads in a drilled hole.

## MECHANICAL COMPREHENSION

1. **D.** The anchorman described in the question essentially serves as the fulcrum. Half the length of the ladder is considered the resistance distance and 10 feet represents the effort distance. Therefore:

$$\text{Effort} = \frac{75 \text{ pounds} \times 12.5 \text{ feet}}{10 \text{ feet}} = 93.75 \text{ pounds}$$

2. **C.** This is the only true statement given.

3. **B.** For every one revolution made by gear 1, gear 2 turns twice. Therefore, if gear 1 is turning at 400 rpm, gear 2 is turning at 800 rpm.

4. **A.** Every other gear in a drive train of this design will turn in the same direction. Since gears 1 and 5 have the same number of teeth, both will turn at equivalent speeds. Choice B is false only because gear 4 will turn faster than gear 2, because of its fewer teeth. Choice C is incorrect because gears 1 and 2 turn opposite to one another, as do gears 3 and 4. Choice D is wrong because the larger the gear (i.e., the more teeth present), the slower it will turn, providing the driver gear size remains constant. This is an example where speed is decreased and there is a corresponding or proportional increase in torque.

5. **A.** Using the Pythagorean theorem ($a^2 + b^2 = c^2$), we can figure the length of guy wire required (which represents the hypotenuse of a right triangle) by squaring the height of the collar plus squaring the base. So, $23^2 + 15^2 = 754$. Since $754 = c^2$, we need to find its square root to determine what $c$ equals. $\sqrt{754} = 27.46$ feet. The question also stated that an extra 8 inches would be required to fasten the ends of each wire. Since we are dealing in units of feet, we need to convert inches to feet; 8 inches $= \frac{8}{12} = 0.67$ feet. Therefore, the total length of one wire is equal to 27.46 feet + 0.67 feet, or 28.13 feet. Four such lengths of wire are required to support the antenna, so 4 × 28.13 feet = 112.52 feet of guy wire is needed.

6. **A.** In this case, strap 1 would be subjected to the greater load factor of the three strap supports shown. Choice B would have been correct if the strap supports were evenly spaced.

7. **C.** For every one revolution made by the driver gear, the driven gear makes approximately two revolutions. This has the effect of increasing the speed of the drive train with corresponding sacrifice of torque. Choice A is true, but the question asked for the overall effect of the gear size disparity shown. This choice did not account for diminished torque. Choices B and D are false on their own merit.

8. **C.** Since pulley A rotates clockwise and pulley D rotates clockwise as well, we can think of this question as being a direct compound proportion. Pulleys A and B are in the ratio $\frac{13}{9}$ and Pulleys C and D are in the ratio $\frac{16}{6}$. Thus:

$$\frac{13}{9} \times \frac{16}{6} = \frac{208}{54}$$

Given that A is turning at 54 rpm, then Pulley D is operating at 208 rpm.

9. **D.** Gears 3, 5, and 7 turn counterclockwise. Gear 2 turns clockwise.

10. **C.** The length of the handle that extends perpendicularly from the windlass's drum is the key to the amount of leverage exerted on the line. The longer the handle, the larger the amount of force that can be exerted on the smaller wheel or in this case, the drum. Choices A, B, and D have little if any bearing on leverage gains.

11. **D.** Since we are dealing with a wheel and axle, we can use the following formula to determine the answer: Force × Circumference of large wheel = Resistance × Circumference of small wheel. We already know that the force is equal to 125 pounds. The circumference of the larger wheel, which represents the handle's turning circumference, is our unknown. Resistance is the amount of tension on the line, which is equal to 400 lbs. The circumference of the smaller wheel (in other words, the windlass drum) is equal to $\pi$ (diameter) or 18.85 inches.

12. **B.** The formula that applies to inclined planes is: Effort × length of inclined plane = resistance × height. Effort is what we are trying to solve for. The resistance is the weight of the drum (460 pounds). According to the diagram, the height of the inclined plane used is 4.25 feet. The length of the inclined plane warrants extra consideration. We can look at the inclined plane as a right triangle. According to the Pythagorean theorem $(a^2 + b^2 = c^2)$, when we square the base and height of a right triangle and add them together, we can determine the hypotenuse (i.e., length of the plane itself) by taking that sum and determining its square root: $9.25^2 + 4.25^2 = 103.625$. To find $c$, or the length of the inclined plane, we need to find the square root of 103.625, which is 10.18 feet.

    If we plug our numbers into the formula above, we can say that $10.18x = 460$ pounds × 4.25 feet. Then, if we solve for $x$, we find that 192 pounds is the total effort required for the task. However, since two people are involved in rolling the drum up the inclined plane, we can assume that each person need only contribute half the total effort required. Therefore, we get 96 pounds of effort per individual.

13. **C.** If each person contributes 150 pounds of effort, then simply divide the effort into resistance to calculate the lift advantage: 780 divided by 150 equals a 5.2:1 advantage.

14. **A.** Since this pulley demonstrates a 2:1 mechanical advantage (because of the two ropes in the pulley arrangement), we simply divide the resistance or weight being lifted by 2. Therefore, 375 pounds divided by 2 = 187.5 lbs of effort required.

15. **A.** To determine the height that the weight will lift, we need to use the following formula. Length of pull = Lift × Mechanical advantage. The mechanical advantage is 2, so $2x = 15$ feet. Divide both sides by 2 to isolate $x$ and determine that the lift is 7.5 feet.

16. **D.** Choice A is incorrect, because wheels 3 and 4 rotate at the same rpm since they are keyed to the same shaft. Therefore, wheel 4 turns at the same speed that wheel 2 does. Choice B is incorrect because wheel 5 turns in a counterclockwise direction. This is the result of twisting the belt drive between wheels 2 and 3. Choice C is incorrect, because wheel 5 not only turns at a greater rpm than wheel 2, it turns in the opposite direction of the driver gear. Wheel 4 is directly responsible for wheel 5's speed enhancement.

17. **B.** The first thing we need to do is convert tons into pounds so that everything is figured in one unit of measure—in this case, pounds. Since there are 2,000 pounds per ton, there are 5,000 pounds in $2\frac{1}{2}$ tons.

    To determine the mechanical advantage of this jackscrew, we need to calculate the handle/lever's turning circumference. Circumference is found by multiplying $\pi \times$ diameter. Since the handle length represents only the radius of a circle, the diameter is found by multiplying the radius by 2. Therefore $38\pi = 119.38$ inch circumference. Now, mechanical advantage can be determined by dividing the screw pitch into the circumference. To divide by a fraction $(\frac{1}{8})$, multiply by its inverse. So: $119.38 \times 8 = 955.04$. To solve for the unknown, we plug what we do know into the formula:

$$\text{Effort} = \frac{\text{Resistance}}{\text{Mechanical Advantage}}$$

Or, 5000 divided by 955.04 = 5.24 lbs of effort is required

18. **D.** Since the drive gear has twice the number of teeth as the driven gear, there is a 50% reduction of torque with a corresponding 50% increase in speed.

19. **C.** To understand this problem better, let's approach it in a quantitative sense. Let's assume for the moment that gear A (the driver gear) is rotating at 1000 rpm. Since we are told that gear A is half the size of gear B, we can figure that rpm are reduced 50% or in other words, gear B will turn at 500 rpm. Gears B and C will turn at the same rate because both gears are keyed to the same shaft. However, gear C is half the size of gear D, so another 50% reduction of speed occurs. In the end, gear D rotates at 250 rpm or $\frac{1}{4}$ the drive gear's speed. Remember, what is sacrificed in speed is gained in torque. Therefore, four times the amount of torque is realized at the expense of speed.

20. **A.** This question involves several mathematical steps. If we are told that we want to raise the level of the third cylinder from 4.5 liters to 9.75 liters, that represents an added volume of 5.25 liters (9.75 liters – 4.5 liters = 5.25). Since the tank has a 13-liter capacity, this reflects a 0.4038 or 40.38% increase in volume. Now that we have the added volume figured as a percentage, we need to calculate comparable volume increases in the other two cylinders. If cylinder 2 were to increase its volume by 40.38%, that would account for 2.826 liters of water. If cylinder 1 also has a 40.38% increase in volume, that accounts for another 2.019 liters. To reflect the total volume of water needed to increase the levels in each tank, we simply add the volume differences together to arrive at the final answer. 5.25 liters + 2.826 liters + 2.019 liters = 10.095, so 10.1 liters of water are required.

21. **D.** Simple machines do not have motors, and are used to create mechanical advantage.

22. **C.** A compound machine is two or more simple machines put together, like a wheelbarrow. D is an example of a compound machine, but C is a better definition and therefore a more correct answer.

23. **C.** The nearer the fulcrum is to the resistance, the easier it is to move the resistance.

24. **A.** Since length of pull = height (lift) × mechanical advantage, any variation on the pull has a direct correlation to the height.

25. **B.** Wedges and inclined planes function in a very similar way.

## ASSEMBLING OBJECTS

1. B.
2. C.
3. A.
4. B.
5. C.
6. B.
7. C.
8. C.
9. A.
10. B.
11. A.
12. B.
13. C.
14. A.
15. C.
16. A.

# CHAPTER 17

# *Practice Test #3*

Take the practice test just as you would any standardized test. Use the answer sheet at the end of this chapter to record your answers. Set a timer for the amount of time allotted for each subtest, take them in the order in which they're given, and try to do your best. Then turn to the answer key later in this chapter to grade your efforts and help you plan your review before taking the next practice test.

## GENERAL SCIENCE

You have 11 minutes to answer the 25 questions on this subtest.

1. The three types of blood cells are

   A. white blood cells, red blood cells, and hemoglobin
   B. erythrocytes, thrombocytes, and leukocytes
   C. platelets, hemoglobin, and white blood cells
   D. erythrocytes, white blood cells, and leukocytes

2. A catalyst is

   A. a substance that assists a chemical reaction but does not undergo a change itself
   B. necessary for a chemical reaction to occur
   C. is another word for reactant
   D. a substance that assists a chemical reaction and is destroyed in the process

3. A positive ion

   A. is an atom with more protons than electrons
   B. is an atom with an even number of protons and electrons
   C. is an atom with more electrons than protons
   D. cannot exist. Only negative ions exist

4. The two most abundant elements in the universe are

   A. hydrogen and oxygen
   B. nitrogen and oxygen
   C. oxygen and helium
   D. hydrogen and helium

5. Meteorologists are interested in the study of

   A. meteors
   B. the earth's atmosphere
   C. measurements
   D. the structure of the earth

6. A blind study is designed to correct for

   A. a researcher's bias in favor of a hypothesis
   B. badly designed tests
   C. a subject's unwillingness to participate
   D. observational errors in conducting tests

7. A nanogram is

   A. 1 millionth of a gram
   B. 1 thousandth of a gram
   C. 1 hundredth of a gram
   D. 1 billionth of a gram

8. Darwin's theory of natural selection (also called "survival of the fittest") means

A. organisms in good health survive
B. a population that adapts to its environment is more likely to thrive
C. predators will always triumph over prey
D. populations change over time, for good or bad

9. Meiosis is a type of cell division that

A. allows a parent cell to produce two daughter cells with only half the genetic material of the parent cell
B. allows a parent cell to produce two daughter cells with the exact same genetic material as the parent cell
C. allows a parent cell to produce two daughter cells with twice the genetic material as the parent cell
D. scientists don't understand very well

10. *Homo sapiens* is the

A. genus name for the domestic dog
B. species name for humans
C. phylum for humans
D. order for the domestic dog

11. Most vertebrates

A. are cold-blooded
B. are asymmetrical
C. have poorly developed sense organs
D. rarely have appendages used for locomotion

12. Your vestibular system

A. is connected to the lunar cycle
B. has no known function
C. is responsible for the acuteness of your hearing
D. helps you maintain your balance

13. Points of articulation in your body are called

A. joints
B. tendons
C. impingements
D. connectors

14. An irregular heartbeat is called

A. high blood pressure
B. arrhythmia
C. bradycardia
D. tachycardia

15. Your esophagus

A. connects your throat to your stomach
B. connects your nasal cavity to your lungs
C. is a sphincter muscle
D. links the small intestine to the large intestine

16. An individual with a dominant gene and a recessive gene for a trait

A. will tend to express the dominant gene
B. will tend to express the recessive gene
C. is more likely to pass on the dominant gene
D. is more likely to pass on the recessive gene

17. A lack of potassium in the diet would affect which part of the body most seriously?

A. bones
B. lungs
C. bladder
D. muscles

18. During the late Jurassic period,

A. dinosaurs flourished
B. humans became a dominant species
C. the earth was just beginning to cool
D. the first humans competed with dinosaurs

19. The most common way for fossils to be formed is through

A. being trapped in amber, like an insect
B. the process of perimineralization
C. being trapped under heavy pressure
D. deliberate burial

20. A body of water that is partly salt but is neither seawater nor fresh water is called

A. a lagoon
B. an estuary
C. brackish
D. saline

21. When a cloud accumulates sufficient water vapor, it

A. creates a cold front
B. causes a tornado
C. rains
D. could rain, sleet, hail, or snow

22. Our solar system contains

    A. eight planets
    B. billions of planets
    C. one planet and one moon
    D. the Milky Way galaxy

23. Scalar measures

    A. quantify magnitude
    B. quantify direction
    C. quantify speed
    D. quantify A and B

24. Kinetic energy takes what three main forms?

    A. potential, actual, and exerted
    B. sound, sight, and movement
    C. momentum, power, and acceleration
    D. vibrational, rotational, and translational

25. Sound waves travel through air

    A. more quickly than through water
    B. more slowly than through water
    C. at the same rate as they travel through water
    D. but can't travel through water

## ARITHMETIC REASONING

You will have 30 questions and 36 minutes to answer them.

1. $132.069 - 130.69 = x$. Which of the following equals $x$?

   A. 0.379
   B. 1.379
   C. 1.739
   D. 1.793

2. $8.53 + 17.671 = x$. Which of the following equals $x$?

   A. 16.524
   B. 23.102
   C. 26.201
   D. 25.012

3. $17 - 14.87 \div 2.5 + 3.61 = x$. Which of the following equals $x$?

   A. 4.46
   B. 0.35
   C. 14.66
   D. 4.64

4. When speaking of an engine's thermal efficiency, the amount of heat transformed into work is compared to the amount of heat produced. This is normally measured in British Thermal Units, or BTU. If an engine produces 72,500 BTU, of which 60,000 BTU are transformed into work, what is the thermal efficiency of this engine expressed as a percentage?

   A. 120.83%
   B. 115.7%
   C. 93.28%
   D. 82.75%

5. On the basis of the principle described in the previous question, how many BTU can we assume are transformed into work if we know that an engine is 61.3% thermally efficient and produces a total of 87,500 BTU?

   A. 47,960.5 BTU
   B. 53,637.5 BTU
   C. 57,960.5 BTU
   D. 82,600 BTU

6. If one gallon of water weighs $8\frac{35}{100}$ pounds, how many gallons of water would weigh 16,000 pounds?

   A. 1916.17 gallons
   B. 2435.07 gallons
   C. 2,789 gallons
   D. 3,916.07 gallons

7. If one side of a hexagonal nut measures $\frac{2}{3}$ centimeter in length, what is the length of all sides added together, or, in other words, its perimeter length?

A. 4 cm
B. 3.75 cm
C. 3.12 cm
D. 2.91 cm

8. If the factory specification of a shaft's diameter is 1.75 inches, but was actually determined to be 1.732 inches with micrometer calipers, what is the difference involved?

A. 0.018 inches
B. 0.0018 inches
C. 0.18 inches
D. 1.8 inches

9. A fire started by an electrical short was quickly put out with a dry chemical extinguisher. If the extinguisher has a capacity of $8\frac{1}{2}$ pounds, and $3\frac{1}{4}$ pounds were left after the fire, what percentage of extinguishing agent was actually used?

A. 45.92%
B. 49.61%
C. 57.52%
D. 61.76%

10. If Lakeside Township experienced a 450% increase of fatalities related to fires when comparing figures from 1990 to the present year, and 14 fatalities were reported in 1990, how many fatalities were there in the present year?

A. 57
B. 58
C. 63
D. 77

11. Assuming that a mechanical device weighs 4.75 pounds and is an alloy comprised of 67% copper, how many ounces of copper are present in this device?

A. 3.1825 ounces
B. 60.79 ounces
C. 54.93 ounces
D. 50.92 ounces

12. An EMT has the need for a 5% boric acid solution to be utilized as a mild antiseptic. How much distilled water should be added to 2 liters of a solution comprising 20% boric acid?

A. 8 liters
B. 7.5 liters
C. 6 liters
D. 5.5 liters

13. A public relations expert made a trip to the city of Creston to conduct a lecture on dealing with bad press. The trip to Creston from his home took 2 hours. After having spent $4\frac{1}{2}$ hours giving the lecture, he returned home using the same route except he had to drive 15 mph slower because of traffic congestion. If the expert was away from home a total of 9 hours, how fast did he drive both ways?

    A. 75 mph there and 60 mph returning
    B. 65 mph there and 50 mph returning
    C. 60 mph there and 45 mph returning
    D. 55 mph there and 40 mph returning

14. According to one agency's staff-duty chain of command, the Chief of Operations is responsible for 3 departments. One third of the complement comprises Public Information Officers, one half work in supply, and 5 individuals serve as Police Liaison Officers. Given this information, how many personnel does the Chief of Operations supervise?

    A. 30
    B. 32
    C. 36
    D. Not possible to determine

15. An insurance adjuster calculated that one room of a home suffered enough flood damage to warrant complete replacement of all the drywall. If this room had the dimensions of 25 feet × 27 feet × 9.6 feet, how many square feet of drywall would be required for the job? (Assume the door and windows account for 48.5 square feet.)

    A. 1673.4 square feet
    B. 1251.4 square feet
    C. 949.9 square feet
    D. 1624.9 square feet

16. Of the participants in a dance class, $\frac{1}{4}$ are male and $\frac{1}{2}$ are under the age of 10. What proportion are likely to be boys under the age of 10?

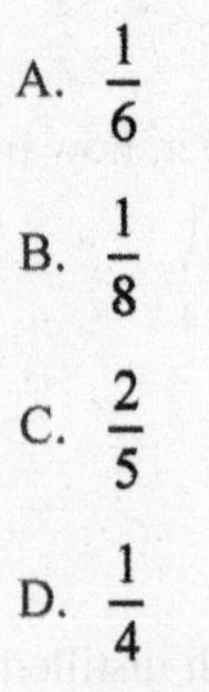

    A. $\frac{1}{6}$
    B. $\frac{1}{8}$
    C. $\frac{2}{5}$
    D. $\frac{1}{4}$

17. If 115 of the patrons of a bakery choose doughnuts and 37 pick croissants, what percentage of the patrons choose donuts?

    A. 7.6%
    B. 32%
    C. 76%
    D. 63%

18. A stylist can cut 16 heads of hair per shift. If a salon gets 120 customers during a day, how many stylists are needed to staff the salon?

    A. 7
    B. 8
    C. 5
    D. 12

19. Jay is contemplating the purchase of a life insurance policy. The policy costs $8 per year per thousand dollars in coverage. Jay can put $50 every six months toward the purchase of the policy. How much policy can he afford?

    A. $12,500
    B. $1,250
    C. $6250
    D. $62,500

20. A chef uses 3 ounces of specialty cheese to create her signature dish. The cheese costs $27.99 per pound. How much does each serving cost?

    A. $5.58
    B. $2.79
    C. $2.15
    D. $6.45

21. If 95% of the people taking a screening test receive accurate test results, but 25 people have to retake an inaccurate test, how many people took the screening test to begin with?

    A. 100
    B. 250
    C. 500
    D. 300

22. What is the next term in the sequence {3, 9, 4, 16, 5}?

    A. 19
    B. 25
    C. 6
    D. 21

23. Given the sequence of $3_n + 3$, what is the fifth term in the sequence?

    A. 18
    B. 6
    C. 11
    D. 9

24. Greta works as a bartender, earning a base pay of $9.75 an hour. She averages a ten percent tip on drinks served and generally serves 15 drinks an hour at an average cost of $4.75 per drink. She also gets a 10% share of the servers' tips on meals that include drink orders. Servers average tips of $75 an hour on meals that include drink orders. In a six-hour shift, how much does Greta earn on average?

    A. $58.50
    B. $101.25
    C. $146.25
    D. $108.75

25. A conference costs $480 to attend. The early bird discount is 15%, and previous attendees can take an additional $25 off. If a previous attendee registers by the early bird deadline, how much does she pay?

   A. $386.75
   B. $306
   C. $408
   D. $383

26. A teacher throws out the highest and lowest test scores before averaging a grade. If a student scored 74%, 86%, 67%, 99%, 93%, and 85%, what grade will she receive in the class?

   A. 85.5%
   B. 84.5%
   C. 84%
   D. 86%

27. A real estate agent sold 116 houses last year. This year the housing market was better and she sold 152 houses. What percent change occurred in sales between last year and this year?

   A. 31%
   B. 131%
   C. 13%
   D. 36%

28. A square rug has a total area of 81 inches. How long is each side?

   A. 7 inches
   B. 8 inches
   C. 9 inches
   D. 8.5 inches

29. If a map is drawn at 1:100 scale, with one inch on the map equaling 100 miles, how far apart are two towns that are 3.7 inches apart on the map?

   A. 370 miles
   B. 37 miles
   C. 3700 miles
   D. 100 miles

30. When Miriam raised the price of her handmade tote bags by 20%, the number of bags she sold declined from 150 per year to 119. What was the percentage decline in sales?

   A. −20%
   B. −31%
   C. −79%
   D. −21%

## WORD KNOWLEDGE

You will have 35 questions to answer in 11 minutes.

1. Bequeath most nearly means

   A. give
   B. resent
   C. tremble
   D. expect

2. The board expected a candid appraisal of each candidate. Candid most nearly means

   A. complete
   B. honest
   C. biased
   D. useful

3. The homeowner was despondent over the inspector's report. Despondent most nearly means

   A. elated
   B. intimidated
   C. discouraged
   D. energized

4. Abdicate most nearly means

   A. indicate
   B. instruct
   C. cede
   D. indict

5. The children bombarded each other with snow balls. Bombarded most nearly means

   A. threatened
   B. pelted
   C. faced
   D. teased

6. The library introduced a moratorium on fines for overdue books. Moratorium most nearly means

   A. ban
   B. extension
   C. increase
   D. decrease

7. Scientists were concerned that the new bacteria would pervade the environment. Pervade most nearly means

   A. affect
   B. destroy
   C. quickly infect
   D. spread throughout

8. Quibble most nearly means

A. discussion
B. import
C. argument
D. triviality

9. The farmer wished the rain would subside. Subside most nearly means

A. increase
B. arrive
C. ebb
D. delay

10. The lawyer made a cogent argument for the defendant's innocence. Cogent most nearly means

A. convincing
B. incoherent
C. creative
D. standard

11. Latent most nearly means

A. hidden
B. delayed
C. obscure
D. grown

12. Deleterious most nearly means

A. charming
B. feverish
C. harmful
D. omitted

13. Marilyn was contrite after she lost her temper. Contrite most nearly means

A. impatient
B. refreshed
C. upset
D. sorry

14. Her feeling of relief was transient. Transient most nearly means

A. temporary
B. important
C. permanent
D. unexpected

15. A meticulous examination of the books turned up the error. Meticulous most nearly means

A. brief
B. thorough
C. expensive
D. unscheduled

16. Tenuous most nearly means

A. soft
B. slight
C. inconsistent
D. inconsiderate

17. Adrian flouted the rules at least once a week. Flouted most nearly means

A. disregarded
B. questioned
C. complained about
D. followed

18. The paradox intrigued the researcher. Paradox most nearly means

A. question
B. puzzle
C. challenge
D. contradiction

19. Malleable most nearly means

A. temperamental
B. hard-headed
C. shapeable
D. suitable

20. Embellish most nearly means

A. adorn
B. enjoy
C. ignore
D. include

21. The new recruit was adroit at his tasks. Adroit most nearly means

A. inexperienced
B. late
C. able
D. shiftless

22. The yoga teacher sought a moment of repose. Repose most nearly means

A. time
B. rest
C. happiness
D. connection

23. The scientist's ideas were vilified at first. Vilified most nearly means

A. ignored
B. understood
C. accepted
D. disparaged

24. Fetid most nearly means

A. weak
B. smelly
C. distant
D. strong

25. The child's manner was ebullient. Ebullient most nearly means

A. sulky
B. enthusiastic
C. calm
D. unhappy

26. The doctor made an egregious error in diagnosis. Egregious most nearly means

A. mild
B. understandable
C. bad
D. novel

27. Parched most nearly means

A. thirsty
B. lacking
C. overdone
D. worn

28. Impetuous most nearly means

A. penniless
B. unfortunate
C. welcoming
D. unthinking

29. The evidence substantiated the victim's claim. Substantiated most nearly means

A. confirmed
B. disproved
C. clarified
D. invalidated

30. Conformity is valued among certain groups. Conformity most nearly means

A. recklessness
B. impertinence
C. sociability
D. compliance

31. Ubiquitous most nearly means

A. unique
B. everywhere
C. approachable
D. fair

32. The members of the unit experienced camaraderie. Camaraderie most nearly means

A. friendship
B. tension
C. cohesion
D. leadership

33. Zenith most nearly means

A. low point
B. arc
C. progression
D. high point

34. Most of Barney's life experiences were the result of vicissitude. Vicissitude most nearly means

A. planning
B. logic
C. chance
D. emotion

35. Puerile most nearly means

A. childish
B. disgusting
C. pungent
D. mature

## PARAGRAPH COMPREHENSION

You'll have 15 questions and 13 minutes to answer them.

1. Once a defendant is arrested and subsequently taken to jail, he or she has the right to appear before a judge within twenty-four hours to seek a release. If a judge is reasonably assured that the defendant will honor a promise to return for the hearing, he or she is released without bail, or, in other words, on personal recognizance. If, on the other hand, a defendant has a dangerous criminal history, he or she may be asked to post significant bail. In either case, the presiding magistrate must render a decision concerning the defendant's disposition very quickly.
   According to this passage,
   A. a defendant has only 24 hours to ask for bail
   B. a defendant always has to pay at least a minimal amount of bail to be released pending a hearing
   C. a judge must allow a defendant to be released if requested
   D. a defendant has the right to appear before a judge within 24 hours to seek a release

2. Mithraism was a major Roman religion that celebrated the cult of Mithra, a Persian sun god. It influenced Christianity. Some Christian rites, such as baptism, communion, and the use of holy water, are Mithraic. So, too, is the celebration of Sunday as a holy day. December 25 was celebrated as Mithras's birthday. Other similarities also existed.
   According to this passage,
   A. The similarities between Christianity and Mithraism are purely coincidental.
   B. Mithraism influenced Christianity.
   C. Some Mithraic rites were influenced by Christianity.
   D. Mithraism was a Greek religion.

3. Ancient medicine was based on the four elements (air, earth, wind, and fire). The human body turned these elements into humors. All people belonged to one of four humors: sanguine, choleric, melancholic, and phlegmatic. People who were sanguine, for example, were thought to have more blood than people who were choleric, who were thought to have more bile. A sanguine person was calm, which was a function of the blood, whereas choleric people were easily angered, which was a function of the bile. To cure a sanguine person of a disease required bloodletting.
   According to this passage,
   A. ancient medicine was based on the four elements
   B. the humors did not relate to temperament
   C. people of different humors were treated the same way
   D. most people belonged to four main humors, but there were others

4. The Hagia Sophia was a cathedral begun in the reign of Justinian (532–537), built in Constantinople (now Istanbul). Known as the Church of the Holy Wisdom, it was one of the most spectacular religious buildings ever built and is the most famous Byzantine building. Although defaced by iconoclasts and then turned into a mosque, it was a model for Muslim architects as well as Christian ones. It is now a museum.
   A good title for this passage would be
   A. A History of the Hagia Sophia
   B. Cathedrals Throughout History
   C. Byzantine Churches
   D. A Modest Museum

5. The Choson Dynasty was a Korean dynasty founded in the fourteenth century. The spread of neo-Confucianism inspired many petty noblemen to demand social and political reform. The movement coalesced in the founding of the Choson dynasty by Yi Songgye in 1392. The dynasty survived until 1910.
According to the passage, the Choson Dynasty

   A. survived in China for more than five hundred years
   B. spread neo-Confucianism throughout Asia
   C. was founded in response to a demand for social and political reform
   D. was short-lived and brutal

6. Cambridge is a city in central England on the Cam River. A center of learning, it is the site of the University of Cambridge, which was founded in the thirteenth century. A number of important ancient structures still stand, including a tenth-century Saxon church, and the Church of the Holy Sepulchre, a round Norman church. King's College Chapel, a mid-fifteenth-century church, is an outstanding example of Gothic architecture.
According to this passage, the city of Cambridge

   A. is more notable for its architecture than its university
   B. is the site of a number of notable old buildings
   C. was established in the thirteenth century
   D. is located in the West Midlands

7. Ancestor worship is the veneration of dead relatives. In many ancient cultures, ancestors were believed to have great power and were thought to influence events and to protect the family. If they were not respected, they could cause harm and misfortune. If treated with appropriate respect, they could assure the well-being of their descendants. Ancestors were sometimes believed to serve as intermediaries between people and God or gods.
From this passage it can be assumed that

   A. ancestor worship precludes belief in other religions
   B. ancestor worship would be unlikely to take the form of prayer or sacrifice
   C. disrespecting one's ancestors could anger one's living family
   D. ancestors would protect the family no matter what

8. The Grand Ole Opry is one of the most prestigious of the barn dance programs, as well as the longest running. Performers on stage at the Grand Ole Opry still say they feel as if they have joined a family. The Grand Ole Opry is held in awe by aspiring singers. To be invited to play there is an honor and a privilege, though it pays very little; to be invited to join is the pinnacle of one's success.
According to this passage,

   A. singing at the Grand Ole Opry is very lucrative
   B. joining the Grand Ole Opry is like joining a family
   C. anyone can join the Grand Ole Opry
   D. mostly actors join the Grand Ole Opry

9. Feast days included the twelve days of Christmas, Easter Sunday, funerals, anniversaries, and saints' days. Even the completion of a time-consuming task, such as harvest, meant one was rewarded with a feast. In Paris, the feast of St. Denis was renowned throughout Europe and lasted the entire month of October. Companies and guilds sponsored feasts on special days, as did members of the aristocracy, which confirmed the lord's generosity and place in the social network. Often feasts had spectators who watched the retinue eat, though they themselves did not partake. Entertainment was always provided and consisted of music, dancers, jugglers, minstrels, acrobats and even animal trainers.
According to this passage,

   A. feasts were all about the food
   B. feasts were only held on feast days
   C. anyone invited to a feast would participate in it
   D. feasts were a form of entertainment

10. The IRS randomly audits business owners (they also randomly audit regular people, just not as often). Although the main reason for this is to determine if a business is underreporting income, two other important reasons include discovering where business owners are making mistakes, in order to educate them, and discovering where business owners find loopholes, in order to close them.
According to the author,

   A. there is only one reason the IRS conducts audits
   B. most businesses cheat on their taxes
   C. the IRS randomly audits regular people more than it does businesses
   D. the IRS audits businesses for several reasons

11. Angkor Wat is a twelfth-century temple complex at Angkor, the capital of the Khmer Empire of Cambodia. It is the largest known religious monument ever constructed. The structure was built to celebrate the king's incarnation as the god Vishnu. It was also meant to serve as his burial chamber. Though now in ruins, it is clear that a central tower was surrounded by four smaller towers. These represented Mount Meru, which, according to Hindu mythology, is where the gods live. The central tower was surrounded by terraces that symbolize the earth. A moat enclosed the complex, signifying the ocean.
According to this passage, which of the following is <u>not</u> true:

   A. the construction of Angkor Wat had religious significance
   B. Angkor Wat can be called a temple complex
   C. Angkor Wat served as a burial chamber
   D. Little is known about Angkor Wat

12. Basques are people of unknown origin inhabiting a territory in north-central Spain. Throughout their history, they have been independent and freedom-loving. They created strict laws that addressed every aspect of social and private life and maintained order and law through assemblies that were democratically elected and which represented the voices of all classes of people. Even after a united Spanish kingdom was founded in the fifteenth century, the Basques maintained their own customs, laws, and foreign relations.
According to this passage,

   A. historically, Basques have been known to be independent and freedom-loving
   B. Basques were eventually completely assimilated into Spanish culture
   C. traditionally, a king ruled over the Basques
   D. Basques had a very relaxed and nomadic way of existence

13. It is an unfortunate fact that many homeowners tragically lose their lives because of apathy expressed toward home fire drills. EDITH, or Exit Drills In The Home, and Learn Not To Burn are two programs recently implemented by fire departments nationwide to counter such attitudes. Both of these programs, developed by the National Fire Protection Association (NFPA), accentuate the installation and maintenance of smoke detection equipment and teach users to establish an evacuation procedure for all occupants and conduct fire drills at regular intervals to practice what has been adopted.
What is EDITH an acronym for, according to the passage?

    A. the name of the person who developed the program
    B. Emergency Dispatch in Time to Help
    C. Exit Drills In The Home
    D. Emergency Doors In The Home

14. If a defendant prefers the jury trial, the attorneys conduct jury selection, referred to as "voir dire." Prospective jurors are interviewed by both counsels and accepted or eliminated depending on the attitudes they exhibit toward the defendant. At the close of jury selection, the trial begins.
According to this passage, the definition of "voir dire" is

    A. court hearing
    B. jury selection
    C. jury trial
    D. judicial process

15. Building inspectors play a key role in preventing substandard building and remodeling processes. Prior to an inspection, the inspector involved should be as well prepared as possible. This includes the ability to recognize potential hazards and to offer reasonable solutions. The inspector must have a thorough understanding of local building codes and how they apply to both commercial and private occupancies. It is equally important to demonstrate a positive attitude that conveys a willingness to work with, not against, a property owner.
A good title for this passage would be

    A. What a Property Owner Should Know about Building Inspection
    B. Keeping Your Property Up to Code
    C. What to Know about Conducting a Building Inspection
    D. Characteristics of a Building Inspection Program

## MATHEMATICS KNOWLEDGE

You'll have 25 questions and 24 minutes to answer them.

1. **If a spherical storage container measured 72.75 centimeters in diameter, how many cubic centimeters of liquid could this tank accommodate (maximum)?**

   A. 5,542.37 cubic centimeters
   B. 107,541.2 cubic centimeters
   C. 201,603.76 cubic centimeters
   D. 500,944.3 cubic centimeters

2. **A chemical storage tank is cylindrical, with a height of 32.5 feet and a diameter of 18.5 feet. If the liquid in this tank were at the 20.7 foot mark, how many gallons are there, assuming 7.48 gallons occupy 1 cubic foot?**

   A. 40,640.51 gallons
   B. 41,620.404 gallons
   C. 43,790.2 gallons
   D. 50,000 gallons

3. **A rectangular packing crate contains 14,364 cubic inches of a given material. If the crate measures 18 inches wide and 38 inches long, what would be the height of this particular container?**

   A. 18.75 inches
   B. 19.5 inches
   C. 20 inches
   D. 21 inches

4. **The coordinates {7, 3} indicate what positions on a graph?**

   A. the position of 7 on the $y$-axis and the position of 3 on the $x$-axis
   B. the position of 7 on the $x$-axis and the position of 3 on the $y$-axis
   C. the positions of 7 and 3 on the $x$-axis
   D. the positions of 7 and 3 on the $y$-axis

5. **A mathematical way to state the expression "The budget for purchasing office supplies cannot exceed $5,000 this year" is:**

   A. $b = \$5,000$
   B. $b < \$5,000$
   C. $b > \$5,000$
   D. $b \leq \$5,000$

6. **If $x = 3$, then what does $2x^2$ equal?**

   A. 3
   B. 9
   C. 18
   D. 36

7. **What is the square of $-5$?**

   A. **−25**
   B. 25
   C. 10
   D. **−10**

8. Solve for $x$: $\frac{1}{5}x > 5$.

A. $\frac{4}{5}$

B. $-5$

C. 5

D. 25

9. If a right triangle has an angle equal to 45°, what is the measurement of the third angle?

A. 90°

B. 45°

C. 180°

D. 55°

10. Solve for $x$: $5x - 2 = 13$.

A. $x = 3$

B. $x = 5$

C. $x = 2$

D. $x = 15$

11. A triangle with no equal sides and no equal angles is a(n):

A. right triangle

B. equilateral

C. scalene triangle

D. isosceles

12. Solve for $x$: $-3x = 18$.

A. $x = 15$

B. $x = 21$

C. $x = 6$

D. $x = -6$

13. Solve for $x$: $\frac{x}{3} = 18$.

A. 54

B. 6

C. 18

D. 27

14. Solve for $x$: $-2x > 4$.

A. $x = 2$

B. $x > 2$

C. $x < -2$

D. $x > -2$

15. The angles of an octagon have a total measurement of:

A. 800°
B. 1080°
C. 980°
D. 360°

16. Sam is mixing together a cleaning solution that requires 4 parts water to 1 part cleaning product. If he is using 6 gallons of water to clean his driveway, how much cleaning product does he need?

A. 2 gallons
B. 1 gallon
C. 1.5 gallons
D. 8 gallons

17. Add the fractions $\frac{x}{5}+\frac{2-x}{3}$.

A. $\frac{1}{4}$

B. $\frac{-2x+10}{15}$

C. $\frac{2x}{8}$

D. $\frac{10}{3x}$

18. Subtract the fractions $\frac{x+2}{5}-\frac{1}{x-3}$.

A. $\frac{x^2-x-11}{5x-15}$

B. $\frac{x+1}{x+2}$

C. $\frac{2x}{5}$

D. $\frac{x+2}{5x-15}$

19. What is not true about the expression $\frac{2x^3-y}{x}$?

A. It is a polynomial
B. It has two unknowns
C. It is a nonlinear expression
D. It has an exponent in one unknown

20. What is the product of $(x+3)(x-4)$?

A. $x^2-1$
B. $2x-1$
C. $x^2-x-12$
D. $x^2-12$

21. What is the root of $x^2-9=0$?

A. 9
B. 3
C. −3
D. Both B and C.

22. The formula for determining the probability of an independent event (such as a coin toss) can generally be represented as:

A. the number of selected outcomes divided by the number of possible outcomes
B. the number of possible outcomes divided by the number of selected outcomes
C. the number of possible outcomes multiplied by the number of selected outcomes
D. the number of selected outcomes divided by the number of events

23. Janice received a scratch-off coupon with seven areas to scratch off. According to the information on the back of the coupon, two of the areas have discount codes and the other five have nothing. If Janice can only scratch off one area, what are her chances of picking a winning discount code?

A. $\frac{1}{7}$

B. $\frac{1}{5}$

C. $\frac{2}{7}$

D. $\frac{1}{2}$

24. Given $y=3x+3$ and $y=x+5$, solve for $x$ and $y$.

A. $x=1, y=8$
B. $x=2, y=11$
C. $x=3, y=8$
D. $x=1, y=6$

25. Given $3x+2y=13$ and $-3x+7y=5$, solve for $x$ and $y$.

A. $x=2, y=5$
B. $x=1, y=4$
C. $x=3, y=2$
D. $x=-3, y=8$

## ELECTRONICS INFORMATION

You'll have 20 questions and 9 minutes to answer them.

1. Which of the following is a good conductor of electricity?

   A. copper wire
   B. glass
   C. air
   D. rubber

2. $1 \mu\Omega$ is the same as:

   A. 1 watt
   B. 1 ohm
   C. 100 oms
   D. $10^{-6}$ ohm

3. An ohm measures

   A. resistance
   B. conductance
   C. power
   D. rate of flow

4. 1 kw is

   A. 1,000 watts
   B. 10 watts
   C. 100 watts
   D. 0.001 watts

5. The formula for measuring resistance is:

   A. $R = \frac{I}{V}$

   B. $G = IV$

   C. $R = VI$

   D. $R = \frac{V}{I}$

6. Power plants generate AC power because

   A. they can't build batteries big enough to store DC power
   B. that's how it's always been done
   C. AC power can be sent out at higher voltages than DC power
   D. DC power can only be generated when the sun is shining

7. A negatively charged object is always attracted to

   A. other negatively charged objects
   B. positively charged objects
   C. neutral objects
   D. none of the above

8. An electric current is which of the following?

A. the flow of electrons from one point to another
B. the combination of unknown elements that create energy
C. movement of any electrically charged material
D. a chemical reaction that produces power

9. In a series circuit, if $R_1$ stops working, what happens to $R_2$?

A. nothing
B. it stops working, too
C. it works harder to compensate
D. it continues working, but not as efficiently

10. What kind of circuit is shown in the figure below?

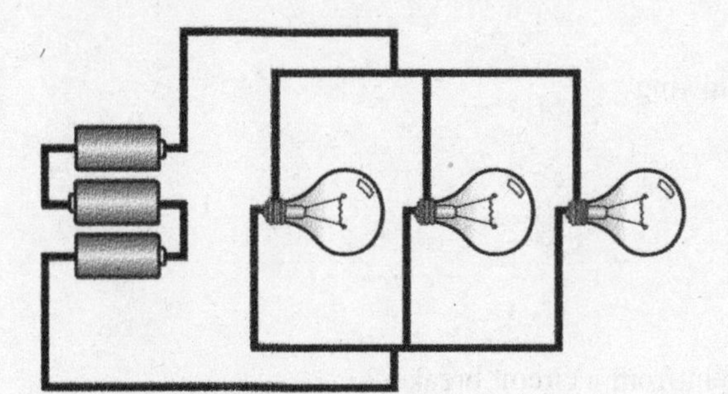

A. series circuit
B. series-parallel
C. parallel circuit
D. integrated circuit

11. A series circuit has 15 volts. $R_1$ has 2 ohms of resistance and $R_2$ has 3 ohms of resistance. What is the current in the circuit?

A. 7.5 amperes
B. 5 amperes
C. 3 amperes
D. 45 amperes

12. A 100-watt bulb left on for half an hour uses how many joules?

A. 180,000 joules
B. 100 joules
C. 1800 joules
D. 1.8 joules

13. In the figure below, if $R_1$ stops working, what happens to $R_2$ and $R_3$?

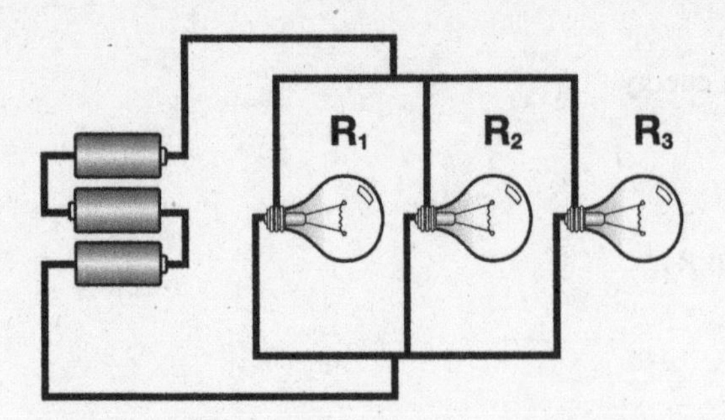


A. nothing
B. they stop working
C. they work harder to compensate
D. they continue working, but not as efficiently

14. An inductor is a component that does which of the following?

A. it stores an electric charge
B. it steps up voltage
C. it steps down voltage
D. it contains electric potential

15. How is a ground fault circuit interrupter (GFCI) different from a circuit breaker?

A. the GFCI is manual
B. the GFCI must be reset
C. the GFCI is wired at the outlet, while the circuit breaker is wired at the panel
D. the GFCI runs directly to the ground rod whereas the circuit breaker does not

16. In a schematic, which of the following is true?

A. circuits are always drawn to scale
B. circuits are always drawn with components proportional
C. connectors are always copper wire unless otherwise indicated
D. standard abbreviations are used to indicate components

17. In the figure below, if the voltage drop across $R_1$ is 1.5V and the voltage drop across $R_2$ is 2V, what is the total voltage drop in the circuit?

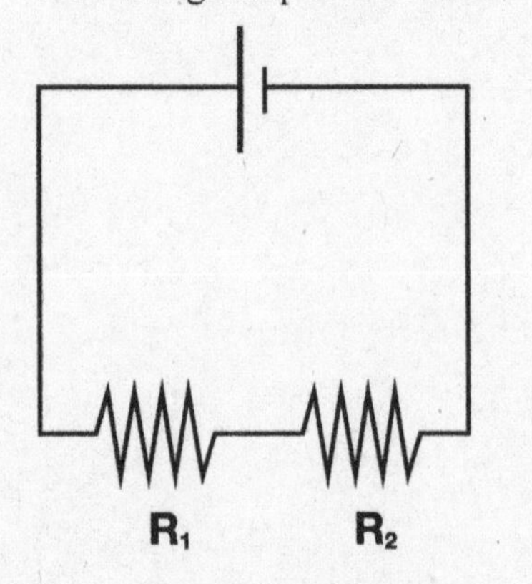

A. 3.5V
B. 0.5
C. 3V
D. 1.33V

18. The symbol for an AC power source on a schematic is which of the following?

A.
B.
C.
D.

19. The symbol could <u>not</u> be which of the following in a circuit?

A. a light bulb
B. the heating element of a toaster
C. an on/off switch
D. the heating element of a stove

20. In the figure below, if the total current is 3 amperes and the total resistance is 5 ohms, what is the voltage?

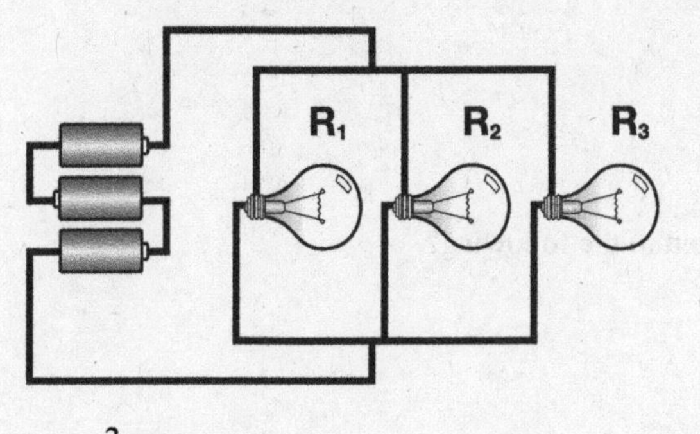


A. $\frac{3}{5}$ volt
B. 15 volts
C. 60 volts
D. 8 volts

## AUTOMOTIVE AND SHOP INFORMATION

You'll have 25 questions and 11 minutes to answer them.

1. If a loose clamp results in a coolant leak, which of the following is a likely consequence?

   A. the brakes will malfunction
   B. the engine will overheat
   C. power-assisted steering will require more force
   D. the air-conditioning won't operate

2. In the figure below, the arrow labeled A is pointing to what car part?

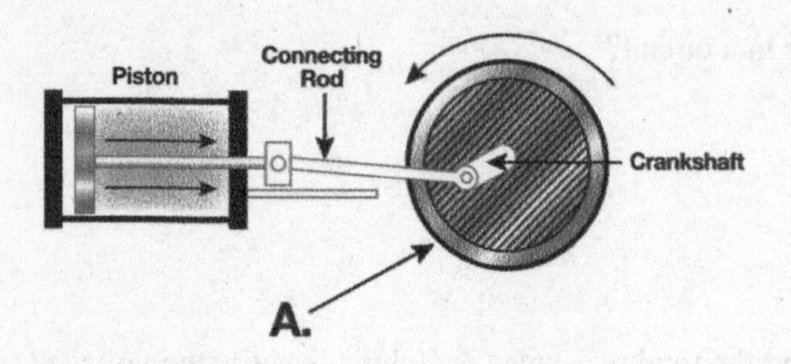


   A. camshaft
   B. disk brake
   C. master cylinder
   D. flywheel

3. In a four-stroke cycle, after the intake stroke comes which of the following?

   A. compression
   B. exhaust
   C. combustion
   D. ventilation

4. In the figure below, which car parts are the arrows pointing to?

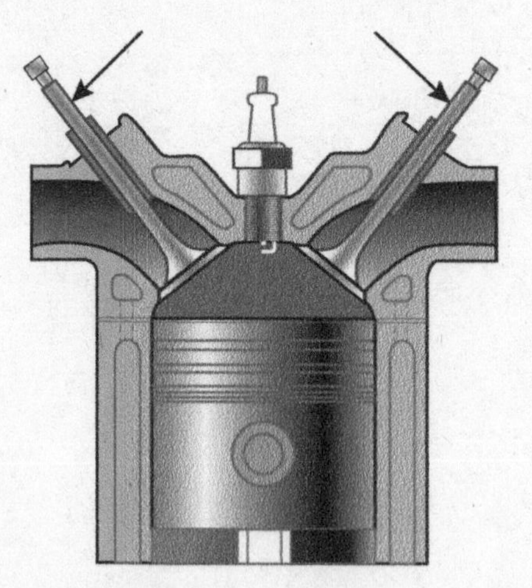

   A. combustion chambers
   B. intake and exhaust valves
   C. spark plugs
   D. pistons

5. Which of the following is true of a continuously variable transmission?

A. it basically has any number of gear ratios
B. it has 6 gear ratios
C. it is found only on manual transmissions
D. it is an old-fashioned transmission rarely found on newer cars

6. "AWD" is an abbreviation for

A. Alternate Wheel Deviation
B. Anti-Wipeout Drive
C. All Wheel Drive
D. All Ways Drive

7. The main components of a vehicle's electrical system are which of the following?

A. thermostat, battery, starter
B. starter, alternator, transmission
C. battery, crankshaft, alternator
D. battery, starter, alternator

8. Most car batteries are which of the following?

A. 220-volt grounded
B. 120-volt cold cranking
C. 12-volt rechargeable
D. 8-volt dry cells

9. A fuel injector replaces which car part?

A. intake manifold
B. carburetor
C. spark plug
D. piston

10. The catalytic converter changes exhaust chemicals into which of the following?

A. carbon monoxide and oxygen
B. carbon monoxide and carbon dioxide
C. carbon dioxide and water
D. oxygen and nitrogen

11. Which of the following is <u>not</u> a method for controlling emissions?

A. PCV
B. hydrometer
C. evaporative controls
D. air injection

12. What tool would be most appropriate to use in cutting thin sheet metal such as tin?

    A. cold chisel
    B. straight snips
    C. side-cutting pliers
    D. end-cutting pliers

13. What is the name of the tool shown in the diagram in the figure below?

    A. torque wrench
    B. crocodile wrench
    C. Stilson wrench
    D. monkey wrench

14. If you wanted to cut down a tree using hand tools, you would probably use which of the following?

    A. pickaxe
    B. hatchet
    C. sickle
    D. wedge felling axe

15. The tool pictured in the figure below is associated with what trade?

    A. plumbing
    B. electrical work
    C. masonry
    D. automotive mechanic

16. If a firefighter needed to gain entry to a premises where the doors were chained and padlocked, what tool illustrated below is most appropriate to be used to cut the chain link or the lock's shackle?

A.

B.

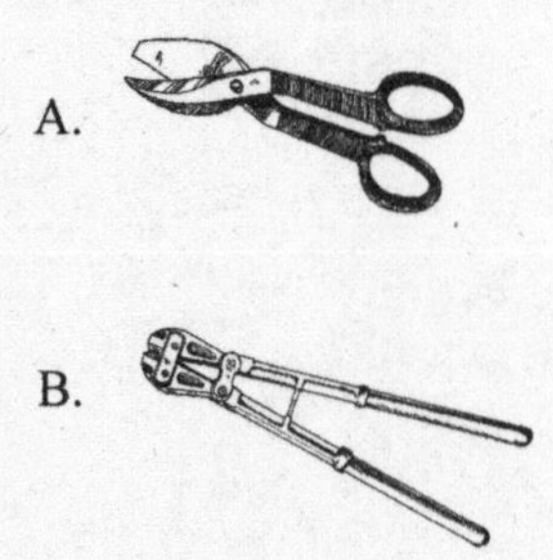

C.

D.

17. Which of the tools illustrated below would best be used to hold a piece of flat metal stock so that its end could be filed smooth?

18. The tool illustrated in the figure below is used for what purpose?

A. to etch glass
B. to pry small pieces of work apart
C. to start holes in wood to accommodate nails or screws
D. to press lines into wood with the aid of a straight edge

19. Which of the following tools below is not used in metal fabrication work?

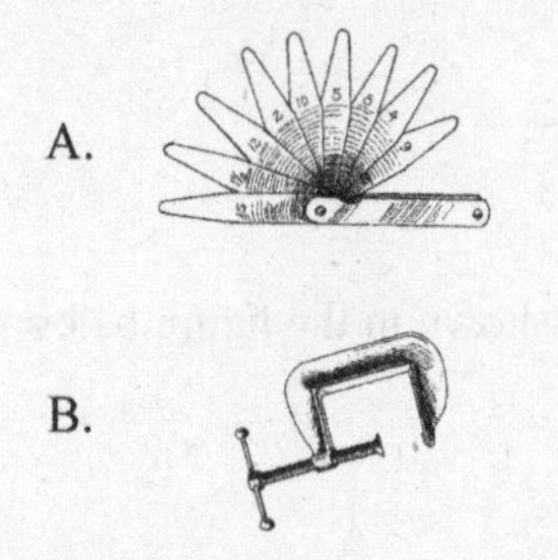


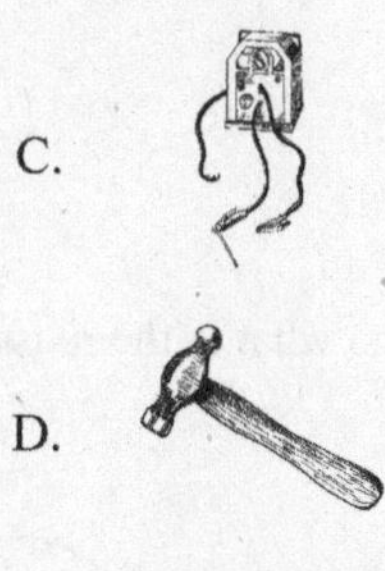


20. What kind of electric power tool is used to create the flared tenon joinery demonstrated in the figure below?

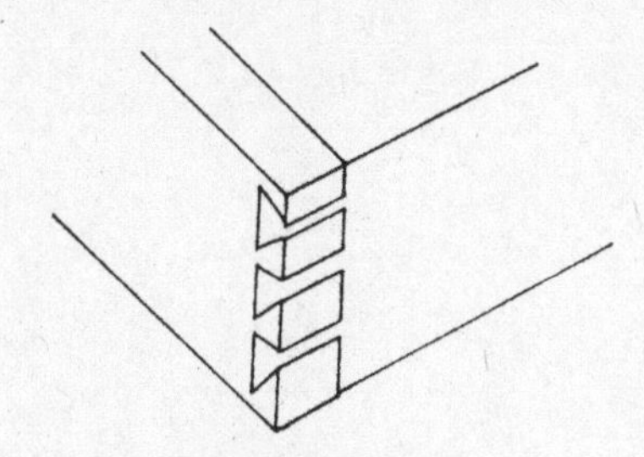

A. tenon saw
B. reciprocating saw
C. portable electric router
D. portable circular saw

21. The device illustrated in the figure below measures what quantity?

A. electrical resistance
B. tire pressure
C. current flow
D. engine cylinder compression

22. If an electrician needed to flare the end of a piece of electrical conduit to create a coupling with another piece of electrical conduit, what kind of tool would be used?

A. a brace with an auger bit
B. a brace with a ream
C. a power drill with a spade bit
D. a power drill with a countersink bit

23. If a length of wood had to be cut perpendicular to its grain, what kind of saw blade would be recommended?

A. rip cut blade
B. saber saw blade
C. crosscut blade
D. friction blade

24. When referring to belt drives, what is the reason a belt is twisted in the manner shown in the figure below?

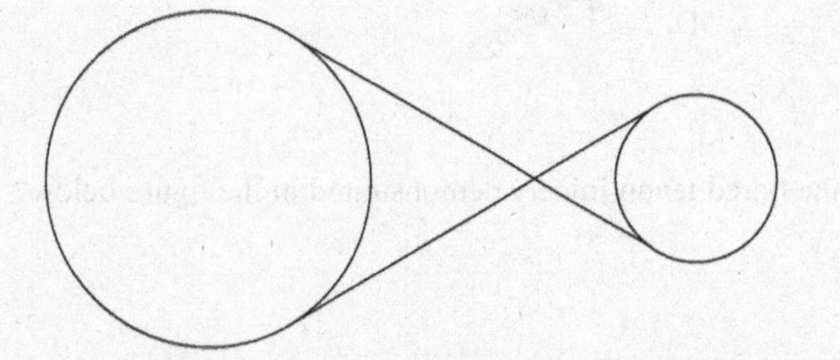

A. It tends to increase torque on the smaller wheel.
B. It tends to increase torque on the larger wheel.
C. It tends to increase the speed of the smaller wheel.
D. It causes the opposing wheel to change direction.

25. Which of the gears listed below demonstrates the unique capability of changing drive train direction?

A. helical gears
B. beveled gears
C. herringbone gears
D. spur gears

## MECHANICAL COMPREHENSION

You'll have 25 questions and 19 minutes to answer them.

1. If a child used a 6-inch-long stick to dislodge a large rock, which location of the fulcrum would provide the greatest lift?

   A. 3.5 inches from the rock
   B. 2 inches from the rock
   C. it makes no difference
   D. the end of the stick held by the child

2. Marcus is moving a crate that weighs 1,200 pounds and is a square with 4-foot sides. The fulcrum of an 8-foot lever rests 18 inches from the crate. If Marcus applies force at the very end of the lever opposite the load, how much effort will he need to exert to lift the crate (rounding up to the nearest pound)?

   A. 277 pounds
   B. 332 pounds
   C. 225 pounds
   D. 300 pounds

3. Joe has to move a crate that weighs 300 pounds. He can use a lever or he can just lift the crate. If he were to use a lever, he would place a 6-foot lever so that the fulcrum rests 2 feet from the crate and applies effort at the very end of the lever opposite the load. What mechanical advantage is gained by using the lever as opposed to lifting the crate directly?

   A. 1:4
   B. 3:1
   C. 4:1
   D. 2:1

4. In the figure below, which of the options gives the greatest mechanical advantage?

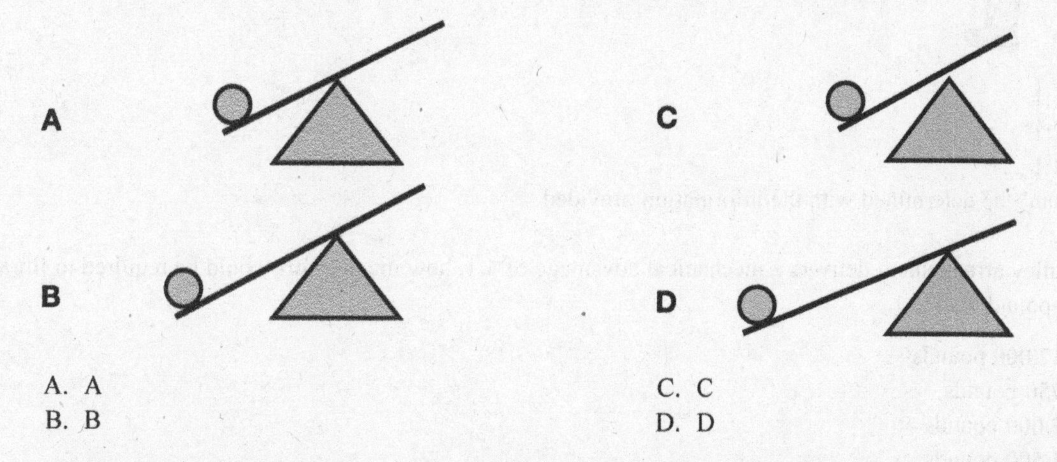


   A. A
   B. B
   C. C
   D. D

5. Two people are struggling to lift a 12-foot telephone pole. The total weight of the pole is 205 pounds. If one person anchors the end of the pole to the ground (serving as the fulcrum), and the other person attempts to lift the flagpole at a point 6 feet from the fulcrum, how much resistance would that person encounter?

   A. 51.25 pounds
   B. 102.5 pounds
   C. 205 pounds
   D. 410 pounds

6. Two people are struggling to lift a 10-foot canoe to store it upright in a shed. The canoe weighs 115 pounds. If one person anchors the end of the canoe to the ground (serving as the fulcrum) while the other person lifts the canoe 5 feet from the fulcrum, what is the mechanical advantage gained by this method?

   A. 1:1
   B. 2:1
   C. there is no advantage gained by using leverage in this manner
   D. can't be determined with the information provided

7. What is the mechanical advantage of the pulley illustrated in the figure below?

   A. 1:1
   B. 2:1
   C. 4:1
   D. can't be determined with the information provided

8. If a pulley arrangement delivers a mechanical advantage of 4:1, how much effort would be required to lift a 3,000-pound load?

   A. 12,000 pounds
   B. 750 pounds
   C. 3,000 pounds
   D. 1,500 pounds

9. If a pulley arrangement delivers a mechanical advantage of 4:1, and the effort end of the cable was pulled 3 feet, how far would the load be lifted?

A. 12 feet
B. 3 feet
C. 9 inches
D. 12 inches

10. For the pulley arrangement shown in the figure below, how much effort is required to lift the load?

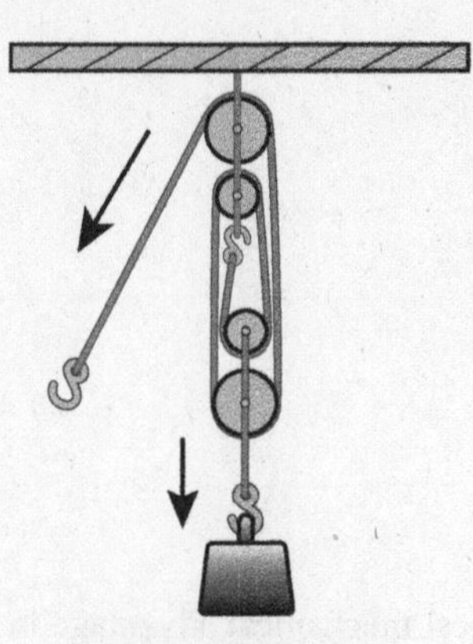


A. 267 pounds
B. 800 pounds
C. 400 pounds
D. 200 pounds

11. If 250 pounds of pulling force were applied to the pulley arrangement shown in the figure below, what would be the maximum load this pulley could lift?

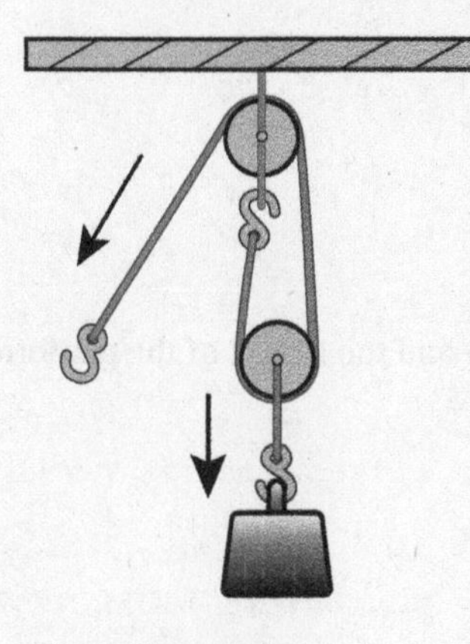

A. 500 pounds
B. 250 pounds
C. 1,000 pounds
D. 750 pounds

12. How long of a pull would be required to lift 1,000 pounds of resistance 2 feet using the pulley arrangement shown in the figure below?

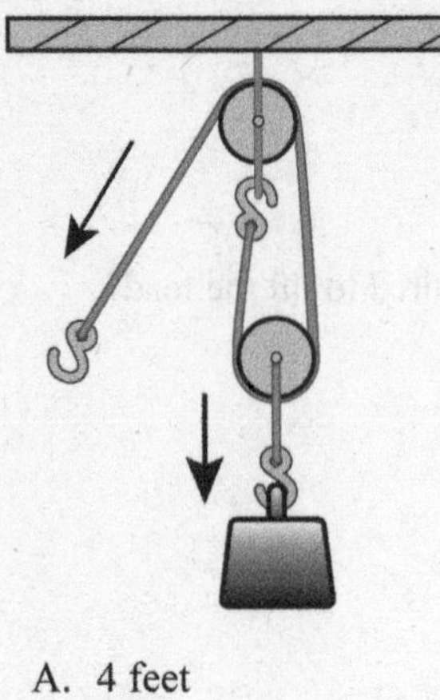

A. 4 feet
B. 2 feet
C. 8 feet
D. 6 feet

13. Which of the inclined plane diagrams in the figure below demonstrates the best mechanical advantage in lifting a heavy object to the height of the platform?

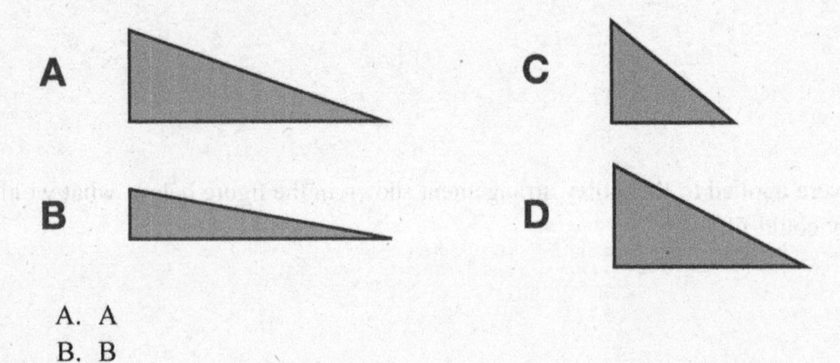


A. A
B. B
C. C
D. D

14. What is the mechanical advantage of an inclined plane if its length is 18 feet and the height of the platform it reaches is 10 feet?

A. 1.8:1
B. 2:1
C. 2.8:1
D. 4:1

15. If someone needed to load a 530-pound barrel into the back of a truck with a bed height of 5 feet, how much effort would be required if an 8-foot ramp were used as an inclined plane?

A. 530 pounds
B. 848 pounds
C. 331.25 pounds
D. 265.33 pounds

16. What is the maximum height that a 360-pound barrel could be lifted if a 14-foot inclined plank having a mechanical advantage of 2:1 was used and only 90 pounds of force is available?

A. 4 feet
B. 3.5 feet
C. 2.25 feet
D. 2 feet

17. What is the mechanical advantage of the incline plane shown in the figure below?

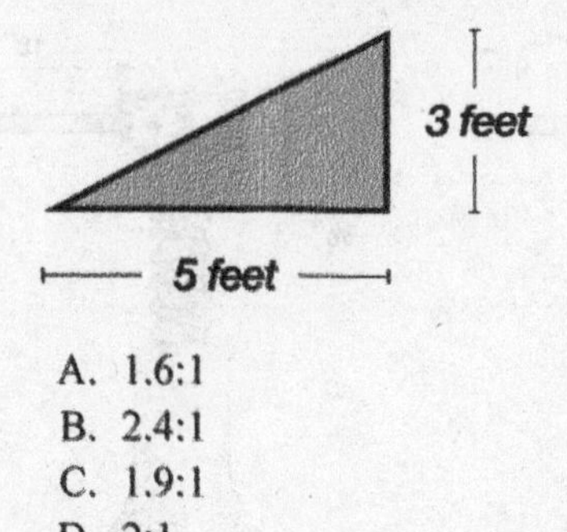


A. 1.6:1
B. 2.4:1
C. 1.9:1
D. 2:1

18. What is the mechanical advantage of using a 10-inch symmetrical wedge with a width (at the widest end) of 5 inches?

A. 3:1
B. 2:1
C. 4:1
D. there is no mechanical advantage

19. Which of the wheel-and-axle configurations shown in the figure below has the greatest mechanical advantage?

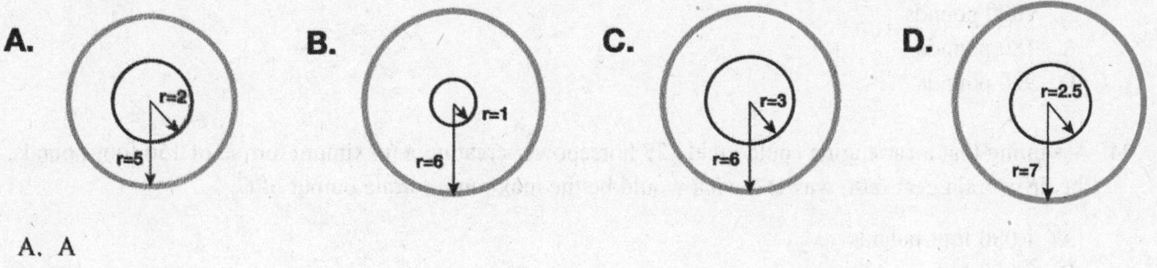


A. A
B. B
C. C
D. D

20. If an axle has a radius of 2 inches and its wheel has a radius of 5 inches, and 75 pounds of force can be applied, how much resistance can the wheel-and-axle move?

A. 115.27 pounds
B. 231.65 pounds
C. 188.4 pounds
D. 365.29 pounds

21. What is the mechanical advantage if resistance is 900 pounds and force is 180 pounds?

A. 3:1
B. 5:1
C. 2:1
D. 4:1

22. Given the various jackscrew configurations shown in the figure below, which has the greatest mechanical advantage?

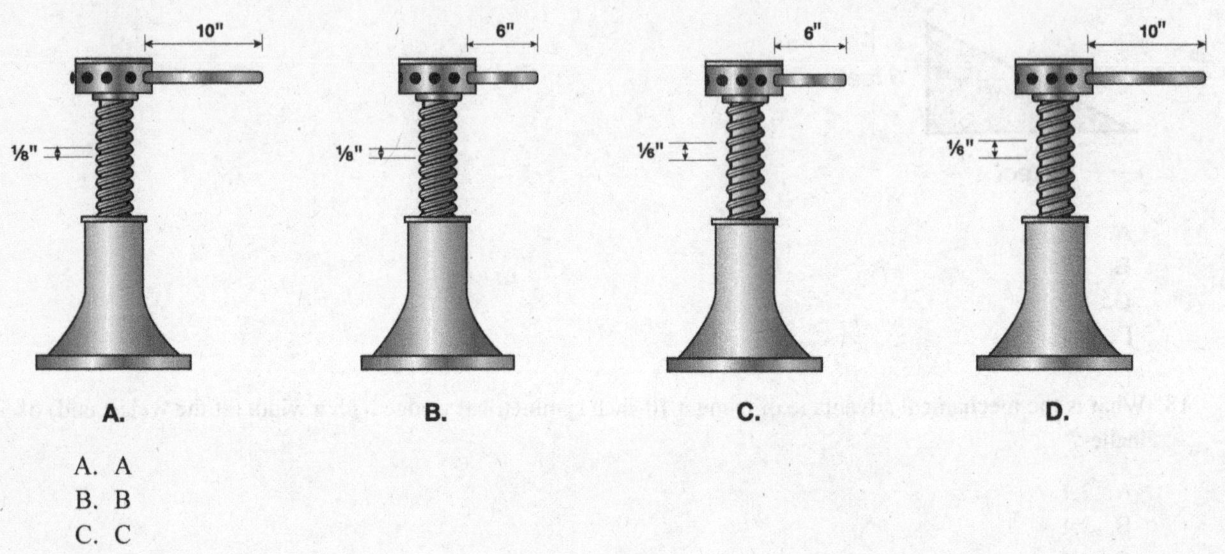


A. A
B. B
C. C
D. D

23. If a jackscrew has a mechanical advantage of 600:1, how much can be lifted if 30 pounds of effort is exerted?

A. 600 pounds
B. 1800 pounds
C. 180 pounds
D. 900 pounds

24. Assuming that a car engine could yield 225 horsepower creating a maximum torque of 150 foot-pounds, and the drive train gear ratio was 1:7, what would be the maximum torque output of $G_L$?

A. 1,000 foot-pounds
B. 1,050 foot-pounds
C. 1,100 foot-pounds
D. 1,150 foot-pounds

25. For a drive train that must change direction, which of the following gears would be used?

A. helical
B. spur
C. beveled
D. herringbone

## ASSEMBLING OBJECTS

You'll have 16 questions and 15 minutes to answer them.

1.

2.

3.

4.

5.

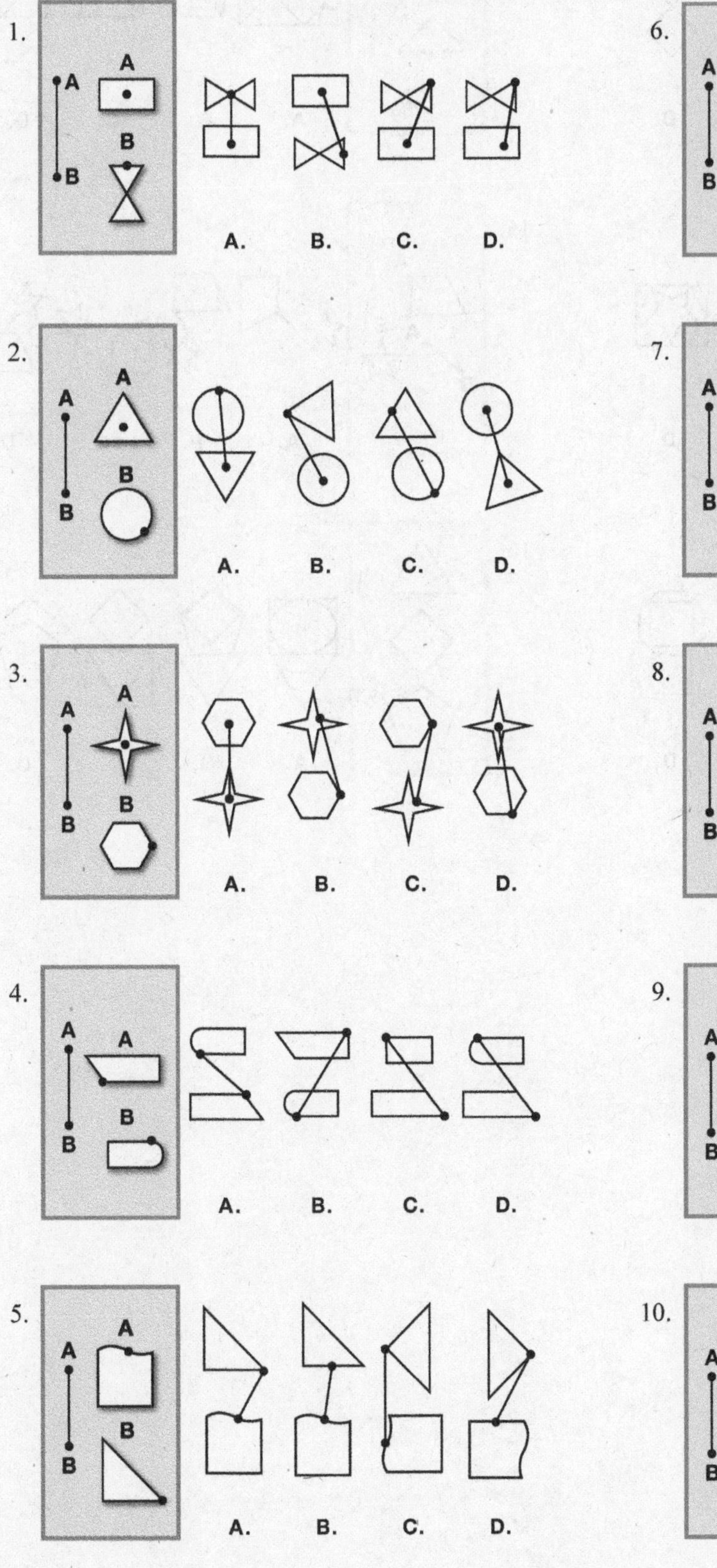


6.

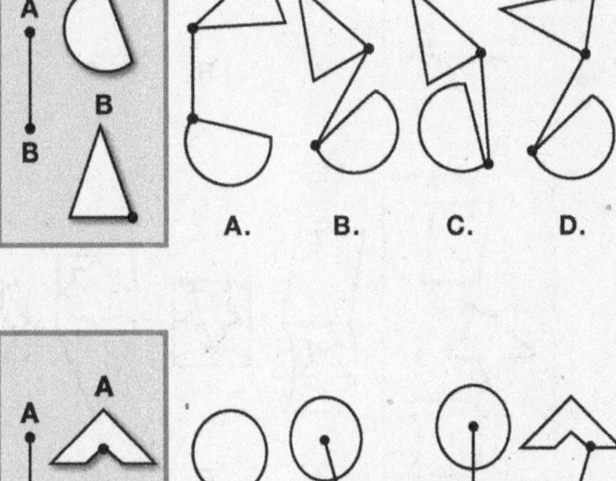


7.

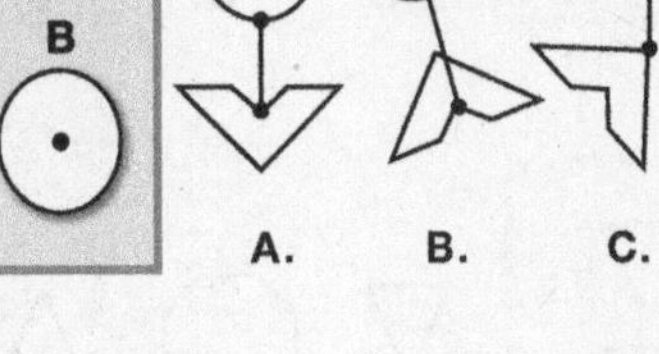


8.

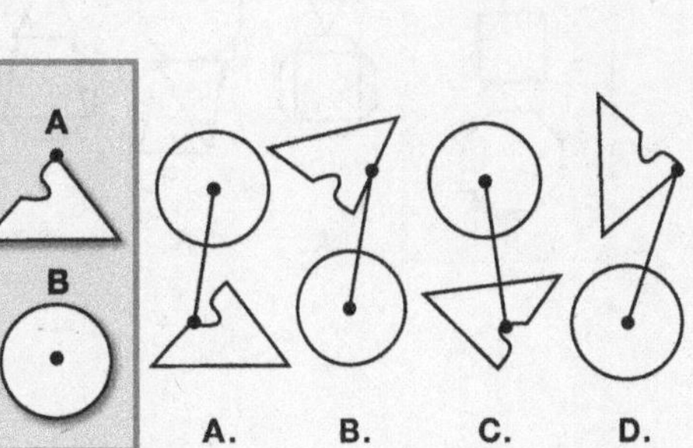


9.

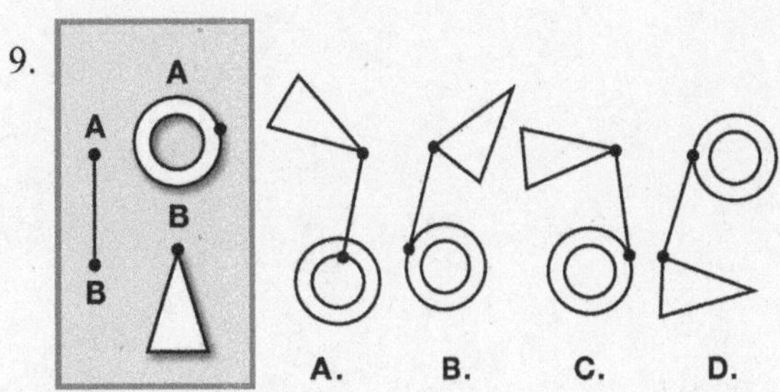


10.

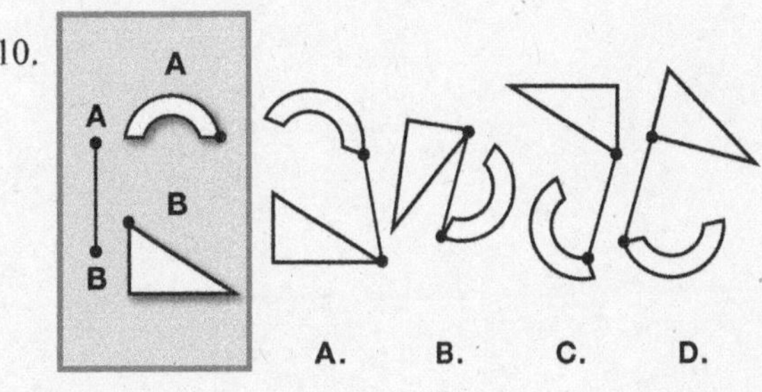

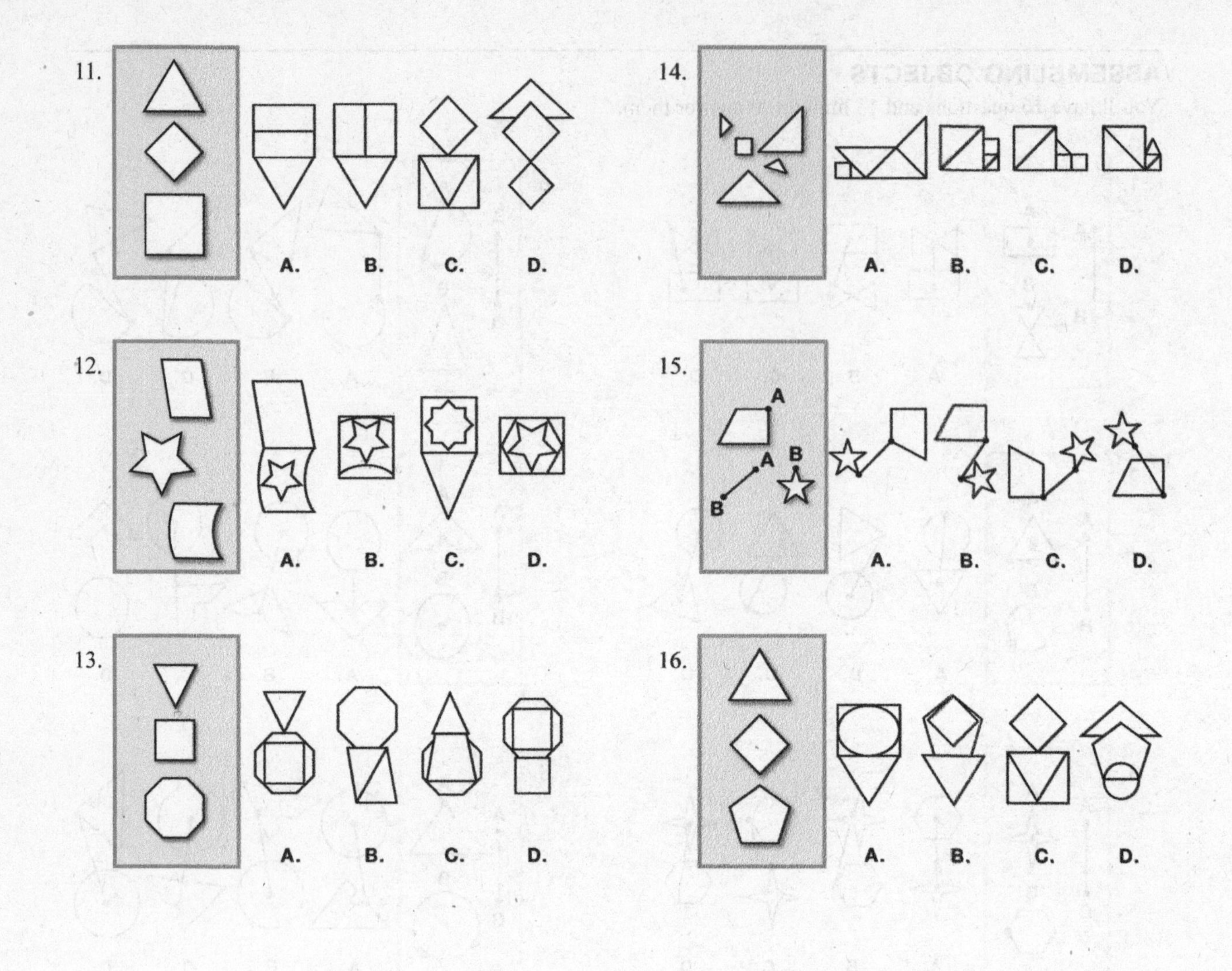
11.
A.
B.
C.
D.
14.
A.
B.
C.
D.
12.
A.
B.
C.
D.
15.
A
A
B
B
A.
B.
C.
D.
13.
A.
B.
C.
D.
16.
A.
B.
C.
D.

## ANSWER SHEET FOR PRACTICE TEST #3

### GENERAL SCIENCE

1. (A) (B) (C) (D)
2. (A) (B) (C) (D)
3. (A) (B) (C) (D)
4. (A) (B) (C) (D)
5. (A) (B) (C) (D)
6. (A) (B) (C) (D)
7. (A) (B) (C) (D)
8. (A) (B) (C) (D)
9. (A) (B) (C) (D)
10. (A) (B) (C) (D)
11. (A) (B) (C) (D)
12. (A) (B) (C) (D)
13. (A) (B) (C) (D)
14. (A) (B) (C) (D)
15. (A) (B) (C) (D)
16. (A) (B) (C) (D)
17. (A) (B) (C) (D)
18. (A) (B) (C) (D)
19. (A) (B) (C) (D)
20. (A) (B) (C) (D)
21. (A) (B) (C) (D)
22. (A) (B) (C) (D)
23. (A) (B) (C) (D)
24. (A) (B) (C) (D)
25. (A) (B) (C) (D)

### ARITHMETIC REASONING

1. (A) (B) (C) (D)
2. (A) (B) (C) (D)
3. (A) (B) (C) (D)
4. (A) (B) (C) (D)
5. (A) (B) (C) (D)
6. (A) (B) (C) (D)
7. (A) (B) (C) (D)
8. (A) (B) (C) (D)
9. (A) (B) (C) (D)
10. (A) (B) (C) (D)
11. (A) (B) (C) (D)
12. (A) (B) (C) (D)
13. (A) (B) (C) (D)
14. (A) (B) (C) (D)
15. (A) (B) (C) (D)
16. (A) (B) (C) (D)
17. (A) (B) (C) (D)
18. (A) (B) (C) (D)
19. (A) (B) (C) (D)
20. (A) (B) (C) (D)
21. (A) (B) (C) (D)
22. (A) (B) (C) (D)
23. (A) (B) (C) (D)
24. (A) (B) (C) (D)
25. (A) (B) (C) (D)
26. (A) (B) (C) (D)
27. (A) (B) (C) (D)
28. (A) (B) (C) (D)
29. (A) (B) (C) (D)
30. (A) (B) (C) (D)

### WORD KNOWLEDGE

1. (A) (B) (C) (D)
2. (A) (B) (C) (D)
3. (A) (B) (C) (D)
4. (A) (B) (C) (D)
5. (A) (B) (C) (D)
6. (A) (B) (C) (D)
7. (A) (B) (C) (D)
8. (A) (B) (C) (D)
9. (A) (B) (C) (D)
10. (A) (B) (C) (D)
11. (A) (B) (C) (D)
12. (A) (B) (C) (D)
13. (A) (B) (C) (D)
14. (A) (B) (C) (D)
15. (A) (B) (C) (D)
16. (A) (B) (C) (D)
17. (A) (B) (C) (D)
18. (A) (B) (C) (D)
19. (A) (B) (C) (D)
20. (A) (B) (C) (D)
21. (A) (B) (C) (D)

22. Ⓐ Ⓑ Ⓒ Ⓓ
23. Ⓐ Ⓑ Ⓒ Ⓓ
24. Ⓐ Ⓑ Ⓒ Ⓓ
25. Ⓐ Ⓑ Ⓒ Ⓓ
26. Ⓐ Ⓑ Ⓒ Ⓓ
27. Ⓐ Ⓑ Ⓒ Ⓓ
28. Ⓐ Ⓑ Ⓒ Ⓓ
29. Ⓐ Ⓑ Ⓒ Ⓓ
30. Ⓐ Ⓑ Ⓒ Ⓓ
31. Ⓐ Ⓑ Ⓒ Ⓓ
32. Ⓐ Ⓑ Ⓒ Ⓓ
33. Ⓐ Ⓑ Ⓒ Ⓓ
34. Ⓐ Ⓑ Ⓒ Ⓓ
35. Ⓐ Ⓑ Ⓒ Ⓓ

## PARAGRAPH COMPREHENSION

1. Ⓐ Ⓑ Ⓒ Ⓓ
2. Ⓐ Ⓑ Ⓒ Ⓓ
3. Ⓐ Ⓑ Ⓒ Ⓓ
4. Ⓐ Ⓑ Ⓒ Ⓓ
5. Ⓐ Ⓑ Ⓒ Ⓓ
6. Ⓐ Ⓑ Ⓒ Ⓓ
7. Ⓐ Ⓑ Ⓒ Ⓓ
8. Ⓐ Ⓑ Ⓒ Ⓓ
9. Ⓐ Ⓑ Ⓒ Ⓓ
10. Ⓐ Ⓑ Ⓒ Ⓓ
11. Ⓐ Ⓑ Ⓒ Ⓓ
12. Ⓐ Ⓑ Ⓒ Ⓓ
13. Ⓐ Ⓑ Ⓒ Ⓓ
14. Ⓐ Ⓑ Ⓒ Ⓓ
15. Ⓐ Ⓑ Ⓒ Ⓓ

## MATHEMATICS KNOWLEDGE

1. Ⓐ Ⓑ Ⓒ Ⓓ
2. Ⓐ Ⓑ Ⓒ Ⓓ
3. Ⓐ Ⓑ Ⓒ Ⓓ
4. Ⓐ Ⓑ Ⓒ Ⓓ
5. Ⓐ Ⓑ Ⓒ Ⓓ
6. Ⓐ Ⓑ Ⓒ Ⓓ
7. Ⓐ Ⓑ Ⓒ Ⓓ
8. Ⓐ Ⓑ Ⓒ Ⓓ
9. Ⓐ Ⓑ Ⓒ Ⓓ
10. Ⓐ Ⓑ Ⓒ Ⓓ
11. Ⓐ Ⓑ Ⓒ Ⓓ
12. Ⓐ Ⓑ Ⓒ Ⓓ
13. Ⓐ Ⓑ Ⓒ Ⓓ
14. Ⓐ Ⓑ Ⓒ Ⓓ
15. Ⓐ Ⓑ Ⓒ Ⓓ
16. Ⓐ Ⓑ Ⓒ Ⓓ
17. Ⓐ Ⓑ Ⓒ Ⓓ
18. Ⓐ Ⓑ Ⓒ Ⓓ
19. Ⓐ Ⓑ Ⓒ Ⓓ
20. Ⓐ Ⓑ Ⓒ Ⓓ
21. Ⓐ Ⓑ Ⓒ Ⓓ
22. Ⓐ Ⓑ Ⓒ Ⓓ
23. Ⓐ Ⓑ Ⓒ Ⓓ
24. Ⓐ Ⓑ Ⓒ Ⓓ
25. Ⓐ Ⓑ Ⓒ Ⓓ

## ELECTRONICS INFORMATION

1. Ⓐ Ⓑ Ⓒ Ⓓ
2. Ⓐ Ⓑ Ⓒ Ⓓ
3. Ⓐ Ⓑ Ⓒ Ⓓ
4. Ⓐ Ⓑ Ⓒ Ⓓ
5. Ⓐ Ⓑ Ⓒ Ⓓ
6. Ⓐ Ⓑ Ⓒ Ⓓ
7. Ⓐ Ⓑ Ⓒ Ⓓ
8. Ⓐ Ⓑ Ⓒ Ⓓ
9. Ⓐ Ⓑ Ⓒ Ⓓ
10. Ⓐ Ⓑ Ⓒ Ⓓ
11. Ⓐ Ⓑ Ⓒ Ⓓ
12. Ⓐ Ⓑ Ⓒ Ⓓ
13. Ⓐ Ⓑ Ⓒ Ⓓ
14. Ⓐ Ⓑ Ⓒ Ⓓ
15. Ⓐ Ⓑ Ⓒ Ⓓ
16. Ⓐ Ⓑ Ⓒ Ⓓ
17. Ⓐ Ⓑ Ⓒ Ⓓ
18. Ⓐ Ⓑ Ⓒ Ⓓ
19. Ⓐ Ⓑ Ⓒ Ⓓ
20. Ⓐ Ⓑ Ⓒ Ⓓ

## AUTOMOTIVE AND SHOP INFORMATION

| | | | | | | | | | | | | | | |
|---|---|---|---|---|---|---|---|---|---|---|---|---|---|---|
| 1. | A | B | C | D | 10. | A | B | C | D | 19. | A | B | C | D |
| 2. | A | B | C | D | 11. | A | B | C | D | 20. | A | B | C | D |
| 3. | A | B | C | D | 12. | A | B | C | D | 21. | A | B | C | D |
| 4. | A | B | C | D | 13. | A | B | C | D | 22. | A | B | C | D |
| 5. | A | B | C | D | 14. | A | B | C | D | 23. | A | B | C | D |
| 6. | A | B | C | D | 15. | A | B | C | D | 24. | A | B | C | D |
| 7. | A | B | C | D | 16. | A | B | C | D | 25. | A | B | C | D |
| 8. | A | B | C | D | 17. | A | B | C | D | | | | | |
| 9. | A | B | C | D | 18. | A | B | C | D | | | | | |

## MECHANICAL COMPREHENSION

| | | | | | | | | | | | | | | |
|---|---|---|---|---|---|---|---|---|---|---|---|---|---|---|
| 1. | A | B | C | D | 10. | A | B | C | D | 19. | A | B | C | D |
| 2. | A | B | C | D | 11. | A | B | C | D | 20. | A | B | C | D |
| 3. | A | B | C | D | 12. | A | B | C | D | 21. | A | B | C | D |
| 4. | A | B | C | D | 13. | A | B | C | D | 22. | A | B | C | D |
| 5. | A | B | C | D | 14. | A | B | C | D | 23. | A | B | C | D |
| 6. | A | B | C | D | 15. | A | B | C | D | 24. | A | B | C | D |
| 7. | A | B | C | D | 16. | A | B | C | D | 25. | A | B | C | D |
| 8. | A | B | C | D | 17. | A | B | C | D | | | | | |
| 9. | A | B | C | D | 18. | A | B | C | D | | | | | |

## ASSEMBLING OBJECTS

| | | | | | | | | | | | | | | |
|---|---|---|---|---|---|---|---|---|---|---|---|---|---|---|
| 1. | A | B | C | D | 7. | A | B | C | D | 13. | A | B | C | D |
| 2. | A | B | C | D | 8. | A | B | C | D | 14. | A | B | C | D |
| 3. | A | B | C | D | 9. | A | B | C | D | 15. | A | B | C | D |
| 4. | A | B | C | D | 10. | A | B | C | D | 16. | A | B | C | D |
| 5. | A | B | C | D | 11. | A | B | C | D | | | | | |
| 6. | A | B | C | D | 12. | A | B | C | D | | | | | |

## ANSWER KEY FOR PRACTICE TEST #3

Use the following answer key to grade your exam. Use the results to guide your review. (See Chapter 5 for strategies on how to do this.)

### GENERAL SCIENCE

1. **B.** The three types of blood cells are erythrocytes, thrombocytes, and leukocytes. Hemoglobin is a component of red blood cells but is not a type of blood cell itself, making answers A and C incorrect. White blood cells and leukocytes are the same thing, making answer D incorrect.

2. **A.** A catalyst is a substance that assists a chemical reaction but does not undergo a change itself. A catalyst is not necessary for a chemical reaction to occur, making answer B wrong. The reactants are the substances coming together to create the reaction, so answer C is incorrect. Catalysts are not destroyed during a reaction, making answer D incorrect.

3. **A.** A positive ion is an atom with more protons than electrons. An atom with an even number of protons and electrons is not an ion at all, making answer B incorrect. An atom with more electrons than protons is a negative ion, making answer C incorrect. Positive ions do exist, making answer D incorrect.

4. **D.** The two most abundant elements in the universe are hydrogen and helium. Hydrogen makes up about 75% of all elements and helium about 25%, with the other elements making up the rest. Nitrogen and oxygen are also very common elements but far less so than hydrogen and helium.

5. **B.** Meteorologists are interested in the study of the earth's atmosphere, especially as it relates to weather and climate. Meteors are more likely to be studied by astronomers (making answer A incorrect). While they may measure things, this is not their primary purpose, making answer C incorrect. Geologists, not meteorologists, are involved in the study of the structure of the earth, making answer D incorrect.

6. **A.** A blind study is designed to correct for a researcher's bias in favor of a hypothesis.

7. **D.** A nanogram is 1 billionth of a gram.

8. **B.** Darwin's theory of natural selection (sometimes called survival of the fittest) means a population that adapts to its environment is more likely to thrive. While it is true that organisms in good health are more likely to survive (answer B), that is not the point of Darwin's theory. Neither is the triumph of predator over prey (answer C). While it is true that populations can change for the worse over time, this is likely to lead to their extinction, not their survival, making answer D incorrect.

9. **A.** Meiosis is a type of cell division that allows a parent cell to produce two daughter cells with only half the genetic material of the parent cell. The type of cell division that allows a parent cell to produce two daughter cells with the exact same genetic material as the parent cell (answer B) is mitosis. Answer C is a type of cell division that doesn't occur, and answer D is not true.

10. **B.** *Homo sapiens* is the species name for humans.

11. **A.** Most vertebrates are cold-blooded. They tend to be symmetrical bilaterally (e.g., having two arms and two legs, one on each side), making answer A incorrect. They also tend to have well-developed sense organs (making answer C incorrect) and they often have appendages used for locomotion (e.g., legs), making answer D incorrect.

12. **D.** Your vestibular system helps you maintain your balance. It has no connection to the lunar cycle, so answer A is incorrect. We understand its function, so answer B is incorrect. While the vestibular system is located in the inner ear, it is not responsible for hearing, making answer C incorrect.

13. **A.** Points of articulation in your body are called joints.

14. **B.** An irregular heart beat is called arrhythmia. High blood pressure (answer A) is a measure of how hard your heart is working, not how it's beating. Bradycardia (answer C) is a slow heart beat, and not necessarily irregular. Tachycardia (answer D) is a fast heart beat, and not necessarily irregular.

15. **A.** Your esophagus connects your throat to your stomach. Your nasal cavity is connected to your lungs via your pharynx, larynx, and trachea, making answer B incorrect. C and D are not true.

16. **A.** An individual with a dominant gene and a recessive gene for a trait will tend to express the dominant gene. An individual with a dominant gene is unlikely to express the recessive gene, meaning answer B is incorrect. An individual with both a dominant and a recessive gene for a trait is equally likely to pass on either gene (there is a 1:2 likelihood that the dominant gene will be passed on and a 1:2 likelihood that the recessive gene will be passed on), making both answers C and D incorrect.

17. **D.** A lack of potassium in the diet would affect your muscles most seriously because they require potassium to function.

18. **A.** During the late Jurassic period (which started about 161 million years ago), dinosaurs flourished. Most species that we recognize as human did not evolve until the Pleistocene, about 2.6 million years ago. The earliest humans did not appear until the Pliocene, about 5.3 million years ago. Thus, answers B and D are incorrect. The earth began to cool once it was formed about 4.5 billion years ago, meaning answer C is incorrect.

19. **B.** The most common way for fossils to be formed is through the process of perimineralization. While an organism could be trapped in amber (answer A) and become a fossil, this is more uncommon than B, making B a more correct answer. Being trapped under heavy pressure (answer C) is more likely to destroy an organism versus create a fossil of it. While fossils have been found of organisms that were deliberately buried (answer D), this is by no means the most common process of fossilization.

20. **C.** A body of water that is partly salt but is neither seawater nor fresh water is called brackish. While a lagoon (answer A) and an estuary (answer B) can contain brackish water, a partly salt body of water isn't necessarily a lagoon or an estuary, making C the better answer. While a body of water with salt in it could be called saline (answer D), the actual term used to described such a body of water is "brackish."

21. **D.** When a cloud accumulates sufficient water vapor, it could rain, sleet, hail, or snow. Water vapor in a cloud does not create a cold front or cause tornados, though clouds with a lot of water vapor can accompany those conditions. Thus, answers A and B are incorrect. While C is correct in that a cloud with sufficient water vapor could rain, answer D is more correct, because such a cloud might cause also snow, sleet, or hail.

22. **A.** Our solar system contains eight planets. There are billions of planets in our galaxy but not our solar system, making answer B incorrect. While earth has one moon, it is not the lone planet in our solar system, making answer C incorrect. Our solar system does not contain the Milky Way galaxy; the Milky Way galaxy contains our solar system, making answer D incorrect.

23. **A.** Scalar measures quantify magnitude only, making B, C, and D incorrect.

24. **D.** Kinetic energy takes the forms of vibrational, rotational, and translational. While it's true that some kinetic energy could be potential as in answer A, that is true of any type of energy, not just kinetic energy, making D a more accurate answer. Answer B is also possibly correct in the sense that you could use kinetic energy to move, but these are not the three main categories scientists use when referring to kinetic energy. While momentum, power, and acceleration (answer C) are related to energy, they have to do with how energy moves objects and aren't specific to kinetic energy, again making D the better answer.

25. **A.** Sound waves travel through air more quickly than through water. The other three answers are incorrect.

## ARITHMETIC REASONING

1. **B.**

$$\begin{array}{r} 132.069 \\ -130.690 \\ \hline 1.379 \end{array}$$

Therefore, $x = 1.379$.

2. **C.**

$$\begin{array}{r} 17.671 \\ +8.53 \\ \hline 26.201 \end{array}$$

Therefore, $x = 26.201$.

3. **C.** Division must be done first: $\mathbf{14.87 \div 2.5} = 5.948$. (This is easiest to calculate as $\mathbf{1487 \div 250}$ then putting the decimal point back into the answer.) Then, $\mathbf{17 - 5.948 + 3.61 = 14.662}$, or 14.66 rounded down to the nearest hundredth.

4. **D.** If we divide the heat transformed into work by the total amount of heat produced and multiply that quotient by 100, we can determine this particular engine's thermal efficiency.

$$\frac{\mathbf{60000\ BTU}}{\mathbf{75000\ BTU}} \bullet \mathbf{100} = x$$

$x = 82.75\%$

5. **B.** By multiplying the total BTU produced by the engine to its thermal efficiency, we can determine the number of BTU that are utilized for work. So, 87,500 BTU × 0.613 = 53,637.5 BTU.

6. **A.** 16,000 pounds divided by $8\frac{35}{100}$ pounds = $x$ gallons of water.

$8\frac{35}{100}$ can also be represented as $\frac{835}{100}$, so:

$$16000 \div \frac{835}{100} = x$$

To divide with fractions, multiply the inverse:

$$16000 \bullet \frac{100}{835} = x$$

$x = 1{,}916.17$ gallons of water.

7. **A.** A hexagonal nut has six sides. We can think of the nut as being a six-sided polygon. Since each side is equal in length, we can simply multiply the length of one side by 6 to determine perimeter length. Therefore, $6 \bullet \frac{2}{3} = \frac{12}{3} = 4$ centimeters.

8. **A.** The difference is equal to the factory specs minus the micrometer reading. 1.750 – 1.732 = 0.018 inches.

9. **D.** What first must be determined is how much dry chemical agent was used to extinguish the fire.

$8\frac{1}{2}$ pounds $-3\frac{1}{4}$ pounds $= x$. The lowest (least) common denominator is 4, so the problem can be restated as $8\frac{2}{4} - 3\frac{1}{4} = x$. Thus, $x = 5\frac{1}{4}$ pounds.

Now, to determine what percentage $5\frac{1}{4}$ pounds represents, simply divide $5\frac{1}{4}$ by the extinguisher's capacity, $8\frac{1}{2}$ pounds. $5\frac{1}{4} = \frac{21}{4}$ and $8\frac{1}{2} = \frac{17}{2}$, so $\frac{21}{4} \div \frac{17}{2}$. To divide fractions, multiply by the inverse: $\frac{21}{4} \bullet \frac{2}{17} = \frac{42}{68}$.

Then multiply by 100 to determine the percentage: $\frac{42}{68} \bullet 100 = \frac{4200}{68} = 61.76\%$ (rounded down to the nearest hundredth).

10. **D.** Since 14 fatalities were recorded in 1990, we can figure the number of fatalities in the present year by setting up the problem as shown, if $x$ = the number of fatalities in the present year:

$$\frac{x - \text{fatalities in 1990}}{\text{fatalities in 1990}} = 4.5$$

Therefore:

$$\frac{x - 14}{14} = 4.5$$

Multiply both sides by 14 to get rid of the fraction and $x - 14 = 63$. Then add 14 to both sides of the equation to isolate $x$ and determine that $x = 77$.

11. **D.** The device weighs 4.75 pounds and is composed of 67% copper, so 3.1825. $4.75 \times 0.67 = 3.1825$ pounds represents the amount of copper present in the device. Since there are 16 ounces per pound, we can multiply 3.1825 by 16, which will give us the amount of copper present. $x = 50.92$ ounces.

12. **C.** The solution to this problem can be set up as 20% of 2 liters + an unknown quantity of 0% (distilled water) = 5%.

$$0.20(2) + x(0\%) = 0.05(x + 2)$$

Thus, $0.40 + 0 = 0.5x + 0.1$. Then, multiply both sides by 100 to get rid of the decimals: $40 = 5x + 10$. Then subtract 10 from both sides: $30 = 5x$. Finally, divide by 5 to isolate $x$. $x = 6$ liters of distilled water.

13. **A.** If the public relations expert was gone from home a total of 9 hours, and he spent $4\frac{1}{2}$ hours of that time conducting a lecture, that would mean his total travel time was $4\frac{1}{2}$ hours.

If $x$ = driving speed getting to Creston (2 hours), then $x - 15$ = driving speed returning home (2.5 hours). Therefore:

$$2 \text{ hours} \bullet x = 2.5 \text{ hours}(x - 15)$$

So:

$$2x = 2.5x - 37.5$$

Multiply both sides by 10 to get rid of the decimals:

$$20x = 25x - 375$$

Subtract 25x from both sides of the equation:

$$-5x = -375$$

Divide both sides by $-5$ to determine that 75 mph was the speed going to the lecture. $75 - 15 = 60$, or the speed returning from the lecture.

14. **A.** Let $\frac{1}{3}x$ represent Public Information Officers; $\frac{1}{2}x$ represent those that work in supply; 5 be the number of Police Liaison Officers; and $x$ be the sum of personnel under the supervision of the Chief of Operations. Therefore, $\frac{1}{3}x + \frac{1}{2}x + 5 = x$.

Using the lowest (least) common denominator, the equation would be restated as $\frac{2}{6}x + \frac{3}{6}x + 5 = x$. Or, $\frac{5}{6}x + 5 = x$.

Subtract $\frac{5}{6}x$ from both sides of the equation to get $5 = x - \frac{5}{6}$. If $x$ is the same is $1x$ (and it is) we could also represent $1x$ as $\frac{6}{6}x$, which means we could subtract $\frac{5}{6}$ from it: $5 = \frac{1}{6}x$. Multiply both sides of the equation by 6 to isolate $x$ and determine that $x = 30$.

15. **D.** A room has four walls plus a ceiling that will require replacement drywall (the floor is not made of drywall). The ceiling accounts for 25 feet × 27 feet or 675 square feet. The two walls measuring 27 feet × 9.6 feet account for 518.4 square feet and the other two walls measuring 25 feet × 9.6 feet account for 480 square feet. Total square feet of drywall required for this room then is 675 sq. ft. + 518.4 sq. ft. + 480 sq. ft. or 1,673.4 sq. ft. However, this number does not take into account the door and windows. The square footage of doors and windows should be subtracted from this total to determine the actual amount of drywall needed. 1,673.4 sq. ft. – 48.5 sq. ft. = 1,624.9 sq. ft. Choice C does not account for the square footage of drywall required for the ceiling. Choice A does not account for the door and window.

16. **B.** Simply multiply the fractions together to reach the likely proportion: $\frac{1}{4} \bullet \frac{1}{2} = \frac{1}{8}$.

17. **C.** The total number of patrons is 152. Divide the number of patrons picking donuts by the total number of patrons (115 ÷ 152) to get a decimal of 0.76 (rounded to the nearest hundredth). Multiply by 100 to determine what percentage this represents: 76%.

18. **B.** Simply divide 120 by 16. The result 7.5 must be rounded up to 8 since stylists can't be divided.

19. **A.** If Jay has $100 per year for the policy ($50 every six months), then he can purchase 12.5 units ($100 divided by $8). Since a unit equals $1000 in coverage, 12.5 units is $12,500 in coverage.

20. **D.** There are 16 ounces in a pound. Determine the cost per ounce (rounding down to the nearest penny): $\$27.99 \div 16 = \$2.15$. Since each serving requires 3 ounces, the total per serving is $6.45.

21. **C.** If 25 people = 5% of the total (100% minus the 95% who received accurate results), we know that they represent $\frac{1}{20}$ of the people who took the test. Therefore $25 \bullet \frac{1}{20} = 500$.

22. **B.** In this sequence, every other number is a whole number that increases by 1 as the sequence continues, and the number that follows it is its square. So the number following 5 must be its square, or 25.

23. **A.** To find the fifth term, let $n = 5$, then simply multiply $3 \times 5$ and add 3, to come up with 18.

24. **C.** Greta's base pay for a six-hour shift works out to $\mathbf{\$9.75 \bullet 6 = \$58.50}$. She earns \$0.475 per drink served and she serves 15 drinks an hour, or 90 drinks in a six-hour shift. So she earns \$42.75 in the tips she generates. Additionally, she gets 10% of the \$75 an hour the servers earn. That's \$7.50 an hour times the 6 hours in her shift, or another \$45. So, on average, Greta earns \$58.50 + \$42.75 + \$45 = \$146.25.

25. **D.** 15% of \$480 is \$72, so $\mathbf{\$480 - \$72 = \$408}$. Subtract the additional \$25 and the total price paid is \$383.

26. **B.** Eliminate the highest (99%) and lowest (67%) scores, leaving 74%, 86%, 93%, and 85%. Add them together (338) and divide by 4 (the number of score being averaged) to reach 84.5%.

27. **A.** To determine the percent change, divide the new value by the old value: $\mathbf{152 \div 116 = 1.31}$. Then multiply by 100 to determine the percentage (131%), and subtract 100% to determine the percent change: 31%.

28. **C.** If the area of a square is one side squared, then the square root of the area will yield the length of one side. $\sqrt{81} = 9$.

29. **A.** This is a simple ratio. If 1= 100, then 3.7 = $\mathbf{3.7 \bullet 100}$, or 370 miles.

30. **D.** To determine a percentage change, divide the new number by the old number: $\mathbf{119 \div 150 = 0.79}$. Multiply by 100 to determine the percentage (79%), then subtract 100% to determine the percentage change: **−21%**.

## WORD KNOWLEDGE

Note: The answers have been provided for the vocabulary section without explanation. If further reference is needed, consult a dictionary.

| | | | |
|---|---|---|---|
| 1. **A.** | 10. **A.** | 19. **C.** | 28. **D.** |
| 2. **B.** | 11. **A.** | 20. **A.** | 29. **A.** |
| 3. **C.** | 12. **C.** | 21. **C.** | 30. **D.** |
| 4. **C.** | 13. **D.** | 22. **B.** | 31. **B.** |
| 5. **B.** | 14. **A.** | 23. **D.** | 32. **A.** |
| 6. **A.** | 15. **B.** | 24. **B.** | 33. **D.** |
| 7. **D.** | 16. **B.** | 25. **B.** | 34. **C.** |
| 8. **D.** | 17. **A.** | 26. **C.** | 35. **A.** |
| 9. **C.** | 18. **D.** | 27. **A.** | |

## PARAGRAPH COMPREHENSION

1. **D.** The passage states that a defendant has the right to appear before a judge within twenty-four hours to seek a release. A is incorrect because the passage does not say the defendant only has 24 hours to ask for bail. B is incorrect because the passage states that a defendant can be released without bail. C is incorrect because the passage says the judge only has to consider the request, not that he or she must grant it.

2. **B.** The passage states that Mithraism influenced Christianity. A is incorrect because the passage clearly states that the rites are Mithraic and that they influenced the development of Christianity. C is incorrect because it is stated that Mithraism influenced Christianity, not the other way around. D is incorrect because Mithraism was a Roman religion.

3. **A.** The passage states that ancient medicine was based on the four elements. B is incorrect because the passage specifically relates humor to temperament (a sanguine person was calm, while choleric people were easily angered). C is incorrect because the passage states that people of different humors were treated in different ways. D is incorrect because the passage states that all people belonged to one of four humors.

4. **A.** The passage describes the history of the Hagia Sophia. B is incorrect because the passage focuses on just one cathedral. C is incorrect for the same reason; the passage focuses on just one Byzantine church. D is incorrect because while the building is now a museum, the passage states that it was one of the most spectacular religious buildings ever built and is the most famous Byzantine building, meaning that "modest" is not a good word to describe it.

5. **C.** The passage states that the spread of neo-Confucianism inspired many petty noblemen to demand social and political reform. A is incorrect because this was a Korean dynasty, not a Chinese dynasty. B is incorrect because it was a reaction to the spread of neo-Confucianism, not a cause of it. D is incorrect because the dynasty survived for many years, and the passage doesn't say anything about how brutal it might or might not have been.

6. **B.** The passage says a number of important ancient structures still stand. A is incorrect because the passage does not convey that judgment. C is incorrect because the passage states that the University of Cambridge was founded in the thirteenth century, not that the city itself was established then. D is incorrect because the city is said to be located in central England.

7. **C.** Since ancestors were thought to have great power to protect the family, disrespecting them could cause one's family to take offense. A is incorrect because the passage doesn't support it; the passage states that ancestors could intercede with God/gods, which implies that people might believe in other religions while still practicing ancestor worship. B is incorrect because veneration implies showing respect through a ritual act such as prayer or sacrifice. D is incorrect because the passage states that if the ancestors were not respected, they could cause harm and misfortune.

8. **B.** The passages states that performers at the Grand Ole Opry say they feel as if they have joined a family. A is incorrect because the passage says that it pays very little. C is incorrect because the passage states that performers are invited and that it is an honor and a privilege (so therefore not something just anyone could do). D is incorrect because the passage talks about singers, not actors.

9. **D.** The passage supports this conclusion the best because the others are inaccurate for one reason or another. A is incorrect because the passage states that entertainment such as music and dancing was always provided. B is incorrect because the passage states that feasts were held for all kinds of reasons, such as the completion of a time-consuming task, like harvest. C is incorrect because the passage states that feasts had spectators who watched the retinue eat, though they themselves did not partake.

10. **D.** The passage states three different reasons why the IRS randomly audits business owners. A is incorrect because the passage does state three different reasons why the IRS conducts audits. B is incorrect because nowhere in the passage does the author imply or state this. C is incorrect because the passage states that regular people are not audited as often as businesses are.

11. **D.** The passage gives a considerable amount of information about Angkor Wat, and the other three answers are incorrect, making D the best answer. A, B, and C are incorrect because they are directly supported in the passage.

12. **A.** The passage states that Basques have always been independent and freedom-loving. B is incorrect because the passage states that even after a united Spanish kingdom was founded, the Basques maintained their own customs, laws, and foreign relations. C is incorrect because the passage states that law and order was maintained through assemblies that were democratically elected and which represented the voices of all classes of people. D is incorrect because the passage states that they created strict laws and says nothing about their having a nomadic existence.
13. **C.** A quick review of the passage will show the correct meaning of the acronym.
14. **B.** The definition is specifically given in the sentence that uses "voir dire."
15. **C.** The passage describes what a building inspector should know and think about before doing an inspection, and how he/she should act during one. A is incorrect because the passage is intended to help building inspectors, not property owners. B is incorrect for the same reason. D is incorrect because while the passage does talk about some characteristics of a good building inspector (demonstrating a positive attitude that conveys a willingness to work with, not against, a property owner) the main point of the passage is to convey the knowledge the inspector needs to have (not just the characteristics he/she needs to possess).

## MATHEMATICS KNOWLEDGE

1. **C.** The formula for the volume of a sphere is $V = \frac{4}{3}\pi r^3$. The radius is half the diameter, so $r = 36.375$. So,

$$V = \frac{4}{3}(3.1416)(36.375^3)$$

According to the order of operations, we do the exponents first:

$$V = \frac{4}{3}(3.1416)(48{,}129.239)$$

Then multiply from left to right. So, V = 201,603.76 cubic centimeters.

2. **B.** The volume of a cylinder is determined by the formula $V = \pi r^2 h$. Since we are calculating the volume of the liquid in the tank (and the tank isn't full), the level of the liquid (20.7 feet) will serve as the height of the cylinder. The radius is equal to half the diameter, or in this case, $r = 9.25$ feet. So, $V = 3.1416(9.25^2)(20.7)$ or 5,564.2252 cubic feet. Therefore, to figure the number of gallons of liquid involved, we multiply this volume by 7.48 gallons (since we know that each cubic foot of space contains this many gallons of liquid). So, 5,564.2252 × 7.48 = 41,620.404 gallons.
3. **D.** The volume of rectangular space is calculated using the formula $V = lwh$. Therefore: $14{,}364 = (18)(38)h$. Or $14{,}364 = 684h$. Divide both sides by 684 to isolate the variable: $h = 21$ inches.
4. **B.** In a set of coordinates, the first number refers to the $x$-axis and the second refers to the $y$-axis.
5. **D.** The way to express "less than or equal to" is with the $\leq$ symbol.
6. **C.** If you know that $x = 3$, then just plug that value in place of $x$ in the expression. Remember to calculate exponents first, so $3^2 = 9$, then multiply by 2 to get 18.
7. **B.** The square of a number is that number multiplied by itself. If you multiply two negative numbers, you get a positive number. Therefore, $-5 \bullet -5 = 25$.
8. **D.** Solve as you would any equation. In this case, multiply both sides by 5 (the reciprocal of the fraction) to isolate $x$. Thus, $x > 25$.

9. **B.** All of the angles of a triangle add up to 180°. A right triangle has one 90° angle, and the problem states that a second angle has 45°. That means the third angle must also be 45° in order for all of the angles to add up to 180°.

10. **A.** To solve for $x$, first add 2 to both sides of the equation to isolate the unknown. Thus $5x = 15$. Then divide both sides of the equation by 5 to determine that $x = 3$.

11. **C.** The definition of a scalene triangle is one with no equal sides and no equal angles. Each of the other answers has a different definition.

12. **D.** Divide both sides by $-3$ to determine that $x = -6$. Since the product of two negative numbers is a positive number, we know that $-3 \bullet -6 = 18$, so our answer is correct.

13. **A.** Multiply both sides by 3 to isolate $x$. Thus, $x = 54$.

14. **C.** To solve the inequality, divide both sides of the inequality by $-2$. The result is $-2$, but remember that when you divide an inequality by a negative number you have to reverse the direction of the inequality sign. So, $x < -2$.

15. **B.** The formula for calculating the total measurement of the angles of a polygon is $180(n-2)°$, and an octagon has 8 sides, so $180 \times 6 = 1080°$.

16. **C.** Since "part" means unit and doesn't specify which unit, as long as the units for water and cleaning product are the same, then the proportion of water to cleaning product is 4:1. So, if Sam is using gallons of water, he is also using gallons of cleaning product. So we know that

$\frac{\text{4 gallons water}}{\text{1 gallon cleaning product}} = \frac{\text{6 gallons water}}{x \text{ gallons cleaning product}}$. Cross-multiplication tells us that $4x = 6$. Divide both sides by 4 to determine that $x = 1.5$ gallons of cleaning product.

17. **B.** To add fractions, remember that $\frac{a}{b} + \frac{c}{d} = \frac{ad + bc}{bd}$. So, plugging in the fractions for this problem yields: $\frac{3x + 5(2 - x)}{15}$, which can be simplified as $\frac{-2x + 10}{15}$.

18. **A.** To subtract fractions, remember that $\frac{a}{b} - \frac{c}{d} = \frac{ad - bc}{bd}$. So, plugging in the fractions for this problem yields $\frac{(x+2)(x-3)-5}{5(x-3)}$. This can be further simplified. Let's start with the denominator. $5(x-3) = 5x - 15$. The numerator is a bit more complicated. First, start by multiplying $(x+2)(x-3)$, which can be written as $x(x-3) + 2(x-3)$. That can be calculated as $x^2 - 3x + 2x - 6$. But the original numerator also had a $-5$, so we need to add that: $x^2 - 3x + 2x - 6 - 5$. Then doing some addition and subtraction, we get $x^2 - x - 11$. That's just the numerator, so put it together with the denominator, and you have $\frac{x^2 - x - 11}{5x - 15}$.

19. **A.** A polynomial cannot be divided by an unknown.

20. **C.** The equation can be restated as $x(x-4) + 3(x-4)$. Then, multiply to get: $x^2 - 4x + 3x - 12$. Do a little addition to get $x^2 - x - 12$.

21. **D.** The solution to a quadratic equation is called its root. In many cases (like this one), a quadratic equation has more than one root. To solve this, add 9 to both sides of the equation to isolate the unknown, making $x^2 = 9$. The square root of 9 is 3, so $x = 3$. But the square root of 9 can also be $-3$, since the product of two negative numbers is a positive. So D is most correct.

22. **A.** The probability of an independent event is generally calculated as the number of selected outcomes (for example, picking heads, which is one outcome) divided by the total number of possible outcomes (in the case of a coin toss, 2).

23. **C.** The number of selected outcomes (picking a winning code) is 2. The number of total possible outcomes is 7. Her chances are then 2 in 7 of picking a winning code.

24. **D.** To solve for two unknowns given that both equations are true, substitute one of the equations for *y* in the other equation. Thus, $x+5=3x+3$. Then subtract *x* from both sides to get $5=2x+3$. Then subtract 3 from both sides to get $2=2x$. Then divide both sides by 2 to get $x=1$. Plug the value of *x* into the equations to determine that $y = 6$.

25. **C.** In this case, you can't solve for both unknowns by substituting one equation for the other. However, you can add one equation to the other to eliminate one of the variables. So,

$$3x+2y+(-3x)+7y=13+5$$

Thus, $9y=18$. Divide both sides by 9 to determine that $y = 2$. Plug that value into the original equation to find *x*: $3x+2(2)=13$. Or, $3x+4=13$. Subtract 4 from both sides of the equation to determine that $3x=9$. Then divide both sides of the equation by 3 to find $x = 3$.

## ELECTRONICS INFORMATION

1. **A.** Metals are in general good conductors of electricity; copper wire is particularly suitable.
2. **D.** $1\mu\Omega$ is one millionth of an ohm.
3. **A.** An ohm is a measure of resistance.
4. **A.** A kw (kilowatt) is 1,000 watts.
5. **D.** This is just an adaptation of Ohm's Law. In this case, resistance equals voltage divided by current.
6. **C.** AC power can be sent out at much higher voltages than DC power, then stepped down before it gets to the electrical panel in your house.
7. **B.** Negative charges are attracted to positive charges.
8. **A.** An electric current is the flow of electrons.
9. **B.** In a series circuit, if the first resistor (such as a light bulb) stops working, then all the others in the circuit quit working, too.
10. **C.** This is a parallel circuit because each resistor (light bulb) is wired independently.
11. **C.** Formula for current (amperes) is voltage divided by resistance. In a series circuit, the total resistance is the sum of $R_1$ and $R_2$. So, 15 volts divided by 5 ohms equals 3 amperes.
12. **A.** A joule is 1 watt per second. A half hour has 1,800 seconds, so 1 watt per half hour is 1,800 joules. 100 watts in a half hour is 180,000 joules.
13. **A.** The series is wired in parallel, so if one resistor (light bulb) quits working, the rest will continue to work.
14. **D.** An inductor contains electric potential. A may seem correct, but an actual charge is stored in a capacitor.
15. **C.** A ground fault circuit interrupter is wired at the outlet, not at the panel. It must be reset, but so, too, must a circuit breaker.
16. **D.** This is the only true statement.

17. **A.** In a series circuit, the total voltage drop is the sum of the voltage drop across each resistor.
18. **D.** This is the symbol for an AC power source.
19. **C.** The symbol is for a resistor. A switch uses a different symbol.
20. **B.** Voltage is simply current times resistance.

## AUTOMOTIVE AND SHOP INFORMATION

1. **B.** A coolant leak will make the cooling system less effective, likely resulting in the engine overheating. The other options are unlikely to happen because of a coolant leak.
2. **D.** The crankshaft connects to the flywheel.
3. **A.** Compression comes after intake. The 4-stroke cycle goes in this order: intake, compression, combustion, exhaust.
4. **B.** The illustration shows a piston and cylinder, and the arrows are pointing to the intake and exhaust valves.
5. **A.** A continuously variable transmission has basically any number of gear ratios, as opposed to a regular transmission, which rarely has more than 6.
6. **C.** If "AWD" is an abbreviation for All Wheel Drive.
7. **D.** The main components of most vehicles' electrical systems are the battery, starter, and alternator.
8. **C.** Most car batteries are 12-volt rechargeable batteries.
9. **B.** Fuel injectors serve the same function as carburetors, to create the correct mixture of fuel and air.
10. **C.** A catalytic converter changes exhaust chemicals into carbon dioxide and water.
11. **B.** A hydrometer is a tool for measuring the specific gravity of electrolytes in batteries. Positive crankcase ventilation (choice A), evaporative controls (choice C), and air injection (choice D) are all methods of emissions control.
12. **B.** Straight snips, better known as tin snips. Side-cutting and end-cutting pliers are used primarily to cut wire.
13. **A.** Torque wrench. Such wrenches can accurately determine the amount of torque that is being applied to a given nut or bolt (e.g., cylinder-head bolts on an engine, as recommended by the manufacturer).
14. **D.** Wedge felling axe. A hatchet has a smaller head designed more to trim wood than to fell trees.
15. **C.** Masonry. A skimmer float is the tool pictured. It is used to create a smooth finish on wet concrete or plaster.
16. **B.** Bolt cutters would be the most appropriate tool used to cut chain link. Straight snips are better used to cut thin sheet metal instead of thick round metal stock. A hacksaw could cut either the lock or the chain; however, it would be significantly slower and more inconvenient to use than bolt cutters.
17. **D.** A machinist's vise would be better suited for this purpose. Channel lock pliers are handheld and can only exert as much pressure on metal stock as an individual's strength will allow. Filing the metal stock with one hand while holding it with the other is neither efficient nor safe. Pipe clamps are better suited for holding boards together for glue bonding. Parallel clamps could conceivably work by holding the metalwork piece to a workbench or something of that order. However, a machinist's vise provides a better grip, thus preventing the metalwork piece from inadvertently shifting.
18. **C.** An awl is principally used to start holes in wood to accommodate screws or nails.

19. **A.** Choices B, C, and D all have various applications in the metalworking trade. A feeler gauge however, is used in the automotive trade. It is specifically used to measure the gap between various items within an engine (e.g., shaft and bearings, spark plug electrodes, etc.).

20. **C.** The joinery shown is a dovetail cut, created by a portable electric router. A tenon saw is a handsaw specifically designed to make similar cuts; however, the question asked for a power tool.

21. **D.** The device illustrated is a compression gauge, which quantifies engine cylinder compression.

22. **B.** This is the principal use for a ream. Choice D would seem to be a possible alternative considering how a countersink bit works on wood; however, it would be inappropriate to use it to flare electrical conduit.

23. **C.** Since the intended use of this saw blade is to cut across the grain of a piece of wood, a crosscut blade would be the better choice. Rip cut blades, on the other hand, are better suited to cut with the grain of wood. A saber saw blade is a form of blade that will fit a saber saw. It does not denote any specific type of blade per se. In other words, a saber saw blade could be a rip cut, crosscut, metal cutting, or other kind of blade.

24. **D.** Regardless of the wheel configuration involved, any time a belt between two wheels is crossed in the manner described, it causes a directional change of the opposing wheel. Instead of both wheels turning clockwise, one wheel will turn counterclockwise. Torque and speed are not affected.

25. **B.** Beveled gears are unlike Choices A, C, and D in that the teeth are cut into the edging of the gear, rather than set perpendicularly to a gear's facing. This angulation allows for the directional change of a drive train.

## MECHANICAL COMPREHENSION

1. **B.** The closer a fulcrum is moved to a heavy object (resistance), the easier it is to apply leverage to move the object.

2. **A.** Effort is determined by multiplying the resistance to lift by the resistance distance, then dividing that product by the effort distance. In this case, we first need to convert inches into feet:

$$\text{Effort} = \frac{1200 \text{ pounds} \times 1.5 \text{ feet}}{6.5 \text{ feet } (8 \text{ feet } - 18 \text{ inches})}$$

   Or Effort = 277 pounds (rounded up to the nearest pound).

3. **D.** The amount of force to lift 300 pounds without use of a lever equals 300 pounds. If Joe uses a lever, his effort will be determined by multiplying the resistance to lift by the resistance distance, then dividing that product by the effort distance. So:

$$\text{Effort} = \frac{300 \text{ pounds} \times 2 \text{ feet}}{4 \text{ feet } (6 \text{ feet} - 2 \text{ feet})}$$

   The amount of force required to lift the load using the lever is 150 pounds. But the question asks about mechanical advantage, so we have one more step. Mechanical advantage is arrived at by dividing resistance by the amount of force required to lift it.

$$\frac{300}{150} = 2$$

   In this case, the lever allows for a 2:1 mechanical advantage.

4. **B.** Greater mechanical advantage is gained by having a longer effort arm (on the lever) and placing the fulcrum closer to the resistance to be lifted.

5. **D.** Effort is determined by multiplying the resistance to lift by the resistance distance, then dividing that product by the effort distance. Since the fulcrum point is at the base of the pole, the entire length of the pole is considered the resistance distance. Therefore:

$$\text{Effort} = \frac{205 \text{ pounds} \times 12 \text{ feet}}{6 \text{ feet}}$$

Effort = 410 pounds of force is required at that point to lift the pole.

6. **C.** First we must determine how much force is required to lift the canoe, which is determined by multiplying the resistance to lift by the resistance distance, then dividing that product by the effort distance:

$$\text{Effort} = \frac{115 \text{ pounds} \times 10 \text{ feet}}{5 \text{ feet}}$$

Thus we determine that Effort = 230 pounds.

Then we can figure mechanical advantage. Mechanical advantage is determined by dividing resistance by the amount of force required to lift $(115 \text{ pounds} \div 230 \text{ pounds})$, so we arrive at a mechanical advantage of less than 1 (0.50). In other words, leverage is actually working against the two individuals trying to lift the canoe.

7. **A.** A single pulley as shown doesn't offer any mechanical advantage.

8. **B.** To determine how much effort is required, simply divide the resistance (3,000 pounds) by the mechanical advantage of the device (4). The answer is 750 pounds of effort.

9. **C.** In a pulley system, there is an inverse relationship between mechanical advantage and lift. That is, the greater the mechanical advantage, the less the lift. In a 1:1 proportion, if 2 feet of pull was applied, the load would be lifted 2 feet. In this case, the amount of pull is divided by the mechanical advantage to determine the lift. Thus, 3 feet of pull divided by 4 equals 0.75 feet of lift (or 9 inches of lift).

10. **D.** The pulley arrangement shown has a mechanical advantage of 4:1. Thus, effort is 200 pounds (resistance divided by mechanical advantage).

11. **A.** The pulley has a 2:1 mechanical advantage. Therefore: 250 pounds of force × 2 = 500 pounds of potential lift.

12. **A.** The mechanical advantage demonstrated by this kind of pulley configuration is 2:1. The length of the pull equals the mechanical advantage times the lift. We know the mechanical advantage is 2 feet and the lift is 2 feet, so the pull must be 4 feet.

13. **B.** The mechanical advantage is determined by the length of the plane divided by the height it is elevated. Since choice B has the longest plane and the lowest height it would have the greater mechanical advantage.

14. **A.** In this case, the mechanical advantage is the length of inclined plane divided by the height of inclined plane, or:

$$\frac{18 \text{ feet}}{10 \text{ feet}} = 1.8:1$$

15. **C.** The formula for effort in this case is Effort = the product of resistance times height divided by the length of the inclined plane. Or:

$$\frac{\text{530 pounds} \times \text{5 feet}}{\text{8 feet}} = \text{331.25 pounds}$$

16. **B.** Effort times effort distance (length of the inclined plane) equals resistance times height (resistance distance). So, we know the effort, the effort distance, and the resistance. We don't know the height (lift). Thus the problem can be stated as:

$$90(14) = 360h.$$

Then, 1,260 divided by 360 (to isolate $h$, or height) equals 3.5. So, the amount of lift possible is 3.5 feet.

17. **C.** Since we must first determine the length of the plane, we have to use the Pythagorean theorem applied to geometric right triangles $(a^2 + b^2 = c^2)$. The square root of the resulting number will give us the length of the third side (that is, the inclined plane). So,

$$a^2 = 3^2 = 9$$
$$b^2 = 5^2 = 25$$

9 + 24 = 34, or $c^2$. To find c, we need to determine the square root of 34, which is 5.83. Now we know the length of the inclined plane. To determine the mechanical advantage, we divide the length of the plane by the height (5.83 feet ÷ 3 feet) and determine that the advantage is (rounded down) 1.9:1.

18. **B.** The mechanical advantage of a wedge is found by dividing the length of the slope by the width of the widest end. Therefore, 10 divided by 5 equals 2, or a mechanical advantage of 2:1.

19. **B.** The mechanical advantage of a wheel and axle can be found by dividing the radius of the wheel by the radius of the axle. Choice B shows a mechanical advantage of 6:1, making it the choice with the greatest mechanical advantage.

20. **C.** If we know that force times the large-wheel circumference equals resistance times the small-wheel circumference (the axle), we can find the solution. Circumference equals pi times the diameter, or $2r\pi$. So the large-wheel circumference is 31.4 inches (rounded down slightly) and the small-wheel circumference is 12.6 inches (rounded up slightly). Thus, we can say: 75(31.4) = 12.5 × resistance or 2,355 = 12.5 × resistance. Divide both sides by 12.5 to determine that resistance = 188.4 pounds.

21. **B.** Divide the resistance by the amount of force used to determine mechanical advantage. 900 divided by 180 equals 5, or a mechanical advantage of 5:1.

22. **A.** The mechanical advantage of a jackscrew can be found by dividing the circumference of the turning handle by the screw pitch. The circumference of the handle can be found by multiplying the length of the handle (which is equivalent to the radius of a circle) by 2 to find the diameter, then multiplying the diameter by $\pi$.

23. **B.** The amount of weight (resistance) that can be lifted is simply effort times mechanical advantage, or 600 times 30 = 1,800 pounds.

24. **B.** Since we know the gear ratio is a 1:7 reduction, its mechanical advantage is 7. Therefore, 7 times 150 foot pounds = 1,050 foot pounds. 1,050 foot pounds is the maximum torque output possible under the conditions given.

25. **C.** Beveled gears can change drive direction.

**ASSEMBLING OBJECTS**

1. B.
2. A.
3. D.
4. A.
5. A.
6. B.
7. B.
8. D.
9. C.
10. B.
11. C.
12. A.
13. A.
14. B.
15. C.
16. B.

# CHAPTER 18

# *Practice Test #4*

**Take the diagnostic test just as you would any standardized test. Use the answer sheet at the end of this chapter to record your answers. Set a timer for the amount of time allotted for each subtest, take them in the order in which they're given, and try to do your best. Then turn to the answer key later in this chapter to grade your efforts and help you plan your review before taking the next practice test.**

## GENERAL SCIENCE

You have 11 minutes to answer the 25 questions on this subtest.

1. An alkaline is a type of

   A. acid
   B. base
   C. neutral substance
   D. caustic material

2. The light waves we see are those

   A. absorbed by the object we're looking at
   B. reflected by the object we're looking at
   C. created by the object we're looking at
   D. unrelated to the object we're looking at

3. Coronary artery disease is caused by

   A. high blood pressure
   B. a defective heart valve
   C. the buildup of plaque inside blood vessels
   D. a weak heart muscle

4. The body's immune system

   A. protects the body from disease
   B. regulates the body's hormone balance
   C. creates red blood cells
   D. is entirely contained in the lymphatic system

5. Velocity can be defined as

   A. rate of speed
   B. rate of motion
   C. change in speed
   D. rate of motion in a particular direction

6. The three main areas of your brain are the

   A. ventricles, spinal cord, and brainstem
   B. brainstem, cerebrum, and cerebellum
   C. cerebrospinal fluid, ventricles, and spinal cord
   D. frontal lobe, ventricles, brainstem

7. A calorie is a measure of

   A. weight gain
   B. weight loss
   C. the amount of energy a food will produce
   D. the nutritional value of a food

8. When tectonic plates come together or collide, they are said to have

A. horizontal shifting
B. transform boundaries
C. divergent boundaries
D. convergent boundaries

9. For the chemical formula $NH_3$ which of the following is *not* true:

A. this is the chemical formula for ammonia
B. this formula is a compound
C. this formula is a molecule
D. this formula is an element

10. Botany is the study of

A. animal life
B. plant life
C. atomic structures
D. mechanical principles

11. Evolution is a process

A. that produces change in a population over a long period of time, and continues to the present day
B. that created biodiversity on earth but is no longer an active process
C. that produces quick change in a population through random genetic mutation
D. caused by radiation

12. The chemical that carries a cell's genetic code is called

A. cytoplasm
B. ribosome
C. DNA
D. phospholipid

13. The largest organ in the human body is

A. the heart
B. the intestines
C. the brain
D. the skin

14. Which of the following are examples of common elements?

A. hydrogen, nitrogen, and oxygen
B. helium, table salt, and sucrose
C. nitrogen, hydrogen, and ammonia
D. hydrogen, nitrogen, and scandium

15. A concentration of more than about 1% white blood cells in an adult's blood indicates

A. general good health
B. the possibility of an infection
C. the presence of a blood disease
D. anemia

16. The systolic pressure is measured

A. when the heart beats
B. when the heart rests
C. as the time between heart beats
D. the number of heart beats per minute

17. The digestive process starts as soon as

A. food reaches the stomach
B. food enters the large intestine
C. you swallow
D. you take the first bite

18. A gamete is a sex cell

A. found only in the testes
B. found only in the ovaries
C. containing half the genetic code of its parent
D. containing the entire genetic code of its parent

19. In order to build more muscle, one could increase protein intake by eating

A. olive oil
B. tomatoes
C. pasta
D. lentils

20. The earth's layers could best be described as going outward from

A. inner core → crust → mantle
B. inner core → outer core → mantle
C. inner core → outer core → crust
D. inner core → outer core → mantle → crust

21. If a person had only seawater to drink,

A. he or she would die of dehydration
B. he or she might dislike the taste but would be fine
C. he or she would be less hungry than usual
D. he or she would sweat more

22. In which marine zone does most marine life exist?

A. epipelagic
B. bathypelagic
C. ocean basin
D. the trenches

23. What is a “shooting star”?

A. a dying sun
B. a collision in the asteroid belt
C. a meteor passing through the earth’s atmosphere
D. a comet

24. Which of the following statements is true of atoms?

A. Electrons are particles with no charge and protons are positively charged particles.
B. Electrons are negatively charged particles and protons are particles with no charge.
C. Electrons are negatively charged particles, protons are particles with no charge, and neutrons can take on a positive or negative charge.
D. Electrons are negatively charged particles, protons are positively charged particles, and neutrons are particles with no charge.

25. A joule is equal to

A. 1 newton of force causing the displacement of 1 meter
B. 1 ton of force exerting pressure on 1 ton of mass
C. 1 newton of force causing displacement in any direction
D. 1 newton of force

## ARITHMETIC REASONING

You will have 30 questions and 36 minutes to answer them.

1. If 23.6 were changed into a percentage of its relationship to the number 1, which of the following would be correct?

   A. 23.6%
   B. 0.236%
   C. 236%
   D. 2,360%

2. Given $\frac{5}{8}=\frac{x}{32}$, which of the following equals $x$?

   A. 10
   B. 20
   C. 25
   D. 30

3. Given $\frac{3}{5}\div\frac{1}{2}=\frac{x}{15}$, which of the following equals $x$?

   A. 18
   B. 16.5
   C. 19.2
   D. 16

4. The formula for translating Fahrenheit temperature readings into Celsius temperature readings is $(F° - 32)\frac{5}{9}$. What would 99° Fahrenheit be if converted to Celsius?

   A. 81.3°
   B. 67.8°
   C. 41.2°
   D. 37.2°

5. How many milliliters are there in 12.38 liters?

   A. 1,238
   B. 123,800
   C. 12,380
   D. 0.001238

6. Assuming there are 1.6 kilometers per mile, what is the distance in miles between two towns that are 96 kilometers apart?

   A. 5 miles
   B. 102.3 miles
   C. 60 miles
   D. 175 miles

7. If a mechanic measures the diameter (i.e., the pitch) of a gear with a micrometer and figures that it is 2.5% larger than the manufacturer's specifications of 5.735 inches, what is the actual pitch of the gear in question?

   A. 5.88 inches
   B. 6.33 inches
   C. 6.721 inches
   D. 7.21 inches

8. If a rectangular area of 47.5 feet by 13.2 feet were roped off for recarpeting, how many square feet would this encompass?

   A. 627 square feet
   B. 593 square feet
   C. 572.5 square feet
   D. 402 square feet

9. If a rectangle measuring 15 meters by 19.8375 meters has the same area as a square, what is the length of the square's side?

   A. 16.37 meters
   B. 17.19 meters
   C. 17.25 meters
   D. 18.88 meters

10. If a 14-quart coolant system contains a 45% antifreeze solution, approximately how many quarts of this solution would have to be drained and replaced with pure antifreeze to achieve a 75% antifreeze solution?

    A. 5.23 quarts
    B. 7.64 quarts
    C. 8.91 quarts
    D. 9 quarts

11. Class A fire extinguishers can protect a maximum area of 557 square meters. A commercial structure had 132,000 square feet of floor space, and the owner wanted to adequately protect this building with Class A fire extinguishers. What would be the required number of extinguishers needed? (Assume there are 10.764 $ft^2$ per $meter^2$.)

    A. 22.02
    B. 23
    C. 23.4
    D. 24

12. The Occupational Safety and Health Administration (OSHA) has established permissible sound exposures in the workplace by using the following equation: $a = -2.81b + 108.9$, where $a$ = maximum decibel levels permissible and $b$ = exposure time in terms of hours. Under these parameters, what would be the maximum permissible sound exposure for a construction worker working an 8-hour shift?

    A. 83.634 decibels
    B. 86.364 decibels
    C. 89.572 decibels
    D. 93.832 decibels

13. One side of a piece of rectangular aluminum is 4 times as long as it is wide. If the perimeter is 420 inches, what is the width of the shorter side?

A. 42 feet
B. 40 feet
C. 3.5 feet
D. 3 feet

14. Of the 250 people attending the career fair, $\frac{1}{4}$ of them were looking for engineering jobs, $\frac{1}{3}$ of them had significant previous experience, and 30 of them were interested in working for Acme Corp. What percentage of people attending the career fair are likely to be looking for engineering jobs, have significant previous experience, and are interested in working for Acme Corp.?

A. 1%
B. 25%
C. 3%
D. 12%

15. A mail carrier can deliver 750 letters in 6 hours. How much mail can she deliver in 20 minutes?

A. 125 letters
B. 63 letters
C. 42 letters
D. 25 letters

16. Juan started training for the triathlon. On his first day of training he ran 4.3 km. On his second day he ran 4.5 km. On his third day he only made 3.9 km. On his fourth day he pushed hard and ran 4.75 km. What was the mean distance he ran?

A. 4.25 km
B. 4.36 km
C. 4 km
D. 4.3 km

17. Brittany had 70 pieces of jewelry left over from her foray into making jewelry. She wanted to give them to her teacher and her two students, with her teacher getting more pieces than her students. She decided to give the jewelry in the proportion of 3:2:2. How many pieces did her teacher get, and how many did each student receive?

A. 21, 14
B. 35, 15
C. 30, 20
D. 60, 10

18. Find $x$. $3^2+(3\bullet 3)-5(2\bullet 2)\div 2=x$.

A. 26
B. −1
C. −32
D. 8

19. Given that $x = 3$ and $y = 2$, solve the following: $x^2 - y + 5$.

A. 7
B. 12
C. 5
D. 6

20. What is the next item in the sequence {10, 8}?

A. 10
B. 6
C. 12
D. 7

21. What is $\frac{1}{3} \bullet \frac{2}{5} \div \frac{1}{4}$?

A. $\frac{2}{3}$

B. $\frac{1}{15}$

C. $\frac{24}{5}$

D. $\frac{8}{15}$

22. After a mandatory training session, employees at a company had 15 accidents in a year versus 42 the year before. What is the percentage change in accidents?

A. −62%
B. 38%
C. −38%
D. 42%

23. If inflation has risen from 3% to 5%, what is the percentage point change?

A. 67
B. 1.67
C. 2
D. 200

24. Which of the following is a prime factor of 42?

A. 2
B. 3
C. 7
D. all of the above

25. What is the greatest common factor of 21 and 33?

A. 21
B. 1
C. 3
D. 2

26. If there are 6 contestants entered in a race, what is the total number of ways in which they could cross the finish line (for example, Runner A, then B, D, E, C, F)?

A. 720
B. 6
C. 36
D. 60

27. If families in a neighborhood earn the following income, what is the median income in the neighborhood? $80,000; $100,00; $55,000; $92,000; $60,000; and $71,000.

A. $76,333
B. $80,000
C. $71,000
D. $75,500

28. If James had $x$ amount of income invested at $y$ interest rate for $z$ period of time, what is the formula that would determine the interest the principal would yield?

A. $I = x + y + z$
B. $I = xyz$
C. $I = \frac{xy}{z}$
D. $I = x(y + z)$

29. Assume an alloy containing 40% zinc is mixed with a 65% zinc alloy to get 500 kg of 55% zinc alloy. What would be the respective quantity of zinc alloy necessary to constitute such a mix?

A. 200 kg of 40% and 300 kg of 65%
B. 300 kg of 40% and 200 kg of 65%
C. 175 kg of 40% and 325 kg of 65%
D. 150 kg of 40% and 350 kg of 65%

30. A government worker has 2 funds dedicated for retirement that total $30,000. One fund is invested in government securities and earns 6%, and the other fund is invested in commercial real estate that currently earns 8%. If it is known that the government securities investment is earning $350 more in annual interest than the real estate investment, how much money does the worker have in each of these investments?

A. $19,642.86 at 6% and $10,357.14 at 8%
B. $21,522.14 at 6% and $8,477.86 at 8%
C. $21,735.37 at 6% and $8,264.63 at 8%
D. $23,181.10 at 6% and $6,818.90 at 8%

## WORD KNOWLEDGE

You will have 35 questions and 11 minutes to answer them.

1. At the board meeting, the department head learned that layoffs were imminent. Imminent most nearly means

   A. postponed
   B. under consideration
   C. impending
   D. ruled out

2. Lacerate most nearly means

   A. cut
   B. lace up
   C. mesh
   D. mash

3. The dog at the pound recoiled every time someone walked by. Recoiled most nearly means

   A. growled
   B. flinched
   C. hid
   D. approached

4. Martin gave a specious excuse for missing his date with Marilyn. Specious most nearly means

   A. convoluted
   B. impressive
   C. false
   D. reasonable

5. Terminus most nearly means

   A. end point
   B. fatal illness
   C. explanation
   D. endeavor

6. The uproarious response to the speaker was unexpected. Uproarious most nearly means

   A. appreciative
   B. uninterested
   C. loud
   D. considerate

7. The administrator had a reputation for being mercurial. Mercurial most nearly means

   A. even-tempered
   B. irresponsible
   C. temperamental
   D. unhappy

8. The old man was lucid most days. Lucid most nearly means

A. coherent
B. irritable
C. pleasant
D. forgetful

9. Inexorable most nearly means

A. avoidable
B. tired
C. influenced
D. unstoppable

10. Obdurate most nearly means

A. offensive
B. unclear
C. stubborn
D. pleasant

11. Marco met most challenges with bravado. Bravado most nearly means

A. boldness
B. timidity
C. fear
D. stubbornness

12. Preschoolers are notable for their capriciousness. Capriciousness most nearly means

A. charm
B. fickleness
C. impatience
D. happiness

13. Vogue most nearly means

A. expression
B. fashionable
C. mode
D. route

14. Wreak most nearly means

A. cause
B. regret
C. despair
D. wish

15. The CPA felt rancor at the thought of the upcoming tax season. Rancor most nearly means

A. stress
B. relief
C. calm
D. bitterness

16. Omitting facts is tantamount to lying. Tantamount most nearly means

A. different from
B. equivalent
C. incomparable
D. worse than

17. The other boys were impressed by Randall's audacity. Audacity most nearly means

A. friendliness
B. mendacity
C. skill
D. daring

18. Quixotic most nearly means

A. idealistic
B. quick
C. uncertain
D. challenging

19. Most of the class found Mr. Martin's digression boring. Digression most nearly means

A. lecture
B. aside
C. question
D. quiz

20. The novice rock climber sprained her ankle. Novice most nearly means

A. professional
B. impatient
C. inexperienced
D. unfortunate

21. Candace had a vitriolic sense of humor. Vitriolic most nearly means

A. biting
B. silly
C. admirable
D. inappropriate

22. Quagmire most nearly means

A. difficulty
B. lecture
C. quadrant
D. appointment

23. Zoe walked at a sedate pace. Sedate most nearly means

A. brisk
B. calm
C. rhythmic
D. halting

24. Perspicacity most nearly means

A. nearness
B. capacity
C. willingness
D. perceptiveness

25. The ornate building caught the buyer's eye. Ornate most nearly means

A. plain
B. decorated
C. dilapidated
D. restored

26. The noxious odor was intermittent. Noxious most nearly means

A. pleasant
B. harmful
C. unidentified
D. slight

27. Officious most nearly means

A. official
B. unpleasant
C. unwanted
D. appreciated

28. Zealot most nearly means

A. believer
B. jealous
C. admirable
D. enthusiastic

29. The vermin seemed to be everywhere on the ship. Vermin most nearly means

A. odor
B. pests
C. unpleasant sound
D. bacteria

30. They reached the nadir of their journey on the twelfth day. Nadir most nearly means

A. culmination
B. destination
C. crossroads
D. low point

31. The commander took the time to upbraid his subordinates. Upbraid most nearly means

A. praise
B. criticize
C. converse
D. fire

32. Wistful most nearly means

A. sad
B. thin
C. pretty
D. wasteful

33. Terry found the lecture enervating. Enervating most nearly means

A. invigorating
B. interesting
C. tiring
D. uncomplicated

34. Hoarse most nearly means

A. lacking
B. slow
C. mute
D. raspy

35. Empathy most nearly means

A. pretense
B. power
C. impatience
D. sympathy

## PARAGRAPH COMPREHENSION

You'll have 15 questions and 13 minutes to answer them.

1. No two fires are alike, and there are many factors to be considered when deciding whether or not to ventilate and what kind of ventilation to use. A few of these considerations are as follows: building type and structure, wind direction, availability of natural openings, and whether or not there is sufficient manpower available to protect surrounding areas in the event that the fire increases in intensity when the building is opened. When used properly, ventilation can be a major aid in combating a fire.
A good title for this passage would be:

    A. Considerations in Using Ventilation in Fire Fighting
    B. Why Fire Fighters Use Ventilation to Fight Fires
    C. No Two Fires Are Alike
    D. The Complexity of Fire Fighting

2. The flash point of a liquid is the temperature required to vaporize a liquid. In layman's terms, any liquid that has a low flash point is particularly susceptible to igniting. Such liquids are identified as volatile.
After reading this passage, one could assume that

    A. the flash point of a liquid is higher than for a solid
    B. liquids with a low flash point are more dangerous than liquids with a high flash point
    C. volatility is not related to flash point
    D. flash point has nothing to do with danger

3. You must file a federal, state, and local (if applicable) tax return for your business each year, whether you made money or not. You must include all the income you received during the year, regardless of whether you claim any business-related expenses or not. This means that even if you don't treat a hobby (for example) like a business, you still have to report and pay taxes on any money you make from it.
The best summary of this passage would be

    A. everyone files income tax returns
    B. you must claim all income on your return, no matter where it came from
    C. income earned from a hobby doesn't need to be reported
    D. filing tax returns is a complex process

4. Throughout human history, obtaining food has been of great concern to all. Gleaning (taking the leftovers in a field that had been harvested) and poaching (killing game on land that didn't belong to you) are common practices that have been made illegal at various places at various times.
The author of this passage

    A. uses definition to help explain how people obtain food
    B. compares and contrasts gleaning and poaching to explain them
    C. defends the practices of gleaning and poaching as defenses against starvation
    D. sides with landowners against the dangerous practices of gleaning and poaching

5. Jimmie Rodgers and the Carter Family were among the first country artists to be widely known and are therefore considered influential in shaping the direction country music first took. Rodgers sang a blues-inspired country music while the Carter Family sang traditional Appalachian music. They relied on direct borrowing, recomposition, and original creation to compose the material—just as oral music has traditionally been composed.
According to this passage, which of the following is <u>not</u> true:

A. early country singers relied on the processes of oral music to compose their songs
B. the Carter family was influential in the development of country music
C. Jimmie Rodgers and the Carter family sang different types of songs
D. very few people ever heard of Jimmie Rodgers

6. Albert the Great was a German philosopher and scientist who was especially important in establishing the study of Aristotle within the parameters of Christian theology. He became an ordained priest of the Dominican Order, and taught at the University of Paris, where he gained a reputation as a teacher. One of his students was Thomas Aquinas.
A good title for this passage would be:

A. The Father of Aristotelian Theology
B. The Man Who Taught Thomas Aquinas
C. A Brief Biography of Albert the Great
D. The Contributions of German Philosophers

7. Annam is an ancient Chinese name for a portion of central Vietnam. The Chinese controlled this territory from the second century B.C. until A.D. 939, when a rebellion drove the Chinese out. Although the Chinese recaptured Annam early in the fifteenth century, they were soon overthrown again. By 1428, Annam functioned as an independent monarchy. The territory was enlarged to include most of Indochina. The country survived in relative peace and prosperity until the late eighteenth century when the French took an interest in it.
According to this passage,

A. Annam was always an independent monarchy
B. Annam never occupied more than a small portion of what is now known as Indochina
C. the French and the Chinese played pivotal roles in the history of Annam
D. Annam was positioned as a trade center throughout much of its history

8. Astrology uses the position of stars and planets to predict the future. It is thought that the exact position of the stars at one's time of birth influences the course of one's life. Other events on earth correspond to the position of the stars and planets in the heavens. Astrology is the forerunner of the science of astronomy.
According to this passage, astrology

A. is a pseudoscience that has created little of value
B. and astronomy are the same thing
C. uses the position of the stars to predict events
D. is used to explain how the cosmos works

9. Three days after the English repulsed invaders at the Battle of Stamford Bridge in the north of England, William of Normandy invaded the south of England. The English king was forced to assemble another army. The Battle of Hastings took place on October 14, 1066. It is unclear how the battle unfolded but it seems to have consisted of a series of attacks by the Normans against the English line. Toward evening, the Normans sent a cavalry charge that was stopped by the English, who broke ranks to plunder the dead soldiers. Seizing the opportunity, William sent his cavalry again and broke through the English line. The king was killed and with his death the battle was lost. William appeared and he was crowned king of England on Christmas Day, 1066.
The author of this passage uses

A. chronological order to organize the material
B. comparison and contrast organization to show the difference between the Normans and the English
C. step-by-step organization to describe how the battle took place
D. a most-important-facts-first approach to explaining the material

10. The Benin Kingdom was a kingdom in West Africa (now Nigeria) that was founded in the twelfth century and lasted for about five hundred years. Its capital was Benin City. The Edo or Bini people settled in the region and were ruled by warrior-kings. Over time, the king assumed an important role in the religion of the Benin Kingdom. The metalsmiths of the kingdom were accomplished artisans. The kingdom exported ivory, pepper, and textiles. By the seventeenth century, the kingdom had begun to decline, and it was taken over by the British in the nineteenth century.
According to this passage, which of the following is not true:
    A. the Benin Kingdom was noted for its metalsmiths
    B. Nigeria is now located where the Benin Kingdom originally flourished
    C. the British took over the Benin Kingdom
    D. the Benin Kingdom did not participate in trade

11. The date of the destruction of the far-flung Roman Empire is usually given as A.D. 476, the year when the last Roman emperor was deposed. There were numerous reasons for the decline and eventual fall of the Roman Empire. Rulers were apathetic, the bureaucracy was monolithic, and the frontier was too large to defend. In the waning years of the empire, economic instability, civil wars, and inflation caused problems.
According to this passage, the fall of the Roman empire can be attributed to
    A. poor military leadership
    B. a combination of many factors
    C. sky-high taxation
    D. the abdication of the last emperor

12. Leonardo of Pisa was an Italian mathematician who lived in the late twelfth and early thirteenth centuries. He introduced Arabic, Indian, and classical mathematical knowledge to Europe, including the use of Arabic numerals and the zero. Although he derived a number of complex theories, he was also absorbed with practical problems such as business mathematics. He wrote on algebra and number theory, and even wrote several treatises on recreational mathematics. His work led to the abandonment of Roman numerals in the west.
According to this passage, Leonardo of Pisa
    A. was notable for introducing the use of Arabic numerals to the west
    B. was a businessman
    C. was noted for his artistic talent
    D. knew only basic arithmetic

13. Chichen Itza was the capital of the Mayan civilization, located in the northern area of the Yucatan Peninsula. The city was named after its inhabitants, the Itza tribe, a branch of Mayans. The city was founded around A.D. 500. Several structures have been uncovered, including platform pyramids decorated with artwork resembling that of the Aztecs. A court for playing a ritual game also stands. In this court, two walls with stone circles projecting from them face opposite each other. Players attempted to send a ball through the stone ring (much like modern basketball). Several temples and what appears to be an observatory have also been found.
According to this passage, the Itza
    A. died out around A.D. 500
    B. practiced astrology
    C. apparently played a game similar to basketball
    D. performed human sacrifice

14. A unanimous decision by jurors is required to convict the defendant. A jury that fails to agree is referred to as a "hung jury." Depending on state discretion, the case will either be dismissed or retried at a later date. Hung juries are usually the consequence of insufficient evidence. The state must prove its charge beyond a reasonable doubt to effect a conviction.
A good title for this passage would be:

    A. When Jurors Can't Agree
    B. What Happens in a Trial
    C. How Juries Deliberate
    D. The Definition of a Hung Jury

15. When the members of a neighborhood watch committee met with the local police, they shared their findings. They claimed that vehicular prowling and larceny seemed to occur more often on weekends between 8:30 P.M. and 1:30 A.M. Malicious mischief and residential burglary seemed to occur more often on weekdays between 6:30 and 10:30 P.M.

    From this passage it can be assumed that

    A. the same people are committing many of the crimes
    B. around the clock vigilance is the best way to prevent these crimes
    C. people should be sure to lock their doors during the day
    D. increasing police patrols daily between the hours of 6:30 P.M. and 1:30 A.M. would probably bring the crime rate down

## MATHEMATICS KNOWLEDGE

You'll have 25 questions and 24 minutes to answer them.

1. A cylinder has a diameter of 22 inches and a height of 66 inches. Assuming there are 231 cubic inches per gallon, how many gallons could this container hold?

   A. 108.61 gallons
   B. 106.8 gallons
   C. 103.75 gallons
   D. 98.93 gallons

2. If an aluminum alloy bar measured 4 feet by 2 inches by 2 inches and weighed 12.3 pounds, how much would a bar of the same material measuring 7 feet by 3 inches by 4 inches weigh?

   A. 64.575 pounds
   B. 56.05 pounds
   C. 43.757 pounds
   D. 26.12 pounds

3. What is <u>not</u> true about the equation $x^2+16=25$?

   A. $x$ represents an unknown
   B. it is a linear equation
   C. it can be solved for $x$
   D. $x$ could be more than one number

4. If $x = 4$, what does $2x^3$ equal?

   A. 4
   B. 24
   C. 128
   D. 512

5. Which of the following represents the equation $6+x+3y^3-(2y)^2$ in standard polynomial form?

   A. it's already in standard form
   B. $x+3y^3-(2y)^2+6$
   C. $y^5+x+6$
   D. $3y^3-(2y)^2+x+6$

6. An angle with a turn of less than 90° is called

   A. an obtuse
   B. an acute angle
   C. a reflex angle
   D. a line

7. Solve for $x$: $x+9=21$

   A. $x = 12$
   B. $x = 30$
   C. $x = 2$
   D. $x = 3$

8. Solve for $y$: $4y = 48$

A. $y = 4$
B. $y = 16$
C. $y = 44$
D. $y = 12$

9. Solve for $x$: $\frac{1}{3}x > 2$

A. $x > 3$
B. $x = 6$
C. $x > 6$
D. $x < 6$

10. Which of the following correctly expresses the equation $2x^2 + 3x = -2$ as a quadratic equation?

A. $2x(2x) + 3x = -2$
B. $5x^2 = -2$
C. $2x^2 = 3x + 2 = 0$
D. it cannot be expressed as a quadratic equation

11. Solve for $x$: $-4x < 2$.

A. $x > -0.5$
B. $x = 2$
C. $x < -0.5$
D. $x > 0.5$

12. On a graph, the points $(x = 1, y = 6); (x = 2, y = 9); (x = 3, y = 12)$ would form:

A. a straight line
B. a parabola
C. a circle
D. an angle

13. The total measurement of the angles of a polygon with five sides is

A. 360°
B. 540°
C. 180°
D. 720°

14. A triangle with one 90° angle is called:

A. an isosceles triangle
B. an equilateral triangle
C. a scalene triangle
D. a right triangle

15. Solve for $y$: $\frac{1}{3}y+9=15$.

A. $y=9$
B. $y=8$
C. $y=18$
D. $y=24$

16. In rush hour traffic, John travels an average of 2 miles every 5 minutes. How far does he travel in 30 minutes?

A. 12 miles
B. 10 miles
C. 15 miles
D. 6 miles

17. Add the fractions $\frac{x}{5}+\frac{x-3}{2}$.

A. $\frac{2x-3}{10}$

B. $\frac{2x-3}{7}$

C. $\frac{7x-3}{10}$

D. $\frac{x^2-3}{7}$

18. Multiply the fractions $\frac{x-2}{5}\times\frac{3}{x}$.

A. $\frac{3x-6}{5x}$

B. $\frac{x-6}{5x}$

C. $\frac{x^2-2x}{15}$

D. $\frac{x}{5x}$

19. If a trapezoid has parallel sides of 4 feet and 2 feet and a height of 4 feet, what is its area?

A. 32 square feet
B. 10 square feet
C. 8 square feet
D. 12 square feet

20. Factor $x^2+9x-36=0$.

A. $(x+3)(x+3)$
B. $(x+12)(x-3)$
C. $(x+9)(x-9)$
D. $(x+18)(x+2)$

21. In a hexagon with equal sides and angles, each angle measures:

A. 720°
B. 120°
C. 45°
D. $63\frac{1}{3}°$

22. If Brianna has a quarter, two dimes, a nickel, and three pennies in her pocket, how likely is it that she will pull out a penny if she randomly picks a coin from her pocket?

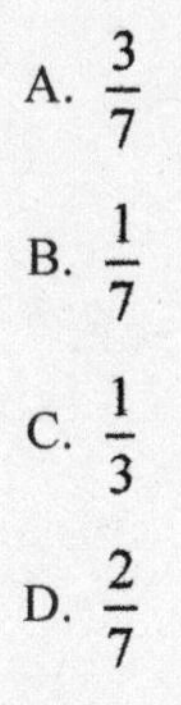

A. $\frac{3}{7}$

B. $\frac{1}{7}$

C. $\frac{1}{3}$

D. $\frac{2}{7}$

23. If Jacob randomly picks a card from a deck that has four suits (spades, diamonds, hearts, and clubs) that occur an equal number of times, what is the likelihood that he will pick a diamond 3 times in a row?

A. $\frac{1}{512}$

B. $\frac{1}{12}$

C. $\frac{1}{4}$

D. $\frac{1}{64}$

24. Given $y = 2x + 3$ and $y = 3x + 1$ find the values for $x$ and $y$.

A. $x = 2, y = 7$
B. $x = 2, y = 6$
C. $x = 1, y = 5$
D. $x = 3, y = 6$

25. Given a cube with a side equal to 3 inches, how much volume does the cube contain?

A. 18 cubic inches
B. 9 cubic inches
C. 6 cubic inches
D. 27 cubic inches

## ELECTRONICS INFORMATION

You'll have 20 questions and 9 minutes to answer them.

1. A semiconductor

   A. has the properties of a conductor
   B. has some of the properties of a conductor and some of the properties of an insulator
   C. has the properties of an insulator
   D. is a small conductor

2. A super capacitor is rated 10F. That means which of the following?

   A. 10 watts
   B. 10 amps
   C. 1 farad
   D. 10 farads

3. A joule is which of the following?

   A. 1 newton of force causing the displacement of 1 meter
   B. 1 volt per second
   C. 1 kilowatt
   D. 1 coulomb per second

4. The formula for conductance is which of the following?

   A. $G = \frac{V}{I}$
   B. $G = \frac{I}{V}$
   C. $G = IV$
   D. $G = AV$

5. The reason a power plant sends AC electricity down the line at such high voltages is for which of the following reasons?

   A. because it needs to travel long distances and loses power to resistance
   B. AC power can only be generated at high voltages
   C. power plants don't use AC power
   D. because the infrastructure currently in use is a poor conductor of electricity

6. A positively charged object has which of the following?

   A. more electrons than neutrons
   B. more electrons than protons
   C. more neutrons than protons
   D. more protons than electrons

7. When a negative charge unites with a positive charge, the result is which of the following?

A. an electric discharge
B. the buildup of static electricity
C. resistance is created
D. none of the above

8. The north pole of a magnet will do which of the following?

A. attract the north pole of another magnet
B. repel the north pole of another magnet
C. repel the south pole of another magnet
D. seek a neutral pole

9. A current of 10 amperes is the equivalent of which of the following?

A. 1 joule per second
B. 10 watts
C. 10 coulombs per second
D. 0.10 watt

10. In a series circuit, the amount of current available to $R_2$ is which of the following?

A. the same as the current available to $R_1$
B. less than the current available to $R_1$
C. unrelated to $R_1$
D. a multiple of the current available to $R_1$

11. A diode is used in a circuit to do which of the following?

A. step down voltage
B. store electric potential
C. turn current on and off
D. keep the current flowing in one direction

12. A rheostat works by doing which of the following?

A. increasing resistance as it is activated
B. reducing resistance as it is activated
C. storing electrical charge
D. amplifying electrical charge

13. An improperly grounded electrical system can cause which of the following problems?

A. an electric shock can injure or kill a person
B. it can start a fire
C. it can damage an appliance
D. all of the above

14. A short circuit is which of the following?

A. a very small circuit
B. electrical current moving in an unintended way
C. a simple closed loop system
D. an open loop system

15. The figure shown below is an example of what type of circuit?

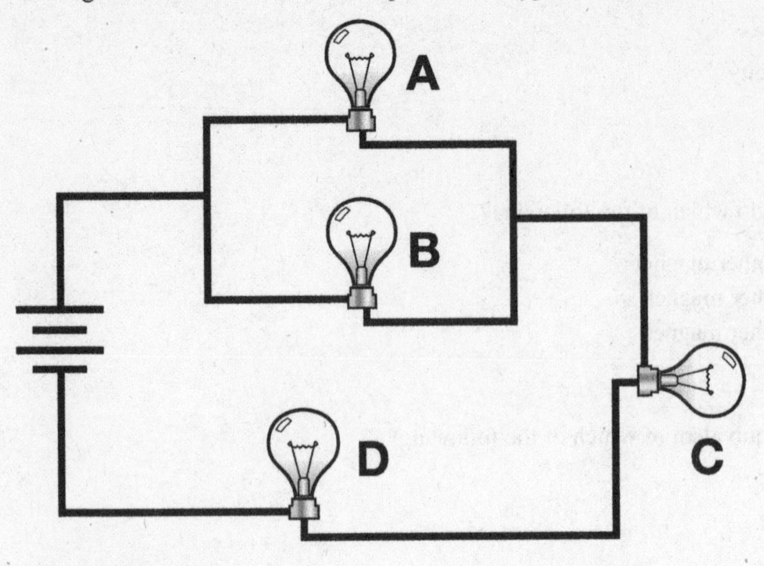


A. series-parallel
B. series
C. integrated circuit
D. parallel

16. A circuit has 15 volts and 3 ohms of total resistance. What is the current?

A. 3 amperes
B. 45 amperes
C. 18 amperes
D. 5 amperes

17. In the figure shown below, $R_1$ has 1.5 ohms of resistance and $R_2$ has 2.5 ohms of resistance. If the total current in the system is 5 amps, what is the voltage?

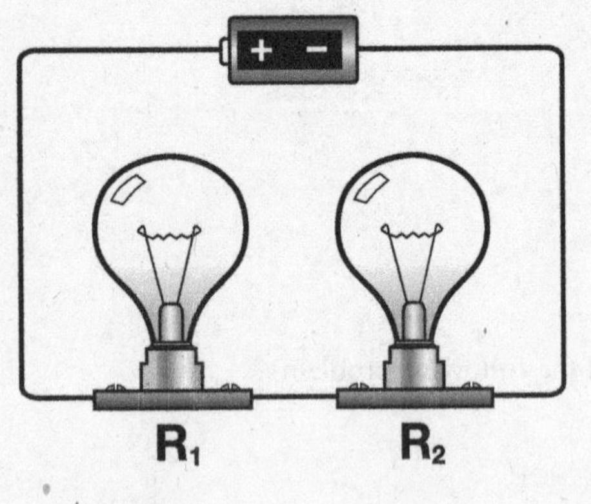


A. 5 volts
B. 4 volts
C. 20 volts
D. 25 volts

18. If the total power input is 75 watts and the total power output is 60 watts, what is the electrical efficiency?

 A. 75%
 B. 60%
 C. 125%
 D. 80%

19. In a schematic, the symbol —⁄— means which of the following?

 A. a closed switch
 B. an open switch
 C. a capacitor
 D. a resistor

20. In the figure below, the component B serves which of the following purposes?

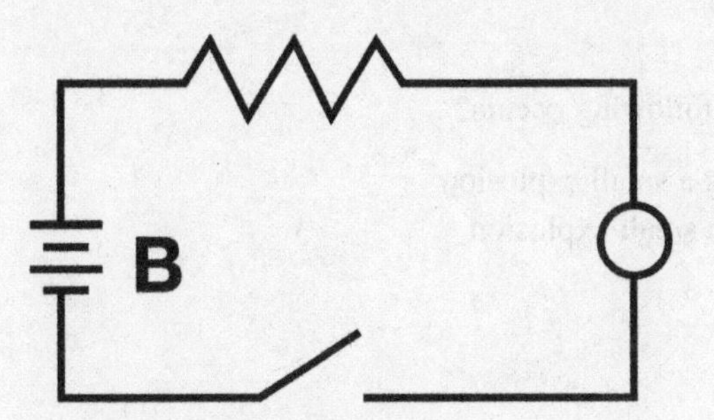


 A. it is the power source
 B. it is an on/off switch
 C. it is a resistor
 D. it steps down the current

## AUTOMOTIVE AND SHOP INFORMATION

You'll have 25 questions and 11 minutes to answer them.

1. Air injection is which of the following?

   A. a type of fuel injection
   B. a type of emissions control
   C. a replacement for a catalytic converter
   D. a process for inflating tires

2. ECU is an abbreviation for which of the following?

   A. Electronic Conversion Unit
   B. Entropic Catalysis Unifier
   C. External Converter Unit
   D. Engine Control Unit

3. In the combustion stroke of a 4-stroke cycle, which of the following occurs?

   A. The fuel-air mixture is ignited in the cylinder, causing a small explosion
   B. The fuel-air mixture is ignited in the piston, causing a small explosion
   C. The fuel-air mixture is compressed in the cylinder
   D. The fuel-air mixture is exhausted

4. What is the purpose of the starter?

   A. It turns on the battery
   B. It starts the engine
   C. It runs the electrical system
   D. It forces the spark plugs to fire

5. The arrow in the figure below shows an example of which of the following car parts?

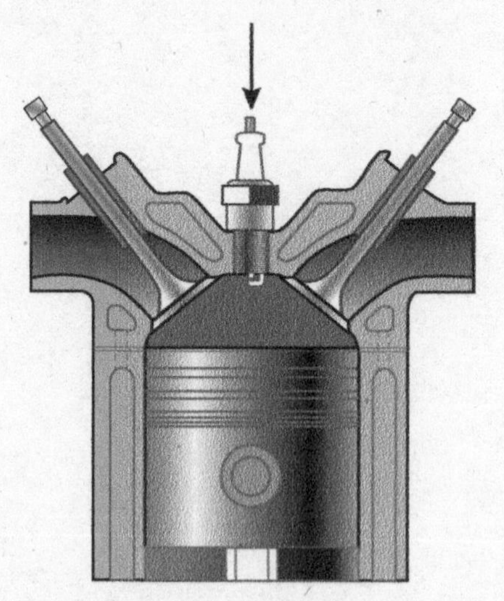

   A. a cylinder head
   B. a fuel injector
   C. a spark plug
   D. an intake valve

6. Which of the following is not true of a fuel-injection system?

   A. it has a valve that squirts a measured amount of fuel into the cylinder
   B. it improves gas efficiency (compared to a carburetor)
   C. it is rare in newer cars
   D. sensors adjust the fuel and air mixture automatically

7. In a vehicle with a carburetor, pushing on the accelerator does which of the following?

   A. opens the throttle
   B. releases the choke
   C. engages the clutch
   D. adjusts the venturi

8. The exhaust manifold funnels exhaust from which car part?

   A. the fuel tank
   B. the cylinder heads
   C. the radiator
   D. the brake system

9. An underinflated tire can cause which of the following problems?

   A. difficulty stopping
   B. difficulty cornering
   C. increased bouncing
   D. both A and B

10. In a 4-wheel drive vehicle, the engine torque is split between the front and rear axle, meaning all 4 tires spin at the same speed. This means which of the following?

    A. greater traction in rough road conditions
    B. more difficulty in cornering
    C. both A and B
    D. neither A nor B

11. Struts, shock absorbers, and tires are components of which of the following systems?

    A. the drive train
    B. the steering system
    C. the electrical system
    D. the suspension system

12. The figure below is an example of which of the following automotive systems?

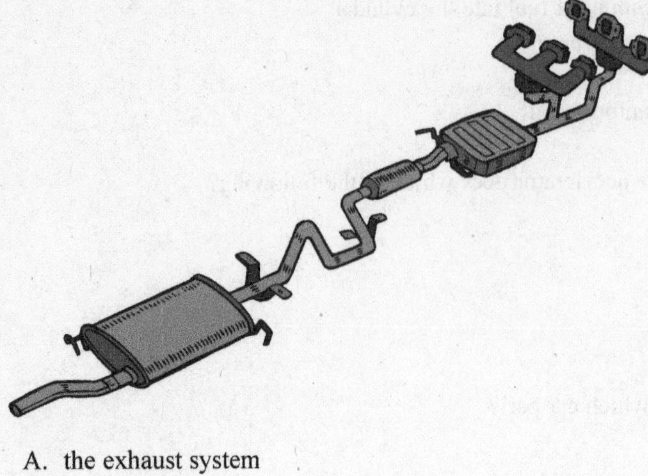

A. the exhaust system
B. the suspension
C. the valve train
D. the drive train

13. Which instrument below could best determine if the interior diameters of two pipes are identical?

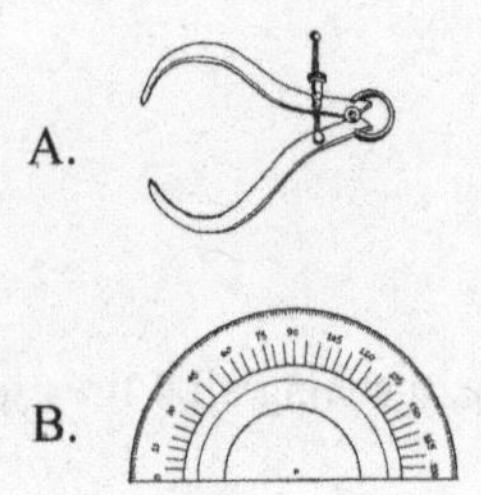


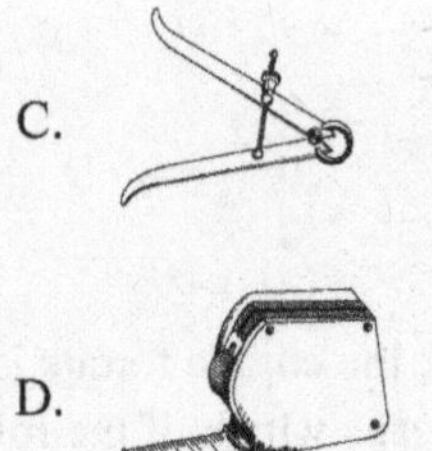


14. The instrument illustrated in the figure below is which of the following?

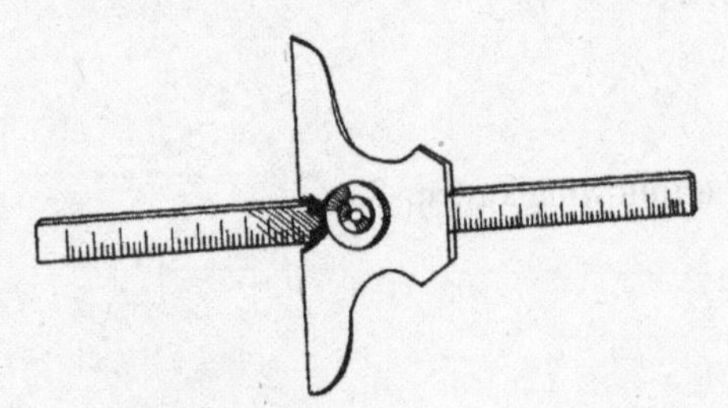

A. depth gauge
B. spring dividers
C. Vernier calipers
D. screw pitch gauge

15. Which of the tools below lacks the ability to miter square?

A. try square
B. combination square
C. carpenter's framing square
D. both A and C

16. If the head of a screw had the kind of configuration illustrated in the figure below, what kind of screwdriver would be required?

A. Phillips screwdriver
B. Torx screwdriver
C. standard screwdriver
D. offset screwdriver

17. Which of the wrenches below is more convenient and can save time when it is necessary to loosen or tighten a bolt in tight quarters?

A. crescent wrench
B. Stilson wrench
C. offset wrench
D. socket wrench

18. What kind of wrench demonstrates an L-shaped hexagonal design that is used to tighten or loosen machined setscrews?

A. Allen wrench
B. torque wrench
C. Stilson wrench
D. offset wrench

19. What kind of file would be better suited to sharpen the dull edges of a saw blade and achieve proper angle set?

A. flat file
B. round file
C. triangular file
D. bench grinder

20. One kind of hose coupling has recessed lugs spaced evenly on its exterior collar. If a person needed to break a coupling of this nature, which of the wrenches shown below would probably be used?

A.

C.

B.

D.

21. The illustration in the figure below is called a Siamese hose adapter. When considering that water enters through the female connective end and exits the male connective end, this device has what kind of an effect on the resulting water flow?

A. It reduces the potential discharge by at least 50%.
B. It splits the water flow, which increases frictional loss.
C. It triples the potential discharge.
D. It combines the potential discharge of two separate hose lines into a master fire stream.

22. Which of the power tools below is best used to put a smooth finish on hardwood?

A.

B.

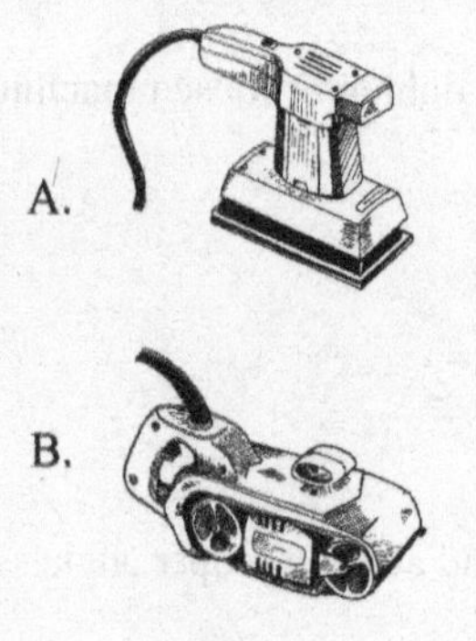

C.

D.

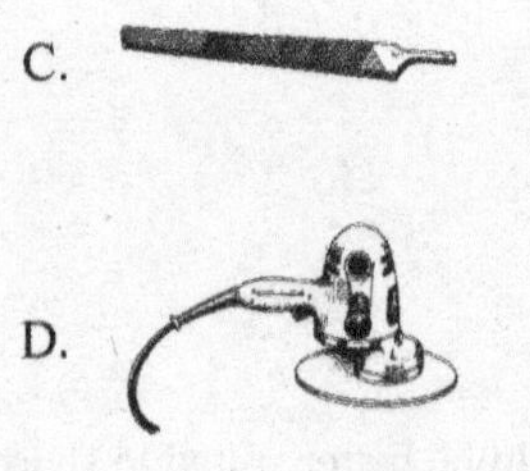

23. Which of the tools illustrated below is best used to sufficiently heat $\frac{1}{2}$-inch copper conduit to take solder when forming a joint?

A.

B.

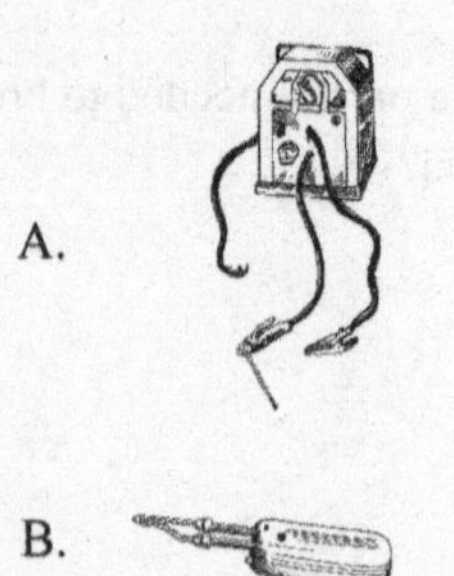

C.

D.

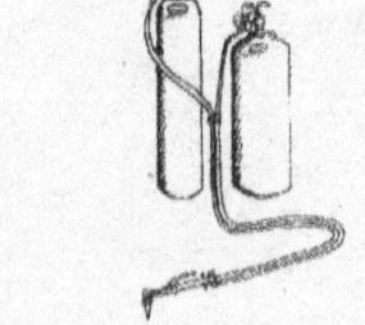

24. What one tool below is not used in the automotive trade?

25. If an individual wanted to dig a hole approximately two feet deep in the soil and was aware that the soil was composed of a mixture of very hard clay and gravel, the best tool suited for the job would be which of the following?

## MECHANICAL COMPREHENSION

You'll have 25 questions and 19 minutes to answer them.

1. Examine the diagram in the figure below. Which statement is correct, assuming that Gear A is turning clockwise?

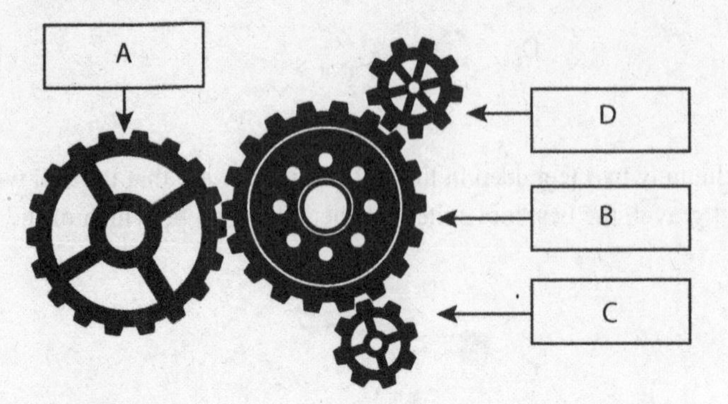


A. Gears B, C, and D are turning counterclockwise.
B. Gears B, C, and D all turn clockwise.
C. Gears C and D turn clockwise and Gear B turns counterclockwise.
D. Gears B and C turn clockwise and Gear D turns counterclockwise.

2. If the diameter of a drive gear is three times that of a connected smaller gear, the output torque is which of the following?

A. the same as the input torque
B. 3 × the input torque
C. $\frac{1}{3}$ the input torque
D. there is not enough information to determine the answer

3. If a drive gear has 40 teeth and a connecting gear (that is, the driven gear) has 10 teeth, which of the following will occur?

A. The output torque is $\frac{1}{4}$ while speed is multiplied by 4.
B. The output torque and speed are both multiplied by 4.
C. The output torque is multiplied by 4 while speed is $\frac{1}{4}$.
D. The output torque is increased 25%.

4. In a drive train, if drive gears $G_1$ and $G_3$ each have 20 teeth, and driven gears $G_2$ and $G_4$ have 25 and 30 teeth respectively, how many revolutions does $G_4$ make for every 1 revolution of $G_1$?

A. 1.875 revolutions
B. about $\frac{1}{2}$ revolution
C. about 5 revolutions
D. about $\frac{1}{5}$ revolution

5. As fluid pressure is increased in an inlet port of a hydraulic apparatus, what happens to the piston?

   A. the pressure has no bearing on it
   B. there is a corresponding perpendicular pressure on the piston
   C. there is an inverse relief of pressure on the piston
   D. there is a corresponding horizontal pressure on the piston

6. Refer to the ocean floor illustrations in the figure below. Assuming that A, B, and C are all 6 feet deep at their deepest point, which of the following can be said?

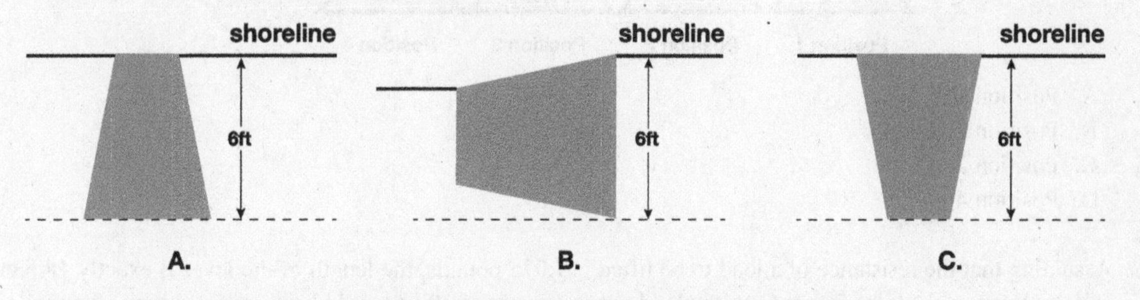


   A. At 6 feet, configurations A and C will exert the same amount of fluid pressure.
   B. A, B, and C will all exert different amounts of pressure at 6 feet, owing to the difference in shoreline.
   C. At 6 feet, configurations B and C will exert the same amount of fluid pressure.
   D. The fluid pressure at 6 feet would be the same in all configurations.

7. A diver going to 33 feet in a freshwater lake experiences which of the following, as compared to diving in the ocean?

   A. slightly lighter water pressure
   B. the water pressure is the same
   C. slightly heavier water pressure
   D. Cannot be determined with the information given.

8. In a confined space like a holding tank, if additional pressure is added to the fluid in the tank, which of the following happens to the pressure?

   A. nothing happens; the movement of the water will dissipate the pressure
   B. the tank will rupture
   C. it is exerted equally in all directions
   D. a greater force is exerted on the bottom of the tank

9. A 2,000-pound statue must be lifted onto its plinth. If a 10-foot lever has a fulcrum placed at its midpoint, how much effort is required to lift the statue?

   A. 200 pounds
   B. 2,000 pounds
   C. 500 pounds
   D. 400 pounds

10. What would be the displacement of a piston that has a bore of 2.75 inches and a stroke of 3.5 inches?

   A. 29.29 cubic inches
   B. 17.59 cubic inches
   C. 32.52 cubic inches
   D. 20.78 cubic inches

11. In the figure below, which is the best position for the fulcrum to gain the greatest mechanical advantage?

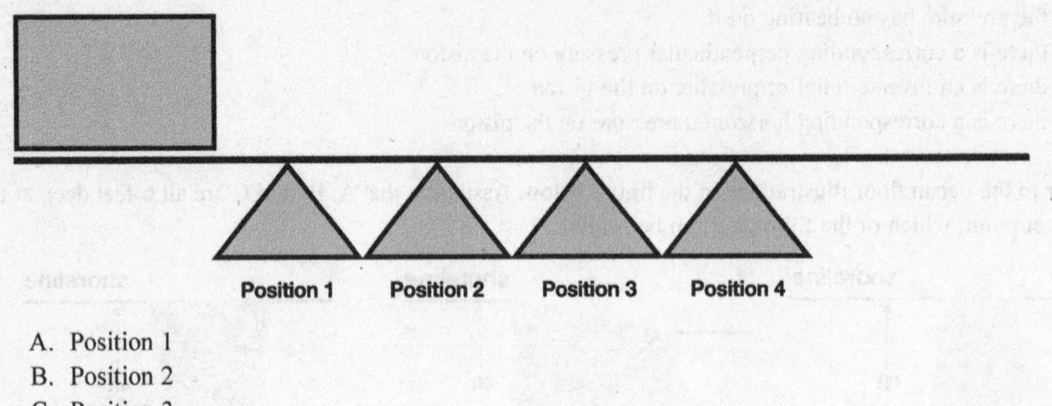


A. Position 1
B. Position 2
C. Position 3
D. Position 4

12. Assuming that the resistance of a load to be lifted is 1,075 pounds, the length of the lever is exactly 18 feet, and the fulcrum is placed 2 feet from the load, what amount of effort would be required at the end opposite the load to attain lift?

A. 90 pounds
B. 537.5 pounds
C. 107.5 pounds
D. 134.375 pounds

13. Assuming that the resistance of a load to be lifted is 500 pounds, the length of the lever is exactly 8 feet, and the fulcrum is placed dead center beneath the lever, the use of the lever as described affords what kind of mechanical advantage for lift?

A. 1:2
B. 1:1
C. 2:1
D. 3:2

14. Which of the following is <u>not</u> an example of a simple machine?

A. corkscrew
B. lever
C. gas-powered weed whacker
D. ramp

15. If two pulleys have a 4:1 ratio and the smaller pulley has a 9.5 inch circumference, how fast would the larger pulley turn if the smaller pulley turned at a rate of 500 rpm?

A. 2,000 rpm
B. 380 rpm
C. 100 rpm
D. 125 rpm

16. In the figure below, assume Gear 1 is the only drive gear. If Gear 1 turns clockwise, which of the following is true?

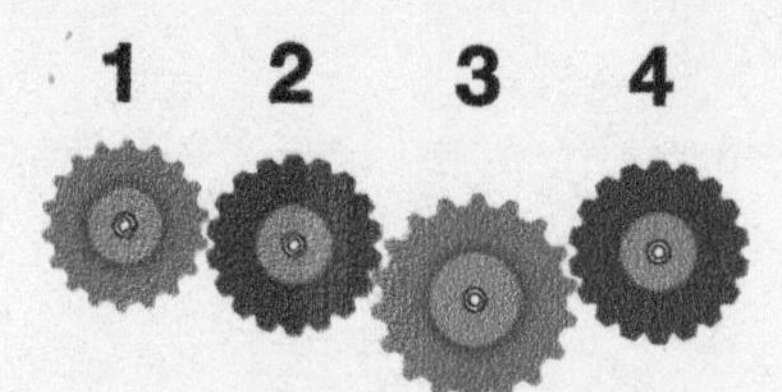


A. The rest of the gears will turn counterclockwise.
B. Gears 2 and 3 will turn counterclockwise and Gear 4 will turn clockwise.
C. Gears 2 and 4 will turn counterclockwise and Gear 3 will turn clockwise.
D. Gears 2 and 3 will turn clockwise and Gear 4 will turn counterclockwise.

17. If a pulley arrangement offers a mechanical advantage of 3:1, how much effort will be needed to lift 960 pounds?

A. 960 pounds
B. 480 pounds
C. 240 pounds
D. 320 pounds

18. In the figure below, which arrangement of pulleys delivers the greatest mechanical advantage?

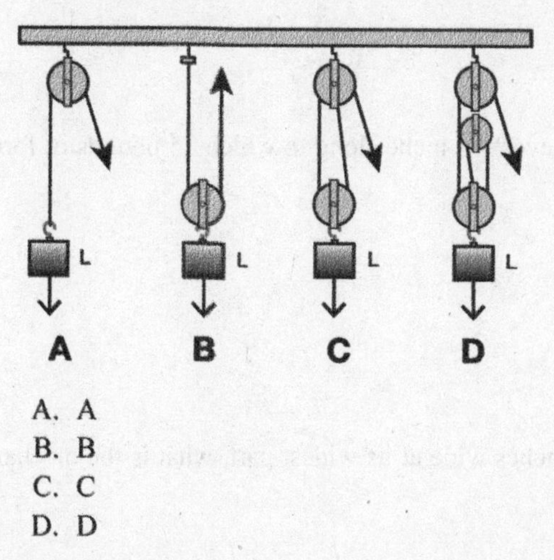


A. A
B. B
C. C
D. D

19. The figure below is an example of what type of simple machine?

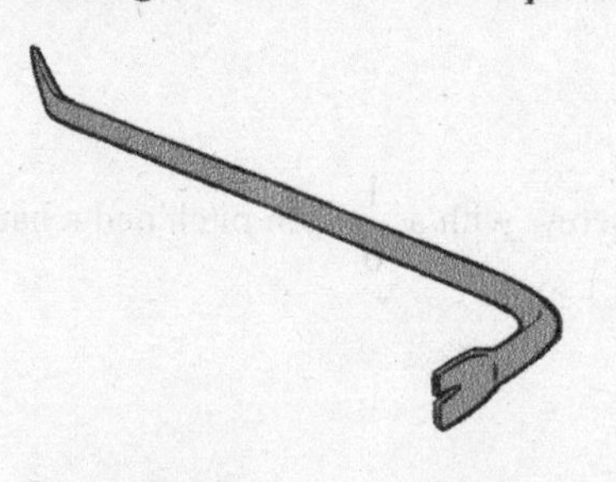

A. a lever
B. an inclined plane
C. a wedge
D. a wheel-and-axle

20. A worker moves a 500-pound barrel up a 10-foot ramp to a truck bed 6 feet off the ground. How much effort is required?

    A. 500 pounds
    B. 300 pounds
    C. 50 pounds
    D. 150 pounds

21. If a tool requires only 75 pounds of effort to move 345 pounds of resistance, what kind of mechanical advantage is gained by using it?

    A. 4.6:1
    B. 4.2:1
    C. 5.1:1
    D. 4:1

22. A jackscrew with a handle of 6 inches and a screw pitch of $\frac{1}{6}$ offers a mechanical advantage of which of the following?

    A. 23:1
    B. 226.2:1
    C. 6.28:1
    D. 2:1

23. If a jackscrew with a pitch of $\frac{1}{8}$ inch possesses a handle (lever) 18 inches long to which 15 pounds of force is applied, how much potential weight could be lifted?

    A. 904.8 pounds
    B. 13,572 pounds
    C. 113 pounds
    D. 9,564 pounds

24. If a symmetrical wedge has a slope of 12 inches and is 4 inches wide at its widest part, what is the mechanical advantage of the wedge?

    A. 3:1
    B. 5:1
    C. 4:1
    D. 2:1

25. How much force or effort would be required to lift 2 tons using a jackscrew with a $\frac{1}{6}$-inch pitch and a handle 15 inches long?

    A. 94 pounds
    B. 667 pounds
    C. 7 pounds
    D. 84 pounds

## ASSEMBLING OBJECTS

You'll have 16 questions and 15 minutes to answer them

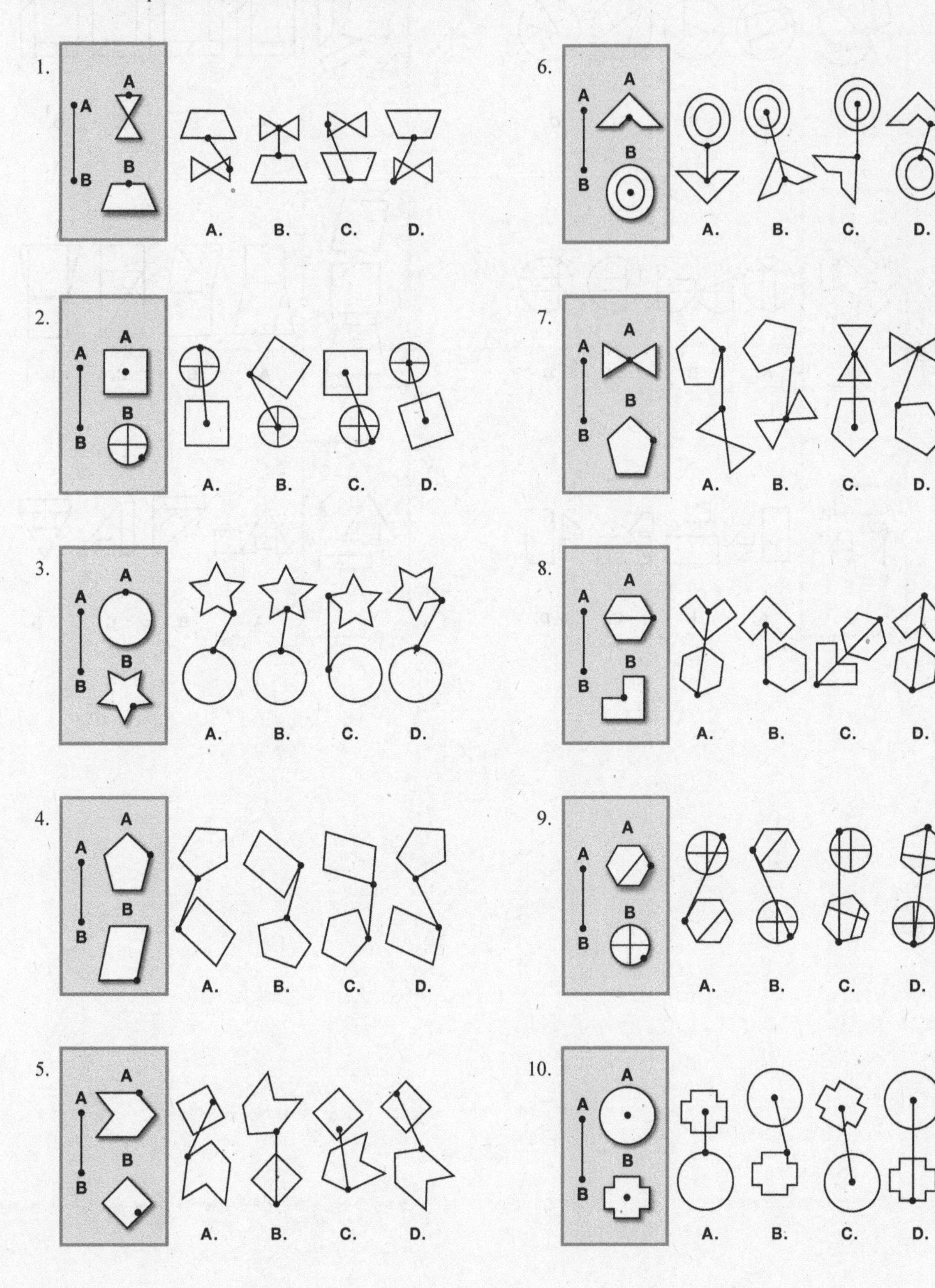

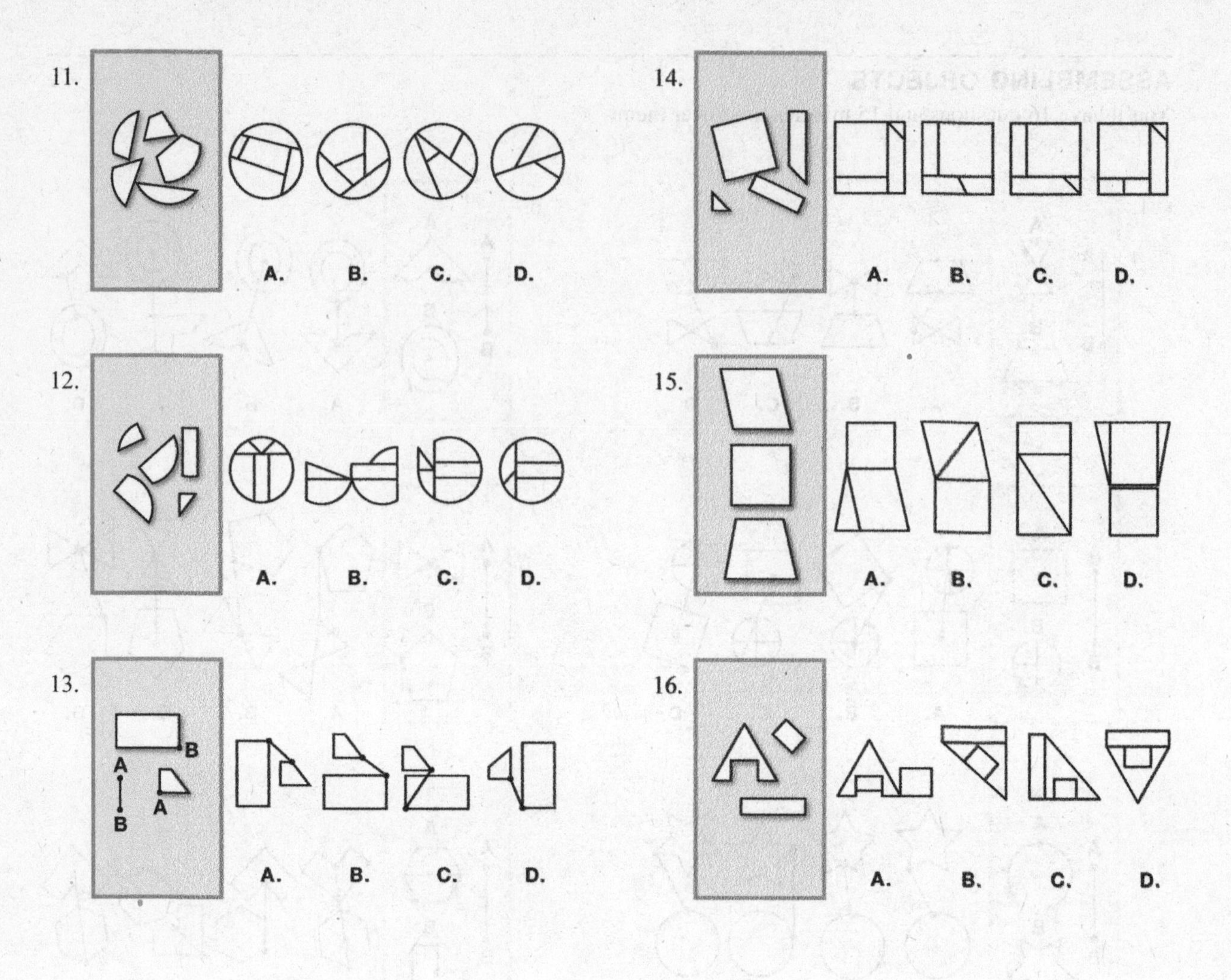
11.
A.
B.
C.
D.
14.
A.
B.
C.
D.
12.
A.
B.
C.
D.
15.
A.
B.
C.
D.
13.
A
B
B
A
A.
B.
C.
D.
16.
A.
B.
C.
D.

## ANSWER SHEET FOR PRACTICE TEST #4

### GENERAL SCIENCE

1. A B C D
2. A B C D
3. A B C D
4. A B C D
5. A B C D
6. A B C D
7. A B C D
8. A B C D
9. A B C D
10. A B C D
11. A B C D
12. A B C D
13. A B C D
14. A B C D
15. A B C D
16. A B C D
17. A B C D
18. A B C D
19. A B C D
20. A B C D
21. A B C D
22. A B C D
23. A B C D
24. A B C D
25. A B C D

### ARITHMETIC REASONING

1. A B C D
2. A B C D
3. A B C D
4. A B C D
5. A B C D
6. A B C D
7. A B C D
8. A B C D
9. A B C D
10. A B C D
11. A B C D
12. A B C D
13. A B C D
14. A B C D
15. A B C D
16. A B C D
17. A B C D
18. A B C D
19. A B C D
20. A B C D
21. A B C D
22. A B C D
23. A B C D
24. A B C D
25. A B C D
26. A B C D
27. A B C D
28. A B C D
29. A B C D
30. A B C D

### WORD KNOWLEDGE

1. A B C D
2. A B C D
3. A B C D
4. A B C D
5. A B C D
6. A B C D
7. A B C D
8. A B C D
9. A B C D
10. A B C D
11. A B C D
12. A B C D
13. A B C D
14. A B C D
15. A B C D
16. A B C D
17. A B C D
18. A B C D
19. A B C D
20. A B C D
21. A B C D

22. Ⓐ Ⓑ Ⓒ Ⓓ
23. Ⓐ Ⓑ Ⓒ Ⓓ
24. Ⓐ Ⓑ Ⓒ Ⓓ
25. Ⓐ Ⓑ Ⓒ Ⓓ
26. Ⓐ Ⓑ Ⓒ Ⓓ
27. Ⓐ Ⓑ Ⓒ Ⓓ
28. Ⓐ Ⓑ Ⓒ Ⓓ
29. Ⓐ Ⓑ Ⓒ Ⓓ
30. Ⓐ Ⓑ Ⓒ Ⓓ
31. Ⓐ Ⓑ Ⓒ Ⓓ
32. Ⓐ Ⓑ Ⓒ Ⓓ
33. Ⓐ Ⓑ Ⓒ Ⓓ
34. Ⓐ Ⓑ Ⓒ Ⓓ
35. Ⓐ Ⓑ Ⓒ Ⓓ

## PARAGRAPH COMPREHENSION

1. Ⓐ Ⓑ Ⓒ Ⓓ
2. Ⓐ Ⓑ Ⓒ Ⓓ
3. Ⓐ Ⓑ Ⓒ Ⓓ
4. Ⓐ Ⓑ Ⓒ Ⓓ
5. Ⓐ Ⓑ Ⓒ Ⓓ
6. Ⓐ Ⓑ Ⓒ Ⓓ
7. Ⓐ Ⓑ Ⓒ Ⓓ
8. Ⓐ Ⓑ Ⓒ Ⓓ
9. Ⓐ Ⓑ Ⓒ Ⓓ
10. Ⓐ Ⓑ Ⓒ Ⓓ
11. Ⓐ Ⓑ Ⓒ Ⓓ
12. Ⓐ Ⓑ Ⓒ Ⓓ
13. Ⓐ Ⓑ Ⓒ Ⓓ
14. Ⓐ Ⓑ Ⓒ Ⓓ
15. Ⓐ Ⓑ Ⓒ Ⓓ

## MATHEMATICS KNOWLEDGE

1. Ⓐ Ⓑ Ⓒ Ⓓ
2. Ⓐ Ⓑ Ⓒ Ⓓ
3. Ⓐ Ⓑ Ⓒ Ⓓ
4. Ⓐ Ⓑ Ⓒ Ⓓ
5. Ⓐ Ⓑ Ⓒ Ⓓ
6. Ⓐ Ⓑ Ⓒ Ⓓ
7. Ⓐ Ⓑ Ⓒ Ⓓ
8. Ⓐ Ⓑ Ⓒ Ⓓ
9. Ⓐ Ⓑ Ⓒ Ⓓ
10. Ⓐ Ⓑ Ⓒ Ⓓ
11. Ⓐ Ⓑ Ⓒ Ⓓ
12. Ⓐ Ⓑ Ⓒ Ⓓ
13. Ⓐ Ⓑ Ⓒ Ⓓ
14. Ⓐ Ⓑ Ⓒ Ⓓ
15. Ⓐ Ⓑ Ⓒ Ⓓ
16. Ⓐ Ⓑ Ⓒ Ⓓ
17. Ⓐ Ⓑ Ⓒ Ⓓ
18. Ⓐ Ⓑ Ⓒ Ⓓ
19. Ⓐ Ⓑ Ⓒ Ⓓ
20. Ⓐ Ⓑ Ⓒ Ⓓ
21. Ⓐ Ⓑ Ⓒ Ⓓ
22. Ⓐ Ⓑ Ⓒ Ⓓ
23. Ⓐ Ⓑ Ⓒ Ⓓ
24. Ⓐ Ⓑ Ⓒ Ⓓ
25. Ⓐ Ⓑ Ⓒ Ⓓ

## ELECTRONICS INFORMATION

1. Ⓐ Ⓑ Ⓒ Ⓓ
2. Ⓐ Ⓑ Ⓒ Ⓓ
3. Ⓐ Ⓑ Ⓒ Ⓓ
4. Ⓐ Ⓑ Ⓒ Ⓓ
5. Ⓐ Ⓑ Ⓒ Ⓓ
6. Ⓐ Ⓑ Ⓒ Ⓓ
7. Ⓐ Ⓑ Ⓒ Ⓓ
8. Ⓐ Ⓑ Ⓒ Ⓓ
9. Ⓐ Ⓑ Ⓒ Ⓓ
10. Ⓐ Ⓑ Ⓒ Ⓓ
11. Ⓐ Ⓑ Ⓒ Ⓓ
12. Ⓐ Ⓑ Ⓒ Ⓓ
13. Ⓐ Ⓑ Ⓒ Ⓓ
14. Ⓐ Ⓑ Ⓒ Ⓓ
15. Ⓐ Ⓑ Ⓒ Ⓓ
16. Ⓐ Ⓑ Ⓒ Ⓓ
17. Ⓐ Ⓑ Ⓒ Ⓓ
18. Ⓐ Ⓑ Ⓒ Ⓓ
19. Ⓐ Ⓑ Ⓒ Ⓓ
20. Ⓐ Ⓑ Ⓒ Ⓓ

## AUTOMOTIVE AND SHOP INFORMATION

1. Ⓐ Ⓑ Ⓒ Ⓓ
2. Ⓐ Ⓑ Ⓒ Ⓓ
3. Ⓐ Ⓑ Ⓒ Ⓓ
4. Ⓐ Ⓑ Ⓒ Ⓓ
5. Ⓐ Ⓑ Ⓒ Ⓓ
6. Ⓐ Ⓑ Ⓒ Ⓓ
7. Ⓐ Ⓑ Ⓒ Ⓓ
8. Ⓐ Ⓑ Ⓒ Ⓓ
9. Ⓐ Ⓑ Ⓒ Ⓓ
10. Ⓐ Ⓑ Ⓒ Ⓓ
11. Ⓐ Ⓑ Ⓒ Ⓓ
12. Ⓐ Ⓑ Ⓒ Ⓓ
13. Ⓐ Ⓑ Ⓒ Ⓓ
14. Ⓐ Ⓑ Ⓒ Ⓓ
15. Ⓐ Ⓑ Ⓒ Ⓓ
16. Ⓐ Ⓑ Ⓒ Ⓓ
17. Ⓐ Ⓑ Ⓒ Ⓓ
18. Ⓐ Ⓑ Ⓒ Ⓓ
19. Ⓐ Ⓑ Ⓒ Ⓓ
20. Ⓐ Ⓑ Ⓒ Ⓓ
21. Ⓐ Ⓑ Ⓒ Ⓓ
22. Ⓐ Ⓑ Ⓒ Ⓓ
23. Ⓐ Ⓑ Ⓒ Ⓓ
24. Ⓐ Ⓑ Ⓒ Ⓓ
25. Ⓐ Ⓑ Ⓒ Ⓓ

## MECHANICAL COMPREHENSION

1. Ⓐ Ⓑ Ⓒ Ⓓ
2. Ⓐ Ⓑ Ⓒ Ⓓ
3. Ⓐ Ⓑ Ⓒ Ⓓ
4. Ⓐ Ⓑ Ⓒ Ⓓ
5. Ⓐ Ⓑ Ⓒ Ⓓ
6. Ⓐ Ⓑ Ⓒ Ⓓ
7. Ⓐ Ⓑ Ⓒ Ⓓ
8. Ⓐ Ⓑ Ⓒ Ⓓ
9. Ⓐ Ⓑ Ⓒ Ⓓ
10. Ⓐ Ⓑ Ⓒ Ⓓ
11. Ⓐ Ⓑ Ⓒ Ⓓ
12. Ⓐ Ⓑ Ⓒ Ⓓ
13. Ⓐ Ⓑ Ⓒ Ⓓ
14. Ⓐ Ⓑ Ⓒ Ⓓ
15. Ⓐ Ⓑ Ⓒ Ⓓ
16. Ⓐ Ⓑ Ⓒ Ⓓ
17. Ⓐ Ⓑ Ⓒ Ⓓ
18. Ⓐ Ⓑ Ⓒ Ⓓ
19. Ⓐ Ⓑ Ⓒ Ⓓ
20. Ⓐ Ⓑ Ⓒ Ⓓ
21. Ⓐ Ⓑ Ⓒ Ⓓ
22. Ⓐ Ⓑ Ⓒ Ⓓ
23. Ⓐ Ⓑ Ⓒ Ⓓ
24. Ⓐ Ⓑ Ⓒ Ⓓ
25. Ⓐ Ⓑ Ⓒ Ⓓ

## ASSEMBLING OBJECTS

1. Ⓐ Ⓑ Ⓒ Ⓓ
2. Ⓐ Ⓑ Ⓒ Ⓓ
3. Ⓐ Ⓑ Ⓒ Ⓓ
4. Ⓐ Ⓑ Ⓒ Ⓓ
5. Ⓐ Ⓑ Ⓒ Ⓓ
6. Ⓐ Ⓑ Ⓒ Ⓓ
7. Ⓐ Ⓑ Ⓒ Ⓓ
8. Ⓐ Ⓑ Ⓒ Ⓓ
9. Ⓐ Ⓑ Ⓒ Ⓓ
10. Ⓐ Ⓑ Ⓒ Ⓓ
11. Ⓐ Ⓑ Ⓒ Ⓓ
12. Ⓐ Ⓑ Ⓒ Ⓓ
13. Ⓐ Ⓑ Ⓒ Ⓓ
14. Ⓐ Ⓑ Ⓒ Ⓓ
15. Ⓐ Ⓑ Ⓒ Ⓓ
16. Ⓐ Ⓑ Ⓒ Ⓓ

## ANSWER KEY FOR PRACTICE TEST #4

Use the following answer key to grade your exam. Use the results to guide your review. (See Chapter 5 for strategies on how to do this.)

### GENERAL SCIENCE

1. **B.** An alkaline is a type of base. They are not acids, they are not necessarily neutral, and they may or may not be caustic, making answers A, C, and D incorrect.

2. **B.** The light waves we see are those reflected by the object we're looking at. Answer A is the opposite of what is true, and therefore incorrect. In general, the objects we're looking at don't create light waves (with the exception, of course, of lights), making C a less correct answer than B. D is incorrect; every object reflects or absorbs some light waves.

3. **C.** Coronary artery disease is caused by the buildup of plaque inside blood vessels. While high blood pressure (answer A) may be associated with coronary artery disease, it does not cause it. Neither a defective heart valve (answer B) or a weak heart muscle (answer D) is the cause.

4. **A.** The body's immune system protects the body from disease. It doesn't regulate the body's hormone balance (answer B)—that's the endocrine system. It creates white blood cells to fight off infection (not red blood cells, as in answer C). And while the lymphatic system contributes to your body's immunity to disease, many organs contribute to the immune system (such as the skin) so it is not entirely contained in the lymphatic system (answer D).

5. **D.** Velocity can be defined as rate of motion in a particular direction. Rate of speed and rate of motion are basically the same thing, but do not completely define velocity, making answers A and B less correct. A change in speed is acceleration, not velocity, making answer C incorrect.

6. **B.** The three main areas of your brain are the brainstem, cerebrum, and cerebellum. The spinal cord is not part of the brain (although it is part of your central nervous system), making answers A and C incorrect. While your brain does have frontal lobe and ventricles, these are not two of the three main areas (although the brainstem is one of them), making D less correct than B.

7. **C.** A calorie is a measure of the amount of energy a food will produce. While the number of calories you take in affect weight gain and loss (answers A and B), a calorie is not the measure of weight gain or loss, making answers A and B incorrect. A calorie does not indicate the nutritional value of a food. Many high-calorie foods have little nutritional value, so answer D is incorrect.

8. **D.** When tectonic plates come together or collide, they are said to have convergent boundaries. While plates that collide can have horizontal shifting, horizontal shifting is also characteristic of plates that are coming apart, making answer A less accurate than D. Transform boundaries (answer B) occur when plates slide past each other. Divergent boundaries (answer C) occur when plates shift apart.

9. **D.** For the chemical formula $NH_3$, answers A, B, and C are correct, but D is not. An element is made up of only one type of atom, and this formula is made up of two elements, nitrogen and hydrogen.

10. **B.** Botany is the study of plant life. The study of animal life (answer A) is biology. The study of atomic structures (answer B) is chemistry, and the study of mechanical principles (answer D) is physics.

11. **A.** Evolution is a process that produces change in a population over a long period of time, and continues to the present day. While answer B is partially correct (evolution created biodiversity), it is not true that evolution is no longer an active process. While answer C is partially correct (random mutation can change a population), evolution is a slow process, not a quick one. While genetic mutation may be caused by radiation (answer D), evolution is not caused by radiation.

12. **C.** The chemical that carries a cell's genetic code is called DNA. The cytoplasm of a cell (answer A) does not contain the genetic code. While ribosomes (answer B) help a cell's RNA carry out its instructions, these are structures, not chemicals, and they don't carry the genetic code of a cell. Phospholipids (answer D) make up the cell membrane and don't carry the genetic code.

13. **D.** The largest organ of the human body is the skin.

14. **A.** Hydrogen, nitrogen, and oxygen are examples of common elements. Table salt and sucrose are not elements, making answer B incorrect. Ammonia is not an element, making answer C correct. While hydrogen, nitrogen, and scandium (answer D) are all elements, scandium is a rare earth element, making it not a "common" element.

15. **B.** A concentration of more than about 1% white blood cells in an adult's blood indicates the possibility of an infection. It does not indicate good health, making answer A incorrect. An abnormal concentration of white blood cells does not generally indicate a blood disease, making C incorrect. Anemia is generally due to a lack of iron in the blood, not an increased concentration of white blood cells, making answer D incorrect.

16. **A.** The systolic pressure is measured when the heart beats. Diastolic pressure is what's measured when the heart rests (answer B). The time between heart beats is not a part of the blood pressure measurement (making answer C incorrect). The number of heart beats per minute (answer D) is your pulse or heart rate.

17. **D.** The digestive process starts as soon as you take the first bite, because the saliva in your mouth begins breaking it down, and your teeth start grinding it to pieces. So, answers A, B, and C are all incorrect because the digestive process has started before all of those events happen.

18. **C.** A gamete is a sex cell containing half the genetic code of its parent. A gamete can be found in the reproductive organs of either sex parent, so answers A and B are incorrect. Since two gametes combine to create one zygote, each gamete contains only half the genetic code of its parent, making answer D incorrect.

19. **D.** In order to build more muscle, one could increase protein intake by eating lentils. Olive oil (answer A) is a good source of fat. Tomatoes (answer B) are a good source of vitamin C. Pasta (answer C) is a good source of carbohydrates.

20. **D.** The earth's layers could best be described as going outward from inner core → outer core → mantle → crust.

21. **A.** If a person had only seawater to drink, he or she would die of dehydration. The other answers are not true.

22. **A.** Most marine life exists in the epipelagic zone. The bathypelagic zone (answer B) is a deeper zone where no sunlight can penetrate, so less life is found here. The ocean basin (answer C) is the bottom ("floor") of the ocean, so even less life is found here. In the trenches (answer D), which are deep cuts in the ocean floor, very little life exists.

23. **C.** A meteor passing through the earth's atmosphere is called a "shooting star."

24. **D.** It is true of atoms that electrons are negatively charged particles, protons are positively charged particles, and neutrons are particles with no charge. Answer A is incorrect because electrons carry a negative charge. Answer B is incorrect because protons carry a positive charge. Answer C is incorrect because protons are positively charged and neutrons have no charge.

25. **A.** A joule is equal to 1 newton of force causing the displacement of 1 meter.

## ARITHMETIC REASONING

1. **D.** 23.6 multiplied by 100 = 2,360%.
2. **B.** Cross-multiply $\frac{5}{8}=\frac{x}{32}$ to determine that $8x = 160$. Then divide both sides by 8 to determine $x = 20$.
3. **A.** To divide fractions, multiply by the inverse: $\frac{3}{5}\bullet\frac{2}{1}=\frac{6}{5}$. Therefore, $\frac{6}{5}=\frac{x}{15}$. Then, multiply both sides by 15 to determine:

$$\frac{90}{5}=\frac{15x}{15}$$

Or, $18 = x$.

4. **D.** Just plug in the known quantity:

$$(99-32)\frac{5}{9}=x$$

Thus,

$$67\bullet\frac{5}{9}=x$$

And $x=\frac{335}{9}$ or 37.2°C.

5. **C.** A milliliter, as the name implies, means $\frac{1}{1000}$ of a liter. Another way to look at it is that there are 1,000 milliliters in 1 liter. Therefore, 12.38 liters × 1000 ml = 12,380 ml.
6. **C.** 96 ÷ 1.6 = 60 miles. To divide decimals, move the decimal point to the right to divide whole numbers (960 ÷ 16).
7. **A.** Since we know that 5.735 inches represents 97.5% of the gear's pitch (100% – 2.5% = 97.5%), then we can set up the following proportion:

$$\frac{97.5}{100}=\frac{5.735}{x}$$

Which shows $97.5x = 573.5$. Divide both sides by 97.5 to determine that $x = 5.88$ inches (rounded).

8. **A.** The square footage of a rectangle is found by multiplying its length by its width. In this case, 47.5 ft × 13.2 ft = 627 square feet.
9. **C.** The area of the rectangle is length times width or 19.8375 meters × 15 meters, which is equal to 297.5625 square meters. Since we know that both areas are equal in size and that the area of a square is the length of one side squared, we can set up the following equation to solve the question: $x^2 = 297.5625$. Therefore, $x=\sqrt{297.5625}=17.25$ meters.
10. **B.** The amount of 100% antifreeze ($1.00x$) plus the amount of 45% antifreeze solution $0.45(14 - x)$ equals the amount of pure antifreeze in 75% solution (0.75 × 14).

$$1x+0.45(14-x)=0.75(14)$$

So,

$$1x+6.3-0.45x=10.5$$

Some subtraction shows us:

$$0.55x=4.2$$

Finally, $x = 7.64$ (rounded) quarts of 100% antifreeze.

11. **B.** First, convert 132,000 square feet into square meters:

$$132{,}000\ \text{ft}^2 \bullet \frac{1\text{m}^2}{10.764\ \text{ft}^2}=12{,}263.1\ \text{m}^2$$

If we know that a Class A fire extinguisher can protect a maximum area of 557 square meters, we simply divide 557 into 12,263.1 to determine the required number of extinguishers, and get 22.02. Since we cannot have 0.02 of a fire extinguisher, we must round up to the next whole number, which is 23. Choices A and C are wrong for this very reason.

12. **B.** Since we know that $b = 8$ hours, we just plug it into the equation: $a=(-2.817)8+108.9$. Then multiply and add to determine $a = 86.364$ decibels.

13. **C.** Let $x =$ the width of the aluminum piece. Then $4x =$ length. We know the total perimeter is 420 inches, so:

$$2(4x)+2(x)=420$$

Some quick multiplication and addition tells us $10x = 420$, or $x = 42$ inches. But that is inches, and we need to know feet, so 42 divided by 12 is 3.5, and so $x = 3.5$ feet.

14. **A.** To determine the likelihood of all three characteristics, first determine the fraction of 250 that 30 people represents (the only one of the numbers not represented as a fraction). That is $\frac{3}{25}$. Then multiply the fractions together: $\frac{1}{3}\bullet\frac{1}{4}\bullet\frac{3}{25}=\frac{3}{300}=\frac{1}{100}$, or 1%.

15. **C.** First, determine the amount of mail the carrier can deliver in one hour: $750\div6=125$. Then, determine that 20 minutes is $\frac{1}{3}$ of an hour, so $125\bullet\frac{1}{3}=\frac{125}{3}$, or (rounded up to the nearest whole letter) 42 letters.

16. **B.** Add all the distances and divide by the number of days he ran, so: $4.3 + 4.5 + 3.9 + 4.75 \div 4 = 4.36$ km.

17. **C.** Let $x =$ one share of the jewelry. Since there are 7 shares (3 + 2 + 2), divide the number of shares into the number of pieces of jewelry to determine that each share receives 10 pieces. Thus, the teacher has three shares or 30 pieces, and each student receives 20 pieces.

18. **D.** Remember the rule of PEMDAS. So, given $3^2+(3\bullet3)-5(2\cdot2)\div2=x$, you'd calculate the parenthesis first. So, $3^2+9-5(4)\div2=x$. Then, do exponents: $9+9-5(4)\div2=x$. Next, multiplication and division, moving from left to right: $9+9-10=x$. Then addition and subtraction: $8=x$.

19. **B.** To solve $x^2-y+5$, simply plug in the values for $x$ and $y$. $3^2-2+5$ or 12.

20. **B.** Given the limited information, all we can tell about the sequence is that it is counting backwards by even numbers, so the most likely answer is 6.

21. **D.** To find $\frac{1}{3}\bullet\frac{2}{5}\div\frac{1}{4}$ do the operations in order. $\frac{1}{3}\bullet\frac{2}{5}=\frac{2}{15}$. Then, $\frac{2}{15}\div\frac{1}{4}$ is the same as $\frac{2}{15}\bullet\frac{4}{1}$, or $\frac{8}{15}$.

22. **A.** To find the percent change, divide the new value by the old value, or $15 \div 42 = 0.38$ (rounded to the nearest hundredth). Then multiply by 100 to determine the percentage: 38%. Then subtract 100 to find the percent change: −62%.

23. **C.** Remember that percentage point change is just the difference between the old percentage and the new. The difference between 3% and 5% is 2 percentage points.

24. **D.** 2, 3, and 7 are all prime numbers and they are all factors of 42.

25. **C.** First, find the factors of 21: 1, 3, 7, 21. Then find the factors of 33: 1, 3, 11, 33. The biggest factor they both share is 3.

26. **A.** To find the permutations, you simply calculate the factorial. 6! is 720, or $6 \times 5 \times 4 \times 3 \times 2 \times 1$.

27. **D.** Remember, the median is the middle number that has an equal amount of numbers above it as below it. In this case, there's an even number of incomes to consider, so you just average the two middle incomes ($71,000 and $80,000) to determine that the median income in the neighborhood is $75,500.

28. **B.** Interest is calculated as the principal amount times the interest rate times the time period.

29. **A.** Let $x$ = kg of 40% zinc alloy. Then, $500 - x$ = kg of 65% zinc alloy.

$$0.40x + 0.65(500 - x) = 0.55(500)$$

Thus,

$$0.40x + 325 - 0.65x = 275$$

Multiply both sides by 100 to get rid of the decimals:

$$40x + 32{,}500 - 65x = 27{,}500$$

Then a little subtraction tells us $-25x = -27{,}500$ and dividing both sides by −25 gives us a positive result: $x = 200$ kg of 40% zinc alloy. $500 - x = 300$ kg of 65% zinc alloy.

30. **A.** Let $x$ = amount of money invested at 6%. Let $\$30{,}000 - x$ = amount of money invested at 8%. The amount of 6% securities equals the amount of 8% securities + $350.

$$0.06x = 0.08(30{,}000 - x) + 350$$

So:

$$0.06x = 2{,}400 - 0.08x + 350$$

Multiply both sides by 100 to get rid of the decimals:

$$6x = 240{,}000 - 8x + 35{,}000$$

Add $8x$ to both sides to move $x$ to one side of the equation. Thus, $14x = 275{,}000$. Divide by 14 to find $x$ = 19,642.86, which represents the amount vested in government securities earning 6%.

$30{,}000 - x = 10{,}357.14$, which represents the remainder of the account earning 8%.

## WORD KNOWLEDGE

Note: The answers have been provided for the vocabulary section without explanation. If further reference is needed, consult a dictionary.

| | | | |
|---|---|---|---|
| 1. **C.** | 10. **C.** | 19. **B.** | 28. **A.** |
| 2. **A.** | 11. **A.** | 20. **C.** | 29. **B.** |
| 3. **B.** | 12. **B.** | 21. **A.** | 30. **D.** |
| 4. **D.** | 13. **B.** | 22. **A.** | 31. **B.** |
| 5. **A.** | 14. **A.** | 23. **B.** | 32. **A.** |
| 6. **C.** | 15. **D.** | 24. **D.** | 33. **C.** |
| 7. **C.** | 16. **B.** | 25. **B.** | 34. **D.** |
| 8. **A.** | 17. **D.** | 26. **B.** | 35. **D.** |
| 9. **D.** | 18. **A.** | 27. **C.** | |

## PARAGRAPH COMPREHENSION

1. **A.** The passage describes what needs to be taken into consideration before deciding to use ventilation to fight a fire. B is incorrect because the passage doesn't explain why ventilation can or should be used in fighting fires. C is incorrect because the purpose of the piece isn't to describe how two fires are different, but what to consider before using ventilation to fight a fire. D is incorrect because while true it is overly general, making A the better answer.

2. **B.** The passage states that liquids with a low flash point are volatile, meaning they are more dangerous than liquids with a high flash point. A is incorrect because the passage doesn't give any information about solids that would enable the reader to draw such a conclusion. C is incorrect because the passage states that volatility is related to flash point. D is incorrect because the flash point has a great deal to do with danger.

3. **B.** The main point of the passage is that you must claim all income on your return, no matter where it came from. A is incorrect because the passage doesn't say "everyone" needs to do this; it is focused on tax returns for business. C is incorrect because the passage specifically states that income earned from a hobby must be reported. D may be true, but it is not what the passage is about.

4. **A.** The passage defines what "gleaning" and "poaching" are and relates them to how important obtaining food is to people. B is incorrect because the author isn't comparing and contrasting anything, merely defining it. C is incorrect because the author doesn't make any such statement. D is incorrect for the same reason.

5. **D.** The passage states that Jimmie Rodgers was widely known. A, B, and C are directly supported in the passage and therefore are incorrect.

6. **C.** The passage describes the main highlights of Albert the Great's life, so this is the best title. A is incorrect because the study of Aristotle was only part of what his life was about. B is incorrect for the same reason. D is incorrect because the passage is only about one German philosopher.

7. **C.** The passage describes how both the French and the Chinese had important roles to play in the history of Annam. A is incorrect because the passage states that the Chinese controlled the territory at various points. B is incorrect because the passage states that Annam was enlarged to include most of Indochina. D is incorrect because nothing in the passage indicates that Annam was a trade center.

8. **C.** The passage specifically states that astrology uses the position of stars and planets to predict the future. A is incorrect because astrology is the forerunner of astronomy. B is incorrect because the passage does not equate the two, merely says that astrology is the forerunner of astronomy. D is incorrect because nothing in the passage indicates that this is how astrology is used.

9. **A.** The story of the battle is told in chronological order. B is incorrect because a comparison/contrast method is not used. C is incorrect because the battle is not described in a step-by-step fashion. D is incorrect because the author does not identify the most important facts first.

10. **D.** The passage states that the Benin Kingdom did export goods, so this answer is correct. A, B, and C are supported in the passage and so are incorrect.

11. **B.** The passage states that there were numerous reasons for the decline and eventual fall of the Roman Empire. A is incorrect because while having a large frontier was a contributing factor, poor military leadership is not named as the reason for the fall of the empire. C is incorrect because taxation is not given as a reason for the fall. D is also incorrect, for the same reason.

12. **A.** The passage states that Leonardo of Pisa introduced Arabic numerals to the west. B is incorrect because nothing in the passage says Leonardo was a businessman. C is incorrect because nothing in the passage says he was an artist. D is incorrect because the passage says he derived a number of complex theories, including algebra.

13. **C.** The passage states that a court has been found where inhabitants apparently played a game similar to basketball. A is incorrect; A.D. 500 was when the city was founded. B is incorrect because while the presence of an observatory suggests familiarity with the skies, it is not specifically stated (they may have been practicing astronomy), making C a better answer. D is incorrect because there's no support for it in the passage.

14. **A.** Most of the passage concerns jurors not agreeing. B is incorrect because the passage doesn't describe what happens in a trial, only what happens when jurors disagree. C is incorrect because the passage doesn't discuss deliberations. D is somewhat correct because the passage does define what a hung jury is, but A is the better answer because the passage does more than give a definition.

15. **D.** The passage specifies when most crimes occur. Logically, increasing police presence during those times would reduce crime. A is incorrect because nothing in the passage suggests that this is true. B is incorrect because the majority of crimes take place within a specific time period. C is incorrect because while it may be a good idea, that's not when the majority of crimes happen.

## MATHEMATICS KNOWLEDGE

1. **A.** The volume of a cylinder is found with the formula $V = \pi r^2 h$. The radius is half the diameter, so for this problem, $r = 11$ inches. So,

$$V = \pi(11^2)66$$

Or, $V = 3.1416(112)(66)$. Thus, the volume of the cylinder is 25,088.82 cubic inches. Since there are 231 cubic inches per gallon, we divide the volume by 231 to determine the number of gallons this container can hold. And $25{,}088.82 \div 231 = 108.61$ gallons.

2. **A.** This question involves a direct compound proportion to solve for the weight of the larger bar. The larger the bar is, the heavier it becomes, so that is considered to be a direct proportion. First, though, we need to convert all the units to inches. So we multiply 4 by 12 to get 48 inches, and 7 by 12 to get 84 inches. Then we can set up the problem to look like this:

$$\frac{48 \bullet 2 \bullet 2}{84 \bullet 3 \bullet 4} = \frac{12.3 \text{ pounds}}{x \text{ pounds}}$$

So

$$\frac{192}{1008} = \frac{12.3}{x}$$

Which can be restated as $192x = 1008(12.3)$. So, $192x = 12{,}398.4$.

Then divide both sides by 192 to isolate the unknown: $x = 64.575$ pounds.

3. **B.** Linear equations cannot have exponents.

4. **C.** Simply plug in 4 as the value of $x$ and do the necessary operations. Remember to start with the exponent first, so $2(4^3) = 2(64)$ or 128.

5. **D.** Polynomials are expressed in standard form by putting them in order from highest to lowest exponent.

6. **B.** The other angles have different measures; a line is an angle of 180°.

7. **A.** To solve the equation, subtract 9 from each side of the equation to isolate $x$. Then, $x = 12$.

8. **D.** Divide both sides of the equation by 4 to isolate the unknown. Then, $y = 12$.

9. **C.** Multiply both sides of the equation by 3 (the reciprocal of the fraction) to isolate $x$. Then, $x > 6$.

10. **C.** A quadratic equation is expressed as $ax^2 + bx + c = 0$.

11. **A.** To solve the inequality, divide both sides by $-4$ to isolate the unknown. Remember that when you divide an inequality by a negative number, you have to change the direction of the inequality sign, so $x > -0.5$.

12. **A.** Each value increases by a linear (not exponential) amount, so the points form a line.

13. **B.** The equation for determining the total measurement of the angles of a polygon is $180(n-2)°$, so $180 \bullet 3 = 540°$.

14. **D.** A right triangle has one right angle; that is, one angle that measures 90°.

15. **C.** To solve this equation, first subtract 9 from each side to isolate the unknown. Then $\frac{1}{3}y = 6$. Next, multiply both sides by the reciprocal (3) of the fraction to isolate $y$. Therefore, $y = 18$.

16. **A.** This is a simple proportion, which we can write as:

$$\frac{2 \text{ miles}}{5 \text{ minutes}} = \frac{x \text{ miles}}{30 \text{ minutes}}$$

We know that $\frac{a}{b} = \frac{c}{d}$ and that $ad = bc$, so if we just plug in our values we get $60 = 5x$. Then divide both sides of the equation by 5 to find $x = 12$.

17. **C.** Fractions are added by following this formula: $\frac{a}{b} + \frac{c}{d} = \frac{ad + bc}{bd}$. So, plugging our values in, we get $\frac{2x + 5(x - 3)}{10}$, or $\frac{7x - 3}{10}$ once simplified.

18. **A.** To multiply fractions, simply multiply the numerators and the denominators. So, $\frac{3(x-2)}{5x}$. Then do the additional operations in the numerator to get the solution $\frac{3x - 6}{5x}$.

19. **D.** The formula for the area of a trapezoid is $A = \frac{1}{2}(a + b)h$ and all of the necessary information is already provided, so just substitute numbers to determine $A = \frac{1}{2}(4 + 2)4$, or $A = 12$ square feet.

20. **B.** The factors of the $c$ variable $(-36)$ that can be subtracted to equal the constant of the $b$ variable are 12,−3. This answer can be tested by multiplying the factors $(x + 12)$ and $(x - 3)$. That operation can be written as $x(x - 3) + 12(x - 3)$. Then multiply: $x^2 - 3x + 12x - 36$. And add: $x^2 + 9x - 36 = 0$.

21. **B.** To determine the total measure of the angles in a polygon, we use the formula $180(n - 2)°$ so for this hexagon we can determine there is a total of 720°. Since there are a total of 6 sides (and therefore 6 angles), we divide the total number of degrees by the number of angles to determine that each angle measures 120°.

22. **A.** The probability is the number of possible outcomes divided by the number of selected outcomes. In this case, there are 7 possible outcomes (the total number of coins) and 3 selected outcomes (the number of pennies she could pick).

23. **D.** To determine the likelihood of an independent event happening several times in a row, multiply the likelihood of that event (1 in 4, in this case, since only 1 card out of every 4 meets the criteria) by the number of events, so $\frac{1}{4} \times \frac{1}{4} \times \frac{1}{4} = \frac{1}{64}$.

24. **A.** To find the solution to two unknowns when given two true equations, substitute one equation for one unknown, so $2x + 3 = 3x + 1$. Then subtract $2x$ from both sides to get $3 = x + 1$. Then subtract 1 from each side to find $x = 2$. Plug that value into the first equation to find $y = 7$. Then substitute these values for $x$ and $y$ in the second equation to confirm the answer is correct.

25. **D.** The volume of a rectangular solid is length times width times height. Since all the sides of a cube are the same length, you simply multiply $3 \times 3 \times 3$ to find a volume of 27 cubic inches.

## ELECTRONICS INFORMATION

1. **B.** A semiconductor both conducts and insulates to help regulate the flow of current through a circuit.

2. **D.** Capacitors are measured in farads (usually very small amounts, like millifarads or microfarads). Super capacitors can be larger, though. A 10F super capacitor can store 10 farads of charge.

3. **A.** A joule is a measure of work.

4. **B.** The formula for conductance is conductance (G) equals current divided by voltage (the inverse of the resistance formula).
5. **A.** Electricity has to travel long distances from the power plant to your house, and it loses energy to resistance. A higher voltage increase efficiency and allows the electricity to travel long distances.
6. **D.** A positively charged object has more protons. A negatively charged object has more electrons.
7. **A.** When a negative and positive charge unite, the result is an electrical discharge.
8. **B.** Unlike poles attract, and like poles repel, so a north pole will always repel another north pole but will attract a south pole.
9. **C.** An ampere is the equivalent of 1 coulomb per second, so 10 amperes = 10 coulombs per second.
10. **B.** In a series circuit, each resistor decreases the amount of current.
11. **D.** A diode is usually made of a semiconductor material with good conductance at one end and poor conductance at the other to move current in one direction.
12. **A.** A rheostat increases resistance, thereby controlling the amount of current available to power the appliance.
13. **D.** All of the possible answers are true of an improperly grounded electrical system.
14. **B.** Current moving in an unintended way is a short circuit—in other words, a type of electrical malfunction.
15. **A.** Some of the wiring is in parallel and some in series, so it's a series-parallel circuit.
16. **D.** The current in a circuit is equal to voltage divided by resistance.
17. **C.** Voltage is current times total resistance, so 20 volts.
18. **D.** Electrical efficiency is determined by power output divided by power input.
19. **B.** This is the symbol for an open switch.
20. **A.** This is the symbol for a battery, so it is the circuit's power source.

## AUTOMOTIVE AND SHOP INFORMATION

1. **B.** Air injection is a type of emissions control. It is used in connection with a catalytic converter, not in place of one.
2. **D.** An ECU is an Engine Control Unit, or sometimes the Electronic Control Unit.
3. **A.** The fuel-air mixture is ignited in the cylinder, causing a small explosion. Choice B is incorrect because the explosion does not occur in the piston.
4. **B.** The starter starts the engine by sending a current through the starter solenoid to the starter engine, which gets the car's motor cranking. Then the starter motor shuts off.
5. **C.** The illustration shows a spark plug.
6. **C.** All of the answers are true except for C. Fuel injection is common on most newer cars.
7. **A.** In a vehicle with a carburetor, pushing on the accelerator would open the throttle, allowing the car to go faster. In cars with fuel-injected systems, the acceleration process is more complex.
8. **B.** The exhaust manifold funnels exhaust from the cylinder heads down a pipe where it passes through the catalytic converter and the muffler out through the tail pipe.

9. **D.** Underinflated tires can cause problems with both stopping and cornering. Additional bouncing (choice C) is the result of overinflated tires.

10. **C.** A 4-wheel drive vehicle has both of these characteristics—better traction in rough road conditions, but more difficulty in cornering.

11. **D.** Struts, shock absorbers, and tires all make up part of the suspension system.

12. **A.** The illustration shows an exhaust system.

13. **C.** Inside calipers would be the most appropriate tool to use. Choice A is an illustration of outside calipers that can be used to compare the outside diameter of two different pipes. Choice B is a protractor, which is used more appropriately to draw or plot angles on a given surface, not to measure various diameters. Choice D can roughly measure internal and external diameters, but it cannot offer the same degree of accuracy that is afforded by calipers.

14. **A.** The instrument shown is a depth gauge. Its principle use is to determine the depth of holes, mortises, or grooves.

15. **D.** A try square and carpenter's framing square are both designed only to determine the true squaring of a given angle (i.e., 90°). A combination square, however, has the versatile feature of determining a miter square.

16. **B.** A Torx screwdriver is needed for this screw.

17. **D.** The socket wrench has the added feature of a ratchet handle, which allows for turning bolts in tight areas. Choices A and B would not be practical under the circumstances given. Choice C is a possibility, but since most lack a ratchet mechanism, it requires more time and effort to loosen the bolt. It is not nearly as convenient as a socket wrench.

18. **A.** Only Allen wrenches have a design of this nature. They are used to tighten or loosen machine setscrews (see example).

19. **C.** A triangular file will serve the purposes described in the question. Choice D is incorrect because the question referred to files only, not electrical tools.

20. **C.** Spanner wrenches are designed with this very purpose in mind. Choice A is an Allen wrench used to tighten or loosen machined setscrews. Choice B is a torque wrench used to apply measured force to nuts or bolts. Choice D is a tap wrench used in conjunction with a tap when cutting internal screw threads.

21. **D.** To further clarify the question, the male end of a hose coupling is the end with exposed threads. When water from two separate hose lines is combined by a Siamese adapter, the discharges of both lines are combined into a master fire stream. A hose coupling with the opposite kind of threading is termed a wye adapter; it serves to divide a master hose stream into two separate, smaller hand lines. The other choices provided are incorrect.

22. **A.** Choice A is an illustration of an orbital sander, which best serves this purpose. Choice B is a belt sander, which is used for coarser work that must be accomplished in an expedient manner. Choice C is not a power tool. Choice D is a disk sander that performs similarly to an orbital sander providing that fine sandpaper is used. The orbital sander, however, can attain the smoothest finish of all the alternatives given.

23. **C.** A propane torch is the most appropriate tool to use for such a job. Choice A fuses metal to metal by utilizing electrical current and a welding rod; solder is not involved. Choice B is a soldering gun; however, it is more appropriately applied to smaller scale projects such as wire or contact terminal connections. Choice D is an acetylene torch, and it can work if used with some finesse. Its primary use is for cutting thick metal workpieces.

24. **B.** Choice B is an illustration of a caulking gun, which is used principally to apply sealants. The other choices, a hydrometer, grease gun, and tire pressure gauge (in that order), have automotive applications discussed earlier in this book.

25. **B.** Choice B, the pickaxe, is principally used to break up hard material like the soil described in the question. Choice A would be more appropriate in loamier (i.e., looser) soils. Both choices C and D are used principally to hew wood.

## MECHANICAL COMPREHENSION

1. **C.** Gear A turning clockwise makes Gear B turn counterclockwise, Gear B makes Gears C and D turn clockwise.

2. **C.** The output torque is inversely proportional to the size of the drive gear as compared to the connected gear. So, a larger drive gear has a lower torque. A drive gear with three times the diameter of the connected gear would have $\frac{1}{3}$ the torque. A drive gear smaller than the connected gear would have a bigger torque.

3. **A.** Since the drive gear has four times as many teeth as the driven gear, there is an inverse reduction of torque with a corresponding increase in speed.

4. **B.** To find the speed of the last gear of a drive train, use the formula:

$$G_L = \frac{\text{number of teeth of drive gears multiplied by each other}}{\text{number of teeth of driven gears multiplied by each other}}$$

So 400 divided by 750 equals about 0.5, or one-half revolution.

5. **B.** Pressure exerted on a piston in a hydraulic apparatus exerts a perpendicular force on a piston.

6. **D.** Fluid pressure is related to depth; in an open container (like the ocean), the pressure is the same at a given depth regardless of the configuration of the container.

7. **A.** The pressure of salt water is slightly heavier than fresh water.

8. **C.** If pressure is exerted on a fluid trapped in a confined space, the pressure is distributed in all directions.

9. **B.** Effort times the effort distance equals resistance times the resistance distance. Since the fulcrum is placed at the midpoint, both distances equal 5 feet. So they cancel each other out, meaning effort = resistance. There is no mechanical advantage to using a lever this way.

10. **D.** What is essentially being described in this question is the volume of a cylinder. The bore represents the diameter of the cylinder and the stroke represents the height of the cylinder. Since volume of a cylinder is $V = \pi r^2 h$, we can easily figure the displacement. The radius is equal to half the diameter or, in this case, 1.375. The square of 1.375 = 1.89 (rounded down). Therefore, $(3.1416)(1.89)(3.5) = x$, or the number of cubic inches of displacement. So, $x = 20.78$ cubic inches (rounding down slightly).

11. **A.** A fulcrum placed at Position 1 would enhance the lift capability of this lever the most. Essentially, the closer a fulcrum is placed to a load or resistance, the easier it becomes to lift with the lever.

12. **D.** Effort times the effort distance equals resistance times the resistance distance. With what we know we can say $16x = 1075 \times 2$. A quick calculation reveals that $x = 134.375$.

13. **B.** Since it requires 825 pounds of effort to lift 825 pounds, no mechanical advantage is gained by using the lever as described. Ratios of 1:1 do not demonstrate mechanical advantage.

14. **C.** Simple machines do not have motors. Choices A, B, and D are all examples of simple machines.

15. **D.** If the pulleys have a 4:1 ratio, then the larger pulley would turn at $\frac{1}{4}$ the rate of the smaller pulley, or 125 rpm.

16. **C.** As a rule of thumb, if gears are directly aligned end to end as shown in the illustration, the odd-numbered gears in the sequence will always turn in the same direction while the even-numbered gears will always turn in the opposite direction.

17. **D.** To determine the effort required, simply divide the resistance by the mechanical advantage.

18. **D.** The system shown in D distributes the weight of the load over various cables, thereby increasing the mechanical advantage.

19. **A.** Choice B is an example of an inclined plane, choice C is a wedge, and choice D is an example of a lever, all of which are classified as simple machines.

20. **B.** When an inclined plane is used, the formula effort times length of the incline plane equals resistance times height can be used. If we plug in the values we know, we come up with $\mathit{Effort}(10) = 500 \times 6$, or $10E = 3000$. Quick division shows that $E = 300$ pounds.

21. **A.** The mechanical advantage is determined by dividing the amount of resistance by the force applied to the tool, or 345 divided by 75.

22. **B.** The circumference of the lever needs to be determined first. Circumference is equal to pi times diameter. We only know the radius (6 inches), so we multiply the radius by 2 to determine the diameter (12 inches). Then multiply the diameter by $\pi$ (3.1416) to determine the circumference, which is 37.7 inches. Divide the circumference by the screw pitch to determine the mechanical advantage: $37.7 \div \frac{1}{6}$. Or, 37.7 inches $\times$ 6 inches = 226.2 (multiply by the inverse to divide by a fraction). So, the mechanical advantage is 226.2:1.

23. **B.** First, determine the circumference of the lever: 18 inch radius $\times$ 2 yields a diameter of 36. 36 $\pi$ (3.1416) = 113.10 inch circumference (rounded up slightly). Then, divide the circumference by the screw pitch ($\frac{1}{8}$ inch) to determine the mechanical advantage. Multiply by the inverse to divide by a fraction: 113.1 $\times$ 8 inches = 904.8, or a mechanical advantage of 904.8:1. Multiply by 15 pounds of force to determine that 13,572 pounds can be lifted by this jackscrew under the conditions given.

24. **A.** The mechanical advantage of a wedge is the length of its slope divided by the width of its widest end (e.g., the nonpointed end).

25. **C.** Tons should be converted to pounds; 2 tons = 4,000 pounds. The handle (which is the lever) has a potential circumference of 94.248 inches (15 inches in length is the radius; multiply that by 2 to determine the diameter, and multiply the diameter by pi to determine the circumference). The mechanical advantage is the circumference divided by the screw pitch. Multiply by the inverse to divide by fractions: 94.248 $\times$ 6 = 565.488, or 565.488: 1 advantage. To determine how much effort is required, divide the resistance (4,000 pounds) by the advantage. So, 7 pounds of effort (rounded down slightly) are required.

### ASSEMBLING OBJECTS

| | | | |
|---|---|---|---|
| 1. B. | 5. A. | 9. B. | 13. D. |
| 2. C. | 6. B. | 10. C. | 14. A. |
| 3. B. | 7. B. | 11. B. | 15. D. |
| 4. B. | 8. A. | 12. C. | 16. D. |

# Refund Policy

In the unlikely event that you use this book but score less than a Category IIIA minimum score of 50 on the Armed Forces Qualification Test (the collection of four ASVAB subtests that determines your eligibility to enlist), your money will be refunded. This guarantee specifically applies to the written exam, not the physical fitness requirement or other requirements to enlist. Scoring well on the ASVAB as a whole and the AFQT in particular is necessary to enlist and do well in the military, but it is no guarantee that you will be accepted. If a test applicant scores above 50 on the written AFQT test, but fails the aforementioned requirements for enlistment, he or she will not be eligible for a refund.

The following conditions must be met before any refund will be made. All exercises in this guide must be completed to demonstrate that the applicant did make a real attempt to practice and prepare to score 50 or better. Any refund must be claimed within ninety days of the date of purchase shown on your sales receipt. Anything submitted beyond this ninety-day period will be subject to the publisher's discretion. The refund amount is limited to the purchase price and may not exceed the cover price of the book.

If you mail this study guide back for a refund, please include your sales receipt and validated test results.

* Requests for refunds should be addressed to Adams Media, ASVAB Exams Division, 57 Littlefield Street, Avon, MA 02322. Please allow approximately four to six weeks for processing.

* On occasion, exam results are not mailed to the test applicant. If this is the case for you, procure a copy of your test score from your recruiter and be sure your name and address are indicated.